THE SANSKRIT LANGUAGE

THE SANSKRIT LANGUAGE

An Introductory Grammar and Reader

Walter Harding Maurer
Professor of Sanskrit
University of Hawai'i at Mānoa

Volume One
Lessons One – Thirty-Two

CURZON

First Published in 1995
by Curzon Press
Richmond, Surrey
http://www.curzonpress.co.uk

Reprinted 2001

Printed and bound in Great Britain by
TJ International, Padstow, Cornwall

British Library Cataloguing in Publication Data
A catalogue record of this book is available from the British Library

Library of Congress Cataloguing in Publication Data
A catalogue record for this book has been requested

ISBN 0–7007–1382–4 (set)

Table of Contents

Volume I

To my wife

Geraldine

without whose insistence

and inspiration

it would not have been written

Foreword

There are numerous grammars, some old, some new, available to the student who wishes to study the elements of the Sanskrit language. Why, then, it may be reasonably wondered, is it desirable to write yet another textbook to join this long line of predecessors? While not wishing in the least to cast praise or dispraise on any of these many introductory works, it seems to me that another grammar is indeed wanted, but a grammar of a different kind, more in conformity with the needs of the majority of students nowadays, who, through no fault of their own, come to the study of Sanskrit with no knowledge or insufficient knowledge of the categories of grammar, the so-called 'parts of speech' and some fundamental concept of the structure of a sentence.

Not only do students need to be provided at the outset of their study with this basic knowledge, but, in their progression through the elements of Sanskrit grammar, they need to have an extended explanation of each new matter that is taken up. For example, it does not suffice to say 'the middle voice is formed in the following way', with perhaps the addition of a few words of explanation concerning the difference in meaning between the active and the middle. It should, in my view, first of all be made abundantly clear what is meant by the term *voice*, why it is called *middle*, how it happens that its meaning in Sanskrit in most instances is indistinguishable from that of the active, along with other particulars of interest. By extended explanations that anticipate the sort of questions that they unconsciously would like to ask, but as beginners find difficult to formulate, students gradually acquire an insight into the language and almost inevitably become fascinated by the way the language works and ultimately infected with what I like to call the 'Bacillus Sanskriticus', an incurable affliction which is notably conducive to further study.

The Sanskrit exercises in most of the existing manuals typically consist of ten or twelve sentences unrelated in content from one to the other, which, so I think, are rather more a practice in decipherment than in reading Sanskrit. Far more desirable and instructive are passages of *connected* material, texts simplified from Sanskrit originals, which are intrinsically interesting and challenging by their degree of difficulty. Reading integrated passages at an early stage in one's study creates a feeling of perceptible progress in learning the language.

The Devanāgarī writing system is complicated and takes time and patience to learn. It is not only the signs themselves and their phonetic values that pose difficulty, but also the concept of voiced and voiceless consonants, aspirated and unaspirated, and the classification of the consonants by organ of speech, matters alien to the beginner, yet so important in grasping the sound changes that have later to be learned. In this work a great deal of attention has accordingly been given to the explanation of the Devanāgarī system, to the traditional method of writing each sign, and to the pronunciation of every sound.

Following the chapter on the system of writing is a short section bearing the forbidding title 'Rattling the Dry Bones of Grammar'. In spite of the repelling title, this section is intended to help the student who has not been exposed to the parts of speech and other elementary aspects of grammar. However, as these matters are treated rather more from the focal point of Sanskrit than that of grammar in general, it is hoped that this section may serve as a bridge to the first lesson for *all* beginners.

Volume I, the instructional manual, contains thirty-two lessons, which my use of this work in its earlier drafts has shown can be comfortably covered in two academic years, sixteen lessons each year, in a class that meets three times a week in fifty-minute sessions. Of course, this pace may be accelerated or decelerated according to a varying frequency and length of sessions and certainly also according to the general background of the students and their receptivity.

The order in which the topics of grammar are treated in these lessons does not correspond, except fortuitously or by absolute necessity of early presentation, to that of any other textbook: the sequence of topics is based upon my own feeling of the degree of importance and frequency of occurrence of the various declensional and conjugational forms and syntactical constructions. Accordingly, I have presented the gerund in Lesson Three, simply because it is of so extremely frequent occurrence that the postponement of it seems to me unrealistic. The formation itself is easily taught and even more easily recognized when it occurs in reading. Similarly, the use of the past passive participle in place of a finite verb in the past tense is taught in Lesson Six, because of its ubiquitousness in the works most likely to be read by students in their early study of the language.

Each lesson begins with a discussion of some topic of grammar, usually including the presentation of a new declension or verb formation, followed by a passage of some length in Sanskrit. Many of these passages have been composed entirely by me, others simplified from Sanskrit originals, as, for example, the stories from the Hitopadeśa. The story of Śakuntalā is skeletonized from Kālidāsa's play, the story of Purūravas and Urvaśī is a composite version I have pieced together from various retellings of the legend. The Churning of the Ocean is drawn chiefly from the Mahābhārata, but its opening part has many threads from the version in the Viṣṇu Purāṇa. The Story of Sagara and His Sons is based on the Rāmāyaṇa. Lessons Twenty-Seven through Thirty-Two contain excerpts from the Bhagavadgītā. All these exercises are provided with detailed grammatical and cultural notes.

The notes are followed by a vocabulary which lists most of the words of the foregoing passage, with omission of those that have recurred repeatedly in the earlier lessons. Through Lesson Sixteen these lists are arranged in the order of their occurrence in the exercise; beginning with Lesson Seventeen, however, the vocabulary entries are arranged in the order of the Devanāgarī alphabet,[1] this being a relatively painless means of familiarizing students with the arrangement of entries in the *Sanskrit-English Lexicon* at the end of Volume Two and, of course, the various Sanskrit dictionaries and wordlists in other grammars.

Throughout I have tried to follow the principle of 'going from the known to the unknown', as the best and clearest means of explaining something new or difficult. So, for example, in introducing the subject of compounds, I start with compounds in English (the 'known') and, after showing how they are put together and how they may be analyzed, proceed to apply the Sanskrit names to the various English types and finally to the analysis of Sanskrit compounds (the 'unknown'). Since it is usual in English to write without intervening space only those compounds that consist of two members, but longer compounds with their members spaced apart (as, for example, 'life insurance company'), students need first to be made aware of *the existence of long compounds* in English that not infrequently extend to considerable length and are really a pervasive feature of modern English. It has been my invariable experience that, once they do become aware of compounds in English, students enjoy analyzing them and experience the same joy in analyzing Sanskrit compounds.

There is, however, an exception to using the principle of 'going from the known to the unknown', *viz.*, when the 'known' (English) is more difficult to grasp or analyze than the 'unknown' (Sanskrit)! This is true, for example, in explaining the locative absolute. The Sanskrit construction is, in fact, easier to grasp than its English counterpart, the nominative absolute, the use of which, incidentally, is by no means as prevalent as it used to be. The difficulty is due in part to the lack of case endings in English which obscures the use of the nominative case in the absolute construction, unless an inflected personal pronoun (he, she, they) is used instead of a noun. The difficulty is due also to the less transparent reason for the use of the nominative in English. In this instance, the Sanskrit use of the locative in its frequent sense of 'with reference to' offers a clearer point of departure for explaining the construction than the English.

There is an aspect of pedagogy, which, while not precisely to be called a principle of instruction, ought to run like a golden thread through the entire fabric of a textbook. I refer to an *affection* for the subject that is taught therein. Of course, this cannot be *taught* like a construction of grammar or the rigmarole of a declension or conjugation: it has to be *conveyed indirectly* by the avoidance of tedium, by the student's sense of progress in something wholly new to him or her, by the clarity of explanation, in short by the methodology that runs its course through the whole work, and it is closely related to the *Bacillus Sanskriticus* I spoke of earlier. It is apparent that, if students enjoy what they are studying, they will apply themselves to it, they will not have to be told how many hours a day to devote

[1]This change in the order of vocabulary entries was made as a result of a suggestion by Timothy Cahill.

to the work assigned. I can but hope that this golden thread, so essential an aspect of pedagogy, may be found shining not too faintly here and there to inspire and impel students to a further study of Sanskrit.

Every lesson through Twenty-Six contains also a passage in English to be translated into Sanskrit. In most instances, the English passage is based on the Sanskrit that precedes it, so that the student may have a pattern to serve as a guide in the translation. The *English-Sanskrit Glossary* in Volume II contains all the words that occur in these passages. English passages have not, however, been included in the last six lessons which contain excerpts from the Bhagavadgītā, the reason for the omission being the undesirability of adding to the greater abundance of matter for translation in those lessons.

Volume II is the product of a unanimous suggestion by my students at the University of Hawai'i at Mānoa who constituted the class with which I tried out my grammar in its first draft. In that draft, what is now denominated Volume II was then a series of appendices to the thirty-two lessons, somewhat loosely connected with them. They felt, with good reason I think, that these appendices along with the *English-Sanskrit Glossary* (then only projected!) and the lengthy *Sanskrit-English Lexicon* could be more conveniently used as a separate work because of the purely referential character of the appendices on the one hand and the great frequency of use of the *Glossary* and *Lexicon* on the other. The paradigms and the survey of sandhi rules are essential for practice and reference, although they are not entirely summary and repetitive, but do contain additional matter.

Included also in Volume II as Appendix I are the first five cantos of the Story of Nala and Damayantī in the critical edition with an introduction and detailed notes extending to 40-odd pages and, forming Appendix IV, an essay entitled 'Sanskrit and its Relationship to the Other Indo-European Languages'.[2]

A peculiar feature of this work is the fairly frequent use of labels for the various functions of the cases, *e.g.*, ablative of separation, dative of purpose, instrumental of description, genitive quasi-dative, ablative of comparison, accusative of the place to which, accusative of duration of time, etc. These expressions, taken, *mutatis mutandis*, from traditional Latin and Greek grammar, seem to me useful in succinctly referring to particular usages and even conducive, so I hope, to their easier comprehension and recollection.

This grammar has been used in a class or perused by several Sanskrit instructors and by others in self-instruction. Some question has occasionally been asked as to why I have used the anusvāra sign for a final *-m* in sentence combination before vowel-initial as well as consonant-initial words, instead of only before the latter in accordance with the usual procedure. I have adopted this practice for *pedagogical reasons*, preferring this expedient to writing *-m* with the virāma sign (-म्) before vowel-initial words, a circuitous procedure which would otherwise

---

[2] I should like to express my thanks to Dr. Albert Lawrence Lloyd, Professor of German, University of Pennsylvania, for his careful perusal of this appendix and the suggestions he made.

have been necessary until the introduction of combinatory Devanāgarī writing in Lesson Twenty-Six. This use of the anusvara is, then, a sort of *compendium scripturae* which in due course is replaced by the standard usage.[3]

I have also been asked why I do not teach the dual from the very beginning, instead of postponing the matter until Lesson Twenty, since, unlike the virtually fossilitic dual in classical Greek, the Sanskrit dual is very much a living form. While I quite agree about the living character of the Sanskrit dual, I feel that the hurdles that the beginning student must surmount are sufficient to deter the addition of yet another hurdle that can more easily be surmounted at a later stage, when familiarity with the commoner forms and constructions has been acquired.

I have learned in the course of writing this book that a textbook is a kind of work, which by its very nature is never really finished: it is something ever in progress, needing addition or modification here or there, further tinkering with this or that detail, to bring greater clarity, cohesion and indeed correctness to it, yet never seeming to be ready to start on its journey.

It is with this permeating sense of incompleteness, perhaps of insufficiency too, that I offer these volumes to those who would not, in their quest to learn Sanskrit, be dissuaded by their inordinate length.

When I came to my *alma mater*, the University of Pennsylvania, during my sabbatical year of 1989-90 to begin this work, which my wife had been pressing me to do for years, I was not only given a comfortable office, but all manner of computerized equipment, which, as a remnant of the older school, I had no idea how to use. Though I was told, upon the confession of my ignorance, that I could become familiar with the use of it within a month or two, I was skeptical about the celerity with which this feat could be accomplished. Without much hesitation, therefore, I decided to spend all the time of my sabbatical on the writing of my introduction to Sanskrit and employ graduate students to do the text-formatting.

Since that crucial decision to avoid the captivating charm of the computer, I have come to know a galaxy of bright students, all having some affiliation with the Department of South Asia Regional Studies, expert not alone in the mysteries of the computer, but also in the Sanskrit language. The first star in the galaxy was Lynken Ghose, now a student of Buddhism at McGill University, then David J. Fern who was, so it would turn out, responsible for a very considerable portion of the work in its first draft, then Jerome H. Bauer, whose special and many-sided skill has suffused itself throughout the two volumes, and Loriliai Biernacki, who worked assiduously on various parts just before leaving for India, and finally Timothy C. Cahill, who contributed immensely not only of his knowledge of the computer, but

---

[3]Upon noting this somewhat deviant use of the anusvāra sign, Timothy Cahill, with his customary insight, called to my attention a *nyāya* regarding the elusive star Arundhatī, which is more easily pointed out by first calling an unimportant nearby star Arundhatī, then rejecting that before pointing out the true Arundhatī (अरुन्धतीं दिदर्शयिषुस्तत्समीपस्थां स्थूलां तारामममुख्यां प्रथममरुन्धतीति ग्राहयित्वा तां प्रत्याख्याय पश्चादरुन्धतीमेव ग्राहयति).

of his learning and fluency in Sanskrit. I owe an incalculable debt to these fine young scholars who it is my firm belief will one day be the principal preceptors of various branches of Indological learning in this country.

I must express my manifold gratitude and appreciation to the Department of South Asia Regional Studies for providing me with the facilities I have mentioned in addition to constant access to the computers and printers used by the graduate students named above – and all this not only during my sabbatical, but repetitively and unstintingly for the past five summers, during which the core of the work done in 1989-90 was supplemented and modified until it was completed in the summer of 1994.

This work in its first draft was used in my elementary Sanskrit class in 1991-92, during which the first sixteen lessons were covered, and with the same students in 1992-93 for the remaining sixteen lessons. These were wonderful students, keen to learn and question, whom it was a joy to teach and to know. All of them contributed in some way to the final form of this work. I cannot and would not wish to single out individuals from this class, lest I do injustice to anyone through failure of memory, but let the names of all be mentioned here: Ok Sun An, Donna Marie J. Anderson, Richard S. Girven, John C. Hodges, In-Sub Hur, Mei-Huang Lee, Gregory P. Merrill.[4]

During the past academic year (1993-94), I used this work in its third draft with another elementary class, the names of whom are here also recorded: Jeffrey T. Giesea, Kurtis G. Hagen, Guy S. Porter, Janice C. Rieger, Dmitri A. Siegel, Ranjan K. Umapathy.

Finally, I come to what is perhaps an unprecedented source of help, though the many involved are quite unaware of their contribution. I refer to the squirrels that make their home in the park behind Independence Hall, where my wife and I habitually ensconced ourselves on weekends. They provided us with endless pleasure and stimulus: we looked forward to seeing them (and offering them food), and we are sure they looked forward to our long sessions there. In our fancy we like to think that, in subsequent summers, they remembered us by their seemingly salutatory movements.

Walter Harding Maurer

University of Pennsylvania
Philadelphia
July 1994

---

[4]Subsequent to this class, Gregory Merrill had occasion to provide a remarkable graduate student of philosophy, y-clept John Smith, with tutorial lessons in Sanskrit, using my grammar in its third draft. I have with pleasure and profound thanks incorporated all their kindly proffered *corrigenda* and suggestions.

Introductory Remarks to the Student of Sanskrit

A study of Sanskrit, the classical language of India, will undoubtedly prove much more interesting and meaningful, if at the outset we may form some conception of the relationship of Sanskrit to *other* languages and the character of its literature. It is unfortunate that the name 'Sanskrit' suggests something exotic -- to many not even a language! -- but, in any case, an alien thing that would occupy only a few thick-lensed scholars interested in curiosities. While it is certainly true that to write a Sanskrit grammar advanced age (not necessarily accompanied by thick spectacles!) is a desirable attribute, the study of Sanskrit transcends the geriatric aspect. In truth there is nothing exotic or alien about Sanskrit, except that many think it so, and it may seem well nigh incredible that this 'exotic' language bears the closest kinship with our own English language as well as with most of the languages of Europe. By kinship I mean precisely *genetic* relationship, not just superficial external resemblances to individual words. Anyone who has studied even a little Latin and one or more of the Romance languages cannot help but observe the close similarity, for example, between the Romance and Latin numerals. Thus, compare French *deux,* Spanish *dos,* Portuguese *dois* and Italian *due,* all meaning 'two', on the one hand, and Latin *duo* on the other. Other perfectly obvious similarities can be illustrated with all the numerals. How is this to be explained? The Latin language, which was in ancient times just one of many interrelated speeches in the Italian peninsula, gradually became the dominant language there, and as Rome's power and conquests grew, Latin was brought by the Roman legions to almost every part of Europe. Latin, thus spread far and wide by conquest and the migration of the Italic peoples, was inevitably affected by the local, indigenous languages. As a result of this process over the centuries, the Latin language was gradually reshaped in accordance with the speech habits of those peoples who fell under the sway of Rome. From this extended process of transformation the Romance languages were born. Spoken Latin, called 'Sermo vulgaris', was, of course, not a unitary unvarying language as we might think from a study of the classical language we learn in school, but it had, like all languages, dialectal variations as well as individual idiosyncrasies from one part of Italy to the other. The Roman poet Catullus had a friend Arrius by name who, much like the cockneys of England, had the habit of putting h's where they didn't belong, and would say, for example, 'Hionian Sea' for 'Ionian' Sea'. That many of the Roman soldiers were addicted to the same habit, is shown by the modern French word *huit* for 'eight' which is the lineal descendant of *hocto,* a common spoken form corresponding to the classical *octo* without *h.*

But what, it may be asked, has this got to do with our assertion that Sanskrit, English and most of the languages of Europe are genetically related? When the Italian merchant Filippo Sassetti visited India in the 16th century, he noted in a letter to Bernando Davanzati that many words in India's classical language Sanskrit were very similar to Italian words of the same meaning. Among examples, he gave the Sanskrit *sarpa* 'snake', which he compared with Italian *serpente.* Two centuries later, in a now famous lecture presented to the Asiatic Society of Bengal Sir William Jones, judge of the Supreme Court in Calcutta, suggested that the similarities between Sanskrit, Latin, Greek, Gothic, Celtic and Persian were due to their coming from the same source. From this assertion and a gradual recognition among scholars of its ineluctable correctness, a new science came into being within a few decades, the science of comparative philology, nowadays generally called 'comparative linguistics'. In remote, prehistoric antiquity there existed a people, probably to the East of Lithuania, who spoke a language which, in the course of their subsequent expansion in many directions, became the languages of most of Europe, Iran and northern India today. To this vast array of languages belong also Icelandic and English, both of which are members of the Germanic family of languages, whose speakers are otherwise concentrated in Germany, the Netherlands and Scandinavia. This immense assemblage of languages, ultimately stemming like a gigantic banyan tree from a single source, is called 'Indo-European' and the people who spoke it are called 'Indo-Europeans' for want of a more specific or ethnic name. Years ago, interestingly enough, the British philologist P. Giles proposed the name 'Wiros' for the ancient Indo-Europeans, a name based on their word for *man* as postulated by scholars.[1] But this suggestion was not widely accepted and is now quite forgotten.

The Indo-European languages are now classified by scholars into a dozen or so families, each of which embraces those languages that belong particularly closely together. According to this classification, English, which is descended from the fusing of several Germanic dialects brought to England in the mid-fifth century A.D., forms one of the numerous languages that constitute the pedigree of the Germanic family. Latin and its Romance descendants, along with the ancient Italic languages Oscan, Umbrian and a few others known only from scattered fragments, make up the Italic family. Of the dozen or so families of Indo-European, the one to which Sanskrit belongs is the so-called Aryan or Indo-Iranian family, which has two principal divisions, the Irano-Aryan and the Indo-Aryan, thus:

[1]*The Cambridge History of India* (1922), vol. I (Ancient India), chapter 3, p. 66 ff.

The Aryan or Indo-Iranian Family

1. *Irano-Aryan*		2. *Indo-Aryan*	
Avestan	Old Persian	Vedic	
(the language of the scriptures of the Zoroastrians, the followers of Zoroaster or Zarathushtra)	(attested in the inscriptions of the Achaemenian dynasty of ancient Persia, 559-330 B.C.)	(the language of the Vedas including the Brāhmaṇas, Āraṇyakas and Upaniṣads)	
	Middle Persian (or Pahlavī, embracing the language of the Arsacid and Sassanian dynasties and the literary works of the Zoroastrians)	Sanskrit (*i.e.*, the classical language of the Mahābhārata, Rāmāyaṇa and and all subsequent texts)	Prakrit (*i.e.*, the spoken language from which ultimately arose the modern languages, Hindī, Urdū, Bengali, Oṛiyā, Gujarātī, Marāṭhī, etc.)
	New or modern Persian (or Fārsī)		

In summation of our brief account of the interrelation of Sanskrit with the Indo-European languages (and hence our own English!), we may select the Sanskrit word *bhrā́tar* 'brother' and compare it with the genetically related word in the other Indo-European languages. The words are arranged under the family to which each language belongs.

1. Aryan (Indo-Iranian)
    Sanskrit *bhrā́tar*
    Avestan *brātar*
    Old Persian *brātar* (from which Modern Persian *bärādär*)

2. Hellenic
    Greek *phrā́tōr* ('member of a clan')

3. Italic
    Latin *frāter*

4. Baltic
   - Lithuanian *broterẽlis* ('little brother')
   - Lettish or Latvian *brãlis* ('little brother'), *brãtarītis* ('dear brother')
   - Old Prussian *brāti*

5. Germanic
   - Gothic *brōthar*
   - Old Norse *brōthir*
   - Old Saxon *brōthar*
   - Old Frisian *brōther*
   - Old High German *bruoder* (whence Modern German *Bruder*)
   - Old English *brōthor* (whence Modern English *brother*)

6. Celtic
   - Old Irish *brāthir*
   - Old Welsh *broder*
   - Old Cornish *broder* (whence Modern Cornish *brawd*)

Gypsy (Romany)
   a) European Gypsy *pral*
   b) English Gypsy *pal* (whence borrowed English 'pal'!)

The language of the Gypsies, collectively called 'Romany', should properly be classed under the Aryan family. This is due to the fact that the people we call Gypsies, in spite of their widely scattered habitats, ultimately originated in India, whence they migrated many centuries ago, partly of their own volition, but, in all probability, partly also because they were displaced and forced to flee due to the numerous invasions to which the subcontinent was constantly subjected.

Astonishing as may seem the close genetic relationship of Sanskrit with English and most of the languages of Europe, equally astonishing will prove to be the vast extent and diversity of Sanskrit literature, especially to those who possess no prior knowledge of it beyond having heard of the Bhagavadgītā and perhaps read a few pages in translation. It must by all means be remembered that Sanskrit is an ancient language, one of the very oldest offshoots of its parent Indo-European, that for the past 3000 or more years it has been a vehicle of expression of Indian civilization and culture. As a spoken language, to be sure, it was in the course of time superseded by its many derivative speeches, just as in Europe spoken Latin was superseded by its descendants. As a literary language, however, Sanskrit never died out, but surprisingly is even nowadays written by a small number of cultivated Hindus, and books and articles are published in it. During its long history thousands of works were composed in Sanskrit, in the earliest times transmitted orally, but later committed to writing on birch-bark or palm-leaves, eventually on paper after about 1000 A.D. It is remarkable that so much of this vast and diverse output has been preserved, saved from the perpetual ravage of hungry insects, but consider how dismayed we would be, were we to know how much has been irrevocably lost!

The oldest literature that has come down to us in Sanskrit is known by the generic name 'Veda', the earliest portion of which, the four Vedas properly known as the Ṛg-, Sāma-, Yajur- and Atharva-veda, is composed in a much more highly inflected language than the later, so-called classical Sanskrit. This earlier stage of Indo-Aryan speech is generally referred to as Vedic to distinguish it clearly from the later. It is not possible to assign dates to these or the later Vedic works (Brāhmaṇas, Āraṇyakas and Upaniṣads), as, in the first place, they were not the production of a single author and so cannot be assigned to a point of time. All that can be said with some element of certainty is that the Ṛgveda, the oldest of the four Vedic collections, must have assumed its *present form* c.1000 B.C., but it would be the purest conjecture to say how long a time was occupied by its composition. Some of the hymns which make up the collection may indeed go back to a very ancient time, perhaps long before the Aryans entered the passages of the northwest, which might have taken place c.1700 B.C.

The four Vedic collections were followed by several strata of derivative treatises concerned with the sacrificial rituals, their origin and their interpretation, culminating in manuals of lofty and mystical character which teach the unity of the self or soul with God, conceived as an absolute or neuter principle. These final treatises of the Vedic period, whose language, though still marked by occasional archaisms, is very nearly classical Sanskrit, are the well-known Upaniṣads, also termed Vedānta 'End of the Veda', both in the literal sense of their standing at the very end of Vedic composition and figuratively as reflecting the highest point to which Vedic speculation and mystic thought had attained.

All this vast literature that is embraced under the name Veda (in the broadest application of the term) is referred to as *Śruti* or 'What is heard', *i.e.,* what has been heard in the sense of communicated orally to the ancient seers by divine inspiration and thereafter transmitted orally from generation to generation; loosely, then, 'revelation'. The subsequent literature is called *Smṛti* 'What is remembered', *i.e.,* passed on from teacher to pupil, hence 'authoritative tradition'. The earliest *Smṛti* literature consists of separate manuals called *sūtras,* which treat of six subjects regarded as essential for the performance of the Vedic ceremonies, understanding the hymns and reciting them correctly. These subjects are: 1. *Kalpa* or Religious Practice, 2. *Śikṣā* or Phonetics, 3. *Chandas* or Metre, 4. *Nirukta* or Exposition (of difficult or rare Vedic words), 5. *Vyākaraṇa* or Grammar, held to be essential for unerring analysis of the language of the hymns, and 6. *Jyotiṣa* or Astronomy, for determining the correct and auspicious time for the performance of the sacrificial acts. Collectively they are known as the Six

Vedāṅgas 'Limbs of the Veda', by which are probably meant not limbs as mere branches or appendages, but rather limbs as essential parts of the body of the Veda, as are the arms and legs to the human body.

A word needs to be said here regarding the format of the manuals called *sūtras,*[2] as much subsequent literature, especially that of a technical character, is modelled on them. *Sūtras* are manuals on a particular subject composed with the greatest economy of words imaginable, only the absolutely basic ideas being actually expressed, the remainder implied. A telegram is the closest analogy, if it were extended to the communication of an entire department of knowledge, but even a tersely worded telegram would be a prolix and wordy document compared to a *sūtra.* Thus, verbs and all adornment are freely omitted, leaving the barest skeleton to convey the essential sense and serve as a thread in the memory to the full expression of the subject.

Occupying a dominant place in Sanskrit literature are the two great epic poems, the Mahābhārata and the Rāmāyaṇa. Although both are written in the classical language, the former is in a simpler, more popular style, while the latter is on a loftier plane, with a good deal of ornamentation and rhetorical figure, the very beginnings of a tendency that continued to be developed and, in the much later literature, carried at times to considerable extreme. The Mahābhārata is an immensely long work, in its complete extent filling out an entire bookshelf, whereas the Rāmāyaṇa is approximately equivalent to the Iliad and Odyssey of Homer combined. Although Indian tradition attributes it to a single author, the Mahābhārata is clearly the product of many authors of many different times, whose separate works are often strung rather loosely together, to contribute in one way or another to the basic theme of the work, *i.e.,* the great war between the Kauravas and the Pāṇḍavas. 'Mahābhārata' is a somewhat abbreviated name for the 'Great [War] of the Bhāratas', the line of kings descended from Bharata, specifically the Kauravas and Pāṇḍavas, sons of the two brothers Dhṛtarāṣṭra and Pāṇḍu. Among the numerous episodes that are told incidentally to the main story is the Bhagavadgītā or 'Song of the Blessed One', a sort of dialog between the Pāṇḍava warrior Arjuna and his charioteer Kṛṣṇa, who is an incarnation of the god Viṣṇu. This dialog takes place just as the two opposing armies are about to clash in battle, whereupon Arjuna becomes dismayed at the thought of slaying his kinsmen. This powerful work, which has been translated countless times and subjected to endless sectarian and scholarly

---

[2]Although there is a wide divergence of opinion on the sense originally intended by the application of the word *sūtra,* literally 'thread', to these manuals, very probably they were called 'threads' simply because, just as the threads, both the vertical and the horizontal, constitute the entire cloth, so do the phrases of which these manuals consist also constitute an entire department of knowledge.

interpretations, has become virtually the bible of modern Hinduism and furnishes spiritual inspiration and solace to millions of Hindus. Another famous episode is the story of Nala and Damayantī, which for the past 150 years or so has served as the first connected text for beginning students in Sanskrit in most Western countries because of its relative simplicity and intrinsic charm.

The Rāmāyaṇa or 'Adventures of Rāma', on the other hand, is the work of an individual author named Vālmīki. As its title indicates, it is a kind of biographical account of the hero Rāma, in great part of his adventures in the Daṇḍaka Forest, where he was obliged to spend an exile of fourteen years, the abduction of his wife Sītā by the demon Rāvaṇa, her ultimate rescue by Rāma with the help of the monkey king Hanumat, and Rāma's restoration to the throne of Ayodhyā. All these and the many other adventures of Rāma and Sītā related in Vālmīki's Rāmāyaṇa are intimately familiar to every Hindu,[3] for whom they have incalculable and unending appeal, and it is scarcely necessary to add that Rāma is universally viewed as the ideal of heroic man and devoted husband, the embodiment of all virtues, as Sītā is of all the most superlative womanly qualities.

Indians are among the best storytellers in the world, and even in early post-Christian times the fame of their beast fable literature had, so tradition has it, come to the ears of the Persian king Khusrū Anūshīrvān, who dispatched to India a physician named Burzūye to procure the collection, apparently called the Pañcatantra, and translate it into medieval Persian (Pahlavī). Burzūye carried out this mission, but unfortunately his translation has not come down to us. Such was its popularity, however, that it was turned into Arabic in the eighth century by the well-known Persian writer Ibn al-Muqaffaʻ. As the Arabic language had by this time been spread from Spain to Persia, the Kalīla wa-Dimnah, as the Pañcatantra was now called, became so widely known that it was translated into the principal languages of that immense area. Through the medium of a Latin version entitled Directorium Vitae Humanae, made from a Hebrew translation of the Arabic (!), these Indian fables finally came to Europe, whence, from an Italian translation of the Latin, they were put into English by Sir Thomas North in 1570. But the story of their migrations does not end with their rendition into English: in due course, by one route or another, these fables, which, in spite of many alterations as they proceeded from translation to translation, remained essentially the same, came to practically every country in the world and, by a full circle, through a later Persian adaptation, they were translated into various languages of India!

---

[3]Perhaps in some measure they are even better known from their retelling in the early Hindī work Rām Carit Mānas 'Lake of Deeds of Rāma' of Tulasi Dās.

The Paññcatantra is a collection of stories in which animals play the role of human beings, as in the fables of Aesop. Apart from this, however, there is scarcely any similarity between them, and the relationship between Aesop's fables and those of the Paññcatantra, if indeed it is other than fortuitous, has never been convincingly set out. The purpose of the Paññcatantra is to teach statecraft, specifically to the dissolute sons of a certain ancient Indian monarch. The fables are set within a simple frame-story, in which a learned Brahman Viṣṇuśarman undertakes to inculcate in these misbehaving princes the sort of behavior at home and abroad that is appropriate to them in the administration of the affairs of the kingdom. He gathers them together on the roof of the palace and relates the stories which make up the collection of five books. The stories are intricately imboxed, one leading into another and that into yet another in a seemingly endless train, so that it is oftentimes difficult to keep the thread of a particular story because of the interposition of subsidiary stories. The original Paññcatantra, which was translated into Pahlavī by Burzūye, is no longer extant, but there are various works bearing the title Paññcatantra which are ultimately derived from it via separate lines of transmission, some of which have become conflated with one another over the centuries. There are also reworkings of the old Paññcatantra material with additions from other similar story collections. Perhaps the best known of these is the Hitopadeśa 'Instruction in Welfare', to which, like the story of Nala and Damayantī, beginning Sanskrit students are generally subjected. The fables in all these derivative versions are, on the whole, composed in fairly simple, straightforward Sanskrit, and it is doubtlessly a source of some comfort to young students in their struggle to acquire the elements of the language to have before them the model of untutored beasts of the forest conversing with one another in fluid Sanskrit!

It is unfortunate that many Western students of Sanskrit do not proceed sufficiently far in their studies to read a play, as the plays are undoubtedly among the fairest gems of Sanskrit literature. The greatness of a Sanskrit play lies, however, not so much in the cleverness or originality of the plot, which is oftentimes based on a familiar episode in one of the epics, but rather in the beauty of the language, the imagery and skillfulness of the ornamentation, the delineation of the characters and such matters a full appreciation of which is not easily attainable in an ordinary university course of two years.

Perhaps the best known Sanskrit play, both in India and the West, is Kālidāsa's Abhijñānaśakuntala 'Śakuntalā [Recognized] through the Signet Ring', in English usually called simply Śakuntalā after the name of the heroine. This play, the story of which was not invented by Kālidāsa, but is found with variations in the Mahābhārata and the Padmapurāṇa, won the high praise of the German poets Goethe and Schiller. The story has several times been made the basis of an opera libretto, although none of these operas seems to have achieved lasting success.[4] Much less widely known outside India, though in many ways far more accessible to Western taste, is Śūdraka's Mṛcchakaṭika 'The Little Clay Cart', so named from an incident in Act Six. Revolving around the love of the impoverished Brahman Cārudatta for the beautiful courtesan Vasantasenā, the Mṛcchakaṭika is replete with human touches and a universal realism that transport it beyond the purely Indian milieu in which it is set.

Although, as indeed with most Indian authors, it is practically impossible to assign dates to Sanskrit dramatists, there is one whose date is fairly accurately known. He is Harṣa or more fully Harṣavardhana, a king who ruled the greater part of northern India in the seventh century A.D. Though he engaged in wars in the course of the expansion of his kingdom, he was yet a man of letters and an excellent poet. Three plays have come down under his name: the Ratnāvalī ('The Necklace'), Nāgānanda ('The Serpent's Joy') and the Priyadarśikā. The last is the oldest Sanskrit play, which, like Hamlet, contains a play within a play. The Nāgānanda is Buddhist in character and may be the very play by Harṣa which the Chinese Buddhist pilgrim Houen Tsang says he witnessed.

A play entirely devoted to political intrigue is Viśākhadatta's Mudrārākṣasa 'The Drama of Rākṣasa and the Signet Ring', the central figure in which is Cāṇakya, the prime minister of Candragupta Maurya, the well-known king who, after the death of Alexander the Great, united most of northern India under his rule. In the consolidation and administration of this enormous kingdom he was assisted by this Machiavellian minister, who is thought to be identical with the author of a cunning work on statecraft called the Arthaśāstra 'Treatise on Polity'.

Second only to Kālidāsa is Bhavabhūti, who lived about a century after King Harṣa. Bhavabhūti wrote two plays dealing with Rāma. The one called Uttararāmacarita concerns Rāma's activities following his return to Ayodhyā and hence the name, which means 'The Later Life of Rāma'. The other is entitled Mahāvīracarita 'The Life of the Great Hero'. Perhaps, however, his most remarkable play is the Mālatīmādhava 'The Drama of Mālatī and Mādhava', the plot of which has a very familiar ring, as the heroine Mālatī is compelled to marry someone she does not love, but is united with her true love by a ruse.

Next to Aśvaghoṣa, who possibly flourished in the second century B.C. and of whose plays only fragments have been preserved, the earliest Sanskrit dramatist was Bhāsa. Although Bhāsa's name was celebrated from ancient times, however, it was generally accepted that all his compositions had been

---

[4]The first of these operas was by the conductor-composer Felix Weingartner in 1884. More recent are those by the pianist Ignacy Jan Paderewski and Franco Alfano, nowadays remembered chiefly for his having completed Puccini's *Turandot*.

irretrievably lost. But about 80 years ago twelve complete plays and a fragmentary play were discovered, which are believed by many to be the works of Bhāsa. The fragment called Daridracārudatta 'The Drama about Poor Cārudatta', consisting of but four acts, seems to have furnished the material for Śūdraka's Mṛcchakaṭika.

A very voluminous branch of Sanskrit literature is constituted by the Purāṇas, a generic name for a group of works traditionally numbering eighteen, but actually far exceeding that number, especially if included are the so-called Upapurāṇas 'Subsidiary (or 'Minor') Purāṇas'. Sometimes referred to as the 'Fifth Veda', they have in fact affiliations to the Mahābhārata and other works. So varied in content and so enormous in bulk are the Purāṇas that it is hard to characterize or define them. According to a persistently prevalent notion, they are supposed to deal with five subjects, *viz.*, primary and secondary creation, genealogy, the periods of time ruled over by the Manus *(Manvantaras)* and history. But this fivefold subject matter, generally speaking, can scarcely be said to dominate any of the Purāṇas. Some of them, like the Agnipurāṇa, are virtually encyclopedias and as such treat of everything imaginable. They are often termed sectarian treatises, *i.e.,* devoted to the worship of Viṣṇu or Śiva, but it cannot be said that every Purāṇa is wholly devoted to the one or the other; for sometimes their loyalty is mixed, and sometimes a Purāṇa may even be non-sectarian.

Held in particular veneration is the Bhāgavatapurāṇa ('the Purāṇa concerning the Blessed One', *i.e.,* Viṣṇu) and especially its tenth chapter which recounts in minutest detail the life of Kṛṣṇa, the incarnation which Viṣṇu assumes in the Bhagavadgītā as Arjuna's charioteer.

There are in the Purāṇas many geographical references and lists of kings, but scholars are far from agreed on their trustworthiness and value. But whatever may be said about these bewilderingly diverse and immense works, there is no doubt that they do contain much that is intrinsically interesting, and all-in-all they tell us a great deal about Hinduism on the more popular level. Their style is in general much like that of the Mahābhārata, straightforward and unadorned, unmarked by the rigid adherence to grammatical rule that is the norm of the classical language.

In sharp contrast to this is the highly ornate poetry of later Sanskrit, called *kāvya,* literally 'the work of a poet (*kavi*)'. In its developed form a *kāvya* is notable, among other things, for its rhetorical figures, polished phraseology, elaborate descriptions, the sonority of its verses, in general for its lofty, courtly style of composition. The plots, which are usually founded on material contained in the Mahābhārata and Rāmāyaṇa, are worked out in a profusion of detail. Several of these *kāvyas* have attained an especially revered status for their perfection and are styled *mahākāvyas* 'great *kāvyas'.* Often regarded as the greatest of the *mahākāvyas* are the Kumārasambhava ('Birth of Kumāra', *i.e.,* Skanda, the war god) and the Raghuvaṃśa ('The

Family of Raghu', *i.e.*, the progenitor of Rāma), both by the renowned Kālidāsa, author of the play about Śakuntalā. Also by Kālidāsa is a short *kāvya,* a lyrical poem entitled Meghadūta ('Cloud Messenger'), by some Indian commentators termed a *mahākāvya* in spite of its brevity and simplicity of plot. The story concerns a certain demigod or *yakṣa,* as he is termed, who for some unspecified dereliction of duty to his overlord Kubera is compelled to leave his domain in the Himālayas and live for a year in the mountains of central India in separation from his wife. At the onset of the rainy season, a time when Indian husbands are reputed to be particularly distraught to be away from their wives, this pathetic *yakṣa* pours forth his plight to a low-hanging cloud which he asks to deliver a message to his wife at the end of its long voyage northward toward the Himālayas. The many sights on the cloud's way are charmingly described and so also the route it is to follow in reaching the *yakṣa's* abode. This short poem is in the opinion of many one of the classics of world literature.

Apart from works of literary character and merit, there are in Sanskrit numerous treatises on technical subjects. Some of these technical treatises, as for example, those concerned with astronomy and mathematics, grew out of the needs of the Vedic sacrifice, which, especially in its later extreme complexity, involved an accurate knowledge of celestial phenomena for determining the precise time of the sacrifice, as well as mathematical knowledge for the measurement and construction of the altar.

The study of grammar too, ultimately owes its origin to the Veda, as it arose from the necessity of analyzing correctly and minutely the words of the Vedic hymns, the mode of construction of the words, the phonetic changes they underwent in combination and the relationship expressed by their varying endings -- in short the rationale of the language in which the hymns were composed. Most remarkable is the grammatical manual of Pāṇini called Aṣṭādhyāyī ('The Eight Chapters'), a work of the fifth century B.C., if not earlier. Composed in the *sūtra* style and hence incomprehensible without a commentary, the Aṣṭādhyāyī is a work of truly miraculous ingenuity: in hardly more than 40 pages when printed in a modern edition, it provides an analysis of the entire structure of the Sanskrit language. This feat is accomplished by the adoption of a meta-language of formulaic words, special uses of the grammatical cases and yet other devices. Pāṇini's grammar is a reflection of the profound and subtle grammatical activity of ancient India, which far exceeded that of any other nation of ancient and medieval times.

Of exceptional importance are the manuals called *dharmaśāstras,* which prescribe in detail the religious and moral conduct that devolves upon the devout Hindu. Best known is the Mānavadharmaśāstra, in English generally called the 'Law Book of Manu', a work of endless fascination and interest in its coverage not only of purely religious observances and customs, but also of the duties of a king, the origin of the world and the four castes, the four ages of the world and the doctrine of transmigration with its concomitant, the law of *karman.* [5]

There are six great Indian philosophical systems, and an enormous literature has sprung up around them, partly in the form of commentaries and subcommentaries on their fundamental texts and partly in the form of relatively independent treatises. Particularly voluminous is the literature that concerns the Vedānta system, due in large measure to the many diverse interpretations that are accorded to its principal doctrine, *i.e.,* the relationship of the individual soul or self, called *ātman,* to the absolute cosmic principle or *brahman.* These philosophical systems have in varying degrees permeated Indian thought through the course of many centuries, and allusions to them, especially to the Vedānta, Sāṃkhya and Yoga, are ubiquitous in Sanskrit literature.

Finally, mention may be made of the Sanskrit medical treatises, not only for the intrinsic interest attaching to them, but for their great value to the study of comparative medicine. A characteristic doctrine, which runs through all these compendia and is generally held to this day by Hindu physicians (*vaidyas*), is that of the three *dhātus* 'elements' of the body, *i.e.,* wind, bile and phlegm, which, when in equilibrium, are responsible for the body's health, but are otherwise the cause of illness. Remarkably similar is the doctrine of the four humors in the teaching of Greek medicine, which prevailed in the West until just a few hundred years ago and is responsible for the characterization of the differing temperaments as sanguine, melancholic, choleric and phlegmatic due to the prevalence of the humors blood, black bile, yellow bile and phlegm respectively. Striking in the Indian treatises is the use of the term *madhuprameha* 'honey(-like) *or* saccharine urine' as applied to diabetes, a significant symptom of the disease unrecognized outside India until recent times.

---

[5] *Karman* (or *karma* without 'n' in less scientific form) literally means 'action', but in its religious usage 'action' plus the 're-action' or consequence which every action is believed to involve. The consequence of one's actions may be experienced immediately or later in life or, if sufficiently pervasive, may only be realized in a subsequent birth of the individual's soul. Thus the 'law of *karman'* is closely connected with the soul's transmigration, and a person's present lot is the consequence of accumulated prior *karman.*

The System of Writing

The script in which Sanskrit is usually written and printed nowadays is called Devanāgarī, a name which means the 'Nāgarī Script of the Gods' or, what is nearly the same thing, the 'Divine Nāgarī Script'.[1] It has been a custom in India from time immemorial to attribute a divine origin to writing, and this is reflected in the names of other Indian scripts too. Thus, the oldest script of all the many in India, apart from the writing system employed by the people of the Ancient Indus Valley civilization, is known as Brāhmī, which means the 'Script of Brahmā', *i.e.,* the script emanating from or bestowed by Brahmā, the god of creation in the Hindu triad of Brahmā, Viṣṇu and Śiva, who embody the great cosmic forces of creation, continuity and dissolution. Another example is the Nandināgarī, the 'Nāgarī Script of Nandi', a rather ambiguous name, since Nandi ('The Gladdener') is a designation of both Viṣṇu and Śiva.

In addition to the Devanāgarī script Sanskrit books are sometimes also printed in the scripts of India's regional languages, Bengali and Malayāḷam probably being the most frequently used. Throughout the centuries, moreover, practically all of India's hundreds of scripts have been used for the writing of Sanskrit manuscripts. But during the course of the past hundred years or so the tendency has become more and more deeply rooted to use Devanāgarī, as though it were a kind of pan-Indian script. This is due in great part to the fact that several of the most widespread regional languages are written in Devanāgarī, as, for example, Marāṭhī and Hindī. But in the manuscriptal tradition too, in spite of the diversity of scripts employed in the transmission of Sanskrit texts, the Devanāgarī has probably been the most predominant.

Although these numerous scripts differ greatly from one another in their outward appearance, all of them are ultimately traceable back to the Brāhmī script mentioned above, the earliest examples of which belong to the fourth century B.C. The Brāhmī script may be fittingly likened to a great banyan tree from whose central stem have been engendered numerous subsidiary trees, which, in the course of many years, have attained a life of their own, some entirely separated from their venerable parent and flourishing in their independent growth.

As a lineal descendent of the old Brāhmī, the Devanāgarī seems first to have attained separate and independent status at least as early as the seventh

---

[1]It is also often more simply called Nāgarī, really the earlier name before the divinizing element Deva- 'god' was prefixed; for further details, *v.* Walter H. Maurer 'On the Name Devanāgarī' in *Journal of the American Oriental Society* Vol. 91, No. 6 (1976), pp. 101-104.

century A.D., from which has been preserved a copperplate inscription of King Dantidurga of the Rāṣṭrakūṭa dynasty of southern Mahārāṣṭra.

Like all the descendants of Brāhmī, the Devanāgarī is essentially a syllabic script. By this is meant that the writing unit is the syllable as opposed to the minimal sounds (consonants and vowels) into which words may be resolved. The Devanāgarī script consists of signs for 13 vowels (and diphthongs) and 33 consonants, which, together with two special signs, make a total of 48. Each of the 33 consonant signs stands for a consonant with the vowel *-a* following it, *e.g.* न (*na*), ग (*ga*), द (*da*), ब (*ba*), म (*ma*), etc. If a vowel other than *-a* is to be expressed, the *-a* is cancelled by the writing in of the appropriate vowel sign, *e.g.* कि (*ki*), की (*kī*), कु (*ku*), कू (*kū*), etc. Thus, a word written in Devanāgarī consists of a series of signs each of which is a *syllable, i.e.,* either a vowel (or diphthong) or a consonant with an inherent *-a* (or with another vowel specifically indicated, which cancels out the *-a*). For example the word *nagarī* (नगरी) 'city' is composed of three syllables *na-ga-rī*, the first two of which are written with the 'naked' signs न (*na*) and ग (*ga*), whereas *-rī*, being vocalized with a vowel other than *-a*, must have the vowel sign for *-ī* written in, thus cancelling out the inherent *-a* of the sign र (*ra*).

The Consonants

In learning Devanāgarī it is best to start with the consonants, then learn the subsidiary signs for the vowels other than *-a*, and lastly the 13 vowel signs that are used when the vowels form syllables by themselves, *i.e.,* when not following a consonant. In reciting the sounds of the Devanāgarī and also for pedagogical purposes, the consonants are traditionally arranged in various groups and sub-groups, as will become clear subsequently. The first and largest group of consonants is that called 'stops' or 'mutes' by Western grammarians. These are sounds, like English *d* or *b*, which involve a momentary stopping of the breath when produced. This stopping of the breath can be simply enough demonstrated if an attempt is made to pronounce a *d* or *b* without any vowel following. The ancient Sanskrit grammarians termed these sounds 'touched sounds', because they are made by some sort of touching, whether due to contact between the tongue and some point in the mouth or due to bringing the lips together. With remarkable astuteness they arranged each group of stops that are articulated at the same point according to the progression of their articulation from the point farthest back on the roof of the mouth (or soft palate) to that farthest forward, *i.e.,* the lips. Within each group of stops or touched sounds there is a further arrangement which does not vary from one group to another, but a consideration of this will become clearer as the consonants of each group are discussed. Here below is a tabulation of the five groups of stops, in which the value of each syllabic sign of the Devanāgarī is given in standard transliteration:

Stops or 'Touched Sounds' of Sanskrit

1. Gutturals	*ka*	*kha*	*ga*	*gha*	*ṅa* [2]
2. Palatals	*ca*	*cha*	*ja*	*jha*	*ña* [2]
3. Cerebrals	*ṭa*	*ṭha*	*ḍa*	*ḍha*	*ṇa* [2]
4. Dentals	*ta*	*tha*	*da*	*dha*	*na* [2]
5. Labials	*pa*	*pha*	*ba*	*bha*	*ma* [2]

The Devanāgarī equivalents of these sounds will be given after the whole system of consonants has been surveyed and the pronunciation of each explained.

1. *The Gutturals*

The word 'guttural' is derived from Latin *gutturālis* 'pertaining to the throat (*guttur*)', and it is just a translation of the Sanskrit term *kaṇṭhya* used by the Indian grammarians to describe the first series of touched sounds articulated rather far back in the mouth, in the throat, as it were. They are produced by raising the back-middle of the tongue so as to touch the roof of the mouth, more precisely the soft portion or soft palate that lies behind the bony vault, as shown in the illustration:

[2] The sounds *ṅa, ña, ṇa, na* and *ma,* called 'nasals', are strictly not stops, because there is no stoppage of breath involved in their production.

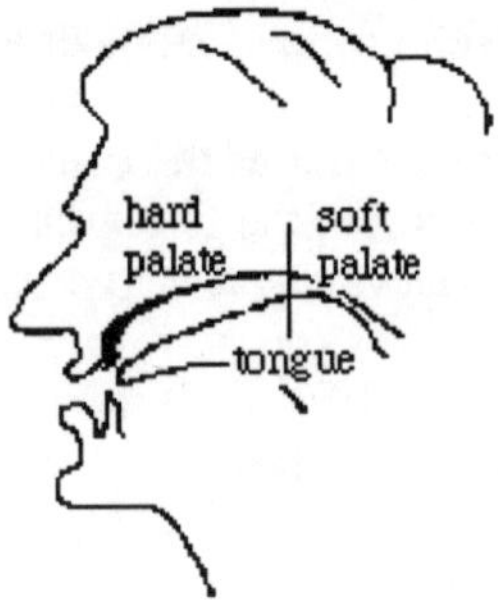

The letters *k* and *g* in English, as in the words *sky* and *go,* are pronounced identically to the Sanskrit consonants *k* and *g* (of *ka* and *ga*), but *c* in English is often also pronounced in the same way as *k* (in s*k*y), as exemplified by English s*c*um. The same sound appears again as *k* in s*k*ull. The spelling of English, where different *written* sounds may in fact represent the same *spoken* sounds, as in these examples, is unfortunately very unhelpful to the student.

The second consonant in the guttural series, *kh*, is the same as *k*, except that there is a clearly audible breath immediately following the *k*, as indicated in the transliteration by the *h*. Whenever a *k* (or *c* pronounced like *k*!) *begins* a word in English, it too, is accompanied by this rather noticeable breath or aspiration. The difference between English and Sanskrit in this matter is that *the aspiration is not indicated in written English*, where its presence is not really significant, no words being distinguished from each other by the presence or absence of this seemingly unimportant breath. But in Sanskrit many words are distinguished from each other by the contrast of aspiration and non-aspiration. For example, *khala* "threshing-floor' and *kala* 'indistinct'.

Since aspiration of consonants, though occurring in spoken English under certain conditions, is not a meaningful phenomenon of which we are normally aware (except when we study Sanskrit!), it will be instructive to describe a simple test for determining the occurrence or absence of this elusive breath. If a sheet of paper is held close to the mouth and the word *kayak* is uttered, emphatically if possible, it will be noticed that the paper is caused to flutter by the breath following the initial *k*. But when *sky* or *skull* is similarly pronounced against the paper, there is no disturbance of the paper at all.

The fourth consonant in the guttural series, *i.e., gh* (of *gha*) bears the same relation to *g* (of *ga*) as *kh* to *k*. It is, then, a *g* with accompanying aspiration. Unfortunately, the sound represented by this *gh* does not occur in

English[3], except for a suggestion of it in compound words like *dog-house* or *log-house*, if the *g* and *h* are pronounced with particular emphasis and exaggeration. This can best be practiced by first pronouncing *dog-house* or *log-house* in the normal way, then repeating it with some dwelling on the *g* and articulating the *h* rather explosively, and after this dropping off the *do-* or *lo-* and saying *ghouse*! In this third, but not yet final attempt care must be taken not to insert a slight vowel-fragment between *g* and *h*: the two sounds must be brought together and pronounced as *one*, *i.e.*, a *g* with a breath. As if all these lingual acrobatics were insufficient to dull the ardor of the most adventuresome beginner, an attempt must now be made to pronounce only *gh* without *-ouse*!

The last sound in the guttural series, *i.e.*, *ṅ* (or *ṅa*), is common enough in English. It is the same as the *n* in *finger* or *tank*, but it should be observed that not every *n* in English, when followed by *g* is pronounced like the Sanskrit *ṅ*. The *n* in *tangible*, for example, is not so pronounced.

While all the sounds in the guttural series are produced by touching the tongue to the soft palate, there is a difference between the way *k* and *kh* are made as compared with *g*, *gh* and *ṅ*. The last three are all accompanied by a tensing of the vocal cords, which are thereby caused to vibrate as the breath passes between them. This tension is technically termed 'voice', and sounds that are accompanied by voice are called 'voiced' sounds. In the case of the nasals (appended to all the classes of stops), like *ṅ*, the voice is made to resonate in the nasal cavity instead of issuing through the mouth. The vibration that accompanies the voiced sounds can be felt by lightly touching the Adam's Apple. But in performing this test care must be taken *not* to pronounce a vowel with the *g*, *gh* or *ṅ*, as vowels are by nature voiced.

It was stated above that in each of the five series of stops or touched sounds, the sounds are arranged according to the same pattern, As should now have become clear, it is meant by this that in each series of stops (produced at the same point of contact) the first two sounds are invariably voiceless and the remaining three voiced. Further, the first and third of each series is without aspiration, *i.e.*, unaspirated, while the second and fourth are the corresponding aspirated sounds. Finally the fifth is the nasal of the particular class. In view of the this identical arrangement within each of the five series, the vertical rows may be captioned or labelled in the following way:

---

[3]A *gh* does occur in very many English words, as, for example, *ghost*, *through*, *though*, *tough*, but the divergent sounds which these spellings with *gh* represent have nothing to do with the aspirated *gh* in Sanskrit.

Voiceless		Voiced		
Unaspirated	Aspirated	Unaspirated	Aspirated	Nasal
k(a)	*kh(a)*	*g(a)*	*gh(a)*	*ṅ(a)*

2. *The Palatals*

In accordance with this scheme the palatals may be presented as follows:

Voiceless		Voiced		
Unaspirated	Aspirated	Unaspirated	Aspirated	Nasal
ca	*cha*	*ja*	*jha*	*ña*

This series is produced by raising the forepart, but not the tip, of the tongue toward the *hard palate*, *i.e.*, the bony arch of the mouth.

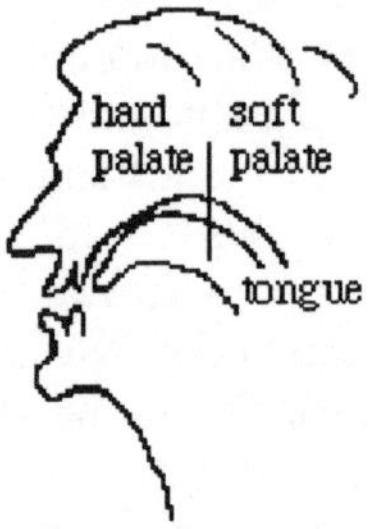

Practically speaking, the unaspirated *c* (of *ca*) is pronounced like the *ch* of English *church* and, almost needless to say, the aspirated counterpart *ch* (of *cha*) is the same sound accompanied by a strong release of breath. This aspirated *ch* occurs in English only in emphatically and emotionally articulated speech, often where contrast between two things is involved, as in 'Bring me the *chair* (pronounced as though written *ch-hair*), not the stool !' It is important to note that the use of *c* in the transliteration of the unaspirated consonant is purely a convention that has nothing to do with English spelling, as English *c* is never pronounced like the *ch* in *church*. This practice of using *c* for the unaspirated sound is due to the fact that, *h* being everywhere utilized in the system of transliteration to mark an aspiration, the unaspirated counterpart of *cha* logically has to be represented by the same sign without *h*.

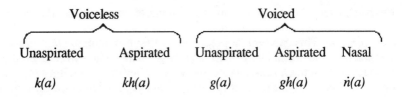

Formerly and even nowadays in the transliteration of the modern vernaculars, however, *ch* and *chh* (!) are often used instead of *c* and *ch*.

The voiced sound *j* (of *ja*) is close to English *j* of *jolly* or the *dg* of *hedge*. Care must be taken to avoid the tendency, common among beginning students, to pronounce the *j* of French *jour*.

The aspirated *jh* is a fairly rare sound in Sanskrit, and one need not therefore expend too great an effort in trying to produce it. Just as in the case of the aspirated voiced sounds in all the series, the sound *jh* is found in English only at word junctures or junctures between the members of compounds, where the last sound of the first word ends in a *j*-sound (however it may be written!) and the next begins with *h*. It will be remembered that *dog-house* and *log-house* served approximately for Sanskrit *gh*; for *jh* perhaps *hedge-hog* may be used. Bear in mind theat the *-dge* is sounded like the *j* in *jolly* .

The palatal nasal *ñ* (of *ña*) is approximated by the *n* in English *pinch* or any *n* followed by *ch*, the nasal in this case being naturally adapted or assimilated to the class of *ch* and articulated at the same point.

3. *The Cerebrals*

Voiceless		Voiced		
Unaspirated	Aspirated	Unaspirated	Aspirated	Nasal
ṭa	*ṭha*	*ḍa*	*ḍha*	*ṇa*

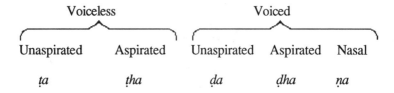

The strange name applied to this important and very distinctively Indian class of sounds requires some explanation. 'Cerebral' means 'pertaining to the brain' (from Latin *cerebrum* 'brain'), but it is really an erroneous translation of the indigenous technical term *mūrdhanya*, literally 'pertaining to the highest point (of the mouth)', applied to this class of sounds as being produced by touching the peak of the mouth with the tip of the tongue. But the Sanskrit word *mūrdhan*, from which *mūrdhanya* is derived, in ordinary parlance happens to mean also 'head', and this apparently gave rise to the notion that the sounds designated *mūrdhanya* were 'head-sounds', and 'cerebral' is but a further misinterpretation of this misconception. An accurate equivalent of the Sanskrit *mūrdhanya* would be 'cacuminal', from Latin *cacūmen* 'peak, highest point', but though this term has been occasionally suggested, it has never won general acceptance. Instead of cerebrals, these sounds are very often called 'linguals' in grammars, but this rather persistent substitute is to be avoided, as 'lingual' simply means 'pertaining to the tongue' (Latin *lingua*), which, being applicable to nearly all sounds in the language, is hardly a desirable substitute for the older term 'cerebrals'. Yet another term in fairly common use is 'retroflex', literally 'turned back' with reference to the fact that the tongue-tip is slightly turned back on itself as it touches the roof of the mouth. This term is perhaps the most suitable of the various terms that are used to name this class of consonants, and it might have been adopted here except for the fact that it is in much less general use than 'cerebral'.

Although the cerebrals are formed, as just stated, by a slightly retroflex action of the tongue-tip as it touches the roof of the mouth -- strictly speaking, the area well above the gum-ridge (the 'alveolar ridge') extending over the upper teeth -- an acceptable approximation to these difficult sounds are the ordinary *t* 's and *d* 's of American English, which are produced by the tongue-tip against the gum-ridge, *i.e.,* on a slightly lower point of contact. In fact, English *t* 's and *d* 's sound precisely like cerebrals to an Indian, who, in taking over into any vernacular language English words like *ticket* or *dumb*, represents them invariably, both in pronunciation and writing, with cerebrals. Conversely, *in English as spoken by Indians* almost every *t* and *d* is spoken as a cerebral, the former usually also without the aspiration that generally accompanies initial voiceless sounds in English.

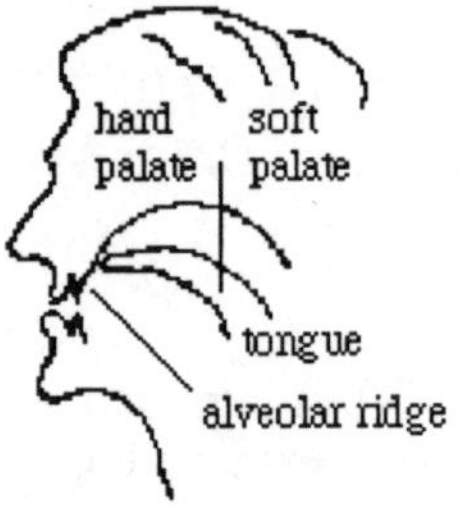

Thus, then, a fairly accurate rendition of the cerebral series by an English speaker is easily attained, the only exception being the voiced aspirate *ḍh*, which, as with the voiced aspirates of all the series of stops, is absent in English. In practicing these sounds the following points must be borne in mind. The aspirated *ṭh* (of *ṭha*) is like any English *t* that begins a word, for example, *tub*. But this *ṭh* must not be associated in any way with the *th* of English *thing* or *this*; the *h* in the transliteration *ṭh* is simply a mark of aspiration as with *kh* and *ch* of the guttural and palatal series. While the *aspirated ṭh* is not difficult to produce, the *unaspirated ṭ* (of *ṭa*) requires the same attention as the *unaspirated* sounds described so far, *viz.*, *kh*, *ch* (and yet to be described: *th* and *ph*!). In the discussion of *kh*, the aspirated counterpart of *k*, it was pointed out that when a *s-* precedes English *k* (or *c* when pronounced as *k*!), the *k* is without aspiration. Thus, the unaspirated sound of Sanskrit *k* may be produced by practicing the English words s*k*ull and s*c*um without the initial *s*-, using the paper-test suggested on p. 16. Unfortunately, there are no similar practice-words in English to help in pronouncing the cerebral *ṭ*, since an English *t* following *s*- is not pronounced with the tongue in the same position as when *t* comes first in a word. It might be helpful to compare the remarks made on p. 22 in the discussion of the voiceless dentals and similarly the remarks concerning the voiceless labials on p. 23.

The voiced *ḍ* (of *ḍa*) is close to any English *d* beginning a word, for example, *dull* or *dub*.The aspirated *ḍh* (of *ḍha*) is approximately to be heard in *mud-house*, which should be practised as indicated for *gh* with the illustrative words *dog-house* and *log-house*.

The nasal *ṇ* (in *ṇa*) is similar to an *n* at the beginning of a word in English, but, as with all the cerebrals, with the tongue-tip somewhat higher than in English and slightly retroflexed. In English *n*, however, is less close to cerebral *ṇ* than are initial *t*, *th* and *d* to their cerebral counterparts.

4. *The Dentals*

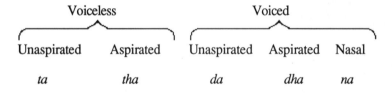

Voiceless		Voiced		
Unaspirated	Aspirated	Unaspirated	Aspirated	Nasal
ta	*tha*	*da*	*dha*	*na*

Notice that the transliteration of the dentals differs from that of the cerebrals in the lack of the subscript dot, but it should not be assumed, therefore, that the dentals are to be exactly equated with English sounds written *t*, *th*, etc. The fact of the matter is that true dentals are scarcely to be found in standard English. It was amply shown above that English *t* 's and *d* 's are really alveolar sounds, close to the Sanskrit cerebrals. The dentals, on the other hand, must be pronounced by placing the tongue-tip *almost between the teeth*, *i.e*, almost in the same position as for English *th* in *thing* or *this* The *th* in these words (voiceless in *thing* and voiced in *this*) is a *true interdental* sound, *i.e.*, produced by placing the tongue between the teeth.

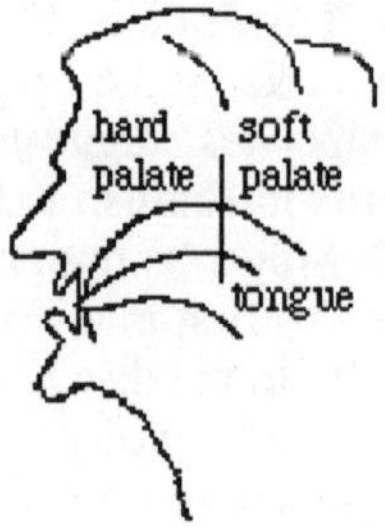

The unaspirated *t* (of *ta*) is approximately like the *t* of English *stub*, or any *t* preceded by an *s*. This is due to the fact that English *s* is a dental sound and a *t* immediately following *s* is articulated also at the teeth. But when *tub* is pronounced, the tongue-tip moves into the alveolar position. Taking these points into consideration, it is best for the student to learn the aspirated *th* by continuing to use *stub* as his guide, but forcing out a breath after the *t*, as might be done when the word is said with great emphasis: *st-h-ub*. Then an effort must be made to say the sound in isolation.

The voiced *d* (of *da*) can probably best be practised by saying a *d* with the tongue-tip between the teeth and similarly with *dh* (of *dha*), using *mud-house* as previously described and also *n* (of *na*).

5. *The Labials*

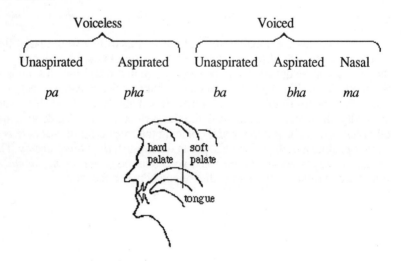

Voiceless		Voiced		
Unaspirated	Aspirated	Unaspirated	Aspirated	Nasal
pa	*pha*	*ba*	*bha*	*ma*

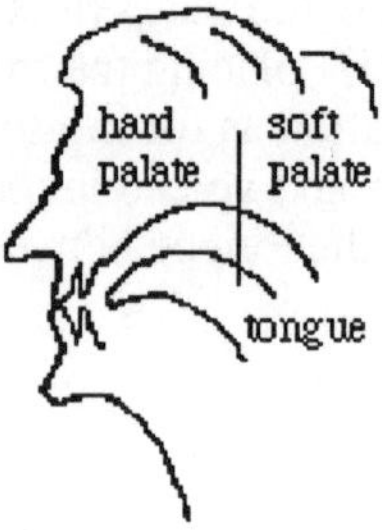

As the name indicates, the labials are lip-sounds, *i.e.,* sounds that are produced by bringing the lips together. The sounds *b* (of *ba*) and *m* (of *ma*) are identical to English *b* and *m* in *bumble* and *mumbo*, *i.e.,* like *b* or *m*.[4] A *p* at the beginning of an English word, being aspirated, as similarly a *k* and *t*, is pronounced exactly like *ph*. Thus, English *pull* is really *p-h-ull*, as may be shown by applying the paper test. The *un*-aspirated *p* (of *pa*) is heard in English only when *p* is preceded by an *s*, as in *spun*, the *p* of which should be contrasted with the strongly aspirated *p* of *pun*. The *bh* (of *bha*) may be learned in the same fashion as the aspirated voiced stops of the other classes by taking a compound word the first member of which ends in *b* and the second of which begins with *h*. A good example of this is *club-house*.

The Semivowels

After the stops or touched sounds the Devanāgarī contains a group of four sounds technically called 'semivowels', *viz., ya* , *ra*, *la*, and *va*. They are called semivowels because they are closely akin to vowels and, as will be seen later on in the grammar, they can be replaced by their cognate vowels under certain conditions, *e.g. y* may become *i*, and *v* may become *u*. They could, perhaps with equal justification and logic, have been called 'semiconsonants' because of their ambivalent nature, being only half consonants. The Sanskrit grammarians call them *'antaḥstha'*, literally '(the sounds) that stand between' *scil.* vowels and consonants. Like the touched sounds, these four semivowels are classified according to the point in the mouth where they are produced, not, however, by contact between the tongue and a particular point, but rather by a slight movement of the tongue toward that point without actual contact. The semivowels are classified as follows:

Palatal	*ya*
Cerebral	*ra*
Dental	*la*
Labial	*va*

The *y* (of *ya*) and *l* (of *la*) are essentially the same as English *y* in *yes* or *young* and *l* in *lump* or *luxury* [5] Labial *v* (of *va*) is generally pronounced as a labio-dental, *i.e.,* with the teeth and lips as *v* in English *valve* or *villain*. But

---

[4]But not a final unaccented *m* as in *bottom*, which is really a vowel *m*.

[5]But not like the *l* in the unaccented syllables of words like *little* or *bottle*, which is really a vowel.

in some parts of India it is pronounced approximately like a *w* when it follows a stop; thus, *dvāra* 'door' may be pronounced *dwāra*. Finally, *r* (of *ra*), although classified as a cerebral is no longer so pronounced. Its current pronunciation is closer to an alveolar sound with a slight flap. There is really no analog in English, so that it must be learned from a teacher. All the semivowels are voiced.

The Sibilants

There are three s-sounds or sibilants, a palatal, cerebral and dental:

Palatal *śa*
Cerebral *ṣa*
Dental *sa*

The palatal *ś* is similar to the *sh* in *she* or *shell*, the dental like the *s* in *sum* or *sultry* (not like the *s* in *sugar*, which is closer to *ś*). Cerebral *ṣ* may be approximated by an English *sh* when followed by *u* or *o*, *viz.*, *shun* or *shot*. Though in writing and for various phonetic reasons Sanskrit *ś* and *ṣ* are sharply distinguished, in some parts of India (*e.g.* Bengal), these two sibilants are not kept apart, both being pronounced like *sh* in English *she*. All the sibilants are voiceless.

The Aspirate

The last consonant in the Devanāgarī system is *ha*. Though in origin and in the kinds of sound changes that take place before it, *h* is voiced, it is pronounced without voice, as an ordinary English *h* at the beginning of a word, *e.g. hum* or *honey*.

The Devanāgarī Signs and Mode of Writing

All the sounds represented by the Devanāgarī system having now been presented and their peculiarities of pronunciation discussed, the individual signs and the method of writing them in traditional fashion must be given.

The student must be reminded that every consonant sign in the Devanāgarī script stands for a particular consonant followed by the vowel *a* or, put slightly differently, each sign is not simply a consonant, but a syllable consisting of a consonant plus *a*. Before the signs are given, it is necessary to say a few words regarding the correct pronunciation of this ubiquitous *a*, which, while not a difficult sound at all, is frequently wrongly pronounced by Western students. The difficulty is that it is *not* pronounced like an English *a* in any of the values the English *a* has in accented syllables,[6] and yet, through association of the *a* used in transliterating Devanāgarī with an English *a*, Western students naturally attach to it the pronunciations typically heard in such words as *garden*, *father* or even *bat*, *mat*, etc. But the Sanskrit *a* is pronounced like the *u* (!) in *bundle* or *dub*, and for this reason early travellers to India from England, in quoting commonly heard words, especially place-names, tended to represent this vowel *a* with a *u*[7]. Thus, they wrote *Punjab* and *Ahmednugur*, where the *u*'s were intended to be pronounced like the *u* in *pun* and similar words. The correct pronunciation of this vowel *a* cannot be sufficiently emphasized, as its extreme frequency is in large measure responsible for the characteristic timbre of Sanskrit.

Every Devanāgarī sign is topped by a horizontal line or headline, which in printed Devanāgarī, where the signs are much closer together, tends to flow together from one sign to another in the same word, thus forming a continuous line surmounting the whole word.[8] But in Devanāgarī as traditionally written each sign has its own headline, and there is a slight space separating one sign from the other. In writing nowadays, however, it has become a common practice to write out all the letters of a word first *exclusive of the headline* and then to draw the headline continuously from one sign to the other, so that each word has an unbroken headline over it. This procedure arose from a need to write quickly, but its adoption should be avoided, at least until the student has thoroughly acquainted himself with the traditional style of writing that is universally seen in Sanskrit manuscripts.

The signs, including the headline, are written from left to right and, in the case of vertical lines from top to bottom. If lined paper is used for practice in writing, the signs may be made directly under these lines, which thus can serve as the headlines, needing only to be gone over with the pen or pencil as each sign is completed. As will be seen below in the steps given for writing each sign, the headline is the final stroke of each sign.

---

[6]But English *a* as well as other English vowels occurring in *un*accented syllables come close to the Sanskrit sound; thus, the *a* of *sofa*, the *o* of *welcome* or the vowel sound of the suffix *-tion*, as in *position*. In fact, English has a strong tendency to pronounce *all* vowels following the principal accented syllable in a muted, indeterminate fashion.

[7]In all vernacular languages of India the vowel *a* is pronounced exactly as in Sanskrit, except in Bengali and Oṛiyā (of the state of Orissa) where it has the sound of a short *o*.

[8]This headline in not found in the parent Brāhmī script, but had its beginning centuries later in some descendants of Brāhmī, where it arose from a slight serif or thickening that was imparted to the upper parts of the vertical lines of the signs, which gradually came to be flared out and extended over the top of every sign.

The Gutturals

Transliteration	Sign	Method of Writing
ka	क	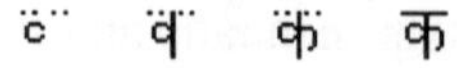
kha	ख	

Note: This method of writing the sign for *kha* is really a very recent phenomenon. In traditional writing the sign consists of two distinct elements, र and व, written closely together (ख), but *not joined* as above. It happens, purely fortuitously, that these two elements र and व are identical to the signs for *ra* and *va*, as will be seen later. Since in quick or careless writing this has often led to confusion, the र and व are linked as shown by a curved stroke extended from the र to the व to prevent the sign from being taken as a sequence of the signs for *ra* and *va*.

ga	ग	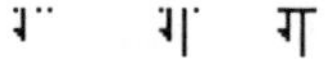
gha	घ	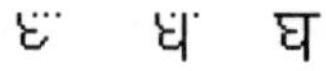
ṅa	ङ	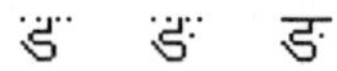

The Palatals

ca	च	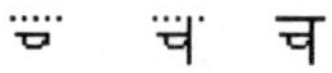
cha	छ	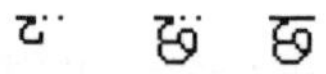
ja	ज	
jha	झ	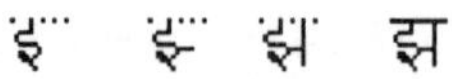
or:	झ	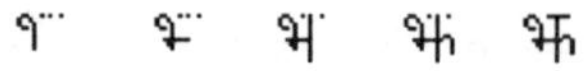

Note: In this last sign (which is rather rare) the headline must not be drawn over the loop which forms the upper left portion, but there should be a slight gap between the loop and the headline.

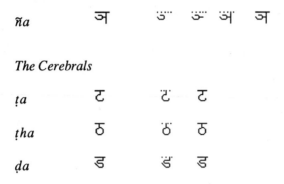

ña ञ 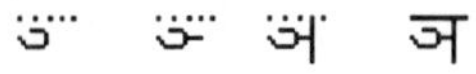

The Cerebrals

ṭa ट 

ṭha ठ 

ḍa ड 

Note: This sign is identical to the guttural nasal ङ (*ṅa*) *except for the dot* on the middle right.

ḍha ढ 

Note: Care must be taken *not* to end the loop with a tail or flourish, thus , as this is nearly identical to the voiced dental द (*da*).

ṇa ण 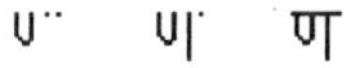

Note: Another sign for this sound, especially in the Mahārāṣṭra region, is  (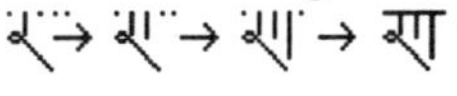). Either may be used, but it would not be proper to use both.

The Dentals

ta त 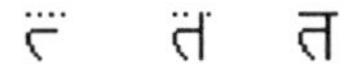

tha थ 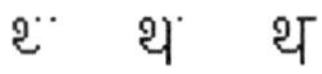

Note: Here again the headline must *not* be drawn over the loop. The loop is essential and should be carefully drawn so as not to confuse this sign with य (*ya*).

da द 

Note: The tail is important and serves to distinguish this sign from ढ (*ḍha*).

dha ध 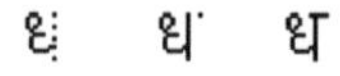

na न 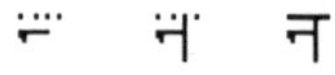

The Labials

pa प 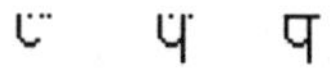

pha फ 

Note: The same as प (*pa*) except for the extra stroke on the right of the vertical line.

ba ब 

bha भ 

Note: भ differs from झ (*jha*) as प (*pa*) from फ (*pha*), *i.e.*, by lacking the extra stroke on the right of the vertical line.

ma म 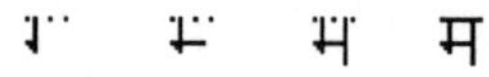

The Semivowels

ya य 

ra र 

la ल 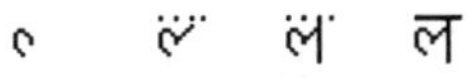

va व 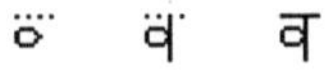

The Sibilants

śa श 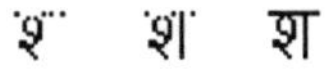

Note: Because of the particular font of Devanāgarī used here, the headline is drawn *over* the loop, contrary to the usual practice.

ṣa ष 

sa स 

Note: The first stroke is identical to र (*ra*).

The Aspirate

ha ह 

Examples of the signs in combination:

1. Words of two syllables

कण (*grain*)
खग (*bird*)
गल (*throat*)
घन (*striking*)
कट (*mat*)
मठ (*ascetic's hut*)
नड (*reed*)
पद (*step*)
चल (*unsteady*)
छद (*cover*)
जन (*people*)
झष (*fish*)
तल (*surface*)
दल (*petal*)
धन (*wealth*)
फल (*fruit*)

बक (*heron*)	भट (*servant*)
मद (*exhilaration*)	यव (*barley*)
रण (*battle*)	वन (*woods*)
मल (*filth*)	शश (*hare*)
शर (*arrow*)	हर (*Śiva*)

2. Words of three syllables

कनक (*gold*)	दशम (*tenth*)
तनय (*son*)	तपन (*burning*)
पतन (*falling*)	नगर (*city*)
दमन (*subduing*)	नमन (*bending*)
शरण (*refuge*)	फलक (*plank*)
बहल (*thick*)	भजन (*worship*)
मनन (*thinking*)	मकर (*sea-monster*)
यवस (*grass*)	रजत (*silver*)
वचन (*word*)	लवण (*salt*)

The Vowels

It was stated earlier that there are 13 vowels, including diphthongs, in Sanskrit, for each of which, when following a consonant, there is a separate sign, except for *-a* which is not written. Every vowel, with but one exception, has both a short and a long counterpart, the long vowel having, technically (or musically) speaking, twice the duration of the short vowel, as may be seen in the correspondence between the *u* in English *put* and *lute*. In the standard transliteration of Devanāgarī a long vowel is topped by a horizontal line called a 'macron', while the short vowel is unmarked. Thus, there are the pairs *a-ā*, *i-ī*, *u-ū*, etc. But although English too, has long vowels corresponding to the short, there is no systematic device for representing them in the orthography, as, for example, through the use of the macron or doubling as in Finnish and some other languages. As long vowels in English are very variously represented in the spelling, the pairing of short and long vowels to illustrate the sound values of the Sanskrit pairs is inevitably confusing to beginners. Thus, for long *ī* double *ee* and *ea* are used as in *meet* and *meat*; for long *ū* a double *oo* as in *noon*, and so on.

The vowels, exclusive of the diphthongs, are as follows:

a-ā, i-ī, u-ū, ṛ-ṝ, ḷ- [ḹ]

a-ā

Though *ā* is treated as the long counterpart of *a*, it has really a quite different quality from that of *a*. While *a* is like the *u* of *tub*, *ā* is like the *a* of *father* or the double *aa* of *bazaar*. The sign for *-ā* after a consonant is a vertical line over which the headline of the preceding consonant sign is extended. Thus, in writing *kā* first क (*ka*) is written, then the vertical ा which cancels out the inherent *-a*, and lastly the headline over both: का and similarly बा (*bā*), ता (*tā*), ला (*lā*), हा (*hā*), etc.

i-ī

Short *i* is pronounced as *i* in *pit* or *middle*; long *ī* as the double *ee* in *peel* or the *ea* in *beat*. Thus, the correspondence between *i-ī* in English is *i-ee* (or *ea*).

The writing of the sign for short *i* in Devanāgarī is peculiar, as it is put *before* the consonant *after* which it is pronounced! The sign consists of a vertical staff (like that for *ā*) with a curve at the top, turned or leaning slightly to the left, thus: ि The righthand end of the curve must be brought down to touch the vertical portion of the following consonant sign. The headline surmounting the two signs, which form a unit, is drawn last. Thus, in writing *ki*, first the vertical staff । is written, then the following consonant sign (after a very slight space) ।क, then the loop, written so as to connect the staff and the vertical part of the consonant sign कि and finally the horizontal line कि, and in the same fashion दि (*di*), गि (*gi*), जि (*ji*), but note that in थि (*thi*), धि (*dhi*) and भि (*bhi*) the headline is broken, as it should not be drawn over the loop of a consonant sign.

The sign for long *ī* is similar to that for short *i*, but it is written *after* the consonant sign to which it is attached, *i.e.,* in its logical position; thus की (*kī*), to be written in the following sequence: क, का, की, की. Note that the loop here is more nearly a semicircle, *i.e.,* it is usually made so as not to lean to the right or left. Other examples are: घी (*ghī*), टी (*ṭī*), ढी (*ḍhī*).

u-ū

The short vowel is identical to *u* in *pull* or *full*; the long *ū* corresponds to the double *oo* in *pool* or *fool*. But observe that sometimes *oo* in English has the value of a short *u*, as in *soot*!

The Devanāgarī signs for these vowels are written beneath the consonant sign and attached to it. The sign for short *u* is a mere hook: ु and for long *ū* it is reversed: ू and thus, when subjoined to क, we have कु (*ku*) and कू (*kū*). In writing these combinations the vowel signs may be written as a continuation of the vertical part of the sign to which they are attached: ◌ वु कु and कु or written after the completion of the consonant sign: ◌ व क कु and finally कु. Other examples are: बु (*bu*), बू (*bū*), मु (*mu*), मू (*mū*), खु (*khu*), खू (*khū*). Note that in the case of the last sign, which consists of two parts, the vowel sign should be attached to the *second* part. Due to the design of this particular font it does not appear that way here.

ṛ-ṝ

To the student it will doubtless seem strange that *r* can be a vowel, yet even in English an *r*-vowel occurs in *un*accented syllables, where, however, it is written *-er*, as in *butter* or *clatter*. An *r*-vowel also occurs in some Slavic languages, such as Czech and Serbian, as evidenced by place names like Brno and Brdy in Czechoslovakia and Brčko and Brza Palanka in Yugoslavia.

The vowel *ṛ* in Sanskrit is no longer pronounced as it seems to have been in ancient times, when the pronunciation may have resembled the *-er* in *butter* or perhaps the *r* in these place names. Nowadays the pronunciation of *ṛ* varies from one part of India to another. Thus, in Mahārāṣṭra it is pronounced as a trilled *r* with a definite *u*-quality (*u* as in *put*) following it, somewhat as the *roo* in English *brook*. But in Bengal it is not distinguished in pronunciation from *ri*, which is often written for *ṛ* in manuscripts originating in Bengal. Thus, the name of the God Kṛṣṇa is pronounced in Mahārāṣṭra almost as though written Kruṣṇa, whereas in Bengal as though written (as it frequently is!) Kriṣṇa. In the light of these and yet other divergent pronunciations, what should the student do? The only answer that can be given is to adopt consistently the one or the other, as none is, in all probability at least, more historically correct than the other.

The short *ṛ* is also a subscript sign in Devanāgarī like the signs for *u-ū*, from which, of course, it has to be carefully distinguished; *ṛ* is, then, also a hook, but, *unlike* the sign for *u* or *ū*, it opens to the right: ृ and is attached to to the vertical bar or lowest part of the sign after which it is pronounced, as in कृ (*kṛ*), written according to the sequence 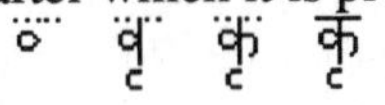 or, alternatively, the vowel may be added after the whole letter has been completed. Additional examples are: भृ (*bhṛ*), गृ (*gṛ*), धृ (*dhṛ*).

The long *ṝ*, which, while far less frequent than *ṛ*, is of considerable importance for its occurrence in certain grammatical endings, is pronounced according to the description above concerning short *ṛ*, but with a prolongation of the sound. The sign for *ṝ* is formed by doubling the sign for short *ṛ*, the one being written directly *under* the other: ॄ as in तॄ (*tṝ*). Other examples need not be given, as *ṝ* usually occurs after त.

ḷ-[ḹ]

The vowel *ḷ*, which, incidentally, occurs in the various forms of only one root-word, is a vocalic *l*, just as *r* is a vocalic *r*. A vocalic *l* is heard in final *un*accented syllables of English words like *bottle*, *myrtle*, which may not be far from the pronunciation in ancient times. Nowadays, however, the pronunciation of *ḷ* is a strange amalgam of *ḷ* and *ṛ*, sounding much like *lru* in Mahārāṣṭra and like *lri* in Bengal! The sign for *ḷ* is a sort of diminutive ल (*la*), but without the headline and with a *ṛ*-like hook ending the vertical line: ॢ . It occurs only after क, thus: कॢ which may be written as follows:

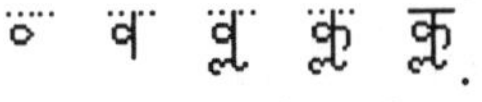

There is no long *ḹ*, although it is found in some Sanskrit grammars, especially those published in India. It arose as a grammatical invention by Indian grammarians, who felt its presence in the sound system necessary to balance out the other pairs of long and short vowels.

The Diphthongs

Four diphthongs are usually listed in Sanskrit grammars, *viz.*, *e*, *ai*, *o* and *au*. But *e* and *o*, though ultimately derived from short diphthongs in the parent Indo-European language and probably still so pronounced in the earliest period of Indo-Aryan speech, gradually lost their diphthongal character and became monophthongs or simple long vowels. Thus, *e* is pronounced as though *ē* (and so transliterated in many early Sanskrit grammars, *i.e.,* like the *a* (!) in English *bagel* or *made*. The *o*, really *ō* (also so transliterated in older books), is like the *o* in English *ogle* or *open*.

The *true* diphthongs *ai* and *au* have no precise equivalents in English.. The *ai* is similar to the *ai* of *aisle*, but the initial element is not a long *ā*, as is the case with *ai* of *aisle*. Rather it is the colorless, somewhat indeterminate Sanskrit *a*. It is this sound that is heard in the name of the religious sect of the Jains (properly Jainas), which to many visitors to India sounds like 'Jayns' and is often so mispronounced by them. But for *practical* purposes the student may pronounce *ai* like the *ai* in *aisle*. The diphthong *au* involves the same difficulty: while similar to the sound written *ow* in English words like *growl* or *town*, the first element of the Sanskrit *au* is really the neutral short *a*, so that it sounds superficially more like the English diphthong *o* in *cold*, just as *ai* sounds superficially like the *ai* in *pain* rather than the *ai* in *aisle*. Again, for practical reasons the student is advised to pronounce *au* like the *ow* in *town*.

e

The sign is a looped slanted line written above the consonant after which it is pronounced and connected to the vertical portion of that sign:  as in के (*ke*), written according to the following sequence: 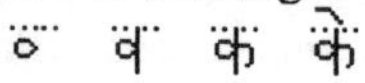 and finally के. So also बे (*be*), दे (*de*), मे (*me,* when as here, there are *two* vertical lines, the sign for *e* is connected to the second), खे (*khe*).

ai

The sign for *ai* consists of two of the signs for *e* with their lower, pointed ends meeting on the headline:  and thus कै (*kai*), written 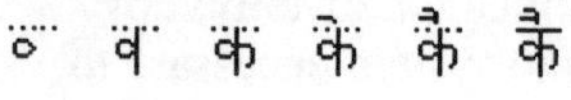 and so also तै (*tai*), दै (*dai*), मै (*mai*), बै (*bai*).

o

The sign for *o* consists of the sign for *e* attached to a vertical staff: ो as in को (*ko*), written ॰ व क का को को and similarly चो (*co*), जो (*jo*), रो (*ro*), गो (*go*).

au

The sign for *au* consists of the two hooks of *ai* attached to a vertical staff: ौ as in कौ (*kau*), written ॰ व क का को कौ कौ and so also यौ (*yau*), पौ (*pau*), ढौ (*ḍhau*).

The following is a list of words of common occurrence in Sanskrit works, which the student should try to transliterate according to the roman equivalents of the Devanāgarī signs. The key is given in Exercise B, but it should be consulted only when absolutely necessary, *i.e.*, when a particular sign has been forgotten and cannot be found in the foregoing explanations. The meanings of the words are not given because, at this stage of the student's progress, no useful purpose would be served by adding yet another burden to his memory. Words and their meanings should properly be learned as one comes upon them in reading, when they have been seen in a meaningful setting. These words, as will be immediately apparent, are of a varying number of syllables, purposely not arranged according to any principle beyond the fact that all the signs occurring in them have been explained. When Exercise A has been completed and checked against errors in B, the words in B should be converted back into Devanāgarī.

Exercise A

गीता। यौवन। कोप। छाया। जननी। जीव। तिथि। देव। दोष।
निधन। नैषध। पति। फल। बाल। पाटव। पूजा। परिदेवित। भारत।
कुतूहल। गभीर। दीपावली। धन। नाग। नारी। चूत। घट। घोष।
भोजन। मनुज। रमणीय। भुवन। रावण। सती। सकाश।हेतु। सोम।
सुकुमार। वीरसेनसुत। महीपति। सखिगणावृत। नृपति मानुष।
तथाविध। दुहितृ। पृथिवीपाल। कुशल। लोक। जीवित। शासन।
अतिथि। विशेष। महाराज। विमान। शूर। सौदामनी। सुसमाहित।
सवितृ। वसुधा। वारि। शोक। मूल। रवि। मति। लालस भूमि।
लोचन। वनिता। शरण। साधु। रामायण। गणिका। कृषि।
कोलाहल। महाभारत। कुसुम। तीर। देवी। तोरण। भूषण। सुरभि।
विराजित। शुभानन। विवाह। नराधिप। मिथुन। विबुध। लघु।
पुरोगम। महाबाहु। वारण। देवदूत। नरपति। मुदित। गुण। देह।
वारण। पीडित। गमन। समय। कृत। राजकूल। वेद। हरि। हीन।
सभा। महायान। वसति। सभा। शोभा।

Exercise B

gītā / yauvana / kopa / chāyā / jananī / jīva / tithi / deva / doṣa / nidhana / naiṣadha / pati / phala / bāla / pāṭava / pūjā / paridevita / bhārata / kutūhala / gabhīra / dīpāvalī / dhana / nāga / nārī / cūta / ghaṭa / ghoṣa / bhojana / manuja / ramaṇīya / bhuvana / rāvaṇa / satī / sakāśa / hetu / soma / sukumāra / vīrasenasuta / mahīpati / sakhigaṇāvṛta / nṛpati / mānuṣa / tathāvidha / duhitṛ / pṛthivīpāla / kuśala / loka / jīvita / śāsana / atithi / viśeṣa / mahārāja / vimāna / śūra / saudāmanī / susamāhita / savitṛ / vasudhā / vāri / śoka / mūla / ravi / mati / lālasa / bhūmi / locana / vanitā / śaraṇa / sādhu / rāmāyaṇa / gaṇikā / kṛṣi / kolāhala / mahābhārata / kusuma / tīra / devī / toraṇa / bhūṣaṇa / surabhi / virājita / śubhānana / vivāha / narādhipa / mithuna / vibudha / laghu / purogama / mahābāhu / kāraṇa / devadūta / narapati / mudita / guṇa / deha / vāraṇa / pīḍita / gamana / samaya / kṛta / rājakūla / veda / hari / hīna / sabhā / mahāyāna / vasati / sabhā / śobhā /

Other Devanāgarī Signs: Anusvāra and Visarga

There are two additional signs in the Devanāgarī script, both traditionally placed after the vowels and diphthongs and before the consonants. They are called anusvāra and visarga respectively. Anusvāra (literally 'after-sound', *i.e.*, a sound that follows another), which consists simply of a dot written above a sign, indicates that the vowel of that syllable is nasalized, *i.e.*, made to resound in the nose, like the vowels in French that are followed by *n* in writing, as in *bon*, *encore*. Anusvāra, which means both the sign itself as well as the sound denoted by it, if properly used, occurs only before the three sibilants (श *śa*, ष *ṣa* and स *sa*), the semivowels and the aspirate ह (*ha*). In transliteration it is represented by *ṁ* or *ṃ*, some scholars preferring the one, others the other symbol. Thus, वंश is transliterated *vaṁśa* or *vaṃśa*, हवींषि *havīṁṣi* or *havīṃṣi*, हिंसा *hiṁsā* or *hiṃsā* and सिंह *siṁha* or *siṃha*. In this book, however, *ṃ* will be consistently used.

Anusvāra is also used to indicate the final *m* of a word when the following word begins with a consonant, *e.g.* नगरं गच्छामि (*nagaraṃ gacchāmi*). In this latter case, however, the anusvāra is pronounced as an *m*, not as a nasalization of the foregoing vowel. This extremely prevalent usage is, as will be explained in a subsequent lesson, merely a so-called *compendium scripturae* (an abbreviated way of writing).

The other sign, visarga, which means literally 'emission (of breath)', precisely resembles in writing and printing the English punctuation mark called a 'colon' and is used at the end of a word for a peculiar sort of breath into which an *-s* or *-r* is liable to be changed under certain conditions. It is transliterated as an *h* with a subscript dot, thus *ḥ*, but its pronunciation is peculiar and requires some extended explanation. Visarga is pronounced as an ordinary English *h* or breath, but with an echo or rebound of the vowel preceding it; thus, मनुः (*manuḥ*) is pronounced *manuh*^{u}, *i.e.,* with a fragment of the preceding *u* after it. Similarly देवः (*devaḥ*) is pronounced *devah*^{a} with a fragmentary *a* thereafter. When the diphthong *ai* precedes visarga, the fragment or echo vowel is *i* (the last part of *ai*!), thus देवैः (*devaiḥ*) pronounced *devaih*^{i}, and similarly when the dipthong *au* precedes visarga, a fragmentary *u* is pronounced, thus गौः (*gauḥ*) pronounced *gauh*^{u}. But the monophthongs *e* and *o* are echoed by a fragmentary *e* and *o*, as कवेः (*kaveḥ*), which is pronounced *kaveh*^{e}, and भानोः (*bhānoḥ*), pronounced *bhānoh*^{o}. Visarga is a very important and frequent sound in Sanskrit, and more will be said about it in a later lesson.

The Virāma

Another sign, while not a phonetic sign and so only a part of the Devanāgarī writing system in a larger sense, is the virāma, a short oblique stroke placed at the foot of a sign to cancel the *-a* that would otherwise be pronounced. Thus, *nagaram* is written नगरम् which, without the little tail attached to म, would be read *nagarama*; similarly कामधुक् with virāma attached to क is read *kāmadhuk*, not *kāmadhuka*.

Conjunct Consonants

When two or more consonants occur together without an intervening vowel, they are combined into a single complex sign, as a means of indicating that the vocalization, whether the inherent *-a* or other written vowel, follows the unitary sign. When two or more consonants are thus combined, all except the last consonant are abbreviated or reduced by the loss of their vertical stroke, and so म (*ma*), ख (*kha*) and त (*ta*) become respectively म्, ख् and त् which are joined *without space* to the following sign. For example, म्ब (*mba*) in लम्बन, ख्य (*khya*) in साख्य, त्न (*tna*) in रत्न and similarly with as many as three consonant signs forming a unit, as ध्न्य (*dhnya*) in बुध्न्य and ब्भ्य in ककुब्भ्याम् where the cluster is vocalized with long *ā*. Theoretically, any number of signs might be thus brought together, but combinations of more than three are exceedingly rare.

When the first of two signs does not have a vertical stroke on its right, as is true of a number of signs, such as ट (*ṭa*) or द (*da*), the second consonant is placed *beneath* and somewhat reduced in size, thus ट्क (*ṭka*) in षट्क (*ṣaṭka*) and ट्ट (*ṭṭa*) in पट्ट (*paṭṭa*) and द्ग (*dga*) in मुद्ग (*mudga*).

In summary, then, when two or more consonants are combined into a single complex sign, the individual signs are arranged horizontally if their fusion can be effected by the omission of the vertical stroke of a preceding sign, otherwise by superposition, in which case they are to be read from the top down. But there are many conjunct consonants of common occurrence whose constituent elements are so altered in combination as to be unrecognizable, as in क्ष (*kṣa*) (also written क्ष), which is a combination of क् (*k*) and ष (*ṣa*) and also ज्ञ (*jña*), made up of ज् (*j*) and ञ (*ña*). These special conjuncts should be learned as they occur in reading. However, a few words must be said here about the form that the semivowel र (*ra*) assumes according to whether it directly precedes or follows a consonant, because it bears no resemblance to the independent sign in either case and is of extremely frequent occurrence..

When र *follows* a consonant as in *pra*, the र is written as a slanted line to the lower left of the consonant sign; thus प्र, also क्र (*kra*), ब्र (*bra*), द्र (*dra*). But त् (*t*) drops most of its characteristic curve in order to accommodate this slanted stroke: त्र (*tra*), to be written . When र follows the palatal श्, the श is abbreviated to श्‍ and the र is written on the vertical stroke: श्र (*śra*). Other special combinations should be learned only as they are encountered.

When र् (*r*) *precedes* a consonant, it is written as a hook, opening to the right, above the consonant sign and connected to its vertical stroke, as in पर्क (*parka*), मर्दन (*mardana*). If it precedes a cluster of two or more consonants, it is written above the last in the series, as in मर्त्य (*martya*) and गार्ग्य (*gārgya*). Another peculiarity is that it is always written to the right of any superscript vowel marks or the anusvāra, as in मर्त्येन (*martyena*), मर्त्यैः (*martyaiḥ*), मर्त्यौ (*martyau*), मर्त्यं (*martyaṃ*) and, as is apparent from these examples, this extreme rightmost position leads to a somewhat awkward displacement of the sign from its place in the sequence of sounds as they are to be read. An extreme example of this sort of displacement is afforded by the rare word कार्त्स्न्य (*kārtsnya*), containing a cluster of four consonants preceded by र्, which, in spite of its being read first, is actually placed over the last! In writing, the र् is drawn simultaneously with the headline, with which it is made to form a part, the pencil or pen backtracking into the shape of the hook, thus: 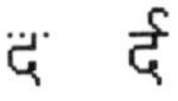 (*rda*).

Here follows a list of conjunct consonants arranged in the order of the Devanāgarī alphabet. They are grouped according to the class to which the initial consonant belongs. The list contains all the consonant combinations that occur in this book in addition to a few of less frequent occurrence. Do not attempt to commit this list to memory: its purpose is merely to show how the combinations are put together. As will become apparent, the method of joining together two or more consonants, with but a few exceptions, follows the rules set out above. Alternative writings do often occur, especially in the case of the more complicated combinations, but these deviations are to be learned by experience.

k-ka क्क; *k-kha* क्ख; *k-ta* क्त / क्‍त; *k-t-ya* क्त्य; *k-t-ra* क्त्र; *k-t-va* क्त्व; *k-ya* क्य; *k-ra* क्र; *k-la* क्ल; *k-va* क्व; *k-ṣa* क्ष / क्‌ष; *k-ṣ-ṇa* क्ष्ण; *k-ṣ-ma* क्ष्म; *k-ṣ-m-ya* क्ष्म्य; *k-ṣ-ya* क्ष्य; *k-ṣ-va* क्ष्व; *kh-y a* ख्य; *g-dha* ग्ध; *g-na* ग्न; *g-ya* ग्य; *gh-na* घ्न; *ṅ-ka* ङ्क; *ṅ-k-ṣa* ङ्क्ष; *ṅ-k-ṣ-va* ङ्क्ष्व; *ṅ-ga* ङ्ग; *ṅ-g-ya* ङ्ग्य; *ṅ-gha* ङ्घ; *ṅ-ya* ङ्य;

c-ca च्च; *c-cha* च्छ; *c-ch-ra* च्छ्र; *c-ña* च्ञ; *c-ya* च्य; *j-ja* ज्ज / ज्ज; *j-j-va* ज्ज्व; *j-jha* ज्झ; *j-ña* ज्ञ; *j-ma* ज्म; *j-ya* ज्य; *j-va* ज्व; *ñ-ca* ञ्च; *ñ-cha* ञ्छ; *ñ-ja* ञ्ज;

ṭ-ṭa ट्ट; *ṭ-ya* ट्य; *ṭh-ya* ठ्य; *ḍ-ya* ड्य; *ḍh-ya* ढ्य; *ṇ-ṭa* ण्ट; *ṇ-ṭha* ण्ठ; *ṇ-ṭh-ya* ण्ठ्य; *ṇ-ḍa* ण्ड; *ṇ-ṇa* ण्ण; *ṇ-ya* ण्य; *ṇ-va* ण्व;

t-ka त्क; *t-k-ṣa* त्क्ष; *t-ta* त्त; *t-t-ya* त्त्य; *t-t-ra* त्त्र; *t-t-va* त्त्व; *t-tha* त्थ; *t-na* त्न; *t-n-ya* त्न्य; *t-pa* त्प; *t-ma* त्म; *t-m-ya* त्म्य; *t-ya* त्य; *t-ra* त्र; *t-r-ya* त्र्य; *t-va* त्व; *t-sa* त्स; *t-s-na* त्स्न; *t-s-n-ya* त्स्न्य; *t-s-ya* त्स्य; *t-tha* त्थ; *th-ya* थ्य; *d-ga* द्ग; *d-gha* द्घ; *d-da* द्द; *d-dha* द्ध; *d-dh-ya* द्ध्य; *d-na* द्न; *d-bha* द्भ; *d-bh-ya* द्भ्य; *d-ma* द्म; *d-ya* द्य; *d-ra* द्र; *d-va* द्व; *dh-na* ध्न; *dh-n-ya* ध्न्य; *dh-ma* ध्म; *dh-ya* ध्य; *dh-ra* ध्र; *dh-va* ध्व; *n-ta* न्त; *n-t-ta* न्त्त; *n-t-ya* न्त्य; *n-t-ra* न्त्र; *n-t-va* न्त्व; *n-da* न्द; *n-d-ra* न्द्र; *n-d-va* न्द्व; *n-dha* न्ध; *n-dh-ra* न्ध्र; *n-na* न्न / न्न; *n-pa* न्प; *n-ma* न्म; *n-ya* न्य; *n-ra* न्र; *n-va* न्व; *n-sa* न्स;

p-ta प्त; *p-t-ya* प्त्य; *p-na* प्न; *p-pa* प्प; *p-ya* प्य; *p-la* प्ल; *p-sa* प्स; *p-s-ya* प्स्य; *b-ja* ब्ज; *b-da* ब्द; *b-dha* ब्ध; *b-dh-va* ब्ध्व; *b-na* ब्न; *b-ba* ब्ब; *b-bha* ब्भ; *b-bh-ya* ब्भ्य; *b-ya* ब्य; *b-ra* ब्र; *bh-na* भ्न; *bh-ya* भ्य; *m-na* म्न; *m-pa* म्प; *m-ba* म्ब; *m-bha* म्भ; *m-ya* म्य; *m-la* म्ल;

y-ya य्य; *l-ka* ल्क; *l-pa* ल्प; *l-ma* ल्म; *l-ya* ल्य; *l-la* ल्ल / ल्ल; *v-ya* व्य;

ś-ca श्च; *ś-c-ya* श्च्य; *ś-na* श्न; *ś-ya* श्य; *ś-ra* श्र; *ś-la* श्ल; *ś-va* श्व / श्व;

ṣ-ka ष्क; *ṣ-ṭa* ष्ट; *ṣ-ṭ-ya* ष्ट्य; *ṣ-ṭ-ra* ष्ट्र; *ṣ-ṭ-va* ष्ट्व; *ṣ-ṭha* ष्ठ; *ṣ-ṇa* ष्ण; *ṣ-pa* ष्प; *ṣ-pha* ष्फ; *ṣ-ma* ष्म; *ṣ-ya* ष्य; *ṣ-va* ष्व;

s-ka स्क; *s-kha* स्ख; *s-ta* स्त; *s-t-ya* स्त्य; *s-t-ra* स्त्र; *s-t-va* स्त्व; *s-tha* स्थ; *s-na* स्न; *s-n-ya* स्न्य; *s-pa* स्प; *s-pha* स्फ; *s-ma* स्म; *s-ya* स्य; *s-ra* स्र; *s-va* स्व;

h-ṇa ह्ण; *h-na* ह्न; *h-ma* ह्म; *h-ya* ह्य; *h-ra* ह्र; *h-la* ह्ल; *h-va* ह्व.

Preconsonantal or Initial Signs for the Vowels

The vowel signs that have been presented so far are, it will be recalled, used when they *follow* a consonant, to which they form mere attachments written to the left, right, above and below the sign, as कि (*ki*), की (*kī*), कै (*kai*), कु (*ku*), etc. As attachments which are written almost as though an integral part of a consonant, they cannot be used to represent a vowel *at the beginning of a word* (or on the very rare occasion when a vowel begins a syllable within a word). When a vowel begins a word, the following signs are used:

अ *a*, as in अत्र (*atra*)

आ *ā*, as in आगमन (*āgamana*)

इ *i*, as in इह (*iha*)

ई *ī*, as in ईश्वर (*īśvara*)[9]
उ *u*, as in उग्र (*ugra*)
ऊ *ū*, as in ऊर्मि (*ūrmi*)
ऋ *ṛ*, as in ऋषि (*ṛṣi*)

(Neither long *ṝ* nor *ḷ* occurs at the beginning of a word).

ए *e*, as in एक (*eka*)
ऐ *ai*, as in ऐरावण (*airāvaṇa*)
ओ *o*, as in ओषधि (*oṣadhi*)
औ *au*, as in औपम्य (*aupamya*)

These independent or initial vowel signs are written in the following manner:

a ३ अ अ
ā ३ अ अ। आ (*i.e.*, with the addition of a vertical stroke to the short vowel sign).
i इ इ
ī इ ई (This hook exactly resembles the sign for र् before a consonant).
u उ उ
ū उ ऊ ऊ
ṛ २ त्र ऋ ऋ
e ए ए ए
ai ए ए ऐ ऐ
o ३ अ अ। ओ ओ
au ३ अ अ। ओ औ औ

[9]Note that when श combines with a following consonant, it takes the abbreviated form श्‍, but nowadays श् (with the vertical stroke omitted) is often used instead.

In Devanāgarī manuscripts individual words were not written separately from one another. This was no doubt partly due to a conscious desire to conserve the writing material, as was true also in the case of Latin and Greek manuscripts. The chief reason, however, is probably the combinatory tendency of the Devanāgarī script, which makes it easier to write words together by utilizing the post-consonantal vowel signs instead of the initial signs (wherever possible) and by joining consonants together at word-junctures. Thus, the words एवम् उक्तस् तु are more easily written एवमुक्तस्तु by writing मु for म् उ and स्तु for स् तु. This natural combinatory tendency of the script and also the frequent fusing together of words by various kinds of vowel contractions and phonetic changes at word-junctures inevitably led to the conception of a sentence as a continuous flow, which the introduction of spaces would have disturbed. In the very earliest books printed in Devanāgarī writing without spaces was continued, but it was not long before the principle arose of introducing a space after words ending in visarga, anusvāra or a vowel or diphthong (when the following word began with a consonant). This is the policy invariably practiced nowadays not only for Devanāgarī, but for all the scripts in India.[10] The writing of words together, even as modified in this way, is a cause of considerable difficulty for the beginner in Sanskrit, however, as in so early a stage of his knowledge of grammatical forms and vocabulary, he does not readily discern the word-junctures that are immediately apparent to him at a later stage. Thus, the following sentence: *munir iha vane vyāghreṣv iṣūn muñcantam ākheṭakam īkṣate*, with words spaced apart according to the practice in transliteration, but written without spaces at all in manuscripts, would appear thus in modern printed Devanāgarī: मुनिरिह वने व्याघ्रेष्विषून्मुञ्चन्तमाखेटकमीक्षते, *i.e.,* with a space only between *iha vane* and *vane vyāghreṣv* because *iha* and *vane* both end in vowels and the following words begin with a consonant.[11]

In view of the general rule that, when a word ends in a consonant and the following word begins with a vowel, they are written together as a unit, the occurrence of the initial vowel signs (as opposed to the attached post-consonantal vowel signs) is practically limited to the first word of a sentence and internally to where, under certain grammatical conditions, two vowels

---

[10] But not so with the Burmese, Thai, Cambodian and Lao scripts, the eastern derivates of Brāhmī, in which words are also not spaced apart, even in newspapers. But this is perhaps due not so much to the continuation of the habit of Indian manuscripts as it is to the monosyllabic structure of these languages, the word-junctures being by nature clearly evident.

[11] In this book, however, the use of combined Devanāgarī writing will be deferred until Lesson Twenty-four.

appear in hiatus at word junctures. Thus, in the example cited above, the *i* of *iha* in *munir iha* is not written with the vowel sign for initial *i*, even though it does begin the word *iha.*

When letters of the Devanāgarī script are referred to, just as when in English we say *bee*, *dee*, *double u*, *aitch*, etc., they are called either by their values as individual signs, *e.g.* क (*ka*), ब (*ba*), न (*na*), etc. or, less commonly, by these syllabic signs with the addition of the word कार (*kāra*), literally 'maker', as ककार (*kakāra*), बकार (*bakāra*), नकार (*nakāra*) '*ka*-maker', '*ba*-maker', '*na*-maker', *i.e.,* 'that which makes *ka* ', etc. The same procedure is followed for the vowels. The only exception to the use of कार is the semivowel र, which is not called रकार (*rakāra*), but, most peculiarly, रेफ (*repha*).[12] These names in कार may refer either to the written symbols or to the sounds indicated by them.

Now that all the signs of the Devanāgarī alphabet and their phonetic values have been given and discussed, it may be helpful to have a synoptic view of the signs and their transliterations according to the sequence followed in Sanskrit dictionaries and also in recitations of the alphabet, which, it will be recalled, differs from our presentation in placing the vowels first, then visarga and anusvāra followed by the other consonants.

Vowels	अ *a*, आ (ा) *ā*, इ (ि) *i*, ई (ी) *ī*, उ (ु) *u*, ऊ (ू) *ū*, ऋ (ृ) *ṛ*, ॠ (ॄ) *ṝ*
Diphthongs	ए (े) *e*, ऐ (ै) *ai*, ओ (ो) *o*, औ (ौ) *au*
Visarga	: *ḥ*
Anusvāra	...˙ *ṃ* or *ṁ*

[12]Literally a 'snarl' or 'growl' and probably so-called from the roll or trill with which it is sounded, like the snarl of a dog! It is of interest to note that the only script in India in which the letters have names, like this one exception in the Devanāgarī, is the Gurmukhī of Pañjābī, in which every letter has its own distinctive name. Thus, *ga* is called *gaggā*, *ṭa* is called *ṭāīṅkā*.

Consonants (stops and nasals)	Voiceless Unaspirated	Voiceless Aspirated	Voiced Unaspirated	Voiced Aspirated	Nasals
Gutturals	क *ka*	ख *kha*	ग *ga*	घ *gha*	ङ *ṅa*
Palatals	च *ca*	छ *cha*	ज *ja*	झ *jha*	ञ *ña*
Cerebrals	ट *ṭa*	ठ *ṭha*	ड *ḍa*	ढ *ḍha*	ण *ṇa*
Dentals	त *ta*	थ *tha*	द *da*	ध *dha*	न *na*
Labials	प *pa*	फ *pha*	ब *ba*	भ *bha*	म *ma*
Semivowels	य *ya*	र *ra*	ल *la*	व *va*	
Sibilants	श *śa*	ष *ṣa*	स *sa*		
Aspirate	ह *ha*				

Accent

Finally, a word must be said about the nature and the position of the accent in Sanskrit. By accent is meant the greater stress or emphasis that is given to one syllable of a word over another. As contrasted with the early Vedic language, classical Sanskrit has what is called a 'stress' accent,[13] as is found, for example, in English, German and the Romance languages with the exception of French, which has a musical or pitch accent, *i.e.*, an accent based not on stress, but a rise or modulation of the voice on a particular syllable. But the stress accent of Sanskrit differs from that of the languages just mentioned in being less forceful, with an even distribution of accent over the syllables that do not bear the main stress, which, therefore, must on no account be slurred or reduced, as is typically the case with unstressed syllables in English.

The position of the accent in Sanskrit is based essentially on the same principle as prevails in Latin: if the second to the last syllable (called the 'penult') consists of a long vowel (or diphthong) or alternatively of a short vowel followed by two or more consonants, it is stressed or accented.[14]

---

[13]Sometimes referred to as an *ictus* accent, the term *ictus*, literally 'a blow', being borrowed from Latin prosody.

[14]A long vowel or diphthong is said to be 'long by nature'; a short vowel followed by two or more consonants is said to be 'long by position'.

Otherwise, the accent falls on the third to the last syllable (called the 'antepenult'). Thus, कुमार (*kumāra*) is accented on the *ā* (the penult) because it is a long vowel; similarly, अतीव (*atīva*) with the accent on the long vowel *ī*, and हितैषिन् (*hitaiṣin*) with the accent on the diphthong *ai*. Accented also on the penult are the following words, because their short penultimate vowel is followed by two consonants (an extremely common case): आदित्य (*āditya*) with the accent on *i*, भवन्ति (*bhavanti*) with the accent on the syllable *ant*, and also गन्धर्व (*gandharva*) with the accent on the syllable *arv*. On the other hand, when the penult is short, the accent is put on the antepenult, as in मनुज (*manuja*), where it falls on the first syllable *ma* and दानव (*dānava*) where it rests on *dā*. If, however, the last three syllables are all short, as is not uncommon, the accent moves back to the *fourth* to the last syllable (the so-called 'ante-antepenult'!), as in चोरयति (*corayati*) and धारयितुम् (*dhārayitum*). In determining the length of the penult (the key syllable!), anusvāra is to be counted as a consonant, hence in शशंस (*śaśaṃsa*) the accent falls on *śaṃs*, as the *a*, though short by nature, is long due to the following anusvāra (*ṃ*) plus *s*.

The stress accent, described above, which has been in use probably for the past 2000 years or more, gradually came to supplant the musical accent of the older language, such as occurs in the hymns of the Ṛgveda and other early Vedic texts. This musical accent, which is marked according to various systems of notation in the different Vedic texts, essentially continued the accentual pattern of the parent Indo-European language and is reflected also in classical Greek[15] and Lithuanian.

[15]But in classical Greek too, the old musical accent had given way to a stress accent, but in contrast with Sanskrit the stress accent in Greek remains on the same syllable as the musical accent. In Sanskrit, however, the position of the stress accent, based as it is on the penultimate rule given above, has nothing to do with the position of the musical accent, except where it happens by coincidence to fall on the same syllable.Thus, *samudra* in the Ṛgveda has the tone on the last syllable, but in the classical language it is accented on the penult (which is long by position); *śarīra* in the Ṛgveda bears the accent on the first syllable, whereas in the later language the stress accent falls on the long *ī* of the penult.

Rattling the Dry Bones of Grammar

A Few Preliminary Remarks

In English the order of words in a sentence can be of cardinal importance. To make this clear, let us take the sentence 'The ascetic sees the god'. If we transpose the words 'ascetic' and 'god' and say 'the god sees the ascetic', the meaning is completely changed, although the words themselves are precisely the same. An analysis of this and similar sentences suggests that in English the agent or performer of an action is put before the word that expresses the action, after which, in turn, the one affected by the action is placed. The agent of an action is called the 'subject' in grammatical parlance, and the one affected by the action of the subject is called the 'object'. The word expressing the action is known as a 'verb'. The example above, which illustrates a simple, basic sentence, consists of the subject 'The ascetic', the verb 'sees' and the object 'the god'.

In Sanskrit it is usual to put the verb at the end of the sentence. In English, however, this word order (subject-object-verb) is found only in poetry, where one might say 'The ascetic the god sees'.

But apart from word order, there is yet another difference between Sanskrit and English that must be explained and understood from the very outset: the subject and object are differentiated by a difference in the *last syllable* or *ending* of the word. Thus, as the subject of a sentence 'ascetic' is *tāpasaḥ*, but as object it is *tāpasam*. Similarly, as the subject 'god' is *devaḥ*, but as object it is *devam*. Since the ending indicates whether a word is the subject or object of a verb, word order in Sanskrit is not fixed or hard and fast, as it is in English. The sentence that has served as an example would normally be in Sanskrit: *tāpasaḥ devaṃ paśyati* ('sees'). The definite article, as grammarians call the word 'the', is generally omitted in Sanskrit, although it can be expressed, as will be seen in due course. It is also possible in Sanskrit, unlike English, to reverse the order of the subject and object and say : *devaṃ tāpasaḥ paśyati*, with no change in meaning. The difference between these two versions of the sentence is a difference of which of the two words (*tāpasaḥ* and *devaṃ*) is emphasized. If the less usual order is adopted and the object is put first, then the object is being especially emphasized. Thus, the second version *devaṃ tāpasaḥ paśyati* implies that it is a god, not anyone else, that the ascetic sees.

The endings of words are a key factor in a Sanskrit sentence, and the student has to pay the closest attention to these final syllables, as we have seen in the words *tāpasaḥ/tāpasam* and *devaḥ/devam*. The verb *paśyati* 'sees' must be changed to *paśyanti*, if more than two persons are doing the seeing.[1] When no subject (or doer) is expressed, the meaning will be 'he(she, it) sees' for *paśyati*, and 'they see' for the plural *paśyanti*. In these instances where the subject is omitted, the context or train of thought tells us whether the subject is he, she, it.[2] We may put the matter in another way by saying that when a particular subject of a Sanskrit verb is expressed, as in *tāpasaḥ paśyati* ('the ascetic sees'), it may be looked upon as defining or replacing the implicit he, she, it.

When the subject of a sentence like *devaḥ* or *tāpasaḥ*, is plural, that is, when it denotes more than two persons or things, the final *-aḥ* is replaced by *-āḥ*. In other words, the 'a' of the ending *-aḥ* is lengthened. So, 'The ascetics see the god' is *tāpasāḥ devaṃ paśyanti*' Bear in mind that a plural subject like *tāpasāḥ* must have its verb in the plural. Notice that in English too, there is a difference in the singular and plural verb forms here: in the singular we have 'sees', but in the plural 'see'. So, whereas in English an 's' is added when the subject is singular, but no ending when it is plural, Sanskrit has *-ati* in the singular, but *-anti* in the plural. Here follow some subject-object-verb sentences with singular and plural subjects to illustrate what has been said above.

महाराजः देशम् रक्षति The king protects the country.
तापसः योगम् आचरति The ascetic practices yoga.
वानरः वृक्षम् आरोहति The monkey climbs the tree.
सर्पः मानुषम् दंशति The serpent bites the man.
बालः आहारम् खादति The child eats the food.
तापसाः देवम् यजन्ति The ascetics worship the god.
शिष्याः ग्रन्थम् पठन्ति The pupils read the book.
नराः विहगम् पश्यन्ति The men see the bird.

A word that denotes a person or a thing is called a 'noun' by the grammarians. In the sentence we have been using as a typical example of the subject-verb-object variety, the words 'ascetic' and 'god' are nouns, as they designate a person. (It is best that we avoid the philosophical argument whether god is a person.) Any word that means a thing in the widest sense of the term is also a noun; for example, house, chair, table, book, etc. A noun is

---

1 In Sanskrit a special form is used when the subject is a pair or two persons or things. Called the 'dual', this will be dealt with later on.

2 Of course, if the verb is plural and no subject is expressed, it must be understood to be 'they'.

often preceded by a word that describes it in some way, for example, 'an *old* house, a *wooden* table, an *interesting* book, etc. These descriptive words are called 'adjectives'. They may also be used when a predication or statement is made about a person or thing (a noun!), generally after 'is' or 'are', 'was' or 'were'. Thus, 'The book is *interesting*', 'the house was *old*', etc. In Sanskrit adjectives, like nouns, have endings which change according to the noun they describe or qualify. Precisely what this somewhat mystifying assertion means will become clear as we proceed with our study of Sanskrit.

As we have seen, the different endings or final syllables of nouns and adjectives are used to indicate whether a word is the subject or performer or whether it designates the one affected by the action. Grammarians call these sense-relationships by the somewhat strange technical name 'cases'. There are various sense-relationships possible among the elements that make up a sentence. Thus far, only two have been mentioned, namely, the relationship of subject or performer of the action and that of the one affected. Other possible relationships are expressed in English by such words as *by*, *with*, *of*, *from*, *to*, *for*, *in*, *at* and by the use of *'s* (apostrophe followed by 's' as in 'the child's toy'). In Sanskrit all these relationships or cases are expressed by the different endings or final syllables of words. The words *by*, *to*, *from* etc. are not expressed separately, then, but their sense is conveyed by the case ending. There are in Sanskrit eight different cases, which, in the order in which they are traditionally given in Sanskrit grammars are: nominative (for the relationship or case of the subject or performer), accusative (for the one affected by the action), instrumental (for the instrument or means by which an action is performed), dative (denoting the idea of 'to' or 'for' someone), ablative (for the idea of 'from' someone or something), genitive (indicating the relationship of 'of' in the broadest sense), locative (for the place 'in' or 'at' which an action takes place) and finally the vocative (used to denote the person addressed, as in '*John*, look at this!'). Though this may sound complicated and perhaps confusing, it is really not so difficult, especially if we bear in mind that English uses the ending *'s* to express the relationship or sense of the genitive case; the only difference is that Sanskrit has many more case endings in order to express the other relationships listed above.[3]

All of these cases would never be found in one and the same sentence, by the very nature of things. The sense relationships expressed by the eight Sanskrit case endings may be shown somewhat artificially by the following English sentence:'O friend, the priest worships Viṣṇu for the king with rice from the field of the peasant in the country'. Thus,

---

[3] The enthusiastic student who takes kindly to the subject of cases will surely be interested to learn that the Finnish language has 15 cases, almost twice as many as Sanskrit!

1. Nominative: 'the priest' as *subject* of 'worships'.
2. Accusative: 'Viṣṇu', the *object* of the verb 'worships'.
3. Instrumental: 'with rice', the *instrument* or *medium* used by the priest in his worship of Viṣṇu.
4. Dative: 'for the king', the person *for whom* the act of worship is performed.
5. Ablative: 'from the field' denoting the place *from which* the rice comes.
6. Genitive: 'of the peasant', which expresses the *of*-relationship, in this instance indicating the possessive relationship (alternatively, we might say 'from the peasant's field').
7. Locative: 'in the country', the place *in which* the act of worship is carried out.
8. Vocative: 'O friend', the one addressed, that is, to whom the whole sentence is spoken.

LESSON ONE

First Beginnings: 1. The Declension of देव and फल. 2. Gender.
3. Writing of Final *-m* (-म्).

I. *The Declension of* देव *and* फल.

In the preliminary remarks it was mentioned that Sanskrit has eight grammatical cases or sense-relationships and these are indicated by the different endings of nouns as well as the adjectives that qualify the nouns. These endings vary considerably, as will be seen in the lessons that follow, depending upon the final vowel (or consonant) of the stem to which they are attached. In grammatical jargon presenting a noun or an adjective in its various cases is called 'declining' it, and this kind of presentation is known as a 'declension'. In this lesson we shall learn the declension of nouns that end in *-a*. At this point it needs to be mentioned that Sanskrit nouns and adjectives when referred to in discussion or listed in dictionaries and short word-lists are given in what is called the 'stem-form', that is to say, not with any particular case-ending, but in a caseless or endingless form which is just a sort of grammatical abstraction on which all the forms may be said to be based. The common word for 'god' that was used in the preliminary remarks is, for example, referred to in the dictionaries as *deva* (देव). The declension of देव in the singular and plural is as follows:

	Singular		Plural		
Nominative:	*devaḥ*	देवः	*devāḥ*	देवाः	(subject of the verb)
Accusative:	*devam*	देवम्	*devān*	देवान्	(object of the verb)
Instrumental:	*devena*	देवेन	*devaiḥ*	देवैः	(by *or* with the god[s])
Dative:	*devāya*	देवाय	*devebhyaḥ*	देवेभ्यः	(to *or* for the god[s])
Ablative:	*devāt*	देवात्	*devebhyaḥ*	देवेभ्यः	(from the god[s])
Genitive:	*devasya*	देवस्य	*devānām*	देवानाम्	(of the god[s] *or* the god's[-s'])
Locative:	*deve*	देवे	*deveṣu*	देवेषु	(in the god[s])
Vocative:	*deva*	देव	*devāḥ*	देवाः	(O god[s])

Note that the vocative happens to be identical to the stem form *deva* (देव).

II. *Gender.*

One other matter that is of first importance in the study of Sanskrit is gender, concerning which a few words require to be said here. All Sanskrit nouns have sex or 'gender', as the grammarians call it. Unfortunately, the gender of a Sanskrit noun does not have anything to do with the actual sex of a person, and things (whether material or abstract) also have gender. There are three genders: masculine, feminine and neuter (by neuter is meant neither masculine nor feminine). In Sanskrit, unlike English, gender is just a grammatical phenomenon. English may be said to have the same three genders, but they are based on the actual gender of the person or thing signified by the noun. Thus, 'wife' is feminine, 'father' is masculine, and 'book' is neuter. But in Old English, that is, our language during the period from c.800 to c.1200 A.D., the earlier forms of 'wife' *(wīf)* and 'book' *(bōc)* were respectively neuter and feminine![1] In other words, they had grammatical, as opposed to natural, gender just as in Sanskrit. In Sanskrit the gender of a noun in general has to be learned, although there are some principles that might be given. Words that end in *-a* are masculine or neuter, never feminine. Their declension differs only in the nominative and accusative singular and plural where neuter words end in *-am* and *-āni* respectively. Thus, the nominative and accusative of the neuter noun *phala* (फल) 'fruit' is *phalam* (फलम्) in the singular and *phalāni* (फलानि) in the plural.

In the preliminary remarks we learned that the action-word or verb normally, although not invariably, appears at the *end* of a Sanskrit sentence. Hence, whereas in English the normal order of words is subject-verb-object, in Sanskrit it is subject-object-verb. For example, the sentence 'The boy sees the book' is to be rendered बाल: पुस्तकं पश्यति. If there is an adjective qualifying either noun ('boy' or 'book'), it must come *before* the noun. Thus, 'The clever boy sees the book' would be निपुण: बाल: पुस्तकं पश्यति. In fact, it is a general rule of Sanskrit word order that any word that qualifies another should precede that word. So, if we should want to speak of 'the teacher's book', that is, not any book but specifically the *teacher's,* we would say आचार्यस्य पुस्तकं not पुस्तकं आचार्यस्य, because the genitive आचार्यस्य ('teacher's') qualifies or limits पुस्तकं ('book').

In translating a Sanskrit sentence into English the first thing to do is find out the verb, which, as has been explained, ordinarily comes last. So far we have learned that the verb ends in *-ati* (for the singular) and *-anti* (for the plural). The next thing to do is to see whether the subject of the verb is

---

[1] Somewhat startling is the fact that *dāra* (दार), one of the many words for 'wife' in Sanskrit, is *masculine* in gender and is used only in the *plural* !

expressed. If it is, it will, of course, be in the nominative case, which, for words of the masculine gender, ends in *-aḥ,* for neuter words in *-am.* If it happens that the subject is *not* expressed, it will be implicit in the verb-form itself, and for the singular 'he, she or it' will be the subject according to the train of thought. Of course, if the sentence is an isolated one, that is, separated from a narrative or context, then it cannot be decided whether the unexpressed subject is 'he, she or it'. But if the verb is *plural,* the implicit subject will have to be translated by 'they'.

After the verb and subject have been determined in this way, and the sentence in its simplest form obtained, an object should be looked for to complete the basic thought. The object, it will be remembered, must be in the accusative case and, so far as we have learned, for a masculine or a neuter word in the singular it must end in *-am,* in the plural it must end in *-ān* for a masculine and *-āni* for a neuter.

Now the enlargement of the sentence, its extension and modification, needs to be ascertained. The sentence in its simplest form consists of the subject, verb and object. This is the mere skeleton, so to speak, all the rest is the flesh upon the skeleton. The enlargement or extension of a sentence consists of all the qualifying words, such as adjectives and the cases other than the nominative, accusative and vocative. These other cases (instrumental, dative, ablative, genitive and locative) introduce other limiting factors into the simple assertion consisting of subject, verb and object. They tell by what means the doer or subject performs the action, for whom it is done, where it is done and so on.

In analyzing a sentence in this fashion, we need not know the meaning of any word: it is just a sort of mechanical process of going from the known (word-order, case endings etc.) to the unknown (the meanings of the words and the idea they express). Let us examine an example in order to see how this process of going from the known to the unknown works, as we try to unravel the meaning of the Sanskrit sentence: तापसः वनस्य मौने ध्यानम् आचरति । The verb, the first thing that should be looked for, is आचरति, as it ends in *-ati* and stands at the end of the sentence. If no noun subject were expressed, we might thus far in our analysis say 'He, she or it does so-and-so'. But as we look at the endings of the other words, we see that तापसः ends in *-aḥ,* the nominative case ending for nouns listed in the dictionary or vocabulary as ending in *-a.* Now the sentence, as it has evolved, can be changed to 'X does so-and-so'. Of the remaining three words only ध्यानम्, because it ends in *-am,* can serve as an object. The sentence now can be extended to 'X (or तापस) performs the action of Y (or ध्यान)'. Of the remaining two words, वनस्य has the very characteristic ending *-asya,* which can only be genitive and must be translated 'of whatever वन means'! Finally,

मौने has to be locative and must mean 'in something or other'. The sentence now, without any of the meanings of the individual words known, can be thus construed: 'A तापस performs the action of ध्यान in the मौन of a वन'. It should be noted in passing that Sanskrit normally does not express the words 'the' or 'a/an', called the definite and indefinite articles respectively, so the use of 'the' and 'a' in the rigmarole above is only provisional, subject to change when the meanings of the words have been obtained and English idiom or our own feeling about the phraseology decides the issue. If now we consult the vocabulary in this lesson and substitute the meanings for तापस, ध्यान, मौन, वन and the verb, the sentence can be rendered thus: 'The ascetic performs meditation in the silence of the forest'. Or if we wish 'An ascetic . . . of a forest'.

III. *A Note on the Writing of Final -m* (-म्).

It is usual in printed books and most MSS to write a final *-m* (-म्) with the anusvāra sign when the next word begins with a consonant. In some parts of India, notably in Bengal, a final *-m* before a consonant is usually replaced both in writing and pronunciation by the nasal belonging to the class of that consonant, but is kept before vowels. Thus, the most accepted practice would be to write, for example: नगरं गच्छामि ('I am going to the city'), but in some parts of India नगरङ्गच्छामि. When the anusvāra is used before a consonant according to the more usual practice, it may be pronounced either as an ordinary *m* or as the nasal of the class of the following consonant, *i.e.,* as though so written.

In this book we shall use the anusvāra sign for *every* final *-m* (-म्) within a sentence as a sort of *compendium scripturae* (abbreviated writing), in this way avoiding the combination of -म with the virāma sign when the next word begins with a vowel. In Lesson Twenty-four, where combined Devanāgarī is introduced, this procedure will be replaced by the standard practice.

IV. *Conversion of Dental -n-* (-न्) *to Cerebral -ṇ-* (-ण्-).

A curious phonetic rule needs to be mentioned here, though, if it were not for the ubiquity of its application, it would be far better to let it die in obscurity in Appendix III. This rule concerns the replacement of dental -न्- (*-n-*) by the cerebral -ण्- (*-ṇ-*). This curious transformation takes place when one of the cerebrals ऋ, ॠ, र् or ष् happens to precede -न-, when the -न- occurs in the same word and is followed by a -म्-, -य्-, -व्-, by any vowel or by another -न्- (in which event both -न्-'s are cerebralized!). This substitution occurs no matter how far away the -न्- is from one of the mischievous letters. But it does not take place if a palatal (except -य्-!), a cerebral or dental comes in between, because these letters are quite against the cerebralizing power of the altering letters. We need to pay some attention to this rule because it often causes the replacement of -न्- when, for example, the endings -एन and -आनाम् are applied. Since, however, this confusing rule is often neglected by Indian scribes and others who should know better, no beginning student need be too deeply disturbed about forgetting to apply it when composing Sanskrit.

Work out the translation of the following sentences according to the principles suggested above:

1. यज्ञस्य प्रभावेण मानुषः स्वर्गं गच्छति[1] ।
2. शूराः युद्धे नृपाय जीवितं त्यजन्ति ।
3. नरः सुखं धनेन न विन्दति ।
4. कृष्णाः अश्वाः क्षेत्रे धावन्ति[2] ।
5. नरेश्वरस्य सूतः रथं आरोहति ।
6. शिष्यः आचार्याय दीर्घं पत्त्रं लिखति ।
7. अश्वः पार्थिवस्य रथं नगरस्य मार्गे[3] वहति ।
8. माल्येन युक्तः शिष्यः कटे सीदति ।
9. ब्राह्मणाः नृपाय अन्नेन देवं यजन्ति ।
10. कृषीवलाः ग्रामस्य दीर्घे मार्गे चलन्ति ।
11. फलैः युक्ताः वृक्षाः उद्याने रोहन्ति ।
12. ब्राह्मणः रामायणस्य[4] अध्यायं नृपाय पठति ।

Notes

1. Verbs of motion like गच्छति ('goes') are used with an accusative of the 'place to which'.

2. Many verbs by reason of their meaning cannot take a direct object. They are called 'intransitive' in contrast to 'transitive' verbs which naturally are construed with an object. In this sentence धावन्ति 'run' is intransitive and has no object. If an accusative were used with this verb, the meaning would be 'run to', that is, the accusative would be of the 'place to which' variety.

3. In Sanskrit one says 'road of the city', whereas the English idiom is 'road to the city'; *cf.* also ग्रामस्य मार्गे in 10.

4. The Rāmāyaṇa is one of the two great Sanskrit epic poems. It relates the life and adventures of the great hero Rāma. It was composed by Vālmīki.

After successfully translating the sentences given above, apply the same principles in translating the following English sentences into Sanskrit.

1. There are (विद्यन्ते) many flowers in the king's[1] garden.
2. Various ascetics practise meditation in the hermitage in the vicinity of the palace.[2]
3. The sun's rays touch the tops of the mountains.
4. The man cuts down the tree near his[3] house.
5. The tiger drinks water from the lake in the forest.
6. The father gives books to the child.
7. The herd of elephants goes to the lake.
8. Herds of deer dwell in the forest.
9. The lord creates beautiful lotuses for the enjoyment[4] of people.
10. The sun illuminates the world for all creatures.[4]

Notes

1. Note that the genitive must precede the noun that it particularizes, exactly as the English genitive in *'s*, as here in the phrase 'in the king's garden'. But note also that when the genitive is expressed in English by means of the preposition 'of', the of-phrase comes after the noun. In this sentence we would have to say 'in the garden of the king'. Thus the genitive may be said to precede the word it 'genitives'.

2. When there are two locative phrases as here, 'in the hermitage' and 'in the vicinity', they should be so arranged that the one that limits more closely comes first. So, here 'in the vicinity of the palace' defines the location of the hermitage and, therefore, should come first. Likewise in sentence 5 'in the forest' should precede 'from the lake'.

3. The possessive adjectives 'his, her, its, their' like the articles 'the' and 'a/an' are normally omitted in Sanskrit. So here we say literally 'in vicinity of house'. This is essentially true also of the modern Indian vernaculars like Hindi, which accounts for the frequent omission of these words in the speech of Indians speaking English.

4. A common use of the dative is to express the purpose of an action, so 'for the enjoyment' and 'for all creatures' in 10.

Vocabulary

Sanskrit

यज्ञ, *m.* sacrifice.
प्रभाव, *m.* power.
मानुष, *m.* a man.
स्वर्ग, *m,* heaven.
गच्छति, goes.
शूर, *m.* a hero.
युद्ध, *n.* battle.
नृप, *m.* king.
जीवित, *n.* life.
त्यजति, abandons, gives up.
नर, *m.* a man.
सुख, *n.* pleasure, happiness.
धन, *n.* wealth.
न, *negative adv.* not
विन्दति, finds.
कृष्ण, *adj.* black.
अश्व, *m.* a horse.
क्षेत्र, *n.* a field.
धावति, runs.

पत्त्र, *n.* a letter.
लिखति, writes.
पार्थिव, *m.* a prince.
नगर, *n.* a city, town.
मार्ग, *m.* a road.
वहति, pulls, draws
माल्य, *n.* a garland.
युक्त, *adj.* provided with (+ *instr.*)
कट, *m.* a mat.
सीदति, sits.
ब्राह्मण, *m.* a Brahman (priest).
अन्न, *n.* food.
यजति, sacrifices, worships (*with acc. of the deity to whom the worship is accorded, instr. of that which is offered and dat. of the one for whom the sacrifice is performed*).
कृषीवल, *m.* a farmer.
ग्राम, *m.* a village.

नरेश्वर, *m.* 'lord of men', a king.
सूत, *m.* a charioteer.
रथ, *m.* a chariot.
आरोहति, mounts.
शिष्य, *m.* a pupil.
आचार्य, *m.* a teacher, preceptor.
दीर्घ, *adj.* long.
चलति, move, go.
फल, *n.* fruit.
वृक्ष, *m.* a tree.
उद्यान, *n.* a garden.
रोहति, grows.
अध्याय, *m.* a chapter.
पठति, recites.

English

many, प्रभूत, *adj.*
flower, पुष्प, *n.*
king, नृप, *m.*
garden, उद्यान, *n.*
various, विविध, *adj.*
ascetic, तापस, *m.*
practise, आचरति
meditation, ध्यान, *n.*
hermitage, आश्रम, *m.*
vicinity, समीप, *n.*
palace, प्रासाद, *m.*
sun, आदित्य, *m.*
ray, कर, *m.*
touch, स्पृशति
top, शिखर, *n.*
mountain, पर्वत, *m.*
man, नर, *m.*, मनुष्य, *m.*,मानुष, *m.*
cut down, अवकृन्तति
tree, वृक्ष, *m.*
house, गृह, *n.*
tiger, व्याघ्र, *m.*
drink, पिबति
water, जल, *n.*
lake, जलाशय, *m.*
forest, वन, *n.*
father, जनक, *m.*
give, यच्छति
book, पुस्तक, *n.*
child, बाल, *m.*
herd, यूथ, *n.*, गण, *m.*
elephant, गज, *m.*
go, गच्छति
deer, मृग, *m.*
dwell, वसति
lord, ईश्वर, *m.*
create, सृजति
beautiful, शोभन, *adj.*
lotus, पद्म, *n.*
enjoyment, भोग, *m.*
people, जन, *m.*
illuminate, प्रकाशयति
world, लोक, *m.*
all, सर्व
creature, भूत, *n.*

LESSON TWO

The Sanskrit Verb.

Thus far we have had two common forms of the verb, the word that expresses the action performed by the subject. These forms end in *-ati* and *-anti* and are used when the subject is singular and plural respectively. A considerable range of nuance is expressed by these forms, which has to be determined from the context when a translation is made. Thus *paśyati* (पश्यति) may mean simply 'He (she, it) sees' or 'is seeing' or 'does see' or 'will see'. Of course, when there is no context, as in the case of an isolated sentence (with no foregoing or following text), then any of these translations may be used. Conversely, it follows that all these variant English verb forms are expressed by one and the same form in Sanskrit, a fact which has to be borne in mind when one is translating from English into Sanskrit.

The action that is expressed by a verb may be viewed as in progress (as in the forms above) or as completed or as to take place at some time in the future. These time spheres are called 'tenses' in grammar. To express these different tenses different endings are used. To form the past tense, the final *-i* of the singular is dropped and the *-ti* of the plural *-anti*, and the short vowel *a-*, called technically the 'augment', is put before. Thus, the present *paśyati*/*paśyanti* (पश्यति/पश्यन्ति) becomes *apaśyat*/*apaśyan* (अपश्यत्/अपश्यन्) This is only one of three past tenses in Sanskrit, all of which have the same meanings and are interchangeable. This particular past tense is called the 'imperfect'; the other two are the 'aorist' and the 'perfect'. These latter will be dealt with in subsequent lessons. Corresponding to the range of meanings of the present tense, the imperfect may be rendered, for example, by 'He (she, it) saw', 'was seeing', 'did see' or 'would see' (in the sense of habitual or repetitive action, as 'He would do this every day', that is, habitually do it).

The four forms we have studied, that is, those ending in *-ati*/*-anti* for the present and *-at*/*-an* (with the augment prefixed!) for the imperfect are all expressive of what the grammarians call the 'third person' by which curious term is meant the one or ones referred to, as denoted by the pronoun 'he, she, it, they' or by a specifically indicated subject, as for example 'the ascetic'. Other endings are substituted to express 'I/we' (the 'first person') and 'you' (the 'second person'). These other endings need not be learned now, as the third person is by far the commonest and hence most needing to be learned. But to show how the forms vary depending on the person and number (singular or plural), all the persons and both numbers are given below along with just one of the possible translations for each.

Present

Singular	Plural
1. *paśyāmi* (पश्यामि) 'I see'	*paśyāmaḥ* (पश्यामः) 'we see'
2. *paśyasi* (पश्यसि) 'you see'	*paśyatha* (पश्यथ) 'you see'
3. *paśyati* (पश्यति) 'he, she, it sees'	*paśyanti* (पश्यन्ति) 'they see'

Imperfect

Singular	Plural
1. *apaśyam* (अपश्यम्) 'I saw'	*apaśyāma* (अपश्याम) 'we saw'
2. *apaśyaḥ* (अपश्यः) 'you saw'	*apaśyata* (अपश्यत) 'you saw'
3. *apaśyat* (अपश्यत्) 'he, she, it saw'	*apaśyan* (अपश्यन्) 'they saw'

Note that 'you' in English is ambiguous, as it can be singular or plural. In older English 'thou' was used for the singular nominative, 'thee' for the accusative, and in the plural 'ye' for the nominative and 'you' for the accusative. In modern times 'thou, thee' and 'ye' have all been displaced by 'you' which is originally the accusative plural!

In an English dictionary a verb is listed by what is called the 'infinitive' form; this same form of entry is also used in dictionaries of the Romance languages, whereas Latin and Greek dictionaries enter a verb under the first person singular. In a Sanskrit dictionary, wordlist or indeed whenever a verb is referred to in a general way (not by a specific form), it is given in a form that is termed its 'root'. Since this constitutes so important and ubiquitous a part of Sanskrit grammar, something needs to be said about it here, especially since this traditional way of listing verbs under their roots will be followed from now on.

Just as nouns are given in their stem form, a sort of endingless abstract from which, by the application of endings, the different cases are made, so verbs are referred to by a grammatical abstraction called a 'root', from which the many forms are made by the addition of endings and other grammatical operations. By a 'root' is meant a kind of basic, irreducible and minimal element that runs like a colored thread throughout all the possible forms of a particular verb.Though the root may be subject to alteration in some forms, the alterations follow certain rules. If we consider the forms *yāti*, *ayāsīt*, *yāsyati*, *yāta*, *yātum*, *yātvā*, *-yāya*, we see that in spite of variations the element '*yā*' remains constant. All these and yet other forms are said to be from the root *yā*. So this unvarying thread, which may be looked upon as the root or source of so many forms - really just a grammatical abstraction - serves as a convenient way of referring to a verb, instead of using a particular form like the first person singular as done in Latin and Greek books. It is customary to indicate a root by means of the root-sign employed in mathematics, but without the horizontal bar, thus, √*yā*, √*pat*, √*dhāv*, etc.

There are approximately 2000 roots in Sanskrit, less than half of which, however, are in fairly common use. These roots were arranged by Indian grammarians at a very ancient time into ten classes, named by them according to the first root listed in each class. So, they speak of a *tud*-class, a *div*-class, and so on. The classes are also numbered from one to ten (in Roman numerals!). The purpose of these classes is to gather together roots which are treated grammatically in the same way. For example, roots of the *div*-class all add the syllable *-ya-*, as does √*paś* 'see', a member of this class, before the endings that denote the persons (first, second and third), thus, (as we have seen!) √*paś+ya+ti→paśyati*. The ten classes fall into two great divisions, called conjugations, according to whether the stem, *i.e.*, the form the root takes before the addition of the personal endings, ends in *-a* or does not. By this dichotomy, roots of the *bhū-*, *div-*, *tud-* and *cur*-classes belong to the one conjugation, and all the rest, namely the *ad-*, *hu-*, *su-*, *rudh-*, *tan-* and *krī*-classes, the stems of which do *not* end in *-a*, belong to the other conjugation. The following tabulation may help to make this clear:

	Root	*Stem*	*Present 3rd Person Singular*
First	I. *bhū*	*bhav-a-*	*bhav-a-ti*
Con-	IV. *div*	*dīv-ya-*	*dīv-ya-ti*
jugation	VI. *tud*	*tud-a-*	*tud-a-ti*
	X. *cur*	*cor-aya-*	*cor-aya-ti*
Second	II. *ad*	*ad-*	*at-ti*
Con-	III. *hu*	*ju-ho-*	*ju-ho-ti*
jugation	V. *su*	*su-no-*	*su-no-ti*
	VII. *rudh*	*ru-ṇa-dh-*	*ru-ṇa-d-dhi*
	VIII. *tan*	*tan-o-*	*tan-o-ti*
	IX. *krī*	*krī-ṇā-*	*krī-ṇā-ti*

Note that all the stems of the first group end in *-a*, whereas those of the second have either *no* addition (like √*ad*) or are amplified in some way. A particular verb form is made by adding the personal endings (*-mi*, *si-*, *ti*, etc.) to the conjugational stem. So, the present second singular of √*paś* 'see' is made by adding *-si* to the stem *paś-ya-* (पश्य-) because this root happens to belong to the *div*-class (which requires the addition of *-ya* to the root). From the root itself it is not possible to know the class to which a root belongs: the class must be determined from the third person singular, which is given after the root in the wordlists or dictionaries. Some dictionaries, instead of giving the third singular, give the class-number, which in less transparent form provides the same information.

All this undoubtedly seems very complicated, but the seeming complication, as will be seen in due course, is largely caused by the newness and unfamiliarity of it all. The only verb forms that the student need be concerned with in this lesson are the third person singular and plural present and imperfect, as typified by *paśyati/-anti* and *apaśyat/apaśyan* of √*paś,* also the general concept of the root as a sort of grammatical abstraction from which the various forms are derived, and finally the meanings that are associated with these two tenses. The scheme of the ten classes and their dichotomy into two conjugations based on whether the stem ends in *-a* or not will become clear in the course of the following lessons.

Of the following two passages that are to be translated into English, the first (A) contains verbs only in the present tense, the second (B) only in the imperfect. All the new words should be sought out in the appended vocabulary.

A. अस्माकं[1] नगरं शोभनं स्थानम्[2] । उच्चाः वृक्षाः मार्गाणां पार्श्वे रोहन्ति । मार्गाः समाः भवन्ति । अतः नृपस्य रथः नगरस्य मार्गेषु शीघ्रं गच्छति । केषुचिद्[3] भागेषु मार्गाः न समाः । तत्र नरेश्वरस्य रथः न गच्छति । यदा यदा[4] नृपः नगरस्य बहिः वनं रथे गच्छति तदा तदा[4] प्रभूताः जनाः गृहेभ्यः नृपस्य दर्शनाय[5] आगच्छन्ति । काले काले बालाः मार्गेषु क्रीडन्ति तदा सूतश्च[6] भयात् शीघ्रं रथं न वहति । नगरस्य मध्ये नृपस्य प्रासादः तिष्ठति । प्रासादस्य समीपे प्रभूतानि गृहाणि विद्यन्ते । गृहाणां कानिचिद् अल्पानि भवन्ति कानिचिद् मध्यमानि कानिचिद् महान्ति[7] । अल्पेषु गृहेषु दरिद्राः जनाः वसन्ति महत्सु[7] गृहेषु सधनाः । इतस्ततः वृषभाः विविधैः फलैः संपूर्णान् शकटान् मार्गेषु वहन्ति । आदित्यस्य तापेन वृषभाः शनैः शनैः एव[8] चलन्ति ।

B. यदा मालवदेशस्य नरेश्वरः वनं रथे अगच्छत् तदा सुन्दरं मृगं शरेण अविध्यत् । यदा मृगः मृतः अपतत् तदा नृपः अनुतापेन संपूर्णः अभवत् ।

सूतं अवदत् । मारणं अतिपापम् । नरः मारणेन स्वर्गं न गच्छति नरकं एव गच्छति इति[1] । ततः नृपः प्रासादं पुनः अगच्छत् । तत्र विषादेन आक्रान्तः एकाकी[2] एव निवेशने अवसत् ।

Notes

A.

1. अस्माकं genitive plural of the pronoun अहम् 'I'; 'the city of us'='our city'. There is also an adjective अस्मदीय 'our' which might have been used here.

2. The Sanskrit equivalents of 'is' and 'are' are freely omitted. Here, then, we must understand the singular 'is': 'Our city [is] a beautiful place'.

3. केषुचिद् locative plural masculine of an indefinite adjective ('some'); कानिचिद्, the nominative plural neuter, occurs below, where it is thrice repeated and may be rendered 'some...others'.

4.When यदा 'when' is repeated, it denotes indefinitely repeated time, expressed in English by appending '-ever' to 'when', *i.e.*, 'whenever'. The following clause which expresses the action that takes place under the circumstances of the 'whenever'-clause -- often, but not necessarily introduced by 'then' -- is normally introduced by an answering तदा तदा, as though to say 'thenever' in correspondence with 'whenever'.

5. दर्शनाय is a 'dative of purpose', literally 'for the seeing of the king' or freely 'in order to see the king'. But in Sanskrit and also the modern vernaculars which have inherited it, this word दर्शन has a special nuance, the 'seeing' of a great and highly respected person being synonymous with the conferral of a sort of benediction. Thus, in modern times, newspapers would often carry a photograph of Mahatma Gandhi amid an enthusiastic crowd, with some such caption as 'Gandhiji offering *darśana* on such-and-such an occasion'. So, in the present passage the people are turning out in the streets for the king's *darśana* in this sense, not merely to see him.

6. In Sanskrit the word च 'and' is a so-called 'enclitic', that is, a word that cannot stand first in a sentence or clause; or, to put it somewhat picturesquely, 'cannot stand on its own legs and leans for support on what precedes'. For this reason it follows the word (or words) it joins. Thus, 'the

flowers and the trees' would in Sanskrit be 'the flowers trees and' (पुष्पाणि वृक्षाणि च). Here तदा सूतश्च 'And then the charioteer...'

7. महान्ति and महत्सु are respectively the nominative neuter plural and locative neuter plural of महत् 'great, big' which belongs to a different declensional pattern from that of the type देव/फल. This pattern will be studied later.

8. एव is an extremely important word in Sanskrit. It has no one specific translation, but its effect is to throw emphasis on the forgoing word, an emphasis which can often be expressed by such English words as 'only, just' or by italics in printing or intonation in speaking.

B.

1. In Sanskrit, when someone's words or thoughts are directly quoted, technically termed 'direct discourse' or *oratio recta* (for the Latinist !), the adverb *iti* (इति) is placed at the end of the quoted words. The quotation may be *preceded* by a verb of saying or thinking (here अवदत्) or, perhaps more usually, *followed* by a verb of this meaning. In this sentence, the words from मारणं through गच्छति (directly before इति) constitute the words of the king to the charioteer. When the verb of saying or thinking follows the adverb इति, there can occasionally be some doubt just where the quoted words begin. In such a case, which is quite rare, only the context can determine the case.

2. एकाकी nominative singular masculine of एकाकिन्, an adjective meaning 'quite alone, all alone'. It belongs to a different declension from देव, as, of course, indicated by the fact that the stem form or dictionary form ends in *-in*, not *-a*.

Vocabulary

A.

नगर, *n.* a city *or* town.
शोभन, *adj.* beautiful.
स्थान, *n.* a place.
उच्च, *adj.* high, tall.
वृक्ष, *m.* a tree.
मार्ग, *m.* a road.

पार्श्व, *n.* side.
√रुह् (रोहति, class I), grow.
सम, *adj.* even, level.
√भू (भवति, class I), be.
अतः, *adv.* therefore.
नृप, *m.* a king.
रथ, *m.* a chariot.
शीघ्रम्, *adv.* quickly.
√गम् (गच्छति, class I), go, walk.
भाग, *m.* a part.
तत्र, *adv.* there.
नरेश्वर, *m.* a king.
बहिः, *adv.* outside; *as postp. with genitive.*
वन, *n.* a forest, woods.
प्रभूत, *adj.* much (singular), many (plural).
जन, *m.* a person; *in plural* people.
गृह, *n.* a house.
दर्शन, *n.* the act of seeing, seeing, looking at, view.
आ-√गम् (गच्छति, class I), come.
काले काले, *redup. adv.* from time to time, sometimes.
बाल, *m.* a child.
√क्रीड् (क्रीडति, class I), play.
तदा, *adv.* at that time, then.
सूत, *m.* a charioteer.
भय, *n.* fear.
√वह् (वहति, class I), pull, draw.
मध्य, *n.* the middle.
प्रासाद, *m.* a palace.
√स्था (तिष्ठति, class I), stand, be situated.
समीप, *n.* vicinity.
विद्यन्ते, there are.
कानिचितद..कानिचितद *indef. adj.* some..others.
अल्प, *adj.* small.
मध्यम, *adj.* middling

दरिद्र, *adj.* poor.
√वस् (वसति, class I), dwell.
सधन, *adj.* rich, wealthy.
इतस्ततः, *adv.* here and there.
वृषभ, *m.* bull.
विविध, *adj.* various.
फल, *n.* fruit.
संपूर्ण, *adj.* full, full of (+ *instr.*).
शकट, *m.* a cart *or* wagon.
आदित्य, *m.* the sun.
ताप, *m.* heat.
शनैः शनैः, *redup. adv.* gradually, slowly.
√चल् (चलति, class I), move.

B.
मालवदेश, *m.* the Mālava country (in west-central India).
सुन्दर, *adj.* beautiful.
मृग, *m.* a deer.
शर, *m.* an arrow.
√व्यध् (विध्यति, class IV), pierce, hit (*as with an arrow*).
मृत, *adj.* dead.
√पत् (पतति, class I), fall.
√भू (भवति, class I), be.
अनुताप, *m.* remorse, regret.
√वद् (वदति, class I), say, say to (+ *acc. of person addressed*).
मारण, *n.* the act of killing, killing.
अतिपाप, *adj.* extremely *or* very evil.
स्वर्ग, *m.* heaven.
नरक, *m.* hell.
इति, *adv.* so, thus; used to mark the end of someone's thoughts or words, like the inverted commas or quotation mark at the beginning and end of direct speech or thought in English.
ततः, *adv.* therefore.
पुनः, *adv.* again.

तत्र, *adv.* there.
विषाद्, *m.* sorrow, despair.
आक्रान्त, *adj.* seized *or* filled with (+ *instr.*)
एकाकिन्, *adj.* alone, by oneself.
निवेशन, *n.* a dwelling; a room *or* chamber.

Translate the following passages into Sanskrit using the Sanskrit exercises as a guide.

A. When the king of the Mālava country drives his chariot in the streets of the city, then the people, provided with garlands, come from their houses to see him (तस्य दर्शनाय). Due to fear of killing people with the chariot, the charioteer drives the chariot ever so slowly.

B. When the king shot a tiger with an arrow in the woods outside the city, then, seized with remorse, he said to the charioteer: 'Charioteer! Go (गच्छ) quickly to the palace! My heart (मम हृदयं) is filled with despair.'

LESSON THREE

The Mysterious Gerund.

There is a particular verb form which is of so frequent and pervasive occurrence in every branch of Sanskrit literature,[1] that some familiarity with it cannot efficaciously be deferred. This verb form is termed the 'gerund'. Although this curious term leaves something to be desired, it has become so firmly rooted in grammars of Sanskrit, that any attempt to find a substitute name or label for it would probably be limited to the innovator and ultimately ill-founded. As with so many grammatical terms, it is best to stick with tradition.

What, then, is this verb form called a 'gerund'? It is really a sort of adjunct or qualifier, usually of the subject, expressing an action performed by the subject prior to that expressed by the verb itself. It is adjectival by nature, as it characterizes the subject as would any adjective, but as it is made from a verb, it denotes an action that has been performed by the subject in addition to that expressed by the verb itself. In a very literal and preliminary translation, a gerund may be rendered, for example, 'having run', 'having read', 'having fallen' etc. But for the most part it is better to substitute a 'when'- or 'since'- clause, or often a full verb connected by 'and' with the verb. While all of this sounds very vague and even complicated, it is really very easy, as a few examples will make clear. But first it must be pointed out that the ending of a gerund is simply *-tvā* (or *-itvā* with an *-i-* interposed between the ending and the root) or *-ya*. The ending *-ya* is only used when the verb root is preceded by an adverbial word like *ud-, ā-, pari-,* etc. The rules by which to determine whether *-tvā* or *-itvā* is added are complicated and rather useless to learn, as there are so many exceptions. It is best to learn the correct gerund form by experience. In any case, it is very easy to recognize a gerund, as any word that ends in *-tvā* or *-itvā* is a gerund! Here are some examples of gerunds as used in sentences:

1. नगरं जित्वा (from √जि 'conquer' + *-tvā*) नृप: प्रासादं अगच्छत् ।

'Having conquered the city, the king went to the palace' or 'When the king conquered the city, he went . . ' or 'The king conquered the city *and* went . . '.

2. दीर्घ कालं वने चलित्वा (from √चल 'wander' + *-itvā*) गजा: जलाशयं अविन्दन् ।

'Having wandered in the woods for a long time, the elephants found a lake' (or with the same variations of phraseology as in no. 1).

---

[1]Except, of course, the type of composition known as the *'sūtra',* which is so telegrammic as to avoid all verb forms whatsoever!

But if a verb has a prefix, *-ya* is used:

3. प्रासादात् आगम्य (from आ + √गम् 'come') नृपः नगरस्य बहिः उद्यानं रथे अवहत् ।

'Having come from the palace, the king drove in his chariot to the garden outside the city.'

4. जलाशयात् आकाशं उत्पत्य (from उत्-√पत् 'fly') विहगाः व्याधस्य शरान् परिहरन्ति (from परि + √हृ) ।

'Having flown up to the sky from the lake, the birds avoid the hunter's arrows'.

It is important to note here that any words that qualify a gerund, such as an accusative or other case or an adverb, must precede, as is normally true of any words that limit or qualify others in a sentence. Thus, in sentence 2 above, the gerund चलित्वा 'having wandered' is limited by दीर्घं कालं 'for a long time' and by वने 'in the woods', which, therefore, must come before चलित्वा. In 4 for the same reason the words जलाशयात् 'from the lake' and आकाशं 'to the sky' precede उत्पत्य. Therefore, when translating a sentence that contains a gerund, always look *before* the gerund for the words that are to be taken with it, *never* after the gerund!

One further note needs to be added here. Although the simple gerund (that is, without a prefixed adverbial element) always ends in *-tvā* or *-itvā,* sometimes there are changes in the final consonant of a root before *-tvā* (not before *-itvā* !). For example, √*yuj* (युज्) 'join, yoke' substitutes *-k* for *-j* when *-tvā* is added, giving *yuk-tvā* (युक्त्वा); similarly from √*tyaj* (त्यज्) we have *tyak-tvā* (त्यक्त्वा). The palatal *ś* as in √*dṛś* (दृश्) 'see' is changed to the cerebral *ṣ,* yielding *dṛṣṭvā* (दृष्ट्वा), a particularly common gerund.

In working out the sentences that follow, remember to find the verb first (*usually* the last word), then a noun subject if expressed (otherwise translate by 'he, she, it' or, if plural, by 'they'), then an object. After the skeleton has been gotten, see if there are any words in *-tvā, -itvā* or *-ya;* if so, translate them provisionally by 'having (whatever the root means)'. This having been done, bring into the translation the embellishments.

A Heavenly Retreat

एकदा कश्चिद् नृपः सूतं अवदत् वनं मां नय[1] सूत इति । नृपस्य वचनं श्रुत्वा सूतः यथा आज्ञापयति देवः[2] इति उक्त्वा शुभान् श्वेतान् अश्वान् रथे अयोजयत् । ततः सर्वैः आभरणैः समुपेतः महाराजः रथं आरुह्य सूतस्य पार्श्वे अतिष्ठत् । तदनन्तरं नगरस्य मध्येन सत्वरं गत्वा वनं अविशत् । तत्र न्यग्रोधपादपस्य[3] अधस्तात् रथं स्थापयित्वा[4] सूतः महाराजं अवदत् अत्र वनं कुत्र अधुना देवः गन्तुं[5] इच्छति इति । तापसानां आश्रमस्य समीपे जलाशयं गन्तुं इच्छामि[6] इति नृपः सूतं प्रत्यवदत्[7] । तथा[8] इति उक्त्वा सूतः जलाशयं रथं अवहत् । जलाशयं आगम्य महाराजः अतीव संतुष्टः अभवत् । तीरस्य समीपे चित्राणि कमलानि दूरे अनेकान् हंसान्[9] अपश्यत् । विहगाः अगायन् । वृक्षाणां षण्डस्य पश्चात् वंशस्य शब्दः उदगच्छत् । ततः महाराजः सूतं अवदत् । अहो रमणीयं अहो सुन्दरं सर्वं अत्र भवति । अत्रैव[10] स्वर्गस्य खण्डं दृष्ट्वा नरः कस्मात् कारणात्[11] स्वर्गं गन्तुं इच्छति इति ।

Notes

1. वनं मां नय 'Take me to the forest!' नय is the imperative of √नी (नयति, class I). The imperative form of the verb is used for giving an order or instruction to do something. In the singular (as here) it has no ending and is therefore identical to the stem. मां is the accusative singular of अहम्, the pronoun of the first person, corresponding to 'me' in English.

2. The words यथा आज्ञापयति देवः 'As the king commands' are the standard reply of a servant to a king in Sanskrit literature.

3. न्यग्रोधपादप 'banyan tree' is a compound word made up of न्यग्रोध 'growing downwards' and पादप 'tree', so literally the 'tree that grows downwards'. Anyone who has seen a banyan, especially an old one, will readily appreciate the descriptive literality of this common word.

4. स्थापयति is a so-called 'causative' verb meaning literally 'causes to stand' *i.e.*, 'stops'. Causative verbs and verbs of class X, both of which have *-aya-* between the root and ending in the present and imperfect, make their gerund by substituting *-itvā* for *-ati;* hence, *sthāpay-itvā* (स्थापयित्वा) here.

5. गन्तुम् is the infinitive, *i.e.*, the 'to-form' of the verb, made from √गम् to which is added the infinitive ending *-tum* (-तुम्); the *-m* (-म्) of √गम् is changed to *-n* (-न्), thus *gantum* (गन्तुम्) 'to go'.

6. इच्छामि 'I wish' is the first person, *i.e.*, the I-form, of इच्छति made by substituting the ending *-mi* (-मि) for *-ti* (-ति) and lengthening the preceding *-a-* to *-ā-*.

7. The imperfect tense of वदति 'says' (from √वद्) is, conforming to the rules we have learned, अवदत्. When the adverb प्रति *'back'* is placed before it, the *-i* is changed to *-y;* hence, *praty-avadat* for *prati-avadat.*

8. तथा as used here is short for तथा भवतु 'So be it!' It is one of several common ways of indicating 'yes' or acquiescence in what another says.

9. *Haṃsas* are mentioned with great frequency in Sanskrit literature. They are a kind of goose which Indians believed is capable of separating pure milk from a mixture of milk and water. This special ability is often alluded to, particularly in comparisons that involve discriminatory ability. For example,

> अनन्तपारं किल शब्दशास्त्रं स्वल्पं तथायुर्बह्वश्च विघ्नाः ।
> सारं ततो ग्राह्यमपास्य फल्गु हंसैर्यथा क्षीरमिवाम्बुमध्यात् ॥
> 'Grammar is surely endless, life is so short, and there are many obstacles. Therefore, one should grasp the essence, leaving aside the trivial, just as do *haṃsas* the milk from water.'

10. अत्रैव is a contraction of अत्र + एव 'right here.'

11. कस्मात् कारणात् 'for what reason, on what account, why?' कस्मात् is ablative singular neuter of the interrogative adjective (and pronoun!) किम् 'who, which, what?' कस्मात् qualifies कारणात्. The ablative here expresses cause.

Vocabulary

एकदा, *adv.* at one time *or* one day, once upon a time.
कश्चिद्, *indef. adj.* a certain.
नृप, *m.* a king.
सूत, *m.* a charioteer.
√वद् (वदति, class I), say to, tell (+ *acc. of person addressed*).
वन, *n.* a forest *or* woods.
माम्, *acc. sing. of pron.* अहम् 'I'.
√नी (नयति, class I), take, lead.
वचन, *n.* speech, words.
श्रुत्वा, *gerund* √श्रु (शृणोति, class V), having heard.
यथा, *conj.* as, just as.
आज्ञापयति, commands; *caus. of* आ-√ज्ञा (जानाति, class IX), understand, perceive.
देव, *m.* a god; a king.
उक्त्वा, *gerund* √वच् (वक्ति, class II), having said *or* spoken.
शुभ, *adj.* beautiful.
श्वेत, *adj.* white.
अश्व, *m.* a horse.
रथ, *m.* a chariot.
योजयति, harnesses, yokes, *caus. of* √युज् (युनक्ति, class VII), join.
ततः, *adv.* then.
सर्व, *adj.* all.
आभरण, *n.* an ornament.
समुपेत, *adj.* provided with (+ *instr.*).
महाराज, *m.* a great king, a supreme sovereign.
आ-√रुह (रोहति, class I), mount, ascend; *gerund* आरुह्य.
पार्श्व, *n.* side.
√स्था (तिष्ठति, class I), stand.
तदनन्तरम्, *adv.* immediately after, thereupon.
नगर, *n.* a city *or* town.

मध्य, *n.* the middle.
सत्वरम्, *adv.* quickly.
गत्वा, *gerund* √गम् (गच्छति, class I), having gone.
√विश् (विशति, class VI), enter.
तत्र, *adv.* there.
न्यग्रोधपादप, *m.* a banyan tree.
अधस्तात्, *postp.* under, beneath (+ *gen.*).
स्थापयित्वा, 'having caused to stand', having stopped, *gerund of caus. of* √स्था 'stand'; *on this v.* note 4.
अत्र, *adv.* here.
कुत्र, *interrog. adv.* where?
अधुना, *adv.* now.
इच्छति, third sing. √इष् (इच्छति, class VI), wish, want.
तापस, *m.* an ascetic.
आश्रम, *m.* a hermitage.
समीप, *n.* vicinity; *loc.* समीपे + *gen.* 'near'.
जलाशय, *m.* a lake.
प्रति-√वद् (वदति, class I), reply to, answer.
तथा, *adv.* in that way, thus, so; *v.* note 8.
√वह् (वहति, class I), draw, pull, drive (*a chariot*).
आगम्य, *gerund* आ-√गम् (गच्छति, class I), having come.
अतीव, *adv.* extremely, very.
संतुष्ट, *adj.* pleased, happy.
तीर, *n.* a bank *or* shore.
चित्र, *adj.* bright, bright colored, variegated.
कमल, *n.* a lotus.
दूरे, *adv.* in the distance, afar.
अनेक, *adj.* 'not one', many.
हंस, *m.* a kind of goose (but *v.* note 9).
विहग, *m.* a bird.
√गा (गायति, class IV), sing.
वृक्ष, *m.* a tree.
षण्ड, *m.* a clump.
पश्चात्, *postp.* behind, in back of (+ *gen.*).

वंश, *m.* a flute.
शब्द, *m.* a sound.
उद्-√गम् (गच्छति, class I), go up (उद्), rise.
अहो, *interjection,* ah! oh! how (+ *adj.*).
रमणीय, *adj.* charming.
सुन्दर, *adj.* beautiful.
खण्ड, *m.* a piece.
दृष्ट्वा, *gerund* √दृश् (no present!) 'having seen'.

Translate the following passage, formulating your phrases as much as possible on the lines of the Sanskrit to English passage. The participial phrases formed with 'having', which occur profusely throughout, are to be rendered by gerunds.

An ascetic, having meditated (ध्यात्वा, gerund of ध्या 'meditate') for a long time, went to a village for alms (भिक्षार्थम्). After he had walked ever so slowly on the side of the road, having seen a banyan tree, stricken by the heat of the sun, he sat down (न्यषीदत् imperfect of नि-सद् , stem नि-षीद with change of स् to ष् and substitution of -ई- for -अ-) there. Thereupon, after seeing beautiful and bright colored flowers near a tree (and) after hearing the sound of a flute in the distance, the ascetic was very pleased. Having seen a farmer on the road (and) having gone up to him (तस्य समीपं) quickly, he said: 'How charming everything here is! Heaven itself is right here!' Having heard the ascetic's words, the farmer, filled with astonishment (विस्मयेन) (and) having stopped his cart (and) having gotten down (अवतीर्य, gerund of अव-तॄ 'descend, get down'), from it (ततः), replied to the ascetic: 'Heaven is not right here, it is in a man's heart (हृदय, *n.*).' Having spoken thus (and) having mounted his cart again, he moved on slowly to the village. After hearing the farmer's words, not having gone to the village, having returned to the forest, the ascetic meditated (अध्यायत्) there for a long time.

LESSON FOUR

Nouns in *-ā*. The Demonstrative तद्.

I. *Nouns in -ā.*

In Lesson One the declension of nouns of the type देव and फल was given in the singular and plural. Some general remarks were also made about the subject of gender in Sanskrit. It was pointed out that there are three genders and especially that the gender of nouns does not necessarily correspond to the gender or sex of the persons or objects denoted by them. All nouns (and adjectives) that end in *-a,* as listed in the dictionary or vocabulary, that is, whose 'stem' ends in *-a,* are either masculine or neuter. The gender has to be learned from practice, but the case endings differ only in the nominative and accusative, where neuter nouns have *-am* in the singular and *-āni* in the plural.

Sanskrit nouns may, however, end in any of the vowels, and, unfortunately for the beginning student, the endings for the different cases tend to vary from the देव/फल type in rather perplexing ways. On the other hand, nouns that end in consonants have a fixed set of endings regardless of the final consonant. An alert student will certainly now ask: 'If the consonant stems have a fixed set of endings, why not learn the consonant stems first?' In answer it has to be said that nouns ending in consonants are, first of all, far rarer than those ending in vowels and, moreover, there are some difficulties involved in the declension of consonant stems that can be best dealt with later in a student's progress.

In this lesson nouns whose stem ends in *-ā* (long *-ā* as distinguished from short *-a*), *all of which are feminine,* are to be taken up. It will be best first to present the declension and then the points that need to be borne in mind. We shall use कन्या 'girl' as the representative or type-word of the *ā*-stems.

Declension of कन्या 'girl'

	Singular		*Plural*	
Nom.	*kanyā*	(कन्या)	*kanyāḥ*	(कन्याः)
Acc.	*kanyām*	(कन्याम्)	*kanyāḥ*	(कन्याः)
Instr.	*kanyayā*	(कन्यया)	*kanyābhiḥ*	(कन्याभिः)
Dat.	*kanyāyai*	(कन्यायै)	*kanyābhyaḥ*	(कन्याभ्यः)
Abl.	*kanyāyāḥ*	(कन्यायाः)	*kanyābhyaḥ*	(कन्याभ्यः)
Gen.	*kanyāyāḥ*	(कन्यायाः)	*kanyānām*	(कन्यानाम्)
Loc.	*kanyāyām*	(कन्यायाम्)	*kanyāsu*	(कन्यासु)
Voc.	*kanye*	(कन्ये)	*kanyāḥ*	(कन्याः)

The following points should be noted:

1. The nominative singular has no ending: *cf.* देव:, फलम्.
2. The accusative singular adds *-m,* just as do देव and फल.
3. The ablative and genitive singular are identical and distinguishable only from the context; in the plural the same is true of the nominative and accusative and the dative and ablative.
4. The dative and ablative plural both end in *-bhyaḥ,* as with देव and फल, *but* देव and फल substitute *-e* (ए) for the final *-a* of the stem, yielding the somewhat curious forms देवेभ्य: and फलेभ्य:.
5. The genitive plural is the same as for देव/फल.
6. The vocative plural is *always* the same as the nominative in *all* declensions.

II. *The Demonstrative* तद्.

A word of extremely common recurrence in Sanskrit is the word for 'this' or 'that', called by Indian grammarians तद्, but त by Western grammarians. It is always troublesome for students to learn, as the forms the various cases take seem so bewilderingly different from the देव/फल and कन्या types. Careful comparison, however, reveals many identical or nearly identical forms.

Declension of तद् (or त)

Singular

	Masculine	*Neuter*	*Feminine*
Nom.	स: [देव:]	तद्	सा [कन्या]
Acc.	तम् [देवम्]	तद्	ताम् [कन्याम्]
Instr.	तेन [देवेन]		तया [कन्यया]
Dat.	तस्मै		तस्यै
Abl.	तस्मात् [देवात्]		तस्या: [कन्याया:]
Gen.	तस्य [देवस्य]		तस्या: [कन्याया:]
Loc.	तस्मिन्		तस्याम् [कन्यायाम्]
Voc.	[no voc.]		

Plural

	Masculine	*Neuter*	*Feminine*
Nom.	ते	तानि [फलानि]	ताः [कन्याः]
Acc.	तान् [देवान्]	तानि [फलानि]	ताः [कन्याः]
Instr.	तैः [देवैः]		ताभिः [कन्याभिः]
Dat.	तेभ्यः [देवेभ्यः]		ताभ्यः [कन्याभ्यः]
Abl.	तेभ्यः [देवेभ्यः]		ताभ्यः [कन्याभ्यः]
Gen.	तेषाम्		तासाम्
Loc.	तेषु [देवेषु]		तासु [कन्यासु]
Voc.		[no voc.]	

In brackets the corresponding cases of देव/फल and कन्या are given to bring out the similarities and serve as a help to remember the forms. Apart from the importance of तद् because of its extremely frequent usage, is its importance as furnishing the pattern for a number of other common words which will appear in subsequent lessons.

तद् is primarily a 'demonstrative', that is, a word that points out. But its demonstrativeness is somewhat indefinite, so that it may point to a nearer or a farther object. Hence, both the meanings 'this' and 'that'. Thus, तद् फलम् may mean either 'this fruit' or 'that fruit'. The noun to which तद् refers may be omitted, in which case तद् functions as a pronoun (a word that stands for a noun); thus, तद् in a context about 'fruit' (फल) means 'this one' or 'that one' in the sense of 'the fruit' (previously referred to). Very often तद् has an attenuated meaning, no different from the English definite article 'the'. So, तद् फलम् can equally mean 'the fruit', if this sense is appropriate to the context and agreeable in English idiom to the translation. Since तद् may be used without a noun, that is, in the place of a noun, it occurs with the greatest frequency as a pronoun of the third person. Thus, the meaning 'that one' easily passes over into 'he, she, it, him, her' (depending on the case and the gender) and 'they, them' in the plural. For example, सा कन्या तं बालं पश्यति 'This (or 'that' or 'the') girl sees this (or 'that' or 'the') boy', but सा तं पश्यति 'She sees him', where सा and तं are made to do duty for सा कन्या and तं बालं. Consider also: तं व्याधं दृष्ट्वा ते विहगाः सहसा समुदपतन् 'When they saw the (or 'this' or 'that') hunter, the (or 'those') birds immediately flew up together'.

Or without either noun expressed, if the context is sufficiently clear: तं दृष्ट्वा ते सहसा समुदपतन् 'When they saw him, they flew up together'.

It should be observed here that in Sanskrit the equivalents of English 'he, she, it' etc. are commonly left out, and it is only the train of thought whereby it can be determined what to supply. In English these words cannot be omitted. For example, we cannot say simply 'sees'; a pronoun (he, she, it) has to be expressed. Similarly, we cannot usually say 'she sees' without some object expressed in the form of a noun or pronoun. But in Sanskrit the pronouns are frequently omitted, if their sense is easily supplied.

It's Harder than It May Seem

कश्चिद् कुमारः कतिपयान् दिवसान् न्यग्रोधपादपस्य छायायां वने ध्यानं आचर्य तापसस्य अल्पां पर्णशालां गत्वा तं तापसं अवदत् । परमं महादेवं दृष्ट्वा स्वर्गस्य आनन्दं अन्वभवम् । अतः किं अधिकेन ध्यानेन इति । क्षणं एव चिन्तयित्वा तापसः तं प्रत्यवदत् । वस्तुतः परमं लोकस्य ईश्वरं न दृष्ट्वा स्वर्गस्य आनन्दं न अनुभूय त्वं ध्यानस्य मध्ये सुप्त्वा तानि द्रव्याणि निद्रायां एव अपश्यः । परमं सत्यं दुर्लभम् । मोक्षस्य लाभः दुष्करः । अतः नरः प्रभूतान् एव वर्षान् ध्यानं कर्तुं अर्हति न कतिपयान् दिवसान् इति । तस्य तापसस्य वचनं श्रुत्वा परं विषादं गत्वा तं ग्रामं प्रत्यागच्छत् यत्र कुलं अवसत् । सः जनकं अवदत् । अविरतं प्रयत्नं विना स्वर्गः दुष्प्रापः इति । जनकः तं प्रत्यवदत् अवश्यमेव पुत्र । तस्मात् कारणात् कतिपयाः एव तं अधिगच्छन्ति इति ।

Vocabulary

कुमार, *m.* a youth, young man.
कतिपय, *adj.* some, a few.
दिवस, *m.* a day.
न्यग्रोधपादप, *m.* a banyan tree.
छाया, *f.* shade, shadow.
ध्यानं, *n.* meditation.
आ-√चर् (चरति), practise, engage in.
पर्णशाला, *f.* a leaf-hut (used by ascetics living in the forest).
√दृश् see (not conjugated in the present and imperfect, where √पश् replaces it), *gerund* दृष्ट्वा.
परम, *adj.* supreme, highest.
महादेव, *m.* *lit.* 'great god', applied to both Viṣṇu and Śiva.
स्वर्ग, *m.* heaven.
आनन्द, *m.* joy, bliss.
अनु-√भू (भवति), experience; *gerund* अनुभूय.
प्रति-√वद् (वदति), reply to, answer.
अतः, *adv.* therefore.
अधिक, *adj.* additional.
क्षण, *m.* an instant.
√चिन्त् (चिन्तयति), think.
वस्तुतः, *adv.* really, actually, indeed.
लोक, *m.* the world.
ईश्वर, *m.* lord.
त्वम् , *second pers. pronoun*, you (*nom. s.*)
मध्य, *n.* the middle.
√स्वप् sleep; *gerund* सुप्त्वा.
द्रव्य, *n.* a thing, article.
निद्रा, *f.* a dream.
सत्य, *n.* truth.
दुर्लभ, *adj.* difficult to attain.
मोक्ष, *m.* release from rebirth, liberation, salvation.
लाभ, *m.* attainment, acquisition.

दुष्कर, *adj.* difficult to do, difficult.
प्रभूत, *adj.* much; *in plur.* many.
वर्ष, *m.* a year.
कर्तुम्, *infinitive of* √कृ (करोति), do, make.
√अर्ह् (अर्हति), should, must (+ *infinitive*).
पर, *adj.* chief, highest.
विषाद, *m.* despair, despondency, dejection.
ग्राम, *m.* a village.
प्रत्य्-आ-√गम् (गच्छति), go back to, return to (+ *acc.*)
यत्र, *adv.* where.
कुल, *n.* a family.
√वस् (वसति), dwell, live.
जनक, *m.* a father.
अविरत, *adj.* uninterrupted, continuous.
प्रयत्न, *m.* an effort.
विना, without (+ *acc.*, which it follows as a *postposition*).
दुष्प्राप, *adj.* difficult to reach *or* attain..
अवश्यं, *adv.* of course, indeed.
पुत्र, *m.* a son.
अधि-√गम् (गच्छति), go to, attain.

Translate the following into Sanskrit:

Once upon a time a certain young man saw the great god Śiva in person (साक्षात्) in a dream and therefore (अतश्च), having thought liberation not hard to obtain, said to his father: 'What is the use of (किं with the instr., literally 'what's with--') much meditation? Attainment of liberation is not difficult!' When his father heard these words, seized with astonishment, he replied to that young man: 'My son, without continuous effort a man does not attain the bliss of heaven. Liberation is not merely a dream. Liberation is actually the highest truth in this world. Only a few ascetics, after meditating for many years on the great god in the silence (मौन, *n.*) of the forest, attain liberation!' Thereupon the young man, having gone to the forest outside his village, sat down in the shade of a banyan tree and having meditated there for a long time, thought: 'Liberation is really hard to attain!'

LESSON FIVE

More about the Sanskrit Verb. Guṇa and Vṛddhi.

In Lesson Two some very general remarks were made about the Sanskrit verb. The concept of the root was taken up in fair detail, and the division of the roots into ten classes by the ancient Indian grammarians was schematically presented. It is important to remember that these ten classes fall into two great groups, generally called the First and Second Conjugations, although it has to be added that in some grammars these numerical denominations are reversed: what is called First here is called Second and vice versa. This interchange of names is of no particular import, however, and need only be borne in mind if one should happen to resort to a grammar where the terms are reversed and some initial confusion result. The important point is that the stems of four of the classes (here embraced under the First Conjugation) end in short *-a,* whereas those of the remaining six classes do not. This short *-a* is technically called the 'thematic vowel', a term borrowed from Greek grammar. The First Conjugation is, therefore, often called the 'Thematic Conjugation', the Second the 'Athematic' or 'Non-thematic'.

In the Thematic Conjugation (or First Conjugation!) all the roots are turned into stems by the addition of a short *-a* or *-ya* or *-aya;* whether it is *-a, -ya* or *-aya* that is added to the root depends on which of the four thematic classes a particular root belongs to, and this can only be learned from a grammar or dictionary. There is nothing about a root which can give the slightest clue whether it is thematic or athematic, or to which one of the ten classes it belongs. Some roots can, in fact, be conjugated in more than one class! A grammar or dictionary gives this information either by including the *number of the class* or, more explicitly, by giving the *third person singular of the present tense.* Thus, if the Roman numeral VI is given, as, for example, after √*tud* 'strike', the student has to form the stem by applying the appropriate rules for that class before attaching the personal endings; if, on the other hand, instead of a numeral, the third singular तुदति (*tudati*) is given, then the student is relieved of this difficulty and by dropping the -ति (*-ti*) can make any form by simply adding the correct personal ending. In the athematic classes the personal endings are added either directly to the root, *i.e.,*with nothing intervening, as in class II, or the personal endings are attached to the root augmented in one of several ways, depending on the class. All this has been shown in the tabulation in Lesson Two. So much, then, by way of review.

It is essential to understand that a verb form of the present or imperfect (the tenses that have been studied so far) consists of a root (unchanged from the dictionary form or changed according to certain rules to be given below), plus a class sign (for example, *-a*, *-ya* or *-aya* in the thematic roots), plus a personal ending. Thus, √*bhū* 'be, become', changed to *bhav-*, plus *-a-*, the sign or marker for class I, which yields *bhav-a-*, to which in turn is attached the required personal ending: *bhav-a-ti*, *bhav-a-si*, *bhav-a-tha*, etc. Herewith are the present and imperfect singular and plural of roots typical of the four thematic classes (I, IV, VI and X). Hyphens are employed in the transliterations, as above, to separate the three elements (root, class sign, personal ending) from one another.

		I	IV	VI	X
		√भू (*bhū*)	√दिव् (*div*)	√तुद् (*tud*)	√चुर् (*cur*)
Present					
Sing.	1.	भवामि *bhav-ā-mi*	दीव्यामि *dīv-yā-mi*	तुदामि *tud-ā-mi*	चोरयामि *cor-ayā-mi*
	2.	भवसि *bhav-a-si*	दीव्यसि *dīv-ya-si*	तुदसि *tud-a-si*	चोरयसि *cor-aya-si*
	3.	भवति *bhav-a-ti*	दीव्यति *dīv-ya-ti*	तुदति *tud-a-ti*	चोरयति *cor-aya-ti*
Plural	1.	भवाम: *bhav-ā-maḥ*	दीव्याम: *dīv-yā-maḥ*	तुदाम: *tud-ā-maḥ*	चोरयाम: *cor-ayā-maḥ*
	2.	भवथ *bhav-a-tha*	दीव्यथ *dīv-ya-tha*	तुदथ *tud-a-tha*	चोरयथ *cor-aya-tha*
	3.	भवन्ति *bhav-anti*	दीव्यन्ति *dīv-y-anti*	तुदन्ति *tud-anti*	चोरयन्ति *cor-ay-anti*
Imperfect					
Sing.	1.	अभवम् *a-bhav-am*	अदीव्यम् *a-dīv-y-am*	अतुदम् *a-tud-am*	अचोरयम् *a-cor-ay-am*
	2.	अभव: *a-bhav-a-ḥ*	अदीव्य: *a-dīv-ya-ḥ*	अतुद: *a-tud-a-ḥ*	अचोरय: *a-cor-aya-ḥ*
	3.	अभवत् *a-bhav-a-t*	अदीव्यत् *a-dīv-ya-t*	अतुदत् *a-tud-a-t*	अचोरयत् *a-cor-aya-t*
Plural	1.	अभवाम *a-bhav-ā-ma*	अदीव्याम *a-dīv-yā-ma*	अतुदाम *a-tud-ā-ma*	अचोरयाम *a-cor-ayā-ma*
	2.	अभवत *a-bhav-a-ta*	अदीव्यत *a-dīv-ya-ta*	अतुदत *a-tud-a-ta*	अचोरयत *a-cor-aya-ta*
	3.	अभवन् *a-bhav-an*	अदीव्यन् *a-dīv-y-an*	अतुदन् *a-tud-an*	अचोरयन् *a-cor-ay-an*

From an examination of these forms the following points may be observed: Whenever the thematic vowel *-a-* is followed by an ending beginning with *m-* + vowel, as in the endings *-mi*, *maḥ* and *-ma*, the *-a-* is lengthened to *-ā-*; thus, भवामि, भवामः and अभवाम. When an ending begins with a vowel, as third plural -अन्ति, first person imperfect -अम् and third plural -अन्, the thematic vowel is dropped, thus, भवन्ति, अभवम् and अभवन्.

The personal endings of the present and imperfect may now be given:

	Present					*Imperfect*			
	Singular		*Plural*			*Singular*		*Plural*	
1.	-मि	(*-mi*)	-मः	(*-maḥ*)	1.	-अम्	(*-am*)	-म	(*-ma*)
2.	-सि	(*-si*)	-थ	(*-tha*)	2.	-ः	(*-ḥ*)	-त	(*-ta*)
3.	-ति	(*-ti*)	-अन्ति	(*-anti*)	3.	-त्	(*-t*)	-अन्	(*-an*)

Even the inattentive student will have noticed that the roots √भू (*bhū*) and √चुर् (*cur*) have been replaced by भव् (*bhav*) and चोर् (*cor*) throughout. On the other hand, √तुद् (*tud*) remains unchanged, and √दिव् (*div*) lengthens the *-i-*. The latter change is of no pervasive importance, as it occurs only in roots ending in *-iv*; these are few in number and, except for √दिव् (*div*), are all uncommon. Roots of class VI like √तुद् (*tud*) normally remain unchanged, but there are a few common ones that insert a nasal before the final consonant; for example, √सिच् (*sic*) 'sprinkle' (सिञ्चति *siñcati*), √लिप् (*lip*) 'smear' (लिम्पति *limpati*), √लुप् (*lup*) 'break' (लुम्पति *lumpati*), etc.[1]

It is only roots of classes I and X where the substitutions भव् (*bhav-*) and चोर् (*cor-*) seen here are the rule. In order to understand more fully the nature of these substitutions, a word needs to be said about a process of vowel modification called 'guṇa' and 'vṛddhi' by the Indian grammarians and 'vowel gradation' or 'ablaut' by Western scholars. The vowel grades in Sanskrit may be tabulated as follows:

Simple	*a*	*i ī*	*u ū*	*ṛ*	*ḷ*
Guṇa	*a*	*e*	*o*	*ar*	*al*
Vṛddhi	*ā*	*ai*	*au*	*ār*	-

[1] The inserted nasal must belong to the same class as the following consonant, otherwise the combination would be difficult to pronounce.

When read vertically, the guṇa and vṛddhi vowels (and diphthongs) are to be viewed as gradations of the pairs of the long and short simple vowels. Thus, for example, the guṇa of *i* and *ī* is *e,* the guṇa of *u* and *ū* is *o;* similarly, the vṛddhi of these same pairs is respectively *ai* and *au.* The rule of vowel gradation for classes I and X is that the guṇa gradation is substituted for the simple grade seen in the root. Since √भू (*bhū*) contains *-ū*, by this rule the *-ū* is replaced by *-o* (the guṇa of *u* or *ū*). By a certain phonetic rule, which will be dealt with in detail in a later lesson, the *-o,* when followed by a vowel, is changed to *av*-, hence, √*bhū* > *bho-* > *bhav*-(*-a-ti*, etc.). In the same way, the *-u-* of √चुर् (*cur*) is replaced by its guṇa counterpart *-o-*, hence, √*cur* > *cor-* (*-aya-ti*, etc.). By the same process, a root ending in *-i* or *-ī*, like √जि (*ji*) 'conquer' and √नी (*nī*) 'lead, guide', replaces *-i/ī* by *-e*, which by phonetic rule is changed to *ay*- when a vowel follows, just as *-o*, as we have seen, is changed to *-av*. Before the appended thematic vowel *-a-*, then, *je* (from √जि) and *ne* (from √नी) are replaced by *jay*- and *nay*-, thus: *jay*-(*-a-ti*, etc.) and *nay*-(*-a-ti*, etc.).

In ordinary Sanskrit prose there is not so much scope for the first and second persons of the verb, except where there are passages of conversation, in which, of course, the I-, we- and you-forms occur plentifully. But there is a frequent use of the first and second persons after verbs of saying, informing, etc. and after verbs of mental action, such as thinking, assuming, etc., where in Sanskrit the original phraseology is used in contrast to the practice in English, which prefers the indirect mode of expression, usually, but not invariably introduced by 'that'. For example, whereas in English we would say: 'He said that he would come', in Sanskrit we should say: 'He said: I will come' or more usually with the verb of saying (or thinking) at the end: 'I will come: he said'. Whatever the order in Sanskrit, the quoted words must be followed by the adverb इति (*iti*), literally 'thus', which serves as a quotation-marker. Since no such marker is used at the beginning of the quoted words, there are occasional passages in which the reader cannot be certain exactly where the quoted words begin. Of extremely common occurrence are the gerunds of verbs of saying and thinking, preceded by इति following quoted words. For example: नगरात् बहिः उद्यानं गन्तुं इच्छामि इति सूतं उक्त्वा नृपः रथं आरोहत् । The words नगरात्...इच्छामि are the exact words of the king, as marked by the adverb इति; the verb of saying is expressed in the form of the gerund उक्त्वा (from √वच्), the object of which (सूतं) immediately precedes it. In idiomatic English, using the *indirect* form, we might translate the sentence: 'When he had said to his charioteer that he wanted to go to the garden outside the city, the king mounted the chariot.'

The Ways to Heaven

कश्चिद् तापसः वृक्षस्य छायायां न्यषीदत् । तस्य समीपं गत्वा एकः[1] दरिद्रः मानुषः तं अवदत् । किमर्थं अत्र निषीदसि इति । तापसः तं दरिद्रं प्रत्यवदत् । ध्यानं आचरामि इति । ततः दरिद्रः तं अपृच्छत् -- किमर्थं ध्यानं आचरसि इति । तदनन्तरं तापसः तं पुनः प्रत्यवदत् -- ध्यानेन विद्यया च नरः स्वर्गं अधिगच्छति इति । दरिद्रः अधुना अचिन्तयत् -- यदि तस्मात् एव[2] स्वर्गस्य अन्यः मार्गः न विद्यते तदा किं करोमि[3] इति । ततः सः तापसं पुनः अवदत् -- त्वां पृच्छामि मनुष्याणां पण्डिततम[4] -- स्वर्गः तेभ्यः एव[5] विद्यते ये[6] ध्यानं आचरन्ति परमां विद्यां च विदन्ति[7] इति । ततः दीर्घं कालं चिन्तयित्वा सः तापसः तं दरिद्रं अवदत् -- बहवः[8] स्वर्गाः विद्यन्ते अधमाः मध्यमाः परमाश्च । ये ध्यानं आचरन्ति परं सत्यं च विदन्ति तेभ्यः एव परमाः स्वर्गाः । अन्ये[9] अधमान् मध्यमान् च स्वर्गान् शुभानां क्रियाणां अनुसारेण अधिगच्छन्ति । अन्ये तु पापैः नरकं गच्छन्ति । तेषु स्वर्गेषु उषित्वा सुकृतानां क्षयं कृत्वा अत्र पुनः जायन्ते इति । तस्य वचनं श्रुत्वा दरिद्रः मन्दभाग्यः भवामि इति चिन्तयित्वा स्वग्रामं अगच्छत् ।

Notes

1. एकः literally 'one', but often, as here, used like the English indefinite article 'a/an'.

2. The ablative is used in Sanskrit with comparative adjectives (bigger, higher, smarter, etc.) where in English we say 'than so-and-so'. It is also used with the word अन्य 'other', as here. Notice that एव, which is always an important word in Sanskrit, throws emphasis upon तस्मात्: 'If there is no other path to heaven than *this* (*i.e.*, the path of meditation and higher knowledge espoused by the ascetic)...'.

3. करोमि is the first person singular present of √कृ 'do', a rather irregular verb of class VIII. It is also a complicated verb whose forms will be learned in due course. But it is so extremely common by reason of its meanings 'do, make' in all the possible senses of these words, that some forms of it have to be presented early in spite of its difficulties. Here the present has future implication, as commonly in Sanskrit. It may be rendered here 'What am I going to do!'

4. पण्डिततम vocative!

5. Be careful of the ubiquitous एव!

6. ये is nominative masculine plural of the relative pronoun यद् 'who, what, which, that', declined precisely like तद्, *i.e.*, if य- is substituted for स- and त- of तद्, we have the declension of यद्.

7. विदन्ति third person plural present of √विद् 'know' which belongs to class II where the personal endings are added directly to the root, thus: विद् + अन्ति → विदन्ति.

8. बह्वः: nominative masculine plural of the adjective बहु 'much, many'.

9. अन्य 'other' is declined almost exactly like तद्; अन्ये is the nominative plural masculine like ते.

Vocabulary

कश्चिद्, *indef. adj.* a certain, a/an.
वृक्ष, *m.* a tree.
छाया, *f.* shade.
नि-√सद् (सीदति, class I), sit down (नि). [The स् becomes ष् after the इ of the prefix.]
समीप, *n.* vicinity; *acc.* समीपं + *gen.* with verbs of motion 'to'.
गत्वा, *gerund* √गम् (गच्छति, class I), having gone.
दरिद्र, *adj.* poor.
मानुष, *m.* a man.

√वद् (वदति, class I), say, say to (+ *acc.*).
किमर्थम्, *interr. adv.* why?
प्रति-√वद् (वदति, class I), 'say back' (प्रति), respond to, answer.
ध्यान, *n.* meditation.
आ-√चर् (चरति, class I), practise.
√प्रछ् (पृच्छति, class VI), ask.
तदनन्तरम्, *adv.* immediately after, thereupon.
विद्या, *f.* knowledge.
नर, *m.* a man.
स्वर्ग, *m.* heaven.
अधि-√गम् (गच्छति, class I), go unto, obtain.
अधुना, *adv.* now.
√चिन्त् (चिन्तयति, class X), think.
यदि . . . तदा, *conj.* if . . . then.
2√विद् (विन्दति, class VI), find; विद्यते, *literally* is found, is; *cf.* French *se trouver,* Italian *trovarsi*.
त्वाम्, *second pers. pronoun,* you (*acc. s.*).
पण्डिततम, *superlative adj.* most learned; as *m.* most learned one.
परम, *adj.* highest, supreme.
1√विद् (वेत्ति, class II), know.
दीर्घ, *adj.* long.
काल, *m.* time.
बहु, *adj.* much, (in *plur.*) many.
अधम, *adj.* lowest.
मध्यम, *adj.* middling, middlemost.
पर, *adj.* highest, supreme.
शुभ, *adj.* good.
क्रिया, *f.* action.
अनुसार, *m.* going after, following; *instr. with gen. as a quasi-postp.* in accordance with [*literally*, 'due to the following of . . .'].
तु, *conj.* but [never occurs first in a sentence.]
पाप, *adj.* evil, bad.
नरक, *n.* hell.
उषित्वा, *gerund* √वस् (वसति, class I), having stayed, having abided.

सुकृत, *n.* a meritorious deed, merit.

क्षय, *m.* destruction; *acc.* क्षयं *with* √कृ 'make a destruction of', bring to an end, exhaust.

√जन् (जायते, *plur.* जायन्ते, class IV), be born.

वचन, *n.* speech, words.

श्रुत्वा, *gerund* √श्रु (शृणोति, class V), having heard.

मन्दभाग्य, *adj.* 'having little (मन्द-) luck', unfortunate.

स्वग्राम, *m.* one's own village.

Translate the following passage into Sanskrit, rephrasing the sentences so as to use as many gerunds as possible:

Once upon a time the king of the Mālava country went in his chariot to the forest near the city. Having come to that forest, the king got down from his chariot and after wandering around for a long time to see[1] the many beautiful flowers there, he decided[2] to return to his palace. At that instant a deer, pierced[3] by a hunter's arrow, came from the middle of the forest and fell dead by the side of the chariot. Stricken with sorrow, the king said to his charioteer: 'Charioteer,[4] go quickly to the palace! I do not wish to stay here now'.[5] Having mounted his chariot, he returned to the palace, entered his chamber and stayed there all[6] alone in silence for a long time.

Notes

1. 'to see': Use either द्रष्टुम्, the infinitive of दृश्, and construe 'the many beautiful flowers' as its object, or use दर्शनाय, dative of the verbal noun दर्शन, *n.* 'seeing, the act of seeing' and put '. . . flowers' in the genitive, *i.e.* 'for (the purpose of) a seeing of . . .'. दर्शनाय was similarly used as a 'dative of purpose' in Lesson Two, exercise A (on which *v.* note A.5).

2. 'he decided': By phonetic rule the -स् of the prefix निस् is changed to -र् before the voiced न्- of नी and the न्- is then cerebralized according to the bewildering rule given in Lesson One, Section IV. The form here, then, will be निरणयत्.

3. 'pierced': The form विद्ध, called a 'past passive participle', is an adjective, though genetically derived from a verb root (व्यध्), and as an adjective must

be in the same case, number and gender as the one that is 'pierced', *viz*. the deer.

4. 'Charioteer': Vocative!

5. Do not forget to add the important word इति at the end of the quoted words!

6. 'all alone': On एकाकिन्, *v*. Lesson Two, note B.2.

Vocabulary

get down, अव-√तॄ (तरति, class I), *gerund* अवतीर्य.
wander, √चर् (चरति, class I), *gerund* चरित्वा, or परि-भ्रम् (भ्रमति, class I), *gerund* परिभ्रम्य.
decide, निस्-√नी (नयति, class I).
pierced, विद्ध, *adj*.
hunter, व्याध, *m*.
dead, मृत, *adj*.
fall, √पत् (पतति, class I).
stay, √स्था (तिष्टति, class I), *infin.*स्थातुम्.
enter, प्र-√विश् (विशति, class VI), *gerund* प्रविश्य.
chamber, निवेशन, *n*.
all alone, एकाकिन्.

LESSON SIX

The Past Passive Participle.

There is a particular verb form that is of so extremely frequent occurrence in Sanskrit works, especially those composed in the later history of the language, that an acquaintance with it cannot long be deferred. This verb form is called the 'past passive participle', and in a literal translation it may be equated with such English locutions as 'having been seen' or 'having been done' as well as with the short form made without 'having been'. These two versions of the past passive participle in English have, of course, different usages, although sometimes they are practically interchangeable. The short version is used in forming the compound past tenses in English in combination with the verb 'has/have/had'; thus, 'he has *seen',* 'they have *done',* 'she had *said',* etc., where the participial value is not so apparent. The short version is also used in forming the English passive voice, as will be seen below. The short as well as the long version is used, sometimes interchangeably, to characterize the noun qualified as having undergone the action the participle expresses. For example, 'The soldiers, having been harassed by the enemy, fled to safer positions'. Here the past participle 'having been harassed' characterizes, or describes the soldiers as having suffered or endured the harassment inflicted by the enemy. The short form 'harassed' might equally well have been employed, though perhaps with some loss of the nuance of prolongation the long form suggests: 'The soldiers, harassed by the enemy, fled' etc. In Sanskrit the use of the past passive participle in the formation of compound tenses of the *has/have/had* type is unknown, but the purely participial or adjectival use, where the short and long English versions are, as we have just seen, virtually interchangeable, is very common, much commoner than in current English, which tends to shy away from these participial constructions in favor of other modes of expression.

Participles, of which Sanskrit has an abundant supply, are adjectives and, like all adjectives in Sanskrit, they must conform to the case, gender and number of the noun or pronoun they qualify. A participle differs from an ordinary adjective, however, in having a verbal character, and this verbal character is due to the fact that a participle is born or derived from a verb root whose characteristics or genes it inherits. Just as its parent verb, a participle has tense (present, past and future!), and it may also take an object, provided that the parent verb is transitive, and finally it also inherits the property of 'voice' in the technical grammatical sense of this word. In this lesson, however, we are concerned only with the *past passive participle,* so that for the time being it will not be necessary or even desirable to enter upon all the details implied in what has just been said about participles in general.

First of all, we should see how the past passive participle is made from the root and then examine its various uses. The past passive participle is formed *directly* from a verb root and has nothing whatever to do with the class to which a root belongs. It is made by adding -त (*-ta*) or -इत (*-ita*) or, most rarely, -न (*-na*) to the unchanged root.[1] Which of these three suffixes is added to the root has really got to be learned. Rules are often given for determining the particular suffix to be added, but there are many exceptions, so that it is best and simplest to learn the past passive participle with each root. But it would be a sheer waste of time and effort for the beginning student to attempt to learn the past passive participles of a large number of roots at the outset. They should be learned, rather picked up, in the course of one's reading. The important point is that it is very easy to *recognize* a past passive participle, whether it is formed with -त, -इत or -न, the inflection by case, gender and number being precisely identical to that of देव/फल and कन्या. Herewith are some examples of past passive participles of very common Sanskrit roots:

a) by adding -त (*-ta*)

√श्रु (*śru*) 'hear': श्रुत (*śruta*) '(having been) heard'
√कृ (*kṛ*) 'do, make': कृत (*kṛta*) '(having been) done *or* made'
√हन् (*han*) 'strike, kill': हत (*hata*) '(having been) struck *or* killed'
√जि (*ji*) 'conquer': जित (*jita*) '(having been) conquered'
√नी (*nī*) 'lead': नीत (*nīta*) '(having been) led'

b) by adding -इत (*-ita*)

√लिख (*likh*) 'write': लिखित (*likhita*) '(having been) written'
√पठ् (*paṭh*) 'recite, read': पठित (*paṭhita*) '(having been) recited *or* read'
√ईक्ष् (*īkṣ*) 'see': ईक्षित '(*īkṣita*) (having been) seen'

c) by adding -न (*na*), but usually with some modification in the root

√म्ला (*mlā*) 'wither': म्लान (*mlāna*) '(having been) withered'

---

[1]This is not strictly or invariably true, as some roots undergo various kinds of weakening processes and phonetic change of their final consonant; thus, from √*vac* 'say' is formed *uk-ta*, from √*sthā* comes *sthi-ta*.

√भिद् (*bhid*) 'split': भिन्न (*bhinna*) '(having been) split' (Note change of -द् to -न् before -न)
√भञ्ज् (*bhañj*) 'break': भग्न (*bhagna*) '(having been) broken' (with loss of nasal and change of ज् to ग्)

Examples of sentences with participles in various cases:

1. व्याधस्य शरेण हतः विहगः आकाशात् अपतत् । 'A bird, struck by the hunter's arrow, fell from the sky.'
2. तापसः व्याधेन हतं विहगं अपश्यत् । 'The ascetic saw the bird killed by the hunter.'
3. सूतेन आदिष्टेन मार्गेण नरः ग्रामं अविन्दत् । 'By the road pointed out by the charioteer, the man found the village.'
4. तृष्णया आविष्टाय नराय कन्या जलं अयच्छत् । 'The girl gave water to the man (who was) overcome with thirst.'

Note that in each of these examples the past passive participle, functioning as does an ordinary adjective, conforms in case, gender and number to the noun it qualifies and, moreover, that, in accordance with the usual rules for word order, the past passive participle is preceded by its own limiting words. Except for the variations in ending required by the construction, the particular use of the past passive participle exemplified here is not different from English.

In English we find the past passive participle also joined with 'is/are/was/were' to form what is called the 'passive voice', in which the grammatical subject undergoes or experiences the action expressed by the verb without participating actively in the action as in the 'active voice'. For example, we may say 'The cat *is seen* by the child', 'The children *are taught* by their teacher', 'The poem *was recited* by the pupil', 'The pots *were broken* by the potter'. The compounds made with 'is/are' denote present time, even though the participle is past! Those made with 'was/were' are, of course, past. These passive locutions occur also in Sanskrit, although Sanskrit has special passive verb forms that are generally employed to express present time. These will be treated in a later lesson. But although the 'was/were' locutions, which are exemplified in the last two sentences, are also regularly found in Sanskrit, the construction differs in that in Sanskrit the equivalent verbs for 'was' and 'were' (आसीत्/अभवत् and आसन्/अभवन्) are *almost always omitted,* thus leaving the participle in effect to function as a verb in the past tense. Thus, the sentence 'The poem was recited by the pupil' would be rendered: काव्यं शिष्येण पठितं [आसीत् or अभवत् 'was' being omitted]. Of course, these words might also be interpreted 'the poem (which was) recited by the pupil'; whether the past passive participle is doing duty as a full-fledged verb or is purely an adjective can only be resolved by the surrounding context.

Since this construction is plentiful enough in English, *except for the dropping of* 'was' or 'were', it should cause the beginner no difficulty. The point where Sanskrit parts company with English idiom is that in sentences cast in the past tense Sanskrit idiom prefers the use of the passive to the active mode of expression that is far more usual in English. There are some works in Sanskrit where the past tense is almost exclusively expressed in this fashion (past passive participle with the performer of the action in the instrumental). The student of historical linguistics will be interested to know that in the modern Indo-Aryan vernaculars the past tense of a transitive verb, if traced back to its oldest form, is simply a past passive participle, although the form is no longer felt as a passive, but merely as a past tense in the active voice.

Since so excessive a use of the passive voice is quite foreign to English idiom, the student must for the most part translate this particular use of the past passive participle by an appropriate active form. Consider the following example:

नृपेण उक्तं सूत रथं योजय उद्यानं गन्तुम् इच्छामि इति । तस्य वचनं श्रुत्वा तेन सूतेन अश्वाः रथे योजिताः । ततः तेन सः नृपः निवेदितः रथः सज्जीकृतः महाराज इति ।

Literally translated:

By the king it [was] said: 'Charioteer, yoke the chariot, I wish to go to the park!' By the charioteer, having heard his words, the horses were yoked to the chariot. Then by him the king [was] informed: 'The chariot [is] readied, your majesty.'

With changes appropriate to English idiom:

The king said, 'Charioteer, yoke the chariot, I wish to go to the park'. Upon hearing his words, the charioteer yoked the horses to the chariot. Then he informed the king that the chariot was readied.

In the case of *in*transitive verbs, *i.e.,* verbs that do not take a direct object, the past passive participle is *passive only in external form, not in meaning*. So सः गतः (for सः गतः अभवत्) means 'He went', literally 'He [was] having gone'. Here गतः is the equivalent of the imperfect अगच्छत्. Since गतः, though passive in form, has an active meaning, the performer of the action of going is expressed by the nominative, not by the instrumental, as would be so if the participle were really passive in meaning. Thus, 'He said' would be तेन उक्तम् [अभवत्], literally 'It [was] said by him', as √वच् 'say' is a transitive verb.

The Brahman and the Mongoose

केनचिद् ब्राह्मणेन श्राद्धं[1] दातुं आह्वानं नरेश्वरात् लब्धम् । यस्मात्[2] तस्य भार्या तस्मिन् काले गृहे न अभवत् तस्मात्[2] बालस्य रक्षार्थं[3] तत्र न अन्यः अतिष्ठत् । यदि सत्वरं न गच्छामि तदा अन्यः कश्चिद्[4] आह्वानं ग्रहीष्यति[5] इति[6] चिन्तयित्वा तेन द्विजेन दीर्घ कालं पालितं नकुलं[7] मम बालस्य रक्षार्थं अवस्थापयामि इति निर्णीतम् । अनन्तरं एकः[8] सर्पः बालस्य समीपं आगम्य नकुलेन दृष्टः व्यापादितः च । श्राद्धं कृत्वा[9] तेन ब्राह्मणेन गृहं प्रत्यागम्य[9] रक्तेन विलिप्तं नकुलं अवलोक्य[9] मम पुत्रः नकुलेन भक्षितः इति चिन्तयित्वा[9] सः नकुलः लगुडेन हतः । सः सहसा एव पञ्चत्वं गतः[10] । ततः ब्राह्मणः पुत्रं शय्यायां सुस्थं दृष्ट्वा महत्[11] पापं मया[12] कृतं इति विदित्वा परमं विषादं गतः ।

(Adapted from Hitopadeśa, Book IV, Fable 13).

Notes

1. A *śrāddha* is a ceremony, incumbent upon every Hindu family, consisting of sacrificial offerings to deceased relatives. It is a supplement to the general funeral ceremony and is intended to pay homage to the deceased as well as to supply them with nourishment.

2. यस्मात् (ablative singular of the relative pronoun यद् expressing cause) to be taken with तस्मात् 'since . . . therefore', literally 'From which (reason) . . . from that (reason)'.

3. रक्षार्थं 'for the sake of the protection', *i.e.,* 'in order to protect'. अर्थं (accusative singular of अर्थ 'object') can be joined to any noun in this way to express purpose. रक्षार्थं is to be construed with the genitive बालस्य, thus, 'for the sake of the protection of his child', or more freely 'to protect his child'.

4. अन्यः कश्चिद् 'someone else'.

5. ग्रहीष्यति 'will get', future tense of √ग्रह् 'get'.

6. Observe the use of इति before the gerund चिन्तयित्वा to show that the preceding words contain the Brahman's thoughts.

7. नकुल 'a mongoose', a word borrowed from the Tamil language and having nothing to do with a goose, signifying a small weasel-like animal that is adept at killing snakes. It is often kept as a pet. The plural of mongoose, by the way, is mongooses (*not* mongeese!).

8. एकः the numeral 'one', which is often used practically as an equivalent of the English indefinite article 'a/an', as here. So, translate एकः सर्पः by 'a serpent'.

9. There are altogether *four* gerunds in this long sentence, all qualifying तेन ब्राह्मणेन which serves as the logical subject of the past passive participle हतः. The construction is: 'By the Brahman, having performed (कृत्वा), having returned (प्रत्यागम्य), having seen (अवलोक्य), [and] having thought (चिन्तयित्वा) . . . the mongoose was struck with a club', *i.e.,* in idiomatic English 'After the Brahman had performed . . . upon returning . . . , he saw . . . and thinking that . . . , he struck the mongoose with a club'.

10. पञ्चत्वं गतः 'went to five-ness', *i.e.,* died. Traditionally, Indians speak of five gross elements (ether, fire, air, water and earth), whence are made all physical things, including the body. When death occurs, the body is said to be resolved into those constituent elements. Hence, 'to go to a condition of five-ness' means 'to die'.

11. महत् 'great' modifying पापं 'sin'. महत् is a consonant stem (as it ends in त्). Consonant stems have *no* ending in the nominative-accusative singular neuter, hence the absence of an ending here before the neuter noun पापं.

12. मया 'by me', instrumental singular of the pronoun अहम् 'I'.

Vocabulary

केनचिद्, *indef. adj.* instrumental masculine singular, a certain.

दातुम्, *infin. of* √दा (ददाति, class III), to give; with श्राद्धं 'to perform a *śrāddha*'.

आह्वान, *n.* an invitation.

नरेश्वर, *m.* a king.

लब्ध, *ppp.* of √लभ् 'get, receive' (the combination *-bh-ta,* formed when making the *ppp.* becomes *-b-dha* by a regular phonetic rule, which requires the aspiration of *-bh* to be thrown forward and the *-t-* to be voiced, *i.e.,* replaced by *-d-*.)

भार्या, *f.* a wife.

काल, *m.* time.

गृह, *n.* a house.

बाल, *m.* a child.

√स्था (तिष्ठति, class I), *etymologically* 'stand', but usually attenuated to 'be'.

यदि, *conditional conj.* if (picked up by तदा 'then' in main clause).

सत्वरम्, *adv.* quickly, right away.

√चिन्त्, (चिन्तयति, class X), think.

द्विज, *m.* 'Twice-born', a term applied to a member of the upper three classes of Hindu society, because upon their investiture with the sacred thread, they are said to go through a second birth. Incidentally, any animal born of an egg, *i.e.,* any oviparous animal, is also called द्विज 'twice-born'.

दीर्घ, *adj.* long.

पालित, *ppp.* √पालय 'protect', a so-called 'denominative' verb, made from the noun पाल 'protector' by addition of the formative element or suffix -य, so literally 'act as a protector' of someone or something, hence 'protect', here 'keep' (as a pet). Denominative verbs, like causatives, are conjugated like verbs of class X; so *pāla-ya* behaves like *cor-aya* (√चुर्), as though consisting of *pāl-aya,* not *pāla-ya.* For further details, *v.* Lesson Twenty-eight.

नकुल, *m.* a mongoose.

मम, genitive singular of the pronoun अहम् 'I'.

अवस्थापयति, *caus.*of अव-√स्था, *literally* 'stand off *or* apart', *hence as caus.* 'causes someone to stand off *or* apart', leaves behind. (Causative verbs are conjugated exactly like verbs of class X).

निस्-√नी (निर्णयति, class I; note substitution of ण for न of the root. This change is due to the cerebralizing influence of the *-r-*), decide; *ppp.* निर्णीत '(having been) decided'.

अनन्तरम्, *adv.* then (like ततः).

सर्प, *m.* a serpent.

समीप, *n.* nearness, presence.

दृष्ट, *ppp.* (√दृश् 'see'), (having been) seen.

व्यापादयति, *caus.* of वि-आ-√पद् fall apart, disintegrate, perish; hence, the *caus.* means 'causes to perish', kills, destroys; *ppp.* व्यापादित.

रक्त, *n.* blood [really a *ppp.* of √रज् (रज्यति, class IV), be colored, be red; *hence, literally* 'colored, red'].

वि-√लिप् (लिम्पति, class VI), smear all over (the adverbial prefix वि means 'here and there'); *ppp.* विलिप्त.

अव-√लोक् (अवलोकयति), see, look at; *ppp.* अवलोकित.

पुत्र, *m.* a son.

√भक्ष् (भक्षयति) eat; *ppp.* भक्षित.

लगुड, *m.* a club *or* cudgel.

√हन् (हन्ति, class II), slay, kill; *ppp.* हत (having been) killed.

सहसा, *adv.* straightaway, immediately [in origin the instrumental singular of the noun सहस् 'might', so *literally* 'with might, forcibly, suddenly'].

शय्या, *f.* a bed.

सुस्थ, *adj.* safe and sound.

महत्, *adj.* great.

पाप, *n.* sin, wrong.

1√विद् (वेत्ति, class II), know; *ppp.* विदित.

विषाद, *m.* despair, dejection, despondency.

Translate the following passage, which is closely patterned on the story of the Brahman and the mongoose. Wherever possible use gerundial constructions and the past passive participle in place of the imperfect tense. Remember that, if the past passive participle is from a transitive verb (and so has truly passive meaning!), the subject or performer of the action must be expressed in Sanskrit by the instrumental, not the nominative.

Once upon a time a certain poor Brahman, having received (लब्ध्वा, gerund of लभ्) an invitation from the king of the country (देश, *m.*) to perform a śrāddha, thought: 'If I don't go to the palace immediately, then someone else will get the śrāddha', and he went to the king's palace. Since his wife had gone to the temple (मन्दिर, *n.*) to worship (पूजार्थम्), therefore no one (न कश्चिद) other than the Brahman (use the ablative after अन्य!) was at home to watch their child. Therefore, he thought: 'I'll leave here our mongoose which has been kept for a long time and go to the palace.' Thereupon a serpent that had gone up to the child was seen by the mongoose and immediately killed. When the Brahman came back home and saw the mongoose smeared with blood, he thought that his son had been eaten by him and struck the mongoose on the head. He died instantly (सपदि). Then, when the twice-born saw his son asleep and safe and sound in his bed, he was in deepest despair and was stricken with remorse for a long time due to his wicked deed (क्रिया).

LESSON SEVEN

Postprandial Exercises.

Too much of a good thing, for example, too much wedding-cake or too many participles and gerunds, can certainly cloy the taste and diminish our pleasure. By almost anyone's estimation the last lesson was a plenteous banquet, even for the hungriest student, and so, rather than add to that rich fare now, we must pause to savor its pleasures and serve no new courses until everything has been thoroughly digested. To this end, the present lesson consists of reading material that amply repeats forms and constructions that have been presented thus far. There follow two stories, which, like that of the preceding tale of the Brahman and the mongoose, are simplified from the Hitopadeśa ('Instruction about What is Salutary'), a collection of beast fables compiled c. 1500 A.D. and intended for the edification of the dissolute and wayward sons of a king of Pāṭaliputra by name Sudarśana. These fables in greater part are drawn from the well-known Pañcatantra of c. 400 A.D., a translation of which was early made into the Pahlavī language, whence it has over the centuries made its way via successive translations into the principal languages of the world.

A. The Lion and the Mouse

एकदा कश्चिद् सिंहः पर्वतस्य कन्दरे[1] अवसत् । निशायां[2] एकेन मूषकेन निद्रां[3] गतस्य तस्य सिंहस्य केसराग्रं छिन्नम्[4] । सः सिंहः प्रातः बुद्ध्वा केसराग्रं छिन्नं विदित्वा[5] परमं क्रोधं[3] गतः । अयं[6] मूषकः क्षुद्रः जन्तुः भवति । ततः तं निहन्तुं न धर्म्यम् । तेन सदृशं एव जन्तुं[7] तं निहन्तुं पुरस्कर्तुं धर्म्यं भवति इति आलोच्य[8] तेन सिंहेन स्वग्रामं गत्वा[8] मार्जारः प्रयत्नात् आनीय[8] कन्दरे धृतः । अनन्तरं यदा यदा[9] तस्य मूषकस्य शब्दः श्रुतः तदा तदा[9] सिंहेन मांसस्य खण्डः मार्जाराय दत्तः । ततः कतिपयान् दिवसान् मार्जारात्[10] भयेन मूषकः बहिः स्वविवरात् न अगच्छत् । एकस्मिन्[11] दिने तु क्षुधया पीडितः मूषकः निर्गम्य मार्जारेण दृष्टः तत्र एव[12] व्यापादितः भक्षितः च ।

(Adapted from Hitopadeśa, Book II, Fable 4).

Notes

1. पर्वतस्य कन्दरे We would probably say 'in a cave *on* the mountain' rather than 'of the mountain'.

2. निशायां 'at night' comes first because it sets the stage, as it were, for the sentence as a whole.

3. Notice how frequently √गम् (गच्छति) is used with the accusative (as here with निद्रां and below with परमं क्रोधं and in the preceding lesson with पञ्चत्वं) to express a condition that is entered into by someone. So, here 'of the lion gone to (a condition of) sleep'. It happens that the English idiom 'gone to sleep' in this particular instance corresponds to the Sanskrit.

4. छिन्नम् past passive participle of √छिद् 'cut, trim, nibble', formed with -न, like many roots ending in -द्. It agrees with the grammatical subject केसराग्रं 'end of his mane', the agent of the action being expressed by एकेन मूषकेन, thus: 'by a mouse . . . the end of the mane of . . . [was] nibbled'.

5. केसराग्रं छिन्नं विदित्वा In connection with verbs of knowing, perceiving and the like, Sanskrit often expresses what is known or perceived not in the form of a 'that'-clause corresponding to the English idiom, but by an accusative with an adjectival modifier, as here with विदित्वा, literally 'having perceived the end of his mane (as) nibbled' which would be in English 'having perceived that the end of his mane had been nibbled'. The 'that' is sometimes omitted in English. If the exact phraseology of what is known or thought by someone is to be expressed, then the adverb इति is placed after the quoted words to serve as an 'end quote' marker, just as in connection with verbs of saying.

6. अयम् is the nominative singular masculine of the demonstrative इदम् 'this', which, like all the demonstratives, may be used as a pronoun or an adjective (as here).

7. तेन सदृशं एव जन्तुं 'a creature exactly (एव) similar to him'. Notice that adjectives denoting likeness or similitude are used with the instrumental of that with which someone or something is likened; where we say 'similar to' Sanskrit says 'similar with'.

8. A typical construction in Sanskrit, especially in narrative prose, much less in poetry, is the use of several gerunds -- six or more are common -- in a single sentence, all preceding the main verb (which may be expressed by a past passive participle, mostly with the equivalent of 'was/were' unexpressed). Each of the gerunds denotes an action that *precedes* that of the following gerund and, of course, also of the main verb itself. The limiting adjuncts of each gerund must come before it. So here: 'Having thought " . . . ", by the lion having gone to his village, a cat, having brought [him] with an effort, [was] kept in the cave.' The three gerunds आलोच्य, गत्वा and आनीय all qualify तेन सिंहेन 'by the lion' which is the *logical,* but *not the grammatical subject* of the verb धृतः [अभवत्]. The sentence in skeletal form may be thus rendered: 'The lion thought " . . . " and, having gone to his village, kept in his cave a cat which he had brought from there with effort.' Or we may keep आलोच्य as a participle and make गत्वा into a full-fledged verb parallel to धृतः, thus: 'Having thought " . . . ", the lion went to his village and kept in his cave a cat which he had brought (from there) with effort.'

9. यदा यदा . . . तदा तदा 'Whenever . . . then'. The doubling expresses frequency of the action over a period of time, which is conveyed by the '-ever' in 'whenever'. In English, however, we would not say 'whenever . . . thenever'.

10. मार्जारात् भयेन 'due to fear of the cat'; words of fearing are construed with the ablative of the person or thing that is feared. This is really an 'ablative of separation', as one recoils *from* what is feared. So, whereas English speaks of 'fear *of* someone or something' (using an objective genitive), Sanskrit speaks of 'fear *from* someone or something'.

11. एकस्मिन् There are several words, some in fairly common use, that are declined wholly or partly like तद्. Among those entirely like तद् are अन्य 'other' and the relative यद्. Among those differing only in having -अम् instead of -अद् in the nominative and accusative neuter singular are सर्व 'all' and एक 'one'. Here एक is used as an indefinite adjective 'certain' or the indefinite sense of 'one'. Thus, एकस्मिन् दिने may be rendered 'on a certain day' or 'one day'. Here the locative case expresses time, so we may call the usage a 'locative of time'.

12. तत्र एव Notice the force of एव (which is always an important word): '*right* there' (not just there!).

Vocabulary

एकदा, *adv.* at one time, at a certain time, once upon a time.
कश्चिद्, *indef. adj.* a certain, a/an.
सिंह, *m.* a lion.
पर्वत, *m.* a mountain.
कन्दर, *n.* a cave.
√वस्, (वसति, class I), stay, abide, dwell.
निशा, *f.* night.
मूषक, *m.* a mouse.
निद्रा, *f.* sleep.
गत, *ppp.* √गम् (गच्छति, class I), having gone.
केसराग्र, *n.* the tip *or* end of the hair *or* mane (a compound made up of केसर, *m.* the hair, mane + अग्र, *n.* the tip *or* end).
अग्र, *n.* the tip *or* end.
छिन्न, *ppp.* √छिद् (छिनत्ति, class VII), cut; nibbled.
प्रातर् (-:) *adv.* early in the morning.
बुद्ध्वा, *gerund* √बुध् (बोधति, class I), having become awake.
विदित्वा, *gerund* 1√विद् (वेत्ति, class II), having known.
क्रोध, *m.* anger.
क्षुद्र, *adj.* small, tiny.
जन्तु, *m.* a creature.
निहन्तुम्, *infin.* नि-√हन् (हन्ति, class II), to strike down (नि), slay.
धर्म्य, *adj.* righteous, proper.
सदृश, *adj.* like, similar to (+ *instr.*).
पुरस्कर्तुम्, *infin.* पुरस्-√कृ (करोति, class VIII), to put in front, appoint, enlist.
आलोच्य, *gerund* आ-√लोच् (लोचयति, class X), having reflected.
मार्जार, *m.* a cat.
प्रयत्न, *m.* effort; *abl.* with effort, with care.
आ-√नी, (नयति, class I), bring.
धृत, *ppp.* √धृ (धारयति, *caus.* √धृ, *without caus. meaning*); held, retained, kept.
अनन्तरम्, *adv.* afterwards, thereupon.
शब्द, *m.* sound, noise.
श्रुत, *ppp.* √श्रु (शृणोति, class V), heard.

मांस, *n.* meat.
खण्ड, *m.* a piece.
दत्त, *ppp.* √दा (ददाति, class III), given.
कतिपय, *adj.* a few.
दिवस्, *m.* a day.
भय, *n.* fear.
बहिः, *adv.* out, outside.
विवर, *m.* an opening, hole.
क्षुधा, *f.* hunger.
पीडित, *ppp.* √पीड् (पीडयति, class X), oppressed, pained, tormented.
निर्गम्य, *gerund* निस्-√गम् (गच्छति, class I), having gone out.
दृष्ट, *ppp.* √दृश् (no present!), having been seen, seen.
व्यापादित, *ppp. caus.* वि-आ-√पद् (पद्यते, class IV), 'caused to fall away', destroyed, killed.
भक्षित, *ppp.* √भक्ष् (भक्षति, class I), eaten.

B. The Brahman and the Three Rogues

एकः[1] द्विजः ग्रामे छागं क्रीत्वा स्कन्धे निधाय नगरस्य मार्गे[2] अगच्छत् । सः त्रिभिः[3] धूर्तैः अवलोकितः । तैः धूर्तैः तस्य छागं चोरयितुं कपटेन निर्णीतम् । ततः तेषां कपटस्य अनुसारेण सः द्विजः एकेन धूर्तेन अभिभाषितः भो ब्राह्मण किमर्थं स्कन्धे श्वानं[4] वहसि इति । तेन द्विजेन प्रत्युक्तं अयं न श्वा अयं छागः यज्ञार्थं[5] छागः इति । अनन्तरं अन्येन धूर्तेन तं अधिगम्य तद् एव उक्तं भो ब्राह्मण किमर्थं स्कन्धे श्वानं वहसि इति । अधुना तस्य द्विजस्य चित्तं व्याकुलं अभवत् । तेन कारणेन छागं भूम्यां[6] निधाय तं पुनः पुनः निरीक्ष्य सः द्विजः अयं न श्वा भवति छागः एव इति उक्त्वा पुनः स्कन्धे स्थापयित्वा प्रस्थितः । ततः तृतीयेन धूर्तेन आगम्य तद् एव वचनं उक्तम् । तदनन्तरं सः द्विजः छागं भूम्यां निधाय अयं निश्चितं न छागः अयं श्वा इति उक्त्वा मार्गे तं त्यक्त्वा स्नात्वा[7] अपगतः ।

(Adapted from Hitopadeśa, Book IV, Fable 10).

Notes

1. एक: On the meaning of एक here, see note 11 above.

2. नगरस्य मार्गे Where we would say 'on the road *to* the city' Sanskrit says 'on the road *of* the city'.

3. त्रिभि: instrumental plural of the numeral त्रि 'three' (*v.* declension on p. 211).

4. श्वानं accusative singular of the consonant stem श्वन् 'dog'. The nominative श्वा occurs below.

5. यज्ञार्थं 'for a sacrifice' *i.e.*, the goat is a sacrificial goat.

6. भूम्यां 'on the ground', *loc. f. sing.* of भूमि, on declension of which *v.* Lesson Ten.

7. The Brahman took a bath in order to wash away the impurity due to having touched a dog.

Vocabulary

द्विज, *m.* 'twice-born', a member of the upper three classes of Hindu society, *viz.*, Brāhmaṇas, Kṣatriyas and Vaiśyas. But usually द्विज is used of the priestly caste of the Brāhmaṇas.

छाग, *m.* a goat.

क्रीत्वा, *gerund* √क्री (क्रीणाति, class IX), having bought.

स्कन्ध, *m.* the shoulder.

निधाय, *gerund* नि-√धा (दधाति, class III), having put down (नि).

धूर्त, *m.* a rogue.

अवलोकित, *ppp. caus.* अव-√लोक् (लोकते, class I), *but without caus. meaning,* seen.

कपट, *m.* fraud, trickery.

निर्णीत, *ppp.* निस्-√नी (नयति, class I), decided.

अभिभाषित, *ppp.* अभि-√भाष् (भाषते, class I), spoken to (अभि), addressed, accosted.

भो, *particle of address,* O, sir. (strictly भोः, the visarga being lost before voiced consonants).
श्वन्, *m.* a dog. [v. note 3]
√वह्, (वहति, class I), carry, bear.
प्रत्युक्त, *ppp.* √वच् (वक्ति, class II), answered.
अनन्तरम्, *adv.* immediately after, thereupon.
अधिगम्य, *gerund* अधि-√गम् (गच्छति, class I), having gone to (अधि), approached.
उक्त, *ppp.* √वच् (वक्ति, class II), said, spoken.
अधुना, *adv.* now.
चित्त, *n.* the mind.
व्याकुल, *adj.* confused, puzzled.
कारण, *n.* reason, cause.
भूमि, *f.* ground, earth.
पुनः पुनः, *adv.* again and again.
निरीक्ष्य, *gerund* निस्-√ईक्ष् (ईक्षते, class I), having contemplated.
स्थापयित्वा, *gerund of caus.* √स्था (तिष्ठति, class I), 'having caused to stand', having put *or* placed.
तृतीय, *ordinal numeral adj.*, third.
प्रस्थित, *ppp.* प्र-√स्था, 'having stood forth', *then* having gone forth.
निश्चितम्, *adv.* surely, certainly.
त्यक्त्वा, *gerund* √त्यज् (त्यजति, class I), having abandoned, having left aside.
स्नात्वा, *gerund* √स्ना (स्नाति, class II), having bathed.
अपगत, *ppp.* अप-√गम् (गच्छति, class I), having gone away (अप).

Translate into Sanskrit:

Thinking (use gerund of √चिन्त्) that heaven is not difficult to attain, a certain Brahman sat down in the shade of a tree full of many fruits and made (अकरोत्) a supreme effort to meditate. After falling asleep in the middle of (his) meditation, he saw the great god Śiva in a dream and, awakened (प्रबोधित) by the fall (पतन, *n.*) of one of the fruits on (his) head (मस्तक, *n.*), he said aloud (प्रकाशम् *or* उच्चैः): 'After experiencing the bliss of heaven and returning to this earth (वासुधा, *f.*), I have gone to the deepest (use परम 'supreme'!) despair!'

LESSON EIGHT

Nouns in *-ī*. The Demonstrative इदम.

I. *Nouns in -ī.*

It has been mentioned that Sanskrit nouns and adjectives may end in any of the vowels or diphthongs. Unfortunately for the learner, the declension of vowel stems varies, sometimes considerably, according to the final vowel; that is to say, there is not one *invariable* set of endings that is attached to the stem in forming all the declensions. We have dealt with stems in *-a,* which may be masculine or neuter, and feminines in *-ā*. There is also a large and important class of feminine nouns in *-ī,* which is best treated at this point because of the transfer of some of its endings to other classes of vowel stems. The somewhat perplexing variations in the declension of these other stems will be more readily understood -- or at least digested! -- if the *ī*-stems are learned first. We may take the very common noun नदी 'river' as our type for this declension.

	Singular		*Plural*	
Nom.	*nadī*	(नदी)	*nadyaḥ*	(नद्यः)
Acc.	*nadīm*	(नदीम्)	*nadīḥ*	(नदीः)
Instr.	*nadyā*	(नद्या)	*nadībhiḥ*	(नदीभिः)
Dat.	*nadyai*	(नद्यै)	*nadībhyaḥ*	(नदीभ्यः)
Abl.	*nadyāḥ*	(नद्याः)	*nadībhyaḥ*	(नदीभ्यः)
Gen.	*nadyāḥ*	(नद्याः)	*nadīnām*	(नदीनाम्)
Loc.	*nadyām*	(नद्याम्)	*nadīṣu*	(नदीषु)
Voc.	*nadi*	(नदि)	*nadyaḥ*	(नद्यः)

In learning anything, it is always best to proceed from the simple to the difficult or from what is obvious to what is obscure, a principle that is not always embraced as firmly as it should. If we apply this reasonable principle in learning this declension, we will see that there are, in spite of marked differences, many similarities to the कन्या declension: the nominative singular has no ending (नदी/कन्या), the accusative singular ends in -म् (नदीम्/कन्याम्), the accusative plural adds -: (नदीः/कन्याः), the instrumental, dative-ablative, genitive and locative plural add the same endings as कन्या (नदी-भिः/कन्या-भिः, नदी-भ्यः/कन्या-भ्यः, नदी-नाम्/कन्या-नाम्, नदी-षु/कन्या-सु, with change of dental स् to cerebral ष् as in देवेषु and फलेषु). Remember that the vocative plural is the same as the nominative in *all* declensions. The instrumental, dative, ablative-genitive and locative singular of the *-ī* declension end in *-ā, -ai, -āḥ* and *-ām,* before which the *-ī* is changed to *-y-;* thus, in transcription for greater clarity in seeing the process: *nadī-ā* → *nady-ā, nadī-ai* → *nady-ai, nadī-āḥ* → *nady-āḥ, nadī-ām* → *nady-ām.* If we compare these particular forms with the corresponding ones of कन्या, we may see that कन्या uses these same peculiar endings, but with an interposed -*y*- to keep the *-ā* of the stem intact, *i.e.,* from contracting with the vowel of the endings: *kanyā-y-ai, kanyā-y-āḥ, kanyā-y-ām,* but in the instrumental the final *-ā* of कन्या is shortened: *kanya-y-ā.*

II. *The Demonstrative* इदम्.

In Lesson Four the declension of the demonstrative pronoun तद् was given. It was pointed out that तद् has an indefinite reference and may mean 'this' or 'that' (more usually the latter), that it frequently means simply 'the', that it may be used as an adjective (for example, 'this *or* that fruit'), or independently as a pronoun, the person or thing referred to being clear from the context. Lastly, the important use of तद् in the appropriate gender as a pronoun of the third person ('he, she, it, her, him, they, them').

There is another demonstrative of common occurrence, more specifically meaning 'this', used both as a pronoun and an adjective. But as a pronoun, it still retains its demonstrative ('pointing out') force; that is to say, it is not used as a pronoun of the third person ('he, she, it' etc.). This pronoun is called इदम् by Indian scholars, but generally अयम् by Western scholars. As will be seen from the declension below, इदम् is the nominative-accusative neuter singular, whereas अयम् is the nominative masculine singular. Here, as in the case of तद् (nominative-accusative neuter singular), we shall employ the Indian mode of reference in favor of consistency.

Declension of इदम् 'this'

Singular

	Masculine	*Neuter*	*Feminine*
Nom.	अयम्	इदम्	इयम्
Acc.	इमम्	इदम्	इमाम्
Instr.	अनेन (*anena/tena*)		अनया (*anayā/tayā*)
Dat.	अस्मै (*asmai/tasmai*)		अस्यै (*asyai/tasyai*)
Abl.	अस्मात् (*asmāt/tasmāt*)		अस्याः (*asyāḥ/tasyāḥ*)
Gen.	अस्य (*asya/tasya*)		अस्याः (*asyāḥ/tasyāḥ*)
Loc.	अस्मिन् (*asmin/tasmin*)		अस्याम् (*asyām/tasyām*)

[no voc.]

Plural

Nom.	इमे	इमानि	इमाः
Acc.	इमान्	इमानि	इमाः
Instr.	एभिः		आभिः (*ābhiḥ/tābhiḥ*)
Dat.	एभ्यः (*ebhyaḥ/tebhyaḥ*)		आभ्यः (*ābhyaḥ/tābhyaḥ*)
Abl.	एभ्यः (*ebhyaḥ/tebhyaḥ*)		आभ्यः (*ābhyaḥ/tābhyaḥ*)
Gen.	एषाम् (*eṣām/teṣām*)		आसाम् (*āsām/tāsām*)
Loc.	एषु (*eṣu/teṣu*)		आसु (*āsu/tāsu*)

[no voc.]

At first sight these forms may seem discouragingly difficult. Close inspection, however, will show that many of the forms are identical to those of तद् if the त् (*t*-) of तद् is dropped. To bring this out more clearly, the forms of तद् which are the same except for the initial *t*- are given in transliteration within parentheses, in juxtaposition with similar forms of इदम्, which are repeated in transliteration.

The Twice-born and His Plate of Barley

पूर्वस्मिन्[1] काले केनचिद्[2] द्विजेन यवैः पूर्णः शरावः प्राप्तः । यतः[3] सः दरिद्रः अभवत् ततः[3] इमं यवपूर्णं[4] शरावं प्राप्य तस्य हृदये प्रभूतः संतोषः जातः[5] । अनन्तरं स्वग्रामं त्यक्त्वा चिरकालीनस्य मित्रस्य कुम्भकारस्य मण्डपिकां गत्वा तत्र रात्र्यां शय्यायां शयित्वा एवं अचिन्तयत् । यदि[6] अहं इमं यवपूर्णं शरावं विक्रीय कतिपयान् कपर्दकान् प्राप्नोमि तदा[6] तैः कपर्दकैः अन्यान् घटान् क्रीत्वा विक्रीय[7] अनेकधा वृद्धेन धनेन प्रभूतानि अन्यानि द्रव्यानि उपक्रीय अनेन प्रकारेण धनस्य संचयं उत्पाद्य चतस्रः पत्नीः परिणयामि[8] । ततः तासु पत्नीषु अधिकरूपवत्यां[9] अधिकं अनुरागं करोमि[10] । यदा यदा[11] ताः अन्याः नार्यः ईर्ष्यया[12] द्वन्द्वं कुर्वन्ति[13] तदा तदा[11] अहं कोपेन आकुलः इत्थं अनेन लगुडेन ताः ताडयामि । इति उक्त्वा शय्यायाः उत्थाय[14] तेन द्विजेन लगुडः क्षिप्तः । अतः तेन लगुडेन तस्य यवपूर्णः शरावः चूर्णितः भाण्डानि च प्रभूतानि भग्नानि । एषां भाण्डानां भङ्गस्य शब्देन कुम्भकारेण आगम्य तद् दृष्ट्वा सः द्विजः तिरस्कृतः मण्डपिकायाः च बहिष्कृतः ।

(Adapted from Hitopadeśa, Book IV, Fable 8).

Notes

1. पूर्वस्मिन् loc. masc. sing. of पूर्व 'former', one of a group of words called 'pronominals' because they are declined wholly or partly like the demonstrative pronoun तद्.

2. केनचिद् instr. masc. sing. of the indefinite adjective कश्चिद् 'a certain, some, a', the first part of which is declined like तद्, except for the nom.-acc. sing., which is peculiar in taking the form किं instead of the expected कद्. So,

in the masc. sing. कश्चिद्, कंचिद्, केनचिद्, कस्मैचिद् etc.; in the fem. काचिद्, कांचिद्, कयाचिद्, कस्यैचिद् etc.

3. यत: . . . तत: 'Because . . . therefore'; in English the correlative 'therefore' is generally omitted, in Sanskrit तत: is rather rarely omitted.

4. यवपूर्ण Instead of saying यवै: पूर्ण 'filled with barley', in this occurrence the two words are brought together into one compound word, just as we might say 'barley-filled' in English. Note that when a compound is thus made in Sanskrit, the first part, here यवै:, loses its case ending, only the stem form यव being used: यव-पूर्ण.

5. जात: past passive participle of √जन् 'be born', commonly employed in this way in the sense of 'arose'. In analyzing it, one may say that it is the typical construction whereby a main verb in the past tense is replaced by a past passive participle with अभवत् or अभवन् ('was/were') unexpressed.

In working out the next two sentences, which have many gerunds, bear in mind that each gerund expresses an action that precedes that of the following gerund, and the actions of all precede that of the principal verb; furthermore, that objects and other qualifiers always *precede* the gerund they qualify.

6. यदि . . . तदा 'If . . . then'. An 'if'-clause (that is, a conditional clause or protasis, as it is more technically termed) is generally introduced in Sanskrit by यदि, and the main predication that depends on the fulfillment of the condition (the 'apodosis') is often prefaced by the answering word तदा 'then' (that is, 'in that case'), the English equivalent of which is mostly omitted.

7. विक्रीय With the gerund the sense of the accusatives preceding क्रीत्वा must be supplied: 'having bought (क्रीत्वा) other pots with these *kapardakas* [and] having sold (विक्रीय) [them]'.

8. परिणयामि 'I'll marry'. The present tense in Sanskrit often has the meaning of an immediate future, a usage found in many languages, including our own English language in its early stage known as Old English, which, like modern English, did not have a true future. In modern English the helping ('auxiliary') verbs 'shall' and 'will' are used to form what is in fact a periphrastic or compound future. परिणयामि means literally 'I (shall) lead around' an expression which has reference to an essential act in the Hindu

wedding ritual, which involves the groom's leading the bride around the sacrificial fire.

9. अधिकरूपवत्यां 'on the one (that is, the wife) who is especially or extraordinarily beautiful', to be taken with अनुरागं करोमि. रूपवत्यां is the loc. fem. sing. of रूपवती '(she) who has beauty (रूप)', an adjective (strictly speaking!) used as a noun, declined like नदी.

10. करोमि literally 'I make', but, like परिणयामि above, with the sense of a future; with अनुरागं 'I shall *bestow* affection'. √कृ (करोति) 'do, make' belongs to class VIII, which entails adding the regular personal endings to the stem करो- (*kar-o*) in the sing. of the present and imperfect but कुर् (*kur-*) before the endings -मः (*-maḥ*) and -म (*-ma*), elsewhere the long stem कुरु- (*kur-u*), thus: करोमि, करोति, अकरोत् (imperfect 3rd sing.), but कुर्मः, अकुर्म (with the short stem) and कुरुत, अकुरुत (with the long stem).

11. यदा यदा . . . तदा तदा On these repetitive correlatives, see p. 101, note 9.

12. ईर्ष्यया An instr. of cause.

13. कुर्वन्ति Third person plur. present of √कृ, made with the long stem कुरु- which, before the vowel of the ending अन्ति becomes कुर्व् (*kuru* + *anti* → *kurv-anti*).

14. उत्थाय 'having stood *or* gotten up', gerund of उद्-√स्था (तिष्ठति), the suffix -य instead of -त्वा being due to the prefixed adverb उद्. Note the change of उद् to उत् and the loss of the -स्- in between (*ud-sthā-ya* → *ut-sthā-ya* → *ut-thā-ya*).

Vocabulary

पूर्व, *adj.* preceding, former.
काल, *m.* time.
यव, *m.* barley
शराव, *m.* a plate, dish.
प्राप्त, *ppp.* प्र-√आप् (आप्नोति, class V), gotten, acquired.
दरिद्र, *adj.* poor.

प्राप्य, *gerund* प्र-√आप् (आप्नोति, class V), get, acquire.

हृदय, *n.* the heart.

संतोष, *m.* joy [to be pronounced as though written सन्तोष].

√त्यज् (त्यजति, class I), leave, abandon; *ppp.* त्यक्त (*tyak-ta,* with the change of ज् to क् and similarly in the *gerund* त्यक्त्वा *tyak-tvā*).

चिरकालीन, *adj.* of a long time, long-standing. [चिर 'long' + काल 'time + formative suffix -ईन 'pertaining to'].

मित्र, *n.* (!) a friend. [Note that the gender is *neuter.*]

कुम्भकार, *m.* a maker of pots.

मण्डपिका, *f.* a shed.

रात्री, *f.* the night.

शय्या, *f.* a bed.

शयित्वा, *gerund* √शी (शेते, class II), lie, lie down.

एवम्, *adv.* so, thus, in this way.

√क्री (क्रीणाति, class IX), buy; with adverbial prefix वि 'sell', *i.e.,* वि (etymologically 'apart') reverses the meaning: *cf.* German *kaufen* 'buy' and *verkaufen* 'sell'.

कपर्दक, *m.* *kapardaka,* a small seashell used as a coin in barter.

घट, *m.* a pot.

अनेकधा, *adv.* in many ways. [formed from अनेक 'many', *literally* 'not one' + -धा an adverb-forming suffix indicating manner].

वृद्ध, *ppp.* √वृध् (वर्धति, class I), increase, grow [*vṛdh* + *-ta* → *vṛd-dha,* the aspiration and voicing moving forward].

द्रव्य, *n.* a thing (in the most general sense).

उप-√क्री (synonymous with the simple √क्री given above).

प्रकार, *m.* manner, way.

संचय, *m.* a heap, accumulation (pronounced as though written सञ्चय).

उद्-√पद् (उत्पादयति, causative of √पद् 'step, go', hence with उद् 'forth', literally 'cause to go forth, produce' (Note that द् of उद् is changed to त् before प्). The gerund of causatives when compounded with an adverbial prefix, loses its *-aya-,* thus *ut-pād-ya.*

चतुर्, *numeral adj.* four (the declension of this numeral is irregular; चतस्रः is acc. fem. plur. here).

पत्नी, *f.* a wife.

अनुराग, *m.* love, affection.

नारी, *f.* a woman, wife.
ईर्ष्या, *f.* jealousy.
द्वन्द्व, *n.* a quarrel.
कोप, *m.* anger.
इत्थम्, *adv.* thus, so (synonym of एवम्).
√तड् (ताडयति, class X), strike, beat.
√क्षिप् (क्षिपति, class VI), throw (remember: class VI roots do *not* allow the replacement of their vowel by the guṇa substitute, which in this case would be *-e-* for *-i-*. Hence, because √क्षिप् belongs to class VI, we cannot make the stem क्षेप [*kṣep-a*], but we must leave it unchanged).
चूर्णित, *ppp.* √चूर्णय (चूर्णयति), smash, break to pieces (*literally* 'reduce to powder', really a denominative verb from चूर्ण 'powder'; *v.* Lesson Twenty-eight for particulars on denominatives).
भाण्ड, *n.* a vessel, pot *or* dish.
भग्न, *ppp.* √भञ्ज् (भनक्ति, class VII), break (formed from the root without nasal + the suffix -न, hence, भज् + -न which becomes भग् with substitution of ग् for ज्, yielding भग्न).
भङ्ग, *m.* the act of breaking, breaking.
तिरस्-√कृ (तिरस्करोति, class VIII), scold, upbraid; *ppp.* तिरस्कृत.
बहिस्-√कृ, put outside, expel (बहिस् becomes बहिष् before *k*-).

Translate the following passage:

In a former time a certain Twice-born, having begged in the city for a long while, acquired[1] a plate full of barley. A very evil rogue saw him near a temple beside a river. The rogue thought thus: 'If I go up to this Twice-born and, having beaten him with this club, get the dish full of barley, then, after cooking the barley, I'll eat it and sell the dish.' Having thought thus, the rogue went up to the poor Brahman that night and struck him on the head with the club. Therefore, the dish fell[2] on the ground from the Twice-born's hand and was smashed.[3] All the barley[4] scattered[3] everywhere. Thereupon a few men, having come due to the sound of the breaking of that dish and seen the Twice-born fallen on the ground, seized that wicked rogue and beat[5] him severely. In the meantime the Twice-born, though[6] severely beaten by the rogue, got up[7] from the ground. These men, stricken with compassion, upon seeing his head bespattered with blood, brought a pot full of water and, after washing the wound of this unfortunate Twice-born, gave[1] him many *kapardakas*.

Notes

1. Use the *ppp.* with the agent (grammatical subject of the English sentence) in the *instr*.
2. Turn 'fell' into a gerund.
3. Use the ppp. in agreement with the subject.
4. Translate 'All the barley' by सर्वे यवाः, *i.e.*, by the plur. to suggest the individual grains. सर्वे is nom. m. plur., declined like तद्. So, as we say ते, so we say सर्वे (not सर्वाः like देवाः).
5. All the verbs except 'beat' should be expressed by gerunds.
6. Use अपि (*lit*.: 'even') to impart the sense of 'though' to the *ppp*. 'beaten'.
7. Translate 'got up' by the *ppp*. of उद्-√स्था.

Vocabulary

city, नगरी (declined like नदी).

beg, √भिक्ष् (भिक्षते, class I), *gerund* भिक्षित्वा.

very evil, अतिपाप (*adj*. declined like देव/कन्या/फल).

beat, √तड् (ताडयति, class X), *gerund* ताडयित्वा.

cook, √पच् (पचति, class I), *gerund* पक्त्वा.

eat, √भक्ष् (भक्षति, class I), *caus*. भक्षयति without *caus*. meaning, *gerund* भक्षयित्वा.

sell, वि-√क्री (क्रीणाति, class IX).

strike, √तुद् (तुदति, class VI - no guṇa in pres. stem!), *ppp*. तुदित.

head, मस्तक, *n*. (declined like फल).

hand, हस्त, *m*. (declined like देव).

scatter, वि-√कॄ (किरति, class VI), ppp. विकीर्ण.

wicked, दुष्ट, really *ppp*. √दुष् (दुष्यति, class IV. 'become bad').

in the meantime, अस्मिन् अन्तरे.

severely, अतीव *or* गाढम्.

get up, उद्-√स्था (तिष्ठति, class I), *ppp*. उत्थित. [for phonetic changes see note 14, p. 110.]

compassion, कृपा (declined like कन्या).

bring, आ-√नी (नयति, class I), *gerund* आनीय.

unfortunate, मन्दभाग्य.

wash, प्र-√क्षल् (क्षालयति, class X), *gerund* प्रक्षाल्य.
wound, व्रण, *m*. (declined like देव).
give, √दा (ददाति, class III), *ppp*. दत्त.

LESSON NINE

The Middle Voice.

In addition to expressing *tense* (the time sphere of an action, whether past, present or future), *person* (the performer or subject, whether as speaker, the one spoken to or spoken about, indicated by the pronouns *I, we, you, he, she, it, they*) and *number* (whether the performer is one individual, two[1] or more), a Sanskrit verb also has the property of expressing the *relationship of the subject to the action performed.* By relationship to the action is meant whether the subject is viewed simply as the performer of the action in a sort of absolute sense without implication of its effects on himself or herself, or whether the subject performs the action with reference to himself or herself (in which case the subject is at once both a doer and a receiver), or, finally, whether the subject is viewed as a participant in an action performed by another.

The property or power inherent in a particular verb form to imply these relationships is known as 'voice', a curious term which must, of course, not be confounded with 'voice' as applied to the tensing of the vocal cords in pronouncing certain consonants. The three kinds of voice that have been referred to are called *active, middle* and *passive* respectively.

The two groups of verb forms we have studied so far, that is, the forms of the present and imperfect, are in the *active* voice. In all of these the subject is the active participant in the action, and nothing is necessarily implied as to the benefits accruing to the subject from the performance of the action, except as may be inferred from the phraseology and the context. The implication of a verb that is in the active voice is that the action is performed on behalf of someone other than the subject, as in यजति 'He sacrifices', which means that 'he' is performing the sacrifice *on behalf of someone other than himself*. The corresponding form in the middle voice, on the other hand, namely यजते, means 'He sacrifices *for himself*'. The English terms 'active' and 'middle' are not really helpful in conveying this distinction, whereas the terms used by the Indian grammarians are perfectly clear and to the point. They call a verb in the active voice परस्मैपद 'a word for another' and the middle आत्मनेपद 'a word for oneself'. One may naturally wonder what the basis of the term 'middle voice' is. This rather strange term, which is deeply rooted in Western grammatical terminology, seems to derive from the fact that the subject of a verb in the middle voice is both a doer and a receiver,

---

[1]In addition to a singular and plural, Sanskrit also has a dual, denoted by special endings. It is found also in the declension of nouns and adjectives. Because of its relative rarity, the study of the dual can be taken up much later.

whereas in the active voice it is only a doer and in the passive a receiver, so that the middle form stands *between* the active and passive. Consider the difference between 'He washes' (active, 'he' is the washer), 'He is washed' (passive, 'he is washed by someone else') and 'He washes himself' (middle, 'he' performs the washing and is affected by its performance).

The middle voice is expressed by a different set of endings from that which has been learned for the present and imperfect active. To show the differences between the two sets of endings, the present and imperfect active of √यज् 'sacrifice' may now be juxtaposed with the same tenses in the middle.

	Active		*Middle*	
		Present		
Singular				
1.	यजामि	(-मि)	यजे	(-ए)
2.	यजसि	(-सि)	यजसे	(-से)
3.	यजति	(-ति)	यजते	(-ते)
Plural				
1.	यजामः	(-मः)	यजामहे	(-महे)
2.	यजथ	(-थ)	यजध्वे	(-ध्वे)
3.	यजन्ति	(-अन्ति)	यजन्ते	(-अन्ते)
		Imperfect		
Singular				
1.	अयजम्	(-अम्)	अयजे	(-ए)
2.	अयजः	(-ः)	अयजथाः	(-थाः)
3.	अयजत्	(-त्)	अयजत	(-त)
Plural				
1.	अयजाम	(-म)	अयजामहि	(-महि)
2.	अयजत	(-त)	अयजध्वम्	(-ध्वम्)
3.	अयजन्	(-अन्)	अयजन्त	(-अन्त)

Note that in both voices, wherever an ending begins with a vowel (-अन्ति, -अम्, -अन् and -ए, -अन्ते, -ए, -अन्त), the thematic vowel of the stem, that is, the final vowel *-a,* is dropped; thus, from √यज् (यजति) the stem of which is यज *(yaj-a)*, the third person plural is यजन्ति *(yaj-anti), not* यजअन्ति

(yaja-anti). Remember that *all* imperfects begin with an अ- *(a-)* called the 'augment'. Finally, when an ending beginning with -म is added, the thematic vowel is replaced by -आ-; hence, यजा-मि *(yajā-mi)*, अयजा-म *(a-yajā-ma)*, यजा-महे *(yajā-mahe)*, अयजा-महि *(a-yajā-mahi)*.

Not every verb root in Sanskrit, however, can be conjugated in both the active and middle voice with the clear differentiation of meaning seen in the case of यजति and यजते above. Many roots occur *exclusively* in one voice only without any obvious basis or rationale, and yet others are found in both the active and middle with no perceptible variation in sense! In fact, the sharp difference in meaning exemplified by यजति/यजते is comparatively rare. The existence of the middle voice is to a large extent a relic of a bygone age when the two voices still stood apart in meaning as well as form. In the spoken languages or Prakrits, the middle voice was quickly lost altogether, except for isolated instances. But although the middle voice is *semantically* not a really significant factor, the grammatical forms are too common to be ignored. They must be learned, therefore, for their common occurrence and also to explain and interpret those cases where a truly middle meaning is involved.[2] In comparative linguistics the middle voice is a factor of considerable importance, as it occurs in several other Indo-European languages, preeminently where, incidentally, the middle sense is often more apparent. To illustrate how fuzzy the line of difference between the active and middle can be, we may take the motto from the Great Seal of India सत्यमेव जयते 'Truth alone (एव) is victorious'. When these words were selected from the Muṇḍaka Upaniṣad to serve as a kind of affirmation not only of the Gandhian ideal of Truth, but also of a notion which runs through much of Indian thought from very ancient times, there was considerable discussion among Indian Sanskrit paṇḍits whether the correct verb form should be जयते (middle) or जयति (active), both voices being allowed for √जि 'conquer'. There would not have been so extended a discussion of the matter, had the issue been clear cut, but the fact is that the difference in use between जयति and जयते is not by any means hard and fast.

---

2 In some tenses, for example, the future and the perfect, middle forms are occasionally used in a passive sense.

The Lion, the Old Hare and the Well

एकदा कश्चिद् सिंहः पर्वतस्य शिखरे महावनस्य[1] समीपे अवसत् । सः सर्वदा मृगाणां[2] वधं कृत्वा अभक्षयत् । ततः सर्वैः मृगैः मेलकं कृत्वा अयं सिंहः विज्ञप्तः[3] । देव किमर्थं सर्वेषां मृगाणां वधं करोषि । वयं एव त्वदाहारार्थं[4] प्रत्यहं एकं एव मृगं उपनयामः इति । सिंहेन उक्तम् । यदि इच्छथ तदा एवं भवतु[5] इति । ततः प्रभृति[6] ते मृगाः प्रत्यहं एव एकं मृगं तस्मै दुर्वृत्ताय सिंहाय उपानयन् । अथ कदाचिद् एकस्य वृद्धस्य शशस्य कालः प्राप्तः[7] । यतः[8] सिंहस्य समीपं मन्दं मन्दं[9] अगच्छत् ततः[8] सः सिंहः महत्या क्षुधया पीडितः कोपात्[10] तं शशकं अवदत् । कुतः विलम्बसे त्वं[11] इति । शशकः तं अभ्यभाषत । क्षमां प्रार्थये । अहं[12] तु न अपराद्धः । मार्गे अन्येन सिंहेन बलात् धृतः पुनः आगमनाय तस्य समीपे शपथं कृत्वा त्वां[13] निवेदयितुं अहं अत्र आगतः इति । तस्य शशकस्य तद् वचनं श्रुत्वा सः सिंहः परं कोपं[14] गत्वा प्रत्यभाषत । सत्वरं अस्य सिंहस्य समीपं मां[15] नय[16] इति । तदनन्तरं सः शशकः तं सिंहं गृहीत्वा गम्भीरं कूपं[17] गत्वा तं अभ्यभाषत । अत्रागम्य पश्य[18] इति उक्त्वा तस्मिन् जले तस्य प्रतिबिम्बं एव अदर्शयत् । ततः सः सिंहः दर्पेण आध्मातः तस्य प्रतिबिम्बस्य उपरि आत्मानं[19] निक्षिप्य पञ्चत्वं गतः ।

(Adapted from Hitopadeśa, Book I, Fable 11).

Notes

1. The word महा 'great' never occurs as a separate word, but must always be prefixed to a noun, forming a single word or compound with it; *cf.* महाराज 'great king' from महा + राजन् 'king' (which loses its final *n)*.

2. We should expect the genitive plural of मृग 'animal' to be मृगानाम्, but that rather complicated phonetic rule, which requires the change of न to ण under certain conditions, has caused the substitution here. The change here is due to the pervasive cerebralizing influence of the vowel -*ṛ*-.

3. विज्ञप्त: past passive participle of the causative of वि-√ज्ञा 'know fully, understand'; the regular causative is विज्ञापयति, with interpolated प्, literally meaning 'causes to know fully, causes to understand', then 'makes a representation to', used of bringing a matter before a potentate (as here in the form of a lion!).

4. त्वदाहारार्थं 'for your food' Remember that अर्थं joined to a noun means 'for the sake of'; आहार means 'food' (literally 'what one takes', a noun derived from आ-√हृ 'take'[3]); त्वद् is an abstraction from the pronoun of the second person ('you') used only before another noun in a compound.

5. एवं भवतु 'So be it', literally 'Let it be so', an extremely common expression of agreement or acquiescence. भवतु is the imperative third singular of √भू (भवति) formed by adding the ending of -तु to the stem.

6. तत: प्रभृति a common adverbial phrase meaning 'from then on, from that time'.

7. प्राप्त: here used actively: 'arrived, came', from प्र-√आप् (आप्नोति) 'reach, get to'; but प्र-√आप् also means 'obtain' and the past passive participle of this would be truly passive, which would require the agent to be in the instrumental: 'by so-and-so such-and-such [was] obtained'. This latter usage was seen in the first sentence of the story about the Brahman and the dish of barley: केनचिद् द्विजेन यवै: पूर्ण: शराव: प्राप्त: (Lesson 8) 'By a certain twice-born a dish full of barley [was] obtained'.

8. यत: . . . तत: 'because . . . therefore'.

9. मन्दं मन्दं The repetition emphasizes the meaning: 'very slowly, ever so slowly'.

---

[3] In speaking English, Indians often say 'take food', where we would simply say 'eat'.

10. कोपात् ablative of cause: 'due to anger'. As in Sanskrit, in English we can also say 'from anger'.

11. त्वं usually the personal pronouns, especially those of the first and second persons, which do not show gender, are omitted. Here त्वं is expressed and placed after the verb for emphasis, as the lion is chiding the hare for being late.

12. अहं The pronoun is expressed here both for emphasis as well as because the verb अस्मि or भवामि is omitted: 'But *I* [am] not to blame'. In the next sentence, अहं is expressed in अहं अत्र आगत: because of the omission of अस्मि/भवामि, not for emphasis. When a participle (as आगत: here) is used as a main verb and the subject is in the first or second person, the pronoun has to be expressed, unless the appropriate form of √अस् or √भू is included. If it is omitted, the pronominal reference would not be clear.

13. त्वां accusative singular of the second person pronoun, object of निवेदयितुं.

14. कोपं This accusative is similar to the usage of पञ्चत्वं in the oft-repeated idiom with √गम्. It is simply an extension of the 'accusative of the place to which' used with verbs of motion.

15. मां The accusative singular of the first person pronoun, parallel in form to त्वां.

16. नय Imperative singular of √नी (नयति) 'lead, take', here serving as the lion's command to the hare. This common form of the verb corresponds precisely to the stem in the four thematic classes; thus, भव, दीव्य, तुद and चोरय respectively for the roots भू, दिव्, तुद् and चुर्.

17. कूपं An 'accusative of the place to which' in its literal application with गत्वा.

18. पश्य v. note 16 on नय for this form.

19. आत्मानं accusative masculine singular of आत्मन्, literally 'soul,' but often, as here, used as a reflexive pronoun of all three persons, genders and numbers (*myself, yourself, himself, ourselves,* and so on). Here, as the context makes clear, it refers to the lion and means 'himself'.

Vocabulary

पर्वत, *m.* a mountain.

शिखर, *n.* a peak *or* top.

सर्वदा, *adv.* always, all the time [formed from सर्व 'all' and the adverbial suffix -दा which denotes 'time when'; *cf.* एकदा 'at one time, once upon a time'].

महावन, *n.* a great forest, jungle.

वध, *m.* killing, slaughter; with √कृ (करोति, class VIII) 'make' as equivalent of √हन् or causative of √मृ 'kill'.

भक्ष् (भक्षति, °ते, class I), eat; *caus.* भक्षयति, *without caus. meaning.*

मेलक, *m.* an assembly.

विज्ञप्त, *ppp.* of causative of वि-√ज्ञा (जानाति, class IX), on which *v.* note 3 to the text.

मृग, *m.* an animal; often, especially in later texts, specifically a 'deer' [for an exactly parallel example of this specialization, *cf.* modern English 'deer' from Old English *dēor* 'animal' and further note that the meaning 'animal' was still current in Shakespeare's time, as may be seen in *King Lear* III. 4. 128: 'rats and mice and such small deer'].

वयम्, *nom. m. plur.* of the pronoun of the first person (अहम्).

प्रत्यहम्, *adv.* every day, daily.

दुर्वृत्त, *adj.* ill-behaved.

उप-√नी (नयति, class I), bring to (someone).

अथ कदाचिद्, *adv. phrase* then one day.

वृद्ध, *adj.* old [really *ppp.* of √वृध् (वर्धति, class I), grow, so *literally* 'grown, grown up'].

शश, *m.* a hare; शशक is a sort of diminutive of शश, but without substantial difference in meaning.

महती, feminine of *adj.* महत् 'great'.

क्षुधा, *f.* hunger.

पीड् (पीडयति, class X), press; oppress; pain; *ppp.* पीडित.

कोप, *m.* anger.

कुतः, *interrogative adv.* why? [interchangeable with the phrasal adverb किमर्थम्].

वि-√लम्ब (लम्बते), hang around, delay, linger.

अभि-√भाष् (भाषते, class I), speak to, address.

क्षमा, *f.* pardon; with प्र-√अर्थय (अर्थयते), seek, request, beg one's pardon.

तु, *conj.* but [this word cannot come first in a sentence].

अपराद्ध, *adj.* guilty [really *ppp.* अप-√राध् (राध्नोति, class V), fail to succeed, do wrong].

बलात्, forcibly [*abl.* of बल, *n.* strength, force].

धृत, *ppp.* √धृ (धारयति, *only caus. in pres., but without caus. meaning*), held, detained.

आगमन, *n.* the act of coming *or* approaching; *with* पुनः, a returning.

शपथ, *m.* an oath; *with* कृ, swear an oath.

निवेदयितुम्, *infin. of caus. of* नि-विद् (वेत्ति, class II), 'to cause to know', to inform.

गृहीत्वा, *gerund* of √ग्रह् (गृह्णाति, class IX), having taken *or* grasped.

गम्भीर्, *adj.* deep.

कूप, *m.* a well.

प्रतिबिम्ब, *m.* reflection.

दर्शय, causative stem of √दृश् (no present!), see, *hence* 'cause to see, show'.

दर्प, *m.* pride, arrogance.

आध्मात, puffed up; *ppp.* of आ-√ध्मा or धम् (धमति, class I), blow up, puff up.

उपरि, *adv.* above; *as postp. with gen.* above, on.

आत्मन्, *m.* soul, individual soul; used commonly also as a reflexive pronoun in the singular of all numbers , persons and genders; *v.* note 19 above.

नि-√क्षिप् (क्षिपति, class VI), throw down, hurl down, cast.

Translate into Sanskrit:

In a former time a certain king went hunting[1] every day in the great forest in the vicinity of his palace. Since many animals were killed by the arrows of this king, therefore, other animals, stricken with despair, having formed an assembly[2], made a representation to that king.[3] They addressed him thus: 'Many animals have been killed in this forest, and soon we all too will go to death[4]— there's no doubt about it![5] Just as all pleasures are surely transitory in this world, likewise the pleasure of hunting is also transitory. From now on kill just[6] one animal every day. In this way you will gain[7] less pleasure, but we shall live.'[8] Thereupon the king, stricken with the deepest remorse, said 'So be it!' and thereafter protected all the animals[9] in that great forest.

Notes

1. मृगयां + √गम् (either in the imperfect 3rd s. or the *ppp*. गत).

2. मेलकं + *gerund* of √कृ .

3. Use the passive construction with विज्ञप्त (*ppp*. of the causative of वि-√ज्ञा), thus: 'by the other animals, ... stricken ... having formed ... that king [was] caused to understand' (*v*. note 3 on the Sanskrit text above).

4. 'we . . . will go to death': मरणं (death), as '*acc*. of place to which (!)' + गमिष्यामः, *fut*. of √गम् (गच्छति, class I).

5. 'There's no doubt about it' अत्र न संशयः, an extremely common phrase in Sanskrit story literature.

6. Express 'just' by एव after 'one'.

7. 'you will gain': use लप्स्यसे, *fut*. middle of √लभ् (लभते, class I), conjugated like the *pres*. middle.

8. 'we shall live': जीविष्यामः, *fut*. of √जीव् (जीवति, class I).

9. Render 'a protection of all the animals [was] made (*ppp*. of √कृ)'.

LESSON TEN

Masculine and Feminine Nouns in *-i* and *-u*.
The Locative Absolute.

I. *Masculine and Feminine Nouns in -i and -u.*

Thus far in our study of the Sanskrit noun we have dealt with stems ending in *-a* and *-ā,* typified on the one hand hand by देव for the masculines and फल for the neuters and on the other hand by कन्या for the feminines; also with feminines in *-ī-* as exemplified by नदी. It was maintained that Sanskrit nouns may end in any of the vowels and diphthongs as well as also most of the consonants. The vowel stems on the whole are of very common occurrence, and that is why they have to be studied before the stems ending in consonants. It is unfortunate for the beginning student, therefore, that the declensions of the vowel stems show so much variation in the case endings, depending on the particular vowel that ends the stem. The consonant stems, to be sure, have an *un*varying set of endings, regardless of the final consonant of the stem, but the more common types involve changes in the form of the stem itself, a phenomenon to be seen also in the conjugation of verbs of the non-thematic classes, and, like them, better introduced somewhat later. In this lesson, then, we shall continue with the vowel stems, dealing with the stems in *-i* and *-u,* which involve some of the commonest nouns in Sanskrit.

The stems in *-i* and *-u* may be of any gender, but the neuters are of so rare occurrence, that no account of them will be made here. While some rules can be given for determining the gender of *i-* or *u-* stem nouns, it is best at this time to learn the gender with each word and defer the rules to a later time, when a general grasp of the whole system of declensions has been acquired. The reason for taking up *both* the *i*-stems and *u*-stems in one lesson is that, as will be seen below, their declensions are parallel throughout, exhibiting only such changes as are due to the difference in the final vowel of the stem, which in the *i*-stems may become *-ay-, -e-,* and *-ī-,* and in the *u*-stems *-av-, -o-,* and *-ū-*. The feminine *i-* and *u*-stems are declined exactly the same as the masculine, except in the instrumental singular and the accusative plural. These exceptions are marked with an asterisk (*) in the table that follows. To be given especial attention, moreover, are the forms of the feminine stems given in parentheses. These are the dative, ablative, genitive and locative singular. They are alternative to the forms to which they have been appended and are completely interchangeable with them. They are in origin the product of analogy with the same cases of stems belonging to the long *ī* declension.

	i-stems		*u*-stems	
	agni (अग्नि) (*m.*) 'fire'	*mati* (मति) (*f.*) 'thought'	*bhānu* (भानु) (*m.*) 'sun'	*dhenu* (धेनु) (*f.*) 'cow'
	Singular		*Singular*	
Nom.	*agniḥ* अग्निः	*matiḥ* मतिः	*bhānuḥ* भानुः	*dhenuḥ* धेनुः
Acc.	*agnim* अग्निम्	*matim* मतिम्	*bhānum* भानुम्	*dhenum* धेनुम्
Instr.	*agninā* अग्निना	**matyā* मत्या	*bhānunā* भानुना	**dhenvā* धेन्वा
Dat.	*agnaye* अग्नये	*mataye (matyai)* मतये (मत्यै)	*bhānave* भानवे	*dhenave (dhenvai)* धेनवे (धेन्वै)
Abl.	*agneḥ* अग्नेः	*mateḥ (matyāḥ)* मतेः (मत्याः)	*bhānoḥ* भानोः	*dhenoḥ (dhenvāḥ)* धेनोः (धेन्वाः)
Gen.	*agneḥ* अग्नेः	*mateḥ (matyāḥ)* मतेः (मत्याः)	*bhānoḥ* भानोः	*dhenoḥ (dhenvāḥ)* धेनोः (धेन्वाः)
Loc.	*agnau* अग्नौ	*matau (matyām)* मतौ (मत्याम्)	*bhānau* भानौ	*dhenau (dhenvām)* धेनौ (धेन्वाम्)
Voc.	*agne* अग्ने	*mate* मते	*bhāno* भानो	*dheno* धेनो
	Plural		*Plural*	
Nom.	*agnayaḥ* अग्नयः	*matayaḥ* मतयः	*bhānavaḥ* भानवः	*dhenavaḥ* धेनवः
Acc.	*agnīn* अग्नीन्	**matīḥ* मतीः	*bhānūn* भानून्	**dhenūḥ* धेनूः
Instr.	*agnibhiḥ* अग्निभिः	*matibhiḥ* मतिभिः	*bhānubhiḥ* भानुभिः	*dhenubhiḥ* धेनुभिः
Dat.	*agnibhyaḥ* अग्निभ्यः	*matibhyaḥ* मतिभ्यः	*bhānubhyaḥ* भानुभ्यः	*dhenubhyaḥ* धेनुभ्यः
Abl.	*agnibhyaḥ* अग्निभ्यः	*matibhyaḥ* मतिभ्यः	*bhānubhyaḥ* भानुभ्यः	*dhenubhyaḥ* धेनुभ्यः
Gen.	*agnīnām* अग्नीनाम्	*matīnām* मतीनाम्	*bhānūnām* भानूनाम्	*dhenūnām* धेनूनाम्
Loc.	*agniṣu* अग्निषु	*matiṣu* मतिषु	*bhānuṣu* भानुषु	*dhenuṣu* धेनुषु
Voc.	*agnayaḥ* अग्नयः	*matayaḥ* मतयः	*bhānavaḥ* भानवः	*dhenavaḥ* धेनवः

Note that the dominant vowel of the *i*-declension is *-i-*, and hence its name. This *-i* remains unchanged in the nominative (अग्नि:), accusative (अग्निम्), instrumental (अग्निना) singular, and likewise in the plural instrumental (अग्निभि:), dative-ablative (अग्निभ्य:) and locative (अग्निषु). The same may be said of the *u*-stems, which have *-u-* in the cases where the *i*-stems have *-i-:* भानु:, भानुम्, भानुना, भानुभि:, भानुभ्य:, भानुषु. In the ablative-genitive and vocative singular both stems replace their final with *-e-/-o-,* the guṇa of *i/u* respectively; hence, अग्ने:/भानो: and अग्ने/भानो. The substitution is also made in the dative singular and nominative plural, where phonetic rule requires that *-e-* change to *-ay-;* so अग्नये, अग्नय: and similarly *-o-* to *-av-* in भानवे and भानव:. In the accusative and genitive plural both stems lengthen their theme vowel: अग्नीन्/भानून् and अग्नीनाम्/भानूनाम्.

The feminines in *-i* and *-u* differ from the masculines only in the instrumental singular (मत्या/धेन्वा) and the accusative plural (मती:/धेनू:).

II. *The Locative Absolute.*

A very common construction in Sanskrit, which unfortunately has a somewhat high-sounding and forbidding name, is the locative absolute. The construction exists also in English under the equally forbidding name 'nominative absolute'. In explaining the Sanskrit construction, however, it will be better not to utilize the principle of proceeding from the known to the unknown, which we have in general been following. The reason for rejecting this principle in this instance is that the construction is more easily understood from the point of view of the use of the locative than the nominative. When the construction and its variant uses in Sanskrit are grasped, then we may compare them with the English nominative absolute, with a fuller understanding of the construction in both languages. In this way, on this particular occasion, we shall have proceeded from the relatively unknown (Sanskrit!) to the known (English).

We are by now sufficiently accustomed to the basic and literal use of the locative to express the place *in* which, *on* which or *at* which something occurs. But the locative is also employed to express the notion of 'with regard to', 'in respect to', 'with reference to' something   a relation that might be called the 'locative of respect' or 'specification'. An example of this usage is 'skilled *in horses',* that is, 'in respect to horses' (अश्वेषु). If with this type of locative a participle is joined   'with regard to so-and-so or such-and-such having been . . . ed'   then the whole phrase consisting of a noun (or, of course, a pronoun) plus a participle may easily pass over into the sense of 'when (or since) so-and-so or such-and-such was or had been . . . ed'. An example or two will make this clear: बहुषु सैनिकेषु युद्धे हतेषु नरेश्वरः अनुशोकेन आविष्टः अभवत् literally 'With regard to many soldiers (बहुषु सैनिकेषु) having been killed (हतेषु) in the battle, the king was stricken with remorse', but idiomatically: 'When (or since) many soldiers had been killed in the battle,' etc. Or with a pronoun: तस्मिन् आगते गुरुः अतीव संतुष्टः अभवत् 'When he (तस्मिन्) came (आगते), the teacher was very happy' (literally: 'With regard to him having come' etc.). Sometimes the locative absolute is used without a noun or pronoun, consisting generally of a verb of saying in the neuter of the locative and following direct speech; thus एवं उक्ते 'When this was said'.

That it is indeed the *nominative* that is used in the English absolute construction is, of course, obscured by the lack of case endings in modern English. It becomes clear, however, if we use an example with a pronoun that changes form, like 'he, she, it' etc.; thus, 'he having gone to sleep, the thief entered without difficulty'.

The Blind Vulture and the Cat

पूर्वस्मिन् काले गङ्गायाः तीरे अन्धः गृध्रः अवसत् । यतः सः अन्धः अभवत् ततः तस्य जीवनाय[1] विहगाः तस्मै प्रत्यहं आहारं अयच्छन् । अथ कदाचिद् कश्चिद् मार्जारः तेषां विहगानां शावकान् भक्षयितुं तत्र आगतः । तं मार्जारं दृष्ट्वा एव[2] सर्वैः विहगैः तस्मात्[3] भयेन आविष्टैः कोलाहलः कृतः । तं कोलाहलं श्रुत्वा तेन अन्धेन गृध्रेण उक्तम् । कः अयं[4] आगच्छति इति । सः मार्जारः तं गृध्रं अवलोक्य हा हतः अस्मि[5] इति भयेन चिन्तयित्वा सविनयं अभ्यभाषत । मार्जारः अहं । त्वां अभिवन्दे इति । एवं उक्त्वा सः गृध्रस्य समीपं उपगम्य तरोः पादे तत्र एव अतिष्ठत् । यदि त्वं मार्जारः भवसि तदा दूरं सत्वरं अपगच्छ । न चेद्[6] त्वां हनिष्यामि[7] इति सः गृध्रः अवदत् । कुतः[8] मां हन्तुं इच्छसि । किं मम मार्जारत्वेन[9] एव मां हनिष्यसि । अहं मम जात्या एव निश्चितं त्वया न वध्यः । अपरं च[10] अहिंसा परमः धर्मः इति वदन्ति साधवः । अन्येषां हिंसायाः[11] निवृत्ताः ते स्वर्गं गच्छन्ति इति धर्मशास्त्रेषु मया श्रुतम् । अन्यद् च किं अरये अपि गृहं आगताय

आतिथ्यं न यच्छसि । चन्द्रः चाण्डालगृहात् अपि ज्योत्स्नां न संहरते । आसु मतिषु गुरवः न विवदन्ते इति मन्ये इति सः मार्जारः तं गृध्रं प्रत्यभाषत । एवं विश्वास्य सः मार्जारः गृध्रस्य अनुज्ञया तरोः कोटरं तस्य वसतिं[12] प्रविष्टः । ततः कतिपयेषु दिनेषु अतीतेषु मार्जारेण शावकाः एकैकशः प्रत्यहं आक्रम्य कोटरं आनीय व्यापादिताः खादिताः च । अन्यैः विहगैः जिज्ञासायां आरब्धायां सः मार्जारः कोटरं त्यक्त्वा अपसृतः । बहूनां शावकानां कङ्कालैः पूर्णं कोटरं दृष्ट्वा अनेन एव शावकाः भक्षिताः इति निश्चित्य तैः विहगैः सः गृध्रः तत्र एव सहसा व्यापादितः ।

(Adapted from Hitopadeśa, Book I, Fable 4).

Notes

1. तस्य जीवनाय 'to keep him alive', literally, 'for the vivifying of him'. The dative is used here, as often, to express purpose.

2. The use of एव here with the *gerund* दृष्ट्वा is noteworthy; the emphasis it throws on दृष्ट्वा can best be conveyed in English by translating 'As soon as he saw'.

3. तस्मात् Remember that words of fearing (here भयेन) are construed with the ablative of what is feared.

4. कः अयं आगच्छति The combination of the demonstrative (अयं) with the interrogative (कः) requires a locution in English like: 'Who is this that is coming'?

5. हा हतः अस्मि 'Alas! I'm a goner!' (literally 'struck down, killed'); हतः is the *past passive participle* of √हन् (हन्ति, class II).

6. चेद् is another word for 'if', much less common than यदि; as it is a so-called 'enclitic' or unaccented word, leaning for support on a preceding

word, it cannot appear first in a sentence, like the conjunction तु 'but'. न चेद् 'if not' is the usual expression for 'otherwise'.

7. हनिष्यामि future first person of √हन् 'kill', formed by adding *-iṣya-* to the root. The conjugation of the future stem is exactly the same as any present of the thematic classes. For further on the future tense and its formation, *v.* Lesson Nineteen.

8. कुतः 'Why?'; there are three common words for 'why?' in Sanskrit: किमर्थम्, कस्मात् and कुतः as here.

9. मम मार्जारत्वेन एव 'merely because I am a cat', literally 'merely (एव) due to the cat-ness (मार्जारत्वेन) of me (मम)'. The addition of -त्व to a stem, as to मार्जार here, renders it an abstract, corresponding to *-ness* (for example, 'weak-ness') or *-hood* ('nation-hood') in English. If we wish to speak of the state or condition of a Buddha, for example, we may say बुद्धत्व. This usage plays an important role in Sanskrit, especially in philosophical texts.

10. अपरं च 'And another thing' *i.e.*, moreover; like अन्यत् च, which has exactly the same meaning, this is an extremely common expression in the Hitopadeśa. It simply indicates that what follows is in a similar vein to what has gone before.

11. हिंसायाः an 'ablative of separation' with निवृत्ताः 'desisting from injury'.

12. तस्य वसतिं 'his abode', in explanation of तोरः कोटरं and hence वसतिं has to be in the same case as कोटरं. In grammatical parlance वसतिं is said to be 'in apposition' to कोटरं.

Vocabulary

पूर्व, *adj.* former, prior [declined like तद् in *loc. sing*. and a few other cases].
गङ्गा, *f.* the Gaṅgā *or* Ganges River.
तीर, *n.* a bank *or* shore.
अन्ध, *adj.* blind.
गृध्र, *m.* a vulture.
यतः . . . ततः 'since . . . therefore'.
जीवन, *n.* existence; subsistence.
विहग, *m.* a bird.
प्रत्यहम्, *adv.* every day.
आहार, *m.* food.
√यम् (यच्छति, class I), offer, give.
अथ, *adv.* now (not as a temporal *adv.* but as a mere continuative).
कदाचिद्, *indef. adv.* one day, once upon a time.
मार्जार, *m.* a cat.
शावक, *m.* the young (of a bird).
√भक्ष् (भक्षति, class I), eat; *infin.* भक्षितुम्, *ppp.* भक्षित.
तत्र, *adv.* in *or* to that place, there.
आगत, *ppp.* आ-√गम् (गच्छति, class I), having come (active in meaning because it is intransitive).
आविष्ट, *ppp.* आ-√विश् (विशति, class VI), entered by, filled with (+ *instr.*).
कोलाहल, *m.* a confused noise, din, hubbub.
आ-√गम् (गच्छति, class I), come.
अव-√लोक् (लोकयति, *caus. but without caus. meaning*!), look at, see; *gerund* अवलोक्य .
हा, *interjection* alas!
√चिन्त् (चिन्तयति, class X), think; *gerund* चिन्तयित्वा.
सविनयम, *adv.* politely.
अभि-√भाष् (भाषते, class I), say to, say (absolutely, *i.e.,* without an object).
अभि-√वन्द् (वन्दते, class I), greet, salute.
उप-√गम् (गच्छति, class I), go to, approach.
तरु, *m.* a tree.
पाद, *m.* foot (of a tree).

√स्था (तिष्ठति, class I), stand; stay, remain.

यदि . . . तदा if . . . then.

दूरम्, *adv.* far away.

सत्वरम्, *adv.* quickly, immediately.

अप-√गम् (गच्छति, class I), go away; *imperative* अपगच्छ go away!

चेद्, *conj.* if.

√हन् (हन्ति, class II), strike down, kill; *infin.* हन्तुम्.

√इष् (इच्छति, class VI), wish, desire.

जाति, *f.* birth; caste.

निश्चितम्, *adv.* surely, certainly.

वध्य, *adj.* to be killed, *i.e.,* should be killed [really *gerundive* √वध् 'kill', not conjugated in pres.].

अहिंसा, *f.* non-injury.

परम, *adj.* highest, supreme.

धर्म, *m.* virtue.

साधु, *adj.* good, noble; *as m.* a good *or* noble person.

अन्य, *pron.* another, other.

हिंसा, *f.* injury.

निवृत्त, *ppp.* नि-√वृत (वर्तते, class I), turned back *or* away, desisting from (+ *abl.*).

धर्मशास्त्र, *n.* a *dharmaśāstra* or treatise on dharma, *i.e.,* the whole body or system of Hindu customary law.

अरि, *m.* an enemy.

अपि, *adv.* even.

आतिथ्य, *n.* hospitality.

चन्द्र, *m.* the moon.

चाण्डाल, *m.* a Cāṇḍāla, a person of the lowest caste of Hindu society.

ज्योत्स्ना, *f.* moonlight.

सम्-√हृ (हरति, °ते, class I), withhold, withdraw.

मति, *f.* an opinion *or* notion.

गुरु, *m.* a teacher, preceptor.

वि-√वद् (वदते, class I), be at variance, argue.

√मन् (मन्यते, class IV), think.

प्रति,-√भाष् (भाषते, class I), answer.

विश्वास्य, *gerund of caus.* वि-√श्वस् (श्वसिति, class II), 'having caused to have confidence', having inspired confidence.
अनुज्ञा, *f.* approval, permission.
कोटर, *n.* a hollow (of a tree).
विसति, *f.* a dwelling, home.
प्रविष्ट, *ppp.* प्र-√विश् (विशति, class VI), having entered.
ततः, *adv.* then.
कतिपय, *indef. adj.* some, a few.
दिन, *n.* a day.
अतीत, *ppp.* अति-√इ (एति, class II), gone by.
एकैकशः, *adv.* one by one.
आ-√क्रम् (क्रामति, class I), come upon, attack; *gerund* आक्रम्य.
आ-√नी (नयति, class I), bring to (+ *acc.*).
व्यापादित, *ppp. caus.* वि-आ-√पद् (पद्यते, class IV), 'having been caused to perish', (having been) killed.
खाद् (खादति, class I), eat; *ppp.* खादित.
जिज्ञासा, *f.* 'a desire to know *or* find out', *hence* an investigation.
आरब्ध, *ppp.* आ-√रभ् (रभते, class I), (having been) begun.
त्यक्त्वा, *gerund of* √त्यज् (त्यजति, class I), having left.
अप-√सृ (सिसर्ति, class III), go off; *ppp.* अपसृत.
कङ्काल, *m. or n.* a skeleton.
निश्चित्य, *gerund of* √निस्-√चि (चिकेति, class III), having ascertained *or* determined. [Roots ending in a short vowel interpose a -त् (-*t*-) before the *gerund* in -य (-*ya*-)].
सहसा, *adv.* straightway.

Translate into Sanskrit using the preceding text as a model:

Once upon a time a vulture, blind due to the maturation of sins done in a prior[1] birth, abided with other birds in the forest. These birds out of compassion gave him food every day for his sustenance. One day a certain cat came[2] there to eat the young of those birds. As soon as he saw the vulture, he was seized with fear of him.[3] When[4] the cat approached that vulture's tree, the vulture addressed him: 'Who are you? From what region have you come here? Why have you entered[5] this forest?' 'I am a cat. I greet you!'

replied the cat. When he heard his words 'I am a cat,' the vulture said: 'If you are a cat, then go quickly!' Then the cat answered the vulture: 'Just because I am a cat[6] you think I want to eat the young of these birds. For this reason you say to me: 'Go quickly!' But I am virtuous, I am attached to non-violence. I don't want to kill anyone.' In this way, having inspired the vulture with confidence,[7] gotten permission from him to stay in the hollow of the tree there, eaten all the young of the birds and left the skeletons in that hollow, he went away. Thereupon, an investigation having been started by all the birds and the skeletons having been seen in the hollow,[8] the vulture was killed by the birds.

Notes

1. Use पूर्व 'prior, preceding', which is declined prenominally, *i.e.*, like तद् (except in the nom.-acc. n.).

2. Express with the *ppp*. of आ-√गम् .

3. Words of fearing take the ablative of the person or thing feared, whereas English uses the genitive (fear of, not fear from). This is a variation of the 'ablative of separation', as one naturally recoils from the object of fear.

4. यदा 'when' ... तदा 'then' (usually omitted in English). In Sanskrit a यदा-clause normally is answered by a तदा-clause.

5. The *ppp*. of प्र-√विश् alone suffices.

6. 'Just because I am a cat': see the Sanskrit text for this important construction.

7. 'inspire with confidence' is expressed by the caus. of वि-√श्वस् , *viz.*, विश्वासयति. The gerund, required here, is formed by dropping the caus. suffix *-aya-*, thus: विश्वास्य .

8. Use the locative absolute here.

LESSON ELEVEN

Changes of Sound between Words.

In the free flow of speech in all languages, a sound at the end of a word is often affected by the sound that begins the next word. For example, in the sentence 'What do you want?' the final *-t* of 'What' becomes a *-d* due to its closeness to the *d-* of 'do'. The words are not kept as separate and distinct as they appear in print. What we say is indeed more like 'Whaddoyouwant?' But one would only say these four words with absolute separation and individuality in chiding someone or in demanding an explanation where none was expected or under some special circumstance where the ordinary flow of speech would not be conducive to the desired effect. In ordinary speech, we commonly say 'Lem me see' for 'Let me see' with a change of *-t* to *-m,* and perhaps more vulgarly 'I wanna go' for 'I want to go', where the *-n-* has exerted its influence on the *t*'s. Many more examples could be adduced. We are, of course, not conscious of these and similar alterations of sounds because we do not write them and do not see them in the writing of others, except in a very limited way in the language of the comic strip or in novels, where some attempt is made to reflect speech habits in certain passages of conversation. If we were to be confronted with a phonetic transcription of what we actually say, we should certainly be greatly surprised and very likely find it nearly undecipherable, even if we had a knowledge of all the phonetic symbols used in such a phonetic transcription.

Like all other languages, Sanskrit too, has changes similar to those illustrated above and many others as well. In conversational Sanskrit, just as in conversational English, these changes may or may not take place, depending on the speed with which one is speaking, the clarity of speech, the degree of coalescence of words and various other factors that are conditioned by particular circumstances in effect at the time of speaking. But Sanskrit *differs* from most other languages in that it makes these changes in *writing*, as though the written or printed page were an exact replica of the spoken word. Of course, this is quite an artificial and mechanical procedure since, as we have just said, the changes are not always or even uniformly made in speaking. The introduction of hard and fast rules for these sound changes is, therefore, founded upon a crystallization of what generally or frequently, but not always, occurs in speech. Since printed Sanskrit texts and, as a rule, also the MSS on which they are based, always exhibit these changes, it is absolutely essential for the student who wishes to read even the simplest of Sanskrit texts to be thoroughly familiar with the rules and experienced in their application. There are, however, some exceptions to the universal application of the rules for sound change. For example, commentaries on Sanskrit works are sometimes written or printed with only occasional phonetic changes, reflecting the more casual style used by Indian pandits when they explain passages of a text to their *śiṣyas*.

In all our practice texts thus far, we have omitted these changes, as it was felt that the beginning student would be able to cope more easily with them and understand why they are made after some basic knowledge of the language had been acquired. Now that we have reached that stage, we may take up one or two of the most common of these changes, gradually introducing the rules for less common changes in subsequent lessons.

The Sanskrit word for the joining together or combining of words is *sandhi,* more properly written *saṃdhi,* literally 'putting together', which is derived from *sam-√dhā* 'put together'.[1] However, not only does sandhi mean the combining of words in a sentence, but it also means the euphonic changes which are made when the words are combined. Sandhi, then, has come to be a collective term for these changes. It has been brought into English, into the technical vocabulary of linguists, who apply it to any such changes that chance to occur, or are required to occur, in any language. Since sandhi has become an English word, we shall use the spelling with -n-, which also reflects the pronunciation.

Sandhi rules are usually treated in Sanskrit grammars under the headings 'internal'and 'external'. The former concerns sound changes made when endings or suffixes are added to roots or stems, hence, internally or within a word. We will not discuss internal sandhi in this chapter. External sandhi, as the term indicates, concerns changes made at word junctures or between words, such as have been exemplified in English above.

Among the most ubiquitous sandhi changes are those that concern a final visarga, or more accurately, from a historical point of view, final *-s,* as in most of its occurrences visarga stands for an original final *-s,* comparatively rarely for *-r.* So, देवः *(devaḥ)* stands for देवस् *(devas),* अग्निः *(agniḥ)* for अग्निस् *(agnis),* गुरुः for गुरुस् *(gurus),* etc., but in पुनः and a few other words the visarga stands for *-r,* so पुनः represents पुनर्. Since, however, we generally write words ending in original *-s* with visarga, its common replacement, it will be more practical to speak of the changes to which visarga is subject rather than *-s.*

Final *-s* in Sanskrit is a very unstable sound, as shown by the fact that in many instances it becomes the mere breath that is indicated by the visarga sign. The frequency of this particular change is reflected by the representation of final *-s* by visarga when words that etymologically or historically end in -s are referred to separately from a context or occur at the

---

[1]The *-m* of *sam* 'together' may be called a 'servile' *-m* and, though written with the anusvāra sign before any consonant, adapts itself to the class of that consonant; so in *saṃdhi*, *-m* becomes *-n* in pronunciation and often also in writing.

end of a sentence. So, we say देवः *(devaḥ)* in referring to the nominative singular of देव *(deva),* and so also when it occurs at the end of an utterance, as in स्वर्गात् अवतरति देवः (The god descends from heaven). The change to visarga occurs also before words beginning with क् *(k),* ख् *(kh),* प् *(p),* फ् *(ph),* श् *(ś),* ष् *(ṣ),* and स् *(s).* So, नरः खादति (The man eats), बालः फलं इच्छति (The child wants the fruit), गुरुः शिष्यं अभिभाषते (The teacher addresses the pupil), etc. These sounds (क् ख् प् फ् श् ष् स्) before which visarga appears are all voiceless, that is, not pronounced with tension or vibration of the vocal cords. But the commonest permutations to which visarga is subject occur before *voiced* sounds, both vowels and consonants. According to the most important rule of sound change in Indo-European, the rule of 'regressive assimilation', when a voiceless sound (like visarga or *-s*) is followed by a voiced sound, the voiced sound gets the upper hand (so to speak), causing the prior voiceless sound to become voiced. To put it another way, the first sound is affected by the second. Thus, *-s* would accordingly become *-z,* as 'z' is the voiced counterpart of 's' in proto-Aryan. In the development of Sanskrit from proto-Aryan this 's' regularly became 'r'.[2] While in many cases in the historical period of Sanskrit visarga does become *-r* before a voiced sound, there are unfortunately some complicated exceptions to this general rule. The exceptions for the most part concern *-ḥ* (or *-s*!) when it is preceded by *-a* or *-ā,* that is the syllables *-aḥ* or *-āḥ.* Since *-aḥ* and *-āḥ* occur extremely commonly as terminal syllables (for example, in देवः and देवाः), it is necessary to discuss the sandhi of *-ḥ* in these instances.

The simpler case is presented by *-āḥ* which loses its visarga when followed by any voiced sound, whether vowel or consonant. Hence, नृपाः जयन्ति (The kings conquer) becomes नृपा जयन्ति, and नराः इच्छन्ति (Men desire) becomes नरा इच्छन्ति. Presumably, these sentences would, in their earlier pre-Sanskrit stage, have been *nṛpāz jayanti* and *narāz icchanti,* the *-z* here not being developed into *-r,* but simply lost.

The sandhi of *-aḥ,* however, is intricate and quite strange. Before all voiced consonants (those appearing in columns 3, 4, 5 in the table of the Devanāgarī alphabet, all the semivowels and the aspirate *h-)* and before *a-,* the syllable *-aḥ* is changed to *-o,* and the *a-* of the next word is omitted, the omission being indicated in recent MSS and modern printed books by a

---

[2]The change from *s* to *r* is not by any means peculiar to Sanskrit. It is also seen in English in *was/were.* Those who have studied Latin will remember that the imperfect of *es-se* (*es-t*) 'be' is *er-am, er-as, er-at,* etc., which are descended from prehistoric **es-am, *es-as, *es-at.* The intermediate *z-* stage actually occurs in Oscan (an ancient Italic language allied to Latin), where the infinitive of *es-* 'be' is *ez-um,* while the sister language Umbrian has *er-om.*

peculiar sign called 'avagraha' (अवग्रह).[3] Thus, बाल: दीव्यति (The child plays) becomes बालो दीव्यति, शिष्य: लिखति (The pupil writes) becomes शिष्यो लिखति, तापस: ध्यायति (The ascetic thinks) becomes तापसो ध्यायति. When *a-* follows, तापस: अटति (The ascetic roams about) becomes तापसो ऽटति and मनुष्य: अत्र तिष्ठति (The man stands here) becomes मनुष्यो ऽत्र तिष्ठति. This is the case when *-aḥ* precedes a voiced *consonant* or the vowel *a-*, but if *-aḥ* is followed by any vowel *except a-*, then the *-ḥ* drops out. Thus,

नर:	(→ नर)	आगच्छति (The man comes)
"	"	इच्छति (The man wishes)
"	"	ईशं यजते (The man worships the god)
"	"	उपगच्छति (The man approaches)
"	"	ऊर्मिं पश्यति (The man sees the wave)
"	"	ऋषिं ईक्षते (The man sees the sage)

When visarga occurs before च् *(c)* or छ् *(ch)*, it becomes श् *(ś)* or, more technically, the visarga is assimilated to the palatals च् or छ् by regressive assimilation, that all-important rule mentioned above. Thus, मुनि: चरति (The ascetic wanders) becomes मुनिश् चरति, विहग: छायायां निषीदति (The bird rests in the shade) becomes विहगश् छायायां निषीदति. This change is especially common before the conjunction च *(ca)*, thus: तत: च गृहं गच्छति (And then he goes home) becomes ततश् च गृहं गच्छति.

Before the voiceless dentals त् *(t)* and थ् *(th)* visarga reverts to *-s*. An example is: तत: (→ ततस्) तं द्विजं मार्गे अपश्यत् (Then he saw the twice-born on the road).

Finally, स: (nominative masculine singular of तद्) drops its visarga before any consonant beginning the following word, *e.g.*, स तरु:, स देव:, etc.

When *-aḥ* stands for *-ar* as in the common *adv.* पुन: for पुनर्, and (though very rarely) *-āḥ* stands for *-ār*, as in द्वार्, the visarga reverts to *-r* before *any* vowel or voiced consonant and the -अ or -आ remains unchanged. The sandhi in these instances, then, does *not* follow that of the sequences *-aḥ/-āḥ* representing *-as/-ās*. Thus, पुनर्, *never* पुनो, before all voiced consonants

[3]An initial *a-* after a preceding word ending in *-e* is also dropped, and the omission indicated by the avagraha sign; *e.g.*, गृध्रस् तरो: कोटरे ऽवसत् 'A vulture lived in the hollow of a tree'.

and the vowel अ-, and *never* पुन (with loss of visarga) before vowels other than अ-; द्वार् विव्रियते *not* द्वा वि°, and similarly द्वार् before all vowels.

Summary of Sandhi of Visarga

I. Visarga preceded by *a* or *ā*.

1. The sequence *-aḥ* is replaced by *-o* before any voiced consonant (*viz.*, before any sound in columns 3, 4, and 5 of the Devanāgarī alphabet, before any semivowel or before *h-*); also before *a-* beginning the following word. The *a-* is omitted and the sign ऽ (called avagraha) is inserted to indicate the omission.
2. *-aḥ* before any vowel, except *a-*, or before any diphthong loses its visarga.
3. The sequence *-āḥ* loses its visarga before *any* initial voiced sound.

II. Visarga preceded by any vowel other than *a* or *ā*.

1. When any vowel, other than *a* or *ā*, precedes final visarga, the visarga is replaced by *-r* before *any* initial voiced sound, whether vowel or consonant.

III. Visarga preceded by *any vowel including a* or *ā*.

1. Visarga before the voiceless palatals *c-* and *ch-* is replaced by *ś-*.
2. Visarga before the dentals *t-* and *th-* is replaced by *s-*.
3. Visarga at the end of a word standing alone or at the end of a sentence or before *k-*, *kh-*, *p-*, *ph-*, *ś-*, *ṣ-*, *s-* (all voiceless sounds) remains.

The Ass, the Dog and the Thief

कश्चिद् रजको वाराणस्यां अवसत् । एकस्मिन् दिवसे निर्भरं प्रसुप्तः । तदनन्तरं द्रव्याणि हर्तुं[1] तस्य गृहं चौरः प्रविष्टः । रजकेन तु न किंचिद् श्रुतम् । तस्य गृहस्य पश्चात् गर्दभो बद्धो ऽतिष्ठत्[2] कुक्कुरश् च उपविष्टः । तं चौरं अवलोक्य गर्दभः कुक्कुरं अभ्यभाषत । तव एव अयं व्यापारः । ततस् त्वं कस्मात् उच्चैः शब्दं कृत्वा प्रभुं न जागरयसि इति । कुक्कुरो ऽवदत् । त्वं किमर्थं अस्य नियोगस्य चर्चां करोषि । अहं

अहर्निशं अस्य प्रभोर् गृहं रक्षामि । यतोऽयं चिरात् निर्वृतो भवति ततो मम उपयोगं न अवगच्छति । अधुना च मम आहारस्य दानेऽपि मन्दादरो भवति । यदि दुःखं न अनुभवन्ति तदा प्रभवो भृत्येषु मन्दादरा भवन्ति इति । ततो गर्दभः कोपात् प्रत्यभाषत । त्वं पापो रक्षकः । ततो यथा प्रभुर् जागर्ति तथा करिष्यामि [3]। इति उक्त्वा तेन शब्द उच्चैः कृतः । तेन शब्देन सहसा प्रबुद्धो निद्राया विमर्दन कोपात्[4] रजक उत्थाय[5] गर्दभं लगुडेन अताडयत् । अतश् च उक्तं यदि भृत्यः प्रभोर् हितस्य इच्छया अन्यस्य कस्यचिद् अधिकारस्य चर्चां करोति तदा विषादं सत्वरं गच्छति इति[6] ।

(Adapted from Hitopadeśa Book II, Fable 3).

Notes

1. हर्तुं Infinitive of √हृ (हरति, class I), 'take', here expressing purpose with प्रविष्टः.

2. Etymologically √स्था (तिष्ठति) means 'stand', but in many of its usages it is practically equivalent to 'be' and often denotes continuation in a particular state, as here with the *ppp.* of √बन्ध् (बध्नाति, class IX) 'bind'; hence, here to be rendered 'stayed tied up'.

3. यथा प्रभुर् जागर्ति तथा करिष्यामि literally 'In what way (यथा) our master wakes up, in that way (तथा) I shall do', idiomatically: 'I'll see to it that our master wakes up.' This use of यथा....तथा with √कृ is very common. Note that करिष्यामि is an *s*-future of √कृ formed from the guṇated form of the root (कर्) + the suffix इष्य. This *s*-future is conjugated precisely like the present of any thematic verb.

4. निद्राया विमर्दन कोपात् Note how, from the point of view of English, these words have to be translated in reverse order: 'due to anger[1] on account of the interruption[2] of his sleep[3]'. The explanation of this order of ideas, which is typical of Sanskrit, is that whatever limits or qualifies must precede what is qualified. So, here कोपात् 'due to anger' is causally explained or qualified by

विमर्देन 'on account of the interruption' (instrumental of cause) and finally the sort of interruption that has induced the washerman's anger is explained by निद्रायाः 'of his sleep'.

5. उत्थाय gerund of उद्-√स्था (उत्तिष्ठति) 'stand up, get up'; we should expect उत्स्थाय, but there is a phonetic rule that requires -स्- between two dentals (द् of उद् and थ् of स्थाय) to be dropped. The sandhi change of the voiced consonant द् of उद् to the voiceless त् before -स्थाय is due to the regressive force of voiceless स् which, even though it is dropped, affects the preceding sound.

6. The moral that is to be drawn from a fable in the Hitopadeśa is always expressed in the form of a poetic couplet. Here for the purpose of simplification it has been turned into prose.

Vocabulary

रजक, *m.* a washerman.
वाराणसी, Vārāṇasī, the city of Benares or Banaras in NE India, a seat of great learning and sacredness in the proximity of the Ganges River.
निर्भरम्, *adv.* in full measure, completely.
प्र-√स्वप्, (स्वपिति, class II), go to sleep; *ppp.* सुप्त.
द्रव्य, *n.* thing, property.
चौर, *m.* a thief.
प्र-√विश्, (विशति, class VI), enter; *ppp.* विष्ट.
गर्दभ, *m.* an ass, donkey.
√बन्ध्, (बध्नाति, class IX), bind; *ppp.* बद्ध.
कुक्कुर, *m.* a dog.
उप-√विश् (विशति, class VI), sit down, be seated; *ppp.* विष्ट.
व्यापार, *m.* business, affair.
उच्चैः, *adv.* aloud. [really an *instr. plur.* of उच्च 'high'. There are also other adverbs made by inflecting an *adj.* in the *instr. plur.* for example, शनैः 'slowly'.]
जागरयति, awakens [*causative of* √जागृ (जागर्ति, class II), be awake].

नियोग, *m.* task, duty. [*literally*, 'what is enjoined upon someone' from √युज् 'join' + नि 'on']

चर्चा, trouble, concern; with √कृ, concern oneself with.

अहर्निशम्, *adv.* night and day.

चिरात् *adv.* for a long time.

निर्वृत, *ppp.* निर्-√वृ ('uncover'), 'content' [the exact semantic development of meaning from 'uncovered' to 'content' is unclear].

प्रभु, *m.* lord, master.

उपयोग, *m.* use.

अव-√गम्, (गच्छति, class I), understand, know.

आहार, *m.* food.

दान, *n.* the act of giving, a gift.

मन्दादर, *adj.* indifferent to (+ loc.).

अनु-√भू, (भवति, class I), experience.

रक्षक, *m.* protector.

भृत्य, *m.* a servant. [*literally* a *gerundive,* 'one who is to be supported'].

सहसा, *adv.* suddenly. [really *instr.* of सहस् 'force, violence', hence, *literally* 'with force *or* violence'].

प्र-√बुध् (बोधति, class I), become awake, wake up; *ppp.* बुद्ध.

निद्रा, *f.* sleep.

विमर्द, *m.* interruption.

हित, *n.* welfare, benefit. [strictly the *ppp.* of √धा 'put, place', hence 'placed *or* put', but pregnantly in the sense of 'well placed *or* put', the participle then being used as a noun].

इच्छा, *f.* desire.

अधिकार, *m.* business, affair.

Translate into Sanskrit:

One day a certain thief entered[1] a house to steal things. Because he was extremely skilled in the art of stealing,[2] he had no fear[3] of the master. Having made a study of the art of stealing, he was able[4] to make himself[5] invisible through the use of various powders. Therefore, just as the stars of the sky are invisible in the light of day,[6] in the same way, thieves, having smeared their bodies with these powders unknown by others, are able[7] to make themselves invisible by day or night. So, this thief, after entering the house through a hole he had made with great effort,[8] opened the door of the master's bed-chamber and having taken all sorts of ornaments made of gold and silver utensils which he saw, put them all in a bag and started[9] to go out. Awakened by the noise, the master immediately got up from bed, grabbed his cane and hurled it in the direction of[10] the source of the noise. Struck on his head, the thief fell on the floor and at that very instant, the effect of the powder having worn off, he became visible again. Having become conscious again, the thief got up from the floor and, when he saw the master of the house provided with the cane and ready to hit him again, he left his bag right there, full of the things he had stolen and fled from the house.

Notes

1. 'entered': use प्रविष्ट, *ppp.* प्र + √विश् (विशति, class VI).

2. 'in the art of stealing': चौर्यशास्त्रे. That a science of thievery was highly developed among the numerous branches of knowledge in India is reflected in a famous scene in Śūdraka's play, the Mṛcchakaṭika ('Little Clay Cart'), which has many of the technical terms, and in a work called Ṣaṇmukhakalpa ('Treatise of the Six-faced One'), by whom is meant Skanda as the deity who presides over this department of knowledge.

3. Use the predicate 'genitive of possession'; thus, तस्य न भयम् .

4. अशक्नोत् , imperfect 3rd s. of √शक् (शक्नोति , class V 'be able').

5. आत्मानम् , acc. m. s. of the *n*-stem आत्मन् 'soul', commonly thus used as a reflexive pronoun regardless of the number and gender of the person or thing referred to.

6. 'in the light of day': दिवसालोके .

7. शक्नुवन्ति , pres. 3rd plur. of √शक् 'to able'.

8. 'with great effort': महता प्रयत्नेन .

9. 'started': use आरब्ध , *ppp.* आ- √रभ् (रम्भते, class I)

10. 'in the direction of': उद्दिश्य, strictly a gerund of उद्-√दिश् used as a virtual postposition, literally 'having aimed toward, with an aiming at'.

LESSON TWELVE

The Romance of Compounds.

One of the most characteristic features of Sanskrit, especially the late classical language, is the use of compound words, that is, words consisting of two or more words strung together into a single word treated as a unit. We have had many examples of verb roots compounded with one or more adverbs placed before, as उपगच्छति (उप + √गम्), समुत्पतति (सम् + उद् + √पत्). What we propose to study in this lesson is nouns and adjectives that are compounded with other nouns and adjectives, the so-called 'nominal' compounds as opposed to verb compounds.

Nominal compounds are not at all peculiar to Sanskrit: most of the Indo-European languages have them, with the exception generally of the Romance languages, and they are particularly common in English and German. In English, however, their presence is often obscured by the fact that only compounds of two words are usually written together. So, we write 'headache', without a space between 'head' and 'ache', but we certainly would never write 'headachepills' as a single entity. Similarly, we might write 'schoolboard' as one word, but not 'schoolboardpresident'. In German all these compounds, regardless of the number of constituents, are written as single words.[1] But if we disregard the *method* of writing compounds, we will find that English, especially modern English, is pervaded with compounds, often of sesquipedalian size. For example, 'Senate Foreign Relations Sub-committee pro-tempore secretary' and 'computer software inventory accessions list'. The longer the compound, the fuzzier the concept that it is intended to express. The prevalence of compounds, most particularly the long aggregates such as have just been exemplified, is one of the chief causes for the obscure and vague English that people write nowadays. The reason for the obscurity of the longer compounds is very simply that, without the little words like 'for, of, in, with, by' etc. that show relationship, it is difficult to perceive quickly the interconnection of one element with another. It is all the more difficult when the matter in question is abstract or technical. Of course, the same problem of disentangling the ideas and interrelating them exists in the very long Sanskrit compounds, as in English. But in the case of Sanskrit there is the important difference that, along with the other aspects of Sanskrit, Indian grammarians at a very early time subjected compounds to a minute analysis, carefully classifying them

---

[1] In exceptional instances compounds in German can attain extraordinary lengths. For example, *Rathausturmuhrreparaturbegutachtungskommissionsstellvertreter* ('A pro-tempore representative on a commission for determining the cost of repairing the clock in the tower of the townhall').

and labelling the different categories to which they belonged. In putting words together into compounds, Indian authors, on the whole, were careful to form them within these categories, and cultivated Indians, who had even a modicum of Sanskrit, knew how to break up compounds and determine the interrelation of one part to the other. In English we are generally quite unaware of the common compounds we use, to say the least of the long and often vague ones that occur ubiquitously in every department of knowledge.

In conformity with the principle of 'going from the known to the unknown', let us first examine a few commonplace compounds of but two members in English and see what the relationship is between the two members and then proceed to the same operation in Sanskrit. In most compounds in both English and Sanskrit, the *last* member is the *principal* member of the whole compound, that is, the person or thing that is under discussion, and the prior member (or members) serves to limit the last by restricting its application or coverage. In 'cavedweller', which consists of two members 'cave' and 'dweller', the last member 'dweller' is the principal one, and the prior member 'cave' tells us that it is not any 'dweller' that is here involved, but a 'dweller *in* a cave', so that 'cave' restricts the application of 'dweller' or limits it to a specific category. We may, for the purposes of analysis, label the prior and latter members A and B respectively and, in accordance with our analysis of the interrelationship of A to B, say that A has the value of a locative. If we were to dissolve the compound, we should, then, say 'dweller *in* a cave'. In 'sunlit' part A 'sun' has an instrumental relation to B, as the sense is 'lit *by* (means of) the sun'. Similarly, in 'jailbreak' part A is ablatival to B, the sense being a 'break *from* jail'.

The most common case relationship implied in part A of compounds, in both English and Sanskrit, is the genitive, as the genitive is by nature an adjectival case that limits a noun to one of a class. For example, 'bedpost' is the 'post of a bed', that is, belonging to a bed and nothing else and so distinguishing this 'post' from all other posts. It would also be possible to say that 'bed' in this compound has a dative relationship to 'post', that is, a 'post for a bed'. It is often possible to dissolve a compound thus into either the genitive or dative type. Other examples include 'bedtime', the 'time for (going to) bed', and 'bathrobe', a 'robe for a bath'.

In many compounds of frequent occurrence, part B is an adjective or a participle. Thus, 'Godforsaken' (forsaken by God), 'gumchewing' (chewing gum), 'panfried' (fried in a pan), 'motheaten' (eaten by moths), 'riverborne' (borne on the river).

But there are compounds, less frequently met with, in which part A is an adjective and B a noun. They are sometimes difficult to identify as compounds in English, because, unless the two words are written together as a unit, the lack of grammatical endings in English blurs the dividing-line between a compound and two separate (though syntactically related) words.

Some examples of this type of compound consisting of adjective and noun are: 'highschool',[2] 'wildlife', 'goodwill', 'gentleman', 'supermarket', blackguard' (pronounced 'blaggard' with regressive assimilation of 'ck' to 'g'!), 'holiday' (=holy day) and 'commonwealth' (properly, public welfare, then extended to other usages, as of a group of countries joined by common consent to form a nation).[3] Since in all these compounds part A is an adjective and B a noun, part A would, of course, have to be in the *same case* as B if the compound were dissolved. In some instances part A may be a noun in what is called 'explanatory apposition' to B, as in 'houseboat', which is a 'boat' (serving as a) 'house', the two being equivalent, but the first ('house') being the narrower concept, put first (like the adjectives above) to limit the scope of 'boat'. The case of A ('house') would be the same as of B ('boat'), if the compound is resolved into its parts, as may be seen more clearly if we make a sentence, using the two elements in de-compounded form: 'He lives in a boat, a house'.

The two classes of compounds we have discussed, namely, the one in which the implied case relationship of A is *different* from that of B, and the other, in which A and B imply the *same* case relationship, are called 'tatpuruṣa' by the Indian grammarians, but the second type is also categorized separately under the name 'karmadhāraya'. The word 'tatpuruṣa' is just an example of this twofold class of compounds, and may mean either 'that man' or 'man of him', so that, depending on which analysis is used, tatpuruṣa can be taken as an example of either class. In grammars by Western scholars, tatpuruṣa is usually restricted to the compounds with a *different* case relationship between the two parts, karmadhāraya being reserved for the adjective+noun type or appositional noun+noun type, where the cases of the two parts would be the *same* in dissolution.

Sanskrit compounds are put together in the same way as their English counterparts exemplified above. The person or thing involved is put last, the part expressing the limiting factor precedes it. Only the final member is inflected with a case ending, all the prior parts, regardless of their number (which, in the long compounds, may be considerable), are put in their stem form. Any two nouns or adjectives standing in grammatical relationship can be combined into a compound. Thus, देवानां पतिः 'lord of the gods' can be

---

2 Years ago written as two words, when it would have been doubtful whether to take them as forming a compound.

3 Some compounds of this type in English, and also in Sanskrit, do not denote anything that has the particular characteristic expressed in A, but a specific species to be distinguished from others; for example, 'bluebird' and 'blackbird' are not simply birds that are blue and black respectively, but are specific species of birds. So also Sanskrit कृष्णसर्प is not just a 'black serpent', but a 'cobra'.

compounded into देवपतिः, which we will call a 'genitive tatpuruṣa', because the case value of देव, if separated from पतिः, would be genitive (देवानां). In the same way, अश्वेषु कोविदः 'skilled in (respect to) horses' can be put into अश्वकोविदः, a locative tatpuruṣa; बाहुभिः युद्धम् a 'fight with the arms' (wrestling) becomes बाहुयुद्धम्; कुमारेण दत्तः 'granted by (the god) Kumāra' becomes कुमारदत्तः. Karmadhārayas, are made in exactly the same fashion whether they are of the adjectival or appositional type. Thus, वराङ्गना 'excellent woman' (वर 'excellent' and अङ्गना 'woman'), कृष्णसर्पः 'cobra' (literally 'black serpent', from कृष्ण 'black' and सर्प 'serpent'). Examples of the appositional type are: कन्यारत्नम् a 'gem of a young girl' (कन्या 'young girl' and रत्न 'gem'), the literal sense here being a 'gem, (defined as or equivalent to) a young girl'; राजर्षिः a 'royal sage', literally, a 'sage, a king', that is, a 'sage, (who is) a king'.

A Panorama of Indian Life

अस्ति नदीतीरे अल्पं समन्ततो वृक्षपरिवेष्टितं देवमन्दिरम् । तत्समीपे केचिद् गुल्मा अपि रोहन्ति । तेषां पुष्पितशाखानां[1] मध्ये बहवो ऽलयः परागान्वेषणे[2] परिपतन्ति । अलिविरावो विहगशब्दैः सुस्वरं मिश्रीभवति । प्रत्यहं नरा नार्यश्च समीपस्थेभ्यो[3] ग्रामेभ्यस् तद् देवमन्दिरं पूजनार्थं आगच्छन्ति । मन्दिराभ्यन्तरे विष्णोः प्रतिमा तिष्ठति । इयं प्रतिमा अतीव कोविदेन[4] मूर्तिकारेण अन्यस्मिन् एव कल्पे कृता इति ग्रामजना वदन्ति । तस्य देवमन्दिरस्य पश्चात् विशाल आश्रमो विद्यते । तत्र कश्चिद् ब्रह्मर्षिर् निरन्तरं ध्याननिमग्नो[5] वसति । तं ऋषिं न को ऽपि अभिभाषते न को ऽपि अभिवादयति । इति मया श्रुतम् । आश्रमस्य तापसाः पर्णशालासु[6] इतस्ततो वसन्ति । ते केवलं मूलैः फलैः पुष्पैश्च उपजीवन्ति । केचन दीर्घकालं ध्यायन्ति । केचन तरुच्छायायां सूक्तानि पठन्ति । अन्ये तापसाः काष्ठानि यज्ञाग्नये अवचिन्वन्ति । केचन काले काले सूक्ष्मेषु व्याकरणविषयेषु

विवदन्ते यथा किं परस्मैपदं आत्मनेपदं वा कस्मिंश्चिद् सूत्रे दोषरहितं इति । अन्ये विविधानि योगासनानि आचरन्ति । नदीतीरे बहवो बाला दीव्यन्ति - केचिद् धावन्ति केचिद् वृक्षस्य पश्चात् गूहन्ति केचिद् गुल्मस्य अधस्तात् शेरते केचिद् अचलाश् छायायां तिष्ठन्ति - ते सर्वे अन्योन्यान् क्रीडायां प्रतारयितुं यतन्ते । अन्ये तु जले निमज्ज्य अल्पकालं परिप्लुत्य तीरं प्रत्यागच्छन्ति । कतिपयास् तु पारं प्रतिकूलं भुजैस्[7] तीर्त्वा परिश्रान्ताः प्रत्यागम्य तीरे न्यग्रोधपादपच्छायायां स्वपन्ति । कदापि तत्र केनचिद् वाद्यमानं वेणुं शृणुयात्[9] । वादके वाद्यविद्यायां न कोविदे सति[10] शब्दा बहुवारं कर्कशा दृश्यन्ते । तस्मात् देवमन्दिरात् न दूरं एको जलाशयो विद्यते । तत्र अनेका हंसा अन्यैर्विहगैः सह विहरन्ति । वर्षागमे तु सर्वे हंसा इमं जलाशयं त्यक्त्वा कैलासपर्वते मानससरोवरं पतन्ति[11] । अन्ये विहगास् तत्र जलाशये तिष्ठन्ति । चातकास् तु मेघान् समुत्पत्य तेषु अनुषज्जन्ते[12] । चातका हि जलविन्दुभिर् उपजीवन्ति इति वदन्ति जनाः । तस्मिन् जलाशये प्रभूता मत्स्या विद्यन्ते इति विदित्वा कैवर्ता मत्स्यान् जालेन ग्रहीतुं दूरत एव आगच्छन्ति । तत्र जलाशयतीरे मत्स्यान् पक्त्वा भक्षयन्ति । अस्य जलाशयस्य समीपे महावनं विद्यते । तद्वने प्रभूता मृगप्रकारा वसन्ति । प्रतिदिवसं व्याधगणास् तान् मृगान् मृगयितुं अरण्यं प्रविशन्ति । तान् व्याधान् दृष्ट्वा एव ते मृगा अपसरन्ति । यतो व्याधानां इषवो ऽतिशीघ्रास् ततो मृगा बहवो म्रियन्ते । केचिद् शरहताः पृथिव्यां पतित्वा तत्र एव म्रियन्ते । केचन पुनः सहसा न म्रियन्ते । व्याधानां तीक्ष्णशरैर् हता अपि[13] ते दूरं अपद्रुत्य गुहां प्रविश्य अल्पकालं जीवित्वा अन्ते पञ्चत्वं गच्छन्ति । अन्ये मृगास् तीव्रं व्रणिता अपि न मृत्वा व्याधेभ्यः पलाय्य अन्यं वनभागं गत्वा तत्र भयसमुपेता जीवन्ति । केचिद् व्याधाः पाशान् नियुज्य मृगान् अल्पान् जन्तून् विशेषतो लब्ध्वा व्यापादयन्ति खादन्ति च । अन्ये तु शरान् विषेण विलिप्य अरण्ये अश्वपृष्ठे गच्छन्ति ।

Notes

In the first sentence there are three compounds: नदीतीरे, वृक्षपरिवेष्टितं and देवमन्दिरम्. Each consists of only two members. Since, as we have now seen, the *last* member is generally the person or thing referred to, it is best to determine its meaning before going backward to the prior member. So, in the first compound, the second member (B) is तीरे, which can be readily assumed to be locative, 'on the shore *or* bank'; A (नदी 'river') can logically be only in genitive relation to B: 'on the shore (or bank) of a river'. We could, of course, use an exactly identical compound in the English translation and say 'on a riverbank'. Of similar interrelation are the two members of देवमन्दिरम्, the third compound. Tatpuruṣas are named after the case value of A, so that we may call these two compounds 'genitive tatpuruṣas'.

वृक्षपरिवेष्टितं has three elements वृक्ष, परि and वेष्टितं), but as परि is a verbal prefix, it must naturally be taken with the participle वेष्टितं. वृक्षपरिवेष्टितं, then, also consists of two members: A वृक्ष 'tree' and B परिवेष्टितं 'surrounded'. The only logical relationship that can be assumed for A is that of the instrumental: 'surrounded by trees'. The compound is, then, an instrumental tatpuruṣa.

1. पुष्पितशाखानां Since पुष्पित 'flowered, provided with flowers', is an adjective and शाखानां a noun, this compound is a karmadhāraya similar to English 'highschool'.

2. परागान्वेषणे In this compound the two members पराग ('pollen') and अन्वेषणे ('searching after') are fused together by the contraction of their final and initial vowels respectively. The sandhi between the members of a compound is the same as that between the words in a sentence, (external sandhi). In analyzing a Sanskrit compound care must be exercised to avoid the natural tendency to base the analysis on a *free* translation of the compound which, in all probability, may reflect a different interrelationship of the members from what is conformable to Sanskrit syntax. Thus, we could translate परागान्वेषणे variously by 'in looking for pollen, in searching after pollen, in the search for pollen, in search of pollen' etc. All of these renditions correctly convey the *sense* of the compound, but only the *last* ('in search of pollen') expresses the relationship between A and B that corresponds to the Sanskrit syntactical point of view: action nouns like अन्वेषण 'the act of searching' are construed with a genitive -- a so-called objective genitive. By objective genitive is meant a genitive that is the object

of the verbal idea of the noun with which it is joined. In परागान्वेषण, पराग is regarded as object of the verbal idea inherent in अन्वेषण. There exists also a subjective genitive, as in 'the coming of the rains' where 'the rains' is subject of the act of coming; thus, वर्षागमने below. Some phrases with the genitive (or their equivalent in the form of genitive tatpuruṣas) are ambiguous (also in Sanskrit!); for example, 'fear of the enemy', by which may be meant someone's fear of the enemy (objective genitive) or the enemy's fear of someone (subject genitive); so also the Sanskrit equivalents शत्रूणां भयम् or शत्रुभयम् as a compound.

3. समीपस्थेभ्यो literally 'being in the vicinity', that is, 'situated in the vicinity'. The whole may be rendered somewhat freely: 'men and women come from the nearby villages'. समीपस्थ is a very important type of tatpuruṣa compound, consisting of the noun समीप 'vicinity' + -स्थ a so-called 'verbal' extracted from √स्था (तिष्ठति 'stand, be'). Theoretically, any Sanskrit root may be used, like √स्था here, as part B of a compound with a meaning equivalent to that of a present participle. For example, स्वयम् 'by itself' + √भू (भवति 'be') → स्वयंभू 'being *or* existing by itself, self-existent' (an epithet of Brahmā); वेद ('the Veda') + √विद् (वेत्ति 'know') → वेदविद् 'knowing the Veda'. Sometimes the root used in this way is slightly altered, by shortening or the addition of -त्, or by some other process, if the final letter of the root does not occur as a stem final in declension, as, for example, -म् (in √गम्), there being no stem in -म् in classical Sanskrit. Either the -म् is dropped, or the root is extended by the addition of अ; thus, ख 'sky' + √गम् may yield either खग or खगम 'going in the sky, a bird'. A -त् is added to roots in a short -i or -u; so, विश्व 'all' + √जि (जयति 'conquer') → विश्वजित् 'all-conquering'. When √स्था is thus used at the end of a compound, as here, the -आ is shortened to accommodate it to the देव/फल type. Of identical make is पादप 'a tree' below, literally 'drinking with its feet, *i.e.,* roots', -प being the verbal of √पा (पिबति, 'drink'), with -आ shortened. If the resultant compound is required to be feminine the -आ is kept, and the compound is declined like सेना.

4. कोविदेन कोविद 'skilled' is an interesting compound. The last part -विद् is simply √विद् 'know' as a 'verbal', extended by -अ, as explained above under

note 3. को- is one of the several *root* forms of the interrogative pronoun किम् which we have often encountered in our reading passages. The various root forms of this pronoun, *viz.*, किम्, का, कु, कद् and को, are commonly used in an *appreciative* or *depreciative* sense at the beginning of compounds, almost like the inseparable prefixes सु and दुः. This usage of the interrogative arises from an exclamatory value, as in English when we say 'Who!' or 'What!' often with depreciatory implication, depending on the tone of the exclamation. So कुदृष्टि means a 'bad *or* false view (दृष्टि)', literally 'What a [ridiculous] view!' and कापुरुष, through the exclamatory 'What a [cowardly] man!' means 'a coward'. Similarly, कोविद, through the exclamatory 'knowing what!' gets the *appreciative* sense of 'knowing a great deal, skilled'. कोविद can be classed as an accusative tatpuruṣa, as the interrogative is object of -विद.

5. ध्याननिमग्नो The element नि, like परि in वृक्षपरिवेष्टितं above, must be taken as an adverbial prefix of the past passive participle मग्न. Thus, the compound consists of ध्यान 'meditation' + निमग्न 'sunk, immersed'. What sort of compound is it?

ध्यान, through the Prakrit or popular form झाण *(jhāṇa),* has come into Japanese as Zen, in Zen Buddhism.

6. पर्णशालासु 'In huts (made) with leaves', a variety of karmadhāraya with the middle word (कृत 'made' or similar word) omitted, and hence called 'Madhyamapadalopin' ('dropping the middle word'). Another common example of this sort of compound is छायावृक्ष 'a shade tree', that is, 'a tree (offering) shade'. If expressed, the omitted member would be प्रद 'giving forth', a 'verbal' of प्र-√दा (ददाति). Note shortening of final आ, as in √स्था in समीपस्थ.

7. भुजैस् तीर्त्वा 'having swum', literally 'having crossed with their arms'.

8. न्यग्रोधपादपच्छायायां 'in the shade of a banyan tree', a genitive tatpuruṣa, of which part A (न्यग्रोधपादप) is also a compound, an appositional karmadhāraya. पादप means any sort of 'tree', but is here limited to a particular species by the preceding member न्यग्रोध, which is specifically the banyan *(Ficus Indica).* न्यग्रोध is also a compound, consisting of the adverb न्यक् 'downward' + रोध 'growing', the verbal of √रुह् (रोहति 'grow'). The

verbal रोध is formed from √रुध्, an earlier form of √रुह्, by the addition of -अ (as described in note 3 above) and the replacement of the root vowel *-u-* by its guṇa substitute. 'The tree that grows downward' is a very apt and succinct description of the banyan, which sends down fibres from its branches which, upon reaching the ground, take root and eventually become independent trees. न्यग्रोध is a type of karmadhāraya, in which A is an adverb (here न्यक्) and B is an adjective.

9. शृणुयात् third person singular optative of √श्रु 'hear', with indefinite 'one' as implied subject, a very common use of the third singular. The optative here has a contingent value: 'one *might* hear (a flute being played by someone)', that is, if one were there to hear it. √श्रु belongs to class V, of the non-thematic verbs, which involves the addition of the element नो/नु to the root. Like all non-thematic verbs, this class of verbs differentiates strong and weak forms, -नो- being added in the strong forms, -नु- in the weak. The optative is made from the weak stem with the mood sign -या- (corresponding to -ई- in the thematic classes); thus, शृ (substituted for श्रु) + -नु- (which becomes -णु- because of the cerebralising influence of the ऋ) + -या- + third singular *secondary* ending: शृ-णु-या-त्.

10. वादके . . . न कोविदे सति a locative absolute construction: 'When (or if) the musician is not skilled . . .'. सति is locative singular masculine of the present participle of √अस् (अस्ति, class II) 'be'.

11. वर्षागमने तु सर्वे हंसा . . . पतन्ति. The annual migration of the *haṃsas* to Lake Mānasa in the Himālayas at the onset of the rains is ubiquitously mentioned in Sanskrit literature.

12. अनुषज्जन्ते for अनुषज्यन्ते, the -य- being changed to -ज- due to the progressive effect of the preceding -ज-. This form is really present passive, made (as will be explained in Lesson Twenty-Seven) by adding the suffix -य- to the root and conjugating the resultant passive stem in the middle voice. The initial स- of सञ्ज् is changed to the cerebral ष- due to the rule that स् (when *not* final) is replaced by ष् when any vowel *except -a* or *-ā* precedes; hence, for example, देवेषु, अग्निषु, भानुषु, नदीषु for *देवेसु, *अग्निसु, *भानुसु, *नदीसु. Although this is principally a rule of *internal* sandhi, it is also

applied, as here in अनुषज्जन्ते, after a verbal prefix ending in *-i* or *-u*; *cf*. नि-षीदति for नि-सीदति from सद्.

13. हता अपि 'although struck'. When अपि follows an adjective or a participle (as here), it usually imparts a concessive sense to it, to be rendered by '(al)though' or 'even though'. The same usage occurs again in व्रणिता अपि in the next sentence.

Vocabulary

नदी, *f.* a river.
तीर, *n.* a shore *or* bank.
अल्प, *adj.* small.
समन्ततः, *adv.* all around.
परिवेष्टित, *ppp.* of परिवेष्टयति, envelopes, surrounds, *caus. of* परि-√विष्ट् (वेष्टते, class I, 'wind around, envelope'); *caus. without caus. meaning.*
देवमन्दिर, *n.* a temple. [देव + मन्दिर, 'dwelling, house']
गुल्म, *m.* a cluster *or* clump of trees, thicket.
पुष्पित *adj.* flowered, bearing flowers, in bloom.
शाखा, *f.* a branch.
अलि, *m.* a bee.
पराग, *m.* the pollen of a flower.
अन्वेषण, *n.* seeking *or* looking for.
परि-√पत् (पतति, class I), fly around.
विराव, *m.* sound; noise; buzzing.
सुस्वरम्, *adv.* very sweetly.
मिश्री-√भू (भवति, class I), become mixed, mingle.
प्रत्यहम् *adj.* every day.
समीपस्थ, *adj.* being *or* situated in the vicinity.
पूजन, *n.* honoring, reverencing, worship.
मन्दिराभ्यन्तर, *n.* 'the interior *or* inside of the temple' [note contraction of vowels between parts A and B].
विष्णु, *m.* Viṣṇu, name of one of the principal deities of Hinduism, a member of the trinity or triad (त्रिमूर्ति) along with Brahmā and Śiva.

प्रतिमा, *f.* an image *or* likeness; a statue.
अतीव, *adv.* exceedingly, very.
कोविद, *adj.* clever, skilful.
मूर्तिकार, *m.* a maker of images *or* statues, sculptor. [मूर्ति, 'image' + कार, 'maker']
कल्प, *m.* age *or* period.
जन, *m.* a person, man; *in plur.* people.
विशाल, *adj.* broad, spacious.
ब्रह्मर्षि, *m.* a priest-sage, one of a particular class of sages.
निरन्तरम् *adv.* without interval, continously.
ध्याननिमग्न, *adj.* immersed *or* sunk in meditation. [ध्यान, meditation' + निमग्न, 'sunk', *ppp.* of नि-√मज्ज् (मज्जति, class I) 'sink down']
अभि-√वद् (वदति, class I), speak to, greet; *caus.* अभिवादयति, salutes *or* greets, *without caus. meaning.*
पर्णशाला, *f.* a leaf-hut, a hut made of leaves, such as inhabited by a forest hermit.
इतस्ततः, *adv. phrase* here and there.
केवलम्, *adv.* only.
मूल, *n.* a root.
उप-√जीवति, class I), live on (+ *instr.*).
दीर्घकालम्, *adv.* for a long time.
√ध्या (ध्यायति, class IV), think on, meditate.
सूक्त, *n.* a Vedic hymn.
√पठ् (पठति, class I), recite.
काष्ठ, *n.* a stick of wood, log.
अव-√चि (चिनोति, class V), collect, gather.
काले काले, *reduplicative adv.* from time to time.
सूक्ष्म, *adj.* subtle.
व्याकरण, *n.* grammar.
विषय, *m.* matter, subject *or* topic.
वि-√वद् (वदते, class I), dispute *or* argue about.
दोषरहित, *adj.* devoid of error. [दोष, 'fault, defect' + रहित *ppp. of* √रह् (रहति, class I), 'separate, leave']
विविध, *adj.* of different sorts, various.

आसन, *n.* sitting; seat; posture.
√दिव् (दीव्यति, class IV), play.
√धाव् (धावति, class I), run.
अधस्तात्, *adv.* below; *as postpos.* under, beneath (+ *gen.*).
√शी (शेते, class II), lie, lie down; rest; *third plur.* शेरते (with irregularly inserted -र्- before -अते; note that in the athematic classes the third plur. middle does not have a nasal, hence here -अते, not -अन्ते).
अचल, *adj.* motionless, immobile.
छाया, *f.* shade.
अन्योन्य, *pron.* one another.
प्र-√तॄ (*caus.,* तारयति), deceive, trick, mislead; *infin.* प्रतारयितुम्.
√यत् (यतते, class I), strive after, try.
नि-√मज्ज् (मज्जति, class I), sink down, immerse; dive.
परि-√प्लु (प्लवति, class I), swim around; *gerund* परिप्लुत्य.
कतिपय, *adj.* some, several.
पार, *n.* the further shore *or* bank, the other side (of a river).
प्रतिकूलम् *adv.* contrarily, in the opposite direction.
भुज, *m.* the arm.
√तॄ (तरति, class I), cross over; *gerund* तीर्त्वा.
परिश्रान्त, *ppp.* of परि-√श्रम् (श्राम्यति, class IV), weary *or* tire oneself.
न्यग्रोधपादप, *m.* a banyan tree.
√स्वप् (स्वपिति, class II), sleep.
वाद्यमान, being played, *pres. pass. part. of the caus. of* √वद् (वदति, class I)
वेणु, *m.* a reed; a flute.
वादक, *m.* a musician.
वाद्यविद्या, *f.* the art of playing a musical instrument. [वाद्य 'a musical instrument' + विद्या 'knowledge']
बहुवारम्, *adv.* many times, often.
कर्कश, *adj.* harsh.
जलाशय, *m.* a 'water-abode', a lake. [जल, 'water' + आशय, 'abode']
अनेक, *adj.* many. [*literally* 'not one', *i.e.,* more than one]
वि-√हृ (हरति, class I), pass one's time, enjoy oneself.
वर्षा, *f. plur.* the rains, the monsoon.
आगम, *m.* approach, coming.

कैलास, *m.* Kailāsa, name of a mountain peak in the Himālaya range.
मानस, *n.* a large lake *or* pond.
चातक, *m.* a particular bird (the *Cucculus melanoleucus),* which is said to subsist on the raindrops.
अनु-√सञ्ज *or* सज् (सजति, class I), stick to, be attached to. [*v.* note 12 on the form अनुषज्जन्ते]
हि, *enclitic conj.* for (expressing the reason for a preceding action).
विन्दु, *m.* a drop.
मत्स्य, *m.* a fish.
√विद् (वेत्ति, class II), know; *gerund* विदित्वा.
कैवर्त, *m.* a fisherman.
जाल, *n.* a net.
√पच् (पचति, class I), cook.
√भक्ष् (भक्षति, class I), eat; *caus.* भक्षयति *identical in mg.*
प्रभूत, *adj.* abundant, much, numerous.
प्रकार, *m.* kind, sort.
प्रतिदिवसम्, *adv.* every day.
व्याध, *m.* a hunter.
√मृग् (मृगयति, class X), hunt, chase.
अरण्य, *n.* a forest.
अप-√सृ (सरति, class I), run off *or* away.
इषु, *m.* an arrow.
शीघ्र, *adj.* fast, quick.
√मृ (म्रियते), die.
तीक्ष्ण, *adj.* sharp.
शर, *m.* an arrow.
अप-√द्रु (द्रवति, class I), run off *or* away.
गुहा, *f.* a cave.
तीव्र, *adj.* severe; violent; intense; तीव्रम्, *acc. n. sing. as adv.* severely.
व्रणित, *adj.* wounded.
√पलाय् (पलायते, class I), run away, flee; *gerund* पलाय्य.
भाग, *m.* a part.
समुपेत, accompanied by *or* provided with, *ppp.* of सम् - उप - √इ (एति, class II).
पाश, *m.* a bond, snare *or* trap.

नि-√युज् (युनक्ति, class VII), fasten on, set (a trap).
जन्तु, *m.* a creature.
विशेषत:, *adv.* especially, in particular.
√लभ् (लभते, class I), get, obtain.
वि-आ-√पद् (पद्यते, class IV), perish; *caus.* व्यापादयति, causes to perish, kills.
√खाद् (खादति, class I), eat.
विष, *n.* poison.
वि-√लिप् (लिम्पति, class VI), smear.
पृष्ठ, the back.

Translate into Sanskrit:

A certain Twice-born, after wandering on the road to the city[1] for a long time, seized with thirst due to the heat of the sun, saw a man asleep in the shade of a tree and, having gone up to him,[2] awakened him and asked: 'Where can I find water?'[3] Thereupon, thinking that the Twice-born was the god who had appeared in his dream,[4] the man immediately replied: 'O god, there is no water right here![5] However, I'll give you the water that is in this pot.'[6] When he heard these words of his, the Twice-born took the pot from the man's hand and, pretending that he was drinking the water,[7] gave the pot right back to him, and after saying 'I am very thankful to you', again proceeded[8] on the road. When he saw that the pot was still full of water, the poor man thought: 'He is surely a god, there's no doubt about it!' and, having gone to a temple in the vicinity in order to worship,[9] was extremely pleased. In the meantime, the Twice-born's thirst went away: he too, was extremely pleased.

Notes

1. 'on the road to the city': Say 'on the road *of* the city'.

2. 'having gone up to him': Verbs of motion are construed with the 'accusative of the place to which', but when a person is involved, it is usual to say 'go to the presence (*or similar word*) of . . . ' and so here translate तस्य समीपं गत्वा.

3. 'Where can I find water': Say 'where do I find (विन्दामि) water'.

4. 'thinking . . . in his dream': Render 'having thought (*gerund*) the Twice-born a god (+एव) come (आगतं) in a dream'.

5. 'there is no water right here': अत्रैव जलं न विद्यते (literally 'is found' from 2विद् 'find').

6. 'I'll give you the water that is in this pot': To be expressed idiomatically, thus: 'What water is in this pot, that I give you' (यद् जलं तस्मिन् घटे तिष्ठति तद् एव भवते ददामि). भवते is the dative singular of the honorific pronoun भवत्, on which *v.* Appendix II, B.1.

7. 'pretending that he was drinking the water': Translate literally 'having shown (संदर्श्य) himself (आत्मानं, reflexive pron.) as drinking (पिबन्तं, pres. participle √पा 'drink')'. संदर्श्य is the gerund of the causative संदर्शयति of सम्-√दृश् 'cause (some one) to see', *i.e.*, show: 'having caused [the man] to see himself . . . ', having shown himself.

8. 'again proceeded': पुनः प्रस्थितः (*ppp.* प्र-स्था as main verb).

9. 'in order to worship': यज्ञार्थं ('for the sake of worship') -अर्थं (-अर्थाय) at the end of a cpd. is often used to express purpose.

LESSON THIRTEEN

The Romance Continued: Analysis of Long Compounds.

In the previous lesson we had a general introduction to compounds, considered the various ways that the first member of a compound may be related to the last, and studied two basic types of compounds differentiated from each other according to the character of the relationship between the two members. The one type, in which part A has a *different* case value from B, we called a tatpuruṣa, and the other, in which the two parts are in adjectival or appositional agreement with each other, we called a karmadhāraya. In both these compounds, the tatpuruṣa and the karmadhāraya, the last member is the center or pivot of attention the person or thing referred to while the prior member narrows it down to a specific instance. In this lesson we propose to continue with these two types of compounds as they are applied in the secondary sense of possession.

Once again it is better to start with English, with something we know, before proceeding to Sanskrit. When we say 'bigmouth', we certainly do not mean simply a 'mouth that is big', or to put it in the technical jargon we have just learned, this is *not* a karmadhāraya compound. What we do mean is 'one who *has* a big mouth'. Similarly, when we say 'redskin', we mean 'one who *has* red skin', *not* simply 'red skin'. Here, then, the point of emphasis is *not* the last member of the compound: we are *not* speaking of a 'mouth' that is big or of 'skin' of a particular color. The focal point or center of attention, which in a tatpuruṣa or karmadhāraya is the *final* member of the compound, is here *outside* the compound. It is the person (or thing) that possesses the characteristic feature of a 'big mouth' or the 'red skin'. It is a remarkable thing that in these two English compounds we have used as examples whether written as one word (*i.e.,* truly as a compound of two members) or as two words (as was generally done years ago) we place a strong accent on the first part in saying them: 'bígmouth' and 'rédskin', whereas, if we say 'big móuth' and 'red skín', the meaning is quite different. In the latter case we mean quite simply a 'mouth that is big' and 'skin that is red' respectively. The accent makes all the difference in meaning. Sometimes to convey the sense of possession more clearly we add an *-ed,* thus: 'bigmouth*ed*', 'redskinn*ed*'.[1] It is tempting to call these compounds, which are just a particular application of a karmadhāraya, 'exocentric', because their focal point is outside (exo-) the members of the compound. But this term is not in use, so the temptation would have to be resisted.

---

[1] But if by 'redskin' is meant a member of the Amerindian peoples, we would not, of course, say 'redskinned', which is strictly an adjective and means only 'possessed of red skin' (as from overexposure to the sun).

In the older stage of Sanskrit, as represented by the language of the Veda, when there still existed a musical tone such as is presumed to have existed in the parent Indo-European, these exocentric or possessively used karmadhārayas were differentiated (as in English!) by the place of the accent. So, for example, a 'mighty horse' (a simple karmadhāraya) was *'bṛhadáśva'*, the accent of the compound being that of the last member *(áśva),* but if this compound were used of one 'possessing mighty horses', the accent (again as in English!) would shift to that of the first member *bṛhád,* and we should say *bṛhádaśva.* In Classical Sanskrit, however, this musical pitch has disappeared, superseded by a purely stress accent, much like that of English, but uttered with a great deal less force. In Classical Sanskrit texts, then, reflecting as they do a stress-accented stage of the language, there are no written accents to tell the reader whether a compound is of the possessive variety.

In Sanskrit any tatpuruṣa[2] or karmadhāraya may be used possessively, if the sense of the parts permits the implication of possession. A tatpuruṣa or karmadhāraya used in this way is called a 'bahuvrīhi' by the Indian grammarians. 'Bahuvrīhi' means 'having much (*bahu-*) rice (*vrīhi*)' and so is just an example of this type of compound used as a name or label, exactly like 'tatpuruṣa' ('that man' or 'man of him'). It is as if we were to call this type of compound in English a 'bigmouth' compound. In fact linguists, who have borrowed a number of technical grammatical terms from Sanskrit, have borrowed the name 'bahuvrīhi' to denote a possessive compound in whatever language such usage is found.

'Bahuvrīhi' can, of course, mean simply 'much rice' (as a karmadhāraya), and, as has been said, only the context in which the word occurs can determine which meaning is actually intended. So, if we say बहुव्रीहिः व्याधये कल्पते '*Much rice* leads to illness', the word बहुव्रीहिः is a karmadhāraya; but if we say बहुव्रीहिः देशः वर्धते 'A country *that possesses much rice* thrives', then बहुव्रीहिः is a bahuvrīhi!

Bahuvrīhis are ubiquitous in Sanskrit, and it would be hard to find a page in which several do not occur. They are very much less common in English, however, which tends to choose other methods of expression. As we have already observed, English freely uses the suffix *-ed,* which practically has come to mean 'provided with, possessed of'. A few Sanskrit bahuvrīhis of frequent occurrence are: प्रजाकाम 'having a desire for progeny' (as a tatpuruṣa, on which it is based, it means a 'desire for progeny'); पाण्डुवर्ण 'having a pale color' (as a karmadhāraya simply a 'pale color')' महाव्रत

[2]Only tatpuruṣas ending in a noun (something that can be possessed!) are meant here. Remember that a tatpuruṣa may have *either* a noun *or* an adjective as its final member (bedpost, panfried).

'having a great vow', that is 'having undertaken a great vow' (as a karmadhāraya, a 'great vow'). Bahuvrīhis are very often formed with a past passive participle and a noun, where the sense of possession is not so apparent. For example, संयतेन्द्रिय 'having controlled (संयत, past passive participle of सम्-√यम् 'hold together, hold in check') sense-organs (इन्द्रिय)',[3] which may be variously rendered 'whose sense-organs are controlled' or 'by whom the sense-organs have been controlled'; कृतकृत्य 'having one's duty done', or similarly to the other example, 'whose duty is done' or 'by whom one's duty has been done'.

A very prevalent kind of bahuvrīhi consists of two nouns, the one (A) in explanatory apposition to the other (B), that is, an 'appositional karmadhāraya' used as a bahuvrīhi. For example, पाटलिपुत्रनामधेयं नगरम् 'a city *having Pāṭaliputra as its name* (नामधेय)'. Here part B (नामधेय) is defined *not* by an adjective, but by a *noun* (पाटलिपुत्र) in apposition to it ('a city, Pāṭaliputra'). This sort of bahuvrīhi is especially common precisely in 'naming formulae' like this. So also, then गृध्रकूटनाम्नि पर्वते 'in a mountain *having Gṛdhrakūṭa as its name* (नामन्); पद्मगर्भाभिधानं सरः 'a pond (सरः) *having Padmagarbha as its name* (अभिधान)'. But often a compound is not used in these naming formulae, but just the name followed by नाम 'by name'; for example, महाविक्रमो नाम सिंहः 'a lion Mahāvikrama by name'. A good example of an 'appositional bahuvrīhi' in English is 'blockhead', literally 'having a head (which is) a block'.

There are many kinds of bahuvrīhis in which certain prefixes (वि-, अ-, उद्, etc.) and common nouns (-आदि, -मात्र, etc.) have a special function and therefore require separate discussion.

So far we have been treating compounds consisting of only two members, but it was noted that compounds can be very long, and a compound of four to six members is common. The basic principle that has to be borne in mind is that, whatever the length of a compound, it is to by analyzed by a division into two members (A and B).[4] If A and B are also compounds, they are to be halved in the same way and so on with yet other imboxed compounds, until all the members have been reduced to their simplest terms. A few examples will make this clear, but there can be no denying the fact that to analyze the longer compounds correctly requires a fair amount of

---

3The final vowel of *saṃyata* is contracted with the initial *i-* of *indriya* into *-e-* by a regular rule of sandhi vowel-coalescence.

4There is an exception to this twofold division in the class of compounds called 'dvandva' which consist of a series of nouns in simple conjunctive relationship.

experience. First, some examples will be given in English in conformity with our oft-related principle of 'going from the known to the unknown'. But the mode of analysis of the English examples will be the same as if the compounds were in Sanskrit.

I. English Compounds

1. 'Information center employees union'

Analysis:

A B
Information center employees | union
The relationship between A and B is genitive, so the compound is a genitive tatpuruṣa ('Union of . . .').[5]

C D
Part A: Information center | employees
The relationship between C and D, the two parts into which A can be logically bisected, is again genitival, so this imboxed compound is also a genitive tatpuruṣa ('employees of . . .')

E F
Part C: Information | center
The relationship between E and F, the two parts of C, can be taken as either dative or genitive ('center for . . .' or 'center of . . .'), so that C is either a dative or genitive tatpuruṣa.

2. 'Endangered wildlife conservation project'

Analysis:

A B
Endangered wildlife conservation | project
The primary bisection is between 'endangered wildlife conservation' and 'project', and the relationship between A and B is probably datival, but genitival is also possible.

C D
Part A: endangered wildlife | conservation

---

[5]Of course, it is possible to divide this compound into 'information center' (A) and 'employees union' (B) ('employees union of '), but there would be a subtle difference in meaning: in the latter analysis the 'employees union' suggests a union of employees embracing more than those employed at the 'information center'; the other analysis implies a union *specifically* of employees of the information center. A good example of the vagueness to which excessive compounding leads.

Part A consists of C (endangered wildlife) and D (conservation), and the relation between the two members C and D is genitival ('conservation of ...').

Part C: endangered[E] | wildlife[F]
Part C consists of E (endangered) and F (wildlife). Since E is a participial adjective qualifying F (wildlife), Part C is a karmadhāraya.

Part F: wild[G] | life[H]
The last imboxed compound F consists of the adjective 'wild' (G) and 'life' (H) which forms a karmadhāraya (in fact, it is one of the examples of a karmadhāraya given in the previous lesson!)

II. Sanskrit Compounds

1. प्रमृष्टमणिकुण्डलाः (नृपाः)
'(kings) having earrings (कुण्डल) having polished gems'

Analysis:
प्रमृष्टमणि[A] | कुण्डलाः[B]
The first bisection has to come between प्रमृष्टमणि ('having polished gems') and कुण्डलाः ('earrings'). The whole compound is a bahuvrīhi describing the kings (नृपाः). It can be taken as an axiom that whenever a compound *ends in a noun* (here कुण्डल) and is used as an adjective, as प्रमृष्टमणिकुण्डलाः is here, then the compound *must* be a bahuvrīhi.

Part A: Since प्रमृष्टमणि ends in a noun, but is adjectival to कुण्डला, it must, according to the principle just stated, be a bahuvrīhi. प्रमृष्ट ('polished') is a past passive participle from प्र-√मृज् (मार्ष्टि) 'rub thoroughly, polish', so that प्रमृष्टमणि is a bahuvrīhi derived from a karmadhāraya (adjective + noun), just as is the whole compound.

2. कनकसूत्रानुसरणप्रवृत्ताः (राजपुरुषाः)
'(royal officials) gone forth for (the sake of) searching for the golden cord'

Analysis:
कनकसूत्रानुसरण[A] | प्रवृत्ताः[B]

The primary division has to be made between कनकसूत्रानुसरण and वृत्ताः. Since A expresses the purpose of B, the compound is a dative tatpuruṣa ('gone forth for the purpose of. . .').

Part A must be bisected between कनकसूत्र and अनुसरण,[6] as कनकसूत्र ('cord of gold') forms a unit by itself. Since अनुसरण 'searching after, tracking down' (literally 'going after') takes a genitive of what is looked for, part A is a genitive tatpuruṣa.

Part C: कनक^D । सूत्र^E

This is a genitive tatpuruṣa ('cord of . . .'). कनक is technically equivalent in value to a 'genitive of material'.

3. तरुकोटरावस्थितकृष्णसर्पः

'a cobra abiding in the hollow of a tree'

Analysis:

तरुकोटरावस्थित^A । कृष्णसर्पः^B

Part B (कृष्णसर्प), literally 'black serpent' (a karmadhāraya, consisting of the adjective कृष्ण and the noun सर्प), forms a unitary conception, a specific serpent, the cobra, which is qualified by what precedes. The whole compound is, then, a karmadhāraya ('a cobra abiding in . . .').

Part A: तरुकोटरावस्थित[7] has to be divided between तरुकोटर ('hollow of a tree') and अवस्थित ('abiding', past passive participle of अव-√स्था (तिष्ठति) 'abide'; though *past* and *passive* in form अवस्थित has *present active* meaning. The relation between तरुकोटर (C) and अवस्थित (D) is locative, hence Part A is a locative tatpuruṣa.

Part C: तरु^E । कोटर^F

The relationship between E and F is genitive, hence, C is a genitive tatpuruṣa ('hollow of . . .').

---

[6]By rule of sandhi the *-a* of सूत्र forms a long vowel by coalescing with the *a-* of अनुसरण.

[7]As in the previous example, there is a contraction of two *a's* here: the final of कोटर and the initial of अवस्थित.

4. भाण्डपूर्णकुम्भकारमण्डपिका
'a potmaker's shed full of vessels'
Analysis:
भाण्डपूर्ण[A] । कुम्भकारमण्डपिका[B]

Since कुम्भकारमण्डपिका forms a unit ('the shed of a potmaker'), the bisection has to be made after भाण्डपूर्ण ('full of vessels'). The whole compound, then, is a karmadhāraya.

Part A: भाण्ड[C] । पूर्ण[D]

This may be taken as an instrumental or genitive tatpuruṣa because, if not compounded, पूर्ण ('full') is construed with a genitive or instrumental ('full of . . .' or 'full with . . .').

Part B: कुम्भकार[E] । मण्डपिका[F]

This is a simple genitive tatpuruṣa ('shed of a . . .').

Part E: कुम्भ[G] । कार[H]

This is also a genitive tatpuruṣa, consisting of कुम्भ ('pot') and कार ('a maker').

The Training of Four Wayward Princes

अस्ति गङ्गातीरे पाटलिपुत्रनामधेयं[1] नगरम् । तत्र सर्वप्रभुगुणसंयुक्तः सुदर्शनो नाम नरपतिर् आसीत्[2] । तस्य भूपतेश्[3] चत्वारः[4] पुत्रा अभवन् । यतस् ते पुत्रा अनधिगतशास्त्रा[5] उन्मार्गवृत्तयश्च[6] ततः स महीपतिर्[7] उद्विग्नचित्तः । किं करोमि इति पुनः पुनर् अचिन्तयत् । एक एव गुणसंयुक्तः पुत्रो वरं न च[8] मूर्खशतम् अपि । एकश् चन्द्रो ऽन्धकारं हन्ति न तु तारागणा अपि । ऋषिभिर् उक्तं तु । न हि सुप्तस्य सिंहस्य मुखे प्रविशन्ति मृगा इति । तेन कारणेन किंचिद् मया कर्तव्यम्[9] । इति विचिन्त्य तेन नृपतिना पण्डितसभा सपदि कारिता । तस्यां सभायां समागतायां[10] नरेश्वरो ऽवदत् । भो भोः पण्डिताः । मम पुत्राः शास्त्रेषु मन्दादराः । पुस्तकानि न अधिगच्छन्ति न पठन्ति ।

अपरं च ते ऽलसा भवन्ति । ते केवलं व्यसनेन निद्रया कलहेन च कालं गमयन्ति । उक्तं च । यथा काचः काञ्चनसंसर्गात् काञ्चनद्युतिं लभते तथा एव मूर्खा अपि गुणसमन्वितजनसंयोगेन गुणान् लभन्ते । किं[11] अस्यां सभायां कश्चिद् पण्डितो मम पुत्रान् विद्यां नीतिं च उपदेष्टुं समर्थः । अस्मिन् अन्तरे कश्चिद् सकलनीतिशास्त्रकोविदो महापण्डितः सभायां उत्थाय नृपतिं अभिवाद्य कृताञ्जलिर् अभ्यभाषत । देव[12] । अहं षण्मासाभ्यन्तरे नीतिशास्त्रोपदेशेन तव पुत्राणां पुनर्जन्म कर्तुं समर्थः । तस्य तद् वचनं श्रुत्वा स भूपतिः संतुष्टचित्तस् तं पण्डितं अवदत् । इदं मया श्रुतम् । कीटो ऽपि पुष्पसङ्गात् गुणसमन्वितानां जनानां शिर आरोहति । पाषाणो ऽपि महद्भिः प्रतिष्ठितो देवत्वं गच्छति । इति उक्त्वा तेन नृपतिना पुत्रास् तस्मै विष्णुशर्मनामधेयाय पण्डिताय समर्पिताः । भूमिपतये विष्णुशर्ममहापण्डितेन इदं स्पष्टीकृतम् । यथा नवभाजनलग्नः संस्कारो भाजनपचनस्य पश्चात् न अन्यथा भवति तथा नीतिः कुमारेभ्य एव मनोहरकथारूपेण उपदिष्टा स्थितिं गच्छति इति । ततस् तेन महापण्डितेन हितोपदेशस्य विविधाः कथाः तेभ्यो ऽनधिगतशास्त्रपुत्रेभ्यः कथिताः ।

(Adapted from the Introduction to the Hitopadeśa).

Notes

1. पाटलिपुत्रनामधेयं is an adjective qualifying नगरम्. Since it is obviously a compound and ends in a noun, what sort of compound is it?

2. आसीत् 'was', imperfect third person singular of √अस् (अस्ति) 'be', a verb of class II, the root class, in which the personal endings are attached directly to the root, hence अस् + ति. The imperfect ought to be simply आस् in both the second and third persons: augment अ- + अस् → आस् + स् (second person) and आस् + त् (third person), both these yielding simply आस् because of a rule that permits a Sanskrit word to end in only *one* consonant, thus requiring that the

स् and त् be dropped. This form आस् occurs in the Ṛgveda, but because of the ambiguity of आस्, which can be *either* second *or* third person, the endings -ईस् and -ईत् of the aorist tense came to be added to आस्, yielding आसीस् and आसीत् respectively, which are distinctly second and third person.

3. तस्य भूपतेश् This is a predicate genitive of possession: literally, 'Of that king there were four sons', that is, 'That king *had* four sons'. Strictly speaking, Sanskrit lacks a verb meaning 'have' in the sense of 'possess', so that the concept of possession is expressed by saying either 'of so-and-so there is such-and-such' or 'to (dative) so-and-so there is such-and-such'.

4. चत्वारः Nominative masculine plural of the cardinal numeral 'four'. The declensions of the cardinal numerals from one to ten are quite irregular, as may be seen in the declension of चतुर् 'four', which has two stems, चत्वार् and चतुर्. In the masculine it runs thus:

Nom. चत्वारः (as here)
Acc. चतुरः
Instr. चतुर्भिः
Dat./Abl. चतुर्भ्यः
Gen. चतुर्णाम्
Loc. चतुर्षु

The feminine is basically formed from the stem चतसृ, thus:

Nom./Acc. चतस्रः (here -ṛ becomes -r before the vowel of the ending)
Instr. चतसृभिः
Dat./Abl. चतसृभ्यः
Gen. चतसृणाम्
Loc. चतसृषु

5. अनधिगतशास्त्राः This is a bahuvrīhi whose part A is a past passive participle of अधि-√गम् (गच्छति) made negative with the prefix अन्- (अ- before consonants).[8] Both this compound and the following (उन्मार्गवृत्तयः) are predicate adjectives to ते पुत्राः, 'were' (अभवन्) being understood: 'Since those

[8]English also has the same negative prefix *a-* (before consonants) and *an-* (before vowels) which is borrowed from Greek, although its use has been widely extended to words of non-Greek origin; thus, pathetic: apathetic, organic: non-organic; but moral: amoral, which is of Latin origin.

sons were . . .'. That both components are bahuvrīhis is externally apparent from the fact that they end in a noun (शास्त्र and वृत्ति). Another external clue that the compound अनधिगतशास्त्राः is a bahuvrīhi is that if it were a karmadhāraya, we should have अनधिगतशास्त्राणि since शास्त्र is neuter. So we may formulate a rule that, when a tatpuruṣa or a karmadhāraya is used as a bahuvrīhi, the original gender of the noun with which it ends must, if necessary, be made to conform to the gender of the noun the bahuvrīhi qualifies. Apart from the bahuvrīhi at hand, this alteration of gender can be clearly illustrated by the compound बहुफल 'having much fruit', which ends in the neuter noun फल. If we wish to speak of a 'country that has much fruit' using the masculine देश for country', then we must say बहुफलः देशः; similarly a 'grove having much fruit' would be बहुफला वनिका, where फल is given the feminine ending -आ. So it may be said that whenever a compound ends in a noun whose gender has been altered, the compound must be a bahuvrīhi.

6. उन्मार्गवृत्तयः A so-called appositional bahuvrīhi, that is, a bahuvrīhi that is based on an appositional karmadhāraya, a karmadhāraya consisting of two nouns, the first (A) being the narrower concept. Here, then, literally 'having wrong ways as their conduct', ill-behaved. उन्मार्ग means an 'away path' or an 'off path', the prefix उद् (changed to उन् by sandhi) implying what is deviant or 'off the straight and narrow'. It is really a karmadhāraya in which the prefix, though in form an adverb ('out, away, off') is used as a quasi-adjective to qualify मार्ग. In English there are a few compounds in which the adverb 'off' is used in this way, thus 'offwhite' (not truly white), 'offchance' (a slight chance, not a real chance).

7. Sanskrit has innumerable words for 'king'. For the most part they are genitive tatpuruṣas meaning literally 'lord of men' (नरपति, नरेश्वर), 'lord of the earth' (भूपति, महीपति), 'men-protecting' (नृप), 'protector of the earth' (पृथिवीपाल) and so on. If one knows the commonest words occurring in these compounds of fairly stereotyped meaning -- नृ, नर (man), भू, भूमी (or भूमि), मही, पृथिवी (earth), -प (protecting), पाल (protector) and पति, ईश्वर (lord) -- there is no need to use the vocabulary or dictionary.

8. वरं न च In Sanskrit, if one wishes to say 'So-and-so is better than so-and-so', there is a frequently used idiom consisting of the neuter of the adjective वर 'most excellent, best' as predicate to the thing that is better (than

something else) followed by न च and the thing that is inferior: 'So-and-so (is) most excellent (वरं) and not (न च) so-and-so'. So here: 'Just one son provided with good qualities (is) most excellent and not even a hundred fools', or freely 'Just one virtuous son is better than even a hundred fools'.

9. मया कर्तव्यम् 'must be done by me' or actively 'I must do'. कर्तव्य is the so-called 'gerundive' (not to be confused with 'gerund'!) or future passive participle of √कृ (करोति) 'do'. It is always difficult to explain this grammatical form, principally because English does hot have a future passive participle, and literal translations made with 'to', such as 'to be done, about to be done', are misleading because they involve an infinitive. Perhaps the awkward locution made with 'going', participle of 'go', in the sense of a future action, may give some sense of the literal meaning: 'going to be done', that is, to be done in the future. The future passive participles or gerundives may be used simply to refer to an action that *will* occur, as, for example, in the fable where the crow tells his wife that a certain cobra that has been ravaging their nest *will be seen and killed* (द्रष्टव्यो व्यापादयितव्यश्च) by the king's men in their search for the prince's lost gold chain. However, for the most part, the gerundive is used to express what *needs* to be done by someone; it is the regular means of expressing 'necessity or duty' in Sanskrit. Thus, किंचिद् मया कर्तव्यम् means 'Something must be done by me' or 'I must *or* have to do something'; मया गन्तव्यम् 'I must go', here the gerundive is used impersonally.

10. The combination of a noun (or pronoun) in the locative with a participle should generally be taken as a possible absolute construction. Here, then, 'When that assemblage had come together, the king . . .'.

11. किं here serves as a question-marker, as often when it begins a sentence.

12. देव 'O king!' or 'Your Majesty!' The word देव means not only 'god', but frequently 'king', as a king was looked upon as a veritable god on earth.

Vocabulary

पाटलिपुत्र, *n.* Pāṭaliputra, the name of an ancient city of India, capital of the Kingdom of Magadha. It is situated on the confluence of the Śoṇa and Gaṅgā (Ganges) rivers and corresponds to Palíbothra of Ptolemy. It is now called Patna.

गङ्गा, *f.* the river Ganges, also frequently called भागीरथी (Bhāgīrathī), because, according to legend, it was brought from heaven to earth by the extreme asceticism of Bhagīratha in order to purify the ashes of his ancestors. In its descent from heaven it was supported by the great god Śiva who is, in consequence, often called by the epithet गङ्गाधर 'bearer of the Ganges'. Note that the well-known Indian scholar Bal Gangadhar Tilak has this as his middle name.

नामधेय, *n.* name, designation.

संयुक्त, *ppp.* of सं-√युज् (युनक्ति, class VII), 'join together, unite'. Often used at the end of an instrumental tatpuruṣa in the sense of 'provided with, possessed of'.

सुदर्शन, *m.* Sudarśana, name of a king of Pāṭaliputra. [Literally 'handsome', applied to the god Śiva among very numerous other epithets, and probably it is in its use as a name of Śiva that it is commonly also employed as a man's name. In this connection it has to be borne in mind that Indian boys are frequently given divine names.]

नाम, *as adv.* by name.

अधि-√गम् (गच्छति, class I),. go up to, approach; *ppp.* अधिगत, negatived by prefixing अन्-, thus: अनधिगत 'unapproached'.

शास्त्र, *n.* literally 'an instrument of teaching', (derived from √शास् 'teach'), a manual of instruction, a book or treatise of any kind.

उन्मार्ग, *m.* a by-way, a wrong *or* evil way.

वृत्ति, *f.* way of behaving, conduct.

मही, *f.* earth [*literally* 'the mighty one', *f.* of the *adj.* मह् 'mighty'].

उद्विग्न, *ppp.* उद्-√विज् (विजते, class VI, 'start, be agitated').

चित्त, *n.* thought; mind.

पुनः पुनः, *adv.* again and again.

मूर्ख, *m.* a fool.

शत, *n.* a hundred.

अपि, *adv.* also, even; *often concessively after adj.,* though.

चन्द्र, *m.* moon.

अन्धकार, *m.* or *n.* darkness.

√हन् (हन्ति, class II), strike, strike down, kill, destroy.

तारा, *f.* star.

गण, *m.* crowd, host, group, troop.

गुण, *m.* quality; good quality, virtue.

सुप्त, *ppp.* √स्वप् (स्वपिति, class II, 'sleep'), asleep, sleeping.

सिंह, *m.* lion.

मुख, *n.* mouth.

सभा, *f.* assembly, assemblage.

सपदि, *adv.* immediately.

कारित, *ppp. of the causative of* √कृ (करोति, class VIII, 'do make'), *literally*, 'caused to be made'.

भो भो, *vocative adv.* O! Oh!

अपरं च, *conj.* moreover [*literally* 'and another (thing)'].

अलस, *adj.* lazy, indolent.

केवलम्, *adv.* only.

व्यसन, *n.* vice.

निद्रा, *f.* sleep.

कलह, *m.* quarreling, contention, strife.

काल, *m.* time.

√गम् (गच्छति, class I), go; *caus.* 'causes to go', (*of time*) passes.

काच, *m.* glass.

काञ्चन, *n.* gold.

संयोग, *m.* contact, connection.

द्युति, *f.* lustre, gleam.

संसर्ग, *m.* contact.

समन्वित, *ppp.* सम्-अनु-√इ (एति, class II, 'go along *or* after, accompany'), accompanied by, endowed with, possessed of.

सभा, *f.* a hall for public assembly; an assembly *or* meeting.

पण्डित, *m.* a learned man, scholar.

विद्या, *f.* knowledge.

नीति, *f.* conduct, right and proper behavior; political and social ethics.

उप-√दिश् (दिशति, class VI), point out, teach, instruct (*infinitive* उपदेष्टुम्).

समर्थ, *adj.* capable, able (+ *inf.*).

महा-, *adj.* great, *as first member of a karmadhāraya compound, not used separately.*

अन्तर, *n.* interim, juncture.

सकल, *adj.* all.

कोविद, *adj.* skilled in (+ *loc.*).

अभि-√वद् (वदति, class I), say to, salute; *caus.* अभिवादयति, salutes [*without caus. meaning*].

अञ्जलि, *m.* the open hands, hollowed and joined in reverent salutation.

षण्मास, *m.* a period of six months, half a year.

अभ्यन्तर, *n.* interval, space.

उपदेश, *m.* instruction.

पुनर्जन्मन्, *n.* a rebirth [a neuter *n*-stem, nom.-acc. जन्म].

संतुष्ट, *ppp.* सम्-√तुष् (तुष्यति, class IV, 'be satisfied *or* pleased'), pleased, content, happy.

कीट, *m.* a worm *or* caterpillar.

सङ्ग, *m.* a sticking to, attachment.

शिरः, *n.* head [an *s*-stem, nom.-acc. शिरः].

आ-√रुह् (रोहति, class I), rise up to, mount, ascend.

पाषाण, *m.* a stone.

महत्, *adj.* great.

प्रतिष्ठित, *ppp.* प्रति-√स्था (तिष्ठति, class I, 'stand, be established'), established, set up.

देवत्व, *n.* state *or* condition of being a god, godhead.

विष्णुशर्मन्, m. Viṣṇuśarman, name of a great sage. [The final -न् disappears as prior member of a cpd. The name may mean 'having Viṣṇu as his protection' (an appositional bahuvrīhi) or 'Viṣṇu's delight' (a genitive tatpuruṣa), depending on the meaning given to शर्मन्.]

समर्पित, delivered, entrusted, *ppp. of* समर्पयति, *causative of* सम्-√ऋ (ऋच्छति, class VI), delivers, entrusts.

स्पष्टीकृत, *ppp.* of स्पष्टी-√कृ (करोति, class VIII), (having been) made clear, explained.

भाजन, *n.* vessel, receptacle, pot.

नव, *adj.* new, fresh; unbaked (of a clay pot).

√लग् (लगति, class I, 'adhere, stick to'); *ppp.* लग्न attached to (as of a design to a pot prior to baking).

संस्कार, *m.* an impression (as of a design applied to an unbaked clay pot *or* of an impression made on the mind in the past, especially in a prior rebirth).

पचन, *n.* cooking, baking (of a raw clay pot to render it hard and permanent).

पश्चात्, *postp. with gen.,* behind, after.

अन्यथा, *adv.* otherwise; *with* √भू become otherwise, become altered.

कुमार, *m.* a child, a boy.

मनोहर, *adj.* captivating, charming.

कथा, *f.* a story, fable.

रूप, *n.* form, shape.

स्थिति, *f.* standing; permanent condition.

√कथय (कथयति), talk, tell, narrate [a so-called 'denominative' verb formed from the interrogative adv. कथम् 'how', hence, literally 'do the how', *i.e.,* 'tell how' etc.]; *ppp.* कथित, told, narrated.

Translate into Sanskrit:

When the rainy season starts in India, the sky is filled with dark clouds. As soon as they see[1] these clouds, the *cātakas* fly up and cling to them.[2] For[3] these birds subsist on the raindrops,[4] so say the people. At this same time[5] the *haṃsas* fly up together to Lake Mānasa (which is) situated-on-Mt. Kailāsa.[6] When the rain ceases, a rainbow usually appears in the sky. It is thought by some people in India that rainbows are due to the effulgence of the crest jewels of serpents abiding-in-anthills.[7] After the rains have ceased,[8] flowers of-various-colors[9] thrive everywhere in the mountains and in the fields.

Notes

1. 'As soon as they see': The idea of 'as soon as' may be expressed by putting the particle एव after the gerund.

2. 'cling to them': The verb अनु-सञ्ज्, like all words meaning 'cling to' or 'stick to' is construed with the locative.

3. Use the co-ordinating causal conjunction हि, but remember it is an enclitic.

4. 'these birds subsist on the raindrops': Since these words are what people *say*, the particle इति must be added at the end of the quotation. Its sense is here represented by the English 'so', but even if this were omitted, इति would have to be expressed.

5. 'At this same time': The sense of 'same' should be conveyed by placing the all-important emphatic particle एव after the demonstrative, thus: तस्मिन् एव काले (or समये).

6. 'situated-on-Mt. Kailāsa': to be expressed by a locative tatpuruṣa ending in -स्थ 'standing, *i.e.*, situated, thus: कैलासपर्वतस्थ (of course, in case-agreement with the Sanskrit for 'Lake Mānasa'). Omit the words 'which is' in parentheses.

7. 'rainbows are . . . anthills': Here again the particle इति must be appended to indicate that these words are quoted; 'abiding-in-anthills' is to be expressed as a locative tatpuruṣa, as the similar expression discussed under note 6.

8. 'After the rains have ceased': Express this temporal clause by a locative absolute.

9. 'of-various-colors': Render by a bahuvrīhi adjective.

LESSON FOURTEEN

The Relative Pronoun and Related Words. A Little More Sandhi.

There is an important pronoun, called the 'relative pronoun', which begins with the syllable य- (*ya-*) and is declined throughout exactly like तद्, except for the substitution of य- for त- (or स-). So, यः, यम्, येन, यस्मै, यस्मात्, यस्मिन् instead of सः, तम्, तेन, तस्मै, तस्मात्, तस्मिन् and likewise throughout the declension. This pronoun, referred to as यद्, corresponds to English 'who, whom, which',[1] *not,* however, as employed in questions, but as introducing a clause that refers to a foregoing noun, which is, therefore, called the 'antecedent' and which it characterizes or particularizes. For example, 'The palace, *in which this king lives,* is situated on the bank of the river.' In this sentence the clause 'in which the king lives', qualifies 'palace', the preceding noun or antecedent, just as any adjective qualifies a noun. This may become clearer if we put the whole relative clause *before* the antecedent, like an adjective: 'The *in-which-this-king-lives* palace is situated on the bank of the river'. Note that the relative clause in our example stands *between* the antecedent 'palace' and the predicate 'is situated' ('The palace, *in which this king lives,* is situated on the bank of the river.'). This English order (antecedent + relative clause + main verb or predicate) is not allowed in Sanskrit. The relative clause in Sanskrit must *precede* the main statement or predicate and, to continue the issue still further, the antedcedent usually directly follows the relative pronoun यद्, (and is therefore no longer *ante*cedent) or, as the grammarians prefer to say, it is 'incorporated' into the relative clause. If, then, we put this example into the Sanskrit order of things, we must say 'The in which this king lives palace, *that* is situated' etc. Another point to be observed is that the 'incorporated antecedent' is picked up by a demonstrative (usually the appropriate form of तद्) at the very beginning of the main statement ('*that* is situated on the bank of the river'). Of course, it goes without having to be said that both the relative pronoun and the referent demonstrative (called the 'correlative') must agree in gender and number with the antecedent. Now let us be daring enough to put this clumsily worded English equivalent into Sanskrit: यस्मिन् प्रासादे अयं नृपः वसति सः अस्याः नद्याः तीरे विद्यते ।[2] Although the beginning student may not yet be wholly

---

[1] Also to English 'that', which is often used in place of the other relatives, as in 'The man that I see.'

[2] Note that in illustrations it is usual to omit sandhi.

convinced of the sense and perfect logic of this alien sequence of words, the fact is that putting the relative clause in first position is based on the same logic as putting an adjective *before* the noun that it qualifies. To put it another way, the basic sentence, from the Sanskrit point of view, is 'That is situated on the bank of the river' and the 'That' is defined or amplified by the preceding words 'In which this king lives'.

Surely another example might conduce to greater clarity, and on this occasion let us start with the unidiomatic, pedagogical format: 'The which flower you see in the girl's hand, *that* is really beautiful'. So, यद् पुष्पं कन्यायाः हस्ते पश्यसि तद् सुन्दरं एव भवति ।

Now that the enigma of relative clauses and their correlatives has been resolved, let us turn to a particular use of the relative construction which is common in Sanskrit commentarial literature where it is employed in the analysis of bahuvrīhi compounds. First, a bahuvrīhi is simply a tatpuruṣa or karmadhāraya applied to someone (or something) *outside* the compound that possesses what is expressed by the elements of the compound. Thus, if the karmadhāraya सुन्दरपुष्पाणि which means 'beautiful flowers', is applied to someone as an attribute of that person, as in सुन्दरपुष्पा कन्या 'a beautiful-flowered girl' (or 'a girl possessing beautiful flowers'), then the karmadhāraya becomes transformed into a bahuvrīhi. In analyzing this compound, an Indian commentator would say: सुन्दराणि पुष्पाणि यस्याः सा कन्या literally 'that girl, of whom (there are) beautiful flowers'. In thus analyzing a bahuvrīhi in the form of a relative clause, there is no scope for the inverted word order discussed earlier. The analysis requires only the formulation of a relative clause expressing in syntactic form the content of the compound, without any predication about the person to whom the bahuvrīhi refers. No verb is needed, as the first part of the bahuvrīhi (सुन्दर- in our example), which is always predicative to the last, is connected to it in the analysis by the verb 'is/are' *un*expressed. We may take another example, formed with a past passive participle in part A: संयतेन्द्रियः तापसः 'An ascetic by whom (or 'whose') sense-organs have been controlled'. This may be analyzed in either of two ways: संयतानि इन्द्रियाणि येन (or यस्य) सः तापसः Whether येन or यस्य is used depends on how the meaning of the compound is viewed: if one wishes to stress the agency of the ascetic in controlling his sense organs, then the instrumental येन should be used; if, on the other hand, it is felt merely as a statement that the ascetic's sense organs are in a controlled condition without regard to the agency of the condition, then the genitive suffices.

Besides the relative pronoun यद्, there are a few other relative words that can fittingly be taken up here. The relative adverb यत्र is formed from य-, the root of the relative यद्, to which is added the adverbial suffix -त्र which denotes the locative relation. So, यत्र may be etymologically rendered 'in which (place)' or 'to which (place)', as in यत्र न्यग्रोधपादपं पश्यसि तत्र तापसः निषीदति 'Where (in which place) you see the banyan tree, *there* an ascetic is seated'. The correlative, as may be seen, is तत्र or a phrase with a demonstrative serving as its equivalent. Needless to say, तत्र 'there' (etymologically 'in *or* to that place') is formed from the root of तद् exactly as यत्र from that of यद्.

यदा 'when' is similarly formed from य- with the suffix -दा which denotes time; so यदा etymologically means 'at which time, on which occasion', hence, 'when'. The correlative is, as is to be expected, तदा 'at that time, then'. To express repeated action or indefinite time यदा is repeated and usually also तदा, thus यदा यदा ... तदा तदा 'whenever ... then'. Thus, यदा रात्रिः आगच्छति तदा वायुः शीतलः भवति 'When the night approaches, the breeze becomes cool'; यदा यदा अरयः अश्वपृष्ठे आक्रमन्ते तदा तदा जयन्ति 'Whenever the enemies attack on horseback, they are victorious'. There is also the conditional adverb यदि 'if', the correlative of which is also तदा or तर्हि; thus, यदि धर्मं एव आचरसि तदा (or तर्हि) संतुष्टचित्तः भविष्यसि 'If you practice dharma alone, (then) you will be content at heart'. Finally, there is the adverb यतस्, literally 'from which' (from the root य- and the adverbial suffix -तस्), mostly used in a causal sense ('because, since, as'), to which the correlative ततस् answers. Examples of this usage have occured in the foregoing reading selection.

In our preliminary discussion on sandhi, mention was made of the 'law of regressive assimilation'. For our next installment of sandhi rules we must revert to this all-important law, which pervades the entire area of Indo-European philology and governs so many of the consonant changes that recur at word junctures as well as within words.

Put in the simplest terms, the law of regressive assimilation states that the *second* of two consonants causes a prior consonant to become like itself, in other words, that its influence works backwards (regressively!) to affect the previous consonant, causing it to become voiced or voiceless or even identical to itself. This is in reality much simpler than it sounds. Thus, in the combination तद् पुस्तकम् the operation of this law causes the -द् of तद् to be replaced by -त् because the following प- is *voiceless*; and similarly तत् फलम्. On the other hand, we would write तद् बलम् because ब- is *voiced,* requiring the prior consonant to be *voiced.* In brief, then, if the following sound is a *voiced consonant* or a *vowel (all vowels are voiced!),* then the preceding consonant must be *voiced.* Conversely, if the following sound is a voiceless consonant, the previous consonant must be voiceless. These changes are called partial assimilation, but in certain instances *full* assimilation takes place, as when तद् जलम् becomes तज् जलम्. Before च- or -छ a final -त् or द् is changed to च्, as in तच् च and तच् छाया.

The Ascetic and the Tiger

एकदा दक्षिणारण्ये[1] कश्चित् तापसो ऽवसत्। पुष्पैः फलैर् मूलैश्च[2] उपाजीवत्। वारं वारं तु वनं त्यक्त्वा समीपस्थग्रामान् आगम्य तत्र भिक्षां अचरत्। यद् भोजनं तस्मै तापसाय दत्तं तत् तेन कृताञ्जलिना आदत्तम्। य आहारस् तेन तेषु ग्रामेषु लब्धः सो ऽन्तिमस्य ग्रामस्य पर्यन्तं आनीय तत्र तेन खादितः। एकस्मिन् दिवसे स्वपर्णशालां प्रत्यागन्तुं तं अरण्यं प्रविश्य[3] स तापसः क्षुधाकुलेन व्याघ्रेण दृष्टः। तस्मिन् एव क्षणे वानरगणेन तं व्याघ्रं अवलोक्य कोलाहलः कृतः। तेषां शब्दैर् उद्विग्नचित्तस् तापस ऊर्ध्वं दृष्ट्वा व्याघ्रं वृक्षशाखायां अवलोक्य परमं भयं अगच्छत्। आदौ भयेन अचलस् तत्र एव स्थित्वा ततः सहसा माया इदं सर्वं[4] इति वेदान्तदर्शने[5] स्वगुरुणा उपदिष्टं स्मृत्वा तीव्रतपोलब्धबलेन[6] वृक्षस्य अधस्तात् मायामृगं[7] जनयित्वा आत्मानं एव अदृष्टरूपं[8] कृत्वा पर्णशालां शनैः शनैर् अपागच्छत्। तदनन्तरं व्याघ्रो मायामृगं दृष्ट्वा वृक्षशाखाया अवप्लुत्य तं मृगं अन्वधावत्। अरण्यस्य पर्यन्तं धावित्वा यो मृगस् तापसप्रभावेन कृतः स सपदि अन्तर्धानं अगच्छत्। मृगः कुत्र गत इति चिन्तयित्वा विस्मयान्वित उच्चैः शब्दं कृत्वा स व्याघ्रस् तस्माद् वनाद् बहिर् गत्वा अन्यद् वनं प्रविश्य तत्र अन्यं मृगं अन्वद्रवत्।

Notes

1. दक्षिणारण्ये 'in a southern (दक्षिण) forest', that is a forest in the Deccan, the part of India south of the Vindhya mountains. Incidentally, 'Deccan' is an Anglo-Indian word from the vernacular descendant of Prakrit दक्खिण.

2. Flowers, roots and fruits are the traditional food of ascetics living in the forests.

3. When a sentence is constructed with the past passive participle, as here with दृष्टः, a gerund normally qualifies the instrumental (व्याघ्रेण), the *logical* subject. However, the gerund here qualifies तापसः, the *grammatical* subject, as is clear from the sense: 'The ascetic, having entered the forest, [was] seen by the tiger'.

4. माया इदं सर्वं 'All this (world) is illusion', the standard doctrine of the Advaita Vedānta system, which regards only Brahman (the Absolute) as reality. The phenomena of ordinary existence have, to be sure, a lower reality, like the visions seen in a dream, which vanish upon awaking. इदं सर्वं 'All this' is the general expression used for the 'world', and is ubiquitous in Sanskrit texts, going back to the Ṛgveda. Sometimes सर्वं is omitted, and इदं alone is used, as in Mānavadharmaśāstra I.5:

आसीदिदं तमोभूतमप्रज्ञातमलक्षणम् ।
अप्रतर्क्यमविज्ञेयं प्रसुप्तमिव सर्वतः ॥

'This (world) was dark, unknown, devoid of characteristic, imponderable, unknowable, as though sunk in sleep everywhere'.

5. वेदान्तदर्शने *Darśana* is the standard term for any one of the great systems of philosophical thought in India. It means literally a 'seeing, view, doctrine', being a noun derived from √दृश् 'see' in its guṇa-form दर्श् and the suffix -अन which denotes an action or process such as is denoted by the English *-ing*.

6. तीव्रतपोलब्धबलेन Between the members of a compound, the general rules of external sandhi apply, so that the -अस् of तपस् here becomes -ओ, as at word-junctures outside a compound before a voiced consonant. The bisection of this compound should be made between लब्ध and बलेन 'by the power (which was) gained by severe austerity (तपस्)'. तीव्रतपोलब्ध is an adjective modifying बलेन, so the compound as a whole is a karmadhāraya. The next bisection is to

be made between तीव्रतपो and लब्ध which forms an instrumental tatpuruṣa 'gained by (means of) severe austerity'. Finally, तीव्रतपो is a karmadhāraya (adjective and noun).

तपस् means 'burning, heat' etymologically, but even from Ṛgvedic times it was, apart from its literal sense, applied to the heat generated by extremely deep thought or concentration. This internal heat or तपस् was viewed as similar to the heat of the sacrificial fire and so capable of inducing the same results through its effect on the operations of the cosmos.

7. मायामृगं 'An illusion-deer', *i.e.,* a deer which is only an illusion, hence, an appositional karmadhāraya, consisting of two nouns, of which the first (माया) defines the second; *cf.* English 'houseboat' (a boat which is a house). Indian ascetics are often said to gain immense powers from their prolonged austerities and bodily mortification, sometimes causing even the gods to fear being unseated or rendered impotent. On these occasions the frightened gods arrange to send a voluptuous maiden to the forest, who by means of her charms and fascinating beauty may deflect an ascetic from continuing to practice his austerities. Since these maidens are generally dispatched by Indra, the chief of the gods, the term इन्द्रसेना 'Indra's missile' is applied to them.

8. अदृष्टरूपं 'having an unseen form'; this adjective is used proleptically, *i.e.,* its sense is not a general attribute of आत्मानं, but its effect must be reserved until after the action of कृत्वा has taken place.Thus, 'having made *himself* having an unseen form', *i.e.,* 'having made *himself* invisible'. The effect of एव is to underline आत्मानं, as it were, to emphasize the contrast between the appearance of the illusion-deer and the ascetic's sudden disappearance from the scene.

Vocabulary

मूल, *n.* a root.

उप- √जीव् (जीवति, class I), live on (+ *instr.*)

वारं वारं *adv. phrase,* sometimes.

समीपस्थ, *adj.* neighboring, nearby. [a *loc.* tatpuruṣa compound 'standing *or* situated in the vicinity', √स्था 'stand' here being used in the value of a present participle]

भिक्षा, *f.* alms; *with* √चर् (चरति, class I), go a-begging, ask for alms.
भोजन, *n.* food.
दत्त, *ppp.* √दा (ददाति, class III), given.
आ- √दा receive [The prefixed adverb आ- often *reverses* the meaning of a verb, especially verbs of motion, as आ- √गम् come, but √गम् go]
आहार, *m.* food.
लब्ध, *ppp.* √लभ् (लभते, class I), received, gotten.
अन्तिम, *adj.* last.
ग्राम, *m.* a villlage.
पर्यन्त, *m.* edge, outskirts.
आ- √नी (नयति, class I), bring [On reversive use of आ-, *v.* note on आ- √दा]
खादित, *ppp.* √खाद् (खादति, class I), eaten.
प्रति-आ- √गम् (गच्छति, class I), come back, return.
क्षुधा, *f.* hunger.
आकुल, *adj.* agitated.
व्याघ्र, *m.* a tiger.
क्षण, *m.* an instant.
वानर, *m.* a monkey.
कोलाहल, *m.* a hubbub, confused noise.
ऊर्ध्वम्, *adv.* upwards, up.
शाखा, *f.* a branch (*of a tree*).
भय, *n.* fear.
आदि, *m.* beginning; आदौ (*loc.*) at first.
अचल, *adj.* unmoving, immobile.
√स्मृ (स्मरति, class I), remember.
तीव्र, *adj.* severe, intense.
तपस्, *n.* heat; fire; asceticism, mortification, austerity.
बल, *n.* strength, power.
अधस्तात्, *postp. with gen.*, under.
√जन् (जायते, class IV), be born; *causative* जनयति causes to be born, produces, creates.
आत्मन्, *m.* the breath; the spirit, soul; oneself (as a reflexive pronoun of all persons and numbers); [*n*-stem, acc. sing. आत्मानम्].

अदृष्ट, *adj.* unseen [*ppp.* √दृश् 'see' with negative prefix अ-; *cf.* अचल 'not moving']
रूप, *n.* form.
शनैः शनैः, *adv.* slowly.
अव- √प्लु (प्लवति, class I), jump down; *gerund* अवप्लुत्य.
अनु- √धाव् (धावति, class I), run after.
अनु- √द्रु (द्रवति, class I), run after.
प्रभाव, *m.* power.
सपदि, *adv.* immediately.
विस्मय, *m.* astonishment.
अन्तर्धान, *n.* disappearance.
उच्चैः, *adv.* loud, clear.

Translate into Sanskrit:

A certain ascetic who lived in a leaf-hut in the southern forest, having returned there one day after begging for alms in the neighboring villages, was seen by a tiger agitated by hunger. At first the ascetic did not see him, but when some monkeys made a hubbub, he looked up and saw the tiger on a branch of a tree. As soon as he saw the tiger, he produced an illusion-deer near the tree by means of the power he had attained through long and severe austerities. Upon seeing the deer, the tiger ran after it. Having returned to his leaf-hut, the ascetic thought: 'The illusion-deer that I produced will soon disappear, and therefore it is certain that the tiger will die due to extreme hunger'. Upon thinking thus, the ascetic's heart was filled with great remorse.*

* The words '*the ascetic's heart was filled with great remorse*' should be expressed by means of a bahuvrīhi compound in predicate relation to 'was' (अभवत्), literally thus, was having-[his]-heart-filled-with-great-remorse'.

LESSON FIFTEEN

The Optative Mood. Vowel Sandhi.

I. *The Optative Mood.*

Thus far in our study of the Sanskrit verb we have had two tenses (present and imperfect), in both the active and middle voice. All these forms are made by attaching certain endings to the verb stem, which, we will recall, is made in the so-called thematic classes by adding the vowel *-a* (the 'thematic vowel') to the root. In class I the vowel of the root is replaced by its guṇa equivalent, in class IV the suffix *-ya* is added, in class VI no change is made and, finally, in class X the suffix *-aya* is added to the root which is generally modified by guṇa or vṛddhi substitution. In this way, we arrive at the stems *bhav-a, dīv-ya, tud-a* and *cor-aya* from the roots √*bhū*, √*div*, √*tud* and √*cur* respectively.

The present and imperfect, both active and middle, are used when a statement of fact is made. These verb forms are said to be in the 'indicative' mood. This term 'indicative' is also applied to the ordinary present and past tenses in English. But when we have to express an action that is contingent upon the occurrence of something else, or that may be or might be the case, but is not actually occurring or did not do so in the past, then we have to use helping verbs like may/might, can/could, would/should. These auxiliary verbs impart various shades of unreality or improbability to a verbal idea. There is, then, a big difference between saying 'It is raining' and 'It may *or* might *or* could rain'. In the latter cases, the occurrence of the rain is not stated as a fact, but as a *possibility* or *probability*, with the implication that rain may take place, if certain conditions, not here expressed, are granted. In Sanskrit a special form of the verb is employed to impart this uncertainty or unreality to the meaning. It is called the 'optative' and is made by appending the mood sign *-ī* to the stem; so, *bhava-ī, dīvya-ī, tuda-ī* and *coraya-ī*. But in Sanskrit, two vowels (here *-a* and *-ī*) cannot stand in juxtaposition, at least not without suffering the worse for it. So the *-a* and the *-ī* fuse together into a new sound *-e*, yielding *bhave*, *dīvye*, *tude* and *coraye*. These are *stems*, specifically *optative stems*, and it must be remembered that a *stem* is *not yet* a word: a stem becomes a word by the addition of endings, personal endings for verbs and case endings for nouns and adjectives. In order to make verb forms in the optative mood, therefore, we must add the personal endings to the optative stem formed as just explained. We have learned *two* sets of endings, primary and secondary, used respectively for the present and imperfect tenses. It is the *secondary endings that are added to the optative stem.* Just to refresh our memory, the secondary endings we learned for the imperfect indicative are:

	Active		Middle	
1.	*-am*	*-ma*	*-e*	*-mahi*
2.	*-ḥ*	*-ta*	*-thāḥ*	*-dhvam*
3.	*-t*	*-an*	*-ta*	*-anta*

The three endings underlined, however, are not employed in making the optative: *-an* is replaced by *-uḥ* (the visarga here represents original *-r*), *-e* by *-a*, and *-anta* by *-ran*. When an ending beginning with a vowel is added to the optative stem, a *-y* - is interposed, the reason for which will become apparent in a moment. Here, then, are the optative forms for the active and middle. Transliteration and hyphens are used in order to render more transparent the interposition of the *-y-* and the separation of stem and ending.

		Active	Middle
Class I			
√*bhū*	S.1.	*bhave-y-am*	*bhave-y-a*
	2.	*bhave-ḥ(-s)*	*bhave-thāḥ(-s)*
	3.	*bhave-t*	*bhave-ta*
	P.1.	*bhave-ma*	*bhave-mahi*
	2.	*bhave-ta*	*bhave-dhvam*
	3.	*bhave-y-uḥ(-r)*	*bhave-ran*
Class IV			
√*div*	S.1.	*dīvye-y-am*	*dīvye-y-a*
	2.	*dīvye-ḥ(-s)*	*dīvye-thāḥ(-s)*
	3.	*dīvye-t*	*dīvye-ta*
	P.1.	*dīvye-ma*	*dīvye-mahi*
	2.	*dīvye-ta*	*dīvye-dhvam*
	3.	*dīvye-y-uḥ(-r)*	*dīvye-ran*
Class VI			
√*tud*	S.1.	*tude-y-am*	*tude-y-a*
	2.	*tude-ḥ(-s)*	*tude-thāḥ(-s)*
	3.	*tude-t*	*tude-ta*
	P.1.	*tude-ma*	*tude-mahi*
	2.	*tude-ta*	*tude-dhvam*
	3.	*tude-y-uḥ(-r)*	*tude-ran*
Class X			
√*cur*	S.1.	*coraye-y-am*	*coraye-y-a*
	2.	*coraye-ḥ(-s)*	*coraye-thāḥ(-s)*
	3.	*coraye-t*	*coraye-ta*
	P.1.	*coraye-ma*	*coraye-mahi*
	2.	*coraye-ta*	*coraye-dhvam*
	3.	*coraye-y-uḥ(-r)*	*coraye-ran*

If the -*y*- were not interposed in the three forms *bhave-y-am*, *bhave-y-uḥ* and *bhave-y-a* (and so on identically with the other classes), they would have become respectively *bhavay-am*, *bhavay-uḥ* and *bhavay-a* through the operation of a rule of internal sandhi.[1] But had this happened, the characteristic -*e*- (the optative-ness of the forms!) would have been virtually effaced. So, by the working of analogy or, as the German scholars call this sort of change, 'the compulsion of the system' (*Systemszwang*), the -*e*- is extended to *all* the forms.

The optative in the parent Indo-European language was probably originally used to express a wish, and it is also employed in this way in Sanskrit; for example, आगच्छेत् 'May he come!' (*i.e.*, 'I wish that he would come').[2] Since this type of expression is non-factual, indeed sometimes is even improbable or unlikely, as in 'If only he would come!' it is easy to see how this particular verb form, unreal in its remotest beginning, came to be used also to express any sort of event that is improbable or probable, but not actual. This optative, which may be called an 'optative of contingency or probability', as in वर्षासु प्रत्यहं वर्षेत् 'In the rainy season it may rain every day', *i.e.*, there is a good possibility that it will do so, is extremely common, much more so than verb combinations with 'may/might, can/could', etc. in English. In fact, many optatives of this kind are more idiomatically rendered in English by ordinary indicatives. Thus, अस्मिन् लोके पूर्वजन्मकृतकर्मभिः दुःखं च सुखं च अनुभवेत् 'In this world one would experience both pain and pleasure due to actions done in a former birth', which might equally well be rendered by the indicative 'experiences' without any change in the sense.

The optative of contingency or probability is of frequent occurrence in conditional sentences, where English idiom again often prefers the more assertive indicative over the more vague combinations with the auxiliaries 'may/might', etc., which generally serve as the literal translations of the Sanskrit optative. For example, यदि अतिथिः अस्यां रात्र्यां आगच्छेत् तदा तस्मै भोजनं पानीयं च यच्छेयम् 'If a guest should come this night, I would offer him food and drink', but we could as well render it more assertively in English by saying 'If a guest comes... I'll offer...'. The optative is often used in 'contrary-to-fact' or 'unreal' conditional sentences, *i.e.*, of the 'were...

---

[1] The rule is that *within a word -e* becomes *-ay* before a vowel. We have seen this change in √*ji* 'conquer', which by guṇa substitution becomes *je*, then, with the addition of the thematic vowel *-a-*, *jay-a* (*jaya-ti*); and similarly √*nī* (*naya-ti*) 'lead'.

[2] It may be noted here that the optative mood takes its name from this original usage, being derived through Middle French from Latin *optātīvus* 'expressing a wish'.

would' type, thus: 'If I were in his place, I would not say that' यदि अहं तस्य स्थाने भवेयं तदा तद् न वदेयम्.[3] In this type of sentence, however, English does not allow the use of the indicative: we cannot say 'If I *am* in his place, I *do not say* that'.

A third use of the optative is in prescriptive sentences, to express what one should or should not do. This usage is a development of the optative of contingency, and sometimes it is not possible or even meaningful to separate the two usages, as, for example, in तापस: प्रत्यहं यजेत 'An ascetic would sacrifice every day', *i.e.*, he does so and is expected to, and so it is equivalent to an indicative in English idiom ('An ascetic sacrifices...'), but the sentence might as well be rendered 'An ascetic *should* sacrifice every day'. The prescriptive optative is used ubiquitously in Hindu legal texts, such as the Mānavadharmaśāstra, almost to the exclusion of the indicative. For example, उद्वहेत द्विजो भार्यां सवर्णां लक्षणान्विताम् (III. 4 cd) 'The Twice-born *should marry* a wife of the same caste (who is) provided with marks of excellence'. The third person singular in the indefinite sense of 'one' is particularly common in this prescriptive usage: न लङ्घयेद् वत्सतन्त्रीं न प्रधावेच् च वर्षति (IV. 38 ab) 'One should not jump over a calf's tethering-rope or run when it is raining'. In sum, then, there are three uses of the optative, namely, to express (1) a wish (the original meaning of the optative), (2) a contingent, probable or improbable idea, and (3) a prescription.

II. *Vowel Sandhi.*

In addition to the assimilation and other substitution of consonants at word junctures, which we have studied so far in our treatment of external sandhi, there are also to be considered important changes that take place when a word *ending* in a vowel appears before a word *beginning* with a vowel. While these rules are not at all difficult to understand, the resulting changes when encountered in a Sanskrit text, can occasion difficulty, which can only be surmounted by practice in reading. Contraction into a single long vowel takes place when two vowels of the same class, whether long or short, come together. Thus, *-ă̄* + *ă̄-* > *-ā-*, *-ĭ̄* + *ĭ̄-* > -ī- and *-ŭ̄* + *ŭ̄-* > -ū-. These contractions are due, of course, to the close liaison of the vowels at word junctures in uninterrupted speech, from which they were generalized and codified for application also in writing. According to this rule अत्र आगच्छन्ति 'They come here' becomes अत्रागच्छन्ति, but it is important to note that, when two vowels stand together due to the loss of visarga (or *-s*), they are *not*

[3] There is a so-called 'conditional mood' in Sanskrit, formed by appending the secondary endings to the future stem, but it is extremely rare.

contracted, but the resulting hiatus remains, as in बाला अत्रागच्छन्ति 'The children are coming here'. The fact that -आ of बाला is not contracted with अ- of अत्र into -आ- should be taken as the *product* of sandhi after which no additional sandhi is allowed. Examples of the other vowel contractions are: यदीहागच्छन्ति for यदि इह आगच्छन्ति 'If they come here'; ततस् तूपायो दृष्टः for ततस् तु उपायो दृष्टः 'But then a way was found'.

If the first of two vowels is -W or -X and the second a dissimilar vowel (*i.e.*, *not* W- or X- respectively), then the -W or -X are replaced by their respective semivowels -*y* and -*v*, as in यद्य् अहं गच्छेयम् for यदि अहं गच्छेयम् 'If I should go' and ततस् त्व् इन्द्रो ऽवदत् for ततस् तु इन्द्रो ऽवदत् 'But then Indra said'. In ordinary writing and printing, incidentally, the virāma sign in यद्य् and त्व् would not be used, but these two words would be written together with the following: यद्यहं and त्विन्द्रो. These and similar coalesced modes of writing, which are confusing to beginners (and sometimes also to the advanced student!), in breaking up the individual words in a sentence, will be gradually introduced in the reading selections that follow. They are purely graphic and have nothing to do with word boundaries or sandhi processes.

When -*a* or -*ā* is followed by a dissimilar vowel, then the guṇa substitute of the *second* vowel replaces *both* vowels; if the second is a guṇa vowel (*e*- or *o*-), then the vṛddhi substitute of the second vowel replaces *both* vowels. If the following vowel is a vṛddhi vowel (*ai*- or *au*-), the prior -*a* or -*ā* coalesces with it. When initial *ṛ*- follows -*a* or -*ā*, the resultant product is -*ar*-. The following tabulation will make this rather complicated exposition clear:

Final	*followed by*	*is replaced by*	
-*a* or -*ā*	*i*- or *ī*-	-*e*-	(guṇa
-*a* or -*ā*	*u*- or *ū*-	-*o*-	substitute)
-*a* or -*ā*	*e*- or *ai*- [4]	-*ai*-	(vṛddhi
-*a* or -*ā*	*o*- or *au*- [4]	-*au*-	substitute)
-*a* or -*ā*	*ṛ*-	-*ar*-	(guṇa of *ṛ*)

Thus,

1) तथा इन्द्रः → तथेन्द्रः,
सेना ईक्षते → सेनेक्षते

2) तेन उक्तम् → तेनोक्तम्
अनेन ऊर्णनाभेन → अनेनोर्णनाभेन

[4] Very few words begin with the diphthongs *ai*- and *au*-.

3) तथा एव → तथैव
तथा ऐरावतः → तथैरावतः
4) इह ओषधिः → इहौषधिः
आत्म-औपम्यं → आत्मौपम्यम्
(in a compound)
5) महा-ऋषिः → महर्षिः
(in a compound)

The Story of Śakuntalā

The legend of Śakuntalā first appears in that voluminous Indian epic, the Mahābhārata, but the story as told there is at best raw and primitive, hardly the sort of material that one would think capable of being woven into one of the world's great dramas. Yet this unsatisfactory work furnished the *ultimate* basis for the अभिज्ञानशकुन्तल ('The Play about Śakuntalā [Who is Recognized] by the Token') of Kālidāsa, universally regarded as India's greatest poet. There is also a much more detailed version in the Padma Purāṇa, but this particular version seems, for various reasons, to have been influenced by Kālidāsa's work. The legend in a quite different form is also to be found in the Kaṭṭhahāri Jātaka, in which Śakuntalā gives birth to the Bodhisattva. Kālidāsa may have derived the idea of the ring, which figures so importantly in his drama, from this Jātaka, as it is not in the Mahābhārata version.

The following exercise is but a greatly skeletonized version of the story as told, with some modifications of detail, in Kālidāsa's drama.

आसीद् राजा[1] दुष्षन्तो[2] नाम सर्वप्रभुगुणैर् अन्वितः । स धर्मेण[3] कृत्स्नां पृथिवीं अपालयत् । तेन चैकदा मृगयार्थं महावनं प्रविश्य बहवः प्राणिनः[4] स्वशरैर्[5] हताः । यान् हरिणान् व्याघ्रान् सिंहान् वृकान् ऋक्षान् चापश्यत् ते सर्वे तेन महाराजेनानुधाविता व्यापादिताश् चाभवन् । महावनस्य मध्ये परमरूपान्वितं[6] हरिणं दृष्ट्वा तं हरिणं अनुधावितुं इच्छामि सारथे सत्वरं गच्छेति सूतं[7] उक्त्वैकं शरं तूणीराद् निष्कृष्य धनुः सज्जीकृत्य रथे उदतिष्ठत् । स हरिणस् तु भयेन शीघ्रतरं धावित्वा रथजवं अतिक्रम्य ब्रह्मर्षेः कण्वस्याश्रमं[8] प्राविशत् । तस्मिन् एव क्षणे महाराजस्य रथस्य शब्दं श्रुत्वाश्रमाद् निर्गम्य

कण्वस्य कृत्रिमा दुहिता[9] शकुन्तला नाम भयाकुलं हरिणं दृष्ट्वा तं नृपतिं अभ्यभाषतायं मृगस् तव न हन्तव्यो[10] महाराजायं आश्रममृग इति । रथे सारथिना स्थापिते[11] नृपती[12] रथाद् अवतीर्य तं न हनिष्यामि मा भैषीर्[13] इति कन्यां अवदत् । तां कन्यां दृष्ट्वैव तद्रूपसंभ्रान्तचित्तो महाराजस् तस्यां[14] अन्वरज्यत् । ततो हृदये अनुरागं धारयितुं असमर्थः स नृपतिस् तां अवदद् यदि त्वं मम भार्या भवेस् तदाहं अतिसंतुष्टो भवेयम् इति । अनन्तरं यः पुत्रस् त्वयि जायेत स युवराजो[15] भवेद् इति तस्यै कन्यायै प्रतिज्ञाय शकुन्तलां परिणीय तस्मिन् वने कतिपयान् मासान् उषित्वा[16] दुष्यन्तो महाराजस् तस्यै स्वनामाभिलिखिताङ्गुलीयकं[17] दत्त्वाश्रमे तां त्यक्त्वा स्वनगरं अगच्छत् । पुत्रजन्मानन्तरं शकुन्तला पूर्वकृतसमयानुरोधेन नरेश्वरप्रासादं गच्छेत्[18] । शकुन्तला तु कण्वाशीर्वादं प्राप्याश्रमं त्यक्त्वा प्रासादं पुत्रेण सह गत्वा महाराजेन कस्यचिद् ऋषेः शापेन[19] विस्मृतैवाभवत्[20] । तस्य शापस्य प्रभावेन शकुन्तला तेन नृपतिना प्रत्याख्याता । यत् तस्यै महाराजेन दत्तं अङ्गुलीयकं तत् प्रासादं प्रति गमने स्वहस्ताच् छचीतीर्थसलिले[21] पतितम् । अन्ततः केनचिद् धीवरेण रोहितमत्स्यं जालेन बद्ध्वा खण्डशश् छित्त्वा तद् महाराजाङ्गुलीयकं दृष्टम् । तेन पुरुषेणेदं अङ्गुलीयकं चोरितमेवेति मत्वा तं गृहीत्वा नागरिको ऽङ्गुलीयकं नृपतये ऽदर्शयत् । तद् दृष्ट्वैव नृपतिः शकुन्तलां आत्मनो[22] विवाहं च स्मृत्वा परमं शोकं अगच्छत् । एतेन प्रकारेण शापाद् मुक्तो दुष्यन्तः शकुन्तलया सह संयुक्तो ऽभवत् ।

Notes

1. राजा nominative masculine singular of the *n*-stem राजन् 'king', a declensional type which will be studied in a later lesson. When preceded by महा-, the न् of the stem is dropped and महाराज is declined like देव.

2. दुष्षन्तो The king's name also frequently appears in printed texts and MSS as दुष्यन्त or even दुष्वन्त; the lack of a clear and certain etymology probably accounts for the divergent forms.

3. धर्मेण The word धर्म is one of the most difficult Sanskrit words to render, as its coverage is so wide and diverse in its nuances. Unless the Sanskrit word is used in English, the translation will have to vary with the context. Here it may be said that *all* Indian kings were supposed to rule by dharma, by which is meant the entire complex body of rules, laws and customs as codified in the law books or dharmaśāstras, such as the Mānavadharmaśāstra. But the English word 'law', because of the particular connotations it carries with it, seems scarcely to suit as the rendition here.

4. प्राणिन: nominative masculine plural of the stem प्राणिन् 'a living creature, animal', formed by adding the ending *-aḥ* to the stem. This is the regular ending of the nominative plural for stems that end in a consonant.

5. स्वशरैर् 'by his arrows'; स्व- is a reflexive possessive adjective, referring to the subject or logical subject of a sentence. Here the logical (*not* the grammatical!) subject is the king to whom the स्व- refers. Incidentally, स्व- may refer to any of the persons, singular or plural (my, our, your, his, her, its, their), so that the translation always must depend on the context alone.

6. परमरूपान्वितं The word रूप means not only 'form' and 'color', but also 'beauty' as in this compound: 'provided with (or 'possessed of') supreme beauty'.

7. The words from तं हरिणं through गच्छ are addressed by the king to his charioteer.

8. ब्रह्मर्षेः कण्वस्याश्रमं 'the hermitage of the priest-sage Kaṇva'; Kaṇva or Kāśyapa ('descendent of Kāśyapa) was the foster father of Śakuntalā whom he found abandoned in the forest where she had been protected by the birds. She was born of the famous sage Viśvāmitra and the heavenly nymph (Apsaras) Menakā who had been dispatched by Indra to deflect Viśvāmitra from the further performance of his austerities, by which it was feared he would soon attain sufficient power to unseat the gods. See also note 6 under तपस् in Lesson Fourteen. Kaṇva raised Śakuntalā as his own daughter in the hermitage referred to here.

9. दुहिता nominative feminine singular of दुहितृ 'daughter', one of a dozen or so words of relationship whose stem ends in -*ṛ*. Their declension and that of partially similarly inflected nouns of agency will be given later.

10. तव न हन्तव्यो 'is not to be killed by you', that is 'should not be killed by you'; हन्तव्य is the gerundive (or future passive participle) of √हन् (हन्ति, class II) 'kill'; on this verb form and its usage, read the extensive note 9 under मया कर्तव्यम् in Lesson Thirteen. Here the genitive तव 'of you' is used to express the agent, whereas in that passage the instrumental (मया) is used. In the story of King Nala and Damayantī the *haṃsa*-bird, when playfully seized by Nala, says to him: हन्तव्यो ऽस्मि न ते राजन् 'I am not to be killed of you, O king!' ते is an alternative genitive of त्वम् 'you'. The use of the genitive to express the agent with a passive participle occurs in English archaic phrases such as 'beloved of him', *i.e.*, 'by him'.

11. रथे सारथिना स्थापिते Locative absolute expressing time: 'When the chariot was stopped (literally 'caused to stand') by the charioteer'; of course, we may render it by an English *nominative* absolute: 'The chariot having been stopped by the charioteer'.

12. नृपती nominative masculine singular; the long vowel is due to compensation for the loss of -र् to which the visarga of नृपतिः would be changed before the voiced र- of रथाद्. Sanskrit does not allow two *r*'s together, so when this would occur, as here, the first -*r* is dropped, and the prior vowel, if short, is lengthened.

13. मा भैषीर् (for भैषीः) 'Do not be afraid'. A negative request or 'prohibition', as it is usually termed, is expressed by the negative adverb मा ('not') and the second person of either the imperfect or aorist *without the augment*. भैषीः is the aorist second singular of √भी (बिभेति) 'fear' without the augment.

14. तस्यां The verb अनु-√रज् (रज्यति, class IV) 'feel affection towards' takes the locative of the person *upon whom* the affection is placed.

15. युवराजो 'crown prince', a karmadhāraya compound formed from two *n*-stems, युवन् and राजन्, both of which drop their न्. This compound, then, like महाराज above, is declined like देव.

16. उषित्वा gerund of √वस् (वसति) 'stay'. Roots beginning with व generally substitute उ for व in certain forms like the gerund, past passive participle, etc., where the musical tone of the old language fell on the subsequent syllable, thus, in this instance, *uṣitvā́* and *uṣitá* (past passive participle). उ and व are cognate sounds, both being labial sounds, hence the possibility of their interchange under certain conditions. This interchange, as well as the similar alternation between य and इ and र and ऋ, is called संप्रसारण.

17. स्वनामाभिलिखिताङ्गुलीयकं Do not be deterred by long compounds! Remember to analyze them by a series of bisections, the second member (part B) of which is usually the principal matter or matter under discussion. Perhaps we might liken these long compounds to a series of boxes of gradually increasing size, each fitting into the next up to the last or biggest (corresponding to the final member of the compound). Here, the first bisection should be made between स्वनामाभिलिखित ('inscribed with his name') and अङ्गुलीयक ('a ring'). The whole is a karmadhāraya, part A being an adjective that qualifies part B. स्वनामाभिलिखित must be divided logically into स्वनाम and अभिलिखित, which form an instrumental tatpuruṣa ('inscribed with...'). Finally, स्वनाम is a karmadhāraya. If we continue our analogy with the boxes, we would say that the biggest box here is अङ्गुलीयक into which fits part A (स्वनामाभिलिखित), and this in turn is made up of स्वनाम and अभिलिखित, the latter of which is the bigger box as स्वनाम is qualificatory of it. Similarly, with स्व in relation to नाम.

18. गच्छेत् an optative of contingency.

19. कस्यचिद् ऋषेः शापेन 'by the curse of a certain sage'. The sage referred to is Durvāsas, who, feeling slighted at the lack of hospitality in his reception at Kaṇva's hermitage, laid down a curse which would keep Śakuntalā's husband from remembering her. Śakuntalā's companion, Anasūyā, succeeds in placating him insofar as he allows Duṣṣanta's memory to return upon his seeing an 'ornament'. The 'ornament' by which this is effected turns out to be the signet-ring.

20. विस्मृतैवाभवत् *i.e.*, विस्मृता एव अभवत् 'was simply (एव) forgotten'.

21. छचीतीर्थसलिले 'in the water of the Śacītīrtha'. The initial श (*śa*) has been changed to छ (*cha*) after च् (*c*) of स्वहस्ताच् ('from her hand') by a sort of optional progressive assimilation, which allows, but does not require, the combination -च् श- to be changed to -च् छ-.

Śacītīrtha is a place of pilgrimage at which Śakuntalā and her escort stopped on their way to King Duṣṣanta's palace. The word *tīrtha* means etymologically 'a crossing-place, a ford', being derived from √तॄ *tṝ* (तरति, class I) 'cross, cross over' and the suffix -थ, also seen in the common word अर्थ (from √ऋ 'go' guṇated to अर् 'that to which one goes, an aim *or* object'). Shallow places where a stream could be crossed early acquired sanctity, especially as shrines or temples were often erected there; hence *tīrtha* soon came to mean also 'a place of worship, a place of pilgrimage'. Śacī is the wife of Indra, and it is to him that is dedicated the sacred precinct called 'Śakrāvatāra' (Indra's Descent') in which the Śacītīrtha is located.

22. आत्मनो genitive masculine singular of आत्मन् here used as a reflexive pronoun 'of himself', that is 'his own'. The student will by now have observed that a final *-o* should be assumed to be a sandhi-substitute for a final *-aḥ*. But very occasionally, a final *-o* will be found to represent a vocative of the *-u* declension, गुरो 'O guru!'.

Vocabulary

आसीत्, 'there was', imperfect third singular of √अस् (अस्ति, class II), be.
राजन्, *m.* a king; *nom.* राजा.
नाम, *adv.* by name.
सर्व, *adj.* all, every.
कृत्स्न, *adj.* whole, entire.
प्रभु, *m.* a ruler *or* lord.
गुण, *m.* a quality.
अन्वित, *ppp.* अनु-√इ (एति, class II), followed by, accompanied by or endowed with (+ *instr.*).
पृथिवी, *f.* the earth [*lit.* 'the broad one' being the *f.* of the *adj.* पृथु 'broad'; strictly the *f.* should be पृथ्वी, but very early an excrescent short *-i-* came to be inserted between थ् and वी, much like the extra vowel in the vulgar pronunciation of 'athᵊletic' in English. But पृथिवी is *correct*

Sanskrit, whereas *ath^{ə}letic* has not become generally accepted in English.]

√पालय (पालयति), 'be a protector of', protect [a denominative verb from पाल 'protector', conjugated like a root of class X].

एकदा, *adv.* at one time, once upon a time.

मृगया, *f.* hunting.

प्र-√विश् (विशति, class VI), enter.

प्राणिन्, *m.* a living creature; an animal.

शर, *m.* an arrow.

हत, *ppp.* √हन् (हन्ति, class II), struck, hit.

हरिण, *m.* a deer.

व्याघ्र, *m.* a tiger.

सिंह, *m.* a lion.

वृक, *m.* a wolf.

ऋक्ष, *m.* a bear.

अनु-√धाव् (धावति, class I), run after, pursue; अनुधावित, *infin.* अनुधावितुम्.

व्यापादित, *ppp. caus. of* वि-आ-√पद् (पद्यते, class IV), 'caused to fall apart', destroyed, killed.

मध्य, *n.* the middle; *loc.* मध्ये *with gen.* in the middle, in.

परम, *adj.* supreme, most excellent.

सारथि, *m.* a charioteer.

सत्वरम्, *adv.* quickly.

सूत, *m.* a charioteer.

तूणीर, *m.* a quiver.

निस्-√कृष् (कर्षति, class I or कृषति, class VI), pull out. (निस्); *gerund* निष्कृष्य.

धनस्, *n.* a bow.

सज्जी-√कृ (करोति), prepare, get ready.

उद्-√स्था (तिष्ठति, class I), stand up (उद्).

भय, *n.* fear.

शीघ्रतरम्, *adv.* faster; *comparative* of शीघ्र, fast.

√धाव् (धावति, class I), run; *gerund* धावित्वा.

जव, *m.* speed.

अति-√क्रम् (क्रामति, class I), go beyond (अति), exceed.

ब्रह्मर्षि, *m.* a priest-sage, priestly sage [a karmadhāraya cpd. of the appositional type: 'a sage (who is) a priest', like English *houseboat* 'a boat (which is) a house'].

क्षण, *m.* an instant, moment.

शब्द, *m.* a sound *or* noise.

निस्-√गम् (गच्छति, class I), go out (निस्).

कृत्रिम, *adj.* artificial, not natural; adopted, foster-.

दुहितृ, *f.* a daughter.

आकुल, *adj.* confused, agitated.

अभि-√भाष् (भाषते), say to, address.

अव-√तॄ (तरति, class I), descend, get down; *gerund* अवतीर्य.

√भी (बिभर्ति, class III), fear; *aorist* अभैषीत्.

कन्या, *f.* a young girl.

संभ्रान्त, *ppp.* सं-√भ्रम् (भ्राम्यति, class IV), very confused, agitated, in a flutter.

चित्त, *n.* the mind *or* heart.

अनु-√रज् (रज्यति, class IV), be afflicted with a strong feeling for, feel an affection for (+ *loc.*).

हृदय, *n.* the heart.

अनुराग, *m.* affection.

√धृ (धारयति, *caus. without caus. meaning*!), hold; hold back, bear; *infin.* धारयितुम् .

असमर्थ, *adj.* unable.

भार्या, *f.* a wife.

अहम्, *pron. of first person.* I.

पुत्र, *m.* a son.

√जन् (जायते, class IV), be born of (+ *loc.*).

अतिसंतुष्ट, *adj.* extremely pleased.

युवराज, *m.* a crown prince, heir-apparent [*literally* 'young king' from युवन् 'young' (with regular loss of न् *as prior member of a cpd.*) + राजन् 'king' (with loss of -न् as final of a *cpd*; *cf.* महाराज].

प्रति-√ज्ञा (जानाति, class IX), promise.

परि-√नी (नयति class I), lead around, *esp.* lead a bride around the fire, *hence*, marry. [present stem परिणय, *gerund* परिणीय, with न → ण due to cerebralizing influence of र]

कतिपय, *adj.* several, some.
मास, *m.* a month.
√वस् (वसति, class I), stay; *gerund* उषित्वा.
नामन्, *n.* a name [-न् is lost *as prior member of a cpd.*].
अभिलिखित *ppp.* अभि-√लिख् (लिखति, class VI), written upon; engraved.
अङ्गुलीयक, *n.* a ring.
√दा (ददाति, class III), give; *gerund* दत्त्वा.
√त्यज् (त्यजति, class I), leave, abandon; *gerund* त्यक्त्वा, *ppp.* त्यक्त.
जन्मन्, *n.* birth.
अनन्तरम् *indecl.* immediately after, used *as postp. at end of a cpd.*
समय, *m.* an agreement.
पूर्वम्, *adv.* previously [*as prior member of cpd.* loses its म्].
अनुरोध, *m.* regard; *as final member of cpd.* according to.
आशीर्वाद, *m.* a blessing, benediction.
प्र-√आप् (आप्नोति, class V), obtain, get; *gerund* प्राप्य.
सह, *postp.* with, along with (+ *instr.*)
शाप, *m.* a curse.
प्रभाव, *m.* power.
प्रत्याख्यात, *ppp.* प्रत्-आ-√ख्या (ख्याति, class II), rejected.
हस्त, *m.* a hand.
सलिल, *n.* water.
√पत् (पतति, class I), fall.
अन्ततः, *adv.* finally.
धीवर, *m.* a fisherman [*literally.* 'a very clever man'].
रोहितमत्स्य, *m.* a kind of fish, *Cyprinus Rohitaka* [apparently so called because it is red (रोहित)].
जाल, *n.* a net.
√बन्ध् (बध्नाति, class IX), bind, fasten, catch; *gerund* बद्ध्वा.
खण्डशः, *adv.* in pieces.
√छिद् (छिनत्ति, class VII), cut; *gerund* छित्त्वा.
पुरुष, *m.* a man.
चोरित, *ppp.* √चुर (चोरयति, class X), stolen.
√मन् (मन्यते, class IV), think, imagine; *gerund* मत्वा.
√ग्रह् (गृह्णाति, class IX), seize, grab; *gerund* गृहीत्वा.

नागरिक, *m.* police superintendent.
दर्शयति, 'causes to see', *i.e.*, shows; *caus.* √दृश् 'see'.
विवाह, *m.* marriage.
√स्मृ (स्मरति, class I), remember; *gerund* स्मृत्वा..
शोक, *m.* sorrow, grief.
प्रकार, *m.* sort, kind; way, manner; एतेन प्रकारेण 'in this way'.
मुक्त, *ppp.* √मुच् (मुञ्चति, class VI), released.
संयुक्त, *ppp.* सं-√युज् (युनक्ति, class VII), joined together, united.

Translate into Sanskrit:

Śakuntalā, the daughter of Menakā and Viśvāmitra, lived in the hermitage of Kaṇva. Having entered the hermitage in pursuit of a deer and having seen Śakuntalā, King Duṣṣanta married her by means of a Gāndharva marriage. After staying several months at the hermitage, the king returned to his palace. Before departing from the hermitage, the king gave Śakuntalā a ring with his name engraved upon it. When Śakuntalā came to the palace with her son, she was rejected by the king, who had forgotten her due to a curse. The ring which had been given to Śakuntalā by Duṣṣanta fell from her hand into the water-of-the-Śacītīrtha. A fisherman found that ring in a fish which he had caught and cut to pieces.[1] As soon as he saw that ring when it was brought to him by the superintendent of the police, the king remembered his marriage to Śakuntalā.[2] The son of Śakuntalā and Duṣṣanta, Bharata by name, was made crown prince. The episode-of-Śakuntalā is found in the Mahābhārata and the Padma Purāṇa, but the play composed by Kālidāsa called Abhijñānaśakuntala is known everywhere in this world.

Notes

1. In translating this sentence, rephrase it thus: 'By a (certain) fisherman, having caught a fish, having cut [it] in pieces, that ring [was] found.'

2. 'his marriage to Śakuntalā': say 'marriage of Śakuntalā', using an objective genitive.

LESSON SIXTEEN

Introduction to Consonant Stems.

It has been stated before that Sanskrit nouns (and adjectives[1]) fall into two great classes, those whose stem ends in a vowel and those whose stem ends in a consonant; or, more simply, vowel stems and consonant stems respectively. We have already studied some of the most important of the vowel stems, and a few sporadic consonant stems have been encountered in the reading exercises. It is now necessary formally to take up the consonant stems, first in the form of an overall survey, then the more important types in detail.

There are two broad categories of consonant stems:

1. those stems that remain *un*changed throughout their declension, except for changes caused by sandhi, and
2. those that exhibit two or three variants of their stem.

The latter class will be treated in Lesson Seventeen. This is undoubtedly a little complicated, but all except the most eager and zealous students will be delighted to learn that the variations follow a fixed pattern and, what is particularly heartening, there is *only one* set of case endings for *all* the consonant stems. Furthermore, the same endings are used for the masculine and feminine, and the neuters differ only in the nominative and accusative. The endings are:

	Singular		*Plural*	
	Masculine & Feminine	*Neuter*	*Masculine & Feminine*	*Neuter*
Nom.	*-s* (-स्)	(no ending)	*-aḥ* (-अ:)	*-i* (-इ)
Acc.	*-am* (-अम्)	(no ending)	"	"
Instr.	*-ā* (-आ)		*-bhiḥ* (-भि:)	
Dat.	*-e* (-ए)		*-bhyaḥ* (-भ्य:)	
Abl.	*-aḥ* (-अ:)		"	
Gen.	"		*-ām* (-आम्)	
Loc.	*-i* (-इ)		*-su* (-सु)	

[1]There is no separate declension of adjectives, their declension being the same as for nouns with the same stem final. When the declension of nouns is referred to, that of adjectives should be understood as included.

In the declension of some consonant stems the vocative is the same as the nominative, in others it varies slightly. But the *vocative plural of all declensions* – vowel and consonant stems alike! – is identical to the nominative plural.

These endings are added directly to the stem. *No change in the final consonant is made before endings that begin with a vowel.* For the sake of clarity, let us first exemplify only *these* forms where the final consonant of the stem remains unaltered by sandhi and subsequently treat the other cases where sandhi changes are involved. We may choose as an example the fairly common noun वाच् (*f.*) 'speech, word'.[2]

	Singular	*Plural*
Nom.	(-- -*s*)	*vāc-aḥ*
Acc.	*vāc-am*	*vāc-aḥ*
Instr.	*vāc-ā*	(-- -*bhiḥ*)
Dat.	*vāc-e*	(-- -*bhyaḥ*)
Abl.	*vāc-aḥ*	(-- -*bhyaḥ*)
Gen.	*vāc-aḥ*	*vāc-ām*
Loc.	*vāc-i*	(-- -*su*)
Voc.	(as nom.)	(as nom.)

The nominative ending -*s*, practically speaking, is a sort of fiction, since it is *always* dropped after a consonant stem due to the rule that no Sanskrit word is permitted to end in more than one consonant.[3] Therefore, to say that 'it is added and then dropped' seems an unnecessary intermediate step for the beginner. In addition to this 'one-consonant' rule, there is another restriction, which limits the consonant that may end a word to one of eight possibilities. The consonants that are allowed to end a word are: *k* (क्), *ṭ* (ट्), *t* (त्), *p* (प्), *ṅ* (ङ्), *n* (न्), *m* (म्) and visarga. If a word does *not* end in one of these eight consonants, then the consonant that ends the word must be reduced to one of these eight. The process of reduction is essentially based on the two principles that a word (occurring separately or at the end of a

---

[2]Transliteration is freely used in the following sections in order to separate the case endings more clearly from the stem and to show the changes in the stem final caused by sandhi.

[3]This assertion is not entirely true, as a word may end in two consonants if the first is -*r*- and the second a *k, ṭ, t* or *p* that belongs to the root or is substituted for the second consonant.

sentence[4]) *cannot end in a voiced or an aspirated consonant.* Though voiced, the nasals, except *ñ* (ञ्), may end a word, but only *ṅ* (ङ्), *n* (न्) and *m* (म्) are generally found. The palatals (च्, छ्, ज्, झ्, ञ्) are entirely excluded from occupying the final place, and so also are *ś* (श्) and *h* (ह्).

Final -*s* (-स्) and -*r* (-र्), as we already know, are replaced by visarga (-:), and the cerebral sibilant -*ṣ* (-ष्) becomes -*ṭ* (-ट्). The process whereby the mutes are reduced to an allowed final can more easily be understood by a glance at the table of mutes or 'touched sounds' that is reflected in the arrangement of the letters of the Devanāgarī alphabet. In repeating it here, we shall omit the inherent -*a,* as we are concerned with final consonants not followed by a vowel.

k	←←	**kh*	**g*	**gh*	*ṅ*
ṭ	←←	**ṭh*	**ḍ*	**ḍh*	*ṇ*
t	←←	**th*	**d*	**dh*	*n*
p	←←	**ph*	**b*	**bh*	*m*

The sounds preceded by an asterisk (*) are *not allowed as finals* because they are *aspirated or voiced or both.* The excluded sounds in each horizontal line are replaced by the first sound in each series, as shown by the arrows. The palatals (omitted from the table) are, as has been said, all excluded as finals. The palatals, including -*ś* (-श्), are replaced by -*k* (-क्), less frequently by -*ṭ* (-ट्). The palatal nasal -*ñ* (-ञ्) is replaced by the guttural -*ṅ* (-ङ्) in accordance with this general substitution of final palatals by gutturals. The semivowels *y* (य्) and *v* (व्) do not occur as finals, and -*l* (-ल्) is extremely rare. The treatment of final -*h* (-ह्) (the aspirate, *not* visarga) is complicated by its varied origin. In most instances it is replaced by -*k* (-क्), occasionally by -*ṭ* (-ट्) and in one instance by -*t* (-त्).

It cannot be pretended that this rigmarole is simple, but it is really not as complicated as it sounds. Let us examine a few examples, but in doing so, let us first finish the declension of *vāc* (वाच्). We have said that it is best to omit the intermediate step of adding -*s* (-स्) to form the nominative, as it has to be dropped to avoid a second consonant. वाच् ends in a palatal, and palatals

[4]When a word occurs *before* another word, that is, *within a phrase or sentence,* it is, of course, subject to the rules of external sandhi, some of which have already been presented. The operation of these rules may, in various ways, modify the allowable final consonants, which, it must be borne in mind, are final only when a word is not followed by another word, that is, the last word in a sentence or by itself.

are generally converted into gutturals; -च्, therefore, is replaced by -क्. The nominative of वाच्, then, is वाक्. The sandhi that occurs before the endings *-bhiḥ* (-भिः), *-bhyaḥ* (-भ्यः) and *-su* (-सु) is external sandhi, that is, the same sandhi that takes place between words in a sentence. The Indian grammarians, in fact, call these endings 'word-endings' (pada-endings), precisely because a final consonant before them is treated as before a word in a sentence. Before the pada-endings, then, the final consonant of a consonant stem must be reduced to one of the eight consonants allowable at the end of a word. The palatal *-c* (-च्) of वाच्, therefore, is replaced by *-k* (-क्), but since *bh-* (भ-) is voiced, the law of regressive assimilation requires that the consonant immediately preceding be voiced also; so, *vāk* (वाक्), now to be regarded as though it were a word in a sentence, must be replaced by *vāg-* (वाग्-) before *-bhiḥ* (-भिः) and *-bhyaḥ* (-भ्यः), yielding *vāg-bhiḥ* (वाग्-भिः) and *vāg-bhyaḥ* (वाग्-भ्यः). But it is retained before the voiceless sibilant of *-su* (-सु), which, however, by a kind of progressive effect has to be cerebralized, becoming *ṣ-* (ष्-), thus, *vāk-ṣu* (वाक्-षु)[5]. Now the complete declension of वाच् can be given:

	Singular		*Plural*	
Nom.	*vāk*	(वाक्)	*vāc-aḥ*	(वाचः)
Acc.	*vāc-am*	(वाचम्)	*vāc-aḥ*	(वाचः)
Instr.	*vāc-ā*	(वाचा)	*vāg-bhiḥ*	(वाग्भिः)
Dat.	*vāc-e*	(वाचे)	*vāg-bhyaḥ*	(वाग्भ्यः)
Abl.	*vāc-aḥ*	(वाचः)	"	"
Gen.	"	"	*vāc-ām*	(वाचाम्)
Loc.	*vāc-i*	(वाचि)	*vāk-ṣu*	(वाक्षु)
Voc.	*vāk*	(वाक्)	*vāc-aḥ*	(वाचः)

Note that the form *vācaḥ* (वाचः) is ambiguous, as it can be ablative or genitive singular, nominative, accusative or vocative plural. Obviously, only the context can decide which is meant in a particular instance.

---

[5]The dental sibilant *-s-* (-स्-) within a word is always cerebralized after *-k-* (-क्-) and after all vowels except *-a-* (-अ-) and *-ā-* (-आ-); so, देवेषु, अग्निषु, भानुषु, but कर्मसु, सेनासु.

The nouns *sraj* (*f.* स्रज्) 'garland', *ṛtvij* (*m.* ऋत्विज्) 'priest', *baṇij* (*m.* बणिज्) 'merchant', and *bhiṣaj* (*m.* भिषज्) 'physician', though ending in *-j* (-ज्), are declined like वाच्, since in these words the palatal -ज् is treated like -च् and replaced by -क् and -ग् (before -भिः and -भ्यः). On the other hand, the final -ज् in the common words सम्राज् (*m.*) 'sovereign' and परिव्राज् (*m.*) 'wandering mendicant' is replaced by the cerebral -ट् (-ड् before -भिः and -भ्यः). While -च् is always replaced by the guttural -क् (-ग्), its voiced counterpart -ज् is sometimes changed to a cerebral. To which class it is changed is *not* an optional matter: *one must know which substitution is the correct one.*

Stems ending in the palatal sibilant *-ś* (-श्) also involve the same double possibility: in some words *-ś* (-श्) is changed to *-k* (-क्), in others to *-ṭ* (-ट्); thus, दिश् (*f.*) 'direction (of the compass)' and words ending in -दृश् 'seeing' and -स्पृश् 'touching' change their -श् into -क्. On the other hand, विश् (*m.*). 'settler' changes it to the cerebral -ट्. Final -ष् is replaced by -ट्, as in द्विष् (*m.*) 'enemy' and प्रावृष् (*f.*) 'rains, monsoon season'. Nouns in -त् and -द् are fairly common, especially सुहृद् (*m.*) 'friend' and विश्वजित् (*m.*) 'all-conquering'.

Herewith are the key-forms of all these words:

1. the nominative singular (which, due to the loss of the ending *-s* (-स्), requires reduction of the final consonant to one of the allowable eight when a word occurs in isolation),

2. the accusative singular (where *no* change is made in the final consonant before the vowel-initial ending),

3. the instrumental plural (where the final consonant before the pada-ending is treated as though it ended a foregoing word), and,

4. the locative plural (for the same reason and because of the retention of *s-* [स्-] of the ending *-su* [-सु] or its conversion to *ṣ-* [ष्-]).

Stem	*Nom. Sing.*	*Acc. Sing.*	*Instr. Plur.*	*Loc. Plur.*
स्रज् (*f.*) 'garland'	*srak* स्रक्	*sraj-am* स्रजम्	*srag-bhiḥ* स्रग्भिः	*srak-ṣu* स्रक्षु
ऋत्विज् (*m.*) 'priest'	*ṛtvik* ऋत्विक्	*ṛtvij-am* ऋत्विजम्	*ṛtvig-bhiḥ* ऋत्विग्भिः	*ṛtvik-ṣu* ऋत्विक्षु
बणिज् (*m.*) 'merchant'	*baṇik* बणिक्	*baṇij-am* बणिजम्	*baṇig-bhiḥ* बणिग्भिः	*baṇik-ṣu* बणिक्षु
भिषज् (*m.*) 'physician'	*bhiṣak* भिषक्	*bhiṣaj-am* भिषजम्	*bhiṣag-bhiḥ* भिषग्भिः	*bhiṣak-ṣu* भिषक्षु
सम्राज् (*m.*) 'sovereign'	*samrāṭ* सम्राट्	*samrāj-am* सम्राजम्	*samrāḍ-bhiḥ* सम्राड्भिः	*samrāṭ-su* सम्राट्सु
परिव्राज् (*m.*) 'mendicant'	*parivrāṭ* परिव्राट्	*parivrāj-am* परिव्राजम्	*parivrāḍ-bhiḥ* परिव्राड्भिः	*parivrāṭ-su* परिव्राट्सु
दिश् (*f.*) 'compass direction'	*dik* दिक्	*diś-am* दिशम्	*dig-bhiḥ* दिग्भिः	*dik-ṣu* दिक्षु
-दृश्[6] 'seeing'	*-dṛk* -दृक्	*-dṛś-am* -दृशम्	*-dṛg-bhiḥ* -दृग्भिः	*-dṛk-ṣu* -दृक्षु
-स्पृश्[6] 'touching'	*-spṛk* -स्पृक्	*-spṛś-am* -स्पृशम्	*-spṛg-bhiḥ* -स्पृग्भिः	*-spṛk-ṣu* -स्पृक्षु
विश् (*m.*) 'settler'	*viṭ* विट्	*viś-am* विशम्	*viḍ-bhiḥ* विड्भिः	*viṭ-su* विट्सु

[6]The roots दृश् 'see' and स्पृश् 'touch' are often used as the last member of an accusative tatpuruṣa compound.

Stem	*Nom. Sing.*	*Acc. Sing.*	*Instr. Plur.*	*Loc. Plur.*
प्रावृष् (*f.*)	*prāvṛṭ*	*prāvṛṣ-am*	*prāvṛḍ-bhiḥ*	*prāvṛṭ-su*
'monsoon'	प्रावृट्	प्रावृषम्	प्रावृड्भिः	प्रावृट्सु
द्विष् (*m.*)	*dviṭ*	*dviṣ-am*	*dviḍ-bhiḥ*	*dviṭ-su*
'enemy'	द्विट्	द्विषम्	द्विड्भिः	द्विट्सु
सुहृद् (*m.*)	*suhṛt*	*suhṛd-am*	*suhṛd-bhiḥ*	*suhṛt-su*
'friend'	सुहृत्	सुहृदम्	सुहृद्भिः	सुहृत्सु
-विद्[7]	*-vit*	*-vid-am*	*-vid-bhiḥ*	*-vit-su*
'knowing'	-वित्	-विदम्	-विद्भिः	-वित्सु
विश्वजित्	*viśvajit*	*viśvajit-am*	*viśvajid-bhiḥ*	*viśvajit-su*
'all-conquering'	विश्वजित्	विश्वजितम्	विश्वजिद्भिः	विश्वजित्सु

Nouns ending in *-s* (-स्) (represented by visarga, one of the allowable finals!) are numerous, especially as the final member of a compound, usually a karmadhāraya functioning as a bahuvrīhi. Thus सुमनः (सु 'good' + मनस् 'mind') as a bahuvrīhi means 'having a good *or* cheerful mind',[8] but oftenest it is used as a feminine noun in the sense of 'a flower'! Nouns ending in *-s* (or visarga) may be preceded by *a, i* or *u,* but those in *-as* (*-aḥ*) are far commoner than those in *-is* (*-iḥ*) or *-us* (*-uḥ*). All these nouns are neuter with but a few exceptions, chief among which are probably अङ्गिरः 'Aṅgiras' (a well-known sage), a masculine noun, and अप्सरः 'a heavenly nymph', which is feminine. It will be in the interest of greater lucidity to give the declension of these type-words in parallel columns before discussing the details about them.

---

[7]As in वेदविद् 'Veda-knowing', धर्मविद् 'Dharma-knowing'.

[8]The karmadhāraya on which it is based happens not to be used.

	manas (*n.*) 'mind'	*havis* (*n.*) 'oblation'	*āyus* (*n.*) 'life'	*Aṅgiras* (*m.*) name of a sage
Singular				
Nom.	*manaḥ*	*haviḥ*	*āyuḥ*	*Aṅgirāḥ*
	(मनः)	(हविः)	(आयुः)	(अङ्गिराः)
Acc.	"	"	"	*Aṅgiras-am*
				(अङ्गिरसम्)
Instr.	*manas-ā*	*haviṣ-ā*	*āyuṣ-ā*	*Aṅgiras-ā*
	(मनसा)	(हविषा)	(आयुषा)	(अङ्गिरसा)
Dat.	*manas-e*	*haviṣ-e*	*āyuṣ-e*	*Aṅgiras-e*
	(मनसे)	(हविसे)	(अयुषे)	(अङ्गिरसे)
Abl.	*manas-aḥ*	*haviṣ-aḥ*	*āyuṣ-aḥ*	*Aṅgiras-aḥ*
	(मनसः)	(हविषः)	(आयुषः)	(अङ्गिरसः)
Gen.	"	"	"	"
Loc.	*manas-i*	*haviṣ-i*	*āyuṣ-i*	*Aṅgiras-i*
	(मनसि)	(हविषि)	(आयुषि)	(अङ्गिरसि)
Voc.	*manaḥ*	*haviḥ*	*āyuḥ*	*Aṅgirah*
	(मनः)	(हविः)	(आयुः)	(अङ्गिरः)
Plural				
Nom.	*manāṃs-i*	*havīṃṣ-i*	*āyūṃṣ-i*	*Aṅgiras-aḥ*
	(मनांसि)	(हवींषि)	(आयूंषि)	(अङ्गिरसः)
Acc.	"	"	"	"
Instr.	*mano-bhiḥ*	*havir-bhiḥ*	*āyur-bhiḥ*	*Aṅgiro-bhiḥ*
	(मनोभिः)	(हविर्भिः)	(आयुर्भिः)	(अङ्गिरोभिः)
Dat.	*mano-bhyaḥ*	*havir-bhyaḥ*	*āyur-bhyaḥ*	*Aṅgiro-bhyaḥ*
	(मनोभ्यः)	(हविर्भ्यः)	(आयुर्भ्यः)	(अङ्गिरोभ्यः)
Abl.	"	"	"	"
Gen.	*manas-ām*	*haviṣ-ām*	*āyuṣ-ām*	*Aṅgiras-ām*
	(मनसाम्)	(हविषाम्)	(आयुषाम्)	(अङ्गिरसाम्)
Loc.	*manaḥ-su*	*haviḥ-ṣu*	*āyuḥ-ṣu*	*Aṅgirah-su*
	(मनःसु)	(हविःषु)	(आयुःषु)	(अङ्गिरःसु)
	(or *manas-su*)	(or *haviṣ-ṣu*)	(or *āyuṣ-ṣu*)	(or *Aṅgiras-su*)
	(मनस्सु)	(हविष्षु)	(आयुष्षु)	(अङ्गिरस्सु)
Voc.	*manāṃs-i*	*havīṃṣ-i*	*āyūṃṣ-i*	*Aṅgiras-aḥ*
	(मनांसि)	(हवींषि)	(आयूंषि)	(अङ्गिरसः)

Note that, in the nominative and accusative singular, neuters have *no* ending, just the stem itself with the final *-s* (-स्) changed to visarga. Except for the neuter vowel stems in *-a,* like फल, which add the ending *-m* (-म्), *all* neuters are without ending in the nominative and accusative singular. The ending of the nominative and accusative plural is *-i* (-इ) but the vowel before the immediately preceding consonant is lengthened. Thus, the stems *manas* (मनस्), *havis* (हविस्) and *āyus* (आयुस्) become *manās* (मनास्), *havīs* (हवीस्) and *āyūs* (आयूस्); the long vowel is then nasalized (indicated by placing the anusvāra sign above the lengthened vowel), and where the *-s* (-स्) is preceded by *-ī* (-ई) or *-ū* (-ऊ), the *-s* (-स्) is cerebralized. The stems are now *manāṃs* (मनांस्), *havīṃṣ* (हवींष्) and *āyūṃṣ* (आयूंष्), which, with the addition of the neuter ending *-i* (-इ), become *manāṃs-i* (मनांसि), *havīṃṣ-i* (हवींषि) and *āyūṃṣ-i* (आयूंषि).

In the locative plural the visarga (representing *-s* !) of the stem remains before *-su* (-सु), which, after the stems in *-iḥ* (-इः) and-*uḥ* (-उः), becomes *-ṣu* (-षु) (हविःषु, आयुःषु). There is an alternative sandhi which allows the assimilation of the visarga to the following sibilant, so that we may optionally write *manas-su* (मनस्सु), *haviṣ-ṣu* (हविष्षु) and *āyuṣ-ṣu* (आयुष्षु).

Note that, exactly as with final *-aḥ* (-अः) in sentence sandhi, so the *-aḥ* of the type stem *manaḥ* (मनः) becomes *-o* (-ओ) before *-bhiḥ* (-भिः) and *-bhyaḥ* (-भ्यः), thus: *mano-bhiḥ* (मनोभिः), *mano-bhyaḥ* (मनोभ्यः); *-iḥ* (-इः) and *-uḥ* (-उः) become *-ir* (-इर्) and *-ur* (-उर्): *havir-bhiḥ* (हविर्भिः), *havir-bhyaḥ* (हविर्भ्यः), *āyur-bhiḥ* (आयुर्भिः), *āyur-bhyaḥ* (आयुर्भ्यः).

As far as the masculine and feminine nouns of the types *aṅgiras* (अङ्गिरस्) and *apsaras* (अप्सरस्) are concerned, note that they add the regular endings given above for all consonant stems (the same for both genders!), which differ from the neuters only in the nominative and accusative. Again in the nominative, the old historical *-s* (*-ḥ*) is lost because of the two-consonant rule, the final vowel preceding the *-s* is lengthened as though to make up for the loss; hence *aṅgirās* (अङ्गिरास्) and *apsarās* (अप्सरास्).

It was noted at the outset of our discussion of *s*-stems that they often occur as the final member of a bahuvrīhi compound. As a bahuvrīhi is an adjective and the masculine or feminine is inevitably commoner than the neuter in this usage, an *s*-neuter in a bahuvrīhi has to be treated as a masculine or feminine and accordingly declined like *aṅgiras* (अङ्गिरस्) and *apsaras* (अप्सरस्). As a sample of this 'switch' of gender, we may give in full the declension of *mahā-yaśaḥ* (महायशः) 'having great glory' or 'whose glory is great'.

<table>
<tr><th></th><th colspan="2">Singular</th><th colspan="2">Plural</th></tr>
<tr><th></th><th>Masculine & Feminine</th><th>Neuter</th><th>Masculine & Feminine</th><th>Neuter</th></tr>
<tr><td>Nom.</td><td>mahāyaśāḥ
(महायशाः)</td><td>mahāyaśaḥ
(महायशः)</td><td>mahāyaśas-aḥ
(महायशसः)</td><td>mahāyaśāṃs-i
(महायशांसि)</td></tr>
<tr><td>Acc.</td><td>mahāyaśas-am
(महायशसम्)</td><td>mahāyaśaḥ
(महायशसः)</td><td>mahāyaśas-aḥ
(महायशसः)</td><td>mahāyaśāṃs-i
(महायशांसि)</td></tr>
<tr><td>Instr.</td><td colspan="2">mahāyaśas-ā
(महायशसा)</td><td colspan="2">mahāyaśo-bhiḥ
(महायशोभिः)</td></tr>
<tr><td>Dat.</td><td colspan="2">mahāyaśas-e
(महायशसे)</td><td colspan="2">mahāyaśo-bhyaḥ
(महायशोभ्यः)</td></tr>
<tr><td>Abl.</td><td colspan="2">mahāyaśas-aḥ
(महायशसः)</td><td colspan="2">"</td></tr>
<tr><td>Gen.</td><td colspan="2">"</td><td colspan="2">mahāyaśas-ām
(महायशसाम्)</td></tr>
<tr><td>Loc.</td><td colspan="2">mahāyaśas-i
(महायशसि)</td><td colspan="2">mahāyaśaḥ-su
(महायशःसु)
or mahāyaśas-su
(महायशस्सु)</td></tr>
<tr><td>Voc.</td><td colspan="2">mahāyaśaḥ
(महायशः)</td><td>mahāyaśas-aḥ
(महायशसः)</td><td>mahāyaśāṃs-i
(महायशांसि)</td></tr>
</table>

The common compound *mahātapaḥ* (महातपः) 'having great austerities' or 'whose austerities are great' is similarly declined. Since it is only the stems in *-as* (*-aḥ*) that lengthen the final vowel in masculines and feminines, words of the *haviḥ* (हविः), *āyuḥ* (आयुः) type, when used as the final member of a bahuvrīhi, are *un*changed in the nominative of all three genders.

The Story of Purūravas and Urvaśī.

The story of the mortal king Purūravas and the divine nymph Urvaśī has its origin in the Ṛgveda, where in a single hymn (X.95) the barest skeleton is given in the form of a dialog between Purūravas and Urvaśī. Further details are forthcoming in the version contained in the Śatapatha Brāhmaṇa (V.1-2), and many other elaborations of the myth are to be found in the Purāṇas, culminating in the well-known play Vikramorvaśīya ('The Play about Urvaśī Won through Valor') by Kālidāsa. The story as presented below is not a condensation of any existing version, but is a composite, in which the threads from various tellings have been brought together.

Note: Before attempting to work out the following reading exercise, the student should go over the rules for external vowel sandhi given in Lesson Fifteen.

आसीद् राजा पुरूरवा नाम बुधस्येलायाश् च पुत्रः[1] । तत ऐल[2] इत्यपि विश्रुतः[3] । याप्सरा उर्वशीति विश्रुता मित्रस्य वरुणस्य च शापेन[4] स्वर्गात् पृथिव्यां अवतीर्णाभवत् तस्यां अप्सरसि स महायशाः सम्राड् अन्वरज्यत् । त्वया सह वस्तुं इच्छेयं[5] इत्य् एताभिर् वाग्भिस् तस्या अनुमतिं तां अयाचत । यदि ममोरणयुगं पुत्रनिर्विशेषपालितं[7] शय्यानिबद्धं रक्षेर् यद्य् अहं त्वां वस्त्रशून्यं एव न पश्येयं अन्ततो यदि केवलं सर्पिर् मम भोजनं तव गृहे भवेत् तदा त्वया सह वसेयं[6] इति तस्मै अनुमतिं दत्त्वा सा तूष्णीं अभवत् । तेषु त्रिषु समयेषु पुरूरवसा स्वीकृतेषु[8] सोर्वशी तेन महातेजसा महीक्षिता सह प्रतिष्ठाने तस्य प्रासादे वस्तुं अगच्छत् । ततस्तस्यां अप्सरसि तेन सह तस्मिन् प्रासादे दीर्घकालं उषितायां केचिद् गन्धर्वाः शापान्ते उर्वश्याः स्वर्गप्रत्यागमने इच्छव उरणयुगं एकस्यां रात्रौ शय्यायाश् चोरयित्वा पलायिताः । उरणयुगस्य शब्दं श्रुत्वोर्वशी बुद्ध्वा पुरूरवसं प्राबोधयत् । शय्याया वासोविरहितः[9] सहसोत्थाय पुरूरवा असिं गृहीत्वा चौरान् अनुधावितः । ततो गन्धर्वैस् तं अवलोक्योज्ज्वला विद्युल्लतोत्पादिता ।

तदनन्तरं तमसि विद्युल्लतया हृते[10] उर्वशी पुरूरवसं नग्नशरीरं दृष्ट्वा युगपद् अन्तर्धानं अगच्छत् । उद्विग्नमना: परविषादं गत्वा पुरूरवा: सर्वस्यां पृथिव्यां उर्वशीं अन्विष्यान्ततः कुरुक्षेत्रं प्राप्य तत्र चतसृभिर्[11] अप्सरोभिः सह कस्मिंश्चित् सरसि स्नातीं[12] तां अविन्दत् । तव पुत्रं[13] गर्भे बिभर्मि[14] । परन्त्व् अधुना परेहि[15] । संवत्सरस्यान्ते इह प्रत्यागच्छेः । तदा तुभ्यं पुत्रं दत्त्वा त्वया सहैकां रात्रीं वत्स्यामि[16] । इत्येवं तयाप्सरसोक्तः पुरूरवास् तथा भवतु[17] । एकस्य वर्षस्यान्ते ऽत्र प्रत्यागमिष्यामीति तस्यै प्रतिज्ञाय स्वनगरं प्रतिष्ठानं गतः । वर्षस्यान्ते तत् कुरुक्षेत्रस्थं सरः प्रत्यागत्य पुरूरवाः परमरूपान्वितं आयुषं इति नाम[18] पुत्रं उर्वश्याः पद्मकराद्[19] आदाय तया सहैकां रात्रीं उषित्वा पुनः स्वनगरं गतः । अतःपरं प्रतिवर्षं[20] तत्र गत्वा पञ्च पुत्रान् आदाय पुरूरवा गन्धर्वास् तुभ्यं वरं दातुं इच्छेयुर् इत्युर्वश्या निवेदितो जीवितशेषं स्वर्गे तया सह गमयितुं अवृणीत ।

Notes

1. बुधस्येलायाश् च पुत्रः 'the son of Budha and Ilā'. 'Budha' is *not* to be confused with 'Buddha' (with two *d* 's!), the founder of Buddhism; *Budha* (literally 'the wise one') is the planet Mercury, regarded in Indian mythology as the son of the moon. His name appears in the Sanskrit word for the weekday 'Wednesday', बुधवार (or बुधवासर) 'Budha's Day', the precise equivalent of the Latin Mercuriī Diēs 'Mercury's Day', of which the English 'Wednesday' is a translation loanword. Old English *Wōdnesdæg,* later *Wednesday,* is literally 'Wōden's Day', Wōden being one of the chief Anglo-Saxon gods, who was equated with the Roman Mercury.

2. ऐल Aila, 'son of Ilā', a metronymic formed from Ilā by substituting the vṛddhi of 'i' which, it will be remembered, is 'ai'; the final vowel *-ā* is replaced by the suffix *-a,* which is widely used to make various kinds of derivatives, not only metronymics or patronymics. For example, बौद्ध *bauddha* from बुद्ध 'Buddha', through the vṛddhi of *u,* means 'connected with or related to the Buddha' and, when used as a noun 'a follower of the Buddha'.

3. ऐल इत्यपि विश्रुत: 'known also as Aila' and in the next sentence उर्वशीति विश्रुत: similarly 'known as Urvaśī'. In the episode of King Nala and Queen Damayantī we read विदर्भराज्ञो दुहिता दमयन्तीति विश्रुता 'The King of Vidarbha has a daughter known as Damayantī'.

4. मित्रस्य वरुणस्य च शापेन 'Due to a curse of Mitra and Varuṇa'; these two great gods appear in the Ṛgveda, Mitra as the personification of the compact and Varuṇa as that of truth. They are often invoked, as are many Ṛgvedic deities, as a conjoint pair called Mitrāvaruṇā (मित्रावरुणा).

5. इच्छेयम् The optative is frequently used to soften an assertion; the indicative इच्छामि would mean straightforwardly 'I wish', but इच्छेयम् means 'I should like'.

6. The conditions, which are set out in the three यदि-clauses for Urvaśī's complying with Purūravas' wish to abide with her, are put in the optative along with the apodosis (तदा . . . वसेयम्) and expressed in the form of a so-called 'future less vivid' condition, that is, of the 'should-would' type: '*If* you *should* watch over my pair of rams . . . , *if* I *should* see you . . . , and *if* my food *should* only be ghee . . . , then I *would* abide with you . . .'.

7. पुत्रनिर्विशेषपालितं 'protected like sons'; part A (पुत्रनिर्विशेष-) is adverbial to B (पालित) and would be in the accusative neuter singular if the two members are expressed syntactically. Compounds whose prior member is adverbial are a variety of karmadhāraya. निर्विशेष 'having no distinction, like' is a type of bahuvrīhi, in which the adverbial prefix निस् (नि:) 'away' has a quasi-adjectival value: 'having an away-distinction' (= having no distinction). In dissolving compounds of this type, the Indian grammarians turn the adverb निस् into an adjective by subjoining गत, the past participle of √गम्, thus, निर्गत 'gone away' and say: निर्गत: विशेष: यस्मात् स: 'he from whom the distinction (is) gone away', hence 'like unto'. Since निर्विशेष is here used adverbially (not applied to a person as in the dissolution just given), the analysis would have to be phrased so as to indicate that the quality of 'not having a distinction' belongs to the *act* of 'protecting' (पालित) *not* to a person. It may be done as follows: निर्गत: विशेष: यस्या: क्रिया यथा स्यात् तथा, literally 'in that manner (तथा) as (यथा) would be (स्यात् optative of √अस् 'be') an action (क्रिया) from which the distinction has gone away'. Analytically, then,

the whole compound पुत्रनिर्विशेषपालितं means '(my pair of rams) protected in that manner as would be an action (of protecting) from which the distinction of sons (पुत्र) has gone away'. This sounds terribly complicated and awkward, but not so in Sanskrit! It is important to understand the Indian method of analyzing the various kinds of compounds, as, apart from the clarity and succinctness involved, these analyses pervade Sanskrit commentarial literature where they often help to shed light on the interpretation of a whole passage.

8. तेषु त्रिषु . . . स्वीकृतेषु A locative absolute: 'when these three . . . had been accepted'. Similarly तस्यां अप्सरसि . . . उषितायां 'When that *Apsaras* . . . had stayed'. त्रिषु is the locative masculine plural of the numeral त्रि 'three'.

9. वासोविरहितः At the junctures of the words that make up a compound the rules of *external* sandhi apply, so here वासो- stands for वासस् (वासः), the final *-as* (or *-aḥ*) becoming *-o* before the voiced sound that follows.

10. तमसि . . . हते Another absolute construction, giving the backdrop for the observation made by Urvaśī.

11. चतसृभिः Instrumental feminine plural of the numeral चतुर् 'four' modifying अप्सरोभिः.

12. स्नातीं Accusative feminine singular of the present active participle of √स्ना (स्नाति, class II) 'swim'. It modifies तां. Render: 'found her swimming along with ...'.

13. The words from तव पुत्रं through वत्स्यामि are spoken by Urvaśī, as shown by the quotation-marker इति with the phrase immediately following: इत्येवं तयाप्सरसोक्तः 'thus addressed by that Apsaras'.

14. बिभर्मि 'I am bearing', present first person singular of √भृ (बिभर्ति, class III) 'bear, carry'. This is an athematic root, to which the endings are added without the interposition of a thematic vowel.

15. परेहि 'go away!' इहि is the imperative (= the mood of asking someone to do something) second singular of √इ (एति, class II) 'go' combined with the

adverb परा 'away, off' (परा + इहि which by sandhi forms परेहि). In thematic verbs the stem without ending serves as the second singular imperative, but in the athematic class it is generally formed by adding -हि to what is called the 'weak' stem. The weak stem of √इ is इ-, hence the imperative इ-हि.

16. वत्स्यामि 'I shall abide', future first singular of √वस् (वसति, class I) 'abide' made by substituting -त् for the -स् before appending the future sign -स्य-.

17. तथा भवतु 'So be it!' the standard reply of consent; भवतु is the imperative third singular of √भू (भवति, class I).

18. आयुषं इति नाम 'by name Āyus'. Normally, आयुस् (आयुः) 'life' is a neuter *s*-stem, but here as a name of Purūravas' son it has to be made into a masculine noun, hence the accusative ending *-am*.

19. उर्वश्याः पद्मकराद् 'from Urvaśī's lotus-like hand'. A woman's hand is often likened to a lotus in Sanskrit literature, by reason of its beauty and softness.

20. प्रतिवर्षं 'every year'. The adverb प्रति which, among other meanings, means 'in' with the implication of repetition, often carries the sense of 'every' when prefixed to a noun inflected in the accusative singular neuter. Thus, प्रतिदिनम् or प्रतिदिवसम् 'every day', प्रतिमासम् 'every month', प्रतिदिशम् 'in every direction', etc.

Vocabulary

पुरूरवः, *m.* Purūravas,[9] name of an ancient king of Pratiṣṭhāna; son of Budha and Ilā, and so called Aila.

बुध, *m.* Budha, name of the planet Mercury; father of Purūravas.

विश्रुत, *ppp.* वि-√श्रु (शृणोति, class V), 'heard of far and wide', famous, known, *then* known as (+ *nom.*).

उर्वशी, *f.* Urvaśī, name of an Apsaras.

---

[9] In transliterating *s*-stems for mention in an English setting it is customary not to change the final *-s* to visarga; so we should write Purūravas, Apsaras, etc.

मित्र, *m.* Mitra, name of a Vedic god, the personification of the compact or agreement between two parties.

वरुण, *m.* Varuṇa, name of a Vedic god, the personification of truth.

शाप, *m.* a curse.

स्वर्ग, *m.* heaven.

अवतीर्ण, *ppp.* अव-√तॄ (तरति, class I), having come down, descended.

अप्सरः, *f.* an Apsaras, one of a class of semi-divine beings, wives of the Gandharvas.

यशः, *n.* fame, glory.

सम्राज्, *m.* (*nom.* सम्राट् with change of ज् to cerebral ट्), a sovereign.

अनु-√रज् (रज्यति, class IV), be enamored of (+ *loc.*).

वाच्, *f.* (*nom.* वाक्), word; speech.

अनुमति, *f.* approval, consent.

√याच् (याचति, °ते, class I), request, ask.

उरण, *m.* a ram; उरणयुग, *n.* a pair of rams.

निर्विशेष, *adj.* not having a distinction, without distinction, like.

पालित, *ppp.* √पालय (पालयति), protected.

शय्या, *f.* a bed, couch.

निबद्ध, *ppp.* नि-√बन्ध् (बध्नाति, class IX), tied to, fastened onto.

वस्त्र, *n.* garment, article of clothing.

शून्य, *adj.* empty, void, deserted; destitute of (+ *instr.,* or as second element in a compound).

अन्ततः *adv.* in the end, finally.

केवलम्, *adv.* only.

सर्पिः, *n.* clarified butter, ghee.

भोजन, *n.* food.

तूष्णीम्, *adv.* silently, in silence; + √भू be silent, remain silent.

त्रि, *numeral* three. [inflected only in the plural: masc. *nom.* त्रयः, *acc.* त्रीन्, *instr.* त्रिभिः, *dat.-abl.* त्रिभ्यः, *gen.* त्रयाणाम्, *loc.* त्रिषु; fem. *nom.-acc.* तिस्रः, *instr.* तिसृभिः, *dat.-abl.* तिसृभ्यः, *gen.* तिसृणाम्, *loc.* तिसृषु; neut. *nom.-acc.* त्रीणि]

समय, *m. lit.* a coming together, *then,* an agreement, arrangement, stipulation, condition.

स्वी-√कृ (करोति, class VIII), make one's own, take, receive, accept.

तेजः, *n. lit.* point *or* tip, *then,* tip of flame, flame; glow, splendor; majesty.

महीक्षित्, *m.* 'earth-ruler', a king.

प्रतिष्ठान, *n.* Pratiṣṭhāna, name of an ancient town, at the confluence of the Gaṅgā (Ganges) and the Yamunā (Jumna) rivers, capital of King Purūravas.

दीर्घकालम्, *adv.* for a long time.

प्रत्यागमन, *n.* return.

इच्छु, *adj.* desirous.

रात्रि, *f.* night. [a later form of रात्री]

पलायित, *ppp.* √पलाय् (पलायते), 'having gone away', having fled, having departed.

बुद्ध्वा, *gerund* √बुध् (बोधति, °ते, class I), having awakened (*intrans.*).

वासः, *n.* clothing, garment.

विरहित, *ppp.* वि-√रह् (रहति, class I), abandoned, given up, relinquished.

प्र-√बुध् *in caus.* प्रबोधयति, awakens (*trans.*).

असि, *m.* a sword.

गृहीत्वा, *gerund* √ग्रह् (गृह्णाति, class IX), having grasped *or* taken.

अनुधावित, *ppp.* अनु-√धाव् (धावति, class I), having run after, having pursued.

उज्ज्वल, *adj.* blazing up.

विद्युल्लता, *f.* forked lightning (*lit.* 'lightning-creeper', a compound of विद्युत् 'lightning' + लता 'creeper'; -त् changed to -ल् by regressive assimilation).

उद्-√पद् (पद्यते, class IV), go forth (उद्), come into existence, be produced; *caus.* उत्पादयति, 'causes to be produced', produces, *ppp.* उत्पादित.

नग्न, *adj.* naked, bare.

शरीर, *n.* body.

युगपद्, *adv.* simultaneously.

अन्तर्धान, *n.* disappearance; *acc. with* √गम्, disappear.

अन्विष्य, *gerund* अनु-√इष् (इच्छति, class VI), having sought after *or* looked for.

सरः, *n.* lake, pool.

√स्ना (स्नाति, class II), swim.

गर्भ, *m.* the womb.

√भृ (बिभर्ति, class II), bear, carry.

परन्तु, *conj.* but.

अधुना, *adv.* now.
परा-√इ (एति, class II), go off, go away.
संवत्सर, *m.* year.
वर्ष, *n.* year.
कुरुक्षेत्र, *n.* Kurukṣetra, name of an extensive plain near Delhi, where the great battle described in the Mahābhārata took place.
आयुः, *m.* Āyus, name of the first son born of Urvaśī to Purūravas.
पङ्कज, *n.* a lotus (*lit.* 'that which is born of *or* in the mud').
कर, *m.* the hand.
अतःपरम्, *adv.* henceforth.
प्रतिवर्षम्, *adv.* every year.
जीवितशेष, *m.* remainder of life.
नि-1√विद् (वेत्ति, class II), *caus.* निवेदयति, causes to know, informs, *ppp.* निवेदित, having been informed.
√गम् (गच्छति, class I), go; *caus.* गमयति causes to go, passes (of time); *infin.* गमयितुम् .
2√वृ (वृणीते, class IX), choose.

Translate the following sentences into Sanskrit, using the preceding narrative as a model for the syntactic constructions:

Purūravas, whose glory was great, the son of Budha and Ilā, was the king of Pratiṣṭhāna. As soon as he saw the Apsaras Urvaśī, who had descended from heaven to earth due to a curse, he felt an affection for her. She told him that she would stay with him if he accepted three conditions. The Gandharvas stole her pair of rams which was tied to the bed and fled. When she heard their bleating, Urvaśī awakened Purūravas. Purūravas pursued the thieves, but when they saw him, they produced a lightning-flash, by which Urvaśī saw her husband naked. One of the three conditions having been thus violated, Urvaśī disappeared right there. Purūravas, greatly agitated, after searching throughout the world for Urvaśī, became disheartened. Finally, he found her in Kurukṣetra in company with other Apsarases. She promised that if he came back in a year, she should present him with a son and thereupon she went to heaven. Having returned there at the end of a year, he received from her a son named Āyus. After returning to Kurukṣetra every year for five years and receiving altogether five sons from Urvaśī, Purūravas got a boon from the Gandharvas and chose to abide in heaven with Urvaśī the rest of his life.

LESSON SEVENTEEN

Changeable Stems With Two Variants: Declension of Stems in *-vat*/*-mat*. The Present Participle in *-at*. Adjectives in *-in*.

In the last lesson we began our study of consonant stems and noted that they fall into two great classes: 1. the unchangeable stems, which show no change in their declension except as required by sandhi when the consonant ending the stem stands in absolutely final position and also before the pada-endings; 2. the changeable stems, which exhibit two or three variants in their declension according to a fixed pattern. In that lesson we discussed only the first or unchangeable class. In this lesson we shall take up the class of changeable stems, which contains some of the commonest and most important in the language.

In order to understand the twofold or threefold variation which the changeable stems undergo in their declension, it is necessary to understand what is meant by the terms 'strong', 'weak', 'middle' and 'weakest' and also something about the rationale behind their use. These strange terms are based on a differentiation of the stem, inherited (at least in part) from the parent Indo-European language, due to a shifting of the accent from the stem of a word to the case ending. In the parent language, when the accent fell on the stem, as distinguished from the case ending, the stem had a fuller form than when the accent shifted to the ending. This pattern, however, is preserved only in a few of the Sanskrit changeable stems; in many the accent[1] is fixed on the first syllable throughout the declension, instead of shifting to the case ending when the stem has a reduced or weaker form. In Sanskrit, the fuller form of the stem or 'strong' stem, as it is called, is found in masculine changeable stems in the nominative and accusative singular and the nominative plural, but in the neuters only in the nominative and accusative plural. The reduced form of the stem, called 'weak', appears in all the other cases. This disposition of the strong and weak stems is invariable for the declension of changeable stems of the twofold type. All stems that end in *-vat* (-वत्) and *-mat* (-मत्) as well as present active participles in *-at* (-अत्) follow this pattern. Let us now see how the strong and weak stems of these two important classes of words are made and give the full declension of an illustrative stem of each class.

---

[1]The accent referred to here is the pitch or tonic accent found in the Ṛgveda and other early texts, but *not* in the later language, which has only a stress accent, the position of which is determined by the length of the penultimate syllable.

I. *Changeable Stems in -vat* (-वत्) and *-mat* (-मत्).

-vat and *-mat* are suffixes, *i.e.,* word-building elements, used to make adjectives of possession from nouns. Thus, from *rūpa* (रूप) 'beauty' + *-vat* (-वत्) is made the adjective *rūpa-vat* (रूपवत्) meaning 'possessing beauty, beautiful, handsome'. So also *bhaga-vat* (भगवत्) from *bhaga* (भग) 'portion, lot, good fortune', hence, literally 'possessing good fortune, fortunate, blessed, lordly' etc. Similarly with the synonymous suffix *-mat* (-मत्) is formed *dhī-mat* (धीमत्) 'possessing understanding *or* insight (धी), wise, insightful.' The stem ending in *-vat/-mat* is the weak stem. The strong stem is made by the insertion of the nasal *-n-* before the *-t,* thus, *rūpavant-* (रूपवन्त्-), *bhagavant-* (भगवन्त्-), *dhīmant-* (धीमन्त्-). From these two stems in *-vat/-vant* and *-mat/-mant* the entire declension in the masculine and neuter is formed. Precisely the same format is followed by *all* adjectives ending in *-vat/-mat.*

Declension of Stems in *-vat* and *-mat.*

	bhagavat 'fortunate'		*dhīmat* 'wise'	
strong stem	*bhagavant-*		*dhīmant-*	
weak stem	*bhagavat-*		*dhīmat-*	
	Singular		*Singular*	
	Masculine	Neuter	Masculine	Neuter
Nom.	**bhagavān* (भगवान्)	*bhagavat* (भगवत्)	**dhīmān* (धीमान्)	*dhīmat* (धीमत्)
Acc.	**bhagavant-am* (भगवन्तम्)	*bhagavat* (भगवत्)	**dhīmant-am* (धीमन्तम्)	*dhīmat* (धीमत्)
Instr.	*bhagavat-ā* (भगवता)		*dhīmat-ā* (धीमता)	
Dat.	*bhagavat-e* (भगवते)		*dhīmat-e* (धीमते)	
Abl.	*bhagavat-aḥ* (भगवत:)		*dhīmat-aḥ* (धीमत:)	
Gen.	*bhagavat-aḥ* (भगवत:)		*dhīmat-aḥ* (धीमत:)	
Loc.	*bhagavat-i* (भगवति)		*dhīmat-i* (धीमति)	
Voc.	*bhagavan*[2] (भगवन्)	*bhagavat* (भगवत्)	*dhīman*[2] (धीमन्)	*dhīmat* (धीमत्)

---

[2] The vocative singular is not, strictly speaking, a strong stem, but a modification of it.

	Plural Masculine	Neuter	*Plural* Masculine	Neuter
Nom.	**bhagavant-aḥ* (भगवन्तः)	**bhagavant-i* (भगवन्ति)	**dhīmant-aḥ* (धीमन्तः)	**dhīmant-i* (धीमन्ति)
Acc.	*bhagavat-aḥ* (भगवतः)	**bhagavant-i* (भगवन्ति)	*dhīmat-aḥ* (धीमतः)	**dhīmant-i* (धीमन्ति)
Instr.	*bhagavad-bhiḥ* (भगवद्भिः)		*dhīmad-bhiḥ* (धीमद्भिः)	
Dat.	*bhagavad-bhyaḥ* (भगवद्भ्यः)		*dhīmad-bhyaḥ* (धीमद्भ्यः)	
Abl.	*bhagavad-bhyaḥ* (भगवद्भ्यः)		*dhīmad-bhyaḥ* (धीमद्भ्यः)	
Gen.	*bhagavat-ām* (भगवताम्)		*dhīmat-ām* (धीमताम्)	
Loc.	*bhagavat-su* (भगवत्सु)		*dhīmat-su* (धीमत्सु)	
Voc.	**bhagavant-aḥ*[3] (भगवन्तः)	**bhagavant-i* (भगवन्ति)	**dhīmant-aḥ*[3] (धीमन्तः)	**dhīmant-i* (धीमन्ति)

The strong stems are preceded by an asterisk (*). All the rest are weak. The nominative singular masculine is peculiar: we would have expected **bhagavan* for **bhagavant-s* with regular loss of all the final consonants but one. In addition to this, the final vowel is lengthened as though to compensate for the loss of the two consonants. The feminine is made by adding the feminine suffix *-ī* to the weak stem; thus, *bhagavat-ī, dhīmat-ī*. This feminine stem is declined precisely like नदी:

Nom.	*bhagavatī*	(भगवती)
Acc.	*bhagavatīm*	(भगवतीम्)
Instr.	*bhagavatyā*	(भगवत्या)
Dat.	*bhagavatyai*	(भगवत्यै)
Abl.	*bhagavatyāḥ*	(भगवत्याः)
Gen.	*bhagavatyāḥ*	(भगवत्याः)
Loc.	*bhagavatyām*	(भगवत्याम्)
Voc.	*bhagavati*	(भगवति)

and so on with perfect regularity.

---

[3]The vocative plural is really the nominative used as a vocative.

II. *The Present Active Participle in -at* (-अत्).

The strong stem of this important verb form may be obtained 'mechanically' by dropping the *-i* of the third person plural present. So, the strong stems of the types of the four thematic classes are *bhavant-* (√*bhū*), *dīvyant-* (√*div*), *tudant-* (√*tud*) and *corayant-* (√*cur*) from *bhavant-i, dīvyant-i, tudant-i* and *corayant-i* respectively. The weak stem is gotten by dropping the *-n-;* thus, *bhavat-, dīvyat-, tudat-, corayat-*. The declension of *bhavat* (भवत्) 'being' in the masculine and neuter is as follows:

	Singular Masculine	Neuter	*Plural* Masculine	Neuter
Nom.	**bhavan* (for *bhavant-s*) (भवन्)	*bhavat* (भवत्)	**bhavant-aḥ* (भवन्त:)	**bhavant-i* (भवन्ति)
Acc.	**bhavant-am* (भवन्तम्)	*bhavat* (भवत्)	*bhavat-aḥ* (भवत:)	**bhavant-i* (भवन्ति)
Instr.	*bhavat-ā* (भवता)		*bhavad-bhiḥ* (भवद्भि:)	
Dat.	*bhavat-e* (भवते)		*bhavad-bhyaḥ* (भवद्भ्य:)	
Abl.	*bhavat-aḥ* (भवत:)		*bhavad-bhyaḥ* (भवद्भ्य:)	
Gen.	*bhavat-aḥ* (भवत:)		*bhavat-ām* (भवताम्)	
Loc.	*bhavat-i* (भवति)		*bhavat-su* (भवत्सु)	
Voc.	**bhavan* (भवन्)	*bhavat* (भवत्)	**bhavant-aḥ* (भवन्त:)	**bhavant-i* (भवन्ति)

The feminine of the participles of the four thematic classes of roots is made by adding the suffix *-ī* to the strong stem; thus, *bhavant-ī, dīvyant-ī, tudant-ī, corayant-ī*. It is declined like नदी.

The present active participle, just like the past passive participle we have so plentifully had in our readings, is an adjectival derivative of a verb. It corresponds to the English form in *-ing*, as in *be-ing, play-ing, strik-ing, steal-ing,* and like the English forms expresses an action that takes place contemporaneously with that of the principal verb, as in 'I saw my friend *going* in the road' मार्गे गच्छन्तं मम सुहृदं अपश्यम्. Like any adjective, a participle has to agree in case, gender and number with the noun it qualifies;

in this example गच्छन्तं qualifies सुहृदं which is accusative, masculine, singular, the direct object of अपश्यम्. It is essential to distinguish the English participle in *-ing* from the verbal noun in *-ing*.[4] The forms being absolutely identical, the only means of distinguishing the one from the other is by the sense of the passage in which they occur. For example, in the sentence 'Meditating requires much practice', 'meditating' is a verbal noun, subject of 'requires'. It might even be replaced by the unequivocal noun 'meditation' without change of the sense. But in 'I see an ascetic meditating under a tree', 'meditating' is a participle -- a verbal adjective -- describing the 'ascetic' whom it characterizes as performing meditation at a given moment.

Here may be mentioned the extremely common adjective महत् 'great', which is originally a present active participle from √मह् (महति) 'be great', hence literally 'being great', but with loss of its participial sense it has come to mean simply 'great'. Its strong stem is महान्त्, instead of the expected महन्त्, due to the influence of the synonomous महा-. Of identical origin is बृहत् 'high, lofty', really the present participle of √बृह् (बृहति) 'be strong *or* great'. The strong stem बृहन्त् is, however, perfectly regular, there being no scope for lengthening the final vowel as in महान्त्.

There is yet another twofold changeable stem of a type that is extremely common, which is easily learned along with the stems already given. It ends in the suffix *-in,* which, like *-vat/-mat,* means 'possessing' whatever the noun to which it is attached means. Thus, from *bala* 'strength' is made *bal-in* 'possessing strength, strong' and from *dhana* 'wealth' is made *dhan-in* 'possessing wealth'. As may be seen, when *-in* is added to a noun, the final vowel of the noun is dropped. This suffix is so productive, indeed much more so than the synonymous *-vat/-mat,* that one may make up possessive adjectives freely from it, reasonably sure that the formations already exist. Since the meaning imparted by both *-in* and *-vat/-mat* is sufficiently clear and does not normally involve any special nuances, the student who knows the meaning of the primary word should be able to determine the sense of the words to which they have been added without resorting to the dictionary.

The declension of the *-in* possessives does not show the same sort of alteration of strong and weak stems as does that of the stems in *-vat/-mat* and

---

[4]In Old English, from which (through Middle English) our modern language is descended, the verbal noun and present participle were formed with quite different suffixes. The verbal noun ended in *-ung,* the participle in *-ende;* for example, *bind-ung* and *bind-ende* 'binding'. In the various dialects of Old English -- and subsequently also in the written language -- these two suffixes became phonetically more and more approximated, until they were both conflated into *-inge,* which with loss of the *-e* has become our modern *-ing,* thus serving as the ending of two unrelated forms.

-at, although there are two degrees of the stem. Before the pada-endings and in the nominative and accusative singular neuter, the *-n* is *dropped,* but retained elsewhere, except in the nominative masculine singular which drops the *-n* and prolongs the *-i*.

III. *Declension of Stems in -in* (-इन्).

balin (बलिन्) 'possessing strength, strong'

	Singular		*Plural*	
	Masculine	Neuter	Masculine	Neuter
Nom.	*balī* (बली)	*bali* (बलि)	*balin-aḥ* (बलिन:)	*balīn-i* (बलीनि)
Acc.	*balin-am* (बलिनम्)	*bali* (बलि)	*balin-aḥ* (बलिन:)	*balīn-i* (बलीनि)
Instr.	*balin-ā* (बलिना)		*bali-bhiḥ* (बलिभि:)	
Dat.	*balin-e* (बलिने)		*bali-bhyaḥ* (बलिभ्य:)	
Abl.	*balin-aḥ* (बलिन:)		*bali-bhyaḥ* (बलिभ्य:)	
Gen.	*balin-aḥ* (बलिन:)		*balin-ām* (बलिनाम्)	
Loc.	*balin-i* (बलिनि)		*bali-ṣu* (बलिषु)	
Voc.	*balin* (बलिन्)	*bali* (or *balin*) (बलि or बलिन्)	*balin-aḥ* (बलिन:)	*balīn-i* (बलीनि)

Note that in the nominative and accusative plural the *i* of the suffix is lengthened as are the vowels *a, i* and *u* in *manāṃsi, havīṃṣi* and *āyūṃṣi.* The feminine is made by adding *-ī* to the full stem; thus *balin-ī* (बलिनी). The feminine stem is declined like नदी.

I. The Story of the Churning of the Ocean

The story of the churning of the ocean (समुद्रमन्थन) first appears in the Mahābhārata, although some scholars claim to find foreshadowings of it in the Ṛgveda. Various versions of this myth, differing from one another in many details and greatly extended and embellished in the later texts, are found also in the Rāmāyaṇa and many of the Purāṇas. The account given below is drawn principally from that in the Mahābhārata (I.15-17), but the earlier portion has many threads from the telling of the story in the Viṣṇu Purāṇa (I.9).

It can hardly be doubted that the churning of the ocean is in its ultimate origin a creation myth, into which, however, much relatively extraneous material was gradually introduced. The churning of the firestick to produce fire, often mentioned and even described in the Ṛgveda (III.29), for example, is a creative act. So also is the churning of milk to produce butter a creative act. In a famous and important hymn of the Ṛgveda (I.32) the great god Indra, in a vestige of an ancient creation myth, is depicted as slaying the serpent-demon Vṛtra in order to release the waters pent up within his belly. These waters contain the elements of the cosmos, the sun, the heaven and the dawn, which had been withheld from man by the negative force personified by Vṛtra. When the great ocean is churned by the gods and the demons (in temporary trucial co-operation!) certain basic prototypal elements rise up from the waters. The stated purpose of the churning of the ocean is to obtain the drink of immortality called 'Amṛta' (अमृत), which, apart from its immortalizing effect, will confer upon the gods sufficient strength to defeat the demons by whom they have been worsted and greatly weakened in prolonged combat. According to the account in the Viṣṇu Purāṇa, the gods had lost their strength, vigor and majesty as a result of a curse upon their chief Indra by the irascible sage Durvāsas, a recurrent figure in Sanskrit literature, whose principal function seems to have been the imposition of curses of particularly maleficent nature. The version of the churning in the Mahābhārata does not contain the episode of Durvāsas' curse to explain the gods' loss of strength to fend off the demons.

पूर्वस्मिन् कल्पे पृथिव्यां परिभ्राम्यन् महातपा[1] मुनिर् दुर्वासा मार्गे आयान्तं ऐरावतस्य नाम गजस्य पृष्ठे निषीदन्तं इन्द्रं दृष्ट्वा तां कयाचिद् विद्याधर्या दत्तां स्रजं देवराजायायच्छत्[2] । त्रैलोक्याधिपतिना तां स्रजं गृहीत्वा स्रग् ऐरावतस्य शिरसि न्यस्ता । स्रजो गन्धेनाकृष्टः स गजः करेण शिरसो[3] ऽपहृत्य पृथिव्यां सहसाक्षिपत् । ततस् तद् अवलोक्य परमं क्रोधं गत्वा महामुनिर् दुर्वासा इन्द्रं अवदत् । हे वासव यस्मात्[4] त्वं अतिदर्पाध्मातो मां न प्रणिपत्य[5] मया दत्तां इमां मालां तव गजस्य शिरसि न्यस्यैवं[5] मय्य् अवमानं करोषि तस्मात् त्रैलोक्यस्य लक्ष्मीर् विनाशं गच्छेद्[6] इति[7] त्वयि शापं वदामि । तेनैवं उक्तो बलवान् इन्द्रो हस्तिनः स्कन्धाद्[8] अवतीर्य तं

अतिक्रुद्धं मुनिं प्रसादयितुं महान्तं यत्नं अकरोत्[9] । परन्तु महेन्द्रस्य वाचं श्रुत्वापि[10] स मुनिर् मां बहु न मन्यसे[11] किं बहुना[12] त्वां न क्षमिष्ये इत्युक्त्वापगतः । ततः प्रभृति सर्वं भुवनत्रयं शक्रेणान्यैर् देवैश्च सह[13] दुर्वाससः शापस्य प्रभावेन निर्लक्ष्मीकं अभवत् । यथैवं लक्ष्म्या वर्चसा तेजसा च विरहितानां देवानां ऐश्वर्यं क्षयं अगच्छत् तथा ते दैत्यैर् अन्यै रक्षोभिश्च युद्धे पराजिताः । तदा पृथिव्यां विप्रा यज्ञेषु मन्दादरा अभवन् तापसाश्च तपांसि नाचरन्[14] । अतः परं दानं सत्यवादं कारुण्यं अन्यान् धर्मान् चावधीरयन्तो नरा लोभेनोपहत-मनसोऽभवन् । ततो बलक्षयेण बलिभिर् द्विड्भिर् विजिता असुरैः सह युद्धेन परिश्रान्ताश्च सर्वे देवा इन्द्राद्या[15] अग्निपुरोगमा भयेनोद्विग्न-चित्ता भगवन्तं समस्तलोकपितामहं ब्रह्माणं[16] एव शरणं प्रापद्यन्त ।

Notes

1. महातपा When the adjective महत् 'great' is used as part A of a karmadhāraya or bahuvrīhi compound, it is replaced by महा. महातपः 'whose austerity (तपः) is great' or 'having great austerity' is a common epithet of a sage or seer (मुनि or ऋषि).

2. देवराजाय 'to the king of the gods'; Indra is the principal god of the Ṛgveda, to whose magnification are dedicated more hymns than to any other. Although he is greatly subordinated in function and power in Classical Sanskrit texts, in the Mahābhārata and other earlier works he is still referred to as 'king of the gods' (or by some equivalent epithet). In the following sentence he is called त्रैलोक्याधिपति 'overlord of the three worlds'.

अयच्छत् √यम् (यच्छति) primarily means 'hold', but it comes to signify 'hold' in almost every sense: hold out (hence 'give' as here), hold up (*i.e.*, 'sustain'), hold back (hence, 'suppress, check, control'), etc.

3. शिरसः 'ablative of separation' with अपहृत्य.

4. यस्मात् 'because' ('ablative of cause') correlative to तस्मात् 'therefore'.

5. प्रणिपत्य, न्यस्य Note that gerunds always *follow* the words that are to be taken with them: 'you, not having paid obeisance to me, having thrown down this garland given by me upon the head of your elephant'.

6. गच्छेत् optative of wish: 'may the lustre of the three worlds go to ruin!'

7. इति marks the preceding words from the vocative हे वासव to गच्छेत् as uttered by Durvāsas in pronouncing his curse upon Indra. Strictly speaking, of course, the curse itself consists only of the words त्रैलोक्यस्य लक्ष्मीर् विनाशं गच्छेत्, all the preceding words specifying the reason for its imposition.

8. हस्तिनः स्कन्धाद्: 'from the shoulder ('ablative of separation') of his elephant'. हस्तिन् is really just a possessive adjective meaning literally 'having a hand (हस्त)' and, when applied to the elephant, has reference to its trunk. When the Indo-Europeans, who were to become the Indo-Aryans, entered India, probably about the middle of the second millennium B.C., they had no word for 'elephant', which they not unnaturally referred to as the 'beast with the hand'. Before long the word 'beast' (मृग) was omitted and हस्तिन् alone was used. In the course of time various indigenous words for elephant (गज, मातङ्ग, etc.) were borrowed into Sanskrit, but हस्तिन् was probably the commonest word. In any case, through the Prakrit form हत्थी the old name हस्तिन् has come down into the modern vernaculars, as, for example, into Hindi as हाथी. Incidentally, apart from हस्तिन् and the indigenous names, Sanskrit has very many other words of an epithetical nature for elephant, as द्विरद 'the two-tusked one', सिन्धुर 'the one that takes pleasure in the river', द्विप 'the one that drinks twice', etc.

9. अकरोत् Imperfect third singular of √कृ 'do', which belongs to the non-thematic classes of roots. These roots have two stems, a strong and a weak, which are found in particular forms. The first, second and third persons of the present and imperfect (among others!) require the strong stem. √कृ makes the strong stem करो, hence अ-करो-त्. This root is one of the commonest in Sanskrit, being used in the sense of 'do, make' in their widest possible application. It is also used, as in this passage, with almost any noun with which it can be sensibly connected to express the performance of the act denoted by the noun. So here महान्तं यत्नं अकरोत्, literally 'made a great effort', means 'tried very hard'.

10. श्रुत्वापि 'even though he heard'; when अपि 'even' is used with an adjective or participle (the gerund is a past active participle!), it often imparts the sense of 'though' or 'although' to the adjectival word, *i.e.*, the sense of concession: 'granting that such-and-such is the case, in spite of it'.

11. मां बहु न मन्यसे 'you do not think highly of me'; बहु is the accusative singular neuter employed as an adverb 'much' or 'highly'.

12. किं बहुना 'Why say more?' or 'What's the use of talking?', a very frequent idiom, especially in the dramas; किं 'what' is used with the instrumental in the sense of 'What's the use of such-and-such', literally 'What's with such-and-such?' So किं बहुना is literally 'What's with much?'

13. सह 'along with, together with'; the idea is that the three worlds including all the gods lost their majesty or glory. One is reminded of the sad plight of Wotan and the other gods in Germanic mythology when the goddess Freia (the goddess of love, corresponding to लक्ष्मी) was snatched away by the giants in payment of their building Valhalla.

14. In this sentence and the following are depicted the general declination and neglect of all spiritual values, customs, routines and virtues, which ultimately lead to the worsting of the forces of good (personified by the gods) by the powers of evil (represented by the Daityas, Dānavas, Rakṣases and Asuras -- all demonic forces).

15. सर्वे देवा इन्द्राद्याः 'All the gods having Indra as first', *i.e.*, 'all the gods beginning with Indra' or idiomatically 'All the gods, Indra, etc.' आद्य 'first' and the noun आदि 'beginning' are used as the final member of an appositional bahuvrīhi in the sense of 'so-and-so, etc.' In some modern vernaculars आदि is put after any list of words in the sense of 'etc.'

16. ब्रह्माणं accusative masculine singular with प्रापद्यन्त. It was natural that the gods in their desperate predicament should turn for help to Brahmā, the creator of all the world, as their end seemed to be near at hand, and who else than he should know what to do? The masculine *n*-stem ब्रह्मन् must be carefully distinguished from the neuter, with which it coalesces in all cases except the nominative and accusative. For further details, see the discussion in the following lesson.

Note: Beginning with this vocabulary, words occuring in the Sanskrit exercises are given in the order of the Devanāgarī alphabet, *not* in the order of their occurrence in the exercise.

Vocabulary

अतः परम्, *adv. phrase,* from then on, henceforth.

अति, *adv.* prefixed to nouns and adjectives to express excess; thus, अतिदर्प 'excessive pride', अतिक्रुद्ध 'excessively angry'.

अधिपति, *m.* an overlord *or* supreme head.

अप-√गम् (गच्छति, class I), go off.

अपहृत्य, *gerund* अप-√हृ (हरति, class I), having taken off *or* away.

अवतीर्य, *gerund* अव-√तॄ (तरति, class I), having descended, alighted, gotten down.

√अवधीर् (अवधीरयति, class X), disrespect, disregard, hold in contempt.

अवमान, *m.* disrespect, contempt.

आकृष्ट, *ppp.* आ-√कृष् (कर्षति, class I), drawn toward, attracted.

आद्य, *adj.* first; *at end of appositional bahuvrīhi* 'having . . . as first, *i.e.,* beginning with, so-and-so etc.

आध्मात, *ppp.* आ-√ध्मा (धमति, class I), puffed up.

आ-√या (याति, class II) 'come'. [The adverbial prefix आ-, as often with verbs of motion, reverses the meaning of the root √या 'go', hence आयाति 'he comes'; the third person plural is आयान्ति, whence the strong stem of the present participle is आयान्त्, the weak stem आयात्.]

उपहत, *ppp.* उप-√हन् (हन्ति, class II), hit, hurt; afflicted, pained.

ऐरावत, *m.* Airāvata, name of Indra's elephant.

ऐश्वर्य, *n.* supremacy, power.

कर, *m.* the trunk (of an elephant).

कल्प, *m.* epoch, age.

कारुण्य, *n.* compassion, kindness.

√क्षम् (क्षमते, class I), forgive, pardon; *fut.* क्षमिष्ये.

क्षय, *m.* ruin, decay, destruction; loss.

क्षिप् (क्षिपति, class VI), throw, cast, toss.

गज, *m.* an elephant.

गृहीत्वा, *gerund* √ग्रह् (गृह्णाति, class IX), having seized, grasped *or* taken. .

ततः प्रभृति, *adv. phrase,* from then on, from that time on.

तपस्, *n.* heat; deep concentration *or* meditation, religious austerity. [from √तप् (तपति, class I) 'burn, give out heat; *cf.* Latin *tepidus* 'warm', whence English 'tepid']

तेजस्, *n.* brilliance, lustre; splendor; majesty. [Etymologically तेजस् means 'sharpness', then 'sharp edge' as of a knife, then 'tip or point' as of a flame, whence the meanings given.]

त्रैलोक्य, *n.* the three worlds.

दान, *n.* the act of giving, charity.

दुर्वासस्, *m.* Durvāsas, a sage famous for his irascible nature and predilection for imposing curses for slight offences. [*literally* 'badly clad, naked']

दैत्य, *m.* Daitya, name of one of a class of demons.

द्विष्, *m.* enemy.

निर्लक्ष्मीक, *adj.* without *or* devoid of splendor, lustre.

न्यस्त, *ppp.* नि-√अस् (अस्यति, class IV), cast *or* thrown down.

परन्तु, *conj.* but.

पराजित, *ppp.* परा-√जि (जयते, class I), (having been) overcome *or* conquered.

परि-√भ्रम्, (भ्राम्यति, class IV), wander about, roam.

परिश्रान्त, *ppp.* परि-√श्रम् (श्राम्यति, class IV), fatigued.

पितामह, *m.* grandsire.

पृष्ठ, *n.* the back.

पुरोगम, *adj.* going before, leading, *then as m. noun,* a leader; *at end of appositional bahuvrīhi* 'having . . . as leader', *i.e.,* led by . . .

पूर्व, *adj.* former, preceding [declined according to the pronominal declension, that is, like तद्, except for the nominative/accusative neuter, which is *pūrvam,* not *pūrvat*].

प्र-णि-√पत् (पतति, class I), fall down (नि) before (प्र) someone out of respect. [नि becomes णि due to the cerebralizing influence of the र् of प्र.]

प्र-√पद् (पद्यते, class IV), go forth, go unto, resort to.

प्रभाव, *m.* power, might.

प्र-√सद् (सीदति, class I), be pleased *or* glad, be gracious to; *hence, causative* प्रसादयति 'causes *or* makes glad *or* gracious to one, appeases, propitiates'; *infin.* प्रसादयितुम्.

बलवत्, *adj.* having *or* possessing strength (बल).

ब्रह्मन्, *m.* the god Brahmā, regarded as the 'grandsire' or creator of the worlds. [On this stem and its declension, *v.* Lesson Eighteen]

भगवत्, *adj.* 'possessing fortune', fortunate; prosperous, glorious; venerable, august, holy.

भुवन, *n.* the world. [A synonym of लोक, *but literally* 'being' from √भू, then a 'living creature, man, mankind']

√मन् (मन्यते, class IV), think.

महत्, *adj.* great.

माला, *f.* a garland. [स्रज् and माला are synonymous.]

यत्न, *m.* effort, exertion.

रक्षस्, *n.* an evil being *or* demon.

लक्ष्मी, *f.* prosperity; beauty, loveliness; splendor, lustre. [Unlike words of the नदी or देवी type, लक्ष्मी adds *-ḥ* in the nominative: लक्ष्मीः].

लोभ, *m.* greed, avarice.

वर्चस्, *n.* vital power, energy; brilliance, lustre.

वासव, *m.* Vāsava, a name of Indra as chief of the Vasus, a class of gods mentioned in the Ṛgveda, but of vague function and character. [वासव means *literally* 'relating to *or* derived from the Vasus' and used as a noun denotes one who is connected with the Vasus in some way, whence the specific application to Indra as their chief.]

विद्याधरी, *f.* one of a class of fairies or supernatural beings, possessed of vague magical powers. [विद्याधरी is the *f.* of विद्याधर, the male counterpart, the literal meaning of which is 'bearing *or* possessing knowledge', *i.e.,* some sort of esoteric or magical knowledge.]

विनाश, *m.* ruin, destruction.

विप्र, *m.* a priest.

विरहित, *ppp.* वि-√रह् (रहति, class I), deprived of, free of, devoid of.

शक्र, *m.* Śakra, a name of Indra. [*Literally* the 'powerful one']

शाप, *m.* a curse.

शिरस्, *n.* the head.

सत्यवाद, *m.* truth-speaking.

समस्त, *adj.* whole, all.

स्कन्ध, *m.* the shoulder.

स्रज्, *f.* a garland.

हस्तिन्, *m.* an elephant. [*Literally* the '(beast) having a hand', *i.e.,* a trunk]

Translate into Sanskrit:

When (यदा) Indra's elephant named Airāvata cast[1] on the ground the garland (स्रज्, *f.*) which had been given to that king of the gods by the ascetic (तपस्विन्) Durvāsas, (then) that great sage, having immediately become extremely angry[2], said thus (एवम्) to the overlord of the three worlds:[3] 'O Vāsava, since (यस्मात्) you show me disrespect and[4] do not think much of me, (therefore) I place this mighty curse upon you:[5] may the three worlds[3] along with you and all the other gods go to ruin!' Due to this mighty curse of Durvāsas all[6] the gods, having lost their strength,[7] were worsted in battle by various demons (रक्षस्, *n.*). As a result, the gods, led by Agni, went for refuge[8] to the blessed great grandsire of all the worlds.

Notes

1. Use the imperfect of नि-√क्षिप् (क्षिपति, class VI). Do not forget the augment (which follows the prefix)!

2. Translate 'having become extremely angry' by 'having gone to extreme anger (*acc.*)'.

3. Translate 'the three worlds' by a *gen.* tatpuruṣa *cpd.* ('triad-of-worlds').

4. Put च ('and') after the words 'do not think much of me'.

5. 'to place a curse upon someone' may be expressed by शापं + √वद् and the *loc.* of the person upon whom the curse is placed.

6. Remember that 'all' (सर्व) is declined pronominally, *i.e.*, like तद्, except in the *nom.-acc. sing. n.*, which is सर्वम्, not *सर्वद्.

7. Translate 'having lost their strength' by 'having gone to a loss of their strength' and *cf.* note 2 above; 'loss of their strength' should be expressed by a *cpd.*

8. The Sanskrit idiom for 'to go to someone for refuge' is प्र-√पद् (पद्यते, class IV) + शरणं ('for refuge') and *acc.* of the person with whom refuge is sought.

LESSON EIGHTEEN

Changeable Stems with Three Variants. Negative Compounds. Dvandva Compounds.

I. *Changeable Stems with Three Variants.*

In the last lesson we entered upon the fascinating subject of changeable consonant stems that exhibit two forms or variants of their stem, a 'strong' and a 'weak'. We learned that the terms 'strong' and 'weak' are used here with reference to a fuller and weaker form of the stem, *originally* due to a shifting of the accent in the parent language and partially inherited in Sanskrit. In this lesson we shall take up the class of changeable stems that show three variants.

In this class the strong stem occurs in the same cases as in the class with two variants. The weak stem, however, is divided into 'weakest' and 'middle', that is, a *third* stem is differentiated before the endings beginning with a consonant -- the so-called 'pada-endings' or 'middle endings' as they are sometimes called. Typical of this class are the stems ending in *-an,* which may be masculine or neuter. The strong is made by *lengthening the preceding -a-,* the weakest by *dropping the -a-,* and the middle by *dropping the -n*. Thus, from *rājan* (राजन्) 'king' we have the three stems *rājān* (राजान्), *rāj-ñ* (राज्ञ्) and *rāja* (राज). Note that by the much rarer rule of *'progressive* assimilation', the *-n,* thus brought into contact with *-j-* by the dropping of the vowel *-a-*, is replaced by the palatal *-ñ-*. Everything about the declension is perfectly clear and regular, *except* that in the nominative singular of masculine nouns the *-n* of the strong stem is dropped, just as the *-n* of the stems in *-in* like *balin* (बलिन्).[1]

Declension of *rājan* (राजन्), *m.* 'king'

	Singular		*Plural*	
Nom.	**rājā*	(राजा)	**rājān-aḥ*	(राजानः)
Acc.	**rājān-am*	(राजानम्)	*rājñ-aḥ*	(राज्ञः)
Instr.	*rājñ-ā*	(राज्ञा)	*rāja-bhiḥ*	(राजभिः)
Dat.	*rājñ-e*	(राज्ञे)	*rāja-bhyaḥ*	(राजभ्यः)

---

[1]In Latin too, the *-n* of correspondingly declined words is lost in the nominative, though elsewhere retained; for example, *sermō,* genitive *sermōn-is*.

Abl.	*rājñ-aḥ*	(राज्ञः)	*rāja-bhyaḥ*	(राजभ्यः)
Gen.	*rājñ-aḥ*	(राज्ञः)	*rājñ-ām*	(राज्ञाम्)
Loc.	*rājñ-i*	(राज्ञि)	*rāja-su*	(राजसु)
Voc.	*rājan*	(राजन्)	**rājān-aḥ*	(राजानः)
	(the stem itself!)		(same as the nom.)	

In the neuter stems, as always when there is a differentiation of strong and weak, only the nominative and the accusative plural are strong. In the nominative and accusative singular (which are strong in masculine *n*-stems) the *middle* stem without ending is used.

Declension of *nāman* (नामन्), *n.* 'name'

	Singular		*Plural*	
Nom.	*nāma*	(नाम)	**nāmān-i*	(नामानि)
Acc.	*nāma*	(नाम)	**nāmān-i*	(नामानि)
Instr.	*nāmn-ā*	(नाम्ना)	*nāma-bhiḥ*	(नामभिः)
Dat.	*nāmn-e*	(नाम्ने)	*nāma-bhyaḥ*	(नामभ्यः)
Abl.	*nāmn-aḥ*	(नाम्नः)	*nāma-bhyaḥ*	(नामभ्यः)
Gen.	*nāmn-aḥ*	(नाम्नः)	*nāmn-ām*	(नाम्नाम्)
Loc.	*nāmn-i*	(नाम्नि)	*nāma-su*	(नामसु)
Voc.	*nāman*	(नामन्)	**nāmān-i*	(नामानि)
	or *nāma*	(नाम)		

Both the masculine and neuter *n*-stems have an *alternative* locative singular made by adding the locative ending *-i* to the ordinary dictionary stem in *-an*, thus, *rājan-i* (राजनि) and *nāman-i* (नामनि) in addition to *rājñ-i* (राज्ञि) and *nāmn-i* (नाम्नि).

Many of the *n*-stems end in *-man,* and when this *-man* happens to be preceded by a consonant, as in *ātman* (आत्मन्) *m.* 'soul' and *janman* (जन्मन्) *n.* 'birth', the weakest cases retain the *-a-* to avoid the impossible accumulation of consonants that would otherwise result. So we say *ātman-ā* (आत्मना) and *janman-ā* (जन्मना) in the instrumental, *not ātmn-ā* and *janmn-ā*.

It is noteworthy here that there are two words *brahman* (ब्रह्मन्), the one masculine, the other neuter, differentiated also by meaning. Since, like *all* neuters, the neuter *brahman* differs from the masculine only in the nominative and accusative, all the remaining cases can be distinguished only by the context.[2] The masculine *brahman* means a 'Brahman priest' or 'the personalized god Brahmā'. The neuter word has a number of meanings ranging from 'prayer, a Vedic hymn, holy life' to 'the Absolute, the substrate of the universe', generally called 'Brahman' in books on Indian culture. The form Brahmā, used above for the personalized creator-god, is simply the nominative case of the masculine word employed to distinguish it from the neuter Brahman. Otherwise in English we would have two Brahmans, distinguishable only by context. This is the convention that is everywhere adopted. With this single exception, *all* Sanskrit nouns are normally quoted or referred to in their stem form.[3]

II. *Negative or Privative Compounds.*

Sanskrit nouns and adjectives are made negative by putting *a-* (अ-) before them, as *a-vidyā* (अविद्या) 'non-knowledge', that is 'ignorance', and *a-bhāva* (अभाव) 'non-existence'. So also before adjectives, as *a-dṛṣṭa* (अदृष्ट) 'not seen, unseen, invisible'. When the word to be made negative begins with a vowel, *an-* (अन्-) is used instead of *a-* (अ-); thus, *an-artha* (अनर्थ) a 'non-object', that is, a 'worthless object', *an-iṣṭa* (अनिष्ट) 'not desired, undesirable', *an-ārya* (अनार्य) 'non-Āryan'.[4] These are all karmadhāraya compounds, the *a-/an-* before a noun (as in *a-vidyā* 'non-knowledge') functioning as an adjective, and before an adjective (as in *an-iṣṭa* 'not desired') serving as an adverb. The majority of words beginning with *a-/an-*, however, are bahuvrīhis based on karmadhārayas; as *an-anta* (अनन्त) 'having a non-end, endless', *a-hetu* (अहेतु) 'having a non-cause, causeless'. Only in exceptional instances is it necessary for the student to resort to the dictionary

---

[2]But in the Vedic language, where the old tonic accents are marked, also by the accent; so *bráhman, n.* and *brahmán, m.*

[3]Some common *n*-stems, which have come into English *not* through learned channels, but through popular borrowings from various vernaculars (principally Hindi), reflect the tendency of the vernaculars to borrow Sanskrit *n*-stems in the *nominative* case; for example, *karma, yogi* and *raja* (for *karman, yogin* and *rājan).*

[4]The same use of *a-/an-* to denote negation is found in numerous English words borrowed from Greek where the cognate *a-/an-* occurs; for example, a-political 'non-political', an-algesia 'not feeling pain', etc.

for words compounded with *a-/an-,* if the meaning of the noun or adjective to which they are prefixed is known.[5]

III. *Dvandva Compounds.*

Two or more nouns connected in sense by 'and' may be made into a compound, as in English *washer-drier, radio-TV,* etc. Compound adjectives with similar parallel relationship of their members are much commoner in English, as *Judaeo-Christian, bittersweet,* and especially the compound decade numerals, as *thirty-five.*[6] Indian grammarians, however, generally look upon adjective pairs as a kind of karmadhāraya, as both adjectives would be in the same case when the compound is resolved and the parts given their appropriate endings. The noun combinations, which are really just lists of two or more items connected in thought by 'and' (Sanskrit च) are called 'dvandva' ('pair') compounds. Examples occurring in the reading exercise in this lesson are: दैत्यदानव 'Daityas and Dānavas', उत्पत्तिस्थितिविनाश 'the coming to be, continuation and destruction (of the universe)'; as part of a longer compound: कारणकार्यहेतु 'the cause of *cause and effect',* अजप्रकृतिपुरुषकारण 'the cause of the unborn (अ-ज) *primal matter* (प्रकृति) *and the soul* (पुरुष)' or possibly, by an alternative analysis, 'the unborn cause of *primal matter and the soul'.*

II. The Churning of the Ocean

तेषां सुराणां वचः श्रुत्वैव ब्रह्मा तान् अवदन् महाभागं महौजसं विष्णुं[1] अनादिं अनन्तं चाहेतुं कारणकार्यहेतुं अजप्रकृतिपुरुषकारणं[2] उत्पत्ति-स्थितिविनाशानां हेतुं आर्तजनोपकारिणं -- तं महेश्वरं शरणं प्रपद्येध्वं इति । एवं उक्त्वा लोकपितामहो देवैः सहितो महोदधेर् उत्तरं तीरं[3]

---

[5]So common is this usage of *a-/an-,* that occasionally a word beginning with *a-* is wrongly assumed to be a negative compound, and by dropping the *a-* a new word of *positive* meaning is created! For example, *asura* (असुर) 'demon' was assumed to be *a* + *sura* a 'non-*sura',* and hence *sura* (सुर) was taken to mean a 'god' as opposed to a 'demon'; similarly, from *asita* (असित) 'black', treated as *a* + *sita* 'not-white', was made सित 'white'.

[6]That the two members of these compound numerals are in conjunct and not dependent relationship is apparent from the now obsolete mode of saying 'five-and-thirty', 'three-and-sixty', etc.

भगवतो विष्णोर् निवासं वैकुण्ठं अगच्छत् । महेश्वरं प्रणिपत्य सर्वलोकपितामह्रो देवार्थं विष्णुं उपकारं[4] अयाचत् । तेषां याच्ञां श्रुत्वोपकारं तेभ्यः प्रतिज्ञाय तान् सुरान् तैः कर्तव्यं अवदत् । भवतां बलं[5] पुनः प्राप्तुं महोदधिं अमृतार्थं[6] मथेध्वम् । यद् अमृतं तस्माद् मथिताद् उदधेर् उत्पत्स्यते[7] तद् भवतां उपबृंहणाय[8] भविष्यति । अपि च[9] दुर्वासिसः शापेन विनष्टस्य तेजसः पुनःप्राप्तये महोदधेर् देव्य् अन्तर्धानगता लक्ष्मीर् आविर्भविष्यति । प्रथमं सकला ओषधीः संगृह्य तत्रोदधौ प्रक्षिप्य[10] ततः पर्वतवरं मन्दरं तद् एव स्थानं आनीय मन्थानं तं गिरिं कृत्वा वासुकिनामानं सर्पाणां राजानं नेत्रं कृत्वासुरैः सह युद्धनिवृत्तिं कृत्वा सहिता महोदधिं मथेध्वं इति[11] । यस्मात् तु मन्दरपर्वतो न केवलं बहुभिर् योजनैर् भूमेर् उपरि समुच्छ्रित[12] आसीत् परन्तु तावद्भिर्[13] योजनैर् अधस्ताद् एव तस्मात् ते देवगणास् तं गिरिं उद्धर्तुं अशक्ता अभवन् । यस्मिन्[14] अनन्तशेषनाम्नि भुजंगमे शय्यारूपे भगवान् शेते स विष्णुना प्रचोदित उत्थाय बृहन्तं मन्दरं उद्धृत्य महोदधिं देवैः सहित आनयत् । ततो ऽनन्तशेषेण मन्दरपर्वते[15] एवं उद्धृते आनीते च ते देवाः समुद्रं अवदन् अमृतार्थं तव जलं मथिष्यामहे इति । अथ महोदधिदेवो यदा ममाप्य् अमृतस्यांशो भवेत् तदा मन्दरभ्रमणाद् दुःसहं मर्दनं सहेयेति प्रत्यभाषत । यथा मन्दरशैलः समुद्रजले न निमज्जति तथा भगवान् विष्णुः कूर्मरूपस्[16] तं मन्दरं आत्मनः पृष्ठे आदायास्याधिष्ठानं अभवत् । तं महान्तं गिरिं कूर्मस्य पृष्ठे स्थिरं एकस्मात् स्थानाच् चाचलं कृत्वा बलवान् इन्द्रो यन्त्रेण[17] शैलस्याग्रं अभ्यपीडयत् । मन्दराचलं सर्पाणां राज्ञा वासुकिना संवेष्ट्य मन्थानं[18] कृत्वा तदा देवा दैत्यदानवैः समेता मथितुं आरब्धाः[19] । यत्र सर्पस्य पुच्छस् तत्र स्थिता देवगणा यत्र च मुखं तत्रासुराः ।

Notes

1. विष्णुं The great god Viṣṇu is a member of the triad (त्रिमूर्ति) consisting of Brahmā, Viṣṇu and Śiva, who are regarded respectively as creator, sustainer and destroyer of the universe in an endless continuum of cycles throughout cosmic time. During the quiescent period between each destruction and re-creation of things, Viṣṇu reclines upon the serpent Anantaśeṣa, whose services, as will be seen subsequently, were drawn upon in transferring Mt. Mandara to the ocean, where it was used as a churning-stick by the gods and demons.

विष्णुं is the object of प्रपद्येध्वं ('You should go to Viṣṇu for help'), which is far separated from it by the long array of epithets extolling his infinite greatness. Because of the long separation between the two, the words तं महेश्वरं ('that great lord') are put just before प्रपद्येध्वं as a sort of recapitulation of what has intervened.

2. अजप्रकृतिपुरुषकारणं There are two ways of interpreting this compound. We may take the adjective अज 'unborn' as qualifying कारण, thus: 'the unborn cause of primal matter and the soul'. Or we may take it as limiting the internal dvandva प्रकृतिपुरुष, thus: 'the cause of the unborn primal matter and soul'. The latter possibility is obviously less desirable, as it involves the logical dilemma of Viṣṇu causing what is said not to have been born.

3. It is not possible to give a specific geographic location for the 'great ocean' (महोदधि) referred to here, still less for its 'northern shore' (उत्तर तीर), beyond its proximity to Vaikuṇṭha, which is scarcely of any value, as it too, has no fixed, clearly definable location.

4. विष्णुं उपकारं अयाचत् 'asked Viṣṇu for help'. In Sanskrit, verbs of requesting take *two* accusatives, one the person of whom the request is made (here Viṣṇu) and the other the matter requested (here his help).

5. भवतां बलं 'your strength'; भवतां is the genitive plural of the second person pronoun भवत् 'you', said to be a polite form, but often used interchangeably

with त्वम्, sometimes in the same sentence. Except for the nominative masculine singular, which is भवान्, this peculiar word is declined exactly like the present participle of √भू, with which, however, it has no connection. It is important, by the way, to note that this pronoun भवत्, when the subject of the sentence, takes the verb in the *third,* not the *second* person.[7]

6. अमृतार्थं 'for the sake of the *Amṛta' i.e.,* the drink of immortality. We may compare the ambrosia of the Greeks which conferred immortality on the gods and upon mortals who tasted of it. On the literal meaning of अमृत and its application in the sense of this nectar, see the note in the vocabulary under this word.

7. उत्पत्स्यते 'will go forth *or* arise', third singular future middle of उद्-√पद् (पद्यते). As will be seen in the following lesson, the future is formed by adding to the root the suffix *-sya-*, as here, or *-iṣya-*, as in the following भविष्यति, आविर्भविष्यति in the next sentence and मथिष्यामहे subsequently.

8. उपबृंहणाय 'dative of purpose or end': literally 'will be for a strengthening of you', *i.e.,* will serve or conduce to this end. A similar usage is the dative पुनः प्राप्तये in the next sentence.

9. अपि च 'and besides *or* moreover', a frequent conjunctive phrase.

10. Apparently the *Amṛta* is the product resulting not only from the act of churning the great ocean, but also from the intermixture of the essences of various herbs the gods are here requested to cast into it.

11. There are six gerunds in this long sentence: संगृह्य, प्रक्षिप्य, आनीय, and three कृत्वा's. Each gerund expresses an action which precedes that of the following gerund, and the whole complex of actions precedes the action denoted by the main verb (मथेध्वम्). Again be careful to take the words *before* each gerund as qualifying it. Do *not* skip around in looking for qualifying elements! The construction of the sentence, then, is: 'You should churn (मथेध्वम्) the great ocean (महोदधिं), [1] first (प्रथमं) having gathered

[7]This use of the third person for direct address, *i.e.,* for the *second* person, may be compared with the English use in such phrases as 'As your honor (or your majesty) *commands*'; *cf.* also the use of the third person in Spanish with *Usted* and in Italian with *Lei.* In German the polite second person pronoun *Sie* takes the verb in the third plural.

(संगृह्य) . . ., [2]having thrown away (प्रक्षिप्य) . . ., [3]then (ततः) having brought (आनीय) . . ., [4]having made (कृत्वा) . . ., [5]having made (कृत्वा) . . ., (and) [6]having made (कृत्वा) . . .'. मन्थानं and (सर्पाणां) राजानं are secondary objects of the first two कृत्वा's which are used in the sense of 'having made *or* transformed into'; thus 'having *made* that mountain (तं गिरिं) *into* a churning-stick (मन्थानं)' and 'having made the king of serpents (सर्पाणां राजानं) *into* a rope (नेत्रं)' for turning the mountain.

12. बहुभिर् योजनैर् . . . सुमच्छ्रितः 'high above the earth by many *yojanas*' ('instrumental of measure').

13. तावद्भिर् याजनैर् 'by so many *yojanas; (i.e.,* by the same amount *below* the earth as above).

14. यस्मिन् The relative clause introduced by यस्मिन् is picked up by the correlative स; thus literally: 'On *what* serpent named Anantaśeṣa the blessed one reclines, *that* one brought the lofty mountain' etc.

15. मन्दरपर्वते locative absolute with the two participles उद्धृते and आनीते (connected with each other by च); thus: 'Then when Mt. Mandara had been thus lifted up and brought by Anantaśeṣa' etc. The gods now tell the great ocean (personalized as a god) of their intention, and the ocean agrees to put up with the friction of the churning if he is given a share of the *Amṛta* !

16. कूर्मरूपस् This is, of course, the tortoise-incarnation of Viṣṇu, one of the ten terrestrial forms he is said to assume at one time or another for specific purposes. Here we see that it is in order to keep Mt. Mandara from sinking into the sea.

17. यन्त्रेण 'by means of an instrument for holding' it in place. This has nothing to do with his thunderbolt or वज्र, but is simply some unspecified instrument by which Indra kept the mountain in a fixed position while it was supported on the back of Viṣṇu (in the form of the tortoise) and vigorously rotated by the gods and demons.

18. मन्थानं secondary object of कृत्वा as explained above under note 11; thus: 'having *made* Mt. Mandara (मन्दराचलं) *into* a churning-stick (मन्थानं).

19. आरब्धा: past passive participle of आ-√रभ् (रभते, class I), literally 'take hold of, get a grip on', *then* 'begin' an enterprise. Ordinarily आ-√रभ् would be considered a *transitive* verb, so that the past passive participle would require the logical subject to be put in the instrumental, thus: 'By the gods, along with the Daityas and Dānavas, the churning *(was) begun'*. But here आ-√रभ् has to be taken as an intransitive verb; literally, then: 'The gods, etc. *(were) having begun* to churn', *i.e.*, 'The gods began to churn'.

Vocabulary

अंश, *m.* a portion *or* part.

अग्र, *n.* a tip, top.

अचल, *adj.* unmoving, immobile. [अ- 'not' + चल 'moving']

अचल, *m.* a mountain. [*Literally* 'the unmoving one', see अचल, *adj.* above]

अज, *adj.* unborn. [अ- + ज 'born' from √जन् (जायते, class IV), 'be born']

अधिष्ठान, *n.* a standing-place *or* base of support.

अनन्तशेष, *m.* Anantaśeṣa, name of the great serpent upon which Viṣṇu reclines during periods of cosmic absorption.

अनादि, *adj.* 'having no beginning', beginningless. [अन्- 'not' + आदि 'beginning']

अभि-√पीड् (पीडयति, class X), press upon.

अमृत, *n.* the nectar or drink of immortality. [*Literally* 'that which is immortal', the thing which produces a certain effect being said to possess it'; *cf.* Shakespeare's 'all the drowsy syrups of the world', 'insane root' and 'sweet oblivious antidote']

अशक्त, *adj.* unable. [अ- 'not' + शक्त, *ppp.* √शक् (शक्नोति, class V) 'be able']

आ-√रभ् (रभते, class I), begin. [*Literally* 'grasp, take hold of', *then* 'undertake, make an effort to do something']

आर्त, *adj.* afflicted, distressed, fallen into misfortune. [*ppp.* आ-√ऋ (ऋच्छति, class VI), *literally* 'come to', but pregnantly with negative implication, 'come to misfortune, gotten *or* fallen into trouble' etc.]

आविस्, *adv.* in view; prefixed to √भू (भवति, class I), 'be in view', become manifest, appear.

उत्तर, *adj.* northern. [*Literally* 'upper, higher']

उत्पत्ति, *f.* arising, birth, origin.

उदधि, *m.* the ocean, sea.

उद्-√हृ (हरति, class I), take up, lift up, raise; *ppp.* उद्धृत, *infin.* उद्धर्तुम्, *gerund* उद्धृत्य. [Note that ह् is replaced by ध्, the combination *ud-hṛ* (उद्-हृ) becoming *ud-dhṛ* (उद्-धृ). Similarly, initial ह् after ग्, ड् and ब् is changed respectively to घ्, ढ् and भ्. These latter changes, however, are only rarely encountered.]

उपकार, *m.* help, assistance.

उपकारिन्, *adj.* helping, assisting.

उपबृंहण, *n.* the act of making strong, invigoration.

उपरि, *postp.* above (+ *gen.*).

ओजस् *n.* strength, power.

ओषधी, *f.* an herb *or* plant.

कर्तव्य, *n.* what has to be done. [*gerundive of* √कृ 'do' used as a noun]

कारण, *n.* cause (as opposed to कार्य 'effect').

कूर्म, *m.* a tortoise.

केवलम्, *adv.* only; न केवलं . . . परन्तु, not only . . . but also.

गण, *m.* a group, crowd, host.

गिरि, *m.* a mountain.

तावत्, *adj.* so much, so many.

दुःसह, *adj.* difficult to bear, intolerable.

नि-√मज्ज् (मज्जति, class I), sink down, submerge.

निवास, *m.* an abode.

निवृत्ति, *f.* a 'turning away from', abstention, cessation.

नेत्र, *n.* a cord *or* rope (by which a churning-stick is made to turn). [*Literally* a 'leader *or* conductor', from √नी (नयति, class I) 'lead']

पुच्छ, *m.* a tail.

पुनःप्राप्ति, *f.* re-gaining.

पुरुष, *m.* soul *or* spirit.

प्रकृति, *f.* primal matter (as opposed to पुरुष 'soul *or* spirit').

प्रक्षिप्य, *gerund* प्र-√क्षिप् (क्षिपति, class VI), having cast *or* thrown away.

प्रचोदित, *ppp. of causative of* प्र-√चुद् (चोदति, class I), driven *or* pressed on, impelled, urged.

प्रतिज्ञाय, *gerund* प्रति-√ज्ञा (जानाति, class IX), having promised.

प्रथमम्, *adv.* firstly, first of all.

बृहत्, *adj.* lofty, high. [Etymologically a present active participle of √बृह् (बृहति, class VI) 'be strong *or* tall', which, like महत्, has lost its verbal character]

भुजंगम, *m.* a serpent. [*Literally* 'going in curves *or* coils (भुज)']

भ्रमण, *n.* turning around, revolution.

√मथ् *or* मन्थ् (मथति, -ते, class I), agitate, stir, churn (as a firestick to produce a fire, or a rod to make butter); *ppp.* मथित, *infin.* मथितुम्.

मन्थान, *m.* a churning-stick.

मन्दर, *m.* Mandara, the name of a sacred mountain.

मर्दन, *n.* crushing; grinding; friction.

महाभाग, *m.* eminent, illustrious; venerable. [*Literally* 'whose lot *or* portion is great', hence 'fortunate' etc.]

यन्त्र, *n.* a means *or* implement for holding, a prop.

√याच् (याचति, class I), ask someone (*acc.*) for something (*acc.*).

याच्ञा, *f.* a request.

योजन, *n.* a measure of distance, said to be about nine miles.

वर, *adj.* choice, excellent; *at end of tatpuruṣa cpd.* best of such-and-such, the best such-and-such.

वासुकि, *m.* Vāsuki; the name of the serpent-king used by the gods and demons when they churned the ocean.

विनष्ट, *ppp.* वि-√नश् (नश्यति, class IV), perished, come to naught.

विनाश, *m.* destruction.

वैकुण्ठ, *m.* Vaikuṇṭha, name of Viṣṇu's heaven.

शय्या, *f.* a bed *or* couch.

√शी (शेते, class II), recline, lie, sleep.

शैल, *m.* a mountain.

संवेष्टच, *gerund of causative of* सम्-√विष्ट् (वेष्टते, class I, 'wind oneself about'), 'having caused to wind itself about', having wound around.

सकल, *adj.* all.

संगृह्य, *gerund* सं-√ग्रह् (गृह्णाति, class IX), having gathered together.

समुच्छ्रित, *ppp.* सम्-उद्-√श्रि (श्रयति, class I), raised up, *hence* high.

समुद्र, *m.* the ocean, sea.

समेत, *ppp.* सम्-आ-√इ (एति, class II), come together with, joined with.

√सह् (सहते, class I), bear, endure, tolerate.
सहित, *adj.* united with *or* accompanied by (+ *instr.*).
सुर, *m.* a god.
स्थिति, *f.* 'standing', *hence,* staying or remaining in a condition, continued existence (of the universe, until its absorption).
स्थिर, *adj.* firm, steady.
स्थान, *n.* a place *or* spot.
हेतु, *m.* cause.

Translate into Sanskrit:

As soon as he heard the words of the gods, the grandsire of all the worlds said thus: 'Go for refuge unto the great lord, of mighty strength,[1] the blessed Viṣṇu, the cause of the origin, continuation and destruction[2] of all the worlds and source of primal matter and spirit!'[3] Thus addressed by the blessed Brahmā, the gods went to the abode of Viṣṇu called Vaikuṇṭha.[4] Worsted by demons and having lost their strength[5] due to the curse of the great sage Durvāsas, filled with extreme despair, the gods venerated the great lord and requested his help. When he heard their request, Viṣṇu told the gods what had to be done by them. 'In order to regain[6] your majesty and strength, you must churn[7] the great ocean for the Amṛta. First, having gathered all the herbs and cast them in that great ocean, then bring the mighty Mt. Mandara to the sea and having made that mountain a churning-stick and having made the great serpent called Vāsuki a cord, churn the great ocean!' Thus addressed by Viṣṇu, when Mt. Mandara had been lifted up with the help of the serpent called Anantaśeṣa and brought to that great ocean,[8] the gods having made a truce with the Daityas and Dānavas, after placing the mountain upon the back of Viṣṇu in the form of a tortoise, began to churn the ocean.

Notes

1. 'of mighty strength': Express by means of a bahuvrīhi.

2. 'the cause of the origin, continuation and destruction' is to be rendered by a tatpuruṣa in explanatory apposition to 'the blessed Viṣṇu'.

3. 'source of primal matter and spirit' similarly to be translated by a compound. Use समुद्भव, *m.* for 'source'.

4. 'called Vaikuṇṭha', as a bahuvrīhi, literally 'having V° as its name' or, as viewed from the usual analysis of Indian commentators, 'whose name is V°'. Use an identical type of compound for 'called Vāsuki' and 'called Anantaśeṣa' below.

5. 'having lost their strength': either बलक्षयगत (in the proper case, of course!) or बलक्षयं गत्वा.

6. 'In order to regain': Express by a 'dative of purpose'.

7. 'you must churn': an optative equivalent to a command.

8. 'when Mt. Mandara had been lifted up … and brought': Use a locative absolute construction for this 'when'-clause.

LESSON NINETEEN

The Future Tense.

In the various reading exercises we have had so far, there have occurred a number of examples of the future tense. These forms were briefly explained in the notes (for example, Lesson 11, note 3 and Lesson 18, note 7), but the matter needs now to be taken up formally.

The future tense is much less common in Sanskrit than in English. In Sanskrit the present tense is frequently used with future implication, provided that an event *soon to take place* is meant, not what is projected well beyond the immediate present. English too, employs the present tense in place of a *shall/will* future, but oddly enough only the *progressive* present forms, made with *am/is/are* in combination with the participle in *-ing,* are so used. These progressive forms may be used to express either immediate or even distant futurity; thus, 'I *am leaving* for home tonight', 'I *am going* to Paris next year'. Otherwise in English the auxiliary verbs *shall/will* before an infinitive without 'to' are used to express the future; thus 'I shall/will go'.

None of the Germanic languages, of which our English is one, has a formal future, that is, a single word made by attaching to a root an element denoting futurity. In Sanskrit, apart from the use of the present tense to express immediate futurity, there are two other means of expressing future time, one of which is a true future made, as just mentioned, by the addition of a special suffix to the root; the other is a combination form, peculiar to Sanskrit, which, because of its comparative rarity, may be left for consideration in a later lesson. The true Sanskrit future is formed from a verb root by the addition of the suffix *-sya* or *-iṣya.* Though some complicated rules may be given that help to determine which of these suffixes to use, it is a waste of time, at least at this juncture, for the student to learn them. The best procedure is quite simply to rely for the correct form on the experience gained from reading and to recognize a future from the presence of the suffixes *-sya* or *-iṣya.* The personal endings are *exactly the same* as those that were learned for the present active and middle. The only other point that need be noted here is that before both of these suffixes the root is usually strengthened by the substitution of guṇa for the root vowel. Thus, from √कृ 'do' , the guṇa of which is *kar-* (कर्), is made the future stem *kar-iṣya* (करिष्य), from √नी 'lead', the guṇa of which is *ne* (ने), the stem is *ne-ṣya* (नेष्य) (the change of *-s-* to *-ṣ-* is required after all vowels *except -a-* or *-ā-, cf.* the locatives देवेषु and सेनासु). These are the future active and middle of √कृ 'do':

Active

Singular		*Plural*	
1. *kar-iṣyā-mi*	(करिष्यामि)	1. *kar-iṣyā-maḥ*	(करिष्यामः)
2. *kar-iṣya-si*	(करिष्यसि)	2. *kar-iṣya-tha*	(करिष्यथ)
3. *kar-iṣya-ti*	(करिष्यति)	3. *kar-iṣy-anti*	(करिष्यन्ति)

Middle

1. *kar-iṣy-e*	(करिष्ये)	1. *kar-iṣyā-mahe*	(करिष्यामहे)
2. *kar-iṣya-se*	(करिष्यसे)	2. *kar-iṣya-dhve*	(करिष्यध्वे)
3. *kar-iṣya-te*	(करिष्यते)	3. *kar-iṣy-ante*	(करिष्यन्ते)

Note that the same rules apply here for the attachment of the endings as for the present: before *-m* the *-a* of *-iṣya* is lengthened, and when the ending begins with a vowel (like *-anti, -e,* etc.) the vowel of the stem is dropped.

Sentences Illustrating the Future Tense:

1. अस्य देशस्य सर्वान् एव द्विषो ऽवजित्य प्रजा मे धर्मानुरोधेन पालयिष्यामीति सूतो राज्ञा निर्वेदितः।
2. यद्य् अतीव वर्षिष्यति तदा ते ग्रामवासिनः स्वगृहेषु वत्स्यन्ति ।
3. समीपस्थे वने मृगयित्वा राजा प्रासादं प्रत्यागमिष्यति ।
4. तापसो बहूनि वर्षाण्य् उग्रतपांसि चरित्वा प्रेत्य मोक्षं प्राप्स्यति ।
5. यद् भविष्यति तद् भविष्यतीति चिन्तयित्वा त्यक्तजीविताः सैनिका युद्धं गच्छन्ति ।

III. The Churning of the Ocean

महोदधौ मथ्यमाने[1] तु धूमेनार्चिर्भिश्च मिश्रिता वाताः सर्पस्य मुखान् निर्गम्य विद्युत्समुपेता मेघाः[2] संभूय श्रमसंतापपरिश्रान्तान् देवान् अभ्यवर्षन् । देवासुरैर् भ्राम्यमानेन[3] गिरिणा विनिष्पिष्टा बहवो जलचराः पञ्चत्वं गताः । अपि च गिरेः शिखराद् विहगैर्

विहगकृतनीडैश्च सह महान्तो वृक्षाः समुद्रस्य जले न्यपतन् । परस्परं संघर्षणात् ते वृक्षा मुहुर्मुहुः प्रज्वलन्तः सर्वाणि पर्वतवासीनि सत्त्वान्य् अदहन् । जले निपतितेभ्यो द्रुमेभ्यो निर्गता नानाविधा निर्यासा महोदधौ च देवैर् विष्णोर् आदेशेन पूर्वं निक्षिप्तानां ओषधीनां विविधा रसाः समुद्रस्याम्भसि समस्रवन् । सर्वैस् तै रसैर् निर्यासैश्च तस्य सागरस्योदकं प्रथमं पय[4] एव संभूय ततो घृतं संभूतम् । परन्तु यद् अमृतं देवासुरैर् इष्टं तन् नोदभवत् । अमृतस्य लाभस्याशां त्यजन्तो देवा विष्णुं शरणं पुनः प्रापद्यन्त । तेषां श्रमं विषादं चावलोक्य महेश्वर इदं वचनं अवदत् । भवद्भ्यो हे देवा अधिकं बलं दास्यामि । महत्तरेण यत्नेन महागिरिं परिवर्तयेध्वम् । इत्युक्ता विष्णुनाधिकबलेन युक्ताश्च देवा दैत्यदानवैः सहिता मन्दरपर्वतं परिवर्तयितुं पुनर् आरब्धाः । तदनन्तरं सागराच् छीतांशुः सोमः[5] समुत्पन्नः । ततो देवी श्रीः[6] पाण्डुरवासिनी[7] घृताद् उद्गता । सुरा[8] देव्य् अपि श्वेत उच्चैःश्रवास्[9] तुरगश्च ततो विष्णोर् दिव्यो मणिः कौस्तुभं[10] समुदपद्यन्त । यत्र देवा अतिष्ठन् तत्र वासुकेः पुच्छसमीपं सोमः श्रीः सुरा देवी तुरगश्चागच्छन् । श्रीर् विष्णोर् भार्याभवत् । कौस्तुभं विष्णोर् उरसि गतम् । अन्ततो धन्वन्तरिनामा देवः[11] श्वेतं अमृतसंपूर्णं कमण्डलुं हस्तेन धारयन् समुद्राद् उत्थितः । अमृतं दृष्ट्वैवासुरैर् महान्तं नादं ममेदं इति[12] मुक्त्वामृतसंपूर्णकमण्डलुर् धन्वन्तरेर् हस्ताद् गृहीतः । तस्मिन् एव क्षणे विष्णुः स्वमाययातीव सुन्दर्या अप्सरसो रूपं कृत्वा तस्याश्चित्तहारिणा वपुषासुरान् अमोहयत् । तस्या अप्सरसो वपुषा वशीकृतमनसो ऽसुरास् तस्यै अमृतं मोहेनायच्छन् । तदाप्सरसो हस्ताद् अमृतं प्राप्य विष्णुना देवेभ्यः समर्पितं देवगणाश्च झटिति तद् ईप्सितं अमृतं अपिबन् । अमृतं पिबत्सु देवेषु[13] राहुनामा दानवो ऽपि देवस्य रूपं कृत्वा चन्द्रमसं सूर्यं च वर्जयित्वान्यैर् अदृष्टो ऽमृतं अपिबत् । तस्य राहोः कण्ठं अनुप्राप्ते ऽमृते[14] तदा देवानां हितकाम्यया चन्द्रमसा सूर्येण चाख्यातम् ।

तच्छ्रुत्वैवामृतं पिबतस्तस्य दानवस्य शिरो विष्णुना चक्रेणावच्छिन्नम् । परन्तु तस्य राहोः शिरः पृथिवीतलं निपत्य पीतस्यामृतस्य प्रभावेनामरत्वं गतम् । ततश् चन्द्रमसे सूर्याय च क्रुद्धेन राहुणा शाश्वतं वैरं द्वन्द्वेन सह कृतं अद्यापि च चन्द्रमसं सूर्यं च गगने ग्रसते[15] । तस्मिन् एव काले ऽम्भसः समीपे दानवानां देवानां चातिमहान् संग्रामः प्रवृत्तः । अस्मिन् महति युद्धे विष्णुनासुरा रुधिरावलिप्ताङ्गा बलवता सुदर्शननाम्ना चक्रेण सहस्रशो निहताः । पराजिताः केचिद् असुराः सागरं केचित् तु महीं प्रविष्टाः । ततो विजयं अवाप्य देवा मन्दरपर्वतं स्वं एव देशं गमयित्वा तं मुदितात्मनापूजयन् ।

Notes

1. मथ्यमाने present passive participle of √मथ् in a locative absolute construction with महोदधौ; thus, 'Now (तु) while the great ocean was being churned'. Note that as the counterpart of the present active participle, the time sphere is contemporaneous with the main verb, so that the 'being churned' takes place at the same time as the falling of the rain expressed by अभिवर्षन्.

2. मेघाः to be taken predicatively with संभूय, thus, 'having become clouds'.

3. भ्राम्यमानेन present passive participle (as मथ्यमाने above) from the causative of √भ्रम् (भ्रमति, class I or भ्राम्यति, class IV), 'cause to move in circular fashion', rotate, turn.

4. पय (*i.e.,* पयः), like मेघाः above, to be taken predicatively with संभूय; thus, 'The water of the ocean first having become milk alone (एव), then became butter'.

5. शीतांशुः सोमः 'The moon whose rays are cool'. In its earliest usage सोम means a certain plant, very probably the mushroom *Amanita Muscaria L.,* whence was extracted a hallucinogenic drink also called soma, to which 120 hymns of the Ṛgveda are devoted. In the post-Ṛgvedic period soma comes to

be identified with the moon (the 'lord of herbs and plants', ओषधीपति), the meaning in this passage. The moon is often said to be 'cool-rayed' in Indian literature, and this epithet शीतांशु and other synonymous words are later used as nouns in the sense of 'moon'.

6. श्री: Śrī is an alternative name of Lakṣmī, the goddess of beauty and fortune.

7. पाण्डुरवासिनी The final member of this accusative tatpuruṣa compound means 'wearing' and is unrelated to the -वासिन् in पर्वतवासीनि '(creatures) dwelling in the mountain', which occurs above; the two -वासिन्'s are from separate homonymous roots: √वस् (वसति, class I), 'dwell, abide' and √वस् (वस्ते, class II), 'wear'.

8. सुरा Ordinarily this word means some sort of spirituous liquor, but here, as a product of the churning, it is personified as a goddess, the wife of Varuṇa, also called Varuṇānī. Though all the many versions of the churning of the ocean mention Surā as one of the products, the appropriateness of her appearance is not easily explained.

9. उच्चैःश्रवास् This horse, Uccaiḥśravas, is said to be the model or prototype of all horses. The name, like many proper names, is really an epithet, the interpretation of which, however, is not without dispute: according to some it means 'long-eared' (literally 'whose ears are on high'), according to others 'sounding *or* neighing loudly' (literally 'whose sounds are on high'). This divarication of opinion is due to the fact that श्रवस् may mean 'sound' ('what is heard' from √श्रु 'hear') or the 'ear' ('the hearer').

10. कौस्तुभं As the text itself tells us, this was Viṣṇu's divine jewel. We shall see subsequently that it becomes an adornment of his chest.

11. धन्वन्तरिनामा देव: 'The god named Dhanvantari'; he was regarded as the physician of the gods and the founder of Indian medicine.

12. ममेदम् इति The इति indicates that मम इदम् ('It's mine!') are the exact words of the roar (नादं) the demons emitted, the moment they saw the Amṛta in the cup held by Dhanvantari.

13. पिबत्सु देवेषु locative absolute expressing the circumstance in which the demon Rāhu was able to drink some of the Amṛta.

14. तस्य राहोः कण्ठं अनुप्राप्ते ऽमृते locative absolute again! The Amṛta drunk by Rāhu had hardly gotten to his throat, when the Sun and the Moon mentioned it to the other gods.

15. In this way are explained the eclipses of the sun and the moon. Rāhu thus wreaks eternal vengeance upon them.

Vocabulary

अङ्ग, *n.* limb; body.

अतीव, *adv.* exceedingly, very.

अधिक, *adj.* additional, extra.

अनुप्राप्त, *ppp.* अनु-प्र-√आप् (आप्नोति, class V), (having) gone up to *or* reached.

अन्ततः, *adv.* in the end, finally.

अनुरोध, *m.* regard, concern; *at end of cpd. in instr.* with regard to, in accordance with.

अभि-√वृष् (वर्षति, class I), rain upon.

अम्भस्, *n.* water.

अर्चिस्, *n.* a flame.

अवच्छिन्न, *ppp.* अव-√छिद् (छिनत्ति, class VII), (having been) cut off.

अवजित्य, *gerund* अव-√जि (जयति, class I), having conquered.

अवलिप्त, *ppp.* अव-√लिप् (लिम्पति, class VI), (having been) smeared.

अवलोक्य, *gerund* अव-√लोक् (लोकयति, class X), having seen *or* perceived.

अवाप्य, *gerund* अव-√आप् (आप्नोति, class V), having attained *or* gained.

आख्यात, *ppp.* आ-√ख्या (ख्याति, class II), (having been) told, mentioned.

आदेश, *m.* order, command.

आशा, *f.* hope.

ईप्सित, *ppp. of desiderative* √आप् (आप्नोति, class V), sought after, desired.

उग्र, *adj.* mighty, severe.

उच्चैःश्रवस्, *m.* Uccaiḥśravas, the name of a horse, prototype of all horses.

उत्थित, *ppp.* उद्-√स्था (तिष्ठति, class I), 'having stood forth (उद्)', arisen.

उद्-√भू (भवति, class I), rise up.

उरस्, *n.* the chest (of the body).

कण्ठ, *m.* the throat.
कमण्डलु, *m.* a pitcher *or* water-jar.
कौस्तुभ, *n.* Kaustubha, the name of a jewel worn by Viṣṇu on his chest.
क्रुद्ध, *ppp.* √क्रुध् (क्रुध्यति, class IV), angered at (+ *dat.*).
गगन, *n.* the sky, heaven.
गमयित्वा, *gerund of caus.* √गम् (गच्छति, class I), 'having caused to go'; having transferred.
गृहीत, *ppp.* √ग्रह् (गृह्णाति, class IX), taken.
√ग्रस् (ग्रसते, class I), swallow.
ग्रामवासिन्, *m.* an inhabitant of a village.
घृत, *n.* clarified butter, ghee.
चक्र, *n.* a wheel; a discus, the circular weapon of Viṣṇu.
चन्द्रमस्, *m.* the moon.
चित्तहारिन्, *adj.* mind- *or* heart-captivating.
जलचर, *m.* 'water-goer', any aquatic animal.
झटिति, *adv.* instantly, at once [one of the very few words beginning with झ्].
तल, *m.* or *n.* the surface (of anything); *often used redundantly at the end of a compound.*
तुरग, *m.* a horse.
त्यक्तजीवित, *adj.* 'having abandoned *or* given up life', at the risk of life.
√त्यज् (त्यजति, class I), give up, abandon.
√दह् (दहति, class I), burn.
द्रुम, *m.* a tree.
द्वन्द्व, *n.* a pair *or* couple.
द्विष्, *m.* an enemy.
धन्वन्तरि, *m.* Dhanvantari, the name of the physician of the gods.
धूम, *m.* smoke.
√धृ (धारयति, class X), hold.
नानाविध, *adj.* of various kinds.
नि-√पत् (पतति, class I), fall down; *ppp.* निपतित.
निर्यास, *m.* exudation, resin (from trees).
निर्वेदित, *ppp. of caus.* निस्- 1√विद् (वेत्ति, class II), (having been) informed.
निहत, *ppp.* नि-√हन् (हन्ति, class II), (having been) struck down *or* slain.
नीड, *m.* or *n.* a nest.

पयस्, *n.* milk.

परस्परम्, *adv.* mutually.

पराजित, *ppp.* परा-√जि (जयते, class I), (having been) conquered.

परि-√वृत् (वर्तते, class I), turn around (*intrans.*); *caus.* परिवर्तयते, 'causes to turn around', rotates, churns; *infin.* परिवर्तयितुम्.

पर्वतवासिन्, *adj.* dwelling in the mountain.

परिश्रान्त, *ppp.* परि-√श्रम् (श्राम्यति, class IV), become completely (परि) weary, fatigued.

पाण्डुरवासिन्, *adj.* wearing a white (garment).

√पालय, (पालयति, denom. verb from पाल 'protector', *hence literally* 'be a protector of', protect), *fut.* पालयिष्यति.

पूर्वम्, *adv.* previously, before.

प्र-√आप् (आप्नोति, class V), attain.

प्रजा, *f.* *(in plur.)* the subjects of a king.

प्र-√ज्वल् (ज्वलति, class I), begin to blaze, burst into flames.

प्रविष्ट, *ppp.* प्र-√विश्)विशति, class VI), (having) entered.

प्रवृत्त, *ppp.* प्र-√वृत् (वर्तते, class I), rolled *or* moved forward; occurred, happened *or* taken place.

प्राप्य, *gerund* प्र-√आप् (आप्नोति, class V), having gotten *or* obtained.

प्रेत्य, *gerund* प्र-√इ (एति, class II), *literally*, 'having gone forth *or* away (प्र)', *i.e.,* having died *or* after death.

मणि, *m.* a gem *or* a jewel.

महत्तर, *adj.* greater (*comparative of* महत्).

माया, *f.* supernatural *or* magical power.

मिश्रित, *adj.* mixed.

मुक्त्वा, *gerund* √मुच् (मुञ्चति, class VI), having released, emitted *or* let go.

मुदित, *ppp.* √मुद् (मोदते, class I), glad, joyful.

√मुह् (मुह्यति, class IV), be confused, lose one's senses; *caus.* मोहयति, 'causes someone to be confused *or* lose his senses', *hence,* deceives, tricks.

मुहुर्मुहुः, *adv.* again and again, repeatedly.

मृगयित्वा, *gerund* √मृगय (मृगयते, a denom. verb), having hunted.

मेघ, *m.* a cloud.

मोह, *m.* confusion, loss of one's senses; bewilderment, delusion.

यत्न, *m.* effort.

युक्त, *ppp.* √युज् (युनक्ति, class VII), joined *or* provided with (+ *instr.*).
रस, *m.* juice *or* essence.
रुधिर, *n.* blood.
लाभ, *m.* getting, acquiring.
वपुस्, *n.* beauty.
वर्जयित्वा, *gerund of caus.* √वृज् (वृणक्ति, class VII), 'having turned away from *or* excluded'; excluding, with the exception of (*i.e.*, as a virtual postposition).
वर्ष, *n.* a year.
वशीकृत, *ppp.* वशी-√कृ (वशीकरोति, class VIII), (having been) made submissive, brought under one's control; controlled, subdued.
√वस् (वसति, class I), abide, stay; *fut.* वत्स्यति (with substitution of -त् for -स् before the future suffix).
वात, *m.* wind.
विजय, *m.* conquest.
विद्युत्, *f.* lightning.
विनिष्पिष्ट, *ppp.* वि-निस्-√पिष् (पिनष्टि, class VII), crushed to bits; (note change of -स् of निस् to -ष् by sandhi; as in अग्निषु from *अग्निसु).
विविध, *adj.* various.
विषाद, *m.* dejection.
√वृष् (वर्षति, class I), rain.
वैर, *m.* enmity, hostility.
शाश्वत, *adj.* continual, eternal.
शिखर, *n.* top, pinnacle.
शीतांशु, *adj.* having cool (शीत) rays (अंशु), *said of the moon.*
श्रम, *m.* fatigue, weariness.
श्री, *f.* light, lustre, splendor; beauty; personified as the name of the goddess of beauty and welfare, also called Lakṣmī.
श्वेत, *adj.* white.
संग्राम, *m.* battle; war.
संघर्षण, *n.* rubbing together, friction.
सत्त्व, *n.* a (living) being, creature.
संताप, *m.* heat, fire; pain, distress.
समर्पित, *ppp. of caus.* सम्-√ऋ (ऋच्छति, class VI), given.
समीपस्थ, *adj.* 'situated in the vicinity', nearby.

समुत्पन्न, *ppp.* सम्-उद्-√पद् (पद्यते, class IV), gone forth, arisen; (note change of -द् of उद् to -त् by 'regressive assimilation').

समुपेत, *ppp.* सम्-उप-√इ (एति, class II), joined *or* provided with (+ *instr.*).

संपूर्ण, *adj.* completely full.

संभूत, *ppp.* सम्-√भू (भवति, class I), having become.

संभूय *gerund* सम्-√भू (भवति, class I, *literally* 'be together', *then* 'take form', become, arise), having become; *ppp.* संभूत.

सम्-√स्रु (स्रवति, class I), flow together.

सहस्रशः, *adv.* by the thousands.

सागर, *m.* the ocean, sea.

सुदर्शन, *n.* Sudarśana, name of Viṣṇu's discus.

सुन्दर, *adj.* (सुन्दरी, *f.*), beautiful.

सुरा, *f.* spirituous liquor; Surā, name of a goddess, also called Varuṇāṇī.

सोम, *m.* the moon.

सैनिक, *m.* a soldier.

हितकाम्या, *f.* desire for (another's) welfare.

Translate into Sanskrit:

Now while the great ocean was being churned[1] by the gods and the Asuras, many trees fell down into the water from the top of the mountain. Moreover, resins that came from those trees[2] were mixed[3] with the essences of the herbs previously cast in the sea by the gods. All this, flowing[4] in the water of the sea, first became milk, then butter. When the Amṛta which was desired by the gods and the Daityas and Dānavas did not come forth, (then) the gods, having gone to despair, giving up hope of getting the Amṛta, again went to Viṣṇu[5] for help[6]. After receiving additional strength from Viṣṇu, the gods with greater effort once again rotated[7] Mt. Mandara together with the Asuras. Thereupon many things gradually came forth from the sea of butter. Finally, the physician of the gods Dhanvantari, bearing in his hand a pitcher full of the Amṛta, stood up from the great ocean. While the gods were drinking the Amṛta,[8] a Dānava named Rāhu,[9] who had assumed[10] the form of a god, unseen by the other gods except the sun and the moon, drank the Amṛta. At that very instant, by Viṣṇu, having been informed[11] by the sun and the moon regarding the matter,[12] Rāhu's head was cut off with his discus called Sudarśana. But because[13] the Amṛta actually drunk[14] by Rāhu had reached his throat, (therefore) his head became immortal. As a result due to his anger at the sun and the moon Rāhu formed eternal hatred with the pair and even today swallows the sun and the moon in the sky.

Notes

1. Use the locative absolute.

2. 'that came from those trees': Use the *ppp.* of निस्-√गम् and for the sake of variation use the synonym द्रुम (*m.*) 'tree' instead of वृक्ष.

3. 'mixed': मिश्रित in the appropriate form.

4. Note that 'flowing' is a present participle, to be formed from √स्रु (स्रवति, class I).

5. 'to Viṣṇu': Use समीपम् with the genitive of Viṣṇu.

6. The purpose ('for') is best expressed by अर्थम् as the terminal member of a compound.

7. 'rotated': Use परिवर्तयति (causative of परि-√वृत्) in the imperfect. Remember that the augment comes before the verb, not before the prefix!

8. 'While the gods were drinking the Amṛta': What construction is to be used here?

9. 'named Rāhu': Use a bahuvrīhi compound, as also below for 'called Sudarśana'.

10. 'who had assumed': Do not use a relative clause, but simply a gerund, literally 'having assumed'.

11. 'having been informed': निवेदित *ppp.* of the causative stem नि-वेदय in the instrumental singular to modify 'by Viṣṇu'.

12. 'regarding the matter': either उद्दिश्य or अधिकृत्य with अर्थम् as object.

13. 'because': यस्मात् कारणात् (etc.) तस्मात् ('therefore').

14. 'actually drunk': Use the ubiquitous emphatic particle एव after 'drunk'.

LESSON TWENTY

The Dual and the Numeral द्व 'two'.
The Declensions of अहम् 'I' and त्वम् 'you'.

I. *The Dual and the Numeral द्व 'two'.*

In addition to a singular and plural of nouns, adjectives and verbs, Sanskrit also has a dual, treatment of which has so far been omitted because it is on the whole not very common, and therefore a consideration of it could be postponed until commoner and more important features of the language had been presented. As the name indicates, the dual is used when two persons or things are involved. Thus, 'two kings' and 'two books', also things occurring in pairs like the 'eyes, ears' etc. (whether the number 'two' is expressed or not!) are expressed by nouns with dual, *not* plural, endings. Also adjectives qualifying these dual nouns must be supplied with appropriate dual endings for case and gender, and the verbs of which these nouns are subject must have dual endings.

Although the dual is inflected in all eight cases, there are only four different endings, which entails considerable ambiguity, the same ending having to do duty for more than one case. The endings are:

	Masculine & Feminine	*Neuter*
Nom.	*-au* (-औ)	*-ī* (-ई)
Acc.	"	"
Voc.	"	"
Instr.	*-bhyām* (-भ्याम्)	
Dat.	"	
Abl.	"	
Gen.	*-oḥ* (-ओः)	
Loc.	"	

These are the invariable endings for all the *consonant* stems. With a few exceptions, the endings are also the same for the vowel stems. As will be pointed out subsequently, some changes take place in the final vowels of vowel stems when the endings are added. Because of these irregularities, it will be easier to take up the duals of consonant stems first, where the endings are uniformly the same for all the declensional types and are added without change in the stem final, except as required by sandhi.

1. Consonant Stems.

Where distinctions of strong and weak stems are made, the nominative, accusative and vocative of masculine and feminine[1] stems are strong cases, the rest weak. When three distinctions are made (strong, middle and weakest), the ending *-bhyām,* which like *-bhiḥ, -bhyaḥ* and *-su* of the plural, is a 'middle' ending, is, of course, added to the middle stem. In neuters the nominative, accusative and vocative are weak when the twofold distinction is made, otherwise weakest. The remaining cases are treated like the masculine and feminine stems. Herewith are examples of the dual inflection of unchangeable and changeable stems.

i. *Unchangeable Stems*

	vāc, f. 'word'	*dviṣ, m.* 'enemy'	*yaśas, n.* 'glory'
Nom.	*vāc-au* (वाचौ)	*dviṣ-au* (द्विषौ)	*yaśas-ī* (यशसी)
Acc.	"	"	"
Voc.	"	"	"
Instr.	*vāg-bhyām* (वाग्भ्याम्)	*dviḍ-bhyām* (द्विड्भ्याम्)	*yaśo-bhyām* (यशोभ्याम्)
Dat.	"	"	"
Abl.	"	"	"
Gen.	*vāc-oḥ* (वाचोः)	*dviṣ-oḥ* (द्विषोः)	*yaśas-oḥ* (यशसोः)
Loc.	"	"	"

[1]But feminine changeable stems hardly exist, and these are declined like the masculine; *e.g., sīman* (सीमन्) 'border'. Feminine adjectives of changeable stems are made by adding *-ī* to the weak or weakest stem and declining them like नदी.

ii. *Changeable Stems*

a) Two Stems

	bhavat, pres. part. √*bhū,* 'being'		*rūpavat, adj.* 'beautiful'	
	Masculine	*Neuter*	*Masculine*	*Neuter*
Nom.	**bhavant-au* (भवन्तौ)	*bhavat-ī* (भवती)	**rūpavant-au* (रूपवन्तौ)	*rūpavat-ī* (रूपवती)
Acc.	"	"	"	"
Voc.	"	"	"	"
Instr.	*bhavad-bhyām* (भवद्भ्याम्)		*rūpavad-bhyām* (रूपवद्भ्याम्)	
Dat.	"		"	
Abl.	"		"	
Gen.	*bhavat-oḥ* (भवतोः)		*rūpavat-oḥ* (रूपवतोः)	
Loc.	"		"	

	dhanin,[2] *adj.* 'having wealth'	
	Masculine	*Neuter*
Nom.	*dhanin-au* (धनिनौ)	*dhanin-ī* (धनिनी)
Acc.	"	"
Voc.	"	"
Instr.	*dhani-bhyām* (धनिभ्याम्)	
Dat.	"	
Abl.	"	
Gen.	*dhanin-oḥ* (धनिनोः)	
Loc.	"	

[2]*dhanin* and other formations of this type in *-in* do not, strictly speaking, have strong and weak forms; the rule here is simply that the *-n* drops out before consonant endings.

b) Three Stems

	rājan, m. 'king'	*brahman, m.* 'priest'	*nāman, n.* 'name'
Nom.	**rājān-au* (राजानौ)	**brahmāṇ-au* (ब्रह्माणौ)	*nāmn-ī* (नाम्नी)
Acc.	"	"	"
Voc.	"	"	"
Instr.	*rāja-bhyām* (राजभ्याम्)	*brahma-bhyām* (ब्रह्मभ्याम्)	*nāma-bhyām* (नामभ्याम्)
Dat.	"	"	"
Abl.	"	"	"
Gen.	*rājñ-oḥ* (राज्ञोः)	*brahmaṇ-oḥ* (ब्रह्मणोः)	*nāmn-oḥ* (नाम्नोः)
Loc.	"	"	"

2. Vowel Stems.

For nouns of the *deva* (देव), *nadī* (नदी), *vadhū* (वधू) types the endings are the same as those given. When *-au* is added to *deva,* the *-a* is fused with *-au,* yielding *devau* (देवौ). The final vowel of *deva* is lengthened before *-bhyām;* thus, *devā-bhyām* (देवाभ्याम्), and *-a* is changed to *-ay* before *-oḥ;* thus, *devay-oḥ* (देवयोः). The *phala* (फल) type requires the neuter termination *-ī* in the nominative, accusative and vocative, which contracts with the final *-a* to yield *phale* (फले). The remaining cases, as always with neuters of all numbers, are the same as the masculine, *viz., phalā-bhyām* (फलाभ्याम्), *phalay-oḥ* (फलयोः).

Nouns of the *nadī* (नदी) and *vadhū* (वधू) types change *-ī* and *-ū* to the semivowels *-y* and *-v* respectively before *-au* and *-oḥ;* thus, *nady-au* (नद्यौ), *nady-oḥ* (नद्योः), *vadhv-au* (वध्वौ), and *vadhv-oḥ* (वध्वोः). Feminines in *-ā* have *-e* in the nominative, accusative and vocative, but are otherwise like *deva* (देव) and *phala* (फल); thus, *sen-e* (सेने), *senā-bhyām* (सेनाभ्याम्), *senay-oḥ* (सेनयोः). Finally, masculine nouns in *-i* and *-u* simply lengthen these vowels in the nominative, accusative and vocative and change them to semi-vowels before *-oḥ;* thus, *agnī* (अग्नी)/*bhānū* (भानू), *agni-bhyām* (अग्निभ्याम्)/*bhānu-bhyām* (भानुभ्याम्), *agny-oḥ* (अग्न्योः)/*bhānv-oḥ* (भान्वोः).

The following tables repeat all these forms for comparative reference:

	deva, m. 'god'	*phala, n.* 'fruit'	*senā, f.* 'army'
Nom.	*devau* (देवौ)	*phale* (फले)	*sen-e* (सेने)
Acc.	"	"	"
Voc.	"	"	"
Instr.	*devā-bhyām* (देवाभ्याम्)	*phalā-bhyām* (फलाभ्याम्)	*senā-bhyām* (सेनाभ्याम्)
Dat.	"	"	"
Abl.	"	"	"
Gen.	*devay-oḥ* (देवयोः)	*phalay-oḥ* (फलयोः)	*senay-oḥ* (सेनयोः)
Loc.	"	"	"

	agni, m. 'fire'	*bhānu, m.* 'sun'	*nadī, f.* 'river'	*vadhū, f.* 'woman'
Nom.	*agnī* (अग्नी)	*bhānū* (भानू)	*nady-au* (नद्यौ)	*vadhv-au* (वध्वौ)
Acc.	"	"	"	"
Voc.	"	"	"	"
Instr.	*agni-bhyām* (अग्निभ्याम्)	*bhānu-bhyām* (भानुभ्याम्)	*nadī-bhyām* (नदीभ्याम्)	*vadhū-bhyām* (वधूभ्याम्)
Dat.	"	"	"	"
Abl.	"	"	"	"
Gen.	*agny-oḥ* (अग्न्योः)	*bhānv-oḥ* (भान्वोः)	*nady-oḥ* (नद्योः)	*vadhv-oḥ* (वध्वोः)
Loc.	"	"	"	"

Although the idea of duality can be expressed by the use of the dual number, sometimes the numeral द्व 'two' is included to underline the notion. The declension of द्व conforms entirely to our expectations and is exclusively in the dual! Differentiation of gender is seen only in the nom./acc., where it conforms to the types देव/सेना/फल, hence द्वौ, द्वे, द्वे exactly like देवौ, सेने, फले. Thus.

	Masculine	*Feminine*	*Neuter*
Nom.	द्वौ	द्वे	द्वे
Acc.	द्वौ	द्वे	द्वे
Instr.		द्वाभ्याम्	
Dat.		द्वाभ्याम्	
Abl.		द्वाभ्याम्	
Gen.		द्वयोः	
Loc.		द्वयोः	

3. Duals of Verb Forms.

The dual forms of the verb are made by adding the dual endings for the three persons directly to the tense stem. The usual rules are followed in applying the personal terminations to the stem. Thus, before *-v* the vowel *-a* is lengthened, as in *bhavā-vaḥ* 'we two are', and before an ending beginning with a vowel, the final vowel of the stem is dropped, as in *bhav-ethe* 'you two are'. The endings are:

Primary

	Active	Middle
1.	*-vaḥ* (-वः)	*-vahe* (-वहे)
2.	*-thaḥ* (-थः)	*-ethe* (-एथे)
3.	*-taḥ* (-तः)	*-ete* (एते)

Secondary

1.	*-va* (-व)	*-vahi* (-वहि)
2.	*-tam* (-तम्)	*-ethām* (-एथाम्)
3.	*-tām* (-ताम्)	*-etām* (-एताम्)

Below are the dual forms of the present, imperfect and optative, active and middle of √*bhū* (*bhavati,* class I) 'be, become':

Present

	Active	Middle
1.	*bhavā-vaḥ* (भवावः)	*bhavā-vahe* (भवावहे)
2.	*bhava-thaḥ* (भवथः)	*bhav-ethe* (भवेथे)
3.	*bhava-taḥ* (भवतः)	*bhav-ete* (भवेते)

Imperfect

	Active	Middle
1.	*a-bhavā-va* (अभवाव)	*a-bhavā-vahi* (अभवावहि)
2.	*a-bhava-tam* (अभवतम्)	*a-bhav-ethām* (अभवेथाम्)
3.	*a-bhava-tām* (अभवताम्)	*a-bhav-etām* (अभवेताम्)

Optative

	Active	Middle
1.	*bhave-va* (भवेव)	*bhave-vahi* (भवेवहि)
2.	*bhave-tam* (भवेतम्)	*bhave-y-āthām* (भवेयाथाम्)
3.	*bhave-tām* (भवेताम्)	*bhave-y-ātām* (भवयेताम्)

It may be worth noting, as a sort of mnemonic device, that the endings of the *second* person tend to have an aspirated dental, whereas the unaspirated dental occurs in the third person: *-thaḥ/-taḥ, -ethe/-ete, -ethām/-etām;* only in *-tam/-tām* is this distinction not found.

II. *Pronouns of the First and Second Person.*

As has been observed before, when a first or second person pronoun occurs as the subject of a verb, it is generally omitted, as the verb endings suffice to make the pronominal reference clear. The nominative of these pronouns is generally expressed only when there is contrast between the persons (I ~ you, you ~ he, etc.) or where special emphasis on the person is required; thus, अहं तत् फलं काङ्क्षामि '*I* want that fruit'. Often in this latter instance, the particle एव is added to underline or italicize (so to speak!) the foregoing word: अहमेव तत् फलं काङ्क्षामि.

While the nominative is not so much used, then, the other cases occur with reasonable frequency. Forms of the singular of अहम् and त्वम् have often occurred in the reading lessons. Now the complete declensions of these pronouns in all the three numbers are presented.

1. अहम् 'I'

	Singular	*Dual*	*Plural*
Nom.	अहम्	आवाम्	वयम्
Acc.	माम् (मा)	आवाम् (नौ)	अस्मान् (नः)
Instr.	मया	आवाभ्याम्	अस्माभिः
Dat.	मह्यम् (मे)	आवाभ्याम् (नौ)	अस्मभ्यम् (नः)
Abl.	मद्	आवाभ्याम्	अस्मद्
Gen.	मम (मे)	आवयोः (नौ)	अस्माकम् (नः)
Loc.	मयि	आवयोः	अस्मासु

2. त्वम् 'You'

	Singular	*Dual*	*Plural*
Nom.	त्वम्	युवाम्	यूयम्
Acc.	त्वाम् (त्वा)	युवाम् (वाम्)	युष्मान् (वः)
Instr.	त्वया	युवाभ्याम्	युष्माभिः
Dat.	तुभ्यम् (ते)	युवाभ्याम् (वाम्)	युष्मभ्यम् (वः)
Abl.	त्वद्	युवाभ्याम्	युष्मद्
Gen.	तव (ते)	युवयोः (वाम्)	युष्माकम् (वः)
Loc.	त्वयि	युवयोः	युष्मासु

Note that in the accusative, dative and genitive of all numbers of both pronouns alternative forms are given in parentheses. These forms in parentheses can be substituted for the other forms *only* if they are not put first in the sentence. The reason for this is that they are without accent of their own and, unable to stand on their own legs, so to speak, they 'lean on' the preceding word for support. Hence, they are called 'enclitic', a word of

Greek origin meaning literally 'leaning on'. We have already had some enclitics, though this technical term has not been applied to them; thus, the conjunctions च 'and' and वा 'or' and also the terminal element चिद् used after the interrogative pronoun किम् to form an indefinite, for example, किंचिद् 'something', कश्चिद् 'someone'. The enclitic forms of the first and second person pronouns are commoner than the accented forms and therefore need especially to be learned.

I. The Story of Sagara and His Sons

The story of Sagara, King of Ayodhyā, and his 60,000 sons, forms part of an extensive myth, which, among other things, involves the descent of the Ganges (Gaṅgā) from heaven to earth and subsequently also to the nether world. The story is told, with variations, in the Mahābhārata, the Rāmāyaṇa and some of the Purāṇas. The condensed version presented below and continued in succeeding lessons is based on that contained in the Rāmāyaṇa.

Indian authors are fond of playing with etymologies, especially of proper names, and it is interesting to note that, among the events antecedent to the narrative below, there is a story that turns on the etymology of the name 'Sagara'. The story is told that, when Sagara's mother was pregnant with him, her rival in the king's affections gave her a poison (गर) designed to prevent the delivery of her child. The child's birth was as a result delayed for seven years, and when he was born, he was given the name 'Sagara', literally 'with poison' (स 'with' + गर 'poison'), because he was born 'with the poison' or drug that had been administered to his mother.

पूर्वस्मिन् काले सगरो नामायोध्याया राजासीत् । स नराधिपो धर्मात्मा सर्वगुणयुक्तो ऽभवत् । तस्य द्वे पत्न्यौ अभवतां एका केशिनी नाम विदर्भराजस्य सुता द्वितीया सुमतिर् नामारिष्टनेमेः सुता । प्रजाकामो ऽपि स राजाप्रजो ऽभवत्[1] । ततः प्रजार्थं परमं यत्नं कुर्वन्[2] भार्याभ्यां सह स महाराजो हिमवन्तं गत्वा दीर्घं तप आचरत् । अथ वर्षशते संपूर्णे सति[3] तत्र वसन् महर्षिर् भृगुर् नाम तेन तपसाराधितस् तस्मै सगराय वरं अयच्छत् । स मुनिस् तं इदं वचो ऽवदत् । सुमहान्

अपत्यलाभस् तव भविष्यति । अपि चाप्रतिमं यशो ऽस्मिन् लोके प्राप्स्यसे । एका पत्नी वंशकरं पुत्रं जनिष्यत्य् अपरा तु षष्टिं पुत्रसहस्राण्य् उत्पादयिष्यति । इत्येतास् तस्य मुनेर् वाचः श्रुत्वैव ते भार्ये विलम्बेन विना तं अपृच्छतां कावयोर्[4] एकं यशस्विनं वंशकरं पुत्रं का षष्टिं पुत्रसहस्राणि जनिष्यति । तज् ज्ञातुं इच्छावहे । वचस् ते मुने सत्यं स्याद् इति । तयोस् तद् वचनं श्रुत्वा स भृगुः प्रत्यभाषत । का वां कं वरं इच्छति[5] । स्वच्छन्दो ऽत्र वर्तते[6] । यद् इच्छेथे तद् भविष्यतीति । तच्छ्रुत्वा केशिन्या ज्येष्ठ सगरपत्न्यैको वंशकरः पुत्रो गृहीतो ऽन्यया पत्न्या सुमत्या षष्टिः पुत्रसहस्राणि गृहीतानि । प्रदक्षिणं[7] तं ऋषिं कृत्वा शिरसा च प्रणम्य स सगरो भार्याभ्यां सह स्वनगरं प्रत्यागच्छत् । अथ काले संपूर्णे सति केशिन्यां एकः पुत्रो ऽसमञ्ज इति ख्यातो ऽजायत । सुमत्यां तु गर्भतुम्बो[8] ऽजायत । तस्माद् गर्भतुम्बान्[9] निर्भिन्नात् षष्टिः पुत्रसहस्राणि विनिःसृतानि । कालेन गच्छता षष्टिः पुत्रसहस्राणि रूपयौवनं प्रत्यपद्यत । एकस्मिन् दिने ऽसमञ्जो दुरात्मा सर्वगुणरहितश्च सन्[10] सुमत्याः पुत्रान् गृहीत्वा सरय्वा नद्या जले प्रक्षिप्य तत्र मज्जतस् तान् पश्यन् प्राहसत् । किन्तु ते सगरस्य सुता नाम्रियन्त[11] । तदनन्तरं यस्माद् अयं असमञ्जः सर्वेषां पौराणां अप्य् अहिते युक्तस् तस्मात् सगरेण पुरान्[12] निर्वासितः ।

Notes

1. It is ubiquitous in Sanskrit literature that a virtuous king, like Sagara in this context, is without progeny. Since a son is needed to continue the family line and furnish a successor in the kingship as well as to perform the funeral ceremony, a childless king is bound to expend whatever efforts may be required to obtain a son. These efforts may entail the performance of various religious ceremonies and also austerities of frequently severe and prolonged character, usually culminating in the granting of a boon, as here by the sage Bhṛgu. Note here that राजाप्रजो is a coalescence of राजा अप्रजः.

2. The present third plural active of √कृ (करोति, class VIII) is कुर्वन्ति. Hence, by dropping the final vowel we obtain कुर्वन्त्, the strong stem of the present active participle, the weak being obtained by dropping the nasal; so कुर्वत्. The form कुर्वन् here is nominative masculine singular from कुर्वन्त्स्, the त् and स् of which have to be dropped because of the rule that a Sanskrit word may not (usually!) end in more than one consonant.

3. सति is locative singular neuter of the present participle of √अस् (अस्ति 'be', class II), the third plural of which being सन्ति, the weak stem is सत् (without the nasal). The construction here is locative absolute, and सति, which could have been omitted as संपूर्ण is itself a participle, is included to throw संपूर्ण more clearly into a predicate relationship; thus, literally 'A hundred years being (सति) fulfilled' and freely 'When a hundred years were completed'. The numeral शत 'a hundred' and the higher numbers like सहस्र 'a thousand' are neuter nouns which take the thing numbered in the same case as the numeral or in the genitive plural. Thus, 'a hundred years' may be शतं वर्षाः or शतं वर्षाणाम्. In this passage a genitive tatpuruṣa compound has been made of the second alternative: वर्षशतम्; *cf.* पुत्रसहस्राणि below.

4. कावयोर् The sandhi is tricky here: the interrogative का has been contracted with आवयोः, genitive dual of अहम्.

5. का वां कं वरं इच्छति Notice the doubling of interrogatives, which may be marginally tolerable in English, but surely not the usual idiom; literally 'Who of you two (वां) wishes what boon', *i.e.,* 'Who wishes the one boon and who the other?'

6. स्वच्छन्दो ऽत्र वर्तते 'Your own wish turns (वर्तते) in this', *i.e.,* 'it is dependent on what you want', freely 'It's up to you!'

7. प्रदक्षिणं तं ऋषिं कृत्वा 'having performed a *pradakṣiṇa* around that seer', *i.e.,* walking about him and keeping him to the right. प्रदक्षिण is an adjective meaning 'standing or placed on the right'; it is used here in the accusative neuter singular as an adverb with √कृ 'make so-and-so standing on the right', hence, 'keep so-and-so on the right'.

8. गर्भतुम्बो *Literally* 'An embryo like a gourd', *i.e.*, in the form of a gourd; to be analyzed गर्भः तुम्बः इव, as a karmadhāraya with the limiting or defining element (तुम्ब) last; *cf.* पुरुषव्याघ्र 'a man like a tiger' (पुरुषः व्याघ्रः इव).

9. गर्भतुम्बान्, *i.e.*, गर्भतुम्बात्, the final -त् having become -न् by total regressive assimilation; it would have been possible to turn -त् into -द्, *i.e.*, merely making it into a voiced sound, but the completely assimilated form is commoner.

10. सन् see note under 3 above.

11. नाम्रियन्त by sandhi for न अम्रियन्त. The verb is imperfect third person plural of √मृ 'die'.

12. पुरान् On the final -न् for -त् see note under 9 above.

Vocabulary

अन्य, *adj.* other.
अपत्य, *n.* offspring, child.
अपर, *adj.* other.
अप्रज, *adj.* literally 'having non-offspring', *i.e.*, not having offspring, without offspring.
अप्रतिम, *adj.* 'having no match', unmatched [formed like अप्रज above].
अयोध्या, *f.* Ayodhyā, an ancient city of India, nowadays usually written Oudh by imitative spelling, located on the Sarayū (सरयू) River. It was the capital of Rāma, hero of the Rāmāyaṇa. The name means literally 'the unfightable *or* irresistible one' (the *f.* of the negatived gerundive of √युध् 'fight').
असमञ्ज, *m.* Asamañja, the son of Sagara by Keśinī. The name means 'unbecoming, good-for-nothing'(!)
अहित, *n.* 'non-welfare', harm.
आ-√राध् (राधयति, *caus.* of राधते, class I), propitiate; honor; *ppp.* आराधित, (having been) propitiated, honored.

उत्-√पद् (पद्यते, class IV), go forth, arise, come into existence, be produced; *caus.* उत्पादयति, 'causes to go forth', causes to come into existence, produces.

केशिनी, *f.* Keśinī, a wife of King Sagara of Ayodhyā, daughter of the king of Vidarbha and mother of the wicked Asamañja. The name means 'she who has (fine) hair'.

ख्यात, *ppp.* √ख्या (ख्याति, class II, 'be known, be named'), named, called.

गर्भ, *m.* embryo, child, offspring.

गृहीत, *ppp.* √ग्रह् (गृह्णाति, class IX), (having been) gotten.

छन्द, *m.* pleasure, desire, will.

√जन् (जायते, class IV), be born; the active forms of this verb, like the future जनिष्यति, are transitive, hence 'beget, bring forth, produce'.

√ज्ञा (जानाति, class IX), know; *infin.* ज्ञातुम्.

ज्येष्ठ, *adj.* best, principal; oldest.

तुम्ब, *m.* a gourd.

दुरात्मन्, *adj.* ill-natured.

द्वितीय, *adj.* second.

निर्भिन्न, *ppp.* निस्-√भिद् (भिनत्ति, class VII), split open;

निर्वासित, *ppp. of caus.* निस्-√वस् (वसति, class I), 'caused to stay abroad', expelled.

पत्नी, *f.* a wife.

पुर, *n.* a city.

पौर, *m.* a townsman, citizen.

प्र-√आप् (आप्नोति, class V), gain, obtain.

प्र-√क्षिप् (क्षिपति, class VI), throw *or* cast out *or* away (प्र).

√प्रछ् (पृच्छति, class VI), ask.

प्रति-√पद् (पद्यते, class IV), step toward, attain, get.

प्र-√नम् (नमति, class I), bow before, make obeisance before (+ *acc.*).

प्र-√हस् (हसति, class I), laugh aloud (प्र).

भृगु, *m.* Bhṛgu, a great sage.

√मज्ज् (मज्जति, class I), sink, submerge.

यशस्विन्, *adj.* possessing glory, glorious.

युक्त, *ppp.* √युज् (युनक्ति, class VII, 'join, connect'), engaged upon (+ *loc.*).

रहित, *ppp.* √रह् (रहति, class I), 'separated from', devoid of.

रूपयौवन, *n.* beauty and youth.
लाभ, *m.* the act of getting, acquisition.
वंशकर, *adj.* making a family, propagating a family *or* dynastic line.
वचस्, *n.* speech; words.
वर, *m.* a gift *or* boon.
वर्ष, *m.* (sometimes *n.*) a year.
विना, *postp.* without (+ *instr.*).
विनिःसृत, *ppp.* वि-निः-√सृ (सिसर्ति, class III), gone forth (निः) hither and thither (वि).
विलम्ब, *m.* delay.
√वृत् (वर्तते, class I), turn, move, take place [*v.* note 6].
शत, *n.* a hundred.
शिरस्, *n.* the head.
षष्टि, *f.* sixty.
सत्य, *adj.* true; as *n.* the truth.
सरयू, *f.* Sarayū, the river beside which is situated the city of अयोध्या.
सहस्र, *n.* a thousand.
सुता, *f.* a daughter.
सुमति, *f.* Sumati, a wife of Sagara, daughter of Ariṣṭanemi and sister of Suparṇa. The name means 'She who has good intelligence (मति), wise'.
सुमहत्, *adj.* very great.
संपूर्ण, *adj.* filled, fulfilled. [strictly *ppp.* √पॄ (पिपर्ति, class III 'fill')]
हिमवत्, *m.* Himavat *or* the Himālaya mountain; the name means 'having snow (हिम)', *i.e.*, 'snowy'.

Translate into Sanskrit, using the past passive participle in lieu of the main verb wherever possible:

Formerly[1] there was a king of Ayodhyā named Sagara. He had all the qualities of a lord[2] and was virtuous by nature. He had[3] two wives, one named Keśinī,[4] the other named Sumati.[4] Sagara was desirous of offspring, but he was without offspring. On this account,[5] in order to make a supreme effort for the sake of offspring the king went to a region of the Himavat along with his wives and performed great austerities there.[6] Finally, a great sage named Bhṛgu, having been favored by the austerities he had performed there for a hundred years, gave that Sagara a boon. According to the words of the sage one of the two wives would give birth to a glorious son who would propagate the family line, the other 60,000 sons. 'What you both wish, that will be!' said the sage. By Keśinī one son was chosen, by Sumati 60,000 chosen. In the course of time, of Keśinī one son named Asamañja was born. But of Sumati a gourd-like embryo (was) born. When this gourd-like embryo was split open, 60,000 sons came forth. Now[7] Keśinī's son named Asamañja was extremely evil-natured. For[8] he cast all Sumati's sons into the Sarayū River. However, by a miracle the sons of Sagara did not die. For this reason[9] Asamañja was banished from the city by Sagara.

Notes

1. 'Formerly': पुरा.

2. 'He had all the qualities of a lord': say 'He was provided with all the qualities of a lord' (*i.e.*, as an instrumental tatpuruṣa compound).

3. Express the notion of possession by the genitive of the personal pronoun and the appropriate form of √भू; literally thus: 'Of him two wives were'.

4. The two expressions 'named Keśinī' and 'named Sumati' are to be expressed by appositional bahuvrīhis. At the end of a feminine bahuvrīhi, either the appropriate case of -नामन् may be used or the specifically feminine derivative -नाम्नी.

5. 'On this account': use ततः (etymologically 'from that') or तेन कारणेन.

6. 'the king went... and performed great austerities': say 'by the king having gone (*gerund*)... great austerities (were) performed (*ppp.*)'. Similarly in the next sentence: 'by a great sage... favored (*ppp.*) by the austerities performed (*ppp.*) there... a boon (was) given'.

7. 'Now': use अथ in its continuative sense.

8. 'For': use हि, a coordinating causal conjunction, as is English 'for' in this sentence. Nowadays, it may be noted, 'for' is generally used as a subordinating conjunction, synonymous with 'since, because' and also 'as'.

9. 'For this reason': तस्य हेतोः.

LESSON TWENTY-ONE

The Perfect Tense. The Imperative.

I. *The Perfect Tense.*

There are four different ways of expressing past time in Sanskrit. Of these we have taken up two: the imperfect tense and the idiomatic use of the past passive participle (with the agent in the instrumental). The other two are the perfect tense and the aorist tense. There is no difference in meaning among these four ways of indicating past tense: they are interchangeable, so that it is purely a matter of style or an author's predilection which method is used.[1] The period when a particular work was written also has a good deal to do with the degree of frequency in the use of this or that method. Thus, the use of the past passive participle is much more prevalent in later Sanskrit works than any of the three past tenses. In this lesson we shall take up the perfect tense, which is commoner than the aorist in the epics and generally in the classical language.

There are two different forms of the perfect tense, the one a particular inflection of a verbal root, the other a combination of an auxiliary or 'helping' verb and a specially formed noun, the so-called 'periphrastic perfect'. Only the former will be dealt with here.

The perfect tense has several peculiar characteristics which, taken together, distinguish it from all other verb forms. First of all, the root is reduplicated, that is, a portion of it is repeated; thus, from √*budh (bodhati)* 'be awake' is made the reduplicated stem *bu-budh*. The personal endings are also somewhat different from those so far learned, and the three persons of the singular exhibit a stronger form of the stem than elsewhere in the perfect. This variation of the stem, like that in the changeable noun stems we have just studied, is due to a shifting of the old tonic accent, no longer extant in classical Sanskrit, from stem to ending.

All of this undoubtedly sounds very complicated, but it is really not difficult. Moreover, *only a few* forms of the perfect are in common use, *viz.*, the third persons of the active and, slightly less so, those of the middle also. In explaining the formation of the perfect, it will be easier and clearer first to give the perfect of a typical verb root in all its forms and then show how these forms are made.

---

[1] In the older language, the language of the Veda, however, the three past tenses (imperfect, perfect and aorist) had clearly differentiated meanings, depending upon the way the past act was viewed and its relationship to the present.

Perfect Tense of √*budh* *(bodhati)* 'be awake'

Active		Middle	
Singular		*Singular*	
1.* *bu-bodh-a*	बुबोध	1. *bu-budh-e*	बुबुधे
2.* *bu-bodh-i-tha*	बुबोधिथ	2. *bu-budh-i-ṣe*	बुबुधिषे
3.* *bu-bodh-a*	बुबोध	3. *bu-budh-e*	बुबुधे
Dual		*Dual*	
1. *bu-budh-i-va*	बुबुधिव	1. *bu-budh-i-vahe*	बुबुधिवहे
2. *bu-budh-athuḥ*	बुबुधथुः	2. *bu-budh-āthe*	बुबुधाथे
3. *bu-budh-atuḥ*	बुबुधतुः	3. *bu-budh-āte*	बुबुधाते
Plural		*Plural*	
1. *bu-budh-i-ma*	बुबुधिम	1. *bu-budh-i-mahe*	बुबुधिमहे
2. *bu-budh-a*	बुबुध	2. *bu-budh-i-dhve*	बुबुधिध्वे
3. *bu-budh-uḥ*	बुबुधुः	3. *bu-budh-i-re*	बुबुधिरे

Note that the strong forms, which are marked with an asterisk (*) as was done with the strong forms of noun stems, have the guṇa substitute 'o' for 'u' of √*budh*. *All* the other forms retain 'u'. The personal endings are, for the most part, the primary endings we have already had: *-se, -vahe, -āthe, -āte, -mahe* and *-dhve*. There are two secondary endings, *-va* and *-ma,* which we have had for the imperfect. The *-athuḥ* and *-atuḥ* of the second and third dual active seem to be amalgamations of the primary endings *-thaḥ* and *-taḥ,* with *-uḥ* of the plural substituted for the *-aḥ;* the origin of the preceding *a-* is obscure. Finally, the *-i-* before the endings beginning with a consonant is not originally part of the endings and some verbs do not take it.

All roots containing a short vowel (except *-a-)* followed by a consonant behave like √*budh;* that is, the root vowel is replaced by its guṇa substitute in the strong forms, but remains unchanged elsewhere. Thus, from √*dṛś* 'see' is made *da-darś-a* (remember that *ar* is the guṇa substitute of *ṛ),* from √*viś* 'enter' is formed *vi-veś-a (e* is the guṇa of *i* and *ī).* But when the root vowel is *-a-* before a consonant, *-ā-* (the vṛddhi of *-a-)* replaces *-a-* in the third person; thus, *ta-tān-a* from √*tan* 'stretch'. This vṛddhi form is also *optionally* allowed in the first person, which has either *ta-tan-a* or *ta-tān-a.* This same rule that concerns medial *-a-* is also true of roots ending in vowels; thus, from √*nī* 'lead' are made 1. *ni-nay-a/ni-nāy-a,* 2. *ni-nay-i-tha* and 3. *ni-nāy-*

a. (Remember: *-e-* > *-ay-* and *-ai-* > *-āy-* before vowels in *internal* sandhi!) Roots in final *-ā,* like √*dā* 'give', √*dhā* 'place', √*pā* 'drink', replace *-ā* by *-au* in the first and third persons; thus, *da-dau* 'I, he, she, it gave.'

Before the peculiarities of the weak stem are discussed, a few words must be said about the reduplication. In its simplest form reduplication involves the repetition of the first part of a root, *i.e.,* the consonant and vowel, as in *bu-budh* and *ta-tan (*√*tan* 'stretch'). The vowel in the repeated or reduplicative syllable must be short; thus, *da-dā (*√*dā* 'give'), *pa-pā (*√*pā* 'drink'), and *ṛ* is replaced by *a;* thus, *ma-mṛ (*√*mṛ* 'die'). An aspirated consonant is repeated without aspiration; thus, *da-dhā (*√*dhā* 'place'), and a guttural by the corresponding palatal. Accordingly, *k-* and *kh-* are replaced by *c-*, as in *ca-kṛ (*√*kṛ* 'do'), *ca-khan (*√*khan* 'dig'); *g-* and *gh-* by *j-*, as in *ja-gam (*√*gam), ja-ghrā (*√*ghrā* 'smell'). Most roots beginning with *va-* reduplicate with *u-*, as *u-vas (*√*vas* 'stay'), *u-vad (*√*vad* 'speak') and *u-vac (*√*vac* 'speak'); similarly, √*yaj* 'sacrifice' reduplicates with *i-;* thus, *i-yaj.* This interchange between *va* and *u* and *ya* and *i* is called *samprasāraṇa;* it is also applied to the interchange of *ra* and *ṛ*, seen, for example, in various forms of √*grah* 'grasp'.

Verb roots that reduplicate with *samprasāraṇa* (*i.e.,* with the reduplicative syllable *u-* or *i-* instead of *va-* or *ya-)* make this same substitution also in the root itself in the weak forms and contract into a simple long vowel the two identical vowels *(u- + u- >* *ū-* and *i- + i- > ī).* Thus, from √*vah (vahati)* 'carry' are made the strong stem *u-vāh /u-vah* and the weak stem *ūh* (for *u- + uh).* To make the matter clearer here is the entire active inflection of √*vah:*

1. **u-vāh-a/u-vah-a*	*ūh-i-va*	*ūh-i-ma*
2. **u-vah-i-tha*	*ūh-athuḥ*	*ūh-a*
3. **u-vāh-a*	*ūh-atuḥ*	*ūh-uḥ*

A few very common roots lose their vowel in the weak forms, causing their initial and final consonants to come together; thus, √*gam (gacchati)* 'go', which has the strong stem *ja-gām/ja-gam,* makes the weak stem *ja-gm.* The third persons of the active, then, are: *ja-gām-a, ja-gm-atuḥ* and *ja-gm-uḥ*. The juxtaposition of the two consonants resulting from the loss of the root vowel occasionally produces rather startling changes due to the requirements of internal sandhi; as, for example, in √*ghas (ghasati)* 'eat', which has the easily identifiable third singular *jaghāsa,* but the remarkable third plural of *jakṣuḥ* (from *ja-ghs-uḥ,* in which the combination *-ghs-* becomes *-kṣ-* due to the de-aspirating and de-voicing of *gh-* before *-s* and the conversion of *-s* to *-ṣ* after *k-)*!

Many roots, mostly containing the vowel *a* followed by a single consonant, form their weak stem by a sort of 'telescoping' of the reduplicative syllable and the root, resulting in a monosyllabic stem that shows no evidence of reduplication. These telescoped stems always consist of the unchanged initial and final consonants of the root connected by *-e-*. Thus, *pet, meth, pec, ten* are the weak stems of √*pat* 'fly', √*math* 'agitate', √*pac* 'cook' and √*tan* 'stretch'. The full perfect active of √*tan* is:

1. **ta-tān-a/ta-tan-a*	*ten-i-va*	*ten-i-ma*
2. **ta-tan-tha*	*ten-athuḥ*	*ten-a*
3. **ta-tān-a*	*ten-atuḥ*	*ten-uḥ*

Many more details concerning the formation of the perfect might be given, but the purpose of this lesson is more expeditiously achieved by presenting only such details as are required to gain an overall view of this important tense, so that forms of it may be readily recognized as they occur in the course of reading. Once the salient features of the formation are clear, it is practically necessary for the beginning student only to bear in mind a general impression of them, and for the time being to learn *only the endings of the third person throughout*.

II. *The Imperative Mood*

There is another group of verb forms made from the present stem -- the same stem from which is formed the present third singular which we learn along with the root. This group of forms is called the *Imperative Mood.* As the name implies, these verb forms are used when requesting or ordering a person to do something, as in English 'Go!' or 'Do this!' Usually the pronoun *you* is omitted in the imperative, but it is used for emphatic requests: 'You do this!' The same rule holds also for Sanskrit. Logically, we expect this mood of the verb to be used only in the second person (singular, dual or plural!), as it involves direct address. Oddly enough, however, in Sanskrit it is possible to have an imperative in the first and also the third person! Here neither a request nor an order is involved, but rather an exhortation or suggestion to do this or that, as, for example, when we say 'Let's go!', 'Let's do this!', 'Let him go!' etc. As we may see from these examples, English has no special verb form for this, but uses the helping verb 'let' to express the idea. This can, of course, lead to ambiguity, since 'Let him go!' might mean either 'I exhort him to go' or 'permit him to go'. Obviously, only the context can determine which idea is intended.

The formation of the imperative in Sanskrit is simple. Only a few additional endings need to be learned, as some of them are identical to those of the imperfect. It will be easier if we first present a verb in the imperative in both the active and middle and then take up the special points that have to be observed.

Imperative Mood of √जि (जयति) 'conquer'

Active

	Singular	*Dual*	*Plural*
1.	*jayā-ni* (जयानि)	*jayā-va* (जयाव)	*jayā-ma* (जयाम)
2.	*jaya* (जय)	*jaya-tam* (जयतम्)	*jaya-ta* (जयत)
3.	*jaya-tu* (जयतु)	*jaya-tām* (जयताम्)	*jay-antu* (जयन्तु)

Middle

1.	*jay-ai* (जयै)	*jayā-vahai* (जयावहै)	*jayā-mahai* (जयामहै)
2.	*jaya-sva* (जयस्व)	*jay-ethām* (जयेथाम्)	*jaya-dhvam* (जयध्वम्)
3.	*jaya-tām* (जयताम्)	*jay-etām* (जयेताम्)	*jay-antām* (जयन्ताम्)

Note that the underlined forms are identical to the imperfect, except that there is no augment. The second singular active is identical to the stem. As usual elsewhere in the verbal system, the thematic vowel is lengthened before *v-* and *m-* as well as before *n-* of *-ni* (first singular active). In translating the imperative, we may use the locutions 'let me, let us' for the first person and 'let him/her/it/them' for the third person, and the simple verb with (or without 'you') for the second, as exemplified above. Examples: गुरुः शिष्यान् उवाच वनं गत्वा मूलानि फलानि च आनयत इति । "The teacher said to his pupils: 'Go to the woods and bring hither roots and fruits!'" (literally 'having gone . . . bring')' अधुना गृहं गच्छाव । "Let's both (dual!) go home now!"; राजा जयतु "Let the king (*or* May the king) be victorious!"

II. The Story of Sagara and His Sons

तस्य दुरात्मनो[1] ऽसमञ्जस्य पुत्रो नाम्नांशुमान् इति विश्रुतो ऽभवत् । स सगरस्य पौत्रः सर्वलोकस्य संमतः । ततः कालेन महता[2] यदा सगरमहाराजो ऽधुनाश्वमेधेन[3] यजेयं इत्य् अचिन्तयत् तदा हिमवतो[4] विन्ध्यपर्वतस्य[5] च मध्ये विद्यमानं[6] देशं अंशुमतोपाध्यायगणेन[7] च सह गत्वाश्वमेधेन यष्टुं[8] समुपचक्रमे । अंशुमान् सगरपितामहाय भक्तो ऽस्य यज्ञस्याश्वचर्यां चकार । ततो देवपतिर् वासवो[9] राक्षसस्य शरीरं आस्थाय[10] तं यज्ञियं अश्वं अपजहार । तद् दृष्ट्वैव सर्व उपाध्यायाः सगरं ऊचुः । अयं यज्ञियो ऽश्वो राक्षसेनापहृतः । चौरं हत्वा तं अश्वं पुनर् आनय । एतद् यज्ञच्छिद्रं नः सर्वेभ्यो ऽशिवं भवेत् । तथा भवता कर्तव्यं यथेदं छिद्रं विलम्बेन विना विरमेद् इति । तेषां तद् वचः श्रुत्वैव षष्टिं पुत्रसहस्राण्य् एतद् वाक्यं उवाच । हे पुत्रकाः सर्वत्र गच्छत सर्वां पृथिवीं विचिनुध्वम् । यदि पृथिवी युष्माभिः खनितव्या तदा तां खनत । यावत् तुरगं न द्रक्ष्यथ तावन्[11] मेदिनीं खनत । युष्मासु तुरगं तुरगतस्करं च मार्गमाणेष्व् अहं इहांशुमतोपाध्यायैश्च सह स्थास्यामीति । तस्य तद् वचनं आकर्ण्य सर्वे राजपुत्राः सर्वत्र तुरगतस्करयोर् अन्वेषणे स्वजनकस्याज्ञया परिबभ्रमुः । ते महीतलं स्वभुजबलेन शूलैश्चापि हलैश्च निर्भिद्य तत् प्रविविशुः । यदा ते नृपात्मजा वसुंधरां विबिभिदुस् तदा सा विविधानां सत्त्वानां हन्यमानानां[12] भयंकरं निनदं ननाद । तेन प्रकारेण ते सर्वे जम्बूद्वीपं[13] खनन्तः परिक्रम्यान्ते रसातलं आजग्मुः ।

Notes

1. दुरात्मनो It will be recalled from the previous episode that Keśinī's son Asamañja was extremely evil and vicious by nature, as exemplified by his attempt to drown his 60,000 step-brothers, the sons of Sagara by Sumati. It is

remarkable indeed that so innately wicked a person could have fathered a son of quite the reverse disposition.

2. कालेन महता 'After much time', 'instrumentals of time at the end of which' are common.

3. अश्वमेधेन The instrumental is regularly used with √यज् (यजति) to express the means whereby a sacrifice is offered. This may be, as here, the particular offering itself or the thing offered, for example, rice, ghee, etc. The god to whom the sacrifice is made, if expressed, is in the accusative; thus, for example: विप्रो घृतेन विष्णुं यजति । 'The priest sacrifices to Viṣṇu with ghee'.

The *aśvamedha* or 'horse sacrifice', which in one form or another reaches back in antiquity to the Ṛgveda, is mentioned with great frequency in Sanskrit literature. Its performance lasted in its many phases for more than a year and required the services of a large number of Brahman priests. The purpose of this long, intricate and costly sacrifice was to confirm a powerful king in his sovereignty and even to extend it to include all the land traversed by the sacrificial horse in the course of its unfettered wanderings, a feature which, of course, might involve warfare with a neighboring monarch who was disinclined to see all or even a part of his kingdom annexed in this way. A number of famous Indian kings are alleged to have performed this elaborate sacrifice, perhaps the best known being Samudragupta of the fourth century A.D., who issued several gold medallions to mark the event.

4. हिमवतो Himavat (literally 'possessing snow', snow-clad, snowy) and Himālaya (literally 'abode of snow') are synonyms. Personified, Himavat/Himālaya is regarded as the father of Pārvatī (wife of Śiva) and Gaṅgā, the great river.

5. विन्ध्यपर्वतस्य The Vindhya Mountains are a comparatively low range of mountains extending across central India, thus dividing the country into a northern half, often called Hindūsthān, and a southern, called the Dekkhan or Deccan in Anglo-Indian spelling.

6. विद्यमानं accusative masculine singular of the present passive participle of √विद् (विन्दति, class VI) 'find', hence literally '(the region) being found', *i.e.*, located (between the Himavat and Vindhya Mountains). This use of √विद् to express location or simple existence is exactly parallel to the idiom in the Romance languages; thus, French *trouver* 'find' in *Le livre se trouve sur la table* 'The book is on the table' and similarly Italian *trovare* in *La bottega si trova in questa città* 'The store is (located) in this city'.

7. उपाध्यायगणेन From what has been said above about the *aśvamedha,* it is apparent why Sagara was accompanied 'by a host of preceptors'.

8. यष्टुं The infinitive of √यज् (यजति, class I) 'sacrifice'; as also in the past passive participle इष्ट (in which the य- is changed to इ- by *saṃprasāraṇa),* when ज् is followed by त्, it is replaced by the cerebral ष् and then by 'progressive assimilation' the त् is changed to ट्, so यज्-तुम् becomes यष्-तुम्, then यष्-टुम् (written यष्टुम्).

9. देवपतिर् वासवो 'Vāsava, lord of the gods' is Indra, who from the time of the Ṛgveda held this exalted position, although in the course of time he was relegated to the background due to the rising prominence of Śiva and Viṣṇu. Indra is called 'Vāsava' (literally 'one who is connected with the Vasus') as chief of the Vasus, a rather vague group of deities often mentioned in the Ṛgveda, but of unspecified function.

10. राक्षसस्य शरीरं आस्थाय Indra is often said to assume various bodily forms for one purpose or another. The Rāmāyaṇa does not state the reason for Indra's theft of the horse, but it may be noted that Indra frequently engages in trickery to deflect anyone engaged in severe austerities or a powerful sacrifice out of fear of a diminution of his powers through their efficacy.

11. तावन् Note the change of त् to न् here by 'regressive assimilation'. The त् of तावत् might have been changed to द्, but the further change to the nasal of the same class is usual.

12. हन्यमानानां As विद्यमानं above (note 6), this is a present passive participle, from √हन् (हन्ति, class II) 'kill', formed by adding the passive suffix -य- to the root and, in turn, the participial suffix -मान.

13. जम्बूद्वीपं Jambūdvīpa is one of the seven continents which, according to Indian tradition, constitute the world. Jambūdvīpa is in the center and the other six continents, which are all circular in shape, are each separated from the other by an ocean, thus forming with their intervening oceans a series of concentric rings. In the center of Jambūdvīpa is Mt. Meru, to the south of which is Bhārata(varṣa) or India. Jambūdvīpa is, however, often loosely used as a synonym for India, as is the case in this context.

Vocabulary

अंशुमत्, *m.* Aṃśumat, grandson of King Sagara.
अन्वेषण, *n.* looking for, searching after.
अप-√हृ (हरति, class I), take away, steal; *perf.* अपजहार.
अशिव, *adj.* unkind; unfriendly; inauspicious.
अश्वमेध, *m.* the horse-sacrifice (on which *v.* note 3 above).
√आकर्णय (आकर्णयति, denom. verb from the bahuvrīhi आ-कर्ण 'having the ear to', *i.e.*, lending an ear to), listen, hear.
आज्ञा, *f.* order, command.
आत्मज, *m.* son.
आ-√नी (नयति, class I), bring to.
आ-√स्था (तिष्ठति, class I), stand on (आ); mount, ascend; resort to; *gerund* आस्थाय.
उपाध्याय, *m.* a teacher *or* preceptor.
कर्तव्य, *gerundive of* √कृ 'do', to be done, having *or* needing to be done.
√खन् (खनति, class I), dig, dig up.
खनितव्य, *gerundive of* √खन्, to be dug, having *or* needing to be dug.
चर्या, *f.* occupation with *or* concern for a thing.
√चिन्त् (चिन्तयति, class X), think.
चौर, *m.* a thief.
छिद्र, *n.* hole; gap.
जनक, *m.* father.
जम्बूद्वीप, *m.* Jambūdvīpa, name of one of the seven continents of Indian tradition; India (*v.* note 13).
तस्कर, *m.* a thief.
तुरग, *m.* a horse.
देश, *m.* region, country, area.
√नद् (नदति, class I), sound; *perf.* ननाद.
निनद, *m.* a sound, noise.
निस्-√भिद् (भिनत्ति, class VII), split open (निः); *gerund* निर्भिद्य.
परि-√क्रम्, (क्रामति, class I), step *or* walk around; *gerund* परिक्रम्य.
परि-√भ्रम् (भ्राम्यति, class IV), roam around; *perf.* परिबभ्राम (*plur.* °बभ्रमुः).
पितामह, *m.* grandfather.
पुत्रक, *m.* little son *or* dear son.

पौत्र, *m.* grandson.

प्रकार, *m.* kind, sort; way, manner.

प्र-√विश् (विशति, class VI), enter; *perf.* प्रविवेश (*plur.* °विविशुः).

भक्त, *ppp.* √भज् (भजति, class I), devoted to.

भयंकर, *adj.* causing *or* inspiring fear, fearful.

भुज, *m.* the arm.

महीतल, *n.* the surface of the earth.

√मार्ग्, (मार्गति, class I), seek after, look for; *present middle participle* मार्गमाण 'seeking after, looking for'.

मेदिनी, *f.* the earth.

यज्ञिय, *adj.* connected with a sacrifice, sacrificial.

यावत् . . . तावत्, *correl. conj.* as long . . . so long, until.

रसातल, *n.* Rasātala, name of one of the seven hells beneath the earth.

राक्षस, *m.* a demon.

राजपुत्र, *m.* a king's son, a prince.

√वच् (वक्ति, class II), say, speak to; *perf.* उवाच (*plur.* ऊचुः).

वचस्, *n.* speech; words.

वसुंधरा, *f.* the earth.

वाक्य, *n.* speech; words.

वासव, *m.* Vāsava, a name of Indra as chief of the Vasus (*v.* note 9).

वि-√चि (चिनोति, चिनुते, class V), investigate, explore; scour.

विन्ध्य, *m.* Vindhya, name of a low range of mountains running across central India (on which *v.* note 5).

वि-√भिद्, split apart (वि); *perf.* °बिभेद (*plur.* °बिभिदुः).

वि-√रम् (रमति, class I), cease.

विलम्ब, *m.* delay.

विविध, *adj.* various.

विश्रुत, *ppp.* वि-√श्रु (शृणोति, class V), *literally* 'heard of far and wide (वि)', *hence* 'famous, well-known, known, called'.

शरीर, *n.* the body.

शूल, *m.* a stake; pike, spear.

षष्टि, *f.* sixty.

सत्त्व, *n.* being, living being, creature.

सम्-उप-√क्रम् (क्रामति, class I), go up to, approach; begin; *perfect middle* समुपचक्रमे.

संमत, *ppp.* सं-√मन् (मन्यते, class IV), lit. 'thought together (सम्), being of the same opinion', *hence* 'agreed, approved, highly honored'.

सर्वत्र, *adv.* everywhere.

सहस्र, *n.* thousand.

हल, *m.* a plow.

हिमवत्, *m.* the Himālaya mountain (*v.* note 4).

Translate into Sanskrit:

That King Sagara had[1] a grandson named Aṃśumat. Although he was the son of the evil-minded Asamañja, nevertheless Aṃśumat was virtuous and respected by all the people.[2] In the course of time, Sagara decided that he would perform an Aśvamedha[3] and, having gone to the region selected for the sacrifice by his preceptors, he began to perform the Aśvamedha. But in the middle of the sacrifice, the king of the gods, assuming[4] the form of a demon, stole the sacrificial horse. Thereupon the preceptors said to Sagara that the thief must be slain and the horse brought back.[5] As soon as he heard these words of theirs, Sagara said to his 60,000 sons: 'Go everywhere in your search for the horse! Dig up the earth, if you have to! Find the horse and bring him back here!' When they heard this command of their father, they immediately began searching for[6] the horse. They roamed everywhere and, when they did not find the horse, they dug up the earth. After splitting open the surface of the earth with pikes and plows, they entered it.

Notes

1. 'That King Sagara had': Say 'of that King Sagara was … '.

2. 'by all the people': Use the *gen.*

3. 'that he would perform an Aśvamedha': Turn into the direct form ('I will …') and add इति at the end of the quoted words.

4. 'assuming': Use the *gerund*, not the present participle, as Indra's assumption of the form of a demon preceded his theft.

5. 'that the thief must be slain' etc.: Again to be expressed in direct form followed by इति.

6. 'began searching for': Say 'began *to* search for' (+ *acc.*).

LESSON TWENTY-TWO

Adjectives in *-añc/-ac* (English *-ward*).

There is a small group of quite commonly used adjectives in Sanskrit, numbering perhaps a dozen or more, which are formed with one of the verbal prefixes *(ava, ud, prati, pra, sam,* etc.) and the element *-añc/-ac* 'turned *or* bent'. All these adjectives mean 'turned *or* bent' in the direction indicated by the adverb with which they begin. Thus, *avāñc* (अवाञ्च्), that is *ava + -añc,* means *literally* 'turned *or* bent down *(ava)'*, hence, 'down-ward'; *praty-añc* (प्रत्यञ्च्) means *literally* 'turned *or* directed back *(prati)'*, hence, 'back-ward'; and so on. The terminal or formative element is really just √*a(ñ)c (añcati* or *acati,* class I) 'bend', used like a suffix. These adjectives present the beginner with a little difficulty because some are declined from *two* stems, others from *three,* that is, some distinguish a strong and a weak stem, others a strong, middle and weakest. The two-stem adjectives retain the nasal in the strong stem and drop it in the weak; thus *prāñc- (pra + -añc)* and *prāc-*. The declension of *prāñc* 'turned *or* bent forth, for-ward' is as follows:

	Singular	*Dual*	*Plural*
Nom.	**prāṅ* (प्राङ्)	**prāñc-au* (प्राञ्चौ)	**prāñc-aḥ* (प्राञ्चः)
Acc.	**prāñc-am* (प्राञ्चम्)	**prāñc-au* (प्राञ्चौ)	*prāc-aḥ* (प्राचः)
Instr.	*prāc-ā* (प्राचा)	*prāg-bhyām* (प्राग्भ्याम्)	*prāg-bhiḥ* (प्राग्भिः)
Dat.	*prāc-e* (प्राचे)	*prāg-bhyām* (प्राग्भ्याम्)	*prāg-bhyaḥ* (प्राग्भ्यः)
Abl.	*prāc-aḥ* (प्राचः)	*prāg-bhyām* (प्राग्भ्याम्)	*prāg-bhyaḥ* (प्राग्भ्यः)
Gen.	*prāc-aḥ* (प्राचः)	*prāc-oḥ* (प्राचोः)	*prāc-ām* (प्राचाम्)
Loc.	*prāc-i* (प्राचि)	*prāc-oḥ* (प्राचोः)	*prāk-ṣu* (प्राक्षु)

Note that, as with all stems ending in a consonant, there are *no* deviations in the endings from one declensional type to the other. As always in *internal* sandhi, no change is made in a final consonant before an ending that begins with a vowel. Before endings with initial *bh-* (भ-), final *-c* (-च्) of these adjectives is replaced by *-g* (-ग्); before *-su* (locative plural) *-c* (-च्) is changed to *-k* (-क्), because *s* (स्), unlike *bh* (भ्) is voiceless. In the nominative singular we should theoretically start with *prāñc-s,* but, as we noted when first discussing stems ending in a consonant, the nominative *-s* (-स्) always drops out because of the rule that a Sanskrit word cannot end in more than a single consonant. For the same reason here we must also drop the *-c* (-च्). This leaves *prāñ* (प्राञ्), but *-ñ* (-ञ्) must be replaced by the *guttural* nasal in accordance with the rule that a final palatal is usually replaced by a guttural. In this way we arrive at *prāṅ* (प्राङ्), and so also with all these adjectives in *-añc* (or *-āñc)* in the nominative masculine singular.

So much, then, for the *masculine.* In the *neuter* only the nominative and accusative plural are strong, all the rest weak:

Neuter

	Singular	*Dual*	*Plural*
Nom.	*prāk* (प्राक्)	*prāc-ī* (प्राची)	**prāñc-i* (प्राञ्चि)
Acc.	*prāk* (प्राक्)	*prāc-ī* (प्राची)	**prāñc-i* (प्राञ्चि)

All the other cases are identical to the masculine.

Adjectives that differentiate three stems differ from the stem just exemplified only in the so-called 'weakest' cases, otherwise they are treated alike. First, let us look at the complete declension of *pratyañc* 'back-ward', a stem of *three* degrees, and see how the variations in the stem are disposed. The three stems are: strong *pratyañc-* (प्रत्यञ्च्-), middle *pratyag-/k-* (प्रत्यग्-/क्-), weakest *pratīc-* (प्रतीच्-).

Masculine

	Singular	*Dual*	*Plural*
Nom.	**pratyaṅ* (प्रत्यङ्)	**pratyañc-au* (प्रत्यञ्चौ)	**pratyañc-aḥ* (प्रत्यञ्चः)
Acc.	**pratyañc-am* (प्रत्यञ्चम्)	**pratyañc-au* (प्रत्यञ्चौ)	*pratīc-aḥ* (प्रतीचः)
Instr.	*pratīc-ā* (प्रतीचा)	*pratyag-bhyām* (प्रत्यग्भ्याम्)	*pratyag-bhiḥ* (प्रत्यग्भिः)
Dat.	*pratīc-e* (प्रतीचे)	*pratyag-bhyām* (प्रत्यग्भ्याम्)	*pratyag-bhyaḥ* (प्रत्यग्भ्यः)
Abl.	*pratīc-aḥ* (प्रतीचः)	*pratyag-bhyām* (प्रत्यग्भ्याम्)	*pratyag-bhyaḥ* (प्रत्यग्भ्यः)
Gen.	*pratīc-aḥ* (प्रतीचः)	*pratīc-oḥ* (प्रतीचोः)	*pratīc-ām* (प्रतीचाम्)
Loc.	*pratīc-i* (प्रतीचि)	*pratīc-oḥ* (प्रतीचोः)	*pratyak-ṣu* (प्रत्यक्षु)

Neuter

Nom.	*pratyak* (प्रत्यक्)	*pratīc-ī* (प्रतीची)	**pratyañc-i* (प्रत्यञ्चि)
Acc.	*pratyak* (प्रत्यक्)	*pratīc-ī* (प्रतीची)	**pratyañc-i* (प्रत्यञ्चि)

It will be remembered that the differentiation of strong and weak stems (as also into weakest and middle) was originally the product of a shift in the position of the old accentuation in Indo-European: where the old tonic accent fell on the stem or the suffix, a stronger form of the stem (or the suffix!) developed, but when the accent moved forward to the case-ending, the weaker (middle) or even the weakest form resulted. The stem with the nasal *(pratyañc-)* is the fullest or strong, that without the nasal *(pratyag-/k-)* is in between or middle, and that with loss of the *-a-* of *pratyañc-* or *pratyag-/k-* and conversion of *-y-* to *-ī-* is the weakest. So, theoretically, we go in the following progression from strong to weakest: *praty-añc-, praty-ac-, praty-c-* (with the loss of *-a-)* and finally *pratī-c-*. Exactly the same progression occurs with other adjectives in *-añc* having three degrees; thus, *ny-añc* (that is, *ni + añc)* 'turned *or* bent down (नि), downwards', of which the middle and weakest stems are *ny-ag-/k-* and *nīc-* respectively.

We have taken up the masculine and neuter of these curious stems, but how is the feminine formed? As with the other changeable consonant stems, the feminine is made from the weak stem or weakest where the threefold distinction exists. To this weak or weakest stem is added the characteristically feminine suffix *-ī,* and the resultant product is declined exactly like any *ī*-stem such as *devī* (देवी) or *nadī* (नदी). Thus, from *prāñc* (प्राञ्च्), of which the weak stem is *prāc-* (प्राच्), is formed the feminine *prāc-ī* (प्राची); from *pratyañc* (प्रत्यञ्च्), where, as we have seen, there are three stems, is formed the feminine *pratīc-ī* (प्रतीची) from the weakest stem *pratīc-* (प्रतीच्-).

It may have been noticed that the *-añc/-ac* stems exemplified so far, while *literally* translated 'turned *or* bent in such-and-such a direction', may also be rendered with an adjective ending in the English suffix -ward ('for-ward, back-ward, down-ward', etc.). It is remarkable that this suffix -ward descends genetically from the proto-Indo-European √**wert/wort/wṛt* ;'turn', akin to Sanskrit √*vṛt* (*vartate,* class I), originally also 'turn' (though with a long semantic train of meanings) and to Latin *vert-ere* with the same meaning. Thus, then, the terminal element -ward in these English directional adjectives corresponds precisely *in meaning* to the terminal element *-añc/-ac,* which we saw is simply a suffixal use of √*añc (ac)* 'turn, bend'.

Four of these adjectives in *-añc/-ac,* are used also to denote the cardinal directions; *viz., prāñc* (प्राञ्च्) 'eastern' (*literally* 'for-ward'), *avāñc* (अवाञ्च्) 'southern' (*literally* 'downward'), *pratyañc* (प्रत्यञ्च्) 'western' (*literally* 'back-ward') and *udañc* (उदञ्च्) 'northern' (*literally* 'turned up *or* out, up-ward'). Their feminines *prācī* (प्राची), *avācī,* (अवाची), *pratīcī* (प्रतीची) and *udīcī* (उदीची) are used for East, South, West and North, either *with or without* the word *diś* (दिश्) or *diśā* (दिशा) 'direction' expressed. In naming the cardinal points, Indians begin with the East, the direction which they face in prayer and sacrifice, whereas in western nations the general tendency is to start with the North. From this habitual orientation the words *prāñc* (प्राञ्च्) 'turned before, for-ward' and *pūrva* (पूर्व) 'being *or* situated in front' come also to mean 'eastern'. *Dakṣiṇa* (दक्षिण), *literally* 'right', in this way means also 'southern', and *pratyañc* (प्रत्यञ्च्) 'turned back, back-ward' can also mean 'western'. However, this orientation to the East has nothing to do with the use of *udañc* (उदञ्च्) 'up-ward' for 'northern' and of *avāñc* (अवाञ्च्) 'downward' for 'southern'. These usages are based on the relative elevation of the region north of the Vindhya Mts. as compared to the lowlands of the Deccan.

III. The Story of Sagara and His Sons

महीतलं प्रविश्य तस्करतुरगौ[1] न दृष्ट्वा सर्वे सगरस्यात्मजाः स्वजनकस्य समीपं[2] प्रतिजग्मुः । अस्माभिः सर्वा पृथिवी परिक्रान्ता । भूमिं निर्भिद्य महीतलं च प्रविश्य न तुरगतस्करं न च तुरगं ददृशिम । अपि च बहवो देवदानवराक्षसपिशाचपन्नगा हताः । किं करिष्याम इति । तेषां तद् वचनं श्रुत्वा सगरस् तान् प्रत्यभाषत । भूयः खनत मा विरमध्वम् । चौरं गृहीत्वात्र मम समीपं आनयत । अश्वेन सह विशेषतो निवर्तध्वम् । गच्छत भद्रं व इति । तस्य तद् वचः श्रुत्वैव नृपात्मजाः पृथिवीं पुनश् चख्नुः[3] । ततो महीं खनन्तो महीतलं धारयन्तं विरूपाक्षनामानं दिक्करिणं[4] ददृशुः । स महागजः प्राच्या दिशः पालकः पर्वतसदृशः शिरसैव सगिरिवनां[5] कृत्स्नां पृथिवीं दधार । यदा यदा[6] स विश्रमार्थं शीर्षं खेदाच् चालयेत् तदा तदा[6] भूमिकम्पो भवेत् । तं दिक्पालं महागजं प्रदक्षिणं कृत्वा ते नृपात्मजा मेदिन्याः प्राञ्चं देशं खनितुं पुनर् आरेभिरे । ततस् तेन प्रकारेण प्राचि देशे पृथिवीं निर्भिद्य तस्करतुरगौ न समाप्यावाचीं दिशां भित्त्वा तत्र महापद्मनामानं दिग्गजं ददृशुः । अयं महागजोऽपि सुमहत्पर्वतोपमः[7] सन् पृथिवीं शिरसा दधार । तं अवलोक्य ते सगरस्य पुत्राः परमं विस्मयं जग्मुः । तं हस्तिनं अपि प्रदक्षिणं कृत्वा मानयित्वा च प्रत्यञ्चं देशं बिभिदुः । तत्र महीतलं शीर्षेण धारयन्तं सौमनसनामानं अचलोपमं अपि दिशागजं दृष्ट्वा तं प्रदक्षिणं कृत्वा निरामयं पृष्ट्वा चोदीचीं[8] दिशं आजग्मुः । तत्र भद्रं नाम हिमपाण्डुरं[9] महागजं अवलोक्य यथायोग्यं पूजयित्वा महीं तत्रापि भित्त्वा तुरगं असमाप्य प्रागुदञ्चं देशं गत्वा तत्र पृथिवीं चख्नुः । तत्स्थाने महर्षिं कपिलं अविदूरतश्च यज्ञियं अश्वं चरन्तं

ददृशुः । तुरगं दृष्ट्वैव ते सगरस्य पुत्राः संतुष्टमनसो बभूवुः । तत्क्षणे कपिलं तुरगतस्करं निश्चित्य[10] ते क्रोधपर्याकुललोचनाः[11] खनित्रलाङ्गलादीन्य्[12] आयुधानि धारयन्तस् तं अभिधावितुं समुपचक्रमिरे । तिष्ठ तिष्ठ[13] त्वयास्माकं अश्वो ऽपहृतः । त्वां ग्रहीष्यामः । संप्राप्तान् नः सगरस्यात्मजान् अवगच्छेत्य् उच्चैर् वदन्तस् तस्याभिमुखं दुद्रुवुः । तेषां तद् वचनं श्रुत्वैव कपिलेन महत्क्रोधाग्निना[14] ते सर्वे भस्मराशीकृताः[15] ।

Notes

1. तस्करतुरगौ A dvandva compound 'the thief and the horse', in the dual because two objects are denoted; if the compound meant more than one thief and one horse, the plural would have been required.

2. स्वजनकस्य समीपं 'to their father', *literally* 'to the presence of their father'. With verbs of motion like √गम् (गच्छति) 'go' the 'accusative of the place to which' is used, but when a person is involved, a locution such as 'to the presence *or* vicinity of' with the genitive of the person is used. Thus, नगरं गच्छामि 'I am going to the city', but मम सुहृदः समीपं गच्छामि 'I am going to my friend'. For another example, *cf.* मम समीपं आनयत further on in the text.

3. चख्नुः √खन् (खनति) is one of several commonly used verbs with medial *-a-* (like √गम्), which drop or 'zero-out' this vowel in the weak forms of the perfect; so, *ca-khan-* becomes *ca-kh-n-*.

4. दिक्करिणं According to the traditional Indian belief, the four quarters of the world (East, South, West and North) and the intermediate compass points (Southeast, Southwest, Northwest and Northeast) are in the care or guardianship of certain of the gods (Indra, Yama, Varuṇa and Kubera; Agni, Sūrya, Vāyu and Soma) who in this capacity are called *lokapālas* 'world guardians' or by a synonymous word. Each deity has an elephant, also termed a *lokapāla* (or similarly), which is said to hold up or support the particular sector of the earth over which the god has his jurisdiction. The elephants are all named, as may be seen in the episode here, but there is, in

fact, considerable variation in the names given in the many Sanskrit texts which mention these elephants. Thus, here the elephant guarding the eastern quarter is called Virūpākṣa, but elsewhere other names are given, for example, Airāvata, Abhramātaṅga, Arkasodara, etc.

5. सगिरिवनां 'along with the mountains and woods', a bahuvrīhi compound of a very common type, formed with the inseparable prefix स- 'with' used like an adjective meaning 'accompanying', hence, *literally* '(the earth) having accompanying mountains and woods', but briefly '(the earth) along with the mountains and woods'. Since स- is used as a virtual adjective in this type of compound, we have to say that it is a bahuvrīhi based on a karmadhāraya (adjective + noun).

6. यदा यदा . . . तदा तदा 'Whenever . . . then'. Note the repetition of the relative यदा with the correlative demonstrative adverb to denote repetition.

7. सुमहत्पर्वतोपमः *literally* 'having a likeness with a very (सु-) large mountain', that is, 'like a very large mountain'. This use of उपमा at the end of a bahuvrīhi is very common.

8. चोदीचीं, that is च उदीचीं.

9. हिमपाण्डुरं 'white as snow', a variety of karmadhāraya in which the first member (हिम-) is an object of comparison.

10. कपिलं तुरगतस्करं निश्चित्य 'feeling certain that Kapila was the thief of the horse', *literally* 'determining Kapila (as) the thief of the horse'. A 'that'-clause following a word of mental action (like निश्चित्य here) is normally expressed idiomatically in this way, that is, with the subject of the mental formulation made into a direct object of the verb and the predicate into an adjective or appositional noun.

11. क्रोधपर्याकुललोचनाः That this compound is a bahuvrīhi and not a karmadhāraya may be determined externally or mechanically, so to speak, by the form of the final member -लोचनाः, which would be -लोचनानि if the compound had not been adapted to the masculine gender to agree with ते ('they'). When a compound thus ends in a noun, but is used as an adjective, which, apart from the help afforded by the sense of the sentence, may be ascertained by a change of gender in the final member, the compound must

be a bahuvrīhi. So, the compound महायशाः must be a bahuvrīhi ('having great glory'), not a karmadhāraya ('great glory'), simply because यशस् ('glory') is a neuter *s*-stem which would only lengthen the final vowel when treated as a masculine -- that is, at the end of a compound used as an adjective.

12. खनित्रलाङ्गलादीनि This is also a bahuvrīhi compound of a frequently recurring variety, in which the noun आदि ('beginning') has virtually the value of 'and so forth' or 'etc.'. The compound here modifies आयुधानि 'implements', and so *literally* the meaning is 'implements having shovels and plows as the beginning', that is, 'implements beginning with shovels and plows' or, more idiomatically, 'implements (such as) shovels and plows, etc.'. So common is this usage that आदि has been borrowed into the vernaculars of northern India in the meaning 'and so forth, etc.'. So far has the origin of this meaning been forgotten, that आदि is written *not* as the final member of a compound with the items that are enumerated, but as a separate word!

13. तिष्ठ तिष्ठ to be translated idiomatically: 'Hold on, hold on!'

14. महत्क्रोधाग्निना 'By the fire of his mighty wrath', that is, 'the fire consisting of his mighty wrath', an appositional karmadhāraya compound.

15. भस्मराशीकृताः The roots भू and कृ are often used as the final member of a compound to mean 'become (भू) *or* make into (कृ)' whatever is denoted by the prior member, the resultant condition being the opposite of the previous condition. In these compounds the final of the prior member, if *-a* or *-i,* is replaced by *-ī,* as भस्मराशी- here.

Vocabulary

अचल, *m.* a mountain.
अप-√हृ (हरति, class I), take away (अप); *ppp.* अपहृत.
अपि च, *conj. phrase,* moreover.
अभि-√धाव् (धावति, class I), run unto *or* against; *infin.* धावितुम्.
अभिमुखम्, *adv.* towards, against (+ *gen.*).
अव-√गम् (गच्छति, class I), understand, know.

अव-√लोक् (लोकयति), see. [strictly a *causative, but without causative meaning!*]

अवाञ्च्, *adj.* turned *or* bent down (अव), downward; southern.

अविदूरतः, *adj.* not far away.

असमाप्य, *negative gerund of* सम्-√आप् (आप्नोति, class V), not having gotten.

आत्मज, *adj.* 'born of oneself', *as m.* a son.

आदि, *m.* a beginning; *used at the end of bahuvrīhi compounds* 'having . . . as the beginning, beginning with . . .', *hence* 'so-and-so, etc.'.

आ-√नी (नयति, class I), bring.

आयुध, *n.* weapon; implement.

आ-√रभ् (रभते, class I), take hold of, undertake, *hence* begin; *perf.* °रेभे, (*plur.* °रेभिरे).

उच्चैः, *adv.* aloud.

उदञ्च्, *adj.* turned *or* bent up (उद्), upward; northern. [weakest stem उदीच्-, middle उदग्-/क्-]

उपमा, *f.* comparison; likeness; *at end of a bahuvrīhi compound* 'having a likeness with ...', like....

कपिल, *m.* Kapila, name of a great sage, identified here with Viṣṇu.

कम्प, *m.* trembling, shaking, quaking.

करिन्, *m.* an elephant [*literally* 'having a hand' with reference to its trunk; exactly equivalent to हस्तिन्].

कृत्स्न, *adj.* whole, entire, all.

क्रोध, *m.* anger, wrath.

√खन् (खनति, class I), dig; *perf.* चखान (*plur.* चख्नुः).

खनित्र, *n.* a digging implement, a spade *or* shovel.

खेद, *m.* fatigue.

√ग्रह् (गृह्णाति, class IX), seize, take, grasp; *gerund* गृहीत्वा.

√चर् (चरति, class I), move, go; wander; graze.

√चल् (चलति, class I), move; *caus.* चालयति, causes to move, moves *(trans.)*.

चौर, *m.* a thief.

जनक, *m.* a father.

तस्कर, *m.* a thief.

तुरग, *m.* a horse.

दिश्, *f.* cardinal point *or* direction.

दिशा, *f.* cardinal point *or* compass direction. [an extension of दिश्]
√दृश् (no present, √पश् is used), see; *perf.* ददर्श, (*plur.* ददृशुः).
देश, *m.* place; region.
√द्रु (द्रवति, class I), run; *perf.* दुद्राव (*plur.* दुद्रुवुः).
√धृ (धारयति), hold up, support. [This root does not have a regular present, धारयति being a *causative without causative meaning!*]
निरामय, *m.* 'freedom from illness (आमय)', health, welfare.
नि-√वृत् (वर्तते, class I), return.
निस्-√चि (चिनोति, class V), decide, settle, conclude as certain.
निस्-√भिद् (भिनत्ति, class VII), split open (निः); *gerund* निर्भिद्य.
पन्नग, *m.* a serpent *or* serpent demon.
परम, *adj.* farthest; extreme.
परि-√क्रम् (क्रामति, class I), step *or* go around; *ppp.* परिक्रान्त.
पर्याकुल, *adj.* agitated.
पाण्डुर, *adj.* white.
पाल, *m.* protector.
पिशाच, *m.* a kind of demon or goblin, often mentioned with *rākṣasas* and other demons.
प्रकार, *m.* sort, kind; manner, way.
√प्रछ् (पृच्छति, class VI), ask about (+ *acc.*); *gerund* पृष्ट्वा.
प्रति-√गम् (गच्छति, class I), go back, return; *perf.* °जगाम (*plur.* °जग्मुः).
प्रति-√भाष् (भाषते, class I), answer.
प्रत्यञ्च्, *adj.* turned *or* bent backward; backward; western.
प्रदक्षिणं-√कृ (करोति, class VIII), move around (an object to be venerated), keeping it to the right.
प्र-√विश् (विशति, class VI), enter.
प्रागुदञ्च्, *adj.* northeastern.
प्राञ्च्, *adj.* turned *or* bent forward, forward; eastern.
भद्र, *m.* Bhadra, name of the elephant guardian of the northern quarter.
भद्र, *adj.* blessed, fortunate; as *n.* happiness, good fortune; भद्रं वः, if you please (used parenthetically).
भस्मराशीकृत, *adj.* made into *or* reduced to a heap of ashes.
√भिद् (भिनत्ति, class VII), split; *gerund* भित्त्वा.
भूमि, *f.* the earth.

भूयः, *adv.* again.
महापद्म, *m.* Mahāpadma, name of the elephant that supports the southern quarter of the earth.
मही, *f.* the earth.
महीतल, *n.* the surface of the earth.
मा, *adv.* not (used with the imperative to express a prohibition).
√मानय (मानयति), honor [a denominative stem from मान, *m.* honor].
मेदिनी, *f.* the earth.
यज्ञिय, *adj.* belonging to *or* connected with the sacrifice, sacrificial.
यथायोग्यम्, *adv.* suitably, properly.
लाङ्गल, *n.* a plow.
लोचन, *n.* the eye.
वचन, *n.* speech; words.
वि-√रम् (रमति, °ते, class I), stop, cease.
विरूपाक्ष, *m.* Virūpākṣa, name of the great elephant that holds up the eastern quarter of the earth. [*literally* 'having variegated *or* deformed eyes']
विशेषतः, *adv.* especially.
विश्रम, *m.* rest, repose.
विस्मय, *m.* astonishment, amazement.
शिरस्, *n.* the head.
शीर्ष, *n.* the head.
सदृश, *adj.* of like appearance, similar to.
सं-√तुष् (तुष्यति, class IV), be satisfied, be pleased; *ppp.* संतुष्ट.
सम्-√आप् (आप्नोति, class V), reach, get; find.
समीप, *n.* nearness; presence.
सम्-उप-√क्रम् (क्रामति, class I), step up to; begin; *perf.* समुपचक्रमे (*plur.* °चक्रमिरे).
सं-प्र-√आप् (आप्नोति, class V), arrive, come; *ppp.* संप्राप्त.
सौमनस, *m.* Saumanasa, name of the guardian elephant of the western quarter.
√हन् (हन्ति, class II), strike, strike down; slay; *ppp.* हत.
हस्तिन्, *m.* an elephant; *v.* under करिन् above.
हिम, *m.* cold; winter; snow.

Translate into Sanskrit:

After entering the earth, the sons of the king, having found neither the horse nor the thief, returned to their father and informed him of all that had happened.[1] Extremely disturbed, King Sagara addressed those sons: 'Go again, dig up the earth again; until you have seen the horse and the thief do not return!'[2] and so saying he sent them to dig up the earth again. Thereupon, while digging up[3] the earth again, they saw the direction-elephant named Virūpākṣa, guardian of the eastern region. This mighty elephant supports the entire surface of the earth only with his head (which is) like a mountain;[4] whenever he moves his head in order to rest[5] due to fatigue, then there is an earthquake. After making a *pradakṣiṇa* around this elephant[6] and inquiring about[7] his health and in the same way seeing and worshipping the other elephants, guardians of the directions, finally they came to the northeastern region. Having dug up the earth there and split it open, they saw the great sage Kapila and not far away the sacrificial horse grazing happily. Assuming[8] this was the thief, the sons of Sagara, their eyes agitated with anger,[9] holding in their hands weapons such as spears and pikes,[10] while saying aloud: 'You took away our horse—we'll seize you!', ran toward him. As soon as he saw them, with the fire of his wrath[11] he reduced them to a heap of ashes.

Notes

1. 'of all that had happened': This phrase should be treated as a noun, object of 'informed' (*caus.* of नि-√विद्); thus, सर्वं यथावृत्तम्, *literally* 'everything as happened'. यथावृत्तम् may be regarded either as an avyayībhāva compound or as a neuter noun abstracted from it; 'him', the other object can be expressed in Sanskrit by the *acc.*, *dat.* or even the *loc.* (*cf.* Nala story, I.66 and note thereon).

2. 'until you have seen ... do not return': With the correlative conjunction यावत् ('as long as')... तावत् ('so long'), Sanskrit idiom requires a negative in the यावत्-clause; thus, 'as long as the horse and the thief have *not* been seen by you, so long do not return'.

3. 'while digging up': to be expressed by a present participle, *not* a gerund, because the action of digging up is contemporaneous with that of the main

verb 'they saw'. The gerund, it should be remembered, expresses an action that *precedes* that of the main verb.

4. 'with his head (which is) like a mountain': Express this by a karmadhāraya compound in the *instr.* Part A will be गिरि (or पर्वत)-सदृश, an *instr.* tatpuruṣa ('similar *with* a mountain').

5. 'in order to rest': a compound ending in -अर्थम् or a 'dative of purpose', as often an equivalent of a phrase introduced by 'in order to'.

6. 'After making a *pradakṣiṇa* around this elephant': इमं गजं (or another one of the many words for 'elephant') प्रदक्षिणं कृत्वा; प्रदक्षिणं in this usage is really an *acc. n. sing.* used as an adverb and इमं गजं is the direct object of कृत्वा .

7. 'inquiring about': Use √प्रछ् which takes a direct object of the thing inquired about.

8. 'Assuming': *v.* note 3 above; similarly 'while saying aloud' below.

9. 'their eyes agitated with anger': Use a bahuvrīhi compound for this absolute expression.

10. 'weapons such as spears and pikes': Phrases like this, where there are mentioned several items of the same class with the implication of additional ones (not mentioned) are expressed by a bahuvrīhi ending in -आदि 'beginning', *literally*, 'having such-and-such as the beginning', but including more of the same.

11. 'with the fire of his wrath': Express by means of an appositional karmadhāraya: 'with the fire (which is) his wrath' (क्रोधाग्निना).

LESSON TWENTY-THREE

Noun Stems in *-ṛ*.

In our treatment of the noun, we have seen that noun stems may end in a vowel or a consonant, thus forming the two great classes into which the Sanskrit noun may be conveniently arranged. In addition to the vowel stems we have studied thus far, there is a large and important group ending in the vowel *-ṛ*. There are also nouns ending in a diphthong (except *-e);* they are few in number and will be taken up later.

There are two groups of nouns that end in the vowel *-ṛ:* the one consists of most of the common words for familial relationships (that is, words for 'mother, brother, sister', etc.), numbering hardly more than nine or ten, most of which end in *-tṛ*, a few in *-ṛ*; the other, which is a very large group and ends exclusively in *-tṛ* or *-i-tṛ,* consists of nouns that denote 'one who does this or that', (for example, 'giver, doer, slayer, winner', etc.).[1] Theoretically, these agent nouns can be made from any root, though in practice, of course, not every root has an agent noun. The suffix *-tṛ* is added to the guṇated root, sometimes with, sometimes without an interposed *-i-*. Thus, *je-tṛ* (जेतृ) 'conqueror' from √जि 'conquer', *kar-tṛ* (कर्तृ) 'doer' from √कृ 'do', but from √रक्ष् 'protect' is formed *rakṣ-i-tṛ* (रक्षितृ).

In the declension of these agent nouns in *-tṛ/-itṛ* a differentiation between strong and weak forms is made: the usual strong cases (nominative-accusative singular and dual, and nominative, but *not* accusative plural) change *-ṛ-* to *-ār-*, that is, they replace *-ṛ-* by its vṛddhi substitute *-ār-*. The endings are the usual endings seen in the declension of consonant stems, except that in the ablative and genitive singular *-uḥ* (for *-ur*!) replaces *-aḥ*, before which *-r* of the stem is lost. There are a few other peculiarities, but it is best first to see the declension, then remark on the deviations. Here is the declension of the agent noun *dā-tṛ* (दातृ) 'giver':

	Singular	*Dual*	*Plural*
Nom.	**dātā* (दाता)	**dātār-au* (दातारौ)	**dātār-aḥ* (दातारः)
Acc.	**dātār-am* (दातारम्)	**dātār-au* (दातारौ)	*dātṝn* (दातॄन्)
Instr.	*dātr-ā* (दात्रा)	*dātṛ-bhyām* (दातृभ्याम्)	*dātṛ-bhiḥ* (दातृभिः)

---

[1]The suffix *-tṛ* in the nouns of relationship seems to be only fortuitously identical to the *-tṛ* used to form agent nouns.

Dat.	*dātr-e* (दात्रे)	*dātṛ-bhyām* (दातृभ्याम्)	*dātṛ-bhyaḥ* (दातृभ्यः)
Abl.	*dāt-uḥ* (दातुः)	*dātṛ-bhyām* (दातृभ्याम्)	*dātṛ-bhyaḥ* (दातृभ्यः)
Gen.	*dāt-uḥ* (दातुः)	*dātr-oḥ* (दात्रोः)	*dātṝ-ṇ-ām* (दातॄणाम्)
Loc.	*dātar-i* (दातरि)	*dātr-oḥ* (दात्रोः)	*dātṛ-ṣu* (दातृषु)
Voc.	*dātar* (दातर्)	*dātār-au* (दातारौ)	*dātār-aḥ* (दातारः)

Note that the nominative singular is *dātā* (दाता) instead of the expected *dātāḥ* (for *dātār[-s])*. The loss of the final *-r* here is parallel to the loss of the final *-n* of *n*-stems, as in *rājā* (राजा) for *rājān*.[2] Where an ending begins with a vowel, as in the weak cases of the singular and the genitive-locative dual, the vowel *-ṛ* is replaced by its cognate semivowel *-r;* thus, instrumental *dātr-ā* (दात्रा) for *dātṛ-ā*. The locative singular *dātar-i* दातरि) is peculiar in replacing the *-ṛ* by its guṇa substitute *(-ar-)* before the ending *-i*. Finally, the accusative and genitive plural are 'analogical' forms, that is to say they replace the expected *dātr-aḥ* and *dātr-ām* by *dātṝn* (दातॄन्) and *dātṝ-ṇām* (दातॄणाम्) which are patterned after these cases in the vowel stems: *devān/devānām* (देवान्/देवानाम्), *agnīn/agnīnām* (अग्नीन्/अग्नीनाम्), *bhānūn/bhānūnām* (भानून्/भानूनाम्).

The feminine of an agent noun in *-tṛ* is made by adding the suffix *-ī* to the stem. Thus, from *dātṛ* (दातृ) is made *dātr-ī*, from *kartṛ* (कर्तृ) 'doer' is formed *kartr-ī* (कर्त्री). The feminine is declined exactly like नदी or देवी.

The nouns of relationship, the other class of stems in *-ṛ*, differ from the agent nouns only in the *strong* forms and, in the case of feminine nouns, in the accusative plural. In the strong forms the final *-ṛ* is replaced by *-ar-*, the guṇa substitute of *-ṛ*, *not* by *-ār-*. In the accusative plural of feminine nouns, the ending *-ṝḥ* replaces *-ṝn* of the masculine nouns. The declensions of *pitṛ* (पितृ) 'father' and *mātṛ* (मातृ) 'mother' are:

---

[2]Apparently in the parent Indo-European language there were two forms of the nominative of *r-* and *n*-stems, the one with *-r/-n,* the other without *-r/-n*. Some languages *generalized* the one form, others the other. Thus, Sanskrit, Old Persian and Avestan generalized the form without *-r/-n;* Greek and Latin both keep the *-r* (as in Greek *dā́tōr,* Latin *dātor)* but, whereas Greek retains the final *-n* (*cf. hēgemṓn, poimḗn*), Latin drops it, as in *sermō* (genitive *sermōn-is), homō* (genitive *homin-is).*

Singular

Nom.	**pitā*	(पिता)	**mātā*	(माता)
Acc.	**pitar-am*	(पितरम्)	**mātar-am*	(मातरम्)
Instr.	*pitr-ā*	(पित्रा)	*mātr-ā*	(मात्रा)
Dat.	*pitr-e*	(पित्रे)	*mātr-e*	(मात्रे)
Abl.	*pit-uḥ*	(पितुः)	*māt-uḥ*	(मातुः)
Gen.	*pit-uḥ*	(पितुः)	*māt-uḥ*	(मातुः)
Loc.	*pitar-i*	(पितरि)	*mātar-i*	(मातरि)
Voc.	*pitar*	(पितर्)	*mātar*	(मातर्)

Dual

Nom.-Acc.-Voc.	**pitar-au* (पितरौ)	**mātar-au* (मातरौ)
Instr.-Dat.-Abl.	*pitṛ-bhyām* (पितृभ्याम्)	*mātṛ-bhyām* (मातृभ्याम्)
Gen.-Loc.	*pitr-oḥ* (पित्रोः)	*mātr-oḥ* (मात्रोः)

Plural

Nom.-Voc.	**pitar-aḥ*	(पितरः)	**mātar-aḥ*	(मातरः)
Acc.	*pitṝn*	(पितॄन्)	*mātṝḥ*	(मातॄः)
Instr.	*pitṛ-bhiḥ*	(पितृभिः)	*mātṛ-bhiḥ*	(मातृभिः)
Dat.-Abl.	*pitṛ-bhyaḥ*	(पितृभ्यः)	*mātṛ-bhyaḥ*	(मातृभ्यः)
Gen.	*pitṝ-ṇ-ām*	(पितॄणाम्)	*mātṝ-ṇ-ām*	(मातॄणाम्)
Loc.	*pitṛ-ṣu*	(पितृषु)	*mātṛ-ṣu*	(मातृषु)

Two words of relationship, *naptṛ* (नप्तृ) 'grandson' and *svasṛ* (स्वसृ) 'sister', replace *-ṛ* by *-ār-* in the strong stems, as in the agent nouns. Thus, *naptā* (नप्ता), *naptār-am* (नप्तारम्), *naptār-au* (नप्तारौ), *naptār-aḥ* (नप्तारः), *naptṝn* (नप्तॄन्); *svasā* (स्वसा), *svasār-am* (स्वसारम्), *svasār-au* (स्वसारौ), *svasṝḥ* (स्वसॄः). The word *bhartṛ* (भर्तृ) 'husband', though classed as a noun of relationship because of its meaning, is in origin an agent noun and is so declined. It is derived from √भृ 'bear, *hence* support, maintain' and literally means 'one who supports *or* maintains.' Derived from the same root is *bhāryā* (भार्या) 'wife', literally 'she who is to be supported *or* maintained'.

IV. The Story of Sagara and His Sons

चिरगतान् पुत्राञ् ज्ञात्वा[1] सगरो राजा तद् वाक्यं अंशुमन्तं नप्तारं उवाच । पुत्रा मे चिरगताः । गच्छ शीघ्रं गच्छ । पितॄणां ते गतिं अन्विच्छ । यत्र यज्ञियस् तुरगो विद्यते तत्र गत्वा हयहर्तारं गृहीत्वा सहयो[2] निवर्तस्व । त्वया तथा क्रियतां यथेदं यज्ञच्छिद्रं अचिराद् विरमेत्[3] । सिद्धार्थो[4] यज्ञं मे निर्वर्तयितुं प्रत्यागच्छ इति महात्मनः पितृपितुर् वचनं श्रुत्वा तथेत्य् उक्त्वा[5] च महातेजा अंशुमान् सशरं[6] धनुर् आदाय[7] सत्वरं जगाम । ततः स महात्मभिः पितृभिः खातं अन्तर्भौमं मार्गं प्रपेदे । तत्र देवदानवरक्षःपिशाचोरगैः पूज्यमानं[8] महान्तं दिशागजं ददर्श । तदनन्तरं स तं महाहस्तिनं प्रदक्षिणं कृत्वा निरामयं च पृष्ट्वा पितॄन् वाजिहर्तारं च परिपप्रच्छ । महामतिस् तु दिशागजस् तच् छ्रुत्वा तं प्रत्युवाच । असमञ्जस्य पुत्र कृतार्थस्[9] त्वं सहाश्वः शीघ्रं प्रत्यागमिष्यसीति । तस्य हस्तिनस् तद् वचनं आकर्ण्य ततः सर्वान् एव दिशागजान् यथाक्रमं यथायोग्यं च प्रष्टुं समुपचक्रमे । सर्वे ते गजा एवं तेन पृष्टास् त्वं सहयः प्रत्यागमिष्यसीति तं ऊचुः । तेषां तैर् वचनैर् अभिचोदितो यस्मिन् स्थाने[10] पितरः सागराः कपिलेन भस्मराशीकृता बभूवुः तत् स्थानं[10] सो ऽविलम्बं विवेद । ततः पितॄन् भस्मराशीकृतान् अवलोक्यांशुमान्[11] परमदुःखवशं गत्वा तेषां वधाच् छोकान्वितश् चुक्रोश । तदा ततो ऽविदूरतश् चरन्तं यज्ञियं अश्वं ददर्श । स पुरुषव्याघ्रस्[12] तेषां राजपुत्राणां जलक्रियां[13] कर्तुकामो ऽपि[14] जलाशयं तत्र नापश्यत् । समन्ततो निपुणां दृष्टिं विसार्य सुपर्णनामानं पितॄणां मातुलं खगमाधिपं ददर्श । ततः सुमतिभ्राता सुपर्णो वैनतेयो महात्मानं महातेजसं अंशुमन्तं तद् वचनं उवाच । मा

शोच[15] पुरुषव्याघ्र । महर्षिणाप्रमेयेण[16] कपिलेन ह्रीमे[17] राजपुत्राः पितरस् ते दग्धाः । लौकिकं एव सलिलं पितॄणां ते भस्मनां पावनार्थं प्रयोक्तुं न शक्नोषि । हिमवतो[18] ज्येष्ठा दुहिता गङ्गेति विश्रुता । तस्यां एव नद्यां तेषां पितॄणां सलिलक्रियां कर्तुं अर्हसि[19] । अस्मिन् भस्मनि तया गङ्गया क्लिन्ने[20] सर्वे ते राजपुत्राः स्वर्गलोकं गमिष्यन्ति । अश्वं आदाय गच्छ पुरुषर्षभ । पितामहस्य यज्ञं निर्वर्तयितुं अर्हसीति । सुपर्णवचनं श्रुत्वैव महातपा अंशुमान् हयं गृहीत्वा सगरस्य राज्ञः समीपं त्वरितं प्रत्याजगाम । तस्य समीपं प्रत्यागम्य यथावृत्तं तथा तं न्यवेदयत् । अंशुमतो वाक्यं श्रुत्वा तेन महीपतिनाश्वमेधो यथाकल्पं निर्वर्तितः । ततो यज्ञं इष्ट्वा[21] नराधिपः स्वपुरं जगाम । किन्तु गङ्गाया आगमे निश्चयं नाधिगत्य सगरो राजा महता कालेन[22] त्रिंशद् वर्षसहस्राणि राज्यं कृत्वा दिवं गतः ।

Notes

1. चिरगतान् पुत्राञ् ज्ञात्वा 'having realized that his sons were gone for a long time'. Note once again this typical, idiomatic construction with a verb of mental action (here ज्ञात्वा), whereby the thought is expressed by an accusative and predicate adjective ('having realized his sons as gone for a very long time'), whereas in English a 'that'-clause is used ('having known that' etc.); *v.* note 10 in Lesson 22.

2. सहयो 'with the horse', equivalent to हयेन सह, a bahuvrīhi compound in which the inseparable prefix स functions as an adjective: 'having an accompanying (स-) horse'.

3. तथा क्रियतां यथेदं . . . विरमेत् *Literally* 'Let it be done in that way (तथा), in which way (यथा) this . . . might come to an end', *i.e.,* 'See to it that this comes to an end'. क्रियतां is the third person singular *passive* imperative of √कृ (करोति, class VIII) 'do'.

4. सिद्धार्थो a bahuvrīhi compound, *literally* 'having an attained object', but here virtually equivalent to a temporal clause: 'When you have attained your object'. It may be noted that Gautama Buddha was also called 'Siddhārtha' in a slightly extended sense: 'He who has fulfilled the object (of his coming)'.

5. तथेत्य् उक्त्वा 'Having said "So [be it]!"', an extremely common formula of assent or acquiescence. Occasionally the fuller form तथा भवतु, with the imperative of √भू expressed, is used.

6. सशरं equivalent to शरैः सह; *v.* note 2 above on this type of compound.

7. आदाय gerund of आ-√दा 'take', hence, *literally* 'having taken', but practically equivalent to 'with, along with'; *v.* अश्वं आदाय below.

8. पूज्यमानं 'being honored *or* worshipped', present *passive* participle of √पूज् (पूजयति, class X).

9. कृतार्थस् identical in meaning to सिद्धार्थ above and also used in the same way as equivalent to a temporal clause.

10. यस्मिन् स्थाने . . . तत् स्थानं Remember the predilection of Sanskrit for putting the relative clause *first* and picking up the noun to which it refers (here स्थाने incorporated into the relative clause) by a demonstrative later, with or without the same noun repeated (in the appropriate case, of course): '*In which place* (his forefathers had been reduced to a heap of ashes), *that place* (he found without delay)', that is, 'He found the place without delay where his forefathers had been reduced to a heap of ashes'.

11. पितॄन् भस्मराशीकृतान् अवलोक्य 'Seeing that his fathers had been reduced to a heap of ashes', *v.* note 1 above.

12. पुरुषव्याघ्रस् *Literally* a 'man-tiger', either in the sense of a 'man like a tiger' or a 'tiger (in the form) of a man', but in either case a way of saying a 'distinguished *or* heroic man'. Words for 'bull' (ऋषभ, पुङ्गव), 'tiger' (व्याघ्र as here, or शार्दूल) and 'lion' (सिंह) are thus compounded with पुरुष or a synonymous word with the greatest frequency.

13. जलक्रियां a 'water-ceremony' to purify the dead, but, as we shall see subsequently, ordinary water of *this world* (लौकिकम् एव सलिलं) is not able to produce this result. Hence the necessity of bringing down the Ganges (Gaṅgā), at this time only a heavenly river, to bathe and purify the ashes.

14. कर्तुकामो ऽपि 'although desirous of performing' (the water-ceremony); कर्तुकाम *literally* 'having a desire to perform' is a bahuvrīhi compound whose first member (कर्तु-) is the infinitive कर्तुम् with its म् dropped. Compounds of this type are thus often made with काम 'desire'.

15. मा शोच 'Do not grieve!' Prohibitions (*i.e.,* negative commands) are made in Sanskrit with the negative particle मा (not न !) either with the imperative (as here) or with the imperfect *minus* the augment; thus मा शोचः.

16. अप्रमेयेण Sages or holy men are often called 'immeasurable' or by an equivalent word or by an expanded epithet of more elaborate but similar import to denote the inexpressible character of their wisdom and the immense power inherent in it.

17. ह्रीमे Be careful of the sandhi here!

18. हिमवतो a predicate possessive genitive: '(On the part) of Himavat (is) an eldest daughter', *i.e.,* 'Himavat has an eldest daughter'.

19. अर्हसि The √अर्ह् 'have the right to' is often used to express necessity; so here 'you should perform' etc.; so also in निर्वर्तयितुं अर्हसि below.

20. अस्मिन् भस्मनि . . . क्लिन्ने a locative absolute.

21. इष्ट्वा gerund of √यज् (यजति, class I). As in the past participle इष्ट, the य- is replaced by इ- by *saṃprasāraṇa.* It may be noted here that in general a gerund shows the same form of the root that is seen in the past passive participle. Thus, the gerund may be formed by changing the final -अ *(-a)* of a ppp. to -वा, so दृष्ट्वा on दृष्ट *(i.e., dṛṣṭ + vā),* पृष्ट्वा on पृष्ट.

22. महता कालेन 'after much time', an 'instrumental of time at the end of which'.

Vocabulary

अचिरात्, *adv.* soon.
अधि-√गम् (गच्छति, class I), go to, attain, arrive at.
अधिप, *m.* overlord, lord; ruler.
अनु-√इ (एति, class II), go along *or* after, accompany; *ppp.* अन्वित accompanied by, filled with.
अनु-√इष् (इच्छति, class VI), seek after, search after.
अन्तर्भौम, *adj.* being in the interior of the earth, subterranean.
अप्रमेय, *adj.* immeasurable.
अभि-√चुद् (चोदति, class I), drive on, impel; *caus. same mg.; ppp. of caus.* चोदित.
√अर्ह् (अर्हति, class I), deserve, be worthy to, be obliged to, have to.
अविदूरतः, *adv.* not very far away.
अविलम्बम्, *adv.* without delay.
आकर्णय, *denom. stem from* *आकर्ण 'having the ear to', *i.e.*, listening, a bahuvrīhi cpd; *gerund* आकर्ण्य.
आगम, *m.* coming, approaching.
उरग, *m.* a serpent. [*literally* 'breast-goer']
कर्तुकाम, *adj.* desiring to do *or* perform.
किन्तु, *conj.* but.
कृतार्थ, *adj.* having one's object *or* goal made, having attained one's object.
√क्रुश् (क्रोशति, class I), cry; lament, weep; *perf.* चुक्रोश.
√क्लिद् (क्लिद्यति, class IV), be *or* become wet; *ppp.* क्लिन्न, moistened.
खगम, *m.* a bird. [*literally* 'sky-goer']
√खन् (खनति, class I), dig, dig up; *ppp.* खात.
गति, *f.* way, path.
√ग्रह् (गृह्णाति, class IX), seize, grasp, take; *gerund* गृहीत्वा.
चिरगत, *adj.* gone for a long time.
छिद्र, *n.* hole; gap.
जलक्रिया, *f.* a water ceremony offered to the dead.
जलाशय, *m.* a pond, a lake.

√ज्ञा (जानाति, class IX), know; come to know, learn; notice; *gerund* ज्ञात्वा.
ज्येष्ठ, *superlative adj.* eldest.
ततः, *adv.* from that *or* there, from that place.
तथा, *adv.* in that manner, so, thus; *as a particle of assent or agreement,* yes, so be it.
त्रिंशत्, *f.* thirty.
त्वरितम्, *adv.* quickly.
√दह् (दहति, class I), burn; *ppp.* दग्ध.
दिव, *n.* heaven.
दुहितृ, *f.* a daughter.
दुःख, *n.* pain, sorrow.
दृष्टि, *f.* seeing; sight; glance.
धनुस्, *n.* a bow.
नप्तृ, *m.* grandson.
निपुण, *adj.* clever; skilful, sharp, acute, keen.
निरामय, *m.* 'freedom from illness', health, welfare.
नि-√विद् (वेत्ति, class II), know; *caus.* निवेदयति, 'causes to know', informs.
नि-√वृत् (वर्तते, class I), turn back, return.
निश्चय, *m.* determination, resolve.
निस्-√वृत् (वर्तते, class I), turn *or* roll out, evolve, develop; be effected *or* accomplished; *caus.* निर्वर्तयति, causes to be accomplished, accomplishes, finishes; *infin. of caus.* निर्वर्तयितुम्; *ppp.* निर्वर्तित.
परि-√प्रछ् (पृच्छति, class VI), ask about, inquire about; *perf.* परिपप्रच्छ.
पावन, *m.* cleansing, purification.
पितामह, *m.* a grandfather.
पितृ, *m.* father; *in plural* forefathers, ancestors.
पितृपितृ, *m.* 'father of one's father', *i.e.*, grandfather.
पुर, *n.* a city.
पुरुषव्याघ्र, *m.* a man-tiger, *i.e.,* a man like a tiger, a man of courage.
√पूज् (पूजयति, class X), honor; worship; *pres. pass. part.* पूज्यमान, being worshipped.
√प्रछ् (पृच्छति, class VI), ask; *ppp.* पृष्ट; *infin.* प्रष्टुम्.
प्रत्य्-आ-√गम् (गच्छति, class I), come back, return.
प्र-√पद् (पद्यते, class IV), step forth, set out for; reach, enter; *perf.* प्रपाद, °पेदे.

प्र-√युज् (युनक्ति, class VII), use; *infin.* प्रयोक्तुम्.
भस्मन्, *n.* ashes.
भ्रातृ, *m.* a brother.
महात्मन्, *adj.* having a great soul, noble.
महामति, *adj.* having great understanding, wise.
मातुल, *m.* a maternal uncle.
यथाकल्पम्, *adv.* in conformity with the ritual (कल्प).
यथाक्रमम् *adv.* according to order, in succession.
यथायोग्यम्, *adv.* according to propriety, properly, suitably.
यथावृत्तम्, *adv.* as happened, *i.e.,* as it happened *or* took place.
रक्षस्, *n.* harm; one who harms, a harmer, a demon.
लौकिक, *adj.* belonging to the world (लोक), worldly; *hence,* not sacred.
√वच् (वक्ति, class II), say, speak to; *perf.* उवाच (*plur.* ऊचुः).
वध, *m.* slaying, slaughter.
वश, *m.* controlling power, influence.
वाजिन्, *m.* a horse.
2√विद् (विन्दति, class VI), find; *perf.* विवेद.
वि-√रम् (रमति, °ते, class I), stop, cease.
विश्रुत, *ppp.* वि-√श्रु (शृणोति, class V), *literally* 'heard far and wide, well-known', *then attenuated to* 'known, called'.
वि-√सृ (सिसर्ति, class III), go in various directions (वि-); *caus.* विसारयति causes to go *or* move in various directions, directs here and there; *gerund of caus.* विसार्य.
वैनतेय, *m.* the son of Vinatā, metronymic for Suparṇa (or Garuḍa), the chief of birds.
√शक् (शक्नोति, class V), can, be able.
शर, *m.* an arrow.
शीघ्रम्, *adv.* quickly.
√शुच् (शोचति, class I), grieve, sorrow.
शोक, *m.* pain, grief.
सत्वरम्, *adv.* quickly, right away.
समन्ततः, *adv.* on all sides, everywhere.
सम्-उप-√क्रम् (क्रामति, क्रमते, class I), 'step up to', approach; begin; *perf.* समुपचक्रमे.

सलिल, *n.* water.

सहस्र. *n.* a thousand.

सागर, *m. in plur.* the sons of King Sagara.

सिद्धार्थ, *adj.* having one's goal *or* end achieved, whose goal has been achieved. [सिद्ध, *ppp.* √सिध् (सिध्यति, class IV, be accomplished *or* realized)]

सुमति, *f.* Sumati, name of a wife of Sagara, sister of Suparṇa, the overlord of birds. She bore Sagara 60,000 sons.

सुपर्ण, *m.* Suparṇa, name of the bird also called Garuḍa, son of Kaśyapa and Vinatā (hence, known by the metronymic Vainateya); Suparṇa was the brother of Sumati, a wife of King Sagara.

स्थान, *n.* place, spot.

स्वर्गलोक, *m.* the heavenly world, heaven.

हय, *m.* a horse.

हर्तृ, *m.* one who takes away, a thief, a robber.

हिमवत्, *m.* Himavat, the Himālaya personified as father of Pārvatī (Śiva's wife, also called 'daughter of the mountain') and Gaṅgā, the Ganges River.

Translate into Sanskrit:

After waiting for a long time for the return of his sons, disturbed in mind,[1] King Sagara summoned his grandson Aṃśumat and said to him: 'My sons have not yet returned. Quickly go to where the earth has been dug up by them.[2] Search after them! Bring back the sacrificial horse with them!' Having entered the place in the earth which had been dug up and split open[3] by his ancestors, he performed a *pradakṣiṇa* around all the mighty direction-elephants, venerated them and inquired after their health. Told by all these elephants that he would return with the horse, impelled by their words, he came without delay to the place where Sagara's sons had been reduced to a heap of ashes by the great sage Kapila. When he saw the heap of ashes, he was deeply sorrowed and wept for a long time. Then, when he saw the sacrificial horse grazing not far away, he was joyful at heart.[4] Although desirous of performing[5] the water-ceremony to purify[6] the ashes of his ancestors, he did not see water there. Thereupon, Vainateya, Sumati's brother, named Suparṇa, came up and informed Aṃśumat: 'In order to purify the ashes of your ancestors you must[7] not use water of this world,[8] but when the ashes have been moistened[9] only in the river Gaṅgā will these princes go to the world of heaven. Therefore, Gaṅgā, Himavat's eldest daughter, must be brought down[10] from heaven to purify their ashes. When he heard these words of Suparṇa, he took the sacrificial horse and, having returned to his grandsire Sagara, he told him all that had happened.[11] Then they began to complete the aśvamedha duly.

Notes

1. 'disturbed in mind': Express with a bahuvrīhi cpd., 'having a disturbed mind'.

2. 'go to where the earth has been dug up by them': Render idiomatically: 'where the earth has been ... there go'.

3. 'which had been dug up and split open': Do not use a relative clause, but participles: 'having been dug up and split open'.

4. 'he was joyful at heart': Express with a bahuvrīhi cpd. similarly constructed to that under note 1 above.

5. 'Although desirous of performing': कर्तुकामो ऽपि, the particle अपि with an adjectival word being sufficient to express the concessive sense.

6. 'to purify': पावनार्थम् with an objective *gen.* (भस्मनाम्); similarly 'in order to purify' in the next sentence.

7. 'you must': अर्हसि with an infinitive.

8. 'water of this world': लौकिकं सलिलम् rather than literally अस्य लोकस्य सलिलम्.

9. 'when the ashes have been moistened': Make this temporal or circumstantial clause into a locative absolute.

10. 'must be brought down': Use the gerundive of the causative of अव-√तॄ, *i.e.*, अवतारयितव्य.

11. 'all that had happened': *v.* note 1 on English exercise in Lesson 22.

LESSON TWENTY-FOUR

Combined Devanāgarī Writing. Sandhi Again.

When Sanskrit books were first printed toward the end of the eighteenth century,[1] they were printed without a space between the words, reflecting the practice traditionally followed in MSS. In the course of time, however, as more and more Sanskrit works appeared in print, limited spacing of words was introduced. According to this latter practice, which has since become universal in printed texts, when there is no vowel contraction or change of consonants between words (sandhi), the words are spaced apart. Otherwise they are joined together to form an uninterrupted series of syllables to the end of the sentence. Since no change takes place in sentence sandhi when a word that ends in a vowel, anusvāra or visarga comes before a word beginning with a consonant, it is only natural that the unaffected words should remain apart. So, we write स जनकः पुत्राय फलं यच्छति ('The father gives a fruit to his son') *not* सजनकःपुत्रायफलंयच्छति with all the words joined together. But when two words are fused together by vowel contraction or when there are consonant changes at word junctures due to sandhi, separation is not allowed between the words. Consequently, a consonant ending one word is made into a conjunct with the consonant beginning the next word. Anusvāra at the end of a word is retained, except when a vowel follows; it is then changed into the म् for which the anusvāra stands, and this म् is vocalized with the vowel that begins the next word. The use of the virāma symbol is avoided, except, of course, when the final letter of a sentence is a consonant, in which case the virāma is needed to indicate the absence of a vowel. To illustrate these various points, let us take the sentence *atha prabhāte sa kṣetrapatir laguḍahastas taṃ pradeśaṃ āgacchan kākenāvalokitaḥ* ('Then at daybreak, the owner of the field, approaching that spot with a cudgel in his hand, was seen by the crow'). The first three words *(atha prabhāte sa)* will be spaced apart from one another and from the fourth word *(kṣetrapatir)* because at each juncture the sequence is vowel and consonant (V+C). The final *-r* of the fourth word *(kṣetrapatir)* is a substitute for visarga due to the voiced consonant (semivowel *l-)* that begins the next word *(laguḍahaṣtas)*. The two consonants (C+C) are to be written as a conjunct: -र्ल-. The same is true of the *-s* and *t-* between *laguḍahastas* and

[1]The first printed Sanskrit work was the *Ṛtusaṃhāra* ('The Cycle of the Seasons') by Kālidāsa. It was edited by Sir William Jones, the famous British orientalist, and printed in Bengali letters in 1792. The first book to be printed in Devanāgarī was the *Hitopadeśa,* edited by William Carey, in 1803.

taṃ, so that they will be written with the conjunct -स्त-. The anusvāra of *taṃ* remains, as it is followed by a consonant (*p-* of *pradeśam).* The *-m* of *pradeśam* replaces *-ṃ* because a vowel follows. The *-m* (म्) will be vocalized with the vowel *ā-* which begins *āgacchan.* The *-n* of *āgacchan* and the *k* of the next word will fall together into a conjunct. If the *-n* and *k-* were not thus joined, a virāma would have to be used, and, as we have seen, this is to be avoided, except at the end of a sentence. *Kākenāvalokitaḥ, i.e. Kākena + avalokitaḥ,* must be kept joined as the two have been fused by vowel contraction. The sentence will now appear as follows in Devanāgarī अथ प्रभाते स क्षेत्रपतिर्लगुडहस्तस्तं प्रदेशमागच्छन्काकेनावलोकितः. Perhaps we might summarize the rule for spacing thus: *when a word ends in a vowel, anusvāra or visarga, and the next word begins with a consonant, the words are spaced apart. Otherwise all words are written together without a space.*

Finally, we should note that the joining of words together in writing (or printing!) or spacing them apart has nothing to do with the syntactical relationship of one word to another in a sentence, except, of course, as may result fortuitously. Nor has it anything to do with a pause or lack of pause in reading, as does a comma in English and other languages that make use of a system of punctuation. It is entirely based on a mechanical application of the rules of spacing we have just explained, and these are, in turn, based, in part at least, on the rules of sandhi and the syllabic character of the writing system, in which is inherent the notion of the syllable as the fundamental unit in a sequence of words. The limited spacing of words that was introduced shortly after the first printed Sanskrit works was undoubtedly due to the influence of the use of spacing in English, but the predilection of the Indian system of writing syllabically retains its preponderant influence in the joining of words.

This peculiar habit of writing words together, which, from the point of view of English, ought not to be combined, is undoubtedly the cause of much difficulty to early students of Sanskrit. For this reason, therefore, we have deferred introducing it, until considerable familiarity has been attained in reading Devanāgarī and coping with the basic grammatical forms and constructions of Sanskrit. As this familiarity is developed and as the initial strangeness of the vocabulary recedes with more and more reading, there will follow a commensurate accommodation with the lack of spacing and the use of conjunct consonants between word junctures.

The Insertion of -ś/-s after -n before c-/ch- and t-/th- at Word Junctures

There is a peculiar rule of sandhi which requires the interposition of a sibilant *ś* or *s* (श् or स्) between a final dental *-n* (-न्) and an initial *c-/ch-* (च्-/छ्-) or *t-/th-* (त्-/थ्-). Which of these two sibilants is inserted depends on the class to which the following consonant belongs.[2] The dental *-n* (-न्) is changed to anusvāra before the inserted sibilant; thus *-n/ś/c-/ch-* (-न्/श्/च्-छ्-) as in *tāṃś caurān anvicchāmi* तांश्चौरानन्विच्छामि ('I am looking for the thieves') for तान् चौरान् अन्विच्छामि. And with the dental sibilant: *alpāṃs tarūn avākṛntat* अल्पांस्तरूनवाकृन्तत् ('He cut down the small trees') for अल्पान् तरून् अवाकृन्तत्.

This seemingly arbitrary rule is really a relic of the past history of Sanskrit. In most instances of the insertion of *-s,* the *-s* was originally part of the preceding word. Thus, the accusative plural of masculine nouns of the *deva*-type originally ended in *-s* (स्), so *devāṃs* (देवांस्);[3] similarly, the accusative plural masculine of *tad* (तद्) was *tāṃs* (तांस्), not *tān* (तान्). The 'insertion' of the sibilant is, then, but a reappearance (under certain conditions!) of this lost sibilant. There are, however, instances of the insertion of a sibilant where it is *not* historically justified, as, for example, when *ś/s* is interposed after a third plural imperfect *-n* (-न्), as in *agacchaṃs te devāḥ* अगच्छंस्ते देवा: ('The gods went') for अगच्छन् ते देवा:. The imperfect third plural originally ended in *-n,* not *-ns,* so that the insertion here is due to a levelling out or generalizing tendency.

V. The Story of Sagara and His Sons

जनाधिपे[1] सगरे कालधर्मं गते[1] जना: सुधार्मिकमंशुमन्तं[2] राजानं रोचयामासु:[3]। तस्य पुत्रो दिलीप इति विश्रुत आसीत्। कालेन गच्छता स राजा तस्मै दिलीपाय राज्यं दत्त्वा हिमवन्तं गत्वा तत्र सुदारुणं तपस्तेपे[4]। वर्षाणां बहूनि सहस्राणि तपांसि तप्त्वा सों[5] ऽशुमांस्तपोधन:[6] स्वर्गं लेभे। दिलीपो ऽपि गङ्गावतरणे निश्चयं नाधिगत्य कथं गङ्गामवतारयिष्यामि कथं मम पितामहेभ्यो जलक्रियां

---

[2]The interposition of the cerebral sibilant *ṣ* (ष्) takes place before *ṭ-/ṭh-* (ट्-/ठ्-), but since very few words begin with *ṭ-/ṭh-* (ट्-/ठ्-), the case is extremely rare.

[3]*cf.* Gothic *dagans,* accusative plural of *dags,* a noun of the same type as Sanskrit *deva,* and *þans,* accusative plural of Gothic *sa* (= Sanskrit *sa*!).

करिष्यामि कथं च तांस्तारयेयमिति[7] चिन्तापरो[8] ऽभवत्। तस्यैवं चिन्तयतः[9] पुत्रो भगीरथो नाम जज्ञे। दिलीपो महातेजा[10] राजा बहुभिर्यज्ञैरिष्ट्वा[11] वर्षसहस्राणि राज्यं कारयित्वापि[12] भगीरथं सुतं राज्ये ऽभिषिच्य व्याधिना कालधर्मं गतः। भगीरथो ऽनपत्यः सन्प्रजाकाम[13] आसीत्। प्रजाकामो गङ्गावतरणे रतश्च स्वराज्यं मन्त्रिष्वाधाय गोकर्णस्थं तपोवनं गत्वा तत्रोर्ध्वबाहुः पञ्चतपा मासाहारो जितेन्द्रियो[14] दीर्घं तप आचचार। भगीरथस्यैतानि घोराणि तपांस्याचरतो वर्षाणां सहस्राण्यतीतानि। ततः सर्वलोकपितामहो भगवानीश्वरो ब्रह्मा तस्मै सुप्रसन्नः सन्देवगणैः[15] सहोपागम्य तं महात्मानं भगीरथं तप आचरन्तमुवाच। भगीरथ महाराज सुप्रसन्नस्ते ऽहं जनाधिप सुतप्तेन तपसा ते वरं वरय सुव्रत। इत्येवमुक्तस्तं[16] महाप्रभुं सर्वलोककृतं[17] महातेजा भगीरथः कृताञ्जलिः स्थितः[18] प्रत्युवाच। यदि मे सुप्रीतो भगवन्यदि मे तपसः फलं भवति तदा गङ्गा स्वर्गात्पृथिवीमवतरेत्[19]। तेषां महात्मनां सगरस्यात्मजानां गङ्गासलिलेन क्लिन्ने भस्मनि[20] सर्वे मे प्रपितामहाः[21] स्वर्गं गच्छेयुः। अपरं च देवास्माकं[22] संतत्यर्थं त्वां याचे। इक्ष्वाकूणां कुलं नो नावसीदेत्। एष मे वरो भवतु। इति तस्य तद्वचनं श्रुत्वैव सर्वलोकपितामहो भगीरथं मधुरा वाचः प्रत्युवाच। एवं भवतु महानेष मनोरथो भगीरथ महारथ। पृथिवी हि राजन्गङ्गायाः पतनं न सहिष्यते। तां धारयितुं शक्नुवन्तं शूलिनो[23] नान्यं पश्यामि। इति महात्मानं भगीरथमुक्त्वा महाप्रभुः सुरगणैः सह परमं दिवं गत्वा हिमवतो ज्येष्ठां दुहितरं गङ्गामाबभाषे।

Notes

1. जनाधिपे . . . गते a locative absolute.

2. सुधार्मिकमंशुमन्तं This is a graphic joining of सुधार्मिकं and अंशुमन्तं. The anusvāra of सुधार्मिकं is replaced by म्, thus सुधार्मिकम्, which is then vocalized with the initial vowel (+ anusvāra) of अंशुमन्तं; hence, सुदार्मिकमंशुमन्तं. The inseparable prefix सु-, literally 'well', is often prefixed to an adjective, as to धार्मिक here, in the sense of 'very'. So also in सुदारुण 'very hard', सुप्रसन्न 'very favorably disposed', सुतप्त 'very hot' and सुप्रीत 'very pleased' below.

3. रोचयामासुः This is a so-called 'periphrastic' perfect. Verbs of the tenth class and causatives, whose stems both end in *-aya,* do not form a reduplicated perfect such as we have studied. Instead they make a compound ('periphrastic') perfect, consisting of a noun in the accusative feminine singular (derived from the stem in *-aya)* and the perfect of √अस् (अस्ति) 'be', very rarely of √भू 'be' or √कृ 'make'. So here from रोचय, the causative stem of √रुच् (रोचते), is derived a feminine *ā*-stem by lengthening the final *-a.* This is inflected in the accusative and to it is annexed the perfect of √अस्, which, in the third plural required by the context, is आसुः. On the writing as one word, see the notes on सुधार्मिकं + अंशुमन्तं above. The periphrastic perfect is to be translated like the reduplicated perfect, *i.e.,* as a simple past tense. The use of the *accusative* of the derivative noun is due to the fact that the periphrasis was originally formed with the perfect of √कृ 'make', the noun being the object of this and hence accusative. So, for example, चोरयां चकार meant literally 'he made a stealing' *i.e.,* he stole. In the later history of this construction √भू or √अस् were substituted for the perfect of √कृ, thus, strictly speaking, invalidating the use of the accusative.

4. तपस्तेपे तपस् and तेपे are combined in writing in order to avoid the use of the virāma sign on the -स् of तपस्. तेपे, as also लेभे in the next sentence, is an example of a 'telescoped' perfect, in which (in the weak forms only) the reduplication is lost and the root vowel replaced by *-e-*. Incidentally, when the object of a verb is made from the same root as the verb, it is called a 'cognate' object. So, तपस् here, which is formed from √तप्, and similarly तपांसि in तपांसि तप्त्वा in the next sentence.

5. The anusvāra on सों is due to its having been taken from the first syllable of the next word अंशुमान्. So, whenever a short *a-* is elided after *-o* (as here after *so* for *sas),* if the elided *a-* has an anusvāra, the anusvāra has to be retracted to the *-o*.

6. ऽशुमांस्तपोधनः: Note the inserted sibilant -स्- between (अं)शुमान् and तपोधनः. Similarly, below in तांस्तारयेयम् for तान् तारयेयम्.

7. All the words from the first कथं through तारयेयम् form the thought (चिन्ता) in which Dilīpa was absorbed.

8. चिन्तापरो 'having concerned thought (चिन्ता) as the chief *or* principal thing', an important kind of bahuvrīhi compound based on an appositional karmadhāraya. पर and परम (both 'highest *or* chief [thing]') are thus used interchangeably after any noun to indicate complete attention to or devotion to what is denoted by the noun; *cf.* also ध्यानपर 'having contemplation as the chief thing *or* object', *i.e.,* engrossed in contemplation; also in: श्वासपरम 'having sighing as chief thing', *i.e.,* addicted to sighing.

9. तस्यैवं चिन्तयतः: These words may be taken either as a genitive absolute (the same as a locative absolute, but much less common): 'While he was thinking thus', or alternatively as a sort of predicate possessive genitive '(on the part) of him thinking thus, a son was born'.

10. महातेजा This is a very frequent epithet of a great, important or noble personage. As explained in the vocabulary, the oldest meaning of तेजस् is a 'point' or 'tip' of something, then specifically the 'tip of a flame', then the 'flame' itself and finally, by a natural transfer, 'splendor, majesty'. We might, then, translate महातेजस् by 'majestic' (literally 'having great majesty').

11. बहुभिर्यज्ञैरिष्ट्वा combined writing for बहुभिर् यज्ञैर् इष्ट्वा, literally 'having sacrificed *or* worshipped with many sacrifices', *i.e.,* having performed many sacrifices. The य- of √यज् is changed to इ by *samprasāraṇa* when the -त of the past passive participle is added; *ij-ta* then becomes *iṣṭa.* The stem of the gerund is always the same as that of the past passive participle, hence *iṣṭvā.*

12. राज्यं कारयित्वापि 'although having reigned'. In this idiom with कृ the causative is often used, though without causative value; कृत्वा might have been used with no difference in meaning. Note the use of अपि to impart the sense of 'although', as regularly after participles or adjectives.

13. सन्प्रजाकाम. सन्, the present participle, nominative masculine singular of √अस् 'be', has nothing to do with प्रजाकाम to which it is joined merely due to the Devanāgarī mode of writing consonants together at word junctures. Syntactically सन् belongs with the previous word (अनपत्य:).

14. तत्रोर्ध्वबाहुः . . . जितेन्द्रियो All these adjectives are descriptive of standard ascetic practices.

15. सन्देवगणै: See the note at 13 above.

16. इत्येवमुक्तस्तं Be careful to disjoin these words correctly! Four words are involved.

17. सर्वलोककृतं An accusative tatpuruṣa compound, of which -कृतं is accusative masculine singular of -कृत्, a verbal formed from √कृ + a meaningless suffixal -त् (to render कृ a more easily declinable stem). It is an accusative tatpuruṣa because सर्वलोक- is object of -कृत्: 'making all the worlds'.

18. स्थित: The past passive participle of an intransitive verb such as √स्था 'stand, be' has an *active* sense, so that स्थित: means literally 'having stood *or* been'. As explained briefly in the vocabulary, however, स्थित usually has a very attenuated meaning, hardly more than सन् ('being') above (see notes 13 and 15). Here in combination with कृताञ्जलि: it underlines the reverential attitude of Bhagīratha while replying to Brahmā, unlike महातेजा which is simply a descriptive adjective.

19. अवतरेत् an optative of wish: 'May Gaṅgā descend!' So also गच्छेयु: and अवसीदेत् farther on.

20. क्लिन्ने भस्मनि a locative absolute: 'When the ashes of those sons … have been moistened by …'.

21. प्रपितामहा: The adverb प्र is prefixed to words of relationship in the sense of 'great-'. So पौत्र is a 'grandson', प्रपौत्र is a 'great grandson'.

22. देवास्माकं Here again the combining of words in Devanāgarī brings together syntactically unrelated words: देव is vocative and the genitive अस्माकं goes with संतत्यर्थं.

23. शूलिनो ablative singular with अन्यं. In English we say 'other *than',* in Sanskrit 'other *from',* an extension of the 'ablative of separation'.

Vocabulary

अञ्जलि, *m.* the open hands placed side by side and raised to the forehead in salutation.

अतीत, *ppp.* √इ (एति, class II), gone beyond, past (as of time).

अधि-√गम्, go to, arrive at; *gerund* अधिगत्य.

अधिप, *m.* 'over-keeper', lord. [अधि + *verbal of* √पा (पाति, class II), protect, keep)]

अनपत्य, *adj.* childless.

अपरं च, *conjunctive adv.* 'and another (thing)', moreover.

अभि-√सिच् (सिञ्चति, class VI), pour upon; consecrate; *gerund* अभिषिच्य.

अवतरण, *n.* descending, descent.

अव-√तॄ (तरति, class I), descend, come down (to earth); *in caus.* अवतारयति, causes to descend, brings down; *fut. of caus.* अवतारयिष्यति.

अव-√सद् (सीदति, class I), settle *or* sink down; come to naught.

आ-√चर् (चरति, class I), go to, set about, practice.

आत्मज, *m.* a son.

आ-√धा (दधाति, class III), place *or* put on (+ *loc.),* entrust to; *gerund* आधाय.

आ-√भाष् (भाषते, class I), call on, invite; *perf.* आबभाषे.

इक्ष्वाकु, *m.* Ikṣvāku, name of the founder of the so-called 'solar' race of kings who ruled Ayodhyā. The word is used in the plural to denote the descendants of Ikṣvāku, among whom were Sagara and his lineage.

इन्द्रिय, *n.* a sense organ.

ईश्वर, *m.* lord.

ऊर्ध्व, *adj.* upright; elevated.

कालधर्म, *m.* law of time; *with* √गम् (गच्छति, class I, go), die (literally 'go to the law of time').

कुल, *n.* family.

क्लिन्न, *ppp.* √क्लिद् (क्लिद्यति, class IV), be *or* become wet.

गोकर्ण, *m.* Gokarṇa, name of a place of pilgrimage sacred to Śiva on the Malabar coast.

घोर, *adj.* awful, dreadful.

√चिन्त् (चिन्तयति, class X), think, reflect.

चिन्ता, *f.* thought; anxious thought, concern.

√जन् (जायते, class IV), be born; *perf.* जज्ञे.

जन, *m.* person; *in plur.* people.

जलक्रिया, *f.* water-ceremony.

ज्येष्ठ, *adj.* eldest.

तपोधन, *adj.* rich in austerities (तपस्).

√तॄ (तरति, class I), cross over, get across, *hence* escape; *caus.* तारयति, causes to get across, escape; liberates.

तेजस्, *n.* tip *or* point; tip of flame; flame; splendor, majesty.

√दा (ददाति, class III), give; entrust; *gerund* दत्त्वा.

दिलीप, *m.* Dilīpa, name of the son of Aṃśumat and father of Bhagīratha.

दिव, *n.* heaven.

दीर्घ, *adj.* long.

दुहितृ, *f.* a daughter.

√धृ (धारयति, *caus. without caus. meaning),* hold in check, withstand, bear; *infin.* धारयितुम्.

निश्चय, *m.* determination, fixed opinion *or* firm resolve, decision.

पञ्चतपस्, *adj.* 'having five (पञ्च) fires', *i.e.,* of an ascetic who sits amid four fires arranged at the cardinal points, with the sun overhead.

पतन, *n.* the act of falling, a fall.

पर, *adj.* highest, chief; *at end of bahuvrīhi* 'having . . . as chief thing, wholly devoted to *or* absorbed in . . .').

परम, *adj.* highest.

प्रजा, *f.* offspring, children.

प्रपितामह, *m.* great-grandfather.

बाहु, *m.* the forearm, arm.

ब्रह्मन्, *m.* Brahmā, name of the universal impersonal spirit Brahman manifested as the creator of the world and member of the त्रिमूर्ति or triad, the other members of which are Śiva and Viṣṇu.

भगवत्, *adj.* fortunate; blessed; august, lordly.

भगीरथ, *m.* Bhagīratha, son of Dilīpa and great grandson of Sagara.

भस्मन्, *n.* ashes.

मधुर, *adj.* honeyed, sweet.

मनोरथ, *m.* wish.

मन्त्रिन्, *m.* a counsellor *or* minister.

महारथ, *m.* a great warrior.

मासाहार, *adj.* 'having (*i.e.,* taking) food [once] a month', eating but once a month.

√यज् (यजति, class I), sacrifice, worship; *gerund* इष्ट्वा.

यज्ञ, *m.* a sacrifice.

√याच् (याचते, class I), ask (a person) for (something).

रत, *ppp.* √रम् (रमते, class I 'take pleasure in'), taking pleasure in, devoted to.

राज्य, *n.* kingdom; + √कृ 'rule'.

√रुच् (रोचते, class I), shine, be bright; appear beautiful, *hence* please; *in caus.* रोचयति, chooses *someone as (with two acc.); perf.* रोचयामास.

√लभ् (लभते, class I), receive, get; *with* स्वर्ग, attain heaven, go to heaven; *perf.* लेभे.

वर, *m.* choice, wish, boon.

2√वृ (वृणीते, class IX), choose; *in caus.* वरयति *same meaning.*

वर्ष, *n.* a year.

विश्रुत, *ppp.* वि-√श्रु (शृणोति, class V), 'heard far and wide (वि-)', *hence* known as, named.

व्याधि, *m.* disease, sickness.

शूलिन्, *adj.* possessing a trident, *epithet of Śiva.*

संतति, *f.* continuation (of one's family), *hence* offspring.

सर्वलोककृत्, *m.* 'making the whole world' *i.e.,* maker *or* creator of the whole world.

सलिल, *n.* water.

√सह् (सहते, class I), withstand; *fut.* सहिष्यते.

सुत, *m.* a son, *properly ppp.* √सू (सूते, class II), produce, bear, generate, *hence literally* 'generated, born' *and as m.* a son.

सुतप्त, *adj.* very hot (तप्त, *ppp.* √तप 'burn'), *hence* very severe (said of austerities).

सुदारुण, *adj.* very hard *or* severe.

सुधार्मिक, *adj.* very virtuous.

सुप्रसन्न, *adj.* very favorably disposed. [सु, *adv.* very + *ppp.* प्र-√सद् (सीदति, class I), be favorable, be kindly disposed]

सुप्रीतः, *adj.* very pleased *or* well-disposed. [सु 'very' + *ppp.* √प्री (प्रीयते, class IV, be pleased, be favorably inclined to)]

सुर, *m.* a god.

सुव्रत, *adj.* 'having a good vow *or* good vows', *hence* strict in observing vows, very religious.

स्थितः *ppp.* of √स्था (तिष्ठति, class I), stand, but with very attenuated meaning, not 'having stood', but simply 'being'.

स्वर्ग, *m.* heaven.

हिमवत्, *m.* Himavat, a name of the Himālaya mountains, regarded as the father of Gaṅgā (the Ganges River).

Translate into Sanskrit:

When the great King Sagara died,[1] the people made Aṃśumat king. In the course of time, after giving the kingdom to his son named Dilīpa, Aṃśumat went to Himavat and when he had performed very intense austerities there for many thousands of years, died and attained heaven. Dilīpa, though concerned as to how he would bring down[2] the river Gaṅgā to purify the ashes of his ancestors with her purifying water, performed many sacrifices and very severe austerities and, after ruling for thousands of years, died of some disease. In the meantime, Bhagīratha, who had been consecrated[3] in the kingdom by his father Dilīpa, being without offspring and therefore desirous of offspring, after entrusting the kingdom to various ministers, went to a penance-grove and with arms upraised, surrounded by the five fires, taking food but once a month and with sense organs controlled, engaged in extremely dreadful austerities. Thousands of years having gone by,[4] the grandsire of all the worlds, very kindly disposed to him because of his austerities, accompanied by hosts of the gods, approached him and offered him a boon. In an attitude of an añjali Bhagīratha replied: 'May Himavat's eldest daughter, the river Gaṅgā, come down[5] from heaven to earth to purify the ashes of my ancestors! Moreover, if there is fruit to my austerities, may our family of the Ikṣvākus not decline!' After replying 'So be it!' the Blessed Lord went to the highest heaven with the gods and summoned Himavat's daughter the river Gaṅgā. But he pondered as to how the earth would withstand[6] Gaṅgā's fall; for none other than Śiva, possessor of the trident, is able to bear Gaṅgā.

Notes

1. When ... Sagara died': Render with a *loc.* absolute.

2. 'though concerned as to how he would bring down': कथं गङ्गानदीम् अवतारयिष्यामि इति चिन्तापरः .

3. 'who had been consecrated': Express by a *ppp.*

4. 'Thousands of years having gone by': *Loc.* absolute!

5. 'May Himavat's eldest daughter ... come down': optative of wish, likewise below 'may our family ... not decline'.

6. 'he pondered as to how the earth would withstand': कथं पृथिवी सहिष्यते ... followed by इति; *cf.* note 2 above.

LESSON TWENTY-FIVE

Non-thematic Verbs.

In our reading exercises we have had many verbs, most of them belonging to the first, fourth, sixth and tenth classes of roots, the so-called भू, दिव्, तुद् and चुर् classes of the Indian grammarians, so named because these particular roots happen to occur *first* in their lists of roots of these classes. In these four classes the present stem, *i.e.*, the stem from which are made the present, imperfect, imperative and optative, ends in *-a*, *-ya* or *-aya*, attached to the root, which often undergoes a modification of its vowel. These four classes are called 'thematic' because the thematic vowel *-a* or a suffix ending in the thematic vowel *(-ya, -aya)* is added to make the present stem. The remaining six classes do *not* add to the root the thematic vowel or a suffix ending in the thematic vowel. Therefore, they are known as 'non-thematic' or 'athematic' roots. Although the non-thematic roots are far less common than the thematic, many of the non-thematic roots are of extremely common occurrence. It behooves us now to treat them systematically and in some detail.

Like the thematic classes, the non-thematic are named after the root that heads each class in the old lists of the Indian grammarians. We speak of an अद् (II), हु (III), सु (V), रुध् (VII), तन् (VIII) and क्री (IX) class. Each of these six classes forms its present stem in a different way: for example, by adding the endings directly to the root, by reduplication and vowel modification, by the addition of certain suffixes, etc. Generally speaking, the personal terminations are the same as for the thematic roots, though there are a few deviations that are easily learned. A major difference between the two great classes of roots is that, whereas the thematic have a single, invariable stem throughout the inflection of the present, imperfect, imperative and optative (active and middle), the non-thematic roots exhibit *strong* and *weak* forms that are disposed in an unvarying pattern throughout the conjugation of the present system.[1] As in the nouns that differentiate a strong and weak stem, this variation originated in a shifting of the old musical accent from the stem to the ending. The difference between strong and weak stems shows up strikingly in the present tense of √अस् 'be' which belongs to the second or root class, called the अद् class. The strong stem is अस् (the whole root) and the weak is simply स् (!), the vowel अ- being altogether lost or 'zeroed out' due to

---

[1]The term 'present system' means the forms that are derived from the *present stem, viz.*, the present, imperfect, imperative and optative, active and middle. All the other forms of the verb, such as the future, aorist, perfect, etc., are made directly from the root, which is variously treated.

the shift of the musical tone on to the following syllable. The old musical tone which was the root cause (no pun intended!) of this phenomenon still exists in the language of the Ṛgveda, in the MSS and printed editions of which it is indicated by special signs. It will be instructive and in the interests of greater lucidity to give the present tense of अस् in transliteration with the principal Vedic accent or musical tone marked with an acute accent (´).

Present Tense of √अस् 'be'

Strong		Weak			
Singular		*Dual*		*Plural*	
**ás-mi*	अस्मि	*s-váḥ*	स्वः	*s-máḥ*	स्मः
**ás-i*[2]	असि	*s-tháḥ*	स्थः	*s-thá*	स्थ
**ás-ti*	अस्ति	*s-táḥ*	स्तः	*s-ánti*	सन्ति

Note that in the singular forms the tone is on the root itself, which therefore has its full form. Throughout the dual and plural, however, the tone moves on to the endings and hence the vowel of the root is lost. Hardly any other root reflects the strengthening and weakening processes in so spectacular a fashion, but the changes from strong to weak are reflected in a weaker form of the vowel of the root or the suffix, as we shall see. In the conjugation of the non-thematic roots the strong forms are found only in the first, second and third singular of the present and imperfect active, and in all the first persons of the imperative, both active and middle, and finally in the third person singular of the imperative active. *All the rest of the forms are made on the weak stem.* In learning to conjugate the non-thematic classes, it is best, from a pedagogical point of view, *not* to start with Class II, the अद् class, since, *the endings being added directly to the root,* there are quite a few internal sandhi changes that occur as two or more consonants are brought together. These phonetic changes are not difficult, but remember! one of our basic principles is to 'swim in shallow water, before swimming in deep water'.

Perhaps the least troublesome of these six classes and hence the best one to begin with is Class V, typified by √सु (सुनोति) 'press'. To form the present stem the suffix *-no-* (-नो-) is added to the unchanged root in the strong forms (as enumerated above), elsewhere *-nu-* (-नु-). The personal

---

[2]We should expect *ás-si,* but apparently even in Proto-Indo-European the two forms **és-si* and **és-i* existed side by side. Sanskrit has kept only the simplified version.

endings are the same as in the thematic classes, except that the *-n-* (-न्-) of the third person plural middle drops out, so that those endings are *-ate* (present), *-ata* (imperfect) and *-atām* (imperative) instead of *-ante, -anta* and *-antām.* One or two other matters that need to be discussed concerning some of the forms will be more expeditiously treated after the full conjugation has been presented.

Present

Active

	Singular	*Dual*	*Plural*
1.	**su-no-mi* (सुनोमि)	*su-nu-vaḥ* (सुनुवः)	*su-nu-maḥ* (सुनुमः)
2.	**su-no-ṣi* (सुनोषि)	*su-nu-thaḥ* (सुनुथः)	*su-nu-tha* (सुनुथ)
3.	**su-no-ti* (सुनोति)	*su-nu-taḥ* (सुनुतः)	*su-nv-anti* (सुन्वन्ति)

Middle

1.	*su-nv-e* (सुन्वे)	*su-nu-vahe* (सुनुवहे)	*su-nu-mahe* (सुनुमहे)
2.	*su-nu-ṣe* (सुनुषे)	*su-nv-āthe* (सुन्वाथे)	*su-nu-dhve* (सुनुध्वे)
3.	*su-nu-te* (सुनुते)	*su-nv-āte* (सुन्वाते)	*su-nv-ate* (सुन्वते)

Imperfect

Active

1.	**a-su-nav-am* (असुनवम्)	*a-su-nu-va* (असुनुव)	*a-su-nu-ma* (असुनुम)
2.	**a-su-no-ḥ* (असुनोः)	*a-su-nu-tam* (असुनुतम्)	*a-su-nu-ta* (असुनुत)
3.	**a-su-no-t* (असुनोत्)	*a-su-nu-tām* (असुनुताम्)	*a-su-nv-an* (असुन्वन्)

Middle

	Singular	*Dual*	*Plural*
1.	*a-su-nv-i* (असुन्वि)	*a-su-nu-vahi* (असुनुवहि)	*a-su-nu-mahi* (असुनुमहि)
2.	*a-su-nu-thāḥ* (असुनुथा:)	*a-su-nv-āthām* (असुन्वाथाम्)	*a-su-nu-dhvam* (असुनुध्वम्)
3.	*a-su-nu-ta* (असुनुत)	*a-su-nv-ātām* (असुन्वाताम्)	*a-su-nv-ata* (असुन्वत)

Imperative

Active

1.	**su-nav-āni* (सुनवानि)	**su-nav-āva* (सुनवाव)	**su-nav-āma* (सुनवाम)
2.	*su-nu* (सुनु)	*su-nu-tam* (सुनुतम्)	*su-nu-ta* (सुनुत)
3.	**su-no-tu* (सुनोतु)	*su-nu-tām* (सुनुताम्)	*su-nv-antu* (सुन्वन्तु)

Middle

1.	**su-nav-ai* (सुनवै)	**su-nav-āvahai* (सुनवावहै)	**su-nav-āmahai* (सुनवामहै)
2.	*su-nu-ṣva* (सुनुष्व)	*su-nv-āthām* (सुन्वाथाम्)	*su-nu-dhvam* (सुनुध्वम्)
3.	**su-nu-tām* (सुनुताम्)	*su-nv-ātām* (सुन्वाताम्)	*su-nv-atām* (सुन्वताम्)

Optative

Active

	Singular	*Dual*	*Plural*
1.	*su-nu-yām* (सुनुयाम्)	*su-nu-yā-va* (सुनुयाव)	*su-nu-yā-ma* (सुनुयाम)
2.	*su-nu-yā-ḥ* (सुनुयाः)	*su-nu-yā-tam* (सुनुयातम्)	*su-nu-yā-ta* (सुनुयात)
3.	*su-nu-yā-t* (सुनुयात्)	*su-nu-yā-tām* (सुनुयाताम्)	*su-nu-y-uḥ* (सुनुयुः)

Middle

1.	*su-nv-ī-ya* (सुन्वीय)	*su-nv-ī-vahi* (सुन्वीवहि)	*su-nv-ī-mahi* (सुन्वीमहि)
2.	*su-nv-ī-thāḥ* (सुन्वीथाः)	*su-nv-ī-y-āthām* (सुन्वीयाथाम्)	*su-nv-ī-dhvam* (सुन्वीध्वम्)
3.	*su-nv-ī-ta* (सुन्वीत)	*su-nv-ī-y-ātām* (सुन्वीयाताम्)	*su-nv-ī-ran* (सुन्वीरन्)

The following points should be noticed: In the present second singular active the ending *-si* (-सि) becomes *-ṣi* (-षि), just as *agni-su* (locative plural of *agni)* becomes *agni-ṣu* (अग्निषु); *cf.* also *su-nu-ṣva* (सुनुष्व). The *-u* of the suffix *-nu* may be *optionally* dropped before *-v* or *-m;* thus, we may write *su-n-vaḥ* (सुन्वः), *su-n-maḥ* (सुन्मः), *su-n-vahe* (सुन्वहे), *su-n-mahe* (सुन्महे), etc. Before vowel endings the *-u* of *-nu* is changed to *-v;* thus, *su-nv-anti* (सुन्वन्ति), *su-nv-ate* (सुन्वते), *su-nv-āthe* (सुन्वाथे), etc.[3] In the non-thematic classes the optative sign is *-yā-* (-या-) in the active, and *-ī-* (-ई-) in the middle; hence, *su-nu-yā-t* (सुनुयात्). In the plural the *-ā* of *-yā-* disappears before the ending *-uḥ* (-उः); thus, *su-nu-y-uḥ* (सुनुयुः). In the second and third dual middle there is an interposed *-y-* (-य्-) between the optative sign *-ī-* (-ई-) and

[3]But if a root ends in a consonant, as does the common √आप् 'reach', this change of *-nu-* to *-nv-* when a vowel follows would yield an unpronounceable assemblage of consonants, and therefore a *-v-* is interposed between *-nu-* and the following vowel; thus, instead of *āp-nv-anti,* we have *āp-nu-v-anti.*

the endings *-āthām* (-आथाम्) and *-ātām* (आताम्). The purpose of this is to keep the optative sign intact. If the *-y-* were not inserted, these verb forms would lose their optative character, becoming *su-nv-y-āthām* and *su-nv-y-ātām.*

All the roots of the eighth or तन् class end in *-n* (-न्), except √कृ 'do'. Since this class adds the suffix *-o-/-u-* (-ओ-/-उ-) to make the present stem, the resultant stem ends in *-no-/-nu-* (-नो-/-नु-), which is not different from a stem of Class V, which we have just exemplified. It will not be necessary, therefore, to present the conjugation of √तन् (तनोति) 'stretch'.

√कृ, the only root of the तन् class that does *not* end in *-n* (-न्), adds the regular class suffix *-o* (-ओ) in the strong forms, before which *-ṛ* (-ऋ) is replaced by its guṇa substitute *-ar* (-अर्); thus, *kar-o-ti* (करोति), *a-kar-o-t* (अकरोत्), etc. However, before the suffix *-u* (-उ) in the weak forms, the root assumes the form *kur-* (कुर्-), as in *kur-u-thaḥ* (कुरुथः), *a-kur-u-tam* (अकुरुतम्), etc. The weak form *kur-* (कुर्-) *without* the suffix *-u* (-उ) appears throughout all the active forms of the optative; so, *kur-yā-t* (कुर्यात्, *kur-yā-va* (कुर्याव), etc. It also appears before the personal endings beginning with *v-* (व्-) and *m-* (म्-), as *kur-vaḥ* (कुर्वः), *kur-maḥ* (कुर्मः), etc.[4] This is really not as complicated as it seems, as a glance at the complete conjugation made from these present stems will show:

Present

Active

	Singular	*Dual*	*Plural*
1.	**kar-o-mi* (करोमि)	*kur-vaḥ* (कुर्वः)	*kur-maḥ* (कुर्मः)
2.	**kar-o-ṣi* (करोषि)	*kur-u-thaḥ* (कुरुथः)	*kur-u-tha* (कुरुथ)
3.	**kar-o-ti* (करोति)	*kur-u-taḥ* (कुरुतः)	*kur-v-anti* (कुर्वन्ति)

---

[4]The dropping of the *-u* should be compared with the optional dropping of the *-u* of the suffix *-nu* of the सु class.

Middle

	Singular	*Dual*	*Plural*
1.	*kur-v-e* (कुर्वे)	*kur-vahe* (कुर्वहे)	*kur-mahe* (कुर्महे)
2.	*kur-u-ṣe* (कुरुषे)	*kur-v-āthe* (कुर्वाथे)	*kur-u-dhve* (कुरुध्वे)
3.	*kur-u-te* (कुरुते)	*kur-v-āte* (कुर्वाते)	*kur-v-ate* (कुर्वते)

Imperfect

Active

1.	**a-kar-av-am* (अकरवम्)	*a-kur-va* (अकुर्व)	*a-kur-ma* (अकुर्म)
2.	**a-kar-o-ḥ* (अकरोः)	*a-kur-u-tam* (अकुरुतम्)	*a-kur-u-ta* (अकुरुत)
3.	**a-kar-o-t* (अकरोत्)	*a-kur-u-tām* (अकुरुताम्)	*a-kur-v-an* (अकुर्वन्)

Middle

1.	*a-kur-v-i* (अकुर्वि)	*a-kur-vahi* (अकुर्वहि)	*a-kur-mahi* (अकुर्महि)
2.	*a-kur-u-thāḥ* (अकुरुथाः)	*a-kur-v-āthām* (अकुर्वाथाम्)	*a-kur-u-dhvam* (अकुरुध्वम्)
3.	*a-kur-u-ta* (अकुरुत)	*a-kur-v-ātām* (अकुर्वाताम्)	*a-kur-v-ata* (अकुर्वत)

Imperative

Active

	Singular	*Dual*	*Plural*
1.	**kar-av-āṇi* (करवाणि)	**kar-av-āva* (करवाव)	**kar-av-āma* (करवाम)
2.	*kur-u* (कुरु)	*kur-u-tam* (कुरुतम्)	*kur-u-ta* (कुरुत)
3.	**kar-o-tu* (करोतु)	*kur-u-tām* (कुरुताम्)	*kur-v-antu* (कुर्वन्तु)

Middle

	Singular	*Dual*	*Plural*
1.	**kar-av-ai* (करवै)	**kar-av-āvahai* (करवावहै)	**kar-av-āmahai* (करवामहै)
2.	*kur-u-ṣva* (कुरुष्व)	*kur-v-āthām* (कुर्वाथाम्)	*kur-u-dhvam* (कुरुध्वम्)
3.	*kur-u-tām* (कुरुताम्)	*kur-v-ātām* (कुर्वाताम्)	*kur-v-atām* (कुर्वताम्)

Optative

Active

	Singular	*Dual*	*Plural*
1.	*kur-yām* (कुर्याम्)	*kur-yā-va* (कुर्याव)	*kur-yā-ma* (कुर्याम)
2.	*kur-yā-ḥ* (कुर्याः)	*kur-yā-tam* (कुर्यातम्)	*kur-yā-ta* (कुर्यात)
3.	*kur-yā-t* (कुर्यात्)	*kur-yā-tām* (कुर्याताम्)	*kur-y-uḥ* (कुर्युः)

Middle

	Singular	*Dual*	*Plural*
1.	*kur-v-ī-ya* (कुर्वीय)	*kur-v-ī-vahi* (कुर्वीवहि)	*kur-v-ī-mahi* (कुर्वीमहि)
2.	*kur-v-ī-thāḥ* (कुर्वीथाः)	*kur-v-ī-y-āthām* (कुर्वीयाथाम्)	*kur-v-ī-dhvam* (कुर्वीध्वम्)
3.	*kur-v-ī-ta* (कुर्वीत)	*kur-v-ī-y-ātām* (कुर्वीयाताम्)	*kur-v-ī-ran* (कुर्वीरन्)

VI. The Story of Sagara and His Sons

तस्मिन्देवदेवे गते[1] स भगीरथो ऽतितीव्रं तपस्तपन्महेश्वरस्य[2] शूलिनः शिवस्य संवत्सरं पूजनमकरोत् । अथ[3] संवत्सरे संपूर्णे सर्वलोकनमस्कृत उमापती[4] राजानमुवाच । सुप्रसन्नस्ते ऽहमस्मि नरश्रेष्ठ तव प्रियं करिष्यामि[5] । शैलराजस्य[6] दुहितरं गङ्गां शिरसा धारयिष्यामि[7] । इत्युक्त्वा तदनन्तरं हिमवतः शिखरमभिरुह्योमापतिराकाशगां नदीं गङ्गामाभाष्य पृथिवीं निपतेत्युदित्वा[8] कैलासस्थं स्वनिवासं[9] प्रत्यागच्छत् । महेश्वरस्य तद्वचनं श्रुत्वा पर्वतस्य ज्येष्ठा दुहिता क्रोधसमन्वितातिमहद्रूपं दुःसहं वेगं च कृत्वा[10] शंकरस्य[11] मूर्ध्नि न्यपतत् । भगवांस्तु तस्यास्तं दर्पं दृष्ट्वा क्रुद्धो भूत्वा तां देवीं तिरोभावयितुं बुद्धिमकरोत् । सा जटामण्डलगह्वरे[12] हिमवद्वनप्रतिमे रुद्रस्य मूर्धनि पतिता[13] तत्रैव बहून्संवत्सरान्भ्रान्त्वापि महीं पतितुं[14] निर्गन्तुं नाशक्नोत् । परमं यत्नं कृत्वापि ततो निर्गन्तुमशक्नुवतीं तां ज्ञात्वा[15] ततः संतुष्टो गङ्गां विससर्ज । तस्यां विसृष्टायां सप्त स्रोतांसि जज्ञिरे । ह्लादिनी पावनी नलिनी च प्राचीं दिशं सुचक्षुस्तु सीता सिन्धुश्च[16] महानदी प्रतीचीं दिशं जग्मुः । तासां नदीनां सप्तमी गङ्गा

स्वयं स्वस्यन्दनमास्थितं भगीरथमन्वगच्छत् । तेन प्रकारेणाकाशगा गङ्गा गगनाच्छंकरस्य शिरस्[17] ततो धरणीम्[17] आगता । यस्माच्छंकरो महानदीं गङ्गां शिरसाधारयत्तस्माद्गङ्गाधर इति विश्रुतः । तदेमं[18] लोकं गङ्गावतरणं दिदृक्षवो[19] ऽमितौजसो देवगणा विमानैर्[20] गगने चलन्तः परमविस्मयं समवाप्नुवन् । गगनं हि विविधैर्मत्स्यैरन्यैश्च कच्छपशिशुमारादिभिर्[21] जलचरैराकीर्णम् । अपरं च जलपतनं भयाक्रान्तपतङ्गानां विरवश्च[22] भयंकरं शब्दमकुरुताम् । जनाः सर्वत्र तं तीव्रं निनादं श्रोतुमशक्नुवन् । क्वचिन्महादेवस्य शीर्षादतिद्रुतं प्रस्रवज्[23] जलं पृथिवीं वेगेनाधूनोत् । क्वचित्सलिलं सलिलेनैव प्रतिहतं कुटिलमसरत्ततश्च सहसोर्ध्वं गच्छत्पुनर्वसुधां पपात । यत्तोयं शंकरशिरसो भ्रष्टं तदेव जलं निर्मलं च गतकल्मषं चेति चिन्तयित्वा सर्वे ते वसुधातलनिवासिनस्तत्पस्पृशुः[24] । ये च स्वर्गाद्वसुधातलं शापात्प्रपतितास्[25] तत्राभिषेकमकुर्वंस्ते तेन तत्क्षणे गतकल्मषाः । तेनाद्भुतेन तोयेन धूतपापाः स्वर्गं पुनराविश्य स्वाँल्लोकान्[26] प्रतिपेदिरे । सर्वे देवा ऋषिगणा दैत्यदानवराक्षसा गन्धर्वयक्षाप्सरसः किन्नरमहोरगा जलचराश्च भगीरथरथम् अनुगच्छन्तीं गङ्गामन्वगच्छन् । यत्र महातेजा महात्मा भगीरथो गतस्तत्रैव यशस्विनी सर्वासां सरितां श्रेष्ठा सर्वपापविनाशिनी जगाम । तत्कालं तु महर्षिर्जह्नुर्यज्ञे व्यापृत आसीत्तस्य[27] च महात्मन[27] एवं यजमानस्य[27] गङ्गा यज्ञवाटं संप्लावयामास[28] । तस्या अवलेपनेनापि क्रुद्धो महर्षिर्गङ्गायाः सर्वं जलमपिबत् । तदद्भुतं दृष्ट्वैव सर्वे देवा अन्ये गगननिवासिनश्च परमविस्मयं गत्वा तमृषिसत्तमं पूजयितुं समुपचक्रमिरे तैश्च गङ्गा महातपस ऋषेर्दुहितृत्वं नीता[29] । तेन संतुष्टो महामुनिर्गङ्गां श्रोत्राभ्यामसृजत् । तस्माज्जह्नुदुहिता गङ्गा जाह्नवीत्यपि विश्रुता । तदा सर्वासां सरितां श्रेष्ठा सागरं संप्राप्य रसातलं सगरस्यात्मजानां भस्मशोधनार्थमाविवेश ।

Notes

1. तस्मिन्देवदेवे गते locative absolute. Who is meant by देवदेव ('the god of gods')?

2. महेश्वरस्य objective genitive with the verbal noun पूजनम्. Instead of this construction (genitive + verbal noun + √कृ), the imperfect अपूजयत् with a direct object might have been used. But these periphrases with √कृ are very common and, incidentally, continue to be so in the modern Indo-Aryan vernaculars.

3. अथ used not in a consecutive or temporal sense, but merely as continuing the narrative, quite like English 'now'.

4. उमापती a sandhi form for उमापतिः. We should naturally expect the visarga to be replaced by *-r* (-र्), but two *r's* are not allowed in sequence between word junctures in Sanskrit: the first is dropped, and the previous vowel is lengthened to compensate for the unfortunate loss. Thus, *-iḥ* + *r-* becomes *-ir* + *r-* (which is not allowed), then *-ī* + *r-*.

5. तव प्रियं करिष्यामि We may render 'I shall do what is pleasing (प्रियं) to you' or 'I shall do you a favor (प्रियं)', depending upon whether प्रियं (literally 'dear' or 'pleasing') is treated as an adjective or a noun. In either case, the genitive तव is used as a dative, a ubiquitous usage which we term a 'genitive quasi-dative'. It may be of interest to note that in the Prakrit languages (which represent a later, more precisely a 'middle', stage of Old Indic), the dative is almost entirely replaced by the genitive due to the spread of this 'genitive quasi-dative' usage.

6. शैलराजस्य The 'king of mountains' is, of course, Himālaya or Himavat, who was the father of उमा (variously called पार्वती, दुर्गा, काली or simply देवी 'the goddess'), Śiva's wife, and of गङ्गा.

7. गङ्गां शिरसा धारयिष्यामि It must be borne in mind that, without Śiva's intervention, the descent of the mighty Gaṅgā would have been a catastrophic disaster for the earth.

8. The words to which उदित्वा refers are पृथिवीं निपत 'fall to earth!' -- a laconic command, to be sure, but, as we shall see, sufficiently clear to गङ्गा to

arouse her anger. After all, she was a *heavenly* river (आकाशगा नदी); why should she not object to becoming a *terrestrial* stream, however mighty?

9. कैलासस्थं स्वनिवासं Kailāsa, one of the high peaks of the Himālayas, is often referred to as the abode or heaven of Śiva, while that of Viṣṇu is called 'Vaikuṇṭha', whose location, however, is variously given.

10. अतिमहद्रूपं दुःसहं वेगं च कृत्वा Because गङ्गा was furious upon being ordered to 'fall to earth', she manifested her displeasure by assuming an 'excessively great form' (अतिमहद् रूपं) and 'unbearable impetuosity' (दुःसहं वेगं), petulant arrogance which Śiva alone was capable of thwarting.

11. शंकरस्य 'Śaṃkara' is one of Śiva's numerous epithets used as a name. It means literally 'effecting *or* conferring a blessing (शम्)' and like the name 'Śiva' (really an adjective meaning 'kind' or 'gracious') is just a euphemistic appellation conferred upon him thereby to avoid incurring the displeasure or wrath of which the malevolent and irascible side of his disposition was capable. Kāma (काम), the god of love and a prime example of his wrath, was once incinerated by a mere glance of Śiva's third eye, when the god's meditation was interrupted by him, as a result of which Kāma was devoid of a body and thenceforth called 'the bodiless one' (अनङ्ग). Śiva's original name was 'Rudra', under which, incidentally, there are three hymns addressed to him in the Ṛgveda.

12. जटामण्डलगह्वरे an adjective to मूर्धनि; thus, 'on the head (of Rudra) impenetrable (गह्वर) due to his knot (मण्डल) of twisted hair (जटा)'. Śiva is regarded, among other things, as the supreme ascetic and is accordingly depicted wearing a coil of twisted hair such as is typically worn by ascetics. Because of this thick braid of hair, his head is here said to be हिमवद्वनप्रतिमे 'like a forest of the Himālaya', impenetrable even to the swift-moving waters of गङ्गा.

13. पतिता Since √पत् 'fall' is an intransitive verb, the past passive participle is *passive only in form,* but *active* in meaning: 'having fallen'. It would have been possible, therefore, to use the gerund पतित्वा here instead of पतिता, as the gerund, as we know, has the value of a past *active* participle.

14. पतितुं infinitive expressing the purpose of निर्गन्तुं 'to go out in order to fall . .'.

15. निर्गन्तुमशक्नुवतीं तां ज्ञात्वा 'having realized her as being unable to go out', *i.e.*, 'realizing that she was not able to get out'. Note again the use of an accusative with modifying adjective as object of a verb of mental action (here √ज्ञा 'know'), where in English a 'that-clause' is used.

16. With the exception of सिन्धु, all these rivers which are supposed to have arisen from गङ्गा are mythical. सिन्धु is, of course, the mighty river (महानदी) Sindhu, called 'Indus' in English.

17. शिरस् and धरणीम् are both 'accusative of the place to which'; thus, 'Gaṅgā came from the heaven *to* Śaṃkara's head, then *to* the earth'.

18. तदेमं Be careful of the sandhi here!

19. गङ्गावतरणं दिदृक्षवो 'desirous of seeing the descent of Gaṅgā'. गङ्गावतरणं is object of the verbal idea contained in the adjective. दिदृक्षु is an adjective (of a fairly common type) made from what is called the 'desiderative' of √दृश् 'see'. 'Desiderative' means 'expressing *or* denoting a wish'. The idea of desiring to do this or that may, of course, be expressed by any one of several verbs meaning 'desire, wish' in combination with the infinitive of the root which expresses what one wishes to do; thus, 'I wish to write a letter' पत्रं लिखितुमिच्छामि. From many verb roots, however, may be formed a special derivative which imparts the notion of desire to the basic sense of the root. So, in the sentence above we may convey the sense of 'I wish to write' by means of a single verb form made from √लिख् by reduplication with *li-* and the addition of *-iṣa*; the new stem *li-likh-iṣa* (लिलिखिष) is conjugated like any thematic root in the present, imperfect, imperative and optative. An alternative way of saying लिखितुमिच्छामि, then, is to use the desiderative of √लिख्, thus: लिलिखिषामि *(li-likh-iṣā-mi)*. In the repeated or reduplicated syllable the initial consonant of the root is repeated exactly as in the perfect, which we studied in Lesson Twenty-One. The vowel of the reduplicative syllable is *-i-*, unless the root contains *-u-*, in which instance the vowel of the reduplicative syllable is also *-u-*. The suffix is *-iṣa* or simply *-sa*. Which is to be used with a particular root is best learned from experience.

From the desiderative stem of any verb may be made with mechanical regularity an adjective meaning 'desirous of doing so-and-so'. This is done by changing the final *-a* to *-u*. The resultant adjective is, of course, declined like any *u*-stem. A desiderative adjective is equivalent in meaning to the present participle of a desiderative root and accordingly may take a direct object (if the root is transitive!), as does दिदृक्षवो here. Furthermore, by substituting *-ā* for the final *-a* of a desiderative stem is made a noun with the meaning 'a desire to do so-and-so'. So, from √गम् 'go' we derive first of all *ji-gam-iṣa* (जिगमिष), the verb stem meaning 'desire to go', *ji-gam-iṣu* (जिगमिषु), the adjective 'desirous of going' and finally *ji-gam-iṣā* (जिगमिषा), 'a desire to go'.[5]

20. विमानैर् A *vimāna* is a chariot or car used by gods or other praeter-natural beings for aerial travel. These sky-chariots seem to have been self-propelled and are often of elaborate, even palatial character. The word *vimāna* is derived from वि-√मा literally 'measure across', then 'traverse', so that it is inherently a means for *traversing* the sky. Sometimes a *vimāna* is given a name, as Puṣpaka (पुष्पक) of the demon Rāvaṇa who kidnapped Rāma's wife Sītā in the Rāmāyaṇa.

21. कच्छपशिशुमारादिभिर् This is a bahuvrīhi of a special, but prevalent type; literally '(with water-creatures) having tortoises and dolphins as their beginning', *i.e.,* tortoises and dolphins, and so forth. In compounds of this type आदि 'beginning' is meant to suggest an unspecified number of things beginning with those mentioned in the forepart of the compound, *i.e.,* those mentioned and the rest of the same sort. Thus, इन्द्रादयो देवाः 'the gods beginning with Indra' (literally 'having Indra as their beginning'), *i.e.,* Indra and all the other gods, or 'the gods Indra, etc.' In these compounds, then, आदि may generally be rendered by 'etc.' or 'and so forth' or some equivalent expression.

22. The च 'and' connects जलपतनं and विरवः which is explained by भयाक्रान्तपतङ्गानां; thus, 'the falling of the water and the clamor of . . .'.

23. प्रस्रवज् (by sandhi for प्रस्रवत्) is the present participle of प्र-√स्रु (स्रवति), modifying जलं ('water flowing forth . .'). Similarly, गच्छत् in the next sentence.

---

[5]Occasionally a desiderative has an extended and specialized meaning as मुमुक्ष (from √मुच् 'release') 'desire to be released (from the cycle of birth and rebirth)', and so मुमुक्षा 'a desire for salvation' and मुमुक्षु 'desirous of *or* striving after salvation'.

24. पस्पृशुः perfect third plural of √स्पृश् (स्पृशति) 'touch'. When a root begins with a sibilant followed by a voiceless consonant, only the latter is repeated in the reduplicative syllable; so here *pa-spṛś-; cf.* also *ta-sthā-* (√स्था) and *ta-stambh-* (√स्तम्भ्).

25. ये च स्वर्गाद्वसुधातलं शापात्प्रपतितास् 'And those who had fallen to earth from heaven due to a curse . .'. It is commonplace in Sanskrit literature to read of some celestial being who is compelled to assume a terrestrial existence for a stipulated time as a result of a curse. Those referred to in this passage are exceptionally fortunate as their wrongs (कल्मष) are removed by being laved in Gaṅgā's waters. Gaṅgā's ability to remove sins is alluded to also in the epithet सर्वपापविनाशिनी farther on.

26. स्वाल्ँलोकान् for स्वान् लोकान्. When -न् is followed by an initial ल-, it is changed to a nasalized ल् by regressive assimilation, and the nasalization (left over from the -न्) is indicated by the symbol ँ which is called चन्द्रबिन्दु 'a dot (बिन्दु) in the moon'.

27. तस्य च महात्मन एवं यजमानस्य may be taken either as a genitive absolute ('and while that noble one was thus sacrificing') or as a sort of possessive genitive with यज्ञवाटं ('the place of sacrifice of him . .'). The construction here is a good illustration of how the genitive absolute originated: as a genitive (with participle) rather loosely attached to a noun, then a more independent construction as the connection with the noun becomes less clearly definable and more tenuous.

28. संप्लावयामास a periphrastic perfect of the causative of सं-√प्लु (प्लवति); see note 3 on रोचयामासुः in Lesson Twenty-four. Remember that causatives and roots of Class X (which are conjugated identically) make their perfect periphrastically.

29. तैश्च गङ्गा महातपस ऋषेर्दुहितृत्वं नीता 'and by them (*i.e.,* all the gods and denizens of heaven) Gaṅgā was made a daughter of the sage whose austerities were great' (*literally* 'was led into the condition of a daughter of the sage'). This use of √नी with an abstract in the accusative (दुहितृत्वं) is parallel to that of the abstract with √गम् as in स पञ्चत्वं गतः 'He went to five-ness', *i.e.,* died.

Vocabulary

अतितीव्र, *adj.* extremely severe.
अतिद्रुतम्, *adv.* extremely quickly.
अतिमहत्, *adj.* extremely great.
अद्भुत, *adj.* wonderful, remarkable.
अनु-√गम् (गच्छति, class I), go after, follow.
अन्ततः, *adv.* finally.
अपरं च, *conjunctive adv.* moreover.
अप्सरस्, *f.* Apsaras, name of one of a class of semi-divine beings, the wives of the Gandharvas.
अभि-√रुह् (रोहति, class I), climb up, ascend; *gerund* अभिरुह्य.
अभिषेक, *m.* sprinkling; consecration.
अमित, *adj.* unmeasured, boundless, infinite.
अवतरण, *n.* the act of descending, descent.
अवलेपन, *n.* proud behavior, arrogance.
आकाश, *n.* sky, heaven.
आकाशग, *adj.* going *or* moving in the heaven. [आकाश + ग, verbal of √गम्]
आ-√कॄ (किरति, class VI), scatter, bestrew; *ppp.* आकीर्ण.
आक्रान्त, *ppp.* √आ-√क्रम् (क्रामति, class I), *literally* come to, approached, *then,* attacked, overcome, seized with (+ *instr. or in cpd.).*
आत्मज *m.* a son.
आ-√भाष् (भाषते, class I), call upon; *gerund* आभाष्य.
आ-√विश् (विशति, class VI), enter; *perf.* विवेश; *gerund* °विश्य.
आ-√स्था (तिष्ठति, class I), stand on, ascend, mount; *ppp.* आस्थित.
उमा, *f.* Umā, name of the daughter of Himavat, also called Pārvatī, Durgā, etc., wife of Śiva and sister of Gaṅgā.
उरग, *m.* a serpent.
ऊर्ध्वम्, *adv.* upwards.
ओजस् *n.* strength, power.
कच्छप, *m.* a tortoise.
कल्मष, *n.* spot, stain; impurity.
किन्नर, *m.* a kind of heavenly musician, often associated with the Gandharvas.
कुटिलम्, *adv.* crookedly, in a meandering fashion.

कैलासस्थ, *adj.* being *or* situated on Kailāsa, a mountain peak of the Himālaya.
√क्रुध् (क्रुध्यति, class IV), become angry; *ppp.* क्रुद्ध.
क्रोध, *m.* anger.
क्वचिद् . . क्वचिद् *adv.* in one place . . in another place.
गगन, *n.* the sky, heaven.
गङ्गाधर, *m.* Gaṅgādhara, epithet and name of Śiva as 'Upholder of Gaṅgā'.
गन्धर्व, *m.* Gandharva, name of one of a class of heavenly musicians.
गह्वर, *adj.* thick, impenetrable.
√चल् (चलति, class I), move, move about.
जटा, *f.* a twist *or* coil of matted hair (such as worn by ascetics).
√जन् (जायते, class IV), be born, arise; *perf.* जज्ञे.
जन, *m.* a man; person; *in plur.* people.
जलचर, *m.* 'water-goer', any aquatic creature.
जह्नु, *m.* Jahnu, name of a sage.
जाह्नवी, *f.* Jāhnavī, name of the Ganges or Gaṅgā as the daughter of the sage Jahnu.
ज्येष्ठ, *superlative adj.* eldest.
तत्क्षणे, *adv.* instantly.
तल, *n.* surface; *often meaningless in part B of a cpd.*
तिरः-√भू *in caus.* तिरोभावयति, 'causes to disappear', conceals; *infin.* तिरोभावयितुम्.
तोय, *n.* water.
दर्प, *m.* imprudence, pride.
दिदृक्षु, *desiderative adj.* desirous of seeing.
दुःसह, *adj.* difficult to bear, unbearable.
धरणी, *f.* the earth.
√धू (धुनोति, class V), shake, cause to shake; *ppp.* धूत.
√धृ *(no present, caus.* धारयति *without caus. meaning),* hold, bear, support; *fut. of caus.* धारयिष्यति.
नमस्-√कृ, do homage to, worship; *ppp.* नमस्कृत.
नर, *m.* a man.
नलिनी, *f.* Nalinī, name of a mythical river, 'The Reedy One'.
निनाद, *m.* sound, noise.
नि-√पत् (पतति, class I), fall down.

निर्मल, *adj.* without impurity, pure.

निवास, *m.* a dwelling-place *or* abode.

निवासिन्, *m.* an inhabitant.

पतङ्ग, *m.* any flying thing, a bird.

पतन, *n.* the act of falling, fall.

पति, *m.* a husband.

परम, *adj.* extreme, supreme.

√पा (पिबति, class I), drink.

पाप, *n.* evil deed, sin.

पावनी, *f.* Pāvanī, name of a mythical river, 'The Purifier'.

√पूज् (पूजयति, class X), worship; *infin.* पूजयितुम्.

पूजन, *n.* the act of worshipping, worship.

प्रति-√पद् (पद्यते, class IV), step toward, attain; get back, return to; *perf.* प्रतिपपाद, °पेदे.

प्रतिमा, *f.* a likeness; *at end of bahuvrīhi cpd.* 'having a likeness with', like.

प्रति-√हन् (हन्ति, class II), strike back, impede; *ppp.* प्रतिहत.

प्र-√पत् (पतति, class I), fall forward (प्र) *or* down.

प्र-√स्रु (स्रवति, class I), flow forth, flow.

प्रिय, *adj.* dear, pleasing; *as n.* a favor.

बुद्धि, *f.* mind; बुद्धिं √कृ, make up one's mind.

भगवत्, *adj.* fortunate *or* blessed.

भय, *n.* fear.

भयंकर, *adj.* causing fear, fearsome.

√भ्रम् (भ्राम्यति, class IV), wander, roam about aimlessly; *gerund* भ्रान्त्वा.

भ्रष्ट, *ppp.* √भ्रश् (भ्रश्यति, class IV), fallen.

मण्डल, *n.* a bunch *or* quantity of anything (as of the hair).

मत्स्य, *m.* a fish.

मूर्धन्, *m.* the head.

यक्ष, *m.* Yakṣa, name of one of a class of semi-divine beings, usually, but not invariably, of a benevolent nature.

यत्न, *m.* effort.

यशस्विन्, *adj.* celebrated, famous, splendid, beautiful.

रसातल, *n.* the lower world *or* hell.

रुद्र, *m.* Rudra, an early epithet and name of Śiva.

रूप, *n.* form.
लोक, *m.* the world.
√वद् (वदति, class I), say, speak *or* say to; *gerund* उदित्वा.
वसुधा, *f.* the earth.
वाट, *m.* an enclosure.
विनाशिन्, *adj.* destroying.
विमान, *n.* an aerial chariot.
विरव, *m.* crying, clamor, noise.
विविध, *adj.* 'having different kinds', of various sorts, different.
वि-√सृज् (सृजति, class VI), let go, release; *perf.* विससर्ज; *ppp.* विसृष्ट.
विस्मय, *m.* astonishment.
वेग, *m.* rush, onset, impetus; vehemence.
व्यापृत, *ppp.* वि-आ-√पृ (पृणोति, class V), busied with *or* engaged in (+ *loc.*).
√शक् (शक्नोति, class V), be able, can.
शंकर, *m.* Śaṃkara, epithet and name of Śiva.
शाप, *m.* a curse.
शिखर, *n.* a top *or* peak.
शिरस्, *n.* the head.
शिशुमार, *m.* a dolphin.
शीर्ष, *n.* the head.
शूलिन्, *adj.* possessing a spear (*i.e.*, a trident); *epithet of Śiva.*
शोधन, *n.* the act of purifying, purification.
शैल, *m.* a mountain.
श्रेष्ठ, *superlative adj.* most excellent, best.
श्रोत्र, *n.* the ear.
संवत्सर, *m.* a year.
सत्तम, *adj.* best (*superlative of* सत्, good).
सं-√तुष् (तुष्यति, class IV), be satisfied; *ppp.* संतुष्ट.
सप्त, *numeral adj.* seven.
सप्तम, *f.* सप्तमी, *ordinal numeral adj.* seventh.
सम्-अव-√आप् (आप्नोति, class V), come to, attain, reach.
सम्-उप-√क्रम् (क्रामति, class I), begin; *perf.* समुपचक्राम, °चक्रमे.
संपूर्ण, *adj.* filled, fulfilled; completed.

सं-√प्लु (प्लवते, class I), flow together; be heaped together; *caus.* संप्लावयति, causes to flow *or* be heaped together, submerges, inundates; *periphrastic perf. of caus.* संप्लावयामास.

सर्वत्र, *adv.* everywhere.

सलिल, *n.* water.

सहसा, *adv.* suddenly, immediately.

सिन्धु, *m.* Sindhu, name of the great river Indus.

सीता, *f.* Sītā, name of a mythical river. [Possibly named after the goddess Sītā, who presided over agriculture and the fruits of the earth]

सुचक्षुस्, *f.* Sucakṣus, name of a mythical river, 'The Fair-eyed'.

सुप्रसन्न, *adj.* well (सु)-disposed, favorably disposed.

√सृ (सरति, class I), run, flow, move.

√सृज् (सृजति, class VI), let go, release.

√स्पृश् (स्पृशति, class VI), touch; *perf.* पस्पर्श, पस्पृशे.

स्यन्दन, *n.* a chariot.

स्रोतस्, *n.* a stream, river.

स्वयम् *intensive pron.* oneself, herself, itself (all genders and numbers).

ह्लादिनी, *f.* Hlādinī, name of a mythical river, 'The Gladdener'.

Translate into Sanskrit:

Making a supreme effort to propitiate the great god Śiva, possessor of the trident, for help in bringing down the river Gaṅgā, Bhagīratha worshipped him for a year, performing additional, very severe austerities. Now[1] at the end of the year, the husband of Umā said to Bhagīratha: 'O best of men, true to your vows, majestic one, I am very kindly disposed to you on account of your very severe austerities. Therefore, I shall hold up the daughter of the king of the mountain with my head.' Thereupon he climbed to the peak of Himavat and, having said to the celestial river 'Fall down to earth!' he returned to his abode in Mt. Kailāsa.[2] But because descending to *earth* from heaven was not at all pleasing to that goddess, she became extremely angry and fell upon Śiva's head with a mighty impact. The great god too, having become angry because of her excessive arrogance, determined to conceal her in the coil of his matted hair (which was) difficult to traverse like the forest of Himavat. When he realized that that goddess, though she made a supreme effort, was unable to go out of it, being satisfied, he released her. Finally, flowing forth with a mighty sound from Śiva's head, Gaṅgā, having descended to earth, followed after Bhagīratha (who was) mounted on a chariot. All the inhabitants of the earth, seeing the descent of Gaṅgā, realized that her water was pure and purifying and after touching it immediately were relieved of their sins.[3] As soon as they saw Gaṅgā flowing forth, gods too, who had descended[4] to earth due to a curse, were freed of their sins[5] and returned to the world of heaven. While following the chariot of the majestic Bhagīratha, Gaṅgā inundated the sacrificial enclosure of the great ascetic and great seer Jahnu (who was) engaged[6] in a sacrifice. Extremely angered at that, he swallowed all Gaṅgā's water. As soon as they saw that miracle, all the gods and other denizens of the sky, Apsarases, Gandharvas, etc.,[7] filled with great astonishment, began to worship that great seer whose austerities were great.[8] Thereupon they made Gaṅgā a daughter of that sage. Pleased by this, Jahnu released Gaṅgā from his ears. For this reason that Gaṅgā is known as 'Jāhnavī'. Now, having reached the ocean, Gaṅgā entered Rasātala to purify the ashes of Sagara's noble sons.

Notes

1. 'Now': Use अथ in its continuative sense.

2. 'to his abode in Mt. Kailāsa': Instead of rendering literally 'to his abode in Mt. Kailāsa', it is more idiomatic to say 'to his abode situated in (Mt.) Kailāsa' (कैलासस्थं स्वनिवासम् – note '*acc.* of place to which').

3. 'relieved of their sins': Express with a bahūvrīhi, धूतपापा:, literally 'whose sins have been shaken off'.

4. 'who had descended': It is not necessary to use a relative clause here, the *ppp*. of अव-√तॄ suffices.

5. 'freed of their sins': Use a bahuvrīhi as in note 3.

6. '(who was) engaged': *v*. note 4.

7. 'Apsarases, Gandharvas, etc.': Remember to express the notion of 'etc.' by -आदि at the end of a bahuvrīhi compound; literally, '(denizens ...) having Apsarases, Gandharvas, as the beginning'. As an adjective, this compound will agree with 'denizens'.

8. 'whose austerities were great': Express by a bahuvrīhi.

LESSON TWENTY-SIX

Non-thematic Verbs Continued.

In the preceding lesson we began our discussion of non-thematic verbs with roots of the Vth and VIIIth classes, *viz.*, the सु and तन् classes. There remain to be discussed the अद्, हु, रुध् and क्री classes. The easiest of these is the क्री or IXth class. The strong form of the present stem is made by adding the suffix *-nā-* (-ना-) to the root, the weak stem by adding *-nī-* (-नी-) which becomes *-n-* (-न्-) before vowels. Thus, √स्तभ् 'make firm' has the strong stem *stabh-nā* (स्तभ्ना), the weak stem *stabh-nī* (स्तभ्नी)/*stabh-n* (स्तभ्न्). A commoner root than √स्तभ् is √बन्ध् 'bind', which drops its radical -न्- throughout the present system, so that the strong and weak stems are *badh-nā* (बध्ना) and *badh-nī* (बध्नी)/*badh-n* (बध्न्) respectively. Although all the forms of the present system are made with perfect regularity from these stems, for the sake of clarity and perhaps also systematicity the entire present system is presented below.

√बन्ध् 'bind'

Present

Active

	Singular	*Dual*	*Plural*
1.	**badh-nā-mi* (बध्नामि)	*badh-nī-vaḥ* (बध्नीवः)	*badh-nī-maḥ* (बध्नीमः)
2.	**badh-nā-si* (बध्नासि)	*badh-nī-thaḥ* (बध्नीथः)	*badh-nī-tha* (बध्नीथ)
3.	**badh-nā-ti* (बध्नाति)	*badh-nī-taḥ* (बध्नीतः)	*badh-n-anti* (बध्नन्ति)

Middle

1.	*badh-n-e* (बध्ने)	*badh-nī-vahe* (बध्नीवहे)	*badh-nī-mahe* (बध्नीमहे)
2.	*badh-nī-ṣe* (बध्नीषे)	*badh-n-āthe* (बध्नाथे)	*badh-nī-dhve* (बध्नीध्वे)
3.	*badh-nī-te* (बध्नीते)	*badh-n-āte* (बध्नाते)	*badh-n-ate* (बध्नते)

Imperfect

Active

	Singular	*Dual*	*Plural*
1.	**a-badh-nā-m* (अबध्नाम्)	*a-badh-nī-va* (अबध्नीव)	*a-badh-nī-ma* (अबध्नीम)
2.	**a-badh-nā-ḥ* (अबध्नाः)	*a-badh-nī-tam* (अबध्नीतम्)	*a-badh-nī-ta* (अबध्नीत)
3.	**a-badh-nā-t* (अबध्नात्)	*a-badh-nī-tām* (अबध्नीताम्)	*a-badh-n-an* (अबध्नन्)

Middle

1.	*a-badh-n-i* (अबध्नि)	*a-badh-nī-vahi* (अबध्नीवहि)	*a-badh-nī-mahi* (अबध्नीमहि)
2.	*a-badh-nī-thāḥ* (अबध्नीथाः)	*a-badh-n-āthām* (अबध्नाथाम्)	*a-badh-nī-dhvam* (अबध्नीध्वम्)
3.	*a-badh-nī-ta* (अबध्नीत)	*a-badh-n-ātām* (अबध्नाताम्)	*a-badh-n-ata* (अबध्नत)

Imperative

Active

1.	**badh-nā-ni* (बध्नानि)	**badh-nā-va* (बध्नाव)	**badh-nā-ma* (बध्नाम)
2.	*badh-āna* (बधान)	*badh-nī-tam* (बध्नीतम्)	*badh-nī-ta* (बध्नीत)
3.	**badh-nā-tu* (बध्नातु)	*badh-nī-tām* (बध्नीताम्)	*badh-n-antu* (बध्नन्तु)

Middle

	Singular	*Dual*	*Plural*
1.	**badh-n-ai* (बध्नै)	**badh-nā-vahai* (बध्नावहै)	**badh-nā-mahai* (बध्नामहै)
2.	*badh-nī-ṣva* (बध्नीष्व)	*badh-n-āthām* (बध्नाथाम्)	*badh-nī-dhvam* (बध्नीध्वम्)
3.	*badh-nī-tām* (बध्नीताम्)	*badh-n-ātām* (बध्नाताम्)	*badh-n-atām* (बध्नताम्)

Optative

Active

1.	*badh-nī-yā-m* (बध्नीयाम्)	*badh-nī-yā-va* (बध्नीयाव)	*badh-nī-yā-ma* (बध्नीयाम)
2.	*badh-nī-yā-ḥ* (बध्नीयाः)	*badh-nī-yā-tam* (बध्नीयातम्)	*badh-nī-yā-ta* (बध्नीयात)
3.	*badh-nī-yā-t* (बध्नीयात्)	*badh-nī-yā-tām* (बध्नीयाताम्)	*badh-nī-y-uḥ* (बध्नीयुः)

Middle

1.	*badh-n-ī-y-a* (बध्नीय)	*badh-n-ī-vahi* (बध्नीवहि)	*badh-n-ī-mahi* (बध्नीमहि)
2.	*badh-n-ī-thāḥ* (बध्नीथाः)	*badh-n-ī-y-āthām* (बध्नीयाथाम्)	*badh-n-ī-dhvam* (बध्नीध्वम्)
3.	*badh-n-ī-ta* (बध्नीत)	*badh-n-ī-y-ātām* (बध्नीयाताम्)	*badh-n-ī-ran* (बध्नीरन्)

The only point that needs to be noted is that the imperative, second singular active, is made with the termination *-hi* (-हि) only when the root ends in a vowel, like √क्री 'buy', the imperative of which is *krī-ṇī-hi* (क्रीणीहि). If, however, the root ends in a consonant, the peculiar ending *-āna* (-आन) is added; hence, *not badh-nī-hi* (बध्नीहि), but *badh-āna* (बधान). The form of the root to which *-āna* is added is not the weak stem, as would be expected, as that would yield *badh-n-āna,* but to the root entirely devoid of the class suffix.

There are not many roots in this class, perhaps the commonest, apart from √क्री 'buy' and √बन्ध् 'bind', are √ग्रह् 'seize', for which *gṛh* (गृह्) is substituted throughout the present system, √स्तभ् 'make firm, support', √प्री 'gladden, propitiate', √लू 'cut' and √वृ 'choose' (only in the middle voice).

The IIIrd or हु class makes its present stem by reduplication, as in the perfect tense. The usual rules for the reduplication of the consonant are followed. In the strong forms the root vowel is replaced by its guṇa substitute, but in the weak forms it remains unchanged.

√हु 'offer, make an oblation'

Present

Active

	Singular	*Dual*	*Plural*
1.	**ju-ho-mi* (जुहोमि)	*ju-hu-vaḥ* (जुहुवः)	*ju-hu-maḥ* (जुहुमः)
2.	**ju-ho-ṣi* (जुहोषि)	*ju-hu-thaḥ* (जुहुथः)	*ju-hu-tha* (जुहुथ)
3.	**ju-ho-ti* (जुहोति)	*ju-hu-taḥ* (जुहुतः)	*ju-hv-ati* (जुह्वति)

Middle

1.	*ju-hv-e* (जुह्वे)	*ju-hu-vahe* (जुहुवहे)	*ju-hu-mahe* (जुहुमहे)
2.	*ju-hu-ṣe* (जुहुषे)	*ju-hv-āthe* (जुह्वाथे)	*ju-hu-dhve* (जुहुध्वे)
3.	*ju-hu-te* (जुहुते)	*ju-hv-āte* (जुह्वाते)	*ju-hv-ate* (जुह्वते)

Imperfect

Active

	Singular	*Dual*	*Plural*
1.	**a-ju-hav-am* (अजुहवम्)	*a-ju-hu-va* (अजुहुव)	*a-ju-hu-ma* (अजुहुम)
2.	**a-ju-ho-ḥ* (अजुहोः)	*a-ju-hu-tam* (अजुहुतम्)	*a-ju-hu-ta* (अजुहुत)
3.	**a-ju-ho-t* (अजुहोत्)	*a-ju-hu-tām* (अजुहुताम्)	*a-ju-hav-uḥ* (अजुहवुः)

Middle

1.	*a-ju-hv-i* (अजुह्वि)	*a-ju-hu-vahi* (अजुहुवहि)	*a-ju-hu-mahi* (अजुहुमहि)
2.	*a-ju-hu-thāḥ* (अजुहुथाः)	*a-ju-hv-āthām* (अजुह्वाथाम्)	*a-ju-hu-dhvam* (अजुहुध्वम्)
3.	*a-ju-hu-ta* (अजुहुत)	*a-ju-hv-ātām* (अजुह्वाताम्)	*a-ju-hv-ata* (अजुह्वत)

Imperative

Active

1.	**ju-hav-āni* (जुहवानि)	**ju-hav-āva* (जुहवाव)	**ju-hav-āma* (जुहवाम)
2.	*ju-hu-dhi* (जुहुधि)	*ju-hu-tam* (जुहुतम्)	*ju-hu-ta* (जुहुत)
3.	**ju-ho-tu* (जुहोतु)	*ju-hu-tām* (जुहुताम्)	*ju-hv-atu* (जुह्वतु)

Middle

	Singular	*Dual*	*Plural*
1.	**ju-hav-ai* (जुहवै)	**ju-hav-āvahai* (जुहवावहै)	**ju-hav-āmahai* (जुहवामहै)
2.	*ju-hu-ṣva* (जुहुष्व)	*ju-hv-āthām* (जुह्वाथाम्)	*ju-hu-dhvam* (जुहुध्वम्)
3.	*ju-hu-tām* (जुहुताम्)	*ju-hv-ātām* (जुह्वाताम्)	*ju-hv-atām* (जुह्वताम्)

Optative

Active

1.	*ju-hu-yā-m* (जुहुयाम्)	*ju-hu-yā-va* (जुहुयाव)	*ju-hu-yā-ma* (जुहुयाम)
2.	*ju-hu-yā-ḥ* (जुहुयाः)	*ju-hu-yā-tam* (जुहुयातम्)	*ju-hu-yā-ta* (जुहुयात)
3.	*ju-hu-yā-t* (जुहुयात्)	*ju-hu-yā-tām* (जुहुयाताम्)	*ju-hu-y-uḥ* (जुहुयुः)

Middle

1.	*ju-hv-ī-y-a* (जुह्वीय)	*ju-hv-ī-vahi* (जुह्वीवहि)	*ju-hv-ī-mahi* (जुह्वीमहि)
2.	*ju-hv-ī-thāḥ* (जुह्वीथाः)	*ju-hv-ī-y-āthām* (जुह्वीयाथाम्)	*ju-hv-ī-dhvam* (जुह्वीध्वम्)
3.	*ju-hv-ī-ta* (जुह्वीत)	*ju-hv-ī-y-ātām* (जुह्वीयाताम्)	*ju-hv-ī-ran* (जुह्वीरन्)

It is important to note that, in addition to dropping the nasal *(-n-)* of the third person plural endings of the middle (as do *all* the non-thematic verbs), verbs of the reduplicating class also drop the nasal in the third plural *active* of the present and imperative. These endings, therefore, are *-ati* (-अति) and *-atu* (-अतु) respectively, *not -anti* (-अन्ति) and *-antu* (-अन्तु). Another peculiarity is that the ending of third plural imperfect active is *not -an* (-अन्), but *-uḥ* (-उः), before which the root vowel takes its guṇa substitute; thus, *a-ju-hav-uḥ* (अजुहवुः). Remember that before a vowel *within* a word *-o-* becomes *-av-*, as does the *-o-* of *bho-* (भो), the guṇa form of √भू, which, throughout the present system, becomes *bhav-* (भव्) before the thematic vowel *-a-*, as in *bhav-a-ti* (भवति). Hence, here *ju-ho-* (जुहो-) becomes *ju-hav-* (जुहव्-) before *-uḥ* (-उः).

Two of the most important Sanskrit roots, *dhā* (धा) 'put, place' and *dā* (दा) 'give', belong to this class. Like the spectacular √अस् 'be', they also lose their vowel in the weak stem; thus, *dadhā-/dadh-* (दधा-/दध्-) and *dadā-/dad-* (ददा-/दद्-). Now the question arises, what happens when consonant-initial endings (like *-thaḥ, -taḥ, -se*, etc.) are added to *dadh-*? We will recall that *no* sandhi change takes place within a word when endings beginning with a vowel, nasal or a semivowel are added to a root ending in a consonant. We cannot have a form like *dadh-thaḥ, dadh-taḥ* or *dadh-tha*. By the rule of regressive assimilation the *-dh* (-ध्) is made voiceless due to the regressive influence of the voiceless *t-/th-* (त्/थ्) of the endings. This gives us *dath-thaḥ, dath-taḥ* and *dath-tha*. Now a curious thing happens: the aspiration or *-h* of the root final *-th* rebounds to the initial *d-*, so that the root now becomes *dhat-* ! The three forms in their final shape are *dhat-thaḥ* (धत्थः), *dhat-taḥ* (धत्तः) and *dhat-tha* (धत्थ). The weak stem with transposed aspiration also occurs before the middle endings *-dhve* (-ध्वे) and *-dhvam* (-ध्वम्); thus, *dhad-dhve* (धद्ध्वे) and *a-dhad-dhvam* (अधद्ध्वम्). Note that the *-d* of *dhad-* (धद्-) remains unchanged before the voiced *dh-* of the endings.

√दा 'give' does not involve any of these interesting complications: since the weak stem *dad-* (दद्-) has no aspiration we have only to keep in mind that the final *-d* (-द्) must be changed to *-t* (-त्) before *t-/th-* (त्-/थ्-) of the endings, otherwise remaining unchanged. The following paradigm will show the changes we have exemplified and others based on the same principles.

√धा 'put, place'
Present

Active

	Singular	*Dual*	*Plural*
1.	**da-dhā-mi* (दधामि)	*dadh-vaḥ* (दध्वः)	*dadh-maḥ* (दध्मः)
2.	**da-dhā-si* (दधासि)	*dhat-thaḥ* (धत्थः)	*dhat-tha* (धत्थ)
3.	**da-dhā-ti* (दधाति)	*dhat-taḥ* (धत्तः)	*dadh-ati* (दधति)

Middle

1.	*dadh-e* (दधे)	*dadh-vahe* (दध्वहे)	*dadh-mahe* (दध्महे)
2.	*dhat-se* (धत्से)	*dadh-āthe* (दधाथे)	*dhad-dhve* (धद्ध्वे)
3.	*dhat-te* (धत्ते)	*dadh-āte* (दधाते)	*dadh-ate* (दधते)

Imperfect

Active

1.	**a-dadhā-m* (अदधाम्)	*a-dadh-va* (अदध्व)	*a-dadh-ma* (अदध्म)
2.	**a-dadhā-ḥ* (अदधाः)	*a-dhat-tam* (अधत्तम्)	*a-dhat-ta* (अधत्त)
3.	**a-dadhā-t* (अदधात्)	*a-dhat-tām* (अधत्ताम्)	*a-dadh-uḥ* (अदधुः)

Middle

	Singular	*Dual*	*Plural*
1.	*a-dadh-i* (अदधि)	*a-dadh-vahi* (अदध्वहि)	*a-dadh-mahi* (अदध्महि)
2.	*a-dhat-thāḥ* (अधत्थाः)	*a-dadh-āthām* (अदधाथाम्)	*a-dhad-dhvam* (अधद्ध्वम्)
3.	*a-dhat-ta* (अधत्त)	*a-dadh-ātām* (अदधाताम्)	*a-dadh-ata* (अदधत)

Imperative

Active

1.	**dadhā-ni* (दधानि)	**dadhā-va* (दधाव)	**dadhā-ma* (दधाम)
2.	*dhehi* (धेहि)	*dhat-tam* (धत्तम्)	*dhat-ta* (धत्त)
3.	**dadhā-tu* (दधातु)	*dhat-tām* (धत्ताम्)	*dadh-atu* (दधतु)

Middle

1.	**dadh-ai*[1] (दधै)	**dadhā-vahai* (दधावहै)	**dadhā-mahai* (दधामहै)
2.	*dhat-sva* (धत्स्व)	*dadh-āthām* (दधाथाम्)	*dhad-dhvam* (धद्ध्वम्)
3.	*dhat-tām* (धत्ताम्)	*dadh-ātām* (दधाताम्)	*dadh-atām* (दधताम्)

[1]The *-ā* of the strong stem *dadhā-* is absorbed by the ending *-ai*, hence, **dadh-ai*.

Optative

Active

	Singular	*Dual*	*Plural*
1.	*dadh-yā-m* (दध्याम्)	*dadh-yā-va* (दध्याव)	*dadh-yā-ma* (दध्याम)
2.	*dadh-yā-ḥ* (दध्याः)	*dadh-yā-tam* (दध्यातम्)	*dadh-yā-ta* (दध्यात)
3.	*dadh-yā-t* (दध्यात्)	*dadh-yā-tām* (दध्याताम्)	*dadh-y-uḥ* (दध्युः)

Middle

1.	*dadh-ī-y-a* (दधीय)	*dadh-ī-vahi* (दधीवहि)	*dadh-ī-mahi* (दधीमहि)
2.	*dadh-ī-thāḥ* (दधीथाः)	*dadh-ī-y-āthām* (दधीयाथाम्)	*dadh-ī-dhvam* (दधीध्वम्)
3.	*dadh-ī-ta* (दधीत)	*dadh-ī-y-ātām* (दधीयाताम्)	*dadh-ī-ran* (दधीरन्)

The conjugation of √दा is identical to that of √धा, except, of course, that the stems of √दा (both strong and weak) have *d-* (द्-) instead of *dh-* (ध्-). The imperative *dhehi* (धेहि) is irregular, as is also its counterpart *dehi* (देहि) of √दा.

In the previous lesson we gave the present tense of √अस् 'be' as a quite spectacular illustration of the differentiation between strong and weak stems due to a shifting of the old tonic accent of the earlier language as reflected in the Ṛgveda, In √अस्, we will recall, the vowel *a-* (अ-) drops out, leaving only the *-s* (-स्) as the weak stem, to which the personal terminations are added. Although the roots धा and दा also lose their vowel in forming the weak stem, they are not reduced to a single consonant, as they retain their reduplicative syllable *da-* (द-). With the exception of √अस्, no weak verb of the IInd or अद् class shows so drastic a reduction in the formation of the weak stem. In fact, some roots, as, for example, those ending in *-ā* (-आ), make *no* distinction of strong and weak stems, except for the accentual distinction found in the Vedic texts, but not surviving in classical Sanskrit. In discussing roots of the अद्

class it will be more conducive to simplicity and ease of learning to begin with these roots that end in -*ā* (-आ) and show *no* variation in their present stem.

√या 'go'

Present

	Singular	*Dual*	*Plural*
1.	*yā-mi* (यामि)	*yā-vaḥ* (यावः)	*yā-maḥ* (यामः)
2.	*yā-si* (यासि)	*yā-thaḥ* (याथः)	*yā-tha* (याथ)
3.	*yā-ti* (याति)	*yā-taḥ* (यातः)	*yā-nti* (यान्ति)

Imperfect

1.	*a-yā-m* (अयाम्)	*a-yā-va* (अयाव)	*a-yā-ma* (अयाम)
2.	*a-yā-ḥ* (अयाः)	etc.	
3.	*a-yā-t* (अयात्)		*a-yā-n* (अयान्) *or* *a-y-uḥ* (अयुः)

More than these forms need not be given however, as the whole present system is formed with perfect regularity. The middle voice does not occur. Only a few roots of this type are found in common use: √स्ना (स्नाति) 'bathe', √वा (वाति) 'blow', √त्रा (त्राति) 'rescue', √भा (भाति) 'shine' and √पा (पाति) 'protect'.

Generally, however, a differentiation of strong and weak stems is made in verbs of the अद् class by a modification of the root vowel. In the strong stem the guṇa substitute replaces the root vowel, which remains unchanged in the weak stem. A simple example is √इ 'go', found only in the active voice.

Present

	Singular	*Dual*	*Plural*
1.	**e-mi* (एमि)	*i-vaḥ* (इव:)	*i-maḥ* (इम:)
2.	**e-ṣi* (एषि)	*i-thaḥ* (इथ:)	*i-tha* (इथ)
3.	**e-ti* (एति)	*i-taḥ* (इत:)	*y-anti* (यन्ति)

Imperfect

1.	**āy-am* (आयम्)	*ai-va* (ऐव)	*ai-ma* (ऐम)
2.	**ai-ḥ* (ऐ:)	*ai-tam* (ऐतम्)	*ai-ta* (ऐत)
3.	**ai-t* (ऐत्)	*ai-tām* (ऐताम्)	*āy-an* (आयन्)

Imperative

1.	**ay-āni* (अयानि)	**ay-āva* (अयाव)	**ay-āma* (अयाम)
2.	*i-hi* (इहि)	*i-tam* (इतम्)	*i-ta* (इत)
3.	**e-tu* (एतु)	*i-tām* (इताम्)	*y-antu* (यन्तु)

Optative

1.	*i-yā-m* (इयाम्)	*i-yā-va* (इयाव) etc.	*i-yā-ma* (इयाम)

Note that in the imperfect the augment *a-* (अ-) coalesces with the - *i-* (-इ-) to form the diphthong *ai-* (ऐ-) which becomes *āy-* (आय्-) before a vowel, hence, *āy-am* (आयम्), *āy-an* (आयन्), but *ai-t* ऐत्), *ai-va* (ऐव), etc.[2] Note also that *i-* (इ) before a vowel becomes *y-* (य्-), as in *y-anti* (यन्ति and *y-antu* (यन्तु).

Roots of the अद् class that end in a consonant, however, involve some difficulty due to the sandhi changes that may take place when endings beginning with a consonant are added. It is important to remember here that *no* change is made in the final consonant of a root when the ending to be added begins with a nasal, *i.e., m-* (म्-), the only one that occurs, or a semivowel, *i.e., v-* (व्-) and *y-* (य्-). The consonants with which some endings begin and which, therefore, can produce sandhi changes are: *s-* (स्-) of the endings *-si* (-सि),*-se* (-से) and *-sva* (-स्व), the *t-* (त्-) and *th-* (थ्-) of *-taḥ* (-तः), *-thaḥ* (-थः), *-tha* (-थ), *-ta* (-त), *-tam* (-तम्) and *-tām* (-ताम्), the *dh-* (ध्-) of *-dhve* (-ध्वे), *-dhvam* (-ध्वम्) and *-dhi* (-धि), and finally the *h-* (ह्-) of *-hi*. (-हि).

A common root of the अद् class that illustrates the kinds of changes that typically occur is √विद् 'know'. A glance at the conjugation of it presented below will show that the law of regressive assimilation, by now so familiar to us, is everywhere at work when the *-d* (-द्) of √विद् comes into contact with the consonants just enumerated.

√विद् 'know'[3]

Present

	Singular	*Dual*	*Plural*
1.	**ved-mi* (वेद्मि)	*vid-vaḥ* (विद्वः)	*vid-maḥ* (विद्मः)
2.	**vet-si* (वेत्सि)	*vit-thaḥ* (वित्थः)	*vit-tha* (वित्थ)
3.	**vet-ti* (वेत्ति)	*vit-taḥ* (वित्तः)	*vid-anti* (विदन्ति)

---

[2]The combination of augment with an initial vowel *always* yields the vṛddhi substitute of the vowel; thus, the imperfect of इष् (इच्छति) 'desire' is *aiccham* (ऐच्छम्), *aicchaḥ* (ऐच्छः), etc.

[3]There is another √विद्, belonging to class VI, whose present is *vindati* (विन्दति), meaning 'find'. The two are usually differentiated by a superscript number above the root-sign: [1]√विद् 'know', [2]√विद् 'find'.

Imperfect

	Singular	*Dual*		*Plural*
1.	**a-ved-am* (अवेदम्)	*a-vid-va* (अविद्व)		*a-vid-ma* (अविद्म)
2.	**a-vet* (अवेत्)	*a-vit-tam* (अवित्तम्)		*a-vit-ta* (अवित्त)
3.	**a-vet* (अवेत्)	*a-vit-tām* (अवित्ताम्)		*a-vid-an* (अविदन्)
			or	*a-vid-uḥ* (अविदुः)

Imperative

1.	**ved-āni* (वेदानि)	**ved-āva* (वेदाव)	**ved-āma* (वेदाम)
2.	*vid-dhi* (विद्धि)	*vit-tam* (वित्तम्)	*vit-ta* (वित्त)
3.	**vet-tu* (वेत्तु)	*vit-tām* (वित्ताम्)	*vid-antu* (विदन्तु)

Optative

1.	*vid-yā-m* (विद्याम्)	*vid-yā-va* (विद्याव)
2.	*vid-yā-ḥ* (विद्याः)	etc.
3.	*vid-yā-t* (विद्यात्)	

The only matter requiring notice is the form *a-vet* (अवेत्), the second and third singular imperfect, which stands for both *a-vet-s* and *a-vet-t*. The *-s* (-स्) and *-t* (-त्) have to be omitted in accordance with the rule which disallows two consonants at the end of a word. With the loss of these characteristic endings of the second and third persons, a single form *a-vet* (अवेत्), ambiguous as to person, is left. For the sake of clarity the second person is sometimes altered to *a-ves* (अवेस्).

Another root of the अद् class which has the same vowel variation as √इ and √विद् is √द्विष् 'hate', but the sandhi changes are somewhat more complicated. A sampling of the significant forms will suffice.

√द्विष् 'hate'

Present

Active

	Singular	*Dual*	*Plural*
1.	**dveṣ-mi* (द्वेष्मि)	*dviṣ-vaḥ* (द्विष्वः)	*dviṣ-maḥ* (द्विष्मः)
2.	**dvek-ṣi* (द्वेक्षि)	*dviṣ-ṭhaḥ* (द्विष्ठः)	*dviṣ-ṭha* (द्विष्ठ)
3.	**dveṣ-ṭi* (द्वेष्टि)	*dviṣ-ṭaḥ* (द्विष्टः)	*dviṣ-anti* (द्विषन्ति)

Middle

1.	*dviṣ-e* (द्विषे)	*dviṣ-vahe* (द्विष्वहे)	*dviṣ-mahe* (द्विष्महे)
2.	*dvik-ṣe* (द्विक्षे)	*dviṣ-āthe* (द्विषाथे)	*dviḍ-ḍhve* (द्विड्ढ्वे)
3.	*dviṣ-ṭe* (द्विष्टे)	*dviṣ-āte* (द्विषाते)	*dviṣ-ate* (द्विषते)

Imperfect

Active

1.	**a-dveṣ-am* (अद्वेषम्)	*a-dviṣ-va* (अद्विष्व)	*a-dviṣ-ma* (अद्विष्म)
2.	**a-dveṭ* (अद्वेट्)	*a-dviṣ-ṭam* (अद्विष्टम्)	*a-dviṣ-ṭa* (अद्विष्ट)
3.	**a-dveṭ* (अद्वेट्)	*a-dviṣ-ṭām* (अद्विष्टाम्)	*a-dviṣ-an* (अद्विषन्)

Middle

	Singular	*Dual*	*Plural*
1.	*a-dviṣ-i* (अद्विषि)	*a-dviṣ-vahi* (अद्विष्वहि)	*a-dviṣ-mahi* (अद्विष्महि)
2.	*a-dviṣ-ṭhāḥ* (अद्विष्ठाः)	*a-dviṣ-āthām* (अद्विाथाम्)	*a-dviḍ-ḍhvam* (अद्विड्ढ्वम्)
3.	*a-dviṣ-ṭa* (अद्विष्ट)	*a-dviṣ-ātām* (अद्विषाताम्)	*a-dviṣ-ata* (अद्विषत)

Imperative

Active

1.	**dveṣ-āṇi* (द्वेषाणि)	**dveṣ-āva* (द्वेषाव)	**dveṣ-āma* (द्वेषाम)
2.	*dviḍ-ḍhi* (द्विड्ढि)	*dviṣ-ṭam* (द्विष्टम्)	*dviṣ-ṭa* (द्विष्ट)
3.	**dveṣ-ṭu* (द्वेष्टु)	*dviṣ-ṭām* (द्विष्टाम्)	*dviṣ-antu* (द्विषन्तु)

Middle

1.	*dveṣ-ai* (द्वेषै)	*dveṣ-āvahai* (द्वेषावहै)	*dveṣ-āmahai* (द्वेषामहै)
2.	*dvik-ṣva* (द्विक्ष्व)	*dviṣ-āthām* (द्विषाथाम्)	*dviḍ-ḍhvam* (द्विड्ढ्वम्)
3.	*dviṣ-ṭām* (द्विष्टाम्)	*dviṣ-ātām* (द्विषाताम्)	*dviṣ-atām* (द्विषताम्)

Optative

Active

1.	*dviṣ-yā-m* (द्विष्याम्)	*dviṣ-yā-va* (द्वियाव)
2.	*dviṣ-yā-ḥ* (द्विष्याः)	etc.

Middle

	Singular	*Dual*
1.	*dviṣ-ī-y-a* (द्विषीय)	*dviṣ-ī-vahi* (द्विषीवहि)
2.	*dviṣ-ī-thāḥ* (द्विषीथा:)	*dviṣ-ī-y-āthām* (द्विषीयाथाम्)
3.	*dviṣ-ī-ta* (द्विषीत)	etc.

Most of the sandhi changes in the conjugation of √द्विष् are due to *progressive* assimilation, the reverse of the sort of the assimilation we have just observed in the paradigm of √विद्. Whenever the dentals *t-* (त्-) and *th-* (थ्-) follow the cerebral *-ṣ* (-ष्), they are assimilated to cerebrals, *i.e.*, they become *ṭ-* (ट्-) and *ṭh-* (ठ्-), as, for example, *dveṣ-ṭi* (द्वेष्टि) from *dveṣ* + *-ti* and *a-dviṣ-ṭam* (अद्विष्टम्) from *a-dviṣ* + *tam.* When the dental *dh-* (ध्-) in the endings *-dhve* (-ध्वे), *-dhvam* (-ध्वम्) and *-dhi* (-धि) follows *-ṣ* (-ष्), the *dh-* (ध्-) is changed to the cerebral *ḍh-* (ढ्-) and the preceding *-ṣ* (-ष्) is replaced by the cerebral *-ḍ* (-ड्); thus, *dviḍ-ḍhve* (द्विड्ढ्वे) from *dviṣ* + *dhve,* and similarly *a-dviḍ-ḍhvam* (अद्विड्ढ्वम्) and *dviḍ-ḍhi* (द्विड्ढि).

One of the commonest roots of the अद् class is √ब्रू 'say'. It is peculiar in interposing *-ī-* (-ई-) between the root and the ending in the strong forms (but only before an ending beginning with a consonant). In the strong form the root vowel is replaced by its guṇa substitute, so that *brū* (ब्रू) becomes *bro* (ब्रो), then *brav-* (ब्रव्-) before a vowel, just as *bho* (भो), the guṇa form of √भू 'be', becomes *bhav-* (भव्-) before the thematic vowel *-a-* (-अ-). The present, imperfect and a few scattered forms of the imperative and optative, which are sufficient for illustration, are as follows:

√ब्रू 'say'

Present

	Singular	*Dual*	*Plural*
1.	**brav-ī-mi* (ब्रवीमि)	*brū-vaḥ* (ब्रूवः)	*brū-maḥ* (ब्रूमः)
2.	**brav-ī-ṣi* (ब्रवीषि)	*brū-thaḥ* (ब्रूथः)	*brū-tha* (ब्रूथ)
3.	**brav-ī-ti* (ब्रवीति)	*brū-taḥ* (ब्रूतः)	*bruv-anti* (ब्रुवन्ति)

Imperfect

1.	**a-brav-am* (अब्रवम्)	*a-brū-va* (अब्रूव)	*a-brū-ma* (अब्रूम)
2.	**a-brav-ī-ḥ* (अब्रवीः)	*a-brū-tam* (अब्रूतम्)	*a-brū-ta* (अब्रूत)
3.	**a-brav-ī-t* (अब्रवीत्)	*a-brū-tām* (अब्रूताम्)	*a-bruv-an* (अब्रुवन्)

Imperative

1.	**brav-āṇi* (ब्रवाणि)	**brav-āva* (ब्रवाव)	**brav-āma* (ब्रवाम)
2.	*brū-hi* (ब्रूहि)	etc.	
3.	**brav-ī-tu* (ब्रवीतु)		*bruv-antu* (ब्रुवन्तु)

Optative

1.	*brū-yā-m* (ब्रूयाम्)	
2.	*brū-yā-ḥ* (ब्रूयाः)	etc.
3.	*brū-yā-t* (ब्रूयात्)	

Note that in the third plural forms the *-ū* (-ऊ) becomes *-uv* (-उव्) before the following vowel; hence, *bruv-anti* (ब्रुवन्ति), *a-bruv-an* (अब्रुवन्), *bruv-antu* (ब्रुवन्तु). The middle of √ब्रू is fairly rare.

There are a few roots that interpose a short *-i-* (-इ-) before consonant-initial endings, except *y-* (य्-). The most important of these are √रुद् 'cry', √श्वस् 'breathe' and √स्वप् 'sleep'. In the imperfect second and third singular the inserted vowel is lengthened, rendering these forms parallel to *abravīḥ* (अब्रवीः) and *abravīt* (अब्रवीत्) of √ब्रू. Here are a few sample forms from these roots:

√रुद् 'cry'

Present

	Singular	*Dual*	*Plural*
1.	**rod-i-mi* (रोदिमि)	*rud-i-vaḥ* (रुदिवः)	etc.
2.	**rod-i-ṣi* (रोदिषि)	*rud-i-thaḥ* (रुदिथः)	
3.	**rod-i-ti* (रोदिति)		*rud-anti* (रुदन्ति)

Imperfect

1.	**a-rod-am* (अरोदम्)	*a-rud-i-va* (अरुदिव)	etc.
2.	**a-rod-ī-ḥ* (अरोदीः)		
3.	**a-rod-ī-t* (अरोदीत्)		*a-rud-an* (अरुदन्)

Imperative

1.	**rod-āni* (रोदानि)	etc.	
2.	*rud-i-hi* (रुदिहि)		
3.	**rod-i-tu* (रोदितु)		*rud-antu* (रुदन्तु)

Optative

	Singular	*Dual*
1.	*rud-yā-m* (रुद्याम्)	etc.

√श्वस् 'breathe'

Present

	Singular	*Dual*	*Plural*
1.	**śvas-i-mi* (श्वसिमि)	*śvas-i-vaḥ* (श्वसिवः)	etc.
2.	**śvas-i-ṣi* (श्वसिषि)	*śvas-i-thaḥ* (श्वसिथः)	
3.	**śvas-i-ti* (श्वसिति)		*śvas-anti* (श्वसन्ति)

Imperfect

1.	**a-śvas-am* (अश्वसम्)	*a-śvas-i-va* (अश्वसिव)	etc.
2.	**a-śvas-ī-ḥ* (अश्वसीः)		
3.	**a-śvas-ī-t* (अश्वसीत्)		*a-śvas-an* (अश्वसन्)

Imperative

1.	**śvas-āni* (श्वसानि)	etc.	
2.	*śvas-i-hi* (श्वसिहि)		
3.	**śvas-i-tu* (श्वसितु)		*śvas-antu* (श्वसन्तु)

Optative

	Singular	*Dual*	
1.	*śvas-yā-m* (श्वस्याम्)	etc.	

√स्वप् 'sleep'
Present

	Singular	*Dual*	*Plural*
1.	**svap-i-mi* (स्वपिमि)	*svap-i-vaḥ* (स्वपिव:)	etc.
2.	**svap-i-ṣi* (स्वपिषि)	*svap-i-thaḥ* (स्वपिथ:)	
3.	**svap-i-ti* (स्वपिति)		*svap-anti* (स्वपन्ति)

Imperfect

1.	**a-svap-am* (अस्वपम्)	*a-svap-i-va* (अस्वपिव)	etc.
2.	**a-svap-ī-ḥ* (अस्वपी:)		
3.	**a-svap-ī-t* (अस्वपीत्)		*a-svap-an* (अस्वपन्)

Imperative

1.	**svap-āni* (स्वपानि)	etc.	
2.	*svap-i-hi* (स्वपिहि)		
3.	**svap-i-tu* (स्वपितु)		*svap-antu* (स्वपन्तु)

Optative

	Singular	*Dual*
1.	*svap-yā-m* (स्वप्याम्)	etc.

Note that the *-i-* (-इ-) is not inserted before the *-yā-* (-या-) of the optative. Instead of the imperfect forms in *-īḥ* (-ई:) and *-īt* (-ईत्), alternatives in *-aḥ* (-अ:) and *-at* -(-अत्) are often found; thus, *arodaḥ* (अरोद:), *aśvasat* (अश्वसत्), etc.

As might well have been guessed, the अद् class contains many interesting roots that do not fit into a single category. It is indeed the least homogeneous of all the classes because of the number and diversity of its types. All beginning students of Sanskrit take especial delight in the roots दुह् 'milk' and दिह् 'smear' because of the intriguing way in which the aspiration *-h* (-ह्) behaves. Obviously it cannot remain intact before consonant-initial endings. It is, in fact, treated as though it were *-gh* (-घ्), which, in contact with *t-* (त्-) and *th-* (थ्-), forms the combination *-gdh-* (-ग्ध्-). This results in such forms as *dogdhi* (दोग्धि), *degdhi* (देग्धि), *dugdhaḥ* (दुग्ध:), *digdhaḥ* (दिग्ध:), *adogdham* (अदोग्धम्), *adigdham* (अदिग्धम्), etc.[4] Incidentally, this same change occurs also in the past passive participle, where the same combination of sounds occurs *(duh + ta);* thus, *dugdha* (दुग्ध). However, before *s-* (स्-) and *dh-* (ध्-) of *-dhve* (-ध्वे) and *-dhvam* (-ध्वम्), but *not* of *-dhi* (-धि), the imperative second singular ending, the aspiration of the *-gh* (as which we treated *-h)* is lost, but rebounds to the *d-* (द्-) which begins both roots! This phenomenon yields, for example: *dhokṣi* (धोक्षि) for *doh + -si*, *dhekṣi* (धेक्षि), *dhugdhve* (धुग्ध्वे), *dhigdhve* (धिग्ध्वे), *adhugdhvam* (अधुग्ध्वम्), but *dugdhi* (दुग्धि) and *digdhi* (दिग्धि) in which the lost aspiration is not assumed by the *d-* (द्-).

Equally intriguing, but much more perplexing, is √लिह् 'lick', the present of which will give some idea of the metamorphoses through which it goes: *leh-mi* (लेह्मि), *lek-ṣi* (लेक्षि), *leḍhi* (लेढि), *lih-vaḥ* (लिह्व:), *līḍhaḥ* (लीढ:), *līḍhaḥ* (लीढ:), *lih-maḥ* (लिह्म:), *līḍha* (लीढ), *lih-anti* (लिहन्ति).

---

[4]The forms *dugdhaḥ* (दुग्ध:) and *digdhaḥ* (दिग्ध:) may be *either* second or third dual because the *-h* (or rather *-gh* !) of these roots causes the conversion of both *t-* and *th-* to *dh-*.

A curious root is √शी 'lie down, sleep', found only in the middle voice, which takes guṇa *throughout* the present system, that is, shows no variation between strong and weak stem, and has the unique anomaly of inserting *-r-* (-र्-) before the endings of all the third persons plural. It will suffice to illustrate only the present: *śay-e,* (शये), *śe-ṣe* (शेषे), *śe-te* (शेते), *śe-vahe* (शेवहे), *śay-āthe* (शयाथे), *śay-āte* (शयाते), *śe-mahe* (शेमहे), *śe-dhve* (शेध्वे), *śe-r-ate* (शेरते).

No introduction to Sanskrit can do without some reference to the common √हन् 'strike', which has the peculiarity of losing its *-n* (-न्) in the weak forms before *t-* (त्-) and *th-* (थ्-) and substituting *ghn-* (घ्न्-) for *han-* (हन्-) before the endings of the third person plural. Herewith are the present and imperfect of this important verb:

Present

	Singular	*Dual*	*Plural*
1.	**han-mi* (हन्मि)	*han-vaḥ* (हन्वः)	*han-maḥ* (हन्मः)
2.	**haṃ-si* (हंसि)	*ha-thaḥ* (हथः)	*ha-tha* (हथ)
3.	**han-ti* (हन्ति)	*ha-taḥ* (हतः)	*ghn-anti* (घ्नन्ति)

Imperfect

1.	**a-han-am* (अहनम्)	*a-han-va* (अहान्व)	*a-han-ma* (अहन्म)
2.	**a-han* (अहन्)	*a-ha-tam* (अहतम्)	*a-ha-ta* (अहत)
3.	**a-han* (अहन्)	*a-ha-tām* (अहताम्)	*a-ghn-an* (अघ्नन्)

Note that in the present second singular the *-n* (-न्) is replaced by anusvāra before the sibilant. In the second and third singular of the imperfect the endings *-s* (-स्) and *-t* (-त्) disappear because of the rule that there can be only one consonant at the end of a word. The imperative second singular *jahi* (जहि) is strangely irregular and needs especially to be noticed.

Before leaving the अद् class we must return to the spectacular √अस् 'be' of which we gave only the present tense. In view of the importance of this root *per se,* but also because of its function as an auxiliary verb, it is necessary to learn the whole of the present. This is not at all a difficult matter if we bear in mind that the strong stem is *as-* (अस्-), the full root, and the weak stem is *s-* (स्-). For the purpose of clarity the present is here repeated.

√अस् 'be'

Present

	Singular	*Dual*	*Plural*
1.	**as-mi* (अस्मि)	*s-vaḥ* (स्वः)	*s-maḥ* (स्मः)
2.	**asi* (असि)	*s-thaḥ* (स्थः)	*s-tha* (स्थ)
3.	**as-ti* (अस्ति)	*s-taḥ* (स्तः)	*s-anti* (सन्ति)

Imperfect

1.	**ās-am* (आसम्)	*ās-va* (आस्व)	*ās-ma* (आस्म)
2.	**ās-ī-ḥ* (आसीः)	*ās-tam* (आस्तम्)	*ās-ta* (आस्त)
3.	**ās-ī-t* (आसीत्)	*ās-tām* (आस्ताम्)	*ās-an* (आसन्)

Imperative

1.	**as-āṇi* (असानि)	**as-āva* (असाव)	**as-āma* (असाम)
2.	*e-dhi* (एधि)	*s-tam* (स्तम्)	*s-ta* (स्त)
3.	**as-tu* (अस्तु)	*s-tām* (स्ताम्)	*s-antu* (सन्तु)

Optative

	Singular	*Dual*	*Plural*
1.	*s-yā-m*	*s-yā-va*	*s-yā-ma*
	(स्याम्)	(स्याव)	(स्याम)
2.	*s-yā-ḥ*	*s-yā-tam*	*s-yā-ta*
	(स्याः)	(स्यातम्)	(स्यात)
3.	*s-yā-t*	*s-yā-tām*	*s-y-uḥ*
	(स्यात्)	(स्याताम्)	(स्युः)

The unexpected form *asi* (असि) was explained in footnote 2 of Lesson Twenty-five. The imperfect *ās-am* (आसम्) is from *a-* (the augment!) and *as-* (the strong stem) + *-am* (the secondary ending). In the dual and plural we would expect *a-s-va, a-s-tam,* etc., but *ās-* (आस्-), the strong stem contracted with the augment, has been extended throughout. The forms *ās-ī-ḥ* (आसीः) and *ās-ī-t* (आसीत्) are substitutions for the older *āḥ* (आः) which stood for *both* the second and third persons, the endings *-s* (-स्) and *-t* (-त्) of *ās-s* and *ās-t* having been lost according to the rule of two (or more) final consonants. Since *āḥ* (आः) is not a distinctive form and also is ambiguous as to person, it was early replaced by *āsīḥ* (आसीः) and *āsīt* (आसीत्) which are patterned after forms like *abravīḥ* (अब्रवीः) and *abravīt* (अब्रवीत्). Finally, note the imperative *edhi* (एधि).[5]

In some ways the VIIth or रुध् class, the last we have to take up to complete our consideration of the ten classes, is even more interesting than the अद् class, although there are relatively few roots in this class, and it is devoid of the peculiarities we have just seen in the अद् class. In the strong stem the syllable *-na-* (-न-) is inserted before the final consonant of the root (all roots in this class end in a consonant), which in the weak stem is reduced to *-n-* (-न्-), *-ñ-* (-ञ्-), *-ṅ-* (-ङ्-) or anusvāra, depending on the class of the consonant with which the nasal comes in contact. There is nothing difficult about determining the nasal: it is just a question of regressive assimilation. Thus, √छिद् 'cut' has the strong stem *chi-na-d* (छिनद्), the weak *chi-n-d* (छिन्द्) with a dental nasal to conform to the *-d* (-द्), which is a dental; √युज्

[5] *e-dhi* is from older **az-dhi* (for **as-dhi* by regressive assimilation!). The strong stem *as-* was substituted for the weak in order to give a clearer form, as **z-dhi* (from **s-dhi)* would have yielded **dhi* (!) in historical Sanskrit. Incidentally, *zdī* (with a long vowel) is attested in the Avesta.

'join' has the stems *yu-na-j* (युनज्) and *yu-ñ-j* (युञ्ज्) with palatal *-ñ-* (-ञ्-) because the following *-j* (-ज्) is a palatal; √पिष् 'grind' forms *pi-na-ṣ* (पिनष्) and *piṃṣ* (पिंष्), with anusvāra because of the following sibilant. Here follows the complete present system of the important √युज् 'join':

√युज् 'join'

Present

Active

	Singular	*Dual*	*Plural*
1.	**yu-na-j-mi* (युनज्मि)	*yu-ñ-j-vaḥ* (युञ्ज्वः)	*yu-ñ-j-maḥ* (युञ्ज्मः)
2.	**yu-na-k-ṣi* (युनक्षि)	*yu-ṅ-k-thaḥ* (युङ्क्थः)	*yu-ṅ-k-tha* (युङ्क्थ)
3.	**yu-na-k-ti* (युनक्ति)	*yu-ṅ-k-taḥ* (युङ्क्तः)	*yu-ñ-j-anti* (युञ्जन्ति)

Middle

1.	*yu-ñ-j-e* (युञ्जे)	*yu-ñ-j-vahe* (युञ्ज्वहे)	*yu-ñ-j-mahe* (युञ्ज्महे)
2.	*yu-ṅ-k-ṣe* (युङ्क्षे)	*yu-ñ-j-āthe* (युञ्जाथे)	*yu-ṅ-g-dhve* (युङ्ग्ध्वे)
3.	*yu-ṅ-k-te* (युङ्क्ते)	*yu-ñ-j-āte* (युञ्जाते)	*yu-ñ-j-ate* (युञ्जते)

Imperfect

Active

1.	**a-yu-na-j-am* (अयुनजम्)	*a-yu-ñ-j-va* (अयुञ्ज्व)	*a-yu-ñ-j-ma* (अयुञ्ज्म)
2.	**a-yu-na-k* (अयुनक्)	*a-yu-ṅ-k-tam* (अयुङ्क्तम्)	*a-yu-ṅ-k-ta* (अयुङ्क्त)
3.	**a-yu-na-k* (अयुनक्)	*a-yu-ṅ-k-tām* (अयुङ्क्ताम्)	*a-yu-ñ-j-an* (अयुञ्जन्)

Imperfect

Middle

	Singular	*Dual*	*Plural*
1.	*a-yu-ñ-j-i* (अयुञ्जि)	*a-yu-ñ-j-vahi* (अयुञ्ज्वहि)	*a-yu-ñ-j-mahi* (अयुञ्ज्महि)
2.	*a-yu-ṅ-k-thāḥ* (अयुङ्क्थाः)	*a-yu-ñ-j-āthām* (अयुञ्जाथाम्)	*a-yu-ṅ-g-dhvam* (अयुिङ्ग्ध्वम्)
3.	*a-yu-ṅ-k-ta* (अयुङ्क्त)	*a-yu-ñ-j-ātām* (अयुञ्जाताम्)	*a-yu-ñ-j-ata* (अयुञ्जत)

Imperative

Active

1.	**yu-na-j-āni* (युनजानि)	**yu-na-j-āva* (युनजाव)	**yu-na-j-āma* (युनजाम)
2.	*yu-ṅ-g-dhi* (युङ्ग्धि)	*yu-ṅ-k-tam* (युङ्क्तम्)	*yu-ṅ-k-ta* (युङ्क्त)
3.	**yu-na-k-tu* (युनक्तु)	*yu-ṅ-k-tām* (युङ्क्ताम्)	*yu-ñ-j-antu* (युञ्जन्तु)

Middle

1.	**yu-na-j-ai* (युनजै)	**yu-na-j-āvahai* (युनजावहै)	**yu-na-j-āmahai* (युनजामहै)
2.	*yu-ṅ-k-ṣva* (युङ्क्ष्व)	*yu-ñ-j-āthām* (युञ्जाथाम्)	*yu-ṅ-g-dhvam* (युङ्ग्ध्वम्)
3.	*yu-ṅ-k-tām* (युङ्क्ताम्)	*yu-ñ-j-ātām* (युञ्जाताम्)	*yu-ñ-j-atām* (युञ्जताम्)

Optative

Active

	Singular	*Dual*	*Plural*
1.	*yu-ñ-j-yā-m* (युञ्ज्याम्)	*yu-ñ-j-yā-va* (युञ्ज्याव)	*yu-ñ-j-yā-ma* (युञ्ज्याम)
2.	*yu-ñ-j-yā-ḥ* (युञ्ज्याः)	*yu-ñ-j-yā-tam* (युञ्ज्यातम्)	*yu-ñ-j-yā-ta* (युञ्ज्यात)
3.	*yu-ñ-j-yā-t* (युञ्ज्यात्)	*yu-ñ-j-yā-tām* (युञ्ज्याताम्)	*yu-ñ-j-y-uḥ* (युञ्ज्युः)

Middle

1.	*yu-ñ-j-ī-y-a* (युञ्जीय)	*yu-ñ-j-ī-vahi* (युञ्जीवहि)	*yu-ñ-j-ī-mahi* (युञ्जीमहि)
2.	*yu-ñ-j-ī-thāḥ* (युञ्जीथाः)	*yu-ñ-j-ī-y-āthām* (युञ्जीयाथाम्)	*yu-ñ-j-ī-dhvam* (युञ्जीध्वम्)
3.	*yu-ñ-j-ī-ta* (युञ्जीत)	*yu-ñ-j-ī-y-ātām* (युञ्जीयाताम्)	*yu-ñ-j-ī-ran* (युञ्जीरन्)

Before *s-* (स्-), *t-* (त्-) and *th-* (थ्-), the *-j* (-ज्) of *yu-na-j* (युनज्) and *yu-ñ-j* (युञ्ज्) is replaced by the voiceless guttural *-k* (-क्) (after which *s-* becomes cerebralized to *ṣ-*). Thus, *yu-na-k-ṣi* (युनक्षि), *yu-na-k-ti* (युनक्ति), *yu-ṅ-k-taḥ* (युङ्क्तः), *yu-ṅ-k-tha* (युङ्क्थ). Before the *dh-* of *-dhve* (-ध्वे), *-dhvam* (-ध्वम्) and *-dhi* (-धि) *-j* (-ज्) is replaced by the voiced guttural *-g* (-ग्); thus, *yu-ṅ-g-dhve* (युङ्ग्ध्वे), *a-yu-ṅ-g-dhvam* (अयुङ्ग्ध्वम्) and *yu-ṅ-g-dhi* (युङ्ग्धि).

Sentences Illustrating Non-thematic Verba:

A. 1. तापसा वने फलपुष्पमूलान्याहारार्थमवाचिन्वन् ।

2. यदा जनः पक्षिणां संगीतं शृणोति[1] तदा हृदये प्रीणीते ।

3. भीमस्य दुहिता दमयन्ती नाम नलं नृपं पतित्वे ऽवृणीत[2] ।

4. यो ऽन्यस्मै ददाति स आत्मने दत्ते[3] ।

5. द्विजोत्तमो[4] भैक्षं चरन्भवति भिक्षां देहीति गृहिणीं ब्रूयात् ।

6. यावच्छत्रूणां[5] सेना तन्नगरमरुणत्तावत्तत्र जना भोजनं प्राप्तुं नाशक्नुवन् ।

7. वनवासिषु तपस्विषु कश्चिच्छरीरं भस्मना देग्धि कश्चित् फलपुष्पमूलान्यवचिनोति कश्चित्काष्ठानि छिनत्ति कश्चिदग्निं मथ्नात्यन्ये तु घृतं[6] वा दुग्धं वाग्नौ जुह्वत्यन्ये सूक्तानां पठनं कुर्वन्त्य्[7] अन्ये समीपस्थसरितो[8] जलं घटेषु बिभ्रति ।

8. यं पाशं व्याधो वृक्षस्याधस्तादयुनक्स एव कंचिन्मृगं दृढमबध्नात् ।

9. अध्यायं पठित्वा शिष्यौ कटे पुस्तके अधत्ताम्[9] ।

10. यः स्वभ्रातरं द्वेष्टि स आत्मानमेव द्वेष्टि । स्वभ्राता ह्यन्य आत्मेत्यृषयो ब्रुवन्ति ।

11. एकमेव सत्यमस्ति[10] तत्तु बहूनि रूपाण्याधत्ते । तस्मान्नरो मायया मोहित एतानि रूपाणि नात्येति । तदेकमेव सत्यं वेदितुं न शक्नोति । यथान्धका नरा हस्तिनं पाणिना परिस्पृश्य हस्तिनो हस्तित्वं[11] नैवाविदुः किन्तु केवलं रज्जुस्तम्भवस्त्रादिरूपं हस्तिनमजानंस्तथैव मायामोहितो नरस्तदेकमेव सत्यं नैव वेत्ति किन्तु जगदादिरूपं सत्यं जानाति ।

12. यस्मात्तद्दिवं विमिमीते तस्माद्विमानमिति बुधा अभिदधति ।

13. यदा यदा वायुर्वाति तदा तदा वृक्षगृहादीनि सर्वाणि द्रव्याणि धुनोति ।
14. यदा कश्चित्सिंहः पर्वतकन्दरे ऽशेत तदा मूषिकः केसराग्रमच्छिनत् ।
15. स्थविरा दण्डिनो राज्ञो निवेशनमवृण्वन् ।
16. यस्मिन्काले चौरो द्रव्याणि हर्तुं स्वामिनो गृहं प्रविवेश तस्य कुक्कुरो मार्जारश्च प्राङ्गणे ऽस्वपिताम् ।
17. पूर्वस्मिन्काले पर्वताः पक्षसमन्विता आसंस्ततश्च ते यथाकामं पर्यपतन् । तदेयं पृथिवी शिथिलासीत्तस्मादिन्द्रः पर्वतेभ्यः पक्षानच्छिनत्तैश्च पर्वतैरदृढां पृथिवीमस्तभ्नात् । ते पक्षा जीमूता अभवन् । ये पर्वतास्तेषां पक्षाणां योनिरासंस्तेषामुपरि ते जीमूताः सर्वदा शेरते[12] ।
18. देवानां पतिरिन्द्रो विविधानां राक्षसानां पर्वतस्थपुराणि महता वज्रेणाभिनत्[13] ।
19. शत्रुभ्यो बिभ्यतः[14] सैनिका युद्धे जेतुं नैव शक्नुवन्तीति जानन्सैनिकशास्त्रकोविदो राजा तेष्वभयमादौ नियुनक्ति ।
20. इह कामान्भुङ्क्ष्व परन्तु तेष्वासक्तो मा भव । कामेष्वनासक्तो यो नरः स परमां शान्तिमस्मिञ्जगति भुनक्ति किं पुनस्तु प्रेत्य भोक्ष्यत इति प्राज्ञा ब्रुवन्ति ।

B. VII. The Story of Sagara and His Sons

ततो यत्र भूमेस्तलं सगरात्मजैः खातमासीत्तत्रैव वसुधां प्रविश्य गङ्गयानुगतो भगीरथस्तान्सर्वान्भस्मीभूतान्पितामहानप्रीणात् । अथ गङ्गाम्भसा प्लाविताः सगरस्य सुता दिव्यमूर्तिधरा स्वर्गं समाप्नुवन् । तदैवं प्लावितान्पितृंस्तान्सर्वान्दृष्ट्वा ब्रह्मा महाप्रभुर्देवगणैः सह महात्मानं भगीरथमिदं वचनमब्रवीत् । भगीरथ महाराज नरशार्दूल महातेजस्तारिता[1] महात्मनः सगरस्य षष्टिः पुत्रसहस्राणि देववद्दिवं[2] याताश्चासन् । यावत्सागरस्य[3] जलं जगति स्थास्यति पार्थिव तावत्सर्वे सगरस्यात्मजा देववद्दिवि स्थास्यन्ति । हिमवतश्चेयं ज्येष्ठा दुहिता तव[4] भविष्यत्यस्मिंश्च लोके त्वन्नामव्युत्पन्नेन नाम्ना भागीरथीति विश्रुता भविष्यति[5] । सर्वेषां पितामहानामत्र सलिलक्रियां कुरुष्व राजन्प्रतिज्ञामपवर्जय च । पितृपिता ते राजन्नंशुमानतियशा धर्मिणां प्रवरः स्वर्गात्पृथिवीं गङ्गामवतारयितुं नाशक्नोत् । तथैव तव पित्रा गुणवता राजर्षिणा महर्षिसमतेजसा मत्तुल्यतपसा क्षत्रधर्मस्थितेन च दिलीपेन राज्ञा गङ्गां पृथिवीं नेतुं प्रार्थयतापि मनोरथो नापवर्जितः[6] । त्वयैव सा प्रतिज्ञा समतिक्रान्ता पुरुषर्षभ । त्वमेवास्मिलँ्लोके महद्यशः प्राप्नोः । त्वमेव गङ्गावतरणमकरोः[7] । गङ्गासलिलेनात्मानं पुनीष्व नरोत्तम । तेषां सर्वेषां पितामहानां सलिलक्रियां कुरुष्व । स्वस्ति[8] ते ऽस्तु । अद्य स्वं लोकं गमिष्यामि । इत्युक्त्वा देवदेवः सर्वलोकपितामहो महायशा यथागतं तथा देवलोकमगच्छत् । अस्मिन्नन्तरे भगीरथः सर्वेषां सागराणां जलक्रियां यथान्यायमकरोत् । ततः कृतोदकक्रियः[9] समृद्धार्थो राजा नरश्रेष्ठः स्वपुरं प्रविश्य स्वराज्यं प्रशशास । लोकस्तं नृपं प्रतिलभ्य नष्टशोको विगतज्वरश्च भूत्वा प्रमुमोद ।

Notes

Excercise A.

1. शृणोति √श्रु 'hear', which belongs to class V, substitutes शृ for श्रु in forming the present stem; thus, शृ + नु + ending. The dental -न्- changes to the cerebral due to the cerebralizing influence of *-ṛ-*, so that we have शृणोति. A similar conversion takes place in the following प्रीणीते and अवृणीत.

2. पतित्वे ऽवृणीत Literally 'chose in husband-ness', *i.e.*, chose as her husband. The suffix -त्व, as we have noted before in discussing the idiom पञ्चत्वं + √गम् 'go to five-ness', *i.e.*, die, may be added to almost any word to make an abstract of it. This suffix corresponds most closely to the English *-ness*, although the applicability of *-ness* is much more limited than that of -त्व. The particular idiom we see here, पतित्वे + ²√वृ 'choose as husband *or* choose in wedlock', is very common. It occurs, for example, in the story of Nala and Damayantī: यथा मे नैषधो वृतः पतित्वे तेन सत्येन देवास्तं प्रदिशन्तु मे 'as the King of Niṣadha was chosen by me as (my) husband, by this truth let the gods point him out to me'.

3. दत्ते Here the middle voice has its true value of being 'a word for oneself' (आत्मनेपद).

4. द्विजोत्तमो 'The highest of the twice-born' is, of course, a Brahman, and it is interesting to note that, according to the Mānavadharmaśāstra or 'Lawbook of Manu' (II. 49), the vocative भवति occupies a different place in this begging formula according to the caste of the one begging: for the Brahman भवति comes first (as here), for the Kṣatriya it comes in the middle (भिक्षां भवति देहि) and for the Vaiśya it is last (भिक्षां देहि भवति). भवति is the vocative singular of भवती, which is the *feminine* counterpart of the honorific pronoun भवत् 'you'. The reason for the feminine may be seen in the word गृहिणी 'mistress of the house' who is addressed by the one begging alms.

5. यावच्छत्रूणां Be careful of the sandhi that couples these words together!

6. घृतं Strictly speaking घृत is the past passive participle of √घृ (जिघर्ति, class III) 'sprinkle', and so it means literally 'what is sprinkled'. Almost any past passive participle may be used as a neuter noun in an abstract sense or, as here, concretely. घृत may be translated 'clarified butter' or 'ghee', an Anglo-Indian word borrowed from one of the modern vernaculars. 'Ghee' is the lineal descendant of Sanskrit घृत through the intermediate Prakrit stages *ghida* (घिद), *ghia* (घिअ), *ghiu* (घिउ); the vernacular *ghī* (घी) is a contraction of the vowels *i* and *u* in *ghiu*. Similarly used is the following word दुग्ध 'milk', the past passive participle of √दुह् (दोग्धि, class II), 'milk'.

7. सूक्तानां पठननं कुर्वन्ति Instead of this roundabout expression (literally 'make a recitation of Vedic hymns'), we might have said simply सूक्तानि पठन्ति. These periphrases formed with √कृ and an abstract of the verbal idea being expressed + a genitive ('make a doing of such-and-such') are, however, extremely common as substitutes for particular verb forms. This same construction has come down into the modern Indo-Aryan vernaculars.

8. समीपस्थसरितो An 'ablative of source' ('from a nearby river'), a natural extension of the 'ablative of separation'.

9. The initial अ of अधत्ताम् is *not* elided because the preceding -ए (-*e*) of पुस्तके is one of three dual endings, *viz*., -*e* and also -*ī* and -*ū*, which, whether ending noun forms or verb forms, do not permit sandhi combination. Thus, according to this rule, *a*- after a dual -*e* is not dropped, and -*ī* and -*ū* are not changed to the semivowels -*y* and -*v*. These three uncombinable vowels are technically known as *pragṛhya* vowels, *pragṛhya* being the gerundive of *pra*-√*gṛh*, literally 'to be restrained', *i.e*., from combination.

10. It is best to translate सत्यम् here by 'reality' rather than 'truth', unless, of course, 'truth' is conceived in this larger sense. The doctrine expounded in this short passage is the Vedāntic view, which regards the phenomenal world as unreal, *i.e.*, not *finally* or *ultimately real,* but a product of illusion (माया), based on imperfect knowledge or ignorance that is projected upon *the one absolute reality* called 'Brahman'. The idea of the simile is that all the blind men who touched the elephant had a different concept of what an elephant is. Each was correct in a limited way (a part of the elephant *is* like a rope, a column, etc.), but *none* had the *whole* or *true* picture of what an elephant is. In the same way those who take the objects of everyday life as real have only

a limited conception of the final reality or substrate of all things, which is Brahman.

11. हस्तिनो हस्तित्वं 'The elephant-ness of the elephant', *i.e.,* the true nature of the elephant, what it is really like.

12. The idea of this little myth, which is often alluded to in Sanskrit literature, is that eons ago when the earth was still unsteady and not fastened down, Indra used the mountains, which had been flying about like birds, as weights to hold the earth in place. Their wings which he cut off became the clouds which still rest on the mountains whence they came. This story is told in the Maitrāyaṇīya Saṃhitā I.10.13 and perhaps implied at Ṛgveda II.12.2, in a eulogy of Indra where it is somewhat laconically said that he 'brought to rest the unquiet mountains'.

13. The thunderbolt or *vajra* (वज्र), whose shape is supposed to be discus-like, is the chief weapon employed by Indra in his endless battles with various demons. It is said to have been fashioned by Tvaṣṭṛ, the artificer of the gods, from the bones of the sage Dadhyañc.

14. शत्रुभ्यो बिभ्यत: It will be remembered that the present active participle can be 'mechanically' formed from the present third person plural active by dropping the final *-i*. Thus, by this process, गच्छन्ति from √गम् yields the strong stem गच्छन्त्; the weak stem is gotten by dropping the nasal न्, thus, गच्छत्. From these two stems the whole declension is made, the strong and weak stems being disposed in the usual way of stems in two variants (*v.* Lesson Seventeen). In the case of roots of the हु class (class III), however, in which the third person plural has *no nasal,* the ending being *-ati, not -anti,* there is no strong stem, only the weak stem in *-at*. The nominative/accusative singular, dual and plural (masculine) of √हु, made from *juhvat,* the only participial stem, is:

	Singular	Dual	Plural
Nom.	*juhvat* (for *juhvat-s)*	*juhvat-au*	*juhvat-aḥ*
Acc.	*juhvat-am*	*juhvat-au*	*juhvat-aḥ*

In view of this, what is the form बिभ्यत: here? The ablative शत्रुभ्य: is due to the fact that verbs of fearing in Sanskrit are construed with the 'ablative of the thing feared' (really an 'ablative of separation'!).

Excercise B.

1. तारिता Although तारिता, which is nominative feminine singular, is in grammatical agreement with षष्टिः 'sixty', its coverage extends to the whole numeral 60,000; thus, 'the 60,000 sons of the noble Sagara have been saved'.

2. दिवं an 'accusative of the place to which' with याताः ('gone to heaven').

3. सागरस्य Be careful to note that this is *sāgarasya* 'of the *ocean',* not *sagarasya* 'of Sagara'!

4. तव 'of you' or 'yours', a predicate possessive genitive with भविष्यति; thus, 'And this eldest daughter of Himavat shall be yours', *i.e.,* your wife.

5. त्वन्नामव्युत्पन्नेन नाम्ना भागीरथीति विश्रुता भविष्यति 'shall be known as "Bhāgīrathī" by a name derived from your name'. भागीरथी is the feminine of an adjective भागीरथ 'relating to Bhagīratha', a derivation made from भगीरथ by vṛddhi substitution of the initial vowel. In this world (अस्मिन् लोके), then, Gaṅgā is known also by a name which connects her with Bhagīratha, through whose prolonged austerities her descent from heaven was effected.

6. तथैव तव पित्रा . . . नापवर्जितः The sentence in its simplest form is तव पित्रा . . . मनोरथो न अपवर्जितः 'by your father . . . the wish (was) not fulfilled'. The various instrumentals are in descriptive apposition to पित्रा; प्रार्थयता is a participle modifying दिलीपेन राज्ञा and is given a concessive value by the addition of अपि ('although desiring'). The infinitive नेतुं amplifies both प्रार्थयता अपि ('although desiring to bring Gaṅgā to earth') and the noun मनोरथो ('the wish to bring Gaṅgā down'). When a word thus performs a double function, it is said to behave 'like the (single) eye of the crow' (काकाक्षिवत्), which the crow moves from one socket to the other according to his visual requirements.

7. गङ्गावतरणमकरोः On this periphrasis with √कृ *v.* note on A.7 above. We could equally have said गङ्गामवातारयः.

8. स्वस्ति From this noun स्वस्ति 'well-being, welfare, prosperity' comes the derivative noun स्वस्तिक which has come into English in the spelling 'swastika'. In Sanskrit this word denotes an auspicious sign made of two bars crossed at right angles with fragments of the periphery of a circle attached to each bar. The *svastika* -symbol is found to pervade most of the civilizations of the ancient world and is believed by many to be of solar origin.

9. कृतोदकक्रियः: That this compound is a bahuvrīhi is immediately apparent from the alteration in the form of the final member, which would ordinarily be क्रिया. The change to क्रियः here shows that the compound which it terminates is used as an adjective requiring a masculine ending. Any adjective compound whose final member is a *noun* must be a bahuvrīhi. Its adjectival quality is all the more apparent when the final member exhibits the sort of alteration seen here.

Vocabulary

अग्र, *n.* front; tip, end.

अति, *adv.* beyond; *as a prefix in compounds*, surpassing, extreme, (*i.e.*, as a quasi-adj.).

अति-√इ (एति, class II), go beyond.

अदृढ, *adj.* unfirm, unsteady.

अद्य, *adv.* now.

अधस्तात्, *adv.* below; *as a postp. with the gen.* under.

अध्याय, *m.* a lesson.

अनुगत, *ppp.* अनु-√गम् (गच्छति, class I), followed.

अन्तर, *n.* occasion, juncture.

अन्धक, *adj.* blind.

अन्ये . . . अन्ये, some . . . others.

अपवर्जित, *ppp. of caus. of* अप-√वृज् (वृणक्ति, class VII), fulfilled.

अप-√वृज् (वृणक्ति, class VII), turn away; *caus.* अपवर्जयति, gets rid of; fulfils.

अभय, *n.* non-fear, lack of fear.

अभि-√धा (दधाति, class III), call, designate.

अम्भस्, *n.* water.

अव-√चि (चिनोति, class V), gather.

अवतरण, *n.* the act of descending, descent.

अव-√तॄ (तरति, class I), descend; *caus.* अवतारयति, causes to descend.

आदि, *m.* beginning.
आ-√धा (दधाति, धत्ते, class III), take on, assume.
आसक्त, *ppp.* आ-√सञ्ज् *or* सज् (सजति, class I), attached to (+ *loc.).*
आहार, *m.* food.
इह, *adv.* here; in this world.
उत्तम, *adj.* highest, best.
उदक, *n.* water.
उपरि, *adv.* above, over; *as postp. with the gen.* above.
कट, *m.* a mat.
कन्दर, *n.* a cave.
कश्चिद् . . . कश्चिद्, *indef. pron.* one . . . another.
काम, *m.* desire.
काल, *m.* time.
काष्ठ, *n.* a piece of wood, a stick *or* log.
किं पुनर्, how much more?
केसर, *m.* the hair; a mane.
क्रिया, *f.* action, performance; rite, ceremony.
क्षत्र, *n.* the second or princely caste, called the 'Kṣatriya caste'.
खात, *ppp.* √खन् (खनति, class I), dug, dug up.
गण, *m.* a host, troop, crowd.
गुणवत्, *adj.* 'possessing excellent qualities', virtuous.
गृहिणी, *f.* the mistress of the house.
घट, *m.* a clay pot *or* jar.
घृत, *n.* clarified butter *or* ghee.
चौर, *m.* a thief.
√छिद् (छिनत्ति, class VII), cut, hew.
जीमूत, *m.* a cloud.
√ज्ञा (जानाति, class IX), know, perceive.
ज्वर, *m.* fever; pain; grief.
तपस्विन्, *m.* an ascetic.
तारित, *ppp. of caus. of* √तॄ (तरति, class I), rescued, saved, liberated.
तुल्य, *adj.* like *or* equal to.
दण्डिन्, *adj.* 'staff-possessing'; *as m.* a guard *or* warden.
दमयन्ती, *f.* Damayantī, the daughter of King Bhīma of Vidarbha.

√दा (ददाति, class III), give.
दिलीप, Dilīpa, the name of Bhagīratha's father.
दिव, *n.* the heaven, sky.
दिव्य, *adj.* divine.
√दिह् (देग्धि, class II), smear, besmear.
दुग्ध, *n.* milk.
दृढम्, *adv.* firmly.
देववद्, *adv.* like gods.
द्रव्य, *n.* a thing, object.
द्विज, *m.* 'twice-born', a member of the upper three castes (Brahman, Kṣatriya and Vaiśya).
√द्विष् (द्वेष्टि, class II), hate.
-धर, *adj.* holding, bearing; wearing (*at end of tatpuruṣa cpd.*).
धर्मिन्, *adj.* virtuous.
√धू (धुनोति, class V), shake.
नल, *m.* Nala, name of a king of Niṣadha; chosen by Damayantī to become her husband.
नष्ट, *ppp.* √नश् (नश्यति, class IV), vanished, perished; *as prior member of cpd.* without, devoid of.
नि-√युज् (युनक्ति, class VII), enjoin something *(acc.)* upon someone *(loc.)*.
निवेशन, *n.* a dwelling.
पक्ष, *m.* a wing.
पक्षिन्, *m.* a bird.
पठन, *n.* the act of reciting, recitation.
पठित्वा, *gerund* √पठ् (पठति, class I), having recited.
परम, *adj.* extreme; highest, supreme.
परि-√पत् (पतति, class I), fly around.
परि-√स्पृश् (स्पृशति, class VI), touch; *gerund* परिस्पृश्य.
पाणि, *m.* the hand.
पार्थिव, *m.* a king.
पाश, *m.* a trap *or* snare.
पुर, *n.* a city.
√पू (पुनाति, class IX), cleanse, purify.
पूर्व, *adj.* former, previous.

प्र-√अर्थय (अर्थयति, *denom. verb from* अर्थ 'object', *literally* 'make an object of something', objectify), desire, wish.

प्रतिज्ञा, *f.* a promise.

प्रति-√लभ् (लभते, class I), get back, regain.

प्रभु, *m.* a master, lord.

प्र-√मुद् (मोदते, class I), become joyful, rejoice greatly.

प्रवर, *adj.* most excellent, chief, best.

प्र-√विश् (विशति, class VI), enter; *gerund* प्रविश्य.

प्र-√शास् (शास्ति, class II), rule, govern.

प्राङ्गण, *n.* a forecourt, courtyard.

प्राज्ञ, *adj.* wise; *as m.* a wise man.

√प्री (प्रीणीते, class IX), be glad *or* content.

√प्री (प्रीणाति, class IX), propitiate.

प्रेत्य, *gerund* प्र-√इ (एति, class II), *literally* 'having gone forth' (*i.e.*, out of this world), having died, *hence freely*, in the next world (opposed to इह 'in this world').

प्लावित, *ppp. of caus. of* √प्लु (प्लवते, class I), submerged, inundated.

√बन्ध् (बध्नाति, class IX), bind, fasten; catch.

बुध, *adj.* wise; *as m.* a wise man, a sage.

√ब्रू (ब्रवीति, class II), say.

भस्मन्, *n.* ashes.

भस्मीभूत, *ppp.* भस्मी-√भू (भवति, class I), became *or* turned to ashes.

भिक्षा, *f.* alms.

√भिद् (भिनत्ति, class VII), split, break in two.

√भी, (बिभेति, class III), fear, *with abl. of thing feared.*

भीम, *m.* Bhīma, name of a king of Vidarbha and father of Damayantī.

√भुज् (भुनक्ति, class VII), enjoy; *fut.* भोक्ष्यते.

√भृ (बिभर्ति, class III), bear, carry.

भोजन, *n.* food.

भैक्ष, *n.* asking alms, begging; *with* √चर् (चरति, class I), go about begging.

√मथ् *or* मन्थ् (मथ्नाति, class IX), stir *or* whirl; *with* अग्निम् produce fire by whirling a wooden stick in a piece of wood.

मनोरथ, *m.* a wish, desire.

मा, *adv.* not (*with imperative*).

मार्जार, *m.* a cat.
माया, *f.* illusion.
मूर्ति, *f.* form, shape.
मूल, *n.* a root.
मूषिक, *m.* a mouse.
मोहित, *ppp. of caus.* √मुह् (मुह्यति, class IV), deluded, deceived, befuddled.
यात, *ppp.* √या (याति, class II), gone.
यथाकामम्, *adj.* according to one's pleasure, at will.
यथागतम्, *adv.* 'as come', by the way one came.
यथान्यायम्, *adv.* according to rule, rightly, fittingly.
यावत् . . . तावत्, *correl. conj.* as long as . . . so long.
√युज् (युनक्ति, class VII), join; set (said of a trap or snare).
युद्ध, *n.* a battle.
योनि, *f.* a source *or* origin.
रज्जु, *m.* a rope *or* cord.
राक्षस, *m.* a demon.
राजर्षि, *m.* a royal sage.
राज्य, *n.* a kingdom.
√रुध् (रुणद्धि, class VII), hold back, obstruct; lay siege to, besiege.
वज्र, *m.* the thunderbolt *or* weapon of Indra.
वनवासिन्, *adj.* forest-dwelling.
वसुधा, *f.* the earth.
वस्त्र, *n.* a garment *or* piece of clothing.
√वा (वाति, class II), blow.
वायु, *m.* the wind.
विगत, *ppp.* वि-√गम् (गच्छति, class I), gone away (वि).
1√विद् (वेत्ति, class II), know; *infin.* वेदितुम्.
वि-√मा (मिमीते, class IX), measure across, traverse.
विमान, *n.* a sky-chariot.
1√वृ (वृणोति, class V), cover; surround; guard.
2√वृ (वृणीते, class IX), choose, select.
व्याध, *m.* a hunter.
व्युत्पन्न, *ppp.* वि-उद्-√पद (पद्यते, class IV), originated *or* derived.
√शक्, (शक्नोति, class V), be able, can.

शत्रु, *m.* an enemy.
शरीर, *n.* the body.
शान्ति, *f.* peace.
शार्दूल, *m.* a tiger.
शास्त्र, *n.* science, *or* art.
√शृ (शृणोति, class V), hear.
शिथिल, *adj.* loose, unsteady.
√शी (शेते, class II), lie, lie down.
शोक, *m.* sorrow.
षष्टि, *f.* sixty.
संगीत, *n.* a song, singing.
सम, *adj.* like, similar *or* equal to.
समतिक्रान्त, *ppp.* सम्-अति-√क्रम् (क्रामति, class I), fulfilled; *literally* 'gone completely (सम्) beyond (अति)'.
समन्वित, *ppp.* सम्-अनु-√इ (एति, class II), accompanied by, endowed with.
सम्-√आप् (आप्नोति, class V), reach, attain.
समृद्ध, *ppp.* सम्-√ऋध् (ऋध्नोति, class V), accomplished, succeeded, fulfilled.
सरित्, *f.* a stream *or* river.
सर्वदा, *adv.* always.
सलिल, *n.* water.
सिंह, *m.* a lion.
सुत, *m.* a son.
सूक्त, *n.* a Vedic hymn.
सैनिक, *m.* a soldier.
√स्तभ् *or* स्तम्भ् (स्तभ्नाति, class IX), make firm.
स्तम्भ, *m.* a post *or* pillar.
स्थविर, *adj.* firm, sturdy.
√स्वप् (स्वपिति, class II), sleep.
स्वर्ग, *m.* heaven.
स्वस्ति, *n.* welfare, blessing.
स्वामिन्, *m.* a lord *or* master.
√हु (जुहोति, class III), offer, make an oblation.
√हृ (हरति, class I), take, take away, steal; *infin.* हर्तुम्.
हृदय, *n.* the heart.

Translate into Sanskrit:

Having entered Rasātala, Bhagīratha, standing in his chariot (which was) followed by Gaṅgā, went to the area (that had been) dug up by those noble ancestors. Immediately the heap of ashes of Sagara's sons was inundated by the purifying water of Gaṅgā. Then, the water-ceremony, having been performed[1] by Bhagīratha according to rule, Sagara's sons assumed a divine form and attained heaven. According to a promise by the god of gods, Gaṅgā became Bhagīratha's wife[2] and thereafter she was known in this world also as Bhāgīrathī. Now that he had performed the water-ceremony and attained his goal,[3] Bhagīratha, his austerities and glory great, the best of men, returned to his own city and ruled his kingdom. The people, having gotten their king back, were very happy.

Notes

1. 'the water-ceremony, having been performed': locative absolute.

2. 'Gaṅgā became Bhagīratha's wife': Say 'Gaṅgā went to a condition of a wife (wife-ness) of Bhagīratha'.

3. The two causal clauses 'Now that he had performed the water-ceremony and attained his goal' may be expressed by bahuvrīhi compounds, as in the Sanskrit text (कृतोदकक्रियः समृद्धार्थः), or, alternatively, by two locatives absolute (कृतायामुदक(*or* जल)क्रियायाम् and अर्थे समृद्धे) or better by the absolute construction for the first and a bahuvrīhi (समृद्धार्थः) in place of the second clause. However, since the subject of the main assertion ('Bhagīratha . . . returned') and the causal clauses ('he had performed' and 'attained') is the same, *viz*., he/Bhagīratha, it may not be expressed in the locative absolute, *i.e*., we cannot say तेन (or भगीरथेन) कृतायाम्, etc.

LESSON TWENTY-SEVEN

1. The Śloka Metre. 2. The Passive System.

I. *Poetry in Sanskrit and the Śloka Metre.*

It may come as a surprise that the greater part of Sanskrit literature is composed *not* in prose but in verse. Even dictionaries and the most technical of treatises are almost always cast in metrical form. While the metres employed in classical Sanskrit are extremely numerous, one particular metre, popularly called the 'śloka metre' or simply 'śloka', is by far the commonest. With occasional exceptions, the entire Mahābhārata and Rāmāyaṇa are composed in the śloka metre. In treating of Sanskrit poetry it is logical, then, that we should begin with this dominant of all metres.

The śloka metre evolved from the *anuṣṭubh* metre of the Ṛgveda, a term by which the former is also sometimes called. The śloka consists of four quarter-verses or *pādas* of eight syllables each, arranged into stanzas of two lines (or verses), each, therefore, containing two *pādas*. The end of the first line is marked by a single vertical stroke or *daṇḍa* (।), the second line by a double *daṇḍa* (॥).

Unlike traditional English metre, which is based not only on the number of syllables per line, as is Sanskrit metre, but also on the position of the stress accent of the metrical feet that make up a line, Sanskrit metre is based *not* on the position of the stress accent, but on the length of the syllables, *i.e.,* the length of the vowels. Thus, the commonest metrical foot in English is the iambus, which consists of two syllables with the stress accent falling on the second, as may be illustrated by the following stanza from Thomas Gray's *Elegy Written in a Country Churchyard.* The stressed syllables are marked here with a superscript acute accent.

Full mány a flówer is bórn to blúsh unséen
And wáste its swéetness ón the désert áir;
Full mány a gém of púrest ráy seréne
The dárk unfáthomed cáves of ócean béar.

This particular metrical line, called the 'iambic pentameter', because it is measured in five (penta-) iambi is the characteristic and dominant verse of English poetry, as is the śloka of Sanskrit.

As we have said, however, in Sanskrit metre it is the length of the syllables, *i.e.,* whether long or short, *not* the position of the accent, that determines the particular kind of metrical foot. An iambus in Sanskrit, then, consists of a short syllable followed by a long, corresponding to the unaccented syllable followed by the accented in English. While all other

Sanskrit metres have a fixed pattern of longs and shorts, *i.e.*, specific and unvarying combinations of metrical feet, the śloka metre allows many substitutions or permutations, although the iambic cadence predominates. Perhaps the commonest pattern is:

. . . . | ˘ – – . || . . . . | ˘ – ˘ . ||

In this scheme the dot (.) represents a syllable of indeterminate length, the breve (˘) represents a short syllable, the horizontal line (¯) a long syllable, the double line (||) marks the end of a *pāda* (which corresponds also to a pause or caesura), the single line (|) follows the metric foot, which, in the śloka metre, consists of four syllables, *i.e.*, two iambi (= a diiambus) taken together or other combination. The first two lines of the Bhagavadgītā may be schematized as follows:

dharmakṣetre | *kurukṣetre* || *samavetā* | *yuyutsavaḥ* ||
– – – – | ˘ – – – || ˘ ˘ – – | || ˘ – ˘ ˘̱ ||
māmakāḥ pāṇ | *ḍavāś caiva* || *kim akurva* | *ta saṃjaya* ||
– ˘ – – | ˘ – – ˘ || ˘ ˘ – ˘ | ˘ – ˘ ˘̱ ||

The last syllable of a line may always be taken as long or short, regardless of its actual quantity. A syllable is long if it contains a long vowel or diphthong or a short vowel followed by two or more consonants. The consonants that determine the vowel quantity need not be in the same word. Anusvāra and visarga are to be treated as ordinary consonants.

Sanskrit poetry is almost always chanted when read or recited in India. The different metres are, of course, chanted differently because of their varying long and short syllables and the number of syllables in a line. Although chanting cannot be taught by a description, no matter how detailed, an approximation to it may be attained by exaggeratedly prolonging the long vowels in reading aloud, while pronouncing the short vowels with especial brevity, but without slurring.

It should not be expected that the *order of words* in Sanskrit poetry should be the same as in prose, any more than is the case with poetry in other languages. One of the elements of poetry is precisely a fresh, unusual arrangement of words. It is certainly more poetical to say 'Into the valley of death rode the six hundred' than to say 'The six hundred rode into the valley of death'. A poet much prefers to say 'Of arms and the man I sing' to the prosaic 'I sing of arms and the man'. A much greater deviation of poetic word order from that of prose may be seen in these lines from Milton's Paradise Lost:

Now came still evening on, and twilight grey
Had in her sober livery all things clad.

Rules cannot be given for the altered word order of poetry, simply because it is not governed by rules, but by the poet's fancy. Often, to be sure, the order of words may not differ notably from the prose order, the essence of the poetry residing in the metre and elevated mode of expression, as for example, in Wordsworth's

There was a roaring in the wind all night;
The rain came heavily and in floods;
But now the sun is rising calm and bright;
The birds are singing in the distant woods . . .

One of the differences between the word order of prose and that of poetry in Sanskrit is especially the position of adjectives and other qualifiers, which may *follow* the noun they modify, often in considerable profusion. In prose, qualifying elements normally precede, although when the number of qualifying elements is large, some or all of them may be placed after the noun. One or more adjectives that qualify the subject (which usually stands in the first *pāda*) are often added in the last *pāda,* almost as though they had occurred to the author as an afterthought to what he has already said in the prior three *pādas*. A simple example of this common phenomenon may be seen in the following stanza from the episode of Nala and Damayantī in the Mahābhārata:

दमयन्ती तु रूपेण तेजसा यशसा श्रिया ।
सौभाग्येन च लोकेषु यशः प्राप सुमध्यमा ॥
'Now Damayantī by her shapeliness, majesty, beauty and charm attained fame in the world -- the fair-waisted.'

Here सुमध्यमा 'fair-waisted', though qualifying दमयन्ती in the first *pāda,* is subjoined to an already completed thought as a sort of pendant. In reading Sanskrit poetry, then, even greater attention has to be given to grammatical endings because of this sort of dislocation and yet other deviations from the order we have become accustomed to in prose.

II. *The Passive System.*

In past lessons we have had numerous instances of the past passive participle of a verb root used as a past tense with the imperfect अभवत्/अभवन् (was/were) implied, in place of an imperfect or perfect active, in conformity with the Sanskrit predilection for the passive voice. Thus, as we know,

Sanskrit authors prefer to say तेन तत्कृतं [अभवत्] 'By him that [was] done' rather than स तदकरोत् or स तच्चकार 'He did that' (*i.e.*, the active construction). The passive construction instead of the active is also used in the present, imperfect, imperative and optative of the verb. The passive of these tenses and moods is made *not* from a participle, but from a special passive stem formed directly from a verb root by the addition of the suffix *-ya-* (-य-), without regard to the class to which the root belongs. To this passive stem (*i.e.*, root + *-ya-*) are added the *middle* endings which we have already learned. The root is subject to various weakening processes among which the most important are:

1. final *-ā* is replaced by *-ī*; thus, √*dhā* → *dhī* + *-ya-* → *dhīya-*.
2. a nasal before a consonant drops out; thus, √*bandh* → *badh* + *-ya-* → *badhya;* √*śaṃs* → *śas* + *-ya-* → *śasya-*.
3. final *-i* and *-u* are lengthened; thus, √*ci* → *cī* + *-ya-* → *cīya-;* √*stu* → *stū* + *-ya-* → *stūya-*.
4. final *-ṛ* is replaced by *-ri;* thus, √*kṛ* → *kri* + *-ya-* → *kriya-*.
5. roots containing *-ya-*, *-va-*, or *-ra-* substitute respectively *-i-*, *-u-*, and *-ṛ-;* thus, √*yaj* → *ij* + *-ya-* → *ijya-;* √*svap* → *sup* + *-ya-* → *supya-;* √*prach* → *pṛch* + *-ya-* → *pṛcchya-*.
6. verbs of the Xth class and causatives make their passive stem from the *present stem* by dropping the syllables *-aya-;* thus √*cur* → *coraya-* + *-ya-* → *cor-ya-* → *corya.*

To the stems exemplified, *viz.*, *dhīya-*, *badhya-*, *śasya-*, *cīya-*, *stūya-*, *kriya-*, *ijya-*, *supya-*, *pṛcchya-*, *corya-* , are added the appropriate middle endings for person, number, tense or mood. It seems superfluous to mention that it is naturally the *third* person that is in most frequent use. The *complete* passive conjugation of √कृ 'do' is presented below only for the sake of illustration and reference.

Present

	Singular	*Dual*	*Plural*
1.	*kri-y-e* (क्रिये)	*kri-yā-vahe* (क्रियावहे)	*kri-yā-mahe* (क्रियामहे)
2.	*kri-ya-se* (क्रियसे)	*kri-y-ethe* (क्रियेथे)	*kri-ya-dhve* (क्रियध्वे)
3.	*kri-ya-te* (क्रियते)	*kri-y-ete* (क्रियेते)	*kri-y-ante* (क्रियन्ते)

Imperfect

1.	*a-kri-y-e* (अक्रिये)	*a-kri-yā-vahi* (अक्रियावहि)	*a-kri-yā-mahi* (अक्रियामहि)
2.	*a-kri-ya-thāḥ* (अक्रियथा:)	*a-kri-y-ethām* (अक्रियेथाम्)	*a-kri-ya-dhvam* (अक्रियध्वम्)
3.	*a-kri-ya-ta* (अक्रियत)	*a-kri-y-etām* (अक्रियेताम्)	*a-kri-y-anta* (अक्रियन्त)

Imperative

1.	*kri-y-ai* (क्रियै)	*kri-y-āvahai* (क्रियावहै)	*kri-y-āmahai* (क्रियामहै)
2.	*kri-ya-sva* (क्रियस्व)	*kri-y-ethām* (क्रियेथाम्)	*kri-ya-dhvam* (क्रियध्वम्)
3.	*kri-ya-tām* (क्रियताम्)	*kri-y-etām* (क्रियेताम्)	*kri-y-antām* (क्रियन्ताम्)

Optative

1.	*kri-ye-y-a* (क्रियेय)	*kri-ye-vahi* (क्रियेवहि)	*kri-ye-mahi* (क्रियेमहि)
2.	*kri-ye-thāḥ* (क्रियेथा:)	*kri-ye-y-āthām* (क्रियेयाथाम्)	*kri-ye-dhvam* (क्रियेध्वम्)
3.	*kri-ye-ta* (क्रियेत)	*kri-ye-y-ātām* (क्रियेयाताम्)	*kri-ye-ran* (क्रियेरन्)

As always in the conjugation of verbs, *-a* is lengthened before *-v* and *-m,* hence, *kriyā-vahe* (क्रियावहे), *a-kriyā-mahi* (अक्रियामहि). The *-a* of *-ya-* is lost before an ending beginning with a vowel; thus, *kriy-ante* (क्रियन्ते), *kriy-etām* (क्रियेताम्). The optative suffix *-ī-* coalesces with *-ya-* to form *-ye-;* in the second and third dual a *-y-* is interposed between *-ye-* and the endings *-āthām* and *-ātām* in order to preserve the optative character of *-ye-,* which would otherwise become *-yay-* by internal sandhi (as *ne* from √*nī* becomes *nay-* before the thematic vowel to yield the present stem *nay-a*); hence, *kriye-y-āthām* (क्रियेयाथाम्) and *kriye-y-ātām* (क्रियेयाताम्). The present passive participle is formed by adding the suffix *-māna* (-मान) to the passive stem; thus, *kriya-māṇa* (क्रियमाण) 'being done', *badhya-māna* (बध्यमान) 'being bound'.

There is no separate passive formation for the future tense; the middle forms are used instead, and it must be gleaned from the context whether a passive sense is involved. This usage is fairly rare, however, being usually replaced by the *future passive participle,* called the 'gerundive'. Of course, just as with the *past* passive participle when employed in lieu of the past tense, the appropriate form of √भू, in this instance भवति/भवन्ति (is/are), is implied. Thus, एतानि पुष्पाणि राज्ञः भृत्येन श्वः चेतव्यानि [भवन्ति] 'These flowers will be gathered tomorrow (श्वः) by the king's servant'. Since English does not have a future passive participle or gerundive, it is not possible to give a literal translation of this Sanskrit form. If, continuing with the above example, we say 'going to be gathered', using 'going' to carry the future sense, the infinitive 'to be gathered' in complement to it is confusing. Obviously, the passive infinitive ('to be gathered' or 'about to be gathered') used in many Sanskrit grammars is even less desirable, as it doesn't suggest a participle at all.

Apart from being used to express simple futurity in this way, the gerundive has another usage, which is, in fact, much commoner and really more important. This other usage is to express *what needs to be done* in the future, an inevitable outgrowth of the simple future, which may imply necessity. 'Going to be gathered' (to continue with this awkward rendition *par faute de mieux* !) readily suggests 'having to be gathered', and so our illustrative sentence might as well mean 'These flowers will have to (*or* must) be gathered. . .', if the surrounding context requires this meaning.

In addition to simple futurity or necessity, a gerundive often implies the sense of 'fit to be . . . *or* worthy to be . . .' Thus, *darśanīya* (दर्शनीय), the gerundive of √*dṛś* 'see', often means 'fit *or* worthy to be seen', and similarly *ramaṇīya* (रमणीय) from √*ram* 'find pleasure in' regularly means 'enjoyable, pleasant, charming'.[1]

The formation of the gerundive is essentially simple and need not long detain us. There are three suffixes in use in the classical language, *viz.*, *-tavya*[2] (as in *ce-tavya* above), *-ya* (as in *kār-ya* from √*kṛ*) and, perhaps the least common, *-anīya* (as in *darś-anīya* and *ram-aṇīya* !). These examples show the kind of change to which the root vowel is generally subjected when a particular one of the three suffixes is added: guṇa before *-tavya* and *-anīya*, but vṛddhi before *-ya*. But there are, of course, various exceptions, which are best learned by encountering them in use. An important one is the change of *-ā* to *-e*, as in *jñe-ya* from √*jñā* 'know' and in *de-ya* from √*dā* 'give'.

Just as the past passive participle, as we have plentifully seen, so also the passive forms in general, including the gerundive, are frequently used impersonally, *i.e.*, without an expressed grammatical subject. In order to understand this clearly, we must recall that, when an active sentence is to be converted into the passive, the subject (nominative) is replaced by the instrumental and an object, if expressed, becomes the subject. Thus, 'The king worships Viṣṇu' (राजा विष्णुं यजते) is changed into 'Viṣṇu is worshipped by the king' (विष्णुः राज्ञा इज्यते). If 'Viṣṇu' is omitted in the active, then the passive version is simply 'It is worshipped by the king' *i.e.*, there is worship being performed by the king (राज्ञा इज्यते). The 'it' in this literal English version is a sort of 'dummy' subject, inserted only because English requires every verb to have a subject. Since no subject is expressed here, we must use this impersonal and meaningless 'it'. Even an *intransitive* verb may be put into the passive in Sanskrit and then, there being no object by the nature of the case, the passive construction has to be impersonal. For example, the sentence 'The citizens are coming together' (नागरिकाः समागच्छन्ति), when changed into the passive in conformity with the Sanskrit predilection, becomes 'It is come together by the citizens' (नागरिकैः समागम्यते). Of course, this is *bad* English, because we cannot use an intransitive verb passively in English; the bad English has only a pedagogical purpose here. Similarly, we may say 'Let it be stayed here!' (अत्र स्थीयताम्). The gerundive, being a passive form, is similarly used with reference to future actions, especially if

---

[1]The English word 'reverend', which literally means 'fit *or* worthy to be respected' (and then as a virtual noun meaning a man of the cloth), is from the Latin *reverendus,* used with precisely the same nuance of meaning as Sanskrit *darśanīya* and *ramaṇīya.*

[2]or *-i-tavya,* just as *-ta,* the suffix of the past passive participle, is often attached with an interposed *-i-*, as in *pat-i-ta* (पतित) from √*pat* 'fly'. Whenever a root forms its infinitive with *-i-tum,* the gerundive is formed with *-i-tavya,* not *-tavya.*

the notion of necessity is implied; thus मया गन्तव्यम् 'I shall go' or 'I must go', literally 'It is *going to be gone* by me'.

Sentences illustrating various uses of the passive:

1. शत्रवो राज्ञा जीयेरन्निति[1] नागरिकैरुच्यते ।
2. अस्य वृक्षस्याधस्ताद् बालेन सुखेन सुप्यते ।
3. कैः सह मया योद्धव्यं द्रष्टुमिच्छामि ततश्च मम रथः सेनयोर्मध्ये स्थाप्यतामित्यर्जुनः सूतं कृष्णमवदत् ।
4. अहो रमणीयमिदं वनमत आवाभ्यामत्र रात्रीं स्थीयतां प्रत्युषे च वनं त्यज्यतामिति सूतं राज्ञोक्तम् ।
5. तैश्चौरैश्चोरितं धनिनो धनं वृक्षस्य कोटरे ऽधीयत ।
6. श्राद्धं[2] दातुमाह्वानां राज्ञो गृहीत्वा ब्राह्मणो मया सत्वरं गन्तव्यमन्यथा कश्चिदन्य इमां क्रियां ग्रहीष्यतीति चिन्तयित्वा राजप्रासादं गतः ।
7. क्षेत्रे लाङ्गलं चालयन्नरः कृष्णसर्पेणादश्यत ।
8. एतानि सूक्तानि मया श्वः पठितव्यानीति गुरुणा शिष्याभ्यां न्यवेद्यत ।
9. मुक्तिर्ध्यानेन विद्यया चैव प्राप्यत इति शास्यते बुधैः ।
10. यदा नलो नृपस्तस्मिन्वने विचरतां हंसानाम्[3] एकं जग्राह तदा स हंसो मानुषीं वाचं कृत्वा न हन्तव्यो ऽस्मि ते[4] राजन्नित्युक्त्वा तेनोत्सृष्ट उदपतत् ।

Notes

1. जीयेरन्निति Remember that a final -न् preceded by a *short* vowel and followed by any vowel beginning the next word is doubled.

2. On the *śrāddha* ceremony, *v.* note 1 in Lesson Six.

3. On the semi-mythic *haṃsas, v.* note 9 in Lesson Three.

4. ते genitive used as an instrumental with the gerundive हन्तव्यो; *cf.* English 'beloved *of* him' for 'beloved *by* him', as noted in note 19 in the following extract.

Vocabulary

अन्यथा, *adv.* otherwise.
अहो, *interjection* Ah, oh! What a!
आह्वान, *n.* an invitation.
उद्-√पत्, (पतति, class I), fly up.
उत्सृष्ट, *ppp.* वि-√सृज् (सृजति, class VI), (having been) released, let go.
कृष्णसर्प, *m.* a cobra.
कोटर, *m.* a hollow (of a tree).
क्रिया, *f.* a ceremony.
क्षेत्र, *n.* a field.
√ग्रह् (गृह्णाति, class IX), get, grasp, take hold of; *fut.* ग्रहीष्यति; *perf.* जग्राह; *gerund* गृहीत्वा.
चौर, *m.* a thief.
√त्यज्, (त्यजति, class I), leave.
√दंश् (दंशति, class I), bite.
धन, *n.* wealth.
धनिन्, *adj.* 'possessing wealth', wealthy.
ध्यान, *n.* meditation.
नागरिक, *m.* an inhabitant of a city *or* town (नगर), a citizen.
नि-√विद् *in caus.* निवेदयति, informs (+ *dat.*).
√पठ्, (पठति, class I), recite.
प्रत्युष, *m.* the daybreak, dawn.
प्रासाद, *m.* a palace.
बुध, *m.* a sage.
मानुष, *adj.* (*f.* मानुषी), human.
मुक्ति, *f.* release, salvation.
रात्री, *f.* the night.

लाङ्गल, *n.* a plow; *with caus. of* √चल् (चलति, class I), plow (a field).
वि-√चर् (चरति, class I), move hither and thither, move about.
शत्रु, *m.* an enemy.
√शास् (शासति, class I), teach.
श्वः, *adv.* tomorrow.
सुखेन, *instr. as adv.* pleasantly, in comfort.
सूक्त, *n.* a Vedic hymn.
√हन् (हन्ति, class II), slay, kill.

The Bhagavadgītā

The Bhagavadgītā ('Song of the Blessed One') or simply the Gītā, as it is oftener called, is a colloquy or dialogue in 18 chapters, mostly in the śloka metre, between the warrior Arjuna and Kṛṣṇa, his charioteer, who is an incarnation of the god Viṣṇu. It is not, strictly speaking, an independent work, but is one of the numerous smaller works embedded in the Mahābhārata, where it forms the third episode of the Bhīṣmaparvan, the sixth of the 18 books that make up the great epic. Though an integral part of the Mahābhārata, it has come to be looked upon as a separate creation that embodies in essence the Hindu view of life and accordingly has attained the status of holy scripture.

The dialogue between Arjuna and Kṛṣṇa takes place on the battlefield in Kurukṣetra just as the great armies of the Pāṇḍavas and Kauravas are about to join in mortal combat in the catastrophic war which is the subject of the Mahābhārata. Arjuna has requested Kṛṣṇa to halt his chariot between the two opposing armies that he may view those who stand ready to do battle with him. As he sees arrayed before him a host of his kinsmen and friends, he is stricken at once with extreme compassion and despair. He recoils from participating in the impending slaughter at the thought of its horrifying consequences to all those who are concerned. His bow slips from his hand, and he sits down in his chariot sick at heart.

This dramatic and powerful incident, which brings to an end the first chapter of the Gītā, leads into a series of long and complex discussions commencing with a discourse on the imperishability and indestructibility of the soul, the duty (*dharma*) of a warrior (*kṣatriya*) to fight in a righteous cause, and, in the progress of Kṛṣṇa's responses to Arjuna's questions, covering a bewildering array of theological and philosophical matters.

The Gītā is written in a simple and straightforward style, with remarkable clarity of presentation. There are, to be sure, difficulties, but they are not grammatical or stylistic: they are due to the interpretation of certain frequently recurring words (such as *yoga*), quite familiar from their usage in various Sanskrit technical treatises, where, however, their meaning is often alien to that in the Gītā.

Neither the name of the author of the Gītā nor the date of its composition is known. As to the latter, there has, of course, been endless speculation, but perhaps we may not be far amiss in postulating the date at c.200 B.C. In the course of the centuries the Gītā has been subject to many scholastic interpretations, and commentaries, both old and new, have always been plentiful, nor are they confined to India. Translations into non-Indian languages run into the hundreds, possibly even the thousands, and new ones are ever appearing, with hardly anything new to say, for it has all been said many times long before.

I. Arjuna's Despair

संजय उवाच ।

अथ व्यवस्थितान्दृष्ट्वा धार्तराष्ट्रान्कपिध्वजः[1] ।
प्रवृत्ते शस्त्रसंपाते[2] धनुरुद्यम्य पाण्डवः ॥२०॥
हृषीकेशं तदा वाक्यमिदमाह महीपते[3] ।
सेनयोरुभयोर्मध्ये रथं स्थापय मे ऽच्युत ॥२१॥
यावद्[4] एतान्निरीक्षे ऽहं योद्धुकामान्[5] अवस्थितान् ।
कैर्[6] मया सह योद्धव्यम्[7] अस्मिन्रणसमुद्यमे ॥२२॥
योत्स्यमानानवेक्षे ऽहं य एते[8] ऽत्र समागताः ।
धार्तराष्ट्रस्य[9] दुर्बुद्धेर्युद्धे प्रियचिकीर्षवः ॥२३॥
एवमुक्तो हृषीकेशो गुडाकेशेन भारत[10] ।
सेनयोरुभयोर्मध्ये स्थापयित्वा रथोत्तमम् ॥२४॥
भीष्मद्रोणप्रमुखतः सर्वेषां च महीक्षिताम्[11] ।
उवाच पार्थ पश्यैतान्समवेतान्कुरूनिति ॥२५॥
तत्रापश्यत्[12] स्थितान्पार्थः पितॄनथ[13] पितामहान् ।
आचार्यान्मातुलान्भ्रातॄन्पुत्रान्पौत्रान्सखींस्तथा ॥२६॥
श्वशुरान्सुहृदश्चैव सेनयोरुभयोरपि[14] ।
तान्समीक्ष्य स कौन्तेयः सर्वान्बन्धूनवस्थितान् ॥२७॥
कृपया परयाविष्टो विषीदन्निदमब्रवीत् ।

अर्जुन उवाच ।
दृष्ट्वेमान्स्वजनान्कृष्ण युयुत्सून्समवस्थितान् ॥२८॥
सीदन्ति मम गात्राणि मुखं च परिशुष्यति ।
वेपथुश्च शरीरे मे रोमहर्षश्च जायते ॥२९॥
गाण्डीवं[15] स्रंसते हस्तात्त्वक्चैव परिदह्यते ।
न च शक्नोम्यवस्थातुं भ्रमतीव च मे मनः ॥३०॥
निमित्तानि च पश्यामि विपरीतानि केशव ।
न च श्रेयो ऽनुपश्यामि[16] हत्वा[17] स्वजनमाहवे ॥३१॥
न काङ्क्षे विजयं कृष्ण न च राज्यं सुखानि च ।
किं नो राज्येन[18] गोविन्द किं भोगैर्जीवितेन वा ॥३२॥
येषामर्थे काङ्क्षितं नो राज्यं[19] भोगाः सुखानि च ।
त एव[20] नः स्थिता योद्धुं प्राणांस्त्यक्त्वा सुदुस्त्यजान् ॥३३॥
आचार्याः पितरः पुत्रास्तथैव च पितामहाः ।
मातुलाः श्वशुराः पौत्राः स्यालाः संबन्धिनस्तथा ॥३४॥
एतान्न हन्तुमिच्छामि घ्नतो ऽपि[21] मधुसूदन ।
अपि त्रैलोक्यराज्यस्य[22] हेतोः किं नु[23] महीकृते ॥३५॥
निहत्य धार्तराष्ट्रान्नः का प्रीतिः स्याज्जनार्दन ।
पापमेवाश्रयेदस्मान्हत्वैतानाततायिनः[24] ॥३६॥
तस्मान्नार्हा वयं हन्तुं[25] धार्तराष्ट्रान्सबान्धवान् ।
स्वजनं हि कथं हत्वा सुखिनः स्याम माधव ॥३७॥
यद्यप्येते न पश्यन्ति लोभोपहतचेतसः[26] ।
कुलक्षयकृतं दोषं मित्रद्रोहे च पातकम् ॥३८॥
कथं न ज्ञेयमस्माभिः[27] पापादस्मान्निवर्तितुम्[28] ।
कुलक्षयकृतं दोषं प्रपश्यद्भिर्[29] जनार्दन ॥३९॥
कुलक्षये[30] प्रनश्यन्ति कुलधर्माः[31] सनातनाः ।
धर्मे नष्टे[32] कुलं कृत्स्नमधर्मो ऽभिभवत्युत ॥४०॥

अधर्माभिभवात्कृष्ण प्रदुष्यन्ति कुलस्त्रियः ।
स्त्रीषु दुष्टासु वार्ष्णेय जायते वर्णसंकरः ॥४१॥
संकरो नरकायैव[33] कुलघ्नानां कुलस्य च ।
पतन्ति पितरो ह्येषां लुप्तपिण्डोदकक्रियाः[34] ॥४२॥
दोषैरेतैः कुलघ्नानां वर्णसंकरकारकैः ।
उत्साद्यन्ते जातिधर्माः[35] कुलधर्माश्च शाश्वताः ॥४३॥
उत्सन्नकुलधर्माणां मनुष्याणां जनार्दन ।
नरके नियतं[36] वासो भवतीत्यनुशुश्रुम ॥४४॥
अहो बत महत्पापं कर्तुं व्यवसिता वयम् ।
यद्[37] राज्यसुखलोभेन हन्तुं स्वजनमुद्यताः ॥४५॥
यदि मामप्रतीकारमशस्त्रं शस्त्रपाणयः[38] ।
धार्तराष्ट्रा रणे हन्युस्तन्मे क्षेमतरं भवेत् ॥४६॥

संजय उवाच ।
एवमुक्त्वार्जुनः संख्ये रथोपस्थ उपाविशत् ।
विसृज्य सशरं चापं शोकसंविग्नमानसः[39] ॥४७॥

(Bhagavadgītā I. 20-47).

Notes

1. कपिध्वजः 'monkey-bannered', an epithet of the warrior Arjuna, whose chariot was distinguished by a banner or pennant (ध्वज) on which a monkey (कपि) was depicted. The compound is modelled after compounds like शस्त्रपाणि 'having a sword in the hand' and लगुडहस्त 'having a cudgel in the hand', the members of which are in reversed order, as पाणि and हस्त are strictly in subordinate or dependant relation to शस्त्र and लगुड and hence should precede.

2. प्रवृत्ते शस्त्रसंपाते a locative absolute expressing the time or circumstance when Arjuna raised his bow (धनुरुद्यम्य): 'when the clash of arms had begun', a somewhat incongruous assertion, however, since from the following lines it is clear that the battle had not yet started.

3. महीपते This vocative, like भारत below, is addressed to the blind king Dhṛtarāṣṭra, to whom the Gītā was communicated by the bard Saṃjaya. Such vocatives are commonplace in the Mahābhārata, as it contains so many long narratives that are related to others and so conducive to these apostrophes. In reading one has to be careful not to confuse these vocatives with others that are embedded in words spoken by persons who are part of the narrative. An example of this is अच्युत in the next line, which is addressed by Arjuna to his charioteer Kṛṣṇa.

4. यावद् There are two possible ways of interpreting यावद् here. It may be used as an adverb with the present indicative निरीक्षे to denote an *intended action:* 'I want to see . . ', or it may be taken as a conjunction meaning 'while' (but 'while I see' would be practically equivalent to 'in order that I may see'). In whichever sense it is taken, its effect continues on to अवेक्षे, with which it must accordingly be supplied.

5. योद्धुकामान् 'desirous to fight', a bahuvrīhi compound *literally* 'having a desire to fight (योद्धुम्)', part A being an apocopated or abbreviated infinitive due to the loss of its final -म्.

6. कैर् This interrogative pronoun does not here introduce an independent question, but an *indirect* question to be taken with यावद् निरीक्षे; thus, 'while I see (or 'I want to see') . . by whom (कैर्) it shall be fought with me', *i.e.,* who shall fight with me. The words योद्धुकामानवस्थितान् strictly belong in the indirect question. If occurring there, they would, of course, be in the instrumental in agreement with कैर् which they define, thus: कैर्योद्धुकामैरवस्थितैः . . ('while I see what ones drawn up, eager to fight, shall fight with me'). This sort of retraction of words from a subordinate clause into the main clause is also seen in the biblical 'Consider the lilies of the field how they grow' (for 'Consider how the lilies of the field grow').

7. कैर्मया सह योद्धव्यम् Instead of saying के मया सह योत्स्यन्ते ('Who will fight with me?'), the passive construction is used here in consonance with the

proclivity of Sanskrit for the passive; thus: 'by whom will it be fought with me?' As has been explained in this lesson, the future passive is normally expressed by means of the gerundive, although occasionally the future middle is used in a passive sense. The gerundive योद्धव्यम् is in the *neuter* nominative singular because there is no grammatical subject with which it can agree, and so the usage becomes impersonal. In English, which *requires* a subject (whether a noun or a pronoun) to be expressed, a meaningless 'it' serves as the subject of impersonal verbs, *e.g.*, '*it* rains', where '*it*' has no meaning, but only a grammatical function.

8. एते Logically, this demonstrative belongs with the antecedent योत्स्यमानान् so as to delimit it more pointedly, thus: '*these* (men) ready to fight, who are come together here', but it has been drawn into the relative clause rather to throw its pointed reference there, as though to say: 'the ones ready to fight, who – these very ones – have come together here'.

9. धार्तराष्ट्रस्य a 'genitive quasi-dative', *i.e.,* a genitive used in the sense of a dative, an extremely prevalent usage in the classical language; *cf.* the same usage of the genitive in कुलघ्नानां and कुलस्य below (*v.* note 33). As has been noted before, in the spoken dialects or Prakrits the genitive almost entirely replaces the dative in all the latter's uses. The 'son of Dhṛtarāṣṭra' meant here is Duryodhana, who is called 'ill-natured *or* malignant' (दुर्बुद्धि) because of his treatment of the Pāṇḍavas.

10. भारत another vocative addressed to King Dhṛtarāṣṭra by Saṃjaya, as noted under 3 above; in Gītā II.14, Arjuna is addressed as भारत.

11. सर्वेषां च महीक्षिताम् 'and (in front) of all the kings'. The sense of प्रमुखतः, although the final member of the tatpuruṣa भीष्मद्रोणप्रमुखतः, is carried over to govern महीक्षिताम् with its adjective सर्वेषां, as though प्रमुखतः were a separate and independent word capable of being thus construed with other words in the verse.

12. तत्रापश्यत् 'He saw in them', तत्र being a substitute for उभयोः सेनयोः 'in both armies'. The full expression occurs in 27b.

13. अथ here a synonym for च, as often.

14. अपि This particle is often subjoined to numerals or numerical words, as to उभयोर् here, to throw a degree of emphasis on them, much as we do in English by using 'all', as in 'all three'.

15. गाण्डीवं Weapons were often given names, as Arjuna's bow 'Gāṇḍīva' here. It will be remembered from the passage in Lesson Nineteen that Viṣṇu's discus is called 'Sudarśana'. Similarly, King Arthur's sword was called 'Excalibur' and the hammer of the god Thor of Norse mythology was named 'Mjölnir' ('The Crusher').

16. अनुपश्यामि There appears to be no perceptible difference in meaning between पश्यामि and अनुपच्यामि, the prefix अनु- serving only for variation of expression.

17. हत्वा A gerund does not always have the value of a past active participle, simply denoting prior action, but not infrequently it expresses an action by which something is achieved, as though it had an instrumental or locative relation with the main verb. So here, the meaning is *not* 'I see no good *(after) having slain* my own people in battle', but 'I see no good *in having slain'* etc. The same use of the gerund occurs below with two more occurrences of हत्वा (*v.* note 24). In this usage we may discern an element of the origin of the gerund as an instrumental of a noun of action; thus, *hatv-ā* 'by a slaying' is from *hatu* 'a slaying' + *-ā* (the instrumental ending).

18. किं नो राज्येन 'of what use to us is a kingdom?', *literally* 'what (is) with a kingdom for us', *i.e.,* what need have we of a kingdom. This use of किम् with the instrumental is extremely common.

19. येषामर्थे काङ्क्षितं नो राज्यं 'for the sake of whom a kingdom (is) desired by us'; नो (= नः) is the genitive used for the instrumental with the past passive participle काङ्क्षितं, just as we may say in somewhat antiquated English 'beloved *of* him' for 'beloved *by* him'. Though the following words भोगाः and सुखानि are also to be taken with काङ्क्षितं, it is put in the neuter singular to agree with the nearest word (राज्यं).

20. त एव (for ते एव) correlative of येषाम् in the preceding line: 'for the sake of whom . . . those very (एव) ones are standing . .'.

21. घ्नतोऽपि present participle accusative plural of √हन् 'slay' modifying एतान्; अपि imparts to the participle a concessive force, implying that even granting that the enemy (consisting of kinsmen and friends) may engage in killing, he (Arjuna) does not wish to do so.

22. त्रैलोक्यराज्यस्य The three worlds are heaven, earth and either the atmosphere or nether world.

23. किं नु 'to say the least of', the meaning given in the vocabulary, is just the English idiomatic equivalent; the literal meaning is 'why, then' and with the following compound with which it goes: 'why, then, for the sake of the earth', idiomatically 'to say the least of for the sake of the earth!'. किं is the accusative neuter singular used adverbally ('why').

24. पापमेवाश्रयेदस्मान्हत्वैतानाततायिनः 'Only sin would accrue to us in slaying these who have their bows extended'. Note the force of the all-important particle एव ('only' here). Observe also the same use of the gerund हत्वा as discussed under note 17 above: the sin would not accrue *after* the slaying, but *on account of* it; similarly हत्वा in the next stanza.

25. नार्हा वयं हन्तुं 'we should not (*or* ought not) slay'; the adjective अर्ह is frequently used with an infinitive in the meaning 'should *or* ought'.

26. लोभोपहतचेतसः Bahuvrīhi adjectives, especially those containing a past passive participle, are often equivalent to clauses expressing various relationships (causal, temporal, conditional) to the sentence in which they stand. This compound has causal value: 'Although these do not perceive . . *because their minds are stricken with greed*'. Similarly used are the compounds लुप्तपिण्डोदकक्रियाः and शोकसंविग्नमानसः, for which *v.* under notes 34 and 39. Only the context, of course, will determine the relationship in each instance. Hence, it is best to start with a literal translation ('having minds stricken with greed' or 'whose minds . . ') to see what relationship may be inferred.

27. कथं न ज्ञेयमस्माभिः This question forms the conclusion to the concessive clause beginning with यद्यप्येते 'Even though these do not perceive . . , how should we not know?'

28. निवर्तितुम् This infinitive is subject of the neuter gerundive ज्ञेयम्; thus, literally 'how (is) to turn away (निवर्तितुम्) not to be known?', *i.e.*, 'how should we not *know* . . . ?'

29. प्रपश्यद्भिर् present participle modifying अस्माभिः in the prior verse, and virtually equivalent to a causal clause: 'inasmuch as we see the harm caused by destroying the family'.

30. कुलक्ष्ये a 'locative of time' and hence equivalent to a temporal clause: 'When the family is destroyed'.

31. कुलधर्माः By this is meant all the ceremonies, such as the elementary sacraments, wedding and funeral rites, and the many customs and observances that are part of the daily routine of a family. They are, therefore, called सनातनाः 'everlasting', being followed as long as the family survives.

32. धर्मे नष्टे locative absolute; so also स्त्रीषु दुष्टासु below. The singular धर्मे is used in a collective sense.

33. नरकायैव an extension of the 'dative of purpose', expressing 'the end to which'; we may translate: 'The intermixture (of castes through intermarriage) leads only (एव!) to hell for the ones who slay the family and for the family'. The reason why caste-mixture leads to hell is explained in the following half-śloka. Note the 'genitives quasi-dative' in कुलघ्नानां and कुलस्य.

34. लुप्तपिण्डोदकक्रियाः to be taken causally as लोभोपहतचेतसः discussed under note 26 above. The offering of rice (पिण्ड) and water (उदक) to the deceased ancestors or Fathers (पितरः) is absolutely essential lest their souls, abiding in subtle bodies following cremation, be unable to enter heaven, but be obliged to wander about as 'departed spirits' (*pretas*).

35. जातिधर्माः Often, but by no means always, the terms वर्ण and जाति are interchanged, as in जातिधर्माः and वार्णसंकरः (41) and वर्णसंकरकारकैः (43).

36. नियतं best taken as a neuter noun corresponding to English 'a sure thing'; thus, 'abiding in hell (is) a sure thing', or we may say 'a certainty'.

37. यद् here a *conjunction* meaning 'because' or 'in that': 'because (*or* in that) we are prepared to slay our own people'. The clause introduced by यद्, taken in either sense, explains or amplifies महत्पापं.

38. शस्त्रपाणय: 'having sword in hand'. On this reversed bahuvrīhi, *cf.* note under 1 above.

39. शोकसंविग्नमानस: This bahuvrīhi may also be taken with causal value as लोभोपहतचेतस: and लुप्तपिण्डोदकक्रिया:, on which *v.* notes under 26 and 34.

Vocabulary

अच्युत, *adj.* 'not fallen, firm, steadfast', epithet of Kṛṣṇa. But the meaning is somewhat doubtful, as √च्यु (च्यवति, °ते, class I), of which च्युत is the *ppp.*, may mean 'fall, waver' and also 'perish'; hence, अच्युत might equally mean 'unwavering, *i.e.*, steadfast' or 'imperishable, immortal'.
अधर्म, *m.* unrighteousness.
अनु-√पश् (पश्यति, class I), discern, see.
अनु-√श्रु (शृणोति, class V), hear repeatedly (अनु); *perf.* °शुश्राव (*plur.* °शुश्रुवु:).
अप्रतीकार, 'not having any counteraction *or* retaliation', *hence* defenseless.
अभिभव, *m.* an overpowering.
अभि-√भू (भवति, class I), 'be against', overpower, control.
अर्ह, *adj.* deserving, worthy; fit (+ *infin.* 'fit to', *i.e.,* 'should').
अव-√ईक्ष् (इक्षते, class I), look upon, see.
अव-√स्था (तिष्ठति, class I), stand, stand up; *infin.* अवस्थातुम्.
अवस्थित, *ppp.* अव-√स्था (तिष्ठति, class I), arrayed.
अशस्त्र, 'not having a sword', without a sword, unarmed.
√अह् (*only used in some forms of the perfect*), said.
अहो बत, *compound interj.* alas!
आचार्य, *m.* a teacher, preceptor.
आततायिन्, *adj.* 'having *or* holding a drawn (bow)', *hence as m.,* a warrior.
आविष्ट, *ppp.* आ-√विश् (विशति, class VI), entered into *or* upon; entered by, filled with (+ *instr.*).

आ-√श्रि (श्रयति, class I), lean *or* rest on; happen to, befall, come to, accrue to.

आहव, *n.* a challenge; war, battle.

उत, *particle,* and, also; even.

उत्तम, *adj.* highest, best; *at the end of a tatpuruṣa* most excellent.

उत्सन्न, *ppp.* उद्-√सद् (सीदति, class I), decayed, ruined.

उदक, *n.* water.

उद्यत, *ppp.* उद्-√यम् (यच्छति, class I), prepared, intent on (+ *infin.*).

उद्-√यम् (यच्छति, class I), hold up, raise; *gerund* उद्यम्य.

उद्-√सद् (सीदति, class I), sink, settle down; go to ruin, decay; *caus.* उत्सादयति, brings to ruin, destroys.

उप-√विश् (विशति, class VI), sit down.

उभय, *adj.* both.

उपहत, *ppp.* उप-√हन् (हन्ति, class II), stricken; corrupted.

कपि, *m.* a monkey.

√काङ्क्ष् (काङ्क्षते, class I), desire.

कारक, *adj.* making *or* causing.

किं नु *interr. phrase* to say the least of.

किम्, *interr. pron.* what; + *instr.* 'what's the use of . . . '.

कुरु, *m.* the Kurus, name of a people of northwest India, descended from their eponymous ancestor Kuru. They are also called by the patronymic Kauravas.

कुल, *n.* the family.

कुलघ्न, *adj.* slaying *or* destroying a family.

कृते, *postp.* for the sake of, for (+ *gen. or in compound*).

कृत्स्न, *adj.* whole, entire.

कृपा, *f.* pity, compassion.

केशव, *m.* 'long-haired', Keśava, epithet and name of Kṛṣṇa; *cf.* गुडाकेश in 24.

कौन्तेय, *m.* a son of Kuntī, mother of Yudhiṣṭhira, Bhīmasena and Arjuna.

क्रिया, *f.* a ceremony.

क्षय, *m.* destruction.

क्षेम, *n.* peace, tranquillity; happiness; a state of comfort; क्षेमतर, *n.* a greater peace (etc.).

गाण्डीव, *n.* Gāṇḍīva, the name of Arjuna's bow.

गात्र, *n.* a limb.

गुडाकेश, *m.* 'thick-haired', an epithet of Arjuna.

गोविन्द, *m.* Govinda, a name of Kṛṣṇa [possibly 'cow-finder' from गो 'cow' + verbal of ²√विद् 'find' or a borrowing of Prakrit गोविन्द which may represent either गोपेन्द्र 'lord of cow-herds' (from गोप 'cow-protector' from गो + verbal of √पा 'protect' + इन्द्र 'lord, chief') or, less probably, गोपीन्द्र 'lord of cowherdesses' (गोपी 'cowherdess', feminine of गोप, + इन्द्र).]

चाप, *m. or n.* a bow.

चिकीर्षु, *adj.* desiring to do, ready to do [*desiderative adj. from* √कृ].

चेतस्, *n.* the mind, heart.

जनार्दन, *m.* Janārdana, a name of Kṛṣṇa. [The name seems *literally* to mean 'agitator *or* tormentor of people', but if so, the application to Kṛṣṇa is obscure.]

जाति, *f.* caste.

जीवित, *n.* life.

ज्ञेय, *gerundive of* √ज्ञा (जानाति, class IX), to be known, having to be known.

तस्मात्, *abl. of* तद् 'on account of this', therefore.

√त्यज् (त्यजति, class I), leave, leave off, abandon; risk; *gerund* त्यक्त्वा.

त्रैलोक्य, *n.* the three worlds.

त्वच्, *f.* the skin.

दुर्बुद्धि, *m.* ill-natured, malignant.

दुष्ट, *ppp.* √दुष् (दुष्यति, class IV), defiled.

दोष, *m.* a fault, defect; sin; harm; evil.

द्रोण, *m.* Droṇa, the name of the preceptor of the Pāṇḍavas and Kauravas.

द्रोह, *m.* injury, treachery.

धनुस्, *n.* a bow.

धर्म, *m.* usage, custom, practice, observance, duty.

धार्तराष्ट्र, *m.* a son of Dhṛtarāṣṭra.

ध्वज, *m.* a banner *or* standard.

नरक, *m. or n.* hell.

नष्ट, *ppp.* √नश् (नश्यति, class IV), having perished *or* died away.

निमित्त, *n.* a sign, indication.

नियत, *ppp.* नि-√यम् (यच्छति, class I), held down, checked, controlled; fixed, certain, sure.

निस्-√ईक्ष् (इक्षते, class I), look upon, survey.

निस्-√वृत् (वर्तते, class I), turn away *or* desist from (+ *abl.*); *infin.* वर्तितुम्.

√पत् (पतति, class I), fall; go to ruin.

पर, *adj.* highest, extreme.

परि-√दह् (दहति, class I), burn thoroughly, scorch; *in passive* be on fire.

परि-√शुष् (शुष्यति, class IV), become dry *or* parched.

पाणि, *m.* the hand.

पाण्डव, *m.* a son of Pāṇḍu (there were *five* sons of Pāṇḍu, here Arjuna is meant).

पातक, *n.* a sin, crime.

पाप, *n.* evil; sin.

पार्थ, *m.* a son of Pṛthā, a metronymic of Arjuna.

पिण्ड, *m.* a ball; a ball of rice.

पौत्र, *m.* a grandson.

प्र-√दुष् (दुष्यति, class IV), decay *or* spoil completely (प्र), deteriorate, be defiled *or* corrupted.

प्र-√नश् (नश्यति, class IV), die away, perish.

प्र-√पश् (पश्यति, class IV), see *or* look ahead, discern, perceive.

प्रमुखतः, *postp.* in front of, before (+ *gen.*).

प्र-√वृत् (वर्तते, class I), *literally* turn *or* move forward, *then* start, take place.

प्राण, *m.* breath; *in plur.* life.

प्रीति, *f.* pleasure, joy.

बन्धु, *m.* a relative, kinsman.

बान्धव, *m.* a relative.

भारत, *m.* a descendant from Bhārata.

भीष्म, *m.* Bhīṣma, the name of a famous warrior in the great war between the Pāṇḍavas and Kauravas, who fought on the side of the latter.

भोग, *m.* enjoyment, joy.

√भ्रम् (भ्रमति, class I), move about, roam; wander; be in a whirl; be agitated *or* confused.

भ्रातृ, *m.* a brother.

मधुसूदन, *m.* 'slayer of Madhu', a name of Kṛṣṇa.

मध्य, *n.* the middle.

मनुष्य, *m.* a man.

महीक्षित्, *m.* 'earth-ruler', a king *or* prince.
महीपति, *m.* 'lord of the earth', a king.
मातुल, *m.* a maternal uncle.
माधव, *m.* Mādhava, a name of Kṛṣṇa.
मानस, *n.* the mind, heart.
मित्र, *n.*(!) a friend.
यावत्, *conj.* while.
√युध् (युध्यते, class IV), fight; *future* योत्स्यते; *infin.* योद्धुम्; *gerundive* योद्धव्य; *desiderative adj.;* युयुत्सु.
युयुत्सु, *adj.* desirous *or* about to fight *(desiderative adj. from* √युध्).
योद्धुकाम, *adj.* desirous to fight.
रण, *n.* battle.
रथोपस्थ, *m.* the seat of a chariot.
रोमहर्ष, *m.* the bristling of the hair of the body, horripilation.
लुप्त, *ppp.* √लुप् (लुम्पति, class VI), broken, broken off; interrupted.
लोभ, *m.* strong desire; greed.
वर्ण, *m.* cover, coat; color; class, caste.
वार्ष्णेय, *m.* Vārṣṇeya, a name of Kṛṣṇa as a descendant of Vṛṣṇi in the fifth degree.
वास, *m.* dwelling, abiding.
विजय, *m.* victory.
विपरीत, *ppp.* वि-परि-√इ (एति, class II), turned around, reversed; perverse, contrary to rule, wrong; adverse, inauspicious.
वि-√सद् (सीदति, class I), sink down, be depressed *or* dejected.
वि-√सृज् (सृजति, class VI), let go, release.
वेपथु, *m.* a quivering, trembling.
व्यवसित, *ppp.* वि-अव-√सो (स्यति, class IV), determined, resolved.
व्यवस्थित, *ppp.* वि-अव-√स्था (तिष्ठति, class I), standing here and there, arranged, arrayed.
शर, *m.* an arrow.
शरीर, *n.* the body.
शस्त्र, *n.* a weapon [not to be confused with शास्त्र !].
शाश्वत, *adj.* eternal, everlasting.
शोक, *m.* sorrow, anguish.

श्रेयस्, *n.* welfare, benefit.

श्वशुर, *m.* a father-in-law.

संविग्न, *ppp.* सं-√विज् (विजते, class VI), agitated, disturbed.

सखि, *m.* a companion, comrade.

संकर, *m.* a mixing together, intermixture.

संख्य, *n.* conflict, battle; field of battle.

संजय, *m.* Saṃjaya, name of the bard of the blind king Dhṛtarāṣṭra who reports to him the happenings on the battlefield in the war between the Pāṇḍavas and the Kauravas. The whole of the Bhagavadgītā is, then, related by Saṃjaya.

√सद् (सीदति, class I), sink, sink down; give way, weaken, falter.

सनातन, *adj.* everlasting, eternal.

समवस्थित, *ppp.* सम्-अव-√स्था (तिष्ठति, class I), fully (सम्) arrayed, in full array.

समवेत, *ppp.* सम्-अव-√इ (एति, class II), having come together, assembled.

समागत, *ppp.* सम-आ-√गम् (गच्छति, class I), having come together, gathered.

सम्-√ईक्ष् (ईक्षते, class I), look upon, behold.

समुद्यम, *m.* a lifting *or* raising up, effort, exertion, enterprise.

संपात, *m.* 'a falling together', collision, clash.

संबन्धिन्, *m.* 'having a connection', *as m.* a relative, kinsman.

सुदुस्त्यज, *adj.* very difficult to abandon *or* risk.

सुहृद्, *m.* a friend.

स्त्री, *f.* a woman.

√स्था (तिष्ठति, class I), stand; *caus.* स्थापयति 'causes to stand', stops, brings to rest.

स्याल, *m.* a brother-in-law.

√स्रंस् (स्रंसते, class I), fall, fall down, slip.

स्वजन, *m.* one's own people, kinsmen.

√हन् (हन्ति, class II), smite, smite *or* strike down; slay, kill; *gerund* हत्वा.

हृषीकेश, *m.* 'lord of the senses', an epithet of Kṛṣṇa.

हेतु, *m.* cause; *gen.* हेतोः *as a quasi-postp.* 'for the sake of, for' (+ *gen.*).

LESSON TWENTY-EIGHT

Causative and Denominative Verbs.
The Anaphoric Pronoun एनद्.

I. *Causative Verbs.*

In many of the foregoing lessons we have had examples of so-called 'causative' verbs, but while the term 'causative' has been used in the notes and vocabularies, hardly anything has been said as to their character and formation.

A causative verb is a particular form of verb in which the subject does not perform the action himself, but causes someone else to perform it. So, whereas सः कटं करोति means 'He makes a mat', the causative सः कटं कारयति means 'He *causes* (someone not here mentioned) to make a mat'. Modern English has only a half dozen or so causative verbs inherited from Old English[1] and therefore, has to employ various roundabout means to express the idea of causing someone to perform an action. One method, as in the above example, is, of course, literally to say 'cause someone to do' such-and-such. Perhaps, however, it is much commoner to say 'have someone do', as, to use the same example, 'He has a mat made'. But often English, due to the absence of causative verbs in its grammatical framework, is indifferent to specifying that a particular action is not actually performed by the grammatical subject, but only promoted or initiated by that subject. For example, we may say: 'The Pharaoh Cheops built the Great Pyramid', although he most certainly did not do so himself, but 'had *or* caused it to be built (by others)'. In Sanskrit, however, which can readily form a causative verb from a root by the application of perfectly simple rules, a causative is always employed when an action is not actually performed by the subject.

Logically, then, a causative verb has *two* subjects or agents: the promoter of the action and the one who performs it. As we have seen, the 'instigator' is put in the nominative case. The actual performer, if expressed, is generally put in the instrumental, although there are many exceptions to this rule. If we expand our example to 'He causes *or* has Devadatta make a mat' (using Devadatta in the sense of the indefinite 'so-and-so' of English), we will have to say सः देवदत्तेन कटं कारयति, *i.e.*, he causes the making of a mat through the instrumentality of Devadatta. Indian grammarians list various categories of verbs that require the immediate agent (here Devadatta) to be put into the *accusative*. It is better, however, to enter upon these exceptions when they are seen in a context. The single exception that ought to be

---

[1]For example, *lay* (cause to *lie*), *set* (cause to *sit*), *fell* (cause to *fall*), *raise* (cause to *rise*), *drench* (cause to *drink,* but now with the specialized meaning to 'wet'), *bait* (cause to *bite*).

mentioned here is that *intransitive* verbs, such as √गम् 'go', when made into causatives, take their immediate agent in the accusative; thus, सेनापतिः सैनिकान् योद्धुं प्रागमयत् 'The general caused the soldiers to go forward to fight'.

The formation of the causative stem from a root is a fairly simple procedure. The suffix *-ay-* with the thematic vowel *-a-, viz., -ay-a-,* is added to the root, the vowel of which is usually 'strengthened' by the substitution of its guṇa or vṛddhi counterpart. If the root ends in a consonant, guṇa is usually substituted, otherwise vṛddhi. Thus, from √*vid* 'know' is made the causative stem *ved-ay-a-* (*vedaya-*) 'cause to know', *i.e.,* inform; from √*tuṣ* 'be pleased', comes *toṣ-ay-a-* (*toṣaya-*) 'cause to be pleased'. *i.e.,* satisfy;[2] but from √*kṛ* 'do' (which ends in a vowel) comes *kār-ay-a-* (*kāraya-*) with vṛddhi of the vowel because it is final; and from √*nī* 'lead' comes *nāy-ay-a-* (*nāyaya-*) 'cause to lead'. Roots ending in *-ā,* as √*dhā* 'put', √*dā* 'give', √*sthā* 'stand', interpose a *-p-* between the *unchanged* root and the suffix *-ay-a,* the causative suffix, then, being in effect *-paya.* So, *dhā-paya-, dā-paya-, sthā-paya.* There are, of course, additional and exceptional formations, but it is the better part of valor to learn these details in the course of reading.

Causative stems are conjugated *precisely* like stems from roots of class X, the *cur* class, and no paradigm, therefore needs to be given.

Causative verbs constitute a derivative conjugation or verbal system, as they express a *modification* (*i.e.,* causation!) of the original sense of a root. In this respect they are like the desiderative stems, which express the sense of desiring whatever is meant by the root. Several examples of desideratives have been encountered in our readings, and, it will be recalled, their formation has been discussed. Derivative stems, *un*like the simple stems of the 10 classes, extend their stem *beyond* the so-called 'present system' (*i.e.,* the present, imperfect, imperative and optative) into the future, the periphrastic perfect, the infinitive, gerund, gerundive in *-i-tavya,* and, with loss of the suffix *-aya-* but retention of the vowel modification of the root (and the *-p-* if present), also into the past passive participle and gerund in *-ya.* Thus, if we use √*sthā* as an example, in addition to the forms *sthā-pay-a-ti* (स्थापयति), *a-sthā-pay-a-t* (अस्थापयत्), *sthā-pay-a-tu* (स्थापयतु) and *sthā-pay-e-t, i.e., -pay-a+ī+t* (स्थापयेत्), all of the 'present system', there can be formed from the full stem the future *sthā-pay-i-ṣya-ti* (स्थापयिष्यति); the periphrastic perfect *sthā-payām-āsa* (स्थापयामास); the infinitive *sthā-pay-i-*

---

[2]It should be noted that very often a Sanskrit causative is not to be rendered into English by 'cause *or* have someone do', but by a different verb, as here with the causative stems *vedaya-* and *toṣaya-*. Similarly, the causative *darśaya-* from √*dṛś* 'see' is usually to be rendered 'show', though literally 'cause to see'.

tum (स्थापयितुम्); gerund in *-i-tvā, sthā-pay-i-tvā* (स्थापयित्वा); the gerundive in *-i-tavya, sthā-pay-i-tavya* (स्थापयितव्य). The truncated stem (*i.e., without* the suffix) is seen in the compound gerund in *-ya, e.g., ava-sthā-p-ya* (अवस्थाप्य), the past passive participle *sthā-p-i-ta* (स्थापित), and the so-called present passive system, thus: *sthā-p-ya-te* (स्थाप्यते), *a-sthā-p-ya-ta* (अस्थाप्यत), *sthā-p-ya-tām* (स्थाप्यताम्), *sthā-p-ye-ta* (स्थाप्येत).

II. *Denominative Verbs.*

Another class of derivative verbs, hence formed *not* from the root, but from nouns, adjectives and very rarely from other parts of speech, is that of the denominative verbs. The name 'denominative' is borrowed from the Latin word *dēnōminātīvus,* which is based on the phrase *dē nōmine* 'from a noun or adjective' (as Latin *nōmen,* literally 'name', is used for both!). *Dēnōminātīvus,* then, means 'coming *or* derived from a noun or an adjective', and, as applied to the class of verbs we are about to consider, means 'verbs that are derived from nouns or adjectives'.

Denominative verbs are omnipresent in modern English, although those who have not studied Sanskrit and therefore do not know what a denominative verb is, are, of course, unaware of their existence. When we speak of 'salting' or 'peppering' our food, we are using the denominative verbs 'to salt' and 'to pepper', which are just the nouns 'salt' and 'pepper' employed (unchanged!) as verbs. Similarly, when we say 'to *winter* an army', 'to *number* the guests', 'to *document* a reference', and so on, we are using the nouns *winter, number* and *document* as verbs.

In Sanskrit, however, which uses *suffixes* to form new stems with a different function and meaning, we cannot simply use a noun as a verb, as we can so easily do in English. The suffix *-ya-* has to be added to a noun stem to make a *denominative stem,* to which, in turn are added the personal endings. This suffix *-ya-* is oftenest added to an unchanged noun stem, as to *namas* (नमस्) 'obeisance', yielding *namas-ya* (नमस्य) → *namasya-ti* (नमस्यति) 'makes *or* pays obeisance', and likewise *gopā-ya-ti* (गोपायति) from *gopā* 'cowherd', hence literally 'he is *or* acts like a cowherd', then generalized to 'watches over, protects'. As might be imagined, there are many special rules according to the final vowel or consonant of the stem. The only alteration that is sufficiently common to merit notice here is the lengthening of final *-a* of a noun or adjective stem, when the denominative is *intransitive,* whereas it is kept short for transitives. Thus, from the adjective *śithila* (शिथिल) 'loose' is made the *intransitive* stem *śithilā-ya* (शिथिलाय) thus, *śithilā-ya-te* (शिथिलायते) 'becomes loose', but *śithila-ya* (शिथिलय) with retained short *-a* of the stem, whence *śithila-ya-ti* (शिथिलयति) in the *active,* means 'makes loose, loosens'. Denominative formations like this can be made almost according to an author's need or desire. I am reminded of a small incident that took place many years ago in Washington, D.C. In the first snow of autumn I chanced to be walking along with a young Indian Sanskrit scholar who had just arrived in the United States. He was so struck by the sight of everything clothed in white, that he said quite instinctively: वाशिङ्टन्-नगरी हिमालयायते 'Washington is like the Himālaya!' Note here that the final *-a* of *Himālaya* is lengthened, and the verb is in the middle because it is intransitive, in conformity with this rule we have just given concerning the polarity of meaning between stems in *-aya-* (inflected in the active) and *-āya-* (in the middle).

The meanings that may attach to a noun or adjective that is converted into a denominative stem are quite varied, as is true also of English denominatives. Among the commonest meanings associated with the denominative noun stem are: be like *or* act like X (राजायते 'acts like a king'), use, make *or* perform X (पृतनायति 'fights' from पृतना 'a fight'), desire X (अश्वायति 'desires a horse *or* horses' from अश्व), regard as *or* treat as X (स्वामीयति 'regards as a lord *or* master' from स्वामिन्). In determining the sense of a particular denominative the context and dictionary must be the guide.

Finally, it must be added, in case it has not already been assumed, that all denominative stems are conjugated precisely like verb stems belonging to the *cur* class, as also are the causatives. All three types, *viz.*, verbs of the *cur* class, causatives and denominatives, have stems ending in *-ya-* and are conjugated alike.[3] It is only by the origin of the stem in each particular case that it can be known to which category a verb belongs.

III. *The Anaphoric Pronoun* एनद्.

एनद् is a pronoun of the third person, only used 'anaphorically', *i.e.*, with reference to someone or something that has been mentioned previously, and hence it is unemphatic and cannot stand first in a sentence. Its declension is very incomplete or defective, forms occurring only in the accusative of all numbers, the instrumental singular, and the genitive and locative dual; thus:

---

[3]Perhaps it may be of some interest that in the Veda the musical tone of Xth class verbs and causatives is on the first vowel of the suffix, *i.e., -áya-,* whereas that of the denominatives rests on the *-yá-*. To make the matter of the Vedic accent somewhat complicated, however, some denominatives have *causative* accent, *i.e., -áya-,* as *mantráyate* (मन्त्रयते) 'takes counsel', from *mantra* (मन्त्र).

		Masculine	*Neuter*	*Feminine*
Singular				
	Acc.	एनम्	एनद्	एनाम्
	Instr.	एनेन		एनया
Dual				
	Acc.	एनौ	एने	एने
	Gen.		एनयोः	
	Loc.		एनयोः	
Plural				
	Acc.	एनान्	एनानि	एनाः

As an example of the use of this common pronoun, we may take Bhagavadgītā II.23 which, with reference to the 'embodied one' (देही) or the individual soul, says:

नैनं छिन्दन्ति शास्त्राणि नैनं दहति पावकः ।
न चैनं क्लेदयन्त्यापो न शोषयति मारुतः ॥
'Swords cut him (एनं) not, fire does not burn him (एनं),
Nor does water render him (एनं) moist, the wind dries him not'.

Examples of sentences with causative and denominative verbs:

1. तस्मिन्महावने बहवः क्षुद्रजन्तवः शशकादयस्[1] तृष्णाकुलेन गजयूथेन जलमन्विच्छता पादाहतिभिश्चूर्णिताः ।
2. दुर्जनेन समं सख्यं प्रीतिं चापि[2] न कारयेत्[3] ।
उष्णो दहति चाङ्गारः[4] शीतः कृष्णायते[5] करम् ॥
3. यत्र विद्वज्जनो नास्ति श्लाघ्यस्तत्राल्पधीरपि ।
निरस्तपादपे देश एरण्डो[6] ऽपि द्रुमायते ॥
4. हे सारथे रथमत्र तस्य न्यग्रोधपादपस्य समीपे स्थापयेति स्वामिनस्तद् वचनमाकर्ण्य[7] सारथिर्यथाज्ञापयति[8] देव इत्यवदत् ।

5. यदा कृमयः पुस्तकस्य पत्त्राणि खादन्ति तदा तस्य बन्धनं शिथिलायेत ।
6. मम पुत्रा अनधिगतशास्त्रा उन्मार्गगामिनश्चेति चिन्तयित्वा स नृपतिरुद्विग्नमनाः पण्डितसभामकारयद्यथा सर्वेषु पण्डितेष्वेकं विन्देद्यः स्वपुत्रान्विद्यां नीतिं च ग्राहयितुं शक्नुयात् ।
7. एकदा कतिपयैर्धीवरैः कंचिज्जलाशयमागत्योक्तमस्माभिरिमां रात्रिं नगर्यामुषित्वा प्रातः प्रत्यागम्य सर्वे मत्स्या जालैर्बद्ध्वा व्यापादयितव्या अत्रैव पक्त्वा भक्षितव्याश्चेति ।[9]
8. यदि कश्चिद्राजा प्रजा धर्मेण न पालयेत्तर्हि स दण्डयितव्यः ।
9. यस्मिन्भावे रागद्वेषमोहानामर्चींषि नरेण तपोभिर्[10] ध्यानेन च निर्वाप्यन्ते स भावो निर्वाणमित्युच्यते ।
10. यस्मात्कारणात्तस्य कृषीवलस्य भोजनपचनार्थं काष्ठस्याभावो ऽभवत्तस्मात् परशुना स्वगृहसमीपस्थं वृक्षमपातयत्[11] ।

Notes

1. शशकादयस् qualifying क्षुद्रजन्तवः 'tiny creatures having hares as the beginning', *i.e.*, tiny creatures, such as hares, etc.

2. चापि hardly 'and also' but merely 'and'; note that प्रीतिं is practically a synonym of सख्यं here. Sanskrit writers are fond of accumulating synonymous or nearly synonymous words in the same sentence.

3. कारयेत् used here without causative meaning, which is not uncommon with √कृ. Note that the subject is indefinite ('one should not make').

4. चाङ्गारः The च is considerably out of its usual position: it connects the two verbs, दहति and कृष्णायते, and should strictly follow the latter.

5. कृष्णायते Theoretically we should expect कृष्णायति in accordance with the general law of polarity for denominatives in *-ayati* and *-āyate* (transitive and intransitive). The 'correct' usage is seen in द्रुमायते in the stanza given under 3.

6. एरण्डो *i.e.,* in the absence of trees one would have to make do with a mere castor-oil plant.

7. आकर्ण्य This denominative is made *not* from a noun, as are almost all the denominatives, but from an *un*used bahuvrīhi *ā-karṇa* 'having the ear to (something or someone)' *or* (as a noun) 'one who has the ear to . . .', so literally the verb means 'be *or* behave like one who has his ear to (something or someone)', *i.e.,* listen.

8. आज्ञापयति causative of आ-√ज्ञा 'attend to'; the transition of meaning from that of the simple verb to the causative is not entirely clear. Perhaps, however, the etymological sense of 'cause (someone) to attend to (something)' is sufficient to suggest the notion of ordering or commanding.

9. The basic construction of sentence 7 is: 'by some fishermen . . . it was said', *i.e.,* some fishermen said; all the words starting with अस्माभिर् and ending with भाक्षितव्याश्च are what they said. All the gerunds in the quoted words qualify अस्माभिर्. Perhaps the construction will become clearer if we supply तान्, *i.e.,* तान्मत्स्यान् before बद्ध्वा and पक्त्वा. Are the two gerundives simply future passives here, or is the sense of necessity ('should be' *or* 'must be') implied, as is so often the case with gerundives?

10. तपोभिर् The plural is used to denote many acts of तपस् over a period of time.

11. अपातयत् Note that this causative can be translated by a *true* English causative: 'felled'.

Vocabulary

अङ्गार, *m.* a coal.
अनधिगत, not approached, unapproached. [अन्- + *ppp.* अधि-√गम्]
अनु-√इष् (इच्छति, class VI), look for, search after.

अभाव, *m.* 'non-existence', absence.
अर्चिस्, *n.* a flame.
आकर्णय (आकर्णयति, *denom. verb*), 'have the ear (कर्ण) to (आ-)', listen to, hear.
आ-√ज्ञा (जानाति, class IX), notice; *caus.* आज्ञापयति, orders, commands.
आहृति, *f.* a blow *or* stroke.
उद्विग्न, *ppp.* उद्-√विज् (विजते, class VI), distressed.
उन्मार्ग, *m.* a by-way, evil way.
उष्ण, *adj.* hot.
एरण्ड, *m.* the castor-oil plant, *Ricinus Communis* or *Palma Christi.*
कतिपय, *adj.* some, a few.
कर, *m.* the hand.
कृमि, *m.* a worm.
कृषीवल, *m.* a peasant *or* farmer.
कृष्णाय (कृष्णायते, *denom. verb*), 'make black (कृष्ण)', blacken.
क्षुद्र, *adj.* small, tiny.
√खाद् (खादति, class I), chew, eat.
गामिन्, *adj.* going, going upon.
चूर्णय (चूर्णयति, *denom. verb*), 'turn *or* reduce to powder (चूर्ण)', crush.
जन्तु, *m.* a living being, creature.
जाल, *n.* a net.
तर्हि, *adv.* then; *correlative to* यदि in *conditional sentence.*
तृष्णा, *f.* thirst.
दण्डय (दण्डयति, *denom. verb*), 'apply a stick *or* punishment (दण्ड)', punish; *gerundive* दण्डयितव्य.
√दह् (दहति, class I), burn.
दुर्जन, *m.* an evil person, scoundrel.
द्रुमाय (द्रुमायते, *denom. verb*), 'pass for *or* be regarded as a tree (द्रुम)'.
द्वेष, *m.* hatred (as opposed to राग).
धी, *f.* intelligence.
धीवर, *m.* a fisherman.
निरस्त, *ppp.* निस्-2√उस् (अस्यति, class IV), thrown out, rooted out.
निर्वाण, *n.* a blowing out, being extinguished; cessation of worldly attachments, passions, etc.

निस्-√वा (वाति, class II), blow out, go out, be extinguished; *caus.* निर्वापयति, 'causes to blow out', extinguishes.

नीति, *f.* conduct, *esp.* right and wise conduct.

√पच् (पचति, class I), cook.

पत्त्र, *n.* a leaf *or* page (of a book). [often wrongly written पत्र]

पाद, *m.* the foot.

पादप, *m.* 'drinking with its feet', a tree.

√पत् (पतति, class I), fall; *caus.* पातयति, 'causes to fall', fells.

परशु, *m.* an axe.

पालय (पालयति, *denom. verb*), 'be a protector (पाल)', protect, watch over.

प्रजा, *f.* subject (of a prince or king).

प्रीति, *f.* friendship.

√बन्ध् (बध्नाति, class IX), bind; catch; *gerund* बद्ध्वा.

बन्धन, *n.* the act of binding, *then concretely* something bound, the binding (of a book).

√भक्ष् (भक्षति, class I), eat; *gerundive* भक्षितव्य.

भाव, *m.* (a way of) being, a condition *or* state.

मत्स्य, *m.* a fish.

मोह, *m.* infatuation.

यथा, *conj.* in order that (+ *opt.*).

यूथ, *n.* a herd.

राग, *m.* affection, passion.

वि-आ-√पद् (पद्यते, class IV), fall away, perish; *caus.* व्यापादयति 'causes to perish', kills; *gerundive* व्यापादयितव्य.

विद्वज्जन, *m.* a wise man.

शशक, *m.* a hare.

शिथिलाय (शिथिलायते, *denom. verb*), 'become loose (शिथिल)'.

शीत, *adj.* cold.

श्लाघ्य, *gerundive of* √श्लाघ् (श्लाघते, class), '(going) to be praised', worthy of praise.

समम्, *adv.* equally with, along with, with (+ *instr.*).

सख्य, *n.* companionship.

सभा, *f.* an assembly.

II. Kṛṣṇa's Reply

संजय उवाच ।
तं तथा कृपयाविष्टमश्रुपूर्णाकुलेक्षणम्[1] ।
विषीदन्तमिदं वाक्यमुवाच मधुसूदनः ॥१॥

श्रीभगवान्[2] उवाच ।
कुतस्[3] त्वा कश्मलमिदं विषमे[4] समुपस्थितम् ।
अनार्यजुष्टम्[5] अस्वर्ग्यमकीर्तिकरमर्जुन ॥२॥
क्लैब्यं मा स्म गमः[6] पार्थ नैतत्त्वय्युपपद्यते ।
क्षुद्रं हृदयदौर्बल्यं त्यक्त्वोत्तिष्ठ परंतप[7] ॥३॥

अर्जुन उवाच ।
कथं भीष्ममहं संख्ये द्रोणं च मधुसूदन ।
इषुभिः प्रतियोत्स्यामि पूजार्हावरिसूदन ॥ ४ ॥
गुरूनहत्वा[8] हि महानुभावाञ् श्रेयो भोक्तुं भैक्षमपीह लोके ।
हत्वार्थकामांस्तु गुरूनिहैव भुञ्जीय भोगान्रुधिरप्रदिग्धान् ॥५॥
न चैतद्विद्मः[9] कतरन्नो गरीयो[10] यद्वा जयेम यदि वा नो जयेयुः ।
यानेव हत्वा न जिजीविषामस्ते ऽवस्थिताः प्रमुखे धार्तराष्ट्राः ॥६॥
कार्पण्यदोषोपहतस्वभावः[11] पृच्छामि त्वा धर्मसंमूढचेताः[11] ।
यच्छ्रेयः[12] स्यान्निश्चितं ब्रूहि तन्मे शिष्यस्ते ऽहं शाधि[13] मां त्वां प्रपन्नम्[14] ॥७॥
न हि[15] प्रपश्यामि ममापनुद्याद् यच्[16] छोकमुच्छोषणमिन्द्रियाणाम्[17] ।
अवाप्य भूमावसपत्नमृद्धं राज्यं सुराणामपि चाधिपत्यम्[18] ॥८॥

संजय उवाच ।
एवमुक्त्वा हृषीकेशं गुडाकेशः परंतपः ।
न योत्स्य इति गोविन्दमुक्त्वा तूष्णीं बभूव ह ॥९॥

तमुवाच हृषीकेशः प्रहसन्निव[19] भारत ।
सेनयोरुभयोर्मध्ये विषीदन्तमिदं वचः ॥ १० ॥

श्रीभगवान् उवाच ।
अशोच्यानन्वशोचस्त्वं प्रज्ञावादांश्च[20] भाषसे ।
गतासूनगतासूंश्च नानुशोचन्ति पण्डिताः ॥ ११ ॥
न त्वेवाहं जातु नासं[21] न त्वं नेमे जनाधिपाः ।
न चैव न भविष्यामः[22] सर्वे वयमतः परम् ॥ १२ ॥
देहिनो[23] ऽस्मिन्यथा देहे कौमारं यौवनं जरा ।
तथा देहान्तरप्राप्तिर्धीरस्[24] तत्र[25] न मुह्यति ॥ १३ ॥
मात्रास्पर्शास्तु[26] कौन्तेय शीतोष्णसुखदुःखदाः[27] ।
आगमापायिनो[28] ऽनित्यास्तांस्तितिक्षस्व भारत ॥ १४ ॥
यं हि न व्यथयन्त्येते पुरुषं[29] पुरुषर्षभ ।
समदुःखसुखं धीरं सो ऽमृतत्वाय कल्पते ॥ १५ ॥
नासतो विद्यते भावो नाभावो विद्यते सतः ।
उभयोरपि दृष्टो ऽन्तस्त्वनयोस्तत्त्वदर्शिभिः[30] ॥ १६ ॥
अविनाशि तु तद्[31] विद्धि येन सर्वमिदं[32] ततम् ।
विनाशम्[33] अव्ययस्यास्य न कश्चित्कर्तुम्[33] अर्हति[34] ॥ १७ ॥
अन्तवन्त इमे देहा नित्यस्योक्ताः शरीरिणः[35] ।
अनाशिनो ऽप्रमेयस्य तस्माद्युध्यस्व भारत ॥ १८ ॥
य एनं[36] वेत्ति हन्तारं यश्चैनं मन्यते हतम् ।
उभौ तौ[37] न विजानीतो[38] नायं हन्ति न हन्यते ॥ १९ ॥
न जायते म्रियते वा कदाचिन् नायं भूत्वा भविता वा न भूयः[39] ।
अजो नित्यः शाश्वतो ऽयं पुराणो न हन्यते हन्यमाने शरीरे[40] ॥ २० ॥
वेदाविनाशिनं[41] नित्यं य एनमजमव्ययम् ।
कथं स पुरुषः पार्थ कं घातयति हन्ति कम्[42] ॥ २१ ॥
वासांसि जीर्णानि यथा विहाय नवानि गृह्णाति नरो ऽपराणि ।

तथा शरीराणि विहाय जीर्णान्यन्यानि संयाति नवानि देही ॥ २२ ॥
नैनं छिन्दन्ति शस्त्राणि नैनं दहति पावकः ।
न चैनं क्लेदयन्त्य्[43] आपो न शोषयति[43] मारुतः ॥ २३ ॥
अच्छेद्यो ऽयमदाह्यो ऽयमक्लेद्यो ऽशोष्य[44] एव च ।
नित्यः सर्वगतः स्थाणुरचलो ऽयं सनातनः ॥ २४ ॥
अव्यक्तो ऽयमचिन्त्यो ऽयमविकार्यो ऽयमुच्यते ।
तस्मादेवं विदित्वैनं नानुशोचितुमर्हसि ॥ २५ ॥
अथ चैनं[45] नित्यजातं[46] नित्यं वा मन्यसे मृतम् ।
तथापि त्वं महाबाहो नैनं शोचितुमर्हसि ॥ २६ ॥
जातस्य हि ध्रुवो मृत्युर्ध्रुवं जन्म मृतस्य च ।
तस्मादपरिहार्ये ऽर्थे[47] न त्वं शोचितुमर्हसि ॥ २७ ॥
अव्यक्तादीनि[48] भूतानि व्यक्तमध्यानि भारत ।
अव्यक्तनिधनान्येव तत्र का परिदेवना ॥ २८ ॥
आश्चर्यवत्पश्यति कश्चिदेनमाश्चर्यवद्वदति तथैव चान्यः ।
आश्चर्यवच्चैनमन्यः शृणोति श्रुत्वाप्येनं वेद न चैव कश्चित् ॥ २९ ॥
देही नित्यमवध्यो ऽयं देहे सर्वस्य भारत ।
तस्मात्सर्वाणि भूतानि न त्वं शोचितुमर्हसि ॥ ३० ॥
स्वधर्ममपि चावेक्ष्य[49] न विकम्पितुमर्हसि ।
धर्म्याद्धि युद्धाच्छ्रेयो ऽन्यत्क्षत्रियस्य[50] न विद्यते ॥ ३१ ॥
यदृच्छया चोपपन्नं[51] स्वर्गद्वारमपावृतम् ।
सुखिनः क्षत्रियाः पार्थ लभन्ते युद्धमीदृशम्[52] ॥ ३२ ॥

(Bhagavadgītā II. 1-32).

Notes

1. अश्रुपूर्णाकुलेक्षणम् 'whose eyes were full of tears and (therefore) agitated'. The compound as a whole is a bahuvrīhi (as it is adjectival and ends in a

noun!). The first part is a karmadhāraya consisting of अश्रुपूर्ण and आकुल, of which the latter expresses the consequence of the former, *i.e.,* full of tears and, as a consequence, agitated. An alternative possibility is to bisect the compound between अश्रुपूर्ण and आकुलेक्षणं, in this way taking आकुल *not* as a consequence of अश्रुपूर्ण, but as a consequence of the agitating or troubling sight that confronted Arjuna as he saw all his relatives in both armies. According to this view we may translate: 'whose eyes troubled (at the sight) were full of tears'.

2. श्रीभगवान् The noun श्री 'lustre, splendor, grace' is very often employed as a sort of honorific prefix to the names or epithets of gods, as before भगवान् 'The Blessed One' here, also before the titles of books as श्रीभगवद्गीता, श्रीमहाभारत. This usage is probably just an abbreviation for the adjective श्रीमत् 'possessing lustre, splendor', *i.e.,* illustrious, which is, in fact, frequently used in place of श्री in such an expression.

3. कुतस् It should be borne in mind that the suffix -तस् in various words like कुतस् here and अतस्, ततस् imparts an ablatival value to the pronoun roots to which it is attached. Thus, कुतस् means 'from what' etymologically. In this passage, then, Kṛṣṇa is asking Arjuna, in effect, what the source of his faintheartedness is.

4. विषमे 'in (a time of) distress'.

5. अनार्यजुष्टम् Remember that the branch of the Indo-Europeans that became the Persians on the one hand and the Indians on the other in the course of their settling down called themselves 'Āryans'. This compound might be construed to mean 'acceptable to non-Āryans' or 'not acceptable to Āryans', depending on whether the negative prefix अन्- is taken only with आर्य ('non-Āryans') or with आर्यजुष्ट ('acceptable to Āryans') which it negates ('*un*-acceptable to Āryans'). Alternatively it is possible to take आर्य in the sense of 'noble', *i.e.*, not as a proper name, a sense which is common enough in the later literature.

6. क्लैब्यं मा स्म गमः In Sanskrit a prohibition, *i.e.,* a command *not* to do this or that, is expressed by the negative adverb मा either with the imperative or with the imperfect or aorist without the augment. गमः is the aorist of √गम्

'go' devoid of augment. The unaugmented imperfect गच्छः or the imperative गच्छ could equally have been used. The meaningless particle स्म is frequently used with the augmentless tenses in this construction. 'Go not to impotence!' is, of course, tantamount to saying 'Do not behave like a eunuch!'

7. परंतप 'scorcher of the foe', a frequent epithet in the Gītā; पर, *literally* 'other' also means the 'other one' in the sense of the one on the other side, hence, one's foe. In this compound पर is put in the accusative (as indicated by the anusvāra!) in spite of the general rule that all members of a compound except the last are in their stem form, *i.e., without* case ending. There are occasional exceptions to this, and some common compounds are found with either form of the prior member, as वनचर or वनेचर 'moving in the woods'. Which is used in a given instance is probably largely a matter of metre or the rhythm of the sentence (the latter a very important consideration of Indian authors). परंतप is not exclusively an epithet of Arjuna, but is applied to other heroes also.

8. अहत्वा Note that putting the negative adverb अ- before a gerund does not cause the suffix -त्वा to be replaced by -य, as is the case with other adverbial prefixes, *e.g.,* निहत्य.

The four stanzas 5-8 are composed in the *triṣṭubh* metre, each pāda of which has eleven syllables in contrast to the eight syllables of the śloka or *anuṣṭubh* metre which we have had so far. Pādas *a* and *b* of stanza 6 have each an extra syllable which changes them to *jagatī*. The shift to the *triṣṭubh* occurs in the Gītā when the poet wishes to impart greater elevation to his thought, as here, when Arjuna relates the consequences of fighting and not fighting, and also in Chapter XI which contains the mystic vision of God.

9. विद्मः present first plural of $^1\sqrt{}$विद् (वेत्ति, class II) 'know'; *v.* Lesson Twenty-Six, p. 350.

10. कतरन्नो गरीयो 'which (of the two) is better for us'; the interrogative pronoun कतरन् (for कतरद् by sandhi) is explained by the two *if*-clauses in the following *pāda* ('if we should conquer or if . . .'). The words कतरन्नो गरीयो are in apposition to एतद् 'this'; thus, 'And we do not know *this, viz.,* which (of the two) is better for us: if we should conquer or if . . .'.

It ought to be noted that the pronoun कतर is declined like तद्, hence the nominative neuter singular कतरद्, *not* कतरम्, as would be so if it were a neuter *a*-stem. In many printed additions of the Gītā, however, कतरं is wrongly given here for कतरन्. The change of the -द् of कतरद् to -न् is due to the nasalizing influence of the न्- of the following नो.

11. Both compounds (कार्पण्यदोषोपहतस्वभावः and धर्मसंमूढचेताः) are bahuvrīhis with implicit causal value; *cf.* notes 26, 34 and 39 in Lesson Twenty-seven.

12. यच्छ्रेयः by sandhi for यद् श्रेयः, with regressive assimilation of -द् to -च् and progressive assimilation of श्- to छ्-.

13. शाधि imperative second singular active of √शास् (शास्ति, class II), for शास्धि, the -स्- of which drops out before the following voiced sound.

14. मां त्वां प्रपन्नम् '(teach) me (who have) come to you'; प्र-√पद् is often used of a pupil approaching a teacher for instruction.

15. हि 'for',[4] a mildly causal conjunction which introduces the reason for Arjuna's declaring himself Kṛṣṇa's pupil and in need of his instruction.

16. यच् subject of अपनुद्याद् and is referent to an understood तद्; thus, 'I foresee not [that तद्] which (यच्) would dispel the sorrow . . .'. अपनुद्याद्, by sandhi for °नुद्यात्, is a so-called 'precative', a name applied to an optative of the *s*-aorist, usually expressing a wish, but here a contingency ('would dispel'). It is formed by adding the optative suffix -या + the original aorist sign -स् to the root. Thus, from √नुद् the first person is नुद्यासम् *i.e., nud-yā-s-am*), second person नुद्यास् or नुद्याः (for *nud-yā-s-s*, with loss of final *-s* by the law requiring only one final consonant) and third person नुद्यात्, the form here, (for *nud-yā-s-t*, with loss of *-s-* and retention of *-t* to suggest the third person, which in secondary forms ends in *-t*).

17. इन्द्रियाणाम् a sort of 'objective' genitive with उच्छोषणम् 'making dry', somewhat on the order of the English genitive in 'His behavior was indicative

---

[4]The conjunction 'for' in English (like हि in Sanskrit) used to be a *mildly* subordinating conjunction, introducing a cause expressed independently of the main assertion. In recent years, however, it has often come to be used as an equivalent of the subordinating conjunctions 'since, because, as'.

of the way the matter should be handled'. On this model we might translate उच्छोषणमिन्द्रियाणां by 'desiccative of the senses', except that it savors of ponderosity. The adjective उच्छोषण is formed from the causative stem उच्छोषय (with loss of the causative suffix *-aya-*) + the suffix *-ana.* √शुष् (शुष्यति, class IV) is an *intransitive* verb meaning 'be dry'; the causative शोषयति 'causes to be dry', *i.e.,* makes dry, is the *transitive* counterpart.

Grief (शोक) is here said to 'dry up' the senses because in times of grief the senses are retracted from the objects toward which they normally gravitate and become inert or inactive: sounds, sights, tastes, etc. are simply not consciously attended to.

18. सुराणामपि चाधिपत्यम् It is not to be supposed that by 'overlordship of the gods' is meant *control* over them. Rather is the sense the 'overlordship that the gods have'; सुराणाम् is, then, a sort of subjective genitive.

19. प्रहसन्निव 'almost bursting into laughter', the idea being *not* that Kṛṣṇa is ridiculing or in any way mocking Arjuna's dilemma, but rather mitigating it, with a lighthearted shrug, so to speak, so as to allay Arjuna's distress. The particle इव is frequently used to tone down an expression or soften its effect.

20. च here with a slightly adversative force, a mild 'yet' or 'but': 'yet (*or* but) you speak words of wisdom'; or perhaps better as a question: 'but do you speak words of wisdom?'

21. न त्वेवाहं जातु नासं 'But surely (एव) never (न . . . जातु) have I not existed (न आसं)', an assertion which is then extended to Arjuna (त्वं 'you') and all the others who are present (इमे जनाधिपाः).

22. न चैव न भविष्यामः 'nor surely (एव) shall we not be' with the adverbial phrase अतः परम् added to emphasize the futurity.

23. देहिनो This may be taken as a predicate 'genitive of possession' or a 'genitive quasi-dative', in either case with the appropriate form of √भू 'be' understood in both the यथा- and तथा-clauses: 'Just as (on the part) of the individual (*or* for the individual) [there are] childhood . . . in this [same] body, so [there is] the acquisition of another body [of the individual]' or freely 'Just as the individual has (*i.e.,* experiences) childhood, youth and old

age in this same body, so he gets another body [and has the same experiences]'. देहिन् means literally 'having *or* possessing a body', hence 'an individual' or 'the soul (as the possessor of the body)'.

24. धीरस् There are two homonymous words धीर, the one, derived from √धी (दीधेति) 'think', meaning 'thoughtful, wise', the other from √धृ (धारयति) 'hold', meaning 'firm, steadfast, resolute'. They can be distinguished only by their use in context. Here the first धीर 'wise' seems clearly meant, whereas in śloka 15 the second is the more probable.

25. तत्र 'in this', with reference to what has just been said about the individual soul experiencing childhood, etc. and then acquiring another body in order to undergo the same states again.

26. मात्रास्पर्शास् Among the many meanings of मात्रा (etymologically 'measure' from √मा 'measure') is 'an element', *i.e.*, a basic constituent of the material world, then 'matter' and 'the material world' generally. Here, then, मात्रास्पर्शास् means 'contacts with the material world'.

27. शीतोष्णसुखदुःखदाः an accusative tatpuruṣa compound formed with the verbal of √दा 'give' and the fourfold dvandva compound (शीतोष्णसुखदुःख) as its object: 'giving (the sensations of) cold, hot, pleasure and pain'.

28. आगमापायिनो literally 'having a coming and a going away', *i.e.*, transitory, evanescent, a dvandva compound (आगम 'coming' + अपाय 'going away') to which the possessive suffix *-in* has been added.

29. पुरुषं This is the noun to which यं ('whom') refers, incorporated into the relative clause and later picked up by the correlative सो. The construction, then, is 'For *what man* (यं . . .पुरुषं) these [contacts with the material world] do not disturb, . . . *he* is fit for immortality'.

30. Two principles of reality are separately stated in stanza 16; *viz.*, 1. what does *not* (already) *exist* does not come into being, *i.e.*, does not, indeed cannot, evolve into anything, and 2. what (already) *exists* does not cease to exist. These principles do not concern the transitory world of material objects referred to in the previous stanza, but the higher, eternal reality of the individual soul and the Absolute or substrate of all things, which are

usually interpreted to mean the 'boundary' or 'dividing-line', but it is not clear why we should speak of a 'boundary' or 'dividing-line' with regard to the two principles: rather it is their *finality* (अन्त) as inescapable truths that is perceived 'by those who see the true nature of things (तत्त्वदर्शिभि:)'.

31. तद् 'that', defined by the following relative clause येन सर्वमिदं ततम् ('by which all this world is diffused'), with reference to the Absolute (Brahman), which runs like a thread through all material things. In this stanza the Absolute and the individual soul are treated as an identical spiritual entity, but the focus shifts thereafter (starting with stanza 18) to the individual soul, the embodied one (शरीरिन्).

32. सर्वमिदं 'all this', a standard expression for 'this world', along with the reversed इदं सर्वम् ('this all') and simply इदम् ('this'); *cf.* note 4 (end) in Lesson Fourteen.

33. विनाशम् ... कर्तुम् Note the periphrasis 'to make ... a destruction of (+ *gen.*)' for the simple 'to destroy' (विनाशयितुम्). These compound expressions consisting of a noun + √कृ are very common, as is also their counterpart in some modern Indian vernaculars.

34. अर्हति here equivalent to शक्नोति 'can', but in most contexts it expresses necessity.

35. शरीरिण: genitive masculine singular of शरीरिन् 'having a body (शरीर)', *i.e.*, the soul; *cf.* देहिनस् in 13. It is qualified by the three adjectives नित्यस्य, अनाशिनो and (अ)प्रमेयस्य.

36. एनं referring to शरीरिण: in stanza 18: 'One who knows him (the embodied one) as the slayer ...'. It is used thus anaphorically repeatedly in the following lines.

37. उभौ तौ correlative to the two relatives (य and यश्) in the preceding line.

38. विजानीतो Be particularly careful about the analysis of this verb form! Start out by assuming that the final -ओ (*-o*) stands for अ: (*-aḥ*) by sandhi, an assumption, by the way, which is true of *most* instances of final *-o*.

39. न जायते, etc. The negative preceding जायते is carried over to म्रियते ('He (the embodied one, *i.e.,* the soul) is not born [n]or does he ever die'. Similarly in the next pāda it is necessary to treat वा as [न] वा with continued carryover of the negation and translate: '[n]or, not having come to be (न ... भूत्वा), will he not be again (अयं ... भविता न भूय:)'. Otherwise there will be one negative too few. For we cannot say: 'or, not having come to be, will he not be again', still less '[n]or, *having come to be,* will he not be again', as this quite definitely postulates that the soul *is born* ('having come to be'!) , which counteracts the initial words of न जायते.

भविता is an example of what is called the 'periphrastic future', which was mentioned in Lesson Nineteen. The form here is the third person singular, and its subject is अयं. In the *third* person this future consists only of an agent noun in *-tṛ/-itṛ* formed from the root whose future is being expressed. The agent noun is always in the nominative case and inflected in the three numbers according to the rules given in Lesson Twenty-three. The third persons, singular, dual and plural, of √हन् (हन्ति) 'kill' (whose agent noun occurs in the accusative हन्तारं in stanza 19) are:

हन्ता 'he (she, it) will slay',

हन्तारौ they two *or* both will slay', and

हन्तार: they (plural) will slay'.

From this it may be seen that भविता is the third singular 'will be' of √भू, the agent noun of which is भवितृ. The other persons of the periphrastic future, though not relevant here, are made exclusively from the *nominative singular* of the agent noun in combination with the appropriate form of the present (!) of √अस् (अस्ति) 'be'. Thus, from √हन्

1.	*hantāsmi* (*hantā-asmi*)	*hantāsvaḥ* (*hantā-svaḥ*)	*hantāsmaḥ* (*hantā-smaḥ*)
2.	*hantāsi* (*hantā-asi*)	*hantāsthaḥ* (*hantā-sthaḥ*)	*hantāstha* (*hantā-stha*)

Note that the *nominative singular* is used throughout as a sort of 'frozen' form without regard to number.

40. हन्यमाने शरीरे locative absolute.

41. वेदाविनाशिनं to be resolved into वेद अविनाशिनं; वेद is a *non*-reduplicated perfect of 1√विद् (वेत्ति) 'know' and, curiously, has *present* meaning.[5] Its subject is the relative pronoun य which is displaced to the middle of its clause, thus: 'Who knows him as indestructible, unborn, imperishable, how can that man … ?'
42. कथं स पुरुष: etc. *literally* '*How* does that man (who knows him as indestructible, etc.) have *whom* killed, [*how*] does he kill *whom* ?' In English we cannot usually accumulate interrogatives in this way, although in conversation it is sometimes done for effect, as: 'What do you want me to say to whom?' In translating this passage it is better to substitute 'anyone' for the second interrogative (कं 'whom'). Note, finally, that घातयति, though a *denominative* in formation (from the noun घात 'a slaying'), has *causative* meaning. For a denominative thus to have causative meaning is not as contradictory as it may at first seem, as the literal sense of a denominative can be 'bring about such-and-such' with the implication that the actual agent is other than the grammatical agent.

43. क्लेदयन्ति and शोषयति are the causatives of √क्लिद् and √शुष् respectively, which are *intransitive* verbs, and so these causatives are in effect just their transitive counterparts ('cause to be moist' = moisten something; 'cause to be dry' = dry something).

44. अच्छेद्यो, अदाह्यो, अक्लेद्यो, अशोष्य All these are negated gerundives that have the secondary sense of 'not being able to be …': 'cannot be cut, cannot be burned' etc. The first two are from the simple roots (छिद् and दह्), the last two are from the causative. The frequent repetition of अयम् in this and the following śloka serves to keep the subject of discussion continually before us. Similarly, the various repetitions of the pronoun एनम्; *e.g.*, in ślokas 26 and 29.

45. अथ च 'But if', answered by तथापि 'even so' in the second line; च here has a slightly adversative force, and अथ serves as a conditional conjunction, equivalent to यदि.

---

[5]It is interesting to note that the precise cognates of the Sanskrit perfect *veda* (वेद) 'knows' in various Indo-European languages also have present meaning; thus, for example, Greek *(w)oĩde,* Gothic *wáit,* Old English *wāt* (as in the now obsolete descendant 'I *wot*'), Old High German *weiz* (whence Modern German *weiss*).

46. नित्यजातं 'constantly [re-]born', modifying एनमं; in its counterpart नित्यं...मृतम् 'constantly dead', *i.e.*, constantly dying, the parts are expressed analytically, whether for variety of expression or *metri causa*.

47. (अ)परिहार्ये ऽर्थे locative absolute.

48. The three adjectives अव्यक्तादीनि, व्यक्तमध्यानि and अव्यक्तनिधनानि are bahuvrīhis modifying भूतानि, literally 'beings have unmanifest beginnings, manifest middles, and unmanifest ends', or freely 'the beginnings of beings are unmanifest, their middles are manifest and their ends are unmanifest'. The import of this seems to be that material things, *i.e.*, the phenomenal world, are constantly evolving out of undifferentiated matter and returning to it, whereas the soul is eternally the same.

49. स्वधर्ममपि चावेक्ष्य 'Moreover (अपि), having looked to your own law, *i.e.*, having taken it under consideration.

50. क्षत्रियस्य probably best taken as a 'genitive quasi-dative'.

51. यदृच्छया चोपपन्नं There are two ways of construing these words, neither of which affects the sense of the stanza. Pādas *a* and *b* may be taken as forming a sentence: 'And [a righteous battle] which has come up by chance (is) an open door to heaven'; or, alternatively, उपपन्नं may be taken with युद्धमीदृशम् in pāda d, thus: '(And happy are the kṣatriyas who get) *such a battle as this befallen by chance*, an open door to heaven'.

52. सुखिनः क्षत्रियाः (etc.) The emphatic word, as beginning the pāda, is सुखिनः, and this emphasis may perhaps be best conveyed in English by translating सुखिनः as though it were predicative to क्षत्रियाः and as though लभन्ते were in a relative clause explanatory of it; thus: 'Happy (are) the warriors (who) get such a battle!'

Vocabulary

अकीर्तिकर, *adj.* causing disgrace (अकीर्ति).
अक्लेद्य, *negative gerundive of* क्लेदयति, *caus.* √क्लिद् (क्लिद्यति, class IV), not able to be made wet *or* moistened.
अचल, *adj.* 'not moving', immobile.

अचिन्त्य, *negative gerundive of* √चिन्त् (चिन्तयति), not able to be thought of, unthinkable, incomprehensible.

अच्छेद्य, *negative gerundive of* √छिद् (छिनत्ति, class VII), not able to be cut.

अज, *adj.* unborn.

अत: परम्, *adv. phrase* from now on, hereafter.

अदाह्य, *negative gerundive of* √दह् (दहति, class I), not able to be burned.

अधिपत्य, *n.* overlordship, sovereignty.

अनाशिन्, *adj.* imperishable.

अनुभाव, *m.* dignity, authority.

अनु-√शुच् (शोचति, class I), grieve for, lament, be sorry for (+ *acc.*).

अन्त, *m.* end, boundary; limit, dividing-line; finality.

अन्तर, *n.* interval, distance between two things; difference; *at end of a cpd.* another (*literally*, 'having such-and-such as a difference').

अन्तवत्, *adj.* 'having *or* possessing an end', perishable.

अप्, *plurale tantum,*[6] water.

अप-√नुद् (नुदति, class VI), push *or* drive away, dispel, remove.

अपर, *adj.* other.

अपरिहार्य, *negative gerundive of* परि-√हृ (हरति, class I), 'not able to be gotten around', unavoidable.

अपवृत, *ppp.* अप-[1]√वृ (वृणोति, class V), uncovered, opened up.

अप्रमेय, *negative gerundive of* प्र-√मा (मिमीते, class III), not able to be measured, immeasurable, unlimited.

अभाव, *m.* non-being, not coming to be.

अमृतत्व, *n.* immortality.

अरिसूदन, *m.* a destroyer of the foe; [*cf.* परंतप above].

अर्थ, *m.* a thing.

√अर्ह् (अर्हति, class I), be able, can.

अर्ह, *adj.* deserving, worthy.

अव-√आप् (आप्नोति, class V), attain, obtain.

अवध्य, *negative gerundive of* √वध् (वधति, class I), not able to be slain.

अवस्थित, *ppp.* अव-√स्था (तिष्ठति, class I), arrayed.

अविकार्य, *negative gerundive of* वि-√कृ (करोति, class VIII), not able to be changed, unchangeable.

---

[6]*plurale tantum* 'only plural', *i.e.,* declined *only* in the plural.

अविनाशिन्, *adj.* imperishable.

अवेक्ष्य, *gerund* अव-√ईक्ष् (ईक्षते, class I), having looked after, regarded.

अव्यक्त, *adj.* unmanifest.

अव्यय, *adj.* imperishable.

अशोच्य, *negative gerundive of* शोचयति, *caus.* √शुच् (शोचति, class I), not to be lamented.

अशोष्य, *negative gerundive of* शोषयति, *caus.* √शुष् (शुष्यति, class IV), not able to be dried.

अश्रु, *n.* a tear.

असत्, *negative part.* √अस् (अस्ति, class II), not being *or* existing; *as n.* that which is not *or* does not exist; the non-existent.

असपत्न, *adj.* without a rival *or* adversary.

असु, *m.* the spirit *or* soul.

अस्वर्ग्य, *adj.* not leading to heaven.

आकुल, *adj.* agitated.

आगमापायिन्, *adj.* coming and going, transitory.

आश्चर्यवत्, *adv.* 'like a miracle', by a miracle, by a lucky chance.

इन्द्रिय, *n.* a sense organ.

इषु, *m.* an arrow.

इह, *adv.* here.

ईक्षण, *n.* the eye.

ईदृश, *adj.* of this sort, such.

उच्छोषण, *adj.* causing to dry up (उद्), drying up, desiccating.

उप-√पद् (पद्यते, class IV), be fit for (+ *loc.*).

उपपन्न, *ppp.* उप-√पद् (पद्यते, class IV), having come to, approached.

उपहत, *ppp.* उप-√हन् (हन्ति, class II), afflicted, affected, distressed.

उभ, *adj.* both.

ऋद्ध, *ppp.* √ऋध् (ऋध्नोति, class V), prosperous.

कतर, *interr. adj.* which (of the two)?

कदाचिद्, *indef. adv.* at any time, ever.

कश्मल, *n.* consternation, faint-heartedness, pusillanimity.

कार्पण्य, *n.* compassion, pity.

कुतः, *interr. adv.* from where, whence? why?

√क्लृप् (कल्पते, class I), be in order, be well ordered *or* regulated, be fit *or* suitable for (+ *dat.*).

कौमार, *n.* childhood.

√क्लिद् (क्लिद्यति, class IV), be wet; *caus.* क्लेदयति, 'causes to be wet', makes wet, moistens.

क्लैब्य, *n.* impotence, unmanliness.

क्षुद्र, *adj.* small; trifling, petty.

गरीयस्, *comparative of* गुरु ('heavy'), heavier; greater; dearer, more precious, better.

घातय, (*denom. verb*), 'bring about *or* cause a slaying', *from* घात 'a slaying'. [*used as caus. of* √हन्]

चेतस्, *n.* the mind.

√छिद्, (छिनत्ति, class VII), split, cut.

√जन् (जायते, class IV), be born.

जनाधिप, *m.* 'lord of the people', a king.

जन्मन्, *n.* birth.

जरा, *f.* old age.

जातु, *adv.* at all, ever.

जीर्ण, *ppp.* √जॄ (जीर्यति), grown old; worn out.

√जीव् (जीवति, class I), live; *desid.* जिजीविषति, wishes to live.

जुष्ट, *adj.* acceptable [strictly, *ppp.* √जुष् (जुषते, class VI), 'taste, relish; accept with pleasure'].

तत, *ppp.* √तन् (तनोति, class VIII), extended, spread, diffused.

तत्त्वदर्शिन्, *adj.* seeing the truth; *as m.* one who sees the truth (*i.e.*, the true nature of reality).

तथापि, *conj. adv.* even so, nevertheless.

√तिज् (तेजते, class I), be *or* become sharp; *desiderative* तितिक्षते, 'desires to become sharp *or* firm', *then* bears with firmness, suffers *or* endures patiently.

तूष्णीम्, *adv.* in silence; *with* √भू become silent.

देह, *m.* the body.

देहिन्, *adj.* 'having *or* possessing a body'; *as m.* the spirit *or* soul (as enveloped in the body); an individual (as possessing a spirit *or* soul).

दोष, *m.* fault, defect.

दौर्बल्य, *n.* weakness.

द्वार, *n.* a door.

धर्म्य, *adj.* righteous.

[1]धीर, *adj.* wise; [2]धीर, *adj.* steadfast, resolute. [*v.* note 24 on these homonymous words]

ध्रुव, *adj.* certain, sure.

नव, *adj.* new.

नित्य, *adj.* constant, eternal, everlasting.

नित्यजात, *adj.* always born, constantly born.

निधन, *m. or n.* end, death.

निश्चितम्, *adv.* positively, truly.

परंतप, *m.* scorcher of the foe. [*v.* note 7 on meaning and form]

परिदेवना, *f.* lamentation, grief, sorrow; concern.

पावक, *m.* fire.

पुराण, *adj.* old, ancient.

पूजा, *f.* honor, respect, worship.

पूर्ण, *adj.* filled with *or* full of (+ *instr.*).

प्रज्ञावाद, *m.* a word of wisdom.

प्रति-√युध् (युध्यते, class IV), fight against (प्रति) (+ *acc.*); *fut.* प्रतियोत्स्यति (active!).

प्रदिग्ध, *ppp.* प्र-√दिह् (देग्धि), smeared, besmeared.

प्रपन्न, *ppp.* उप-√पद् (पद्यते, class IV), having come to, approached.

प्रमुखे, *adv.* opposite, in front.

प्र-√हस् (हसति, class I), burst into laughter.

प्राप्ति, *f.* the act of gaining, getting, obtaining, attaining, acquisition.

भगवत्, *adj.* 'possessing (good) fortune', blessed, heavenly, august.

भाव, *m.* being, coming to be.

√भुज् (भुनक्ति, class VII), enjoy; *infin.* भोक्तुम्.

भूत, *n.* a being, creature.

भूयः, *adv.* again.

भैक्ष, *n.* asking alms, begging.

भोग, *m.* joy.

मध्य, *m. or n.* the middle.

√मन् (मन्यते, class IV), think.

मात्रास्पर्श, *m.* material contact, contact with material objects.

मारुत, *m.* the wind.

√मुह् (मुह्यति, class IV), be confused *or* bewildered.

√मृ (म्रियते, prob. in origin a passive), die.

मृत, *ppp.* √मृ (म्रियते), dead.

मृत्यु, *m.* death.

यदृच्छया, *adv.* by chance, perchance.

यद्वा . . . यदि वा, *alternative conditional conj.* if ... or if, whether ... or.

यौवन, *n.* youth.

राज्य, *n.* a kingdom.

रुधिर, *n.* blood.

वासस्, *n.* a garment.

वि-√कम्प् (कम्पते, class I), tremble, waver.

वि-√ज्ञा (जानाति, class IX), understand, know.

1√विद् (वेत्ति, class II), know; *perf.* वेद 'knows' (*i.e.,* with present meaning!); *gerund* विदित्वा, having known.

विनाश, *m.* destruction.

विषम, *adj.* uneven, rugged, rough; *as n.* difficulty, distress.

वि-√हा (जहाति, class III), leave apart *or* aside, discard.

व्यक्त, *adj.* manifest.

√व्यथ् (व्यथते, class I), be disturbed *or* agitated; *caus.* व्यथयति, 'causes to be disturbed *or* agitated; disturbs, agitates.

शरीर, *n.* the body.

शरीरिन्, *adj.* 'having *or* possessing a body', embodied; *as m.* the soul.

शस्त्र. *n.* a cutting implement, a knife *or* sword.

शाश्वत, *adj.* eternal, everlasting.

√शास् (शास्ति, class II), teach, instruct.

√शुष् (शुष्यति, class IV), be dry; *caus.* शोषयति, 'causes to be dry'.

श्रेयस्, *comparative adj*. more beautiful, better

संख्य, *n.* conflict, battle; field of battle.

सत्, *present participle* √अस् 'be', being *or* existing; *as n.* that which is *or* exists; the existent.

सनातन, *adj.* everlasting, eternal.

सम, *adj.* even, like, equal, the same.

समुपस्थित, *ppp.* सम्-उप-√स्था (तिष्ठति, class I), approached, come to; befallen.

संमूढ, *ppp.* सम्-√मुह् (मुह्यति, class IV), perplexed, bewildered.

सम्-√या (याति, class II), go together, join.

सर्वगत, *adj.* 'gone to all', omnipresent.

स्थाणु, *adj.* firm.

सुखिन्, *adj.* 'having *or* possessing pleasure', happy.

सुर, *m.* a god.

स्वभाव, *m.* 'one's being', inherent nature.

ह, *enclitic particle,* indeed, to be sure, *but often a verse-filler and meaningless, esp. at the end of a verse.*

हन्तृ, *m.* one who slays, a slayer.

हृदय, *n.* the heart.

LESSON TWENTY-NINE

Comparison of Adjectives. Verbal Prefixes.

I. *Comparison of Adjectives.*

Apart from expressing a neutral or positive sense, adjectives in English can express higher degrees of their meaning by the addition of the suffixes *-er* and *-est,* as in *quick, quick-er, quick-est* and *long, long-er, long-est,* or by putting before them the adverbs *more* and *most,* as in *clever, more clever, most clever* instead of *clever-er, clever-est.* With some adjectives only one of these methods is allowable; thus, we cannot say *more long, most long* or (*good*), *more good, most good,* but we must say (*good*), *better, best.* What is allowable is a matter of usage, partly a heritage from Old English through Middle English and partly the product of analogical formations (as in the case of *clever*). In general it may be said that the old monosyllabic words take *-er/-est,* the longer words *more/most.*

The forms made with the suffix *-er* and the adverb *more* are said to be in the 'comparative degree', because, when they are used, a comparison with something or someone else is involved explicitly or implicitly. For example, 'King Nala was more skillful in horses than other kings'. Here Nala's skill is compared with that of other kings. When the 'than'-phrase is omitted, a comparison is implied from the context: 'This book is long, but that one is longer'.

The forms in *-est* and those preceded by *most* are in the 'superlative degree'. Here too, a comparison is expressed or implied. If, for example, we say 'He is the oldest king', the idea is that he is older than all the other kings. Sometimes genitive or locative phrases accompany the superlative: 'Menakā was the most beautiful of (*or* among) the Apsarases'. Very often, however, the superlative is used absolutely, *i.e.*, merely to express a very high degree of some quality without reference to anything or anyone else, as in 'He was most kind to do this'.

In Sanskrit too, the comparative and superlative of adjectives are formed by suffixes, but there are *two pairs* of suffixes, whereas English has only the one (*-er/-est*).[1] The Sanskrit pairs are: (*-ī-*)*yas*/*-iṣṭha* and *-tara*/*-tama*. We shall now discuss each pair separately.

---

[1]It may be of interest to note in passing, that in Old English the comparison of some adjectives was accompanied also by mutation of the root vowel, as *lang* ('long'), *leng-ra, leng-est, eald* ('old'), *ield-ra, ield-est.* The latter has come into Modern English as *old, elder, eldest* with the mutation preserved, but *elder* and *eldest* have become somewhat obsolescent and restricted in usage, *older* and *oldest* having largely taken their place. We would not say, for example, 'He is *elder* than I'.

1. Comparatives and Superlatives in (*-ī-*)*yas* and *-iṣṭha.*

This method is less common than the pair *-tara/-tama,* but is the regular and only method for some of the commonest adjectives and so logically should be taken up first. No rule, unfortunately, can be given for determining what adjectives take (*-ī-*)*yas/-iṣṭha* instead of *-tara/-tama.* They are relatively few and easily learned in the course of reading. A very few adjectives take the shorter suffix *-yas,* and some of these, like नव 'new', take either (नव्यस् or नवीयस्). Herewith are the most important adjectives that take (*-ī-*)*yas/-iṣṭha:*

1. *-yas/-iṣṭha*

Positive	*Comparative*	*Superlative*
प्रिय 'dear'	प्रेयस्	प्रेष्ठ
[श्री] 'beautiful'	श्रेयस्	श्रेष्ठ
स्थिर 'firm'	स्थेयस्	स्थेष्ठ
नव 'new'	नव्यस्	नविष्ठ
[ज्या] 'strong' or 'old'	ज्यायस्	ज्येष्ठ

2. *-īyas/-iṣṭha*

Positive	*Comparative*	*Superlative*
गुरु 'heavy'	गरीयस्	गरिष्ठ
लघु 'light'	लघीयस्	लघिष्ठ
वर 'choice'	वरीयस्	वरिष्ठ
दीर्घ 'long'	द्राघीयस्	द्राघिष्ठ
दूर 'far'	दवीयस्	दविष्ठ
[वृद्ध] 'old'	वर्षीयस्	वर्षिष्ठ
[अल्प] 'small'	कनीयस्	कनिष्ठ
[युवन्] 'young'	"	"

Note that some of the comparatives and superlatives above are from a different root than the positive, *e.g.,* कनीयस्/कनिष्ठ 'smaller/smallest' and 'younger/youngest' have obviously no genetic connection with अल्प 'small' and युवन् 'young' (*cf.* English *better/best,* the comparative and superlative of *good,* with which *better/best* have no connection except a semantic one).

श्रेयस्/श्रेष्ठ are from a theoretical positive श्री 'beautiful', but श्री occurs only as a noun in Sanskrit.

Comparatives in *-yas* and *-īyas* have a special declension consisting of two stems, a strong in -(*-ī-*)*yāṃs* and a weak in *-yas*.

Declension of ज्यायस् 'older; stronger'

	Singular		*Dual*		*Plural*	
	masc.	*neut.*	*masc.*	*neut.*	*masc.*	*neut.*
Nom.	*ज्यायान्	ज्यायस्	*ज्यायांसौ	ज्यायसी	*ज्यायांसः	*ज्यायांसि
Acc.	*ज्यायांसम्	ज्यायस्	*ज्यायांसौ	ज्यायसी	ज्यायसः	*ज्यायांसि
Instr.	ज्यायसा		ज्यायोभ्याम्		ज्यायोभिः	
Dat.	ज्यायसे		ज्यायोभ्याम्		ज्यायोभ्यः	
Abl.	ज्यायसः		ज्यायोभ्याम्		ज्यायोभ्यः	
Gen.	ज्यायसः		ज्यायसोः		ज्यायसाम्	
Loc.	ज्यायसि		ज्यायसोः		ज्यायःसु or ज्यायस्सु	
Voc.	ज्यायन्		*ज्यायांसौ	ज्यायसी	*ज्यायांसः	*ज्यायांसि

The feminine is made from the weak stem by the addition of -ई and is declined like नदी. Note that the declension is a consonant stem of two degrees and is perfectly regular in all respects. In the nominative masculine singular the -स् of the strong stem is lost because of the rule that a Sanskrit word can end in but one consonant. The anusvāra which precedes it is then replaced by dental -न्. Before the भ-endings, -अस् becomes -ओ and before -सु it may become -अः (ज्यायःसु) or optionally remain (ज्यायस्सु).

The superlative in *-iṣṭha* is declined precisely like the देव/सेना/फल type; so, ज्येष्ठः, ज्येष्ठा, ज्येष्ठम्, etc.

2. Comparatives and Superlatives in *-tara* and *-tama*.

These suffixes *-tara* and *-tama* are the ones usually used for forming comparative and superlative stems, except from the adjectives listed above and a few others.[2] These suffixes are added directly to the stem of the positive, to the weak stem of adjectives of two degrees, to the middle stem when there are three degrees. They are of unrestricted use, even being added to nouns. Examples are the following:

Positive	*Comparative*	*Superlative*
सुन्दर 'beautiful'	सुन्दरतर	सुन्दरतम
शुचि 'pure'	शुचितर	शुचितम
मृदु 'soft'	मृदुतर	मृदुतम
धनिन् 'wealthy'	धनितर	धनितम
विद्वस् 'wise'	विद्वत्तर	विद्वत्तम
रूपवत् 'beautiful'	रूपवत्तर	रूपवत्तम

Attached to a noun:

वीर 'a hero'	वीरतर 'more a hero' *i.e.*, 'a greater hero'	वीरतम 'most a hero' *i.e.*, 'the greatest hero'

Adjectives in *-tara/-tama* are declined according to the type देव/सेना/फल; thus, रूपवत्तरः, रूपवत्तरा, रूपवत्तमम्, etc.

As we have seen, the object of comparison, when expressed, is preceded by *than* in English. In Sanskrit the object of comparison is put in the ablative, a use we may label an 'ablative of comparison'. Thus, किं तस्माद् दुःखतरम् 'What (is) more painful than that (*literally* from that)'. अन्य 'other' is also construed with an 'ablative of comparison', as in नलादन्यः को राजा स्वराज्याद् द्यूतेन भ्रश्येत् 'What king other than Nala would fall from his kingdom due to gambling?'

[2] Some of the adjectives in *(-ī-)yas/-iṣṭha* also allow their comparison to be made in *-tara/- tama;* so प्रिय, प्रियतर, प्रियतम (instead of प्रेयः प्रेष्ठ).

II. *Verbal Prefixes.*

In the course of our readings we have had numerous examples of verb forms preceded by one or more adverbs, more accurately termed 'verbal prefixes'. Commonest is the prefixation of but one verbal prefix, but two are also common. Rarely are three found. There are about twenty of these prefixes, most of which have occurred in the readings. Since the matter of these prefixes has not been taken up in any detail, a summary of them and some particulars regarding their use can now be suitably given, especially as they have been seen in use sufficiently frequently. Herewith is a list, arranged not in order of frequency, but simply according to the Devanāgarī alphabet, along with their chief meanings:

अति	across, beyond, past, over, to excess.
अधि	above, over, on, upon, up to.
अनु	after, along.
अन्तर्	between, among, within.
अप	away, off.
अपि	on.
अभि	to, unto, against.
अव	down, off.
आ	to, unto.
उद्	up, out.
उप	to, unto, toward.
नि	down, in, into.
निस्	out, away.
परा	to a distance, forth, away.
परि	about, around.
प्र	forward, forth.
प्रति	back, in the opposite direction, against, toward.
वि	apart, asunder, separately, hither and thither, here and there, away.
सम्	together, with.

In general, but especially with the help of a context, it is not difficult to discover the modification of its basic meaning a root undergoes when provided with one or more of these prefixes. For example, विहगः पतति means simply 'The bird flies'; विहग उत्पतति (उद् 'up') 'The bird flies *up*';

विहगाः समुत्पतन्ति (सम् 'together') 'The birds fly *up together*'. Similarly with verbs of motion in general, the modification of meaning is readily apparent; so, from √गम् 'go' are derived the following combinations:

अधि-गम्	go up to, *then* attain.
अनु-गम्	go after, follow.
अन्तर्-गम्	go within, enter.
अभि-गम्	go unto, visit.
अव-गम्	go down.
उद्-गम्	go out.
प्रति-गम्	go back, return.
वि-गम्	go asunder.
सं-गम्	go together, unite.

With verbs of motion like √गम् or of giving like √दा, the prefix आ usually reverses the meaning; thus आगच्छति means 'comes', *not* 'goes to' and आददाति means 'receives', *not* 'gives to'. Often the change of meaning when a prefix is added is on the figurative plane, and in such cases a context is, of course, needed. Thus, √पद् 'step, go' with प्रति *may* mean 'go toward', but also 'go toward *in the sense of* accede, yield *or* consent'. Similarly, वि-√ग्रह् *may* mean quite literally 'hold apart, separate', but more usually 'quarrel, fight'. Sometimes a verbal prefix changes the meaning rather considerably; *e.g.*, अव-√गम्, apart from its literal meaning 'go down', means 'understand', a meaning as distinct from its parts as is the English 'under-stand'!

When two prefixes are used, the first of the two imparts a further modification to the sense, as with समुत्पतन्ति 'They fly *up together*' above. The order of the prefixes, when there are two or three, is determined by the basic sense and the modification of it, the dominant change being effected by the prefix closest to the verb, as in सम्-उत्-पत्, where *flying up* is the principal notion and the *together-ness* secondary. Similarly, we would naturally say वि-परा-√इ(एति) 'go away separately', *not* परा-वि-इ, as the going away or off precedes the separation of those going off. The prefix आ, however, *always* stands directly before the verb, a position probably imposed by its fundamentally localizing meaning, which sets the stage, as it were, for any further modification. A good example is provided by आ-√गम् 'come' into its further modification प्रति-आ-√गम् 'come *back*, return'.

There are a number of other prefixes, generally of less common occurrence, which have a much more restricted use, *i.e.,* are used only with certain verbs, notably √कृ and √भू, *e.g.,* तिर: 'crosswise, sideways' (with √कृ 'scold'!), बहि: 'outside' (with √कृ 'put outside, expel'), अलम् 'enough, fitting, ready' (with √कृ 'make ready, *then* adorn'), प्रादु: and आवि: synonyms meaning 'in view' (with √कृ 'bring into view', with √भू or √अस् 'be in view *or* visible'). Of considerable importance is the prefix श्रद्, an old noun, no longer in separate use, meaning literally 'heart', used only before √धा 'put, place', hence literally 'put *or* place one's heart (in someone)', *i.e.,* bestow one's trust upon someone. Somewhat similar to this is the use of the noun नमस् 'homage, obeisance' with √कृ in the sense of 'pay homage *or* obeisance to'. नमस्, however, is not by any means restricted to this particular application (like श्रद् to √धा), but is an extremely commonly used noun. Generally, the combination of नमस् with √कृ is restricted to the gerund नमस्कृत्य 'having paid homage'.

As will be recalled from our readings, the augment of the imperfect (and also of the aorist yet to be studied!) is not placed before a verbal prefix. The augment (in classical Sanskrit) is an inseparable part of the past tense, and nothing is allowed to be interposed between it and the remaining part of the form. The verbal prefixes are, after all, merely adverbs which have come in the course of time to be associated with verbs to modify their meaning.

Finally, some of the verbal prefixes are often used merely in an intensive sense, especially परि, प्र, वि and सम्, and hardly affect the meaning of a verb, if at all, whether otherwise provided with a prefix or not. For example, संतुष्यति (√तुष्) 'is quite pleased *or simply* pleased'; similarly, प्रहृष्यति (√हृष्) 'is very glad *or* glad'. Intensively used prefixes are particularly common with the past passive participles; thus, संतुष्ट and प्रहृष्ट.

Examples of Comparative and Superlative Adjectives and Verbal Prefixes.

1. किं क्षत्रियाय धर्म्याद्युद्धात्प्रेयो भवेत्[1] ।
2. य: क्षत्रियो धर्म्यं युद्धं युध्यते स वीरतम: सहसा भवति ।

3. अस्मिन्वने तपस्विनो ऽन्येभ्यस्तीव्रतराणि तपांस्याचरन्तीत्यस्माकं ग्रामे श्रूयते[2] ।
4. धर्मशास्त्रानुसारेण ज्यायान्कनीयांसमभिवादयेत्[3] । अभिवादात्परं ज्यायांसमभिवादयन्कनीयानसौ नामाहमस्मीति स्वं नामाभिदध्यात्[4] ।
5. अयं मार्गस्तस्माद्विषमतरः । तस्मात्तत्र सत्वरं चरन्तो रथा महत्तरं शब्दं कुर्वन्ति ।
6. सुकृतानि कर्माणि श्रेयसे दुष्कृतानि नरकाय कल्पन्त इत्यृषिभिरुच्यते ।
7. यस्माद्[5] इदं पुस्तकं द्राघीयोभिर्[6] वाक्यैर्दुर्ज्ञेयाभिर्वाग्भिश्च संपूर्णं तस्मात्कारणाद्[5] अन्यस्मात् प्रयत्नतरेणावगम्यते ।
8. शिष्यौ गुरोः पुरतः कटे निषीदन्तौ बहूनि सूक्तानि पठित्वोत्थाय तं नमस्कृत्यानुज्ञातौ गृहं प्रतिनिवृत्तौ ।
9. तस्मिन्वने बहून्मृगान्व्यापाद्य[7] ते व्याधास्तस्माद्देशादपागच्छन् । तद्वनं त्यक्त्वैवान्यदाविश्य तत्र परिभ्राम्यन्तो विविधांस्तिरश्चो[8] दृष्ट्वाप्येकमपि पाशैर्न बद्ध्वा शरैर्न वा निहत्य स्वग्रामं प्रत्यागच्छन् ।
10. नलं त्यक्त्वैव[9] ते हंसा वनात्समुत्पत्य विदर्भनगरीमागम्य दमयन्त्याः समीपे निपेतुः । यदा सखीगणवृता दमयन्ती तान्सर्वेषां पक्षिणां श्रेष्ठान्कनकालंकृतान्हंसानपश्यत् तदा संतुष्टमानसैकं हंसं ग्रहीतुं शीघ्रमुपचक्रमे । अनन्तरं ते सर्वे सर्वत्र वने विससृपुः । एकैकशस्तु ताः कन्यास्तान्समुपाद्रवन् । ततो यं हंसं सा दमयन्त्युपाधावत्स मानुषीं वाचं कृत्वा तामब्रवीत् ।

Notes

1. भवेत् an optative of contingency, with some vague conditional circumstance understood. In English we would probably use the indicative or the auxiliary 'could'.

2. श्रूयते Remember that the final short *-u* of a root (श्रु, स्तु, etc.) is lengthened before the passive suffix *-ya-*.

3. Note that in India the time-honored rule in salutations is that the elder greets the younger, who then replies ; *cf.* Mānavadharmaśāstra II, 120 ff.

4. The younger should say 'I am so-and-so (असौ) by name', with which words he should declare his own name.

5. यस्माद् . . . तस्मात्कारणाद् 'Because . . . for this reason'.

6. द्राघीयोभिर् Sometimes the comparative is employed more or less absolutely, in which case we may translate by 'rather'; so here, 'rather long'. Of course, a comparison is still implied, *i.e.,* 'longer (than in other books)'.

7. व्यापाद्य Note the loss of the causative sign *-aya-* when *-ya* is added to a compound stem (here वि-आ-पादय).

8. तिरश्चो (for तिरश्चः) accusative plural of तिर्यच्, the strong, weakest and middle stems of which are तिर्यञ्च्-, तिरश्च्- and तिर्यक्-/ग्- respectively.

9. In working out this sentence it needs to be known that the *haṃsa* birds here referred to had previously been in the presence of King Nala, on whose behalf, one of them, in return for his sparing its life, promised to speak to Damayantī of the neighboring kingdom of Vidarbha. The *haṃsa* would speak of Nala in such a way that she could think of no one other than Nala. But in order to learn what precisely the *haṃsa* said to Damayantī you will have to wait until you read the first *sarga* (canto) of Appendix I!

Vocabulary

अनुज्ञात, *ppp.* अनु-√ज्ञा (जानाति, class IX), granted leave *or* permission to.
अनुसार, *m.* 'a going after', following; अनुसारेण (+ *gen.* or as part of a tatpuruṣa cpd.), according to.
अभि-√धा (दधाति, class III), mention.
अभि-√वद् *in caus.* अभिवादयति, greet someone.
अभिवाद, *m.* greeting, salutation.
अव-√गम् (गच्छति, class I), understand.
असौ, *nom. m. sing. denom. pron.* अदः that; so-and-so.
आ-√चर् (चरति, class I), practice.
आ-√विश् (विशति, class VI), enter.
उप-√क्रम् (क्रामति, class I), step up to, approach; *perf.* °चक्रमे.
उप-√धाव् (धावति, class I), run up to.
ऋषि, *m.* a seer *or* sage.
एकैकशः, *adv.* one by one, one at a time.
कट, *m.* a mat.
कनक, *n.* gold.
कनीयस्, *comparative adj.* younger; *superlative* कनिष्ठ, youngest.
कारण, *n.* cause, reason.
√क्लृप् (कल्पते, class I), conduce to (+ *dat.*).
गण, *m.* a crowd, group, host.
√ग्रह् (गृह्णाति, class IX), seize, take hold of; *infin.* ग्रहीतुम्.
√चर् (चरति, class I), move, go.
ज्यायस्, *comparative adj.* older, elder; *superlative* ज्येष्ठ, oldest, eldest.
तपस्विन्, *m.* an ascetic.
तिर्यच्, *adj.* 'bent *or* directed across', horizontal; *as m.* a beast (as moving horizontally).[strong stem तिर्यञ्च्, middle तिर्यक् /-ग्, weakest तिरश्च्]
तीव्र, *adj.* fierce, rigorous (of austerities).
तपस्, *n.* heat, fire; self-inflicted torture, mortification, asceticism.
दुर्ज्ञेय, *adj.* 'difficult to be known', difficult. [ज्ञेय *gerundive of* √ज्ञा 'know']
दुष्कृत, *adj.* 'ill-done', evil.
देश, *m.* a place, region, area.
द्राघीयस्, *comparative adj.* of दीर्घ, long; *superlative* द्राघिष्ट, longest.

धर्मशास्त्र, *n.* compendium of Hindu law, a law book.
धर्म्य, *adj.* righteous.
न . . . न वा, *adv.* neither . . . nor.
नरक, *n.* hell.
नाम, *acc. of* नामन् *as adv.* by name.
नि-√सद् (सीदति, class I), sit down. [in निषीदति note cerebral ष् after *i*-.]
निहत्य, *gerund* नि-√हन् (हन्ति, class II), having struck down, killed.
पक्षिन्, *adj.* 'having *or* possessing wings (पक्ष)', winged; *as m.* a bird.
√पठ् (पठति, class I), recite.
परम्, *adv.* after (*as postp. with abl.).*
परि-√भ्रम् (भ्राम्यति, class IV), roam *or* wander about.
पाश, *m.* a snare *or* trap.
पुरतः, *adv.* before, in the presence of (*as postp. with gen.*).
पुस्तक, *n.* a book.
प्रतिनिवृत्त, *ppp.* प्रति-नि-√वृत् (वर्तते, class I), (having) returned.
प्रयत्न, *m.* an effort.
प्रिय, *adj.* dear; *comparative* प्रेयस्, dearer, *superlative* प्रेष्ठ, dearest.
बद्ध्वा, *gerund* √बन्ध् (बध्नाति, class IX), having bound, tied; having caught (with a trap).
महत्, *adj.* great.
मानस, *n.* the mind *or* heart.
मानुष (*f.* मानुषी), *adj.* human.
वाक्य, *n.* a sentence.
वाच्, *f.* a word.
वि-आ-√पद् (पद्यते, class IV), 'fall away', perish; *caus.* 'cause to perish', kill, *gerund* व्यापाद्य.
विदर्भनगरी, *f.* the city of Vidarbha, *i.e.,* Kuṇḍina, capital of Vidarbha, south of the Vindhya Mts., whose king was Bhīma, father of Damayantī.
विविध, *adj.* of different sorts, various.
विषम, *adj.* uneven.
वि-√सृप् (सर्पति, class I), move apart, separate, scatter; *perf.* °ससर्प (*plur.* °ससृपुः) .
वीर, *m.* a man, a hero.
वृत, *ppp.* ¹√वृ (वृणोति, class V), 'covered', enclosed, surrounded.

व्याध, *m.* a hunter.
शब्द, *m.* noise, sound.
शर, *m.* an arrow.
शिष्य, *m.* a pupil.
शीघ्रम्, *adv.* quickly.
श्रेयस्, *comparative adj.* more beautiful; better; *superlative* श्रेष्ट, most beautiful, best; *as n.* welfare, prosperity.
सखी, *f.* a female companion.
सत्वरम्, *adv.* quickly.
सम्-उप-√द्रु (द्रवति, class I), run up to together.
संपूर्ण, *adj.* quite full. [पूर्ण, *ppp.* √पॄ 'fill']
सहसा, *adv.* immediately.
सुकृत, *adj.* 'well-done', meritorious.
सूक्त, *n.* a Vedic hymn.

III. A Warrior's Highest Duty: A Righteous War.

श्रीभगवान् उवाच ।
अथ चेत्त्वमिमं धर्म्यं संग्रामं न करिष्यसि[1] ।
ततः स्वधर्मं कीर्तिं च हित्वा[2] पापमवाप्स्यसि ॥ ३३ ॥
अकीर्तिं चापि भूतानि कथयिष्यन्ति ते ऽव्ययाम् ।
संभावितस्य[3] चाकीर्तिर्मरणादतिरिच्यते[4] ॥ ३४ ॥
भयाद्रणादुपरतं मंस्यन्ते त्वां महारथाः[5] ।
येषां च त्वं बहुमतो भूत्वा यास्यसि लाघवम्[6] ॥ ३५ ॥
अवाच्यवादांश्च बहून्वदिष्यन्ति तवाहिताः ।
निन्दन्तस्तव सामर्थ्यं ततो[7] दुःखतरं नु किम् ॥ ३६ ॥
हतो[8] वा प्राप्स्यसि स्वर्गं जित्वा[8] वा भोक्ष्यसे महीम् ।
तस्मादुत्तिष्ठ कौन्तेय युद्धाय कृतनिश्चयः ॥ ३७ ॥
सुखदुःखे समे कृत्वा[9] लाभालाभौ जयाजयौ ।
ततो[10] युद्धाय युज्यस्व[11] नैवं पापमवाप्स्यसि ॥ ३८ ॥

एषा[12] तेऽभिहिता सांख्ये बुद्धिर्योगे[13] त्विमां[12] शृणु ।
बुद्ध्या युक्तो यया[14] पार्थ कर्मबन्धं[15] प्रहास्यसि ॥ ३९ ॥
नेहाभिक्रमनाशोऽस्ति प्रत्यवायो न विद्यते[16] ।
स्वल्पमप्यस्य धर्मस्य[17] त्रायते महतो भयात्[18] ॥ ४० ॥
व्यवसायात्मिका बुद्धिरेकेह कुरुनन्दन ।
बहुशाखा ह्यनन्ताश्च बुद्धयोऽव्यवसायिनाम्[19] ॥ ४१ ॥

IV. Action without the Fruits of Action.

श्रीभगवान् उवाच ।
कर्मण्येवाधिकारस्ते मा[20] फलेषु कदाचन ।
मा कर्मफलहेतुर्भूर्मा ते सङ्गोऽस्त्वकर्मणि ॥ ४७ ॥
योगस्थः कुरु कर्माणि सङ्गं त्यक्त्वा धनंजय ।
सिद्ध्यसिद्ध्योः समो भूत्वा समत्वं योग उच्यते[21] ॥ ४८ ॥
दूरेण ह्यवरं कर्म बुद्धियोगाद्धनंजय ।
बुद्धौ शरणमन्विच्छ कृपणाः फलहेतवः ॥ ४९ ॥
बुद्धियुक्तो जहातीह उभे[22] सुकृतदुष्कृते ।
तस्माद्योगाय युज्यस्व योगः कर्मसु कौशलम् ॥ ५० ॥
कर्मजं बुद्धियुक्ता हि फलं त्यक्त्वा मनीषिनः ।
जन्मबन्धविनिर्मुक्ताः पदं गच्छन्त्यनामयम्[23] ॥ ५१ ॥
यदा ते मोहकलिलं बुद्धिर्व्यतितरिष्यति ।
तदा गन्तासि[24] निर्वेदं श्रोतव्यस्य श्रुतस्य च[25] ॥ ५२ ॥
श्रुतिविप्रतिपन्ना[26] ते यदा स्थास्यति निश्चला ।
समाधावचला बुद्धिस्तदा योगमवाप्स्यसि ॥ ५३ ॥

(Bhagavadgītā II. 33-41, 47-53).

Notes

1. करिष्यसि √कृ has an immense range of meanings, far exceeding the English equivalents 'do' or 'make'. In this instance neither of these meanings is idiomatic: we cannot say 'If you won't do *or* make this righteous battle', but rather 'If you won't engage in this righteous battle'. Oddly, however, we may say 'do battle', where 'battle' is not qualified!

2. हित्वा gerund of √हा (जहाति, class III), here used in an instrumental or causal sense, as explained in Lesson 27, note 17 thus: 'then (ततः) by (*or* on account of) laying aside your duty and fame . . .'.

3. संभावितस्य best taken as a 'genitive quasi-dative': 'for one honored', *i.e.,* for one who has been honored. सम्-√भू (भवति) means literally 'be together', *then* 'take shape *or* form, be born'; but the transition to 'honor', the usual meaning of the causative and so of the participle here, has not yet been sufficiently explained.

4. मरणादतिरिच्यते *literally* 'is left over', with a comparative implication: 'is more than', here pejoratively 'is worse than death'. Hence, मरणाद् is an 'ablative of comparison', such as that employed after comparative adjectives.

5. Note the typical construction after a verb of mental action (here मंस्यन्ते): *literally* 'The warriors will think you (as) desisted from battle out of fear', but idiomatically in English '*that* you desisted' etc.

6. The meaning of this line is perfectly clear, but the construction is somewhat irregular. The irregularity lies in the use of the gerund भूत्वा instead of a finite verb, *i.e.,* अभवः. Thus, we expect the wording to be येषां च त्वं बहुमतो [ऽभवो] यास्यसि लाघवम्, *literally* 'and of (*i.e.,* by) whom you *were* (अभवः) highly esteemed, to the disdain [of these] you will go', freely 'and you will become the disdain of those by whom you were highly esteemed'.

7. ततो The adverb ततः is made from त-, the root of the demonstrative तद्, to which has been attached the ablatival suffix -तः. The etymological meaning of ततः, then, is 'from this *or* that' (or, with plural value 'from these *or* those'). Since ततः has the value of an ablative, it may be employed in any of the uses of the ablative. Here ततो is an 'ablative of comparison' with the

comparative adjective दुःखतरं 'more painful than that' (with reference to the criticism that will be brought against Arjuna's skill).

8. हतो (past passive participle of √हन्) and जित्वा (gerund of √जि) are here each the equivalent of a conditional clause with प्राप्स्यसि स्वर्गं and भोक्ष्यसे महीम् respectively: 'Either, if you are slain, you will attain heaven or, if you conquer, you will enjoy the earth'.

9. समे कृत्वा 'regarding, *or* holding (as) the same'; समे (which is accusative dual neuter to agree with सुखदुःखे, but is to be taken, with appropriate change of gender, also with the following masculine dvandva compounds लाभालाभौ and जयाजयौ) is used factitively with कृत्वा, *i.e.,* as completing its meaning, just as when we say 'to *hold* these truths as *self-evident'*.

10. ततो here functioning as an 'ablative of cause': 'on account of this', *i.e.,* therefore.

11. युद्धाय युज्यस्व passive imperative, *literally* 'be yoked for battle', *i.e.,* be prepared to engage in it.

12. एषा, though modifying बुद्धिर्, refers back to the foregoing discussion, while the demonstrative इमां, with which बुद्धिं is to be supplied, has forward reference; that is to say, it looks ahead to the other point of view, *viz.*, the yoga, the discussion of which follows.

13. In this line occur three of the most troublesome words in the Gītā: सांख्य, बुद्धि and योग. The first of these (सांख्य) is often treated as though it were identical to the particular system of orthodox philosophy bearing the name Sāṃkhya, quite a few technical terms of which (*e.g., buddhi, prakṛti, puruṣa, guṇa,* etc.) also occur in the Gītā. Very probably in the Gītā we are dealing with a Sāṃkhya that is pre-classical or, at any rate, of earlier character, before the solidification of usage had set in. In any case, *buddhi* in the Gītā certainly does not mean the highest of the internal organs, the ground of all intellectual processes, as it does in the orthodox Sāṃkhya system. It means rather a particular 'focal point *or* attitude of mind'.

The word *yoga* in the Gītā is difficult not only because of the wide and diverse range of meanings it has, but also because it is often associated by commentators with specific kinds of yoga, *e.g.*, Haṭha and Kuṇḍalinī, which are alien to the thought of the Gītā. The difficulty is not solved by retaining the word *yoga* in translation, as we often do with *dharma, karman* and some other terms. The reason for this is that, although *yoga* has become practically a household word in English, it has come with a long train of the very implications that are foreign to its usage in the Gītā. *Yoga,* as used in the Gītā, denotes 'intense, effortful activity toward a particular end', hence 'disciplined activity'. In fact it is probable that from this sense of bending or directing every effort toward a particular end the technical meaning of *yoga* has evolved, both as a system of concentrated thought culminating in union with the Absolute as well as the physical exercises contributory to that concentration. The idea that *yoga* has the sense of 'union' with the Absolute because it is derived from √*yuj* 'join, unite' is doubtless a latter interpretation of its true meaning.

In the first half of the prior śloka (38), Kṛṣṇa asks Arjuna to regard pleasure and pain, gain and loss, and victory and defeat with equal indifference (समे कृत्वा). In this śloka (39), Kṛṣṇa says, in effect, that this mental attitude (बुद्धि) of indifference to the effects of what he does is laid down in the Sāṃkhya and then he proceeds to declare that this Sāṃkhyan attitude, if subjected to the discipline of *yoga*, will lead to the absence of the bondage that is inevitably the effect or consequence of all actions, the re-action of actions that are performed in the usual fashion of purposefulness and personal concern. Furthermore, actions performed with this disciplined mental attitude will not lose any of the effort underlying them nor will they 'back-track', *i.e.*, lose their direction or momentum. In short, they will be as effective and productive as actions performed in the usual way, *i.e.*, with attachment to the results.

14. यया instrumental of the relative यद्, here used as an adjective qualifying बुद्ध्या 'disciplined with which mental attitude'. It is better thus to translate युक्तो by 'disciplined' than by the attenuated 'provided with' (a common meaning of the participle युक्त), because the author wishes not to speak merely of being 'provided with this mental attitude', but to show that it is the result of disciplined, intense effort (*yoga*).

15. कर्मबन्धं 'bondage of action', a subjective genitive, *i.e.,* bondage due to action, caused by action.

16. In stanza 40 Kṛṣṇa continues to refer to the 'mental attitude' with which one must be disciplined in order to get rid of bondage arising from one's actions. 'In this (mental attitude, इह)', he says, 'there is no loss of the effort put in (अभिक्रम, *literally* 'start') nor any retrogression (प्रत्यवाय:)'. Why?

Because the mental attitude he advocates involves *pure* action unconcerned or unconnected with reward or result. This, we are told in 41, is the only attitude in this discipline (इह) that is based on resolution.

17. धर्मस्य, here, with reference to the Yoga, probably 'prescription' or 'rule of action'.

18. महतो भयात् 'from the great fear', probably from fear of continued rebirth.

19. The meaning of this somewhat obscure stanza seems to be: '[There is] one mental attitude in this, *i.e.*, in this discipline, [which is] of the nature of resolution, O descendant of Kuru: the mental attitudes of the irresolute are certainly of many kinds and endless'.

20. With मा must be understood the *third* person of the augmentless aorist भूत् to express a prohibition ('let it not be'), which is easily supplied from the occurence of the *second* person भूर् , *i.e.*, भूः, ('be not' [motivated by action and the fruit of action]) in the next line. In the last *pāda* the imperative अस्तु is alternatively used to express a prohibition. Here and in the following we are given one of Kṛṣṇa's cardinal precepts, *viz.*, that one should indeed engage in action, but in doing so, not be motivated by thought of the fruits that may accrue therefrom. On the other hand, one should not be attached to non-action.

21. समत्वं योग उच्यते In these succinct words we are given a definition of *yoga* (as used in the Gītā), *viz.*, that it is equanimity or indifference (समत्वं) toward the attainment or non-attainment of one's goal in a particular enterprise. In stanza 50 we are further told that *yoga* or discipline of the mental attitude is 'skillfulness' (कौशलम्) in actions.

22. Note the absence of sandhi between इह and उभे. This sort of hiatus occasionally occurs between pādas, where, in any case, there is a slight pause or caesura.

23. पदं गच्छन्त्यनामयम् 'they go to a place free of disease', a vague assertion which may imply some sort of heaven or, more probably, a beatific state of the soul now no longer subject to rebirth.

24. गन्तासि periphrastic future of √गम्, second person singular; on this form, *v.* note 39 (under भविता), Lesson 28, and the section on the future in Appendix II.

25. श्रोतव्यस्य श्रुतस्य च genitives dependent on निर्वेदं 'aversion to what shall be heard and has been heard', with reference to the continued course of oral scriptural tradition, no longer felt to be needful or meaningful to the disciplined person who is free of all attachments and beyond the cycle of rebirth and its consequences.

26. श्रुतिविप्रतिपन्ना 'averse to tradition'; this adjective, which modifies बुद्धिस् in the next line, simply recapitulates the contents of pādas *c* and *d* of 52.

Vocabulary

अकर्मन्, *n.* non-action, inaction.
अकीर्ति, *f.* disgrace (the opposite of कीर्ति).
अचल, *adj.* 'not moving', motionless.
अति-√रिच् (रिच्यते, class IV), 'be left over', be more than, *with negative connotation* be less than, inferior to, *or* be worse than (+ *abl.*).
अथ, *conj.* now then.
अधिकार, *m.* concern, interest.
अनन्त, *adj.* having no end, endless.
अनामय, *adj.* 'not having disease', free of disease.
अनु-√इष् (इच्छति, class VI), seek after, look for.
अभिक्रम, *m.* attempt; effort.
अभिहित, *ppp.* अभि-√धा (दधाति, class III), declared, stated.
अव-√आप् (आप्नोति, class V), attain, incur; *fut.* आप्स्यति.
अवर, *adj.* inferior.
अवाच्य, *negative gerundive of* √वच् (वक्ति, class II), 'not to be spoken', unspeakable, what should not be said.
अव्यय, *adj.* imperishable.
अव्यवसायिन्, *adj.* 'not possessing resolution (व्यवसाय), irresolute.
असिद्धि, *f.* non-attainment, failure.
अहित, *m.* an enemy, foe.

आत्मिक, *as final element of bahuvrīhi cpd.* 'having ... as its nature', *i.e.,* characterized by *or* based on . . .

इह, *adv.* here; in this world.

उद्-√स्था (तिष्ठति, class I), stand up, arise.

उपरत, *ppp.* उप-√रम् (रमति, class I), having ceased *or* desisted from (+ *abl.*).

√कथय (कथयति, *denom. verb* from कथम् , *hence, literally* 'tell the *how*'), say, talk about.

कदाचन, *indef. adv.* at any time, ever.

कर्मज, *adj.* born of *or* originating in action.

कलिल, *m.* quagmire.

कीर्ति, *f.* fame, glory, reputation.

कुरुनन्दन, *m.* scion *or* offspring of the Kurus.

कृपण, *adj.* wretched.

कौन्तेय, *m.* son of Kuntī, metronymic of Arjuna.

कौशल, *n.* skillfulness.

चेद्, *conj.* if (enclitic only).

जन्मन्, *n.* birth.

जय, *m.* victory.

√त्रा (त्रायते, class IV), save, rescue.

दूरेण, *instr. as adv.* by far.

धनंजय, *adj.* Dhanaṃjaya 'winner of booty', an epithet and name of Arjuna.

धर्म्य, *adj.* righteous.

नाश, *m.* destruction, loss.

√निन्द् (निन्दति, class I), blame, find fault with.

निर्वेद, *m.* indifference.

निश्चय, *m.* decision.

निश्चल, *adv.* 'not moving', immobile, firm.

नु, *adv.* indeed.

पद, *n.* a place.

प्र-√आप् (आप्नोति, class V), attain, obtain.

प्र-√हा (जहाति, class III), abandon, cast aside, get rid of; *fut.* हास्यति.

प्रत्यवाय, *m.* 'going backward', reverse course, backsliding, reversal.

बन्ध, *m.* bondage.

बहुमत, *adj.* highly regarded (*literally* 'much thought of', as *ppp.* √मन् with *adv.* बहु).
बुद्धि, *f.* mental attitude (*v.* note 13).
भय, *n.* fear.
√भुज् (भुनक्ति, class VII), enjoy; *fut.* भोक्ष्यते.
भूत, *n.* a creature, a person.
√मन् (मन्यते, class IV), think; *fut.* मंस्यते.
मनीषिन्, *adj.* wise.
मरण, *n.* death.
महत्, *adj.* great.
महारथ, *m.* a great warrior.
मही, *f.* 'the great one', the earth.
मोह, *m.* delusion, infatuation.
√या (याति, class II), go; *fut.* यास्यति.
युक्त, *ppp.* √युज् (युनक्ति, class VII), disciplined (as derived from the same root as योग 'discipline'; *v.* note 14).
योग, *m.* intense, effortful action, discipline (*v.* note 13).
योगस्थ, *adj.* abiding in discipline.
रण, *m.* or *n.* battle.
लाघव, *n.* 'lightness', making light *or* little of; disdain.
लाभ, *m.* getting, attainment; gain.
√वद् (वदति, class I), say; *fut.* वदिष्यति.
वाद, *m.* a saying, a word.
वि-अति-√तॄ (तरति, class I), cross over (अति) completely (वि); *fut.* तरिष्यति.
विनिर्मुक्त, *ppp.* वि-निस्-√मुच् (class VI), delivered, liberated, free from.
विप्रतिपन्न, *ppp.* वि-प्रति-√पद् (पद्यते, class IV), 'having stepped back (प्रति) away (वि)', averse.
व्यवसाय, *m.* resolution.
शरण, *n.* refuge, shelter.
शाखा, *f.* a branch.
श्रुति, *f.* tradition, the Veda.
सङ्ग, *m.* attachment.
संग्राम, *m.* battle, war.
सम, *adj.* same, equal, indifferent.

समत्व, *n.* state *or* condition of being equal *or* indifferent.
समाधि, *f.* (higher) concentration.
संभावित, *ppp. of caus.* सं-√भू (भवति, class I), honored (*v.* note 3).
सांख्य, *n.* the Sāṃkhya doctrine (*v.* note 13).
सामर्थ्य, *n.* ability, skill.
सिद्धि, *f.* attainment, success.
स्वर्ग, *m.* heaven.
स्वल्प, *adj.* small, little; *as n.* a small amount, a little.
हत, *ppp.* √हन् (हन्ति, class II), (having been) slain.
√हा (जहाति, class III), abandon, leave aside, give up.
हित्वा, *gerund* √हा (जहाति, class III), having abandoned *or* disregarded.
हेतु, *m.* 'impeller', cause, impulse, motivation.

LESSON THIRTY

1. The Aorist Tense. 2. Adverbs Formed by Suffixes. 3. Monosyllabic Nouns in *-ī* and *-ū*.

I. *The Aorist Tense.*

As we have noted on several other occasions, but without going into the details, there are *three* past tenses in Sanskrit: the *imperfect, perfect* and *aorist*. In the classical language these three tenses simply express past time without any special implication, *viz.*, whether the past notion is progressive, repetitive, habitual, conative, etc. or whether it is absolutely past without reference to the present (*e.g.*, 'he came' in contrast to 'he has come'), and so on. Some of these distinctions were made in the Vedic language, but in the later language all of them have been lost, so that in translating an imperfect, perfect or aorist, it is only context and idiom that can determine the particular type of past tense that is required in English. In addition to these three past tenses, there is also the ubiquitous use of the *past passive participle*[1] with the agent expressed by the instrumental (*e.g.*, 'The pot [was] made by the potter' instead of 'The potter made the pot'), of which we have had plentiful exemplification throughout the readings. Which of these methods of expressing past time is used depends upon an author's predilection, on his feeling for the rhythm of a particular form within a sentence, metrical constraints and perhaps finally the time when he flourished, the aorist tending to be more prevalent in later works. The time when an author lived is especially important in the case of *later* classical Sanskrit, when the use of the passive participle was dominant.

A word should be said about the name 'aorist': it is borrowed from classical Greek grammar, where it is applied to a past tense whose formation corresponds to that of the Sanskrit tense we are about to take up.[2]

The aorist is unfortunately a rather complicated tense as far as its formation is concerned. There are *seven* (!) different forms, often with variation of the stem in the active and middle. Moreover, it is not possible to know which one of these seven forms a particular root will have, just as it is

---

[1]There is also a past *active* participle that is sometimes used in place of an active past tense. It is formed by adding the suffix *-vat* (feminine *-vatī*) to the past passive participle; *e.g.*, नलो हंसं वने दृष्टवान् (nominative masculine singular to agree with नलो) 'Nala saw the *haṃsa* in the woods'. As an example of the feminine: दमयन्ती नलं राजानं पतित्वे वृतवती 'Damayantī chose King Nala as her husband' ([2]√वृ 'choose').

[2]The Greek word *a-óristos* means 'undetermined, undefined' and was given to this tense because it expressed a past action undetermined as to its duration, *i.e.*, a mere 'snapshot' view of a past act as contrasted with the sort of 'motion picture' or continuous past act that is expressed (in Greek!) by the imperfect.

not possible to know to which of the ten classes of verbs a particular root will belong. Some roots have more than one aorist, just as some roots may belong to more than one of the ten classes. Such matters are to be learned from experience. What we have to do is to see in a general way how the different aorist stems are made and conjugated. From this knowledge it will be possible easily to recognize an aorist in a given passage and extract the root, then, if necessary, find out its meaning in the glossary or dictionary. The seven types of aorist fall into two large and quite distinct groups:

1. those that add to the root an *s*-suffix, which may take one of four forms, *viz.*, *-sa-*, *-s-*, *-iṣ-*, or *-siṣ-* , and
2. those that are formed from a root with or without the addition of the thematic vowel *-a*, the former thematic class sometimes also with a special kind of reduplication.

The initial *s-* of *-sa-* and the unitary suffix *-s-* are, of course, subject to conversion to *-ṣ-* according to the usual rule (*i.e.*, that if a vowel *other* than *-a-* or *-ā-* or the consonant *-k-* precedes, *-s-* becomes *-ṣ-*). As it happens, the suffix *-sa-* always appears as *-ṣa-* because the *only* roots that take this suffix end in *-ś* and *-h*, both of which are converted by sandhi into *-k* before the addition of a suffix, and this immediately preceding *-k* requires the conversion to *-ṣa-*. Thus, √*diś* 'point out' + *-sa-* becomes *dik-sa-*, then *dik-ṣa-*. The suffix *-siṣ-* is not involved in this initial cerebralization because it is *only* added to roots ending in *-ā* (like √या 'go'), which does not cause the conversion.

In spite of their greater complexity, it is desirable to treat first those aorists formed with the *s*-suffixes, partly because the difficulties involved in the formation of the different stems are more or less homogeneous and partly because they are much commoner than the other type. The *s*-aorists are often called the 'First Aorist', whereas the other types made with or without the thematic vowel are called the 'Second Aorist', terms again arbitrarily transferred from Greek grammar. For the same reason, the First Aorist is occasionally called the 'Sigmatic Aorist', from the letter *sigma* (*i.e.*, the Greek 's') which constitutes the characteristic of the suffix. When this term is used, the other type is naturally called the 'Non-sigmatic' or 'Asigmatic Aorist'.

1. *The First or Sigmatic Aorist.*
   a) *sa*-type.

As we have just observed, it is only to roots ending in *-ś* or *-h* to which the suffix *-sa-* may be added. The combination of *-ś*/*-h* + *-sa-* always becomes *-kṣa-*. The endings are the secondary ones as seen in the First Conjugation with *three* exceptions (in the middle voice), as will be seen from the following example.

√दिश् 'point out' Stem: अदिक्ष- (*a-dik-ṣa-*)

Active

	Singular	*Dual*	*Plural*
1.	अदिक्षम्	अदिक्षाव	अदिक्षाम
2.	अदिक्षः	अदिक्षतम्	अदिक्षत
3.	अदिक्षत्	अदिक्षताम्	अदिक्षन्

Middle

	Singular	*Dual*	*Plural*
1.	अदिक्षि	अदिक्षावहि	अदिक्षामहि
2.	अदिक्षथाः	अदिक्षाथाम्	अदिक्षध्वम्
3.	अदिक्षत	अदिक्षाताम्	अदिक्षन्त

Note that with the exception of the middle first singular (*a-dik-ṣ-i*) and the second and third dual (*a-dik-ṣ-āthām, a-dik-ṣ-ātām*), the inflection corresponds exactly to the imperfect of a verb of class VI of the thematic verbs.[3] The endings *-āthām* and *-ātām,* however, belong to the *non-thematic* verbs, so their occurrence here is not expected. In the thematic verbs the ending *-i* of the first singular middle is contracted with the thematic vowel of the stem, as in अभवे (from *abhava-* + *-i*). The occurrence of *-i* instead of *-e,* then, is exceptional. It has to be explained by assuming the dropping of the *-a* of *-sa-* before *-i.* Only a few roots take the *sa*-aorist, the most important, apart from √दिश्, are √दुह् 'milk' (अधुक्षत्), √गुह् 'hide' (अघुक्षत्), √रुह् 'ascend' (अरुक्षत्) and √विश् 'enter' (अविक्षत्). Note that in अधुक्षत् and अघुक्षत्, the final *-h* of the roots, which has been lost before the suffix *-sa-,* reappears in the aspiration of the *d-* (*a-duh-* → *a-duk-* → *a-dhuk-*) and *g-* (*a-guh-* → *a-guk-* → *a-ghuk-*).

b) *s*-type.

The three remaining *s*-aorists, *viz.,* the *-s-*, *-iṣ-* and *-siṣ-* types, agree in taking the endings *-īs* (*-īḥ*), *-īt* in the second and third singular and *-ur* (*-uḥ*) in the third plural of the active. All the other endings are the same as appear in the imperfect of the non-thematic verb. Roots that take the suffix *-s-* may end in a vowel or a consonant. Since all the vowel-final roots that take this suffix

---

[3]Class VI is specified because the correspondence to VI is closer than to IV, the stem of which ends in *-ya-*, or to I and X, both of which, unlike the *sa*-aorist, normally have modifications of the root vowel.

end in a vowel other than *-a,* the suffix is in effect *-ṣ-*. The root vowel is replaced by its vṛddhi substitute in the active and the guṇa in the middle.

√नी 'lead' Stems: अनैष्- (*a-nai-ṣ-*) and अनेष्- (*a-ne-ṣ-*)

Active

	Singular	*Dual*	*Plural*
1.	अनैषम्	अनैष्व	अनैष्म
2.	अनैषीः	अनैष्टम्	अनैष्ट
3.	अनैषीत्	अनैष्टाम्	अनैषुः

Middle

	Singular	*Dual*	*Plural*
1.	अनेषि	अनेष्वहि	अनेष्महि
2.	अनेष्ठाः	अनेषाथाम्	अनेढ्वम्
3.	अनेष्ट	अनेषाताम्	अनेषत

Note that in the second plural middle the *-ṣ-* is lost and the *dh-* of the ending *-dhvam* is converted to a cerebral.

If a root ends in a consonant, the root vowel remains unchanged in the middle. As an example may be taken √छिद् 'split'.

Active

	Singular	*Dual*	*Plural*
1.	अच्छैत्सम्	अच्छैत्स्व	अच्छैत्स्म
2.	अच्छैत्सीः	अच्छैत्तम्	अच्छैत्त
3.	अच्छैत्सीत्	अच्छैत्ताम्	अच्छैत्सुः

Middle

	Singular	*Dual*	*Plural*
1.	अच्छित्सि	अच्छित्स्वहि	अच्छित्स्महि
2.	अच्छित्थाः	अच्छित्साथाम्	अच्छिद्ध्वम्
3.	अच्छित्त	अच्छित्साताम्	अच्छित्सत

Here it needs to be remarked that whenever the *-s-* occurs between two dentals, it drops out, as in *a-cchit-tām* for *a-cchit-s-tām*. Note also that the *-d* of √छिद् is retained only in the second plural middle *a-cchid-dhvam,* elsewhere having been replaced by *-t* due to the voiceless *-s-* that follows. When this *-s-* drops out, the fate of the final *-d* depends, of course, on whether the sound that follows is voiced or not; hence *a-cchit-thāḥ,* but *a-cchid-dhvam.* A fair number of very common roots form their aorist with the suffix *-s-*. Among these perhaps the most noteworthy are: √कृ 'do' (अकार्षीत्), √दह् 'burn' (अधाक्षीत् with lost aspirate thrown back), √दृश् 'see' (अद्राक्षीत्), √प्रछ् 'ask' (अप्राक्षीत्), √भी 'fear' (अभैषीत्), √श्रु 'hear' (अश्रौषीत्), √सृज् 'release' (अस्राक्षीत्), √स्पृश् 'touch' (अस्प्राक्षीत्), √स्वप् 'sleep' (अस्वाप्सीत्), √हृ 'take' (अहार्षीत्). √मन् 'think' occurs only in the middle अमंस्त (note the change of न् to anusvāra), and √रम् 'take pleasure in' has अरंसीत् and अरंस्त with change of म् to anusvāra. Finally, the important √वस् 'dwell' has अवात्सीत्, which substitutes त् for स् of the root.

c) *iṣ*-type.

Although the *iṣ*-aorist was very common in the Vedic language, most of these old forms have been displaced by other aorist types or have disappeared altogether, the imperfect or perfect having to function in its stead. Of the few that have survived only one or two are found in both the active and middle, in view of which it is better to illustrate the two voices with different roots. For the active voice we may take √वद् 'speak', which, like a few other roots with medial *-a-,* lengthens its vowel. For the middle will serve √शी 'lie down', the vowel of which takes guṇa, *i.e., -ī-* → *e* → *-ay-* before the suffix *-iṣ-*.

√वद् 'speak' Stem: अवादिष्- (*a-vād-iṣ-*).

		Active	
	Singular	*Dual*	*Plural*
1.	अवादिषम्	अवादिष्व	अवादिष्म
2.	अवादीः	अवादिष्टम्	अवादिष्ट
3.	अवादीत्	अवादिष्टाम्	अवादिषुः

In the second person the secondary ending *-s* is irregularly contracted with the suffix to form *-īs* (*-īḥ*), and in the third person the ending *-t* is combined with similar irregularity into *-īt*. Otherwise, by the ordinary rule of sandhi of final *-ṣ* (as expected with the dropping of the endings *-s* and *-t* to avoid two final consonants), we should have had two identical forms ending in *-iṭ* (with the required conversion of final *-ṣ* to *-ṭ*), which do not correspond to any verbs and are indistinctive. Like √वद् are conjugated √मद् 'exhilarate' (अमादीत्) and 1√विद् 'know' (अवेदीत् with guṇa of the root vowel).

√शी 'lie down' Stem: अशयिष्- (*a-śay-iṣ-*).

	Middle		
	Singular	*Dual*	*Plural*
1.	अशयिषि	अशयिष्वहि	अशयिष्महि
2.	अशयिष्ठाः	अशयिषाथाम्	अशयिढ्वम्
3.	अशयिष्ट	अशयिषाताम्	अशयिषत

Similarly conjugated are the aorists of √जन् 'be born' (अजनिष्ट) and √वृध् 'thrive' (अवर्धिष्ट).

d) *siṣ*-type.

This type is conjugated only in the active voice and confined to a half dozen roots ending in *-ā*. The commonest and hence the most important is probably √या 'go'. There are no peculiarities about its inflection.

√या 'go' Stem: अयासिष्- (*a-yā-siṣ-*).

	Active		
	Singular	*Dual*	*Plural*
1.	अयासिषम्	अयासिष्व	अयासिष्म
2.	अयासीः	अयासिष्टम्	अयासिष्ट
3.	अयासीत्	अयासिष्टाम्	अयासिषुः

The second and third persons singular are ambiguous as to aorist type, as the same forms of the *s*-aorist also end in *-sīḥ* and *-sīt* (*-s-* + *-īs* and *-īt*). Unless attested in other forms than the second and third persons singular, therefore, it is not possible to assign a root with certainty to the *s*-aorist or *siṣ*-aorist. Thus, for example, अवासीत् 'blew' could be either aorist of √वा 'blow'. On the other hand, अहासीत् of √हा 'abandon' has to be classed as a *siṣ*-aorist because it occurs in forms other than the second and third persons.

2. *The Second or Non-Sigmatic Aorist.*

In the Second Aorist are included three types: a) a so-called 'Root Aorist' which, as its name suggests, adds the personal endings directly to the root, b) a thematic aorist which involves the interposition of the thematic vowel *-a-* between the root and the endings, and c) a reduplicating aorist which is also thematic.

a) Root type.

Relatively few roots belong to this type, although most of them are of common usage. With the exception of √भू 'be', they all end in *-ā*. The regular secondary endings are employed, except in the third plural where *-ur* (*-uḥ*) replaces *-an* (as in the *s*-aorists). Only the active voice occurs.

√स्था 'stand'

	Active		
	Singular	*Dual*	*Plural*
1.	अस्थाम्	अस्थाव	अस्थाम
2.	अस्थाः	अस्थातम्	अस्थात
3.	अस्थात्	अस्थाताम्	अस्थुः

√भू is peculiar in having the ending *-an* instead of *-ur* (*-uḥ*) in the third plural, and it interposes a *-v-* between the root and endings that begin with a vowel in order to keep the root free of sandhi change throughout.

√भू 'be'

	Active		
	Singular	*Dual*	*Plural*
1.	अभूवम्	अभूव	अभूम
2.	अभूः	अभूतम्	अभूत
3.	अभूत्	अभूताम्	अभूवन्

b) Thematic or *a*-form.

The thematic vowel *-a* is added to the unmodified root, so that this aorist is conjugated exactly like an imperfect of class VI. Because it is formally indistinguishable from an imperfect of class VI, care has to be taken in identifying it. This can only be done by knowing the class to which a form in question belongs. So, for example, अगमत् 'he went' must be taken as an aorist, as √गम् (गच्छति) is a root of class I whose imperfect is अगच्छत्. There are no special endings. A dozen or more common roots take this aorist. Though it occurs in both voices, the middle is not common.

√सिच् 'sprinkle'

Active

	Singular	*Dual*	*Plural*
1.	असिचम्	असिचाव	असिचाम
2.	असिचः	असिचतम्	असिचत
3.	असिचत्	असिचताम्	असिचन्

Middle

	Singular	*Dual*	*Plural*
1.	असिचे	असिचावहि	असिचामहि
2.	असिचथाः	असिचेथाम्	असिचध्वम्
3.	असिचत	असिचेताम्	असिचन्त

Among the most important roots belonging to this aorist are: √आप् 'reach' (आपत्), √क्रुध् 'be angry' (अक्रुधत्), √गम् 'go' (अगमत्), √दृश् 'see' (अदर्शत् with irregular strengthening of the root by guṇa), √रुध् 'obstruct' (अरुधत्), √रुह् 'ascend' (अरुहत्), √वृत् 'turn, move, exist' (अवृतत्), √शक् 'be able' (अशकत्). Two roots, *viz.*, पत् 'fly' and वच् 'say', are reduplicated and obscure the root by a weakening process. Thus, √पत् forms *a-pa-pt-a-t* with zeroing out of the root vowel, and √वच् has *a-voc-a-t,* in which *-voc-* is the product of the contraction of the reduplicative syllable *va-* + *-uc,* the root reduced by *samprasāraṇa* of *va-*.

c) Reduplicated type.

This aorist, apart from a couple of roots, is the 'standard' aorist of roots of class X and causatives. The vowel of the reduplicative syllable, which is *-i-* if the root contains *-a-*, *-ā-*, *-ṛ-* or *-ḷ-*, lengthens its vowel, unless it is long by position, *i.e.,* unless the root begins with two consonants. This produces a prevailing rhythm of short (augment) + long (reduplicative syllable) + short (root). To achieve this rhythm roots with long vowels like √राध् 'succeed' are occasionally shortened; thus, *a-rī-radh-a-t*. The inflection of the reduplicated aorist is in all respects identical to an imperfect of a thematic verb.

√जन् 'be born' Stem: अजीजन- (*a-jī-jan-a-*)
'cause to be born, produce'

Active

	Singular	*Dual*	*Plural*
1.	अजीजनम्	अजीजनाव	अजीजनाम
2.	अजीजनः	अजीजनतम्	अजीजनत
3.	अजीजनत्	अजीजनताम्	अजीजनन्

Middle

	Singular	*Dual*	*Plural*
1.	अजीजने	अजीजनावहि	अजीजनामहि
2.	अजीजनथाः	अजीजनेथाम्	अजीजनध्वम्
3.	अजीजनत	अजीजनेताम्	अजीजनन्त

II. *Adverbs Formed by Suffixes.*

There is a fairly large number of adverbial words in Sanskrit that are formed by means of suffixes from pronoun roots ('pronominal roots'), most commonly the demonstrative तद्, the relative यद् and the interrogative किम्. There are also a few adjectives, *e.g.,* अन्य, सर्व, from which adverbs are made by the same suffixes. All these derivatives are of the commonest occurrence and have accordingly appeared frequently in our readings. The roots of तद् and यद्, as they appear in these 'adverbs by suffixes', are त- and य-, *i.e.,* with the -द् omitted. The interrogative किम् is replaced by the two variant roots कु- and क-.

The adverb-forming suffixes that are added to these roots are *-tas* (*-taḥ*) 'from', *-tra* 'in', *-thā* denoting manner, and *-dā* denoting time. In the following table these four suffixes are arranged horizontally and the various roots and stems to which they are added are given vertically at the left, so that if any root (or stem) is carried across from left to right, its formation into an adverb by addition of the suffix above may be seen. The literal, etymological meaning may be quickly determined by combining the sense conveyed by a particular suffix with the meaning of the pronominal root or adjective stem.

Adverb-forming Suffixes

	1.	2.	3.	4.
Pronoun roots	-तस् (-तः) 'from'	-त्र 'in'	-था 'manner, way'	-दा 'time'
अ- 'this'	अतः	अत्र	अथ	---
त- 'that'	ततः	तत्र	तथा	तदा
य- 'which' (relative)	यतः	यत्र	यथा	यदा
कु- क- 'which?, what?'	कुतः	कुत्र	कथम्	कदा
Adjective stems				
अन्य 'other'	अन्यतः	अन्यत्र	अन्यथा	अन्यदा
सर्व 'all, every'	सर्वतः	सर्वत्र	सर्वथा	सर्वदा
एक 'one'	---	एकत्र	---	एकदा

Sometimes the suffix -था, denoting manner, takes the form -थम्, as in कथम् 'in what way, how?'. The expected form कथा occurs in the Veda. There is also a pronominal root इ- which appears in इतः 'from this', a synonym of अतः, and in इत्थम् 'in this way, thus', earlier इत्था.[4] This same pronominal root इ- also appears in the common adverb इह 'here',

---

[4]Probably formed from इद्, the prehistoric nom./acc. neuter of अयम्, which was supplanted by the extended इदम् (*id-am*), just as तु, the original form of the second person pronoun, was supplanted by त्वम् (*tu-am*).

synonymous with अत्र, but formed with an otherwise unproductive suffix -ह. Finally, note that in अथ the suffix -था has been shortened.

The suffix -तः has a much wider and more general application than the other three, being added to the roots of the pronouns of the first and second persons, singular and plural and also freely to noun stems in place of the ablative ending. Thus, as added to the roots of the personal pronouns: मत्तः (*mat-taḥ* 'from me'), अस्मत्तः (*asmat-taḥ* 'from us'), त्वत्तः (*tvat-taḥ* 'from you'), and युष्मत्तः (*yuṣmat-taḥ* 'from you', plural). Instead of saying पर्वतात् 'from the mountain', we may say पर्वततः; similarly, for जन्मनः 'from birth', we often find जन्मतः.

Since the adverbs in -तः have an ablative sense and in -त्र a locative value, they are often used as quasi-adjectives qualifying nouns in the ablative and locative. Thus, अत्र पर्वते serves for अस्मिन्पर्वते 'on this mountain', ततो देशात् for तस्माद्देशाद् 'from that region', and so on. This usage is more commonly to be encountered in works couched in a more popular, less rigid style, such as the Hitopadeśa, although it is by no means rare in compositions of more elevated character.

In determining the meaning of these adverbs, several points must be borne in mind. While the etymological meaning always lurks in the background, so to speak, often the sense in a particular context is more removed, to a somewhat different plane or focal point. For example, ततः means etymologically 'from that (place)', but more often the reference is transferred from the spatial to the temporal sphere, so that instead of 'from that (place)', the meaning will be 'from that (time)', *i.e.,* then, thereupon. Very frequently ततः is used in the sense of an 'ablative of cause', *i.e.,* 'from that' with the implication 'resulting from that, in consequence of that, on account of that, therefore'. In sum, then, we may see that ततः has in effect the following meanings:

1. from that (place), from there;
2. from that (time), then, thereupon;
3. resulting from that, on that account, therefore.

Only the context can determine which of these meanings is appropriate. Similarly, तत्र etymologically means 'in *or* on that (place) *or* there', but the reference may be to something in the *dual* or *plural:* 'in *or* on those two, among them'. A common meaning is 'with regard to this *or* that (matter)' (remember that the locative has also the sense of 'with regard to, with reference to'!). The suffixes of manner and time (-था and -दा) normally have their literal meanings; thus, तथा 'in that way, thus', यथा 'in which way', कदा 'at what time, when?' अन्यथा 'in another way, otherwise', अन्यदा 'at another time', एकदा 'at one time, once upon a time', etc.

III. *Monosyllabic Nouns in -ī and -ū.*

Nouns of but *one* syllable (roots used as nouns) end in -*ī* and -*ū*. However, unlike the polysyllabic types नदी (which was studied in Lesson Eight) and वधू, these *mono*syllabic nouns take the *same endings as the consonant stems,* although there are some alternative forms due to borrowings from the नदी/वधू type. Here below are the complete declensions of the very common nouns धी 'thought' and भू 'earth'. The alternative forms, which are probably more common, are given after the 'regular' forms.

धी, *f.* 'thought'

	Singular	*Dual*	*Plural*
Nom.	धीः *dhī-ḥ*	धियौ *dhiy-au*	धियः *dhiy-aḥ*
Acc.	धियम् *dhiy-am*	धियौ *dhiy-au*	धियः *dhiy-aḥ*
Instr.	धिया *dhiy-ā*	धीभ्याम् *dhī-bhyām*	धीभिः *dhī-bhiḥ*
Dat.	धिये/ धियै *dhiy-e/dhiy-ai*	धीभ्याम् *dhī-bhyām*	धीभ्यः *dhī-bhyaḥ*
Abl.	धियः/धियाः *dhiy-aḥ/dhiy-āḥ*	धीभ्याम् *dhī-bhyām*	धीभ्यः *dhī-bhyaḥ*
Gen.	धियः/धियाः *dhiy-aḥ/dhiy-āḥ*	धियोः *dhiy-oḥ*	धियाम्/धीनाम् *dhiy-ām/dhī-n-ām*
Loc.	धियि/धियाम् *dhiy-i/dhiy-ām*	धियोः *dhiy-oḥ*	धीषु *dhī-ṣu*

भू, *f.* 'earth'[5]

	Singular	*Dual*	*Plural*
Nom.	भूः *bhū-ḥ*	भुवौ *bhuv-au*	भुवः *bhuv-aḥ*
Acc.	भुवम् *bhuv-am*	भुवौ *bhuv-au*	भुवः *bhuv-aḥ*
Instr.	भुवा *bhuv-ā*	भूभ्याम् *bhū-bhyām*	भूभिः *bhū-bhiḥ*
Dat.	भुवे/भुवै *bhuv-e/bhuv-ai*	भूभ्याम् *bhū-bhyām*	भूभ्यः *bhū-bhyaḥ*
Abl.	भुवः/भुवाः *bhuv-aḥ/bhuv-āḥ*	भूभ्याम् *bhū-bhyām*	भूभ्यः *bhū-bhyaḥ*
Gen.	भुवः/भुवाः *bhuv-aḥ/bhuv-āḥ*	भुवोः *bhuv-oḥ*	भुवाम्/भूनाम् *bhuv-ām/bhū-n-ām*
Loc.	भुवि/भुवाम् *bhuv-i/bhuv-ām*	भुवोः *bhuv-oḥ*	भूषु *bhū-ṣu*

Note that the endings are identical to those added to consonant stems. Wherever an ending begins with a vowel (*-am, -ā, -e,* etc.) the root vowels *-ī* and *-ū* are 'broken' into *-iy* and *-uv*. In the dative, ablative-genitive and locative singular the alternative endings *-ai, -āḥ* and *-ām* are borrowed from the नदी/वधू type (नद्यै ~ धियै, नद्याः ~ धियाः, नद्याम् ~ धियाम् and similarly वध्वै ~ भुवै, वध्वाः ~ भुवाः, वध्वाम् ~ भुवाम्). In the genitive plural too, धीनाम् and भूनाम् are alternative forms based on नदीनाम् and वधूनाम्.

[5]As an adjective at the end of a compound भू may mean 'being, existent'.

Sentences Illustrating the Aorist and Adverbs Formed by Suffixes.

1. ततो यदा वणिग्भूपतेर्वचनमश्रौषीत्तदा तथा भवत्विति प्रतिभाष्य स प्रासादं त्यक्त्वा तेनेप्सितानि द्रव्याण्यानेतुमपागमत् ।
2. दमयन्त्या रूपं तेजो यशश्च श्रुत्वा[1] नलस्य राज्ञो हृदये हृच्छयः सहसावर्धिष्ट । तदा कामं हृदयेन धारयितुमशक्नुवन्नलः प्रासादसमीपस्थं वनं गत्वा तत्रावात्सीत् ।
3. नद्यां स्नात्वा बालौ ततः समीपस्थे क्षेत्रे दीर्घं कालं संक्रीड्य परं श्रमं गत्वा वृक्षस्य च्छायायाम्[2] अशयिषाताम् ।
4. यतः पुत्रः सूर्यास्तङ्गमनस्य[3] प्राक् कर्तव्यं कर्म नाकार्षीत्ततः पितातीवाक्रुधत् ।
5. यश्चौरो मत्तः सौवर्णाङ्गुलीयकमहार्षीत्स नागरिकैर् अस्मात्पुरादन्यत्र गृहीतः ।
6. तत्र जलाशये मत्स्यं गृहीत्वा कश्चित्पक्षी न्यग्रोधपादपस्थं स्वनीडमपप्तत् ॥
7. पितरि सर्पेण व्यापादिते पक्षिशावकाः सर्वेभ्यो वनवासिभ्यो[4] ऽभैषुः ।
8. अयं पुरुषो ऽस्मिन्राज्ये कवितमो ऽत्र न संशय इति मन्त्री स्वस्वामिनमवोचत् ।
9. अरयो नगरं महत्या सेनयारुधन् । यतस्तु नगरवासिनो ऽन्ते पराजिता अपि गृहेषु च गुहासु च प्रभूतमाहारमघुक्षंस्ततस्त्रीन्[5] मासानाक्रामतां[6] शत्रूणां गणान् सहितुमशकन् ।
10. आदौ सर्वमिदं[7] तमोभूतं[8] प्रसुप्तमिवासीत्[9] । ततो भगवान्स्वयंभूरव्यक्तः[10] प्रादुर्भूय सर्वत्र तमो नुदन्नपो [11] ऽस्राक्षीत् । तास्वप्सु बीजमधात् । ततस्तद्बीजं हैममण्डमभूत् । तस्मिन्नण्डे ब्रह्मा[12] सर्वलोकपितामहो ऽजनिष्ट । तत्र भगवान्

परिवत्सरमुषित्वा स्वयमेवात्मनो ध्यानात्[13] तदण्डं द्विधाकार्षीत्[14] । स तस्याण्डस्य शकलाभ्यां दिवं भूमिं चामास्त ।

11. यदा मेनकानाम्न्यप्सराः शकुन्तलामृषिणा विश्वामित्रेणाजीजनत् तदा सा पुनः स्वर्गमारुहत् ।
12. यमग्निं विद्युल्लताः[15] प्रावृष आदावजीजनन्स समीपस्थवनस्य भागमधाक्षीत् । ततो विष्फुलिङ्गा दवाग्नेर्वायुबलेनेतस्ततो विसृप्ताः केषांचिन्निर्धनिनां कृषीवलानां सस्यान्यनीनशन् ।
13. एकदा कश्चन भूपतिः कुत्र मे सर्वेभ्यो ऽन्येभ्यो महत्तरं प्रासादं कारयिष्यामीत्यमंस्त[16] । तां पर्यालोचनां विदित्वा तस्य नृपस्य मन्त्रिणो महाराज प्रथममिमं प्रासादं तुङ्गतरं च सुन्दरतरं च स्थेयांसं च करोतु भवांस्ततः परमन्यत्र प्रासादो भवता कर्तव्य इति तमवादिषुः ।
14. हे ऋषे कथं भवान्मोक्षमार्गमविददित्येको दरिद्रो मुनिमप्राक्षीत् । अहं मोक्षमार्गमद्यापि नैवाविदे परन्तु तमन्विच्छामीत्यृषिः प्रत्यवादीत् ।
15. तत्र देशे[17] संजाते काष्ठच्छेदे[18] कश्चित्कृषीवलो नृपतेरुपवने रोहन्तं वृक्षं परशुनावाच्छित्त । यद्यपि राजपुरुषाः स वृक्षो ऽस्माकं महाराजाय प्राणेभ्य एव प्रेयान्केनचिदवच्छिन्न इत्यद्राक्षुस्तथापि तं कृषीवलमवित्त्वा दण्डयितुं नाशकन् ।

Notes

1. श्रुत्वा Usually a gerund serves as the adjunct to the subject of a sentence or the *logical* subject, such as the instrumental of the personal agent with past passive participle ('By him, having done such-and-such, it [was] said'). Here, however, श्रुत्वा qualifies नलस्य 'Of Nala, having heard' etc.

2. च्छायायाम् After a short vowel, छ्, whether within a word or at a word-juncture, is doubled. When an aspirated consonant (here छ्) is doubled, the *un*aspirated counterpart is prefixed; hence, च्, + छ् (च्छ्), *not* छ् +छ्.

3. सूर्यास्तङ्गमनस्य 'the setting of the sun'. अस्तङ्गमन literally means 'going home (अस्तम्)' and is used of the setting of any celestial body. Since अस्त is actually in the accusative case (*i.e.,* not the stem form), the compound is truly an explicit accusative tatpuruṣa! The noun अस्त 'home' is restricted to use only with verbs of motion and is not a general word for 'home'.

4. वनवासिभ्यो an ablative with a verb of fearing.

5. त्रीन् accusative masculine plural of त्रि 'three' qualifying मासान् in an 'accusative of duration of time' construction.

6. आक्रामताम् Be careful of this form!

7. सर्वमिदं 'all this', *viz.,* this world, the standard expression from Vedic times. This passage has been greatly simplified from Mānavadharmaśāstra I.5-13.

8. तमोभूतं The past passive participle of भूत with present (!) meaning ('being' *not* 'been') is often thus compounded with a noun ('being darkness') as a means of converting the noun into an adjective; here 'being darkness' means simply 'dark'. Damayantī, in the story of Nala and Damayantī, is referred to as रत्नभूतां 'being a gem', *i.e.,* gem-like.

9. प्रसुप्तमिवासीत् 'was as though (इव) sound asleep *or* sunk in sleep'. Note here that the verbal prefix प्र- has *not* its literal meaning, but an intensifying force, hence the translation '*sound* asleep' or '*sunk* in sleep'.

10. स्वयंभूरव्यक्त: The primal force (the neuter Brahman) is said to be 'self-existent' (स्वयंभू:), *i.e.,* existent by itself, because, if it is the source of all (सर्वमिदम्), it cannot have been brought into existence by another than itself; if so, we should have to deal with an infinite and meaningless regress. It is 'unmanifest' (अव्यक्त:) because it has not at this point revealed itself.

11. अपो, *i.e.,* अप:, accusative plural of the curious noun अप् 'water', used only in the plural. The locative plural अप्सु occurs in the next sentence.

12. ब्रह्मा Brahman, the impersonal source of all, has now become a personal creator-god, hence the masculine ब्रह्मा as distinguished from the neuter absolute: 'The grandsire of all the worlds (*i.e.*, the Self-existent or neuter Brahman) was born in that egg (as) Brahmā (*i.e.*, the immediate creator).'

13. स्वयमेवात्मनो ध्यानात् 'by himself alone (एव) through his own (आत्मन:) meditation'. स्वयम् is an intensive pronoun either employed as an adjective qualifying the subject ('he himself') or as equivalent to an instrumental ('by himself') as here. आत्मन् is commonly thus used as a reflexive pronoun. Incidentally, this entire account of creation should be compared to the remarkable hymn X.129 of the Ṛgveda.

14. द्विधाकार्षीत् 'made it into two parts', broke it in two.

15. विद्युल्लता: *literally* 'creepers *or* tendrils (in the form) of lightning', a figurative expression for 'flashes of lightning' fancied to resemble the tendrils of a plant because of their irregular shape. The compound is made up of विद्युत् a root noun, *literally* 'that which shines far and wide (वि + √द्युत् 'shine') + लता 'a creeper *or* tendril'.

16. The words from कुत्र through कारयिष्यामि are the thoughts of the king. The main sentence is एकदा कश्चन भूपति: . . . अमंस्त.

17. तत्र देशे equivalent to तस्मिन्देशे.

18. संजाते काष्ठच्छेदे What construction is this?

Vocabulary

अङ्गुलीयक, *n.* a ring.

अण्ड, *n.* an egg.

अन्ते, *adv.* 'in the end', finally (*loc.* अन्त, 'end').

अप्, *f.* (*plural only*), water.

अप-√गम् (गच्छति, class I), go off *or* away; *aorist* अगमत्

अरि, *m.* an enemy.

अव-√छिद् (छिनत्ति, class VII), cut down; *aorist* अच्छैत्सीत्, अच्छित्त; *ppp.* छिन्न.

अवित्त्वा, *negative gerund of* 2√विद् (विन्दति), not having found.

अव्यक्त, *adj.* unmanifest.

अस्तङ्गमन, *n.* setting (of a celestial body).

आ-√क्रम् (क्रामति, class I), attack.

आदि, *m.* beginning.

आ-√रुह् (रोहति, class I), ascend; *aorist* अरुहत् *and* अरुक्षत्.

आहार, *m.* food.

इतस्ततः, *adv.* here and there.

ईप्सित, *ppp. of the desiderative of* √आप् (आप्नोति, class V), sought for, desired (*literally* 'desired to be obtained').

उपवन, *n.* a grove.

उषित्वा, *gerund* √वस् (वसति, class I), having stayed, having abided.

कवि, *m.* a poet.

कृषीवल, *m.* a cultivator, farmer, peasant.

कर्तव्य, *gerundive* √कृ (करोति, class VIII), having *or* needing to be done.

कर्मन्, *n.* work.

काम, *m.* love.

काष्ठ, *n.* wood, firewood.

√क्रुध् (क्रुध्यति, class IV), become angry; *aorist* अक्रुधत्.

क्षेत्र, *n.* a field.

√गुह् (गूहति, class I), hide, conceal; *aorist* अघुक्षत्.

गुहा, *f.* a cave.

गृहीत, *ppp.* √ग्रह् (गृह्णाति, class IX), (having been) seized.

चौर, *m.* a thief.

छेद, *m.* dearth, want, lack.

√जन् (जायते, class IV), be born; *aorist* अजनिष्ट, *aorist of caus.* अजीजनत्.

जलाशय, *m.* 'water-abode', a lake.

ततःपरम्, *adverbial phrase*, thenceforth.

तमस्, *n.* darkness.

तमोभूत, *adj.* 'being darkness', *hence,* in the dark, dark.

तुङ्ग, *adj.* tall.

तेजस्, *n.* majesty.

√त्यज् (त्यजति, class I), leave; *gerund* त्यक्त्वा.

√दण्ड् (दण्डयति, *denom. verb from* दण्ड, 'stick', *literally* 'apply a stick to'), punish.

दरिद्र, *adj.* poor.

दवाग्नि, *m.* a forest-fire.

√दह् (दहति, class I), burn; *aorist* अधाक्षीत्.

दिव, *n.* the heaven, the sky.

द्रव्य, *n.* a thing, an object.

द्विधा, *adv.* in two parts, in twain.

√धृ (धारयति, *no pres., caus. without caus. meaning!*), hold, sustain, support, bear; *infin.* धारयितुम्.

ध्यान, *n.* meditation.

√नश् (नश्यति, class IV), perish; *aorist of caus.* अनीनशत्.

नागरिक, *m.* a policeman.

निर्धनिन्, *adj.* without wealth, poor.

नीड, *n.* a nest.

√नुद् (नुदति, class VI), drive away, dispel.

पक्षिन्, *adj.* 'possessing wings', winged; *as m.* a bird.

√पत् (पतति, class I), fly; *aorist* अपप्तत्.

पर, *adj.* highest, extreme.

परशु, *m.* an ax.

पराजित, *ppp.* परा-√जि (जयति, class I), (having been) conquered.

परिवत्सर, *m.* a full year.

पर्यालोचना, *f.* a plan.

पुर, *n.* a city.

√प्रछ् (पृच्छति, class VI), ask; *aorist* अप्राक्षीत्.

प्रति-√भाष् (भाषते, class I), 'speak back', answer.

प्रथमम्, *adv.* first, firstly.
प्रभूत, *adj.* much.
प्रसुप्त, *ppp.* प्र-√स्वप् (स्वपिति, class II), sound asleep.
प्राक्, *adv.* before (*as postp. + gen.*).
प्राण, *m.* breath; life (*in plur.*).
प्रादुस्-√भू (भवति, class I), be in view *or* visible; *gerund* प्रादुर्भूय.
प्रावृष्, *f.* the rains, the rainy season *or* monsoon.
प्रासाद, *m.* a palace.
प्रेयस्, *adj.* dearer, *comparative of* प्रिय.
बीज, *n.* a seed.
भाग, *m.* a part.
√भी (बिभेति, class III), fear; *aorist* अभैषीत्.
भूपति, *m.* 'lord of the earth', a king.
मत्स्य, *m.* a fish.
√मन् (मन्यते, class IV), think; *aorist* अमंस्त.
मन्त्रिन्, *m.* a minister.
√मा (मिमीते, class III), measure; form; *aorist* अमास्त.
मास, *m.* a month.
मेनका, *f.* Menakā, an apsaras, mother of Śakuntalā by the sage Viśvāmitra.
मोक्ष, *m.* liberation *or* freedom (from rebirth).
यद्यपि . . . तथापि, *concessive conj.* although . . . nevertheless.
यशस्, *n.* glory, fame.
√रुध् (रुणद्धि, class VII), obstruct, lay siege to; *aorist* अरुधत्.
√वच् (वक्ति, class II), say, speak; *aorist* अवोचत्.
वचन, *n.* speech, words.
वणिज्, *m.* a merchant.
√वद् (वदति, class I), say; *aorist* अवादीत्.
वनवासिन्, *adj.* 'forest-dwelling', *as m.* a forest-dweller, denizen of the forest.
√वस् (वसति, class I), stay, abide, dwell; *aorist* अवात्सीत्.
2√विद् (विन्दति, class VI), find; *aorist* अविदत्, अविदत; *gerund* वित्त्वा.
विद्युल्लता, *f.* a lightning-flash.
विष्फुलिङ्ग, *m.* a spark.
विसृप्त, *ppp.* वि-√सृप् (सर्पति, class I), 'having moved apart', scattered, spread.

√वृध (वर्धते, class I), grow, thrive; *aorist* अवर्धिष्ट.
√शक् (शक्नोति, class V), be able, can; *aorist* अशकत्.
शकल, *n.* a piece; a half (of an eggshell).
√शी (शेते, class II), lie down; *aorist* अशयिष्ट.
श्रम, *m.* fatigue.
√श्रु (शृणोति, class V), hear; *aorist* अश्रौषीत्.
शावक, *m.* the young of an animal *or* bird.
संशय, *m.* doubt.
संजात, *ppp.* सम्-√जन् (जायते, class IV), having arisen.
समीपस्थ, *adj.* situated in the vicinity, nearby, near.
सम्-√क्रीड् (क्रीडति, class I), play together.
सर्प, *m.* a serpent.
सस्य, *n.* crop; grain.
√सह् (सहति, class I), hold out against, withstand; *infin.* सहितुम्.
सहसा, *adv.* immediately.
सुन्दर, *adj.* beautiful.
सूर्य, *m.* the sun.
√सृज् (सृजति, class VI), let go, release; create; *aorist* अस्राक्षीत्.
सौवर्ण, *adj.* golden.
स्थेयस्, *adj.* firmer, *comparative of* स्थिर.
√स्ना (स्नाति, class II), bathe.
स्वयंभू, *adj.* 'self-existent', an epithet of Brahman as the ultimate principle.
स्वर्ग, *m.* heaven.
स्वामिन्, *m.* a lord *or* master.
√हृ (हरति, class I), take; *aorist* अहार्षीत्.
हृदय, *n.* the heart.
हृच्छय, *adj.* 'lying in the heart', *as m.* love.
हैम, *adj.* golden.

V. The Man Whose Mental Attitude is Firmly Established

अर्जुन उवाच ।
स्थितप्रज्ञस्य[1] का भाषा[2] समाधिस्थस्य[3] केशव ।
स्थितधीः किं प्रभाषेत किमासीत व्रजेत किम् ॥ ५४ ॥

श्रीभगवान् उवाच ।
प्रजहाति यदा कामान् सर्वान् पार्थ मनोगतान् ।
आत्मन्येवात्मना तुष्टः[4] स्थितप्रज्ञस्तदोच्यते ॥ ५५ ॥
दुःखेष्वनुद्विग्नमनाः[5] सुखेषु विगतस्पृहः[5] ।
वीतरागभयक्रोधः[5] स्थितधीर्[5] मुनिरुच्यते ॥ ५६ ॥
यः सर्वत्रानभिस्नेहस्तत्तत्[6] प्राप्य शुभाशुभम् ।
नाभिनन्दति न द्वेष्टि तस्य प्रज्ञा प्रतिष्ठिता ॥ ५७ ॥
यदा संहरते चायं कूर्मो ऽङ्गानीव सर्वशः[7] ।
इन्द्रियाणीन्द्रियार्थेभ्यस्तस्य प्रज्ञा प्रतिष्ठिता ॥ ५८ ॥
विषया[8] विनिवर्तन्ते[9] निराहारस्य देहिनः[10] ।
रसवर्जं[11] रसो ऽप्यस्य[10] परं दृष्ट्वा निवर्तते ॥ ५९ ॥
यततो ह्यपि कौन्तेय पुरुषस्य विपश्चितः ।
इन्द्रियाणि प्रमाथीनि हरन्ति[12] प्रसभं मनः ॥ ६० ॥
तानि सर्वाणि संयम्य युक्त आसीत मत्परः[13] ।
वशे हि यस्येन्द्रियाणि तस्य प्रज्ञा प्रतिष्ठिता ॥ ६१ ॥
ध्यायतो विषयान्पुंसः[14] संगस्तेषूपजायते ।
सङ्गात्संजायते कामः कामात्क्रोधो ऽभिजायते ॥ ६२ ॥
क्रोधाद् भवति सम्मोहः सम्मोहात्स्मृतिविभ्रमः ।
स्मृतिभ्रंशाद् बुद्धिनाशो बुद्धिनाशात्प्रणश्यति[15] ॥ ६३ ॥
रागद्वेषवियुक्तैस्तु विषयानिन्द्रियैश्चरन् ।
आत्मवश्यैर्विधेयात्मा प्रसादमधिगच्छति ॥ ६४ ॥

प्रसादे सर्वदु:खानां हानिरस्योपजायते ।
प्रसन्नचेतसो ह्याशु बुद्धि:[16] पर्यवतिष्ठते ॥ ६५ ॥
नास्ति बुद्धिरयुक्तस्य न चायुक्तस्य भावना[17] ।
न चाभावयत: शान्तिरशान्तस्य कुत: सुखम् ॥ ६६ ॥
इन्द्रियाणां हि चरतां यन्मनो ऽनुविधीयते ।
तदस्य हरति प्रज्ञां वायुर्नावम्[18] इवाम्भसि ॥ ६७ ॥
तस्माद् यस्य महाबाहो निगृहीतानि सर्वश: ।
इन्द्रियाणीन्द्रियार्थेभ्यस्तस्य प्रज्ञा प्रतिष्ठिता ॥ ६८ ॥
या निशा सर्वभूतानां तस्यां जागर्ति[19] संयमी ।
यस्यां जाग्रति भूतानि सा निशा पश्यतो मुने: ॥ ६९ ॥
आपूर्यमाणमचलप्रतिष्ठं[20] समुद्रमाप: प्रविशन्ति यद्वत् ।
तद्वत् कामा यं प्रविशन्ति सर्वे स शान्तिमाप्नोति न कामकामी[21] ॥ ७० ॥
विहाय कामान् य: सर्वान् पुमांश्चरति नि:स्पृह:[22] ।
निर्ममो[22] निरहंकार:[22] स शान्तिमधिगच्छति ॥ ७१ ॥
एषा ब्राह्मी स्थिति: पार्थ नैनां प्राप्य विमुह्यति ।
स्थित्वास्यामन्तकाले[23] ऽपि ब्रह्मनिर्वाणम्[24] ऋच्छति ॥ ७२ ॥

(Bhagavadgītā II. 54-72).

Notes

1. स्थितप्रज्ञस्य This, with its synonym स्थितधी: in the next line and other equivalent expressions farther on in this passage, is difficult to render in English: 'whose mental attitude is firmly *or* well established' seems awkward, but is perhaps the closest to conveying the intended meaning. प्रज्ञा in this compound is, then, a synonym of बुद्धि, so that स्थितप्रज्ञ is practically a synonym of बुद्धियुक्त in II.50 and the analytic expression बुद्ध्या युक्तो यया 'disciplined with which mental attitude' in 39.

2. भाषा here does *not* mean 'language' (the usual meaning!), but 'definition' or 'description'.

3. समाधिस्थस्य *literally* 'abiding *or* remaining in deep concentration', *i.e.,* firmly concentrated.

4. आत्मन्येवात्मना तुष्टः *i.e.,* relying entirely upon himself, content within himself alone.

5. Each of these compounds ends in a noun (मनः, स्पृहा, क्रोध and धी), but is used adjectivally. What sort of compound thus ends in a noun, but functions as an adjective? An *external* clue to the adjectival function of अनुद्विग्नमनाः and विगतस्पृहः is the *change of gender* of the terminal member, *i.e.,* मनः is a neuter word, but the lengthening of the final vowel indicates a gender change (remember masculine and feminine nouns in *-as* have their nominative in *-ās,* as अङ्गिरास् and अप्सरास्); स्पृहा is a feminine noun as indicated by its final *-ā,* but in this compound it is converted into a masculine to qualify the subject of उच्यते.

6. तत्तत् The repetition of the demonstrative implies distribution. We may translate this common usage by 'this or that'; thus, 'The one who, without desire in all instances (सर्वत्र), having gotten *this or that* pleasant or unpleasant thing (*i.e.*, good or bad fortune), neither takes delight in the good fortune nor hates the bad fortune', शुभं and अशुभं being extracted from शुभाशुभम् as objects of नाभिनन्दति and न द्वेष्टि respectively.

7. सर्वशः The suffix -शस् (-शः) is added to numerals or to words of numeral character to form adverbs: as एकशः 'singly', पञ्चशः 'by fives', and here सर्वशः 'wholly, entirely'.

8. विषया 'objects of the senses', *i.e.,* the objects to which the sense organs (इन्द्रियाणि) gravitate (as does the ear to sounds, the eye to colors, the nose to smells, etc.). विषय is properly a 'field *or* domain' of something; from the field or proper domain of a particular sense organ, it easily shifts to the object of the sense organ.

9. विनिवर्तन्ते the prefix वि- here simply intensifies the meaning of 'turning away (वि-)', and it is in fact omitted in the next line where निवर्तते is used with the same meaning.

10. देहिनः and अस्य are most easily taken as 'genitives quasi-dative', as they belong more closely to the verbs than to the nouns विषया and रसो. Thus, 'The sense objects turn away (*or* fade away) *for* the individual who refrains from food . . ., flavor too, turns away *for* him, when he sees the highest'. Similar is the genitive पुरुषस्य in the next śloka, and an even clearer example is अस्य in 65.

11. रसवर्जं It is said that 'flavor' (रस), *i.e.,* the object of the sense of taste, is the very last of the sense objects to recede, as the desire for food is the hardest to suppress and tends to rebound even after long fasts. But, as we see in this passage, when the स्थितप्रज्ञ sees the highest (Brahman), even this most resistant sense object relaxes its hold.

12. हरन्ति, *literally*, 'take away, charm' in the sense of 'distract' and practically 'overpower, become master of'.

13. मत्परः 'having me (मत्-, stem form of अहम्) as the chief thing (-पर)', *i.e.,* completely devoted to or intent upon me. This is a bahuvrīhi based on an appositional karmadhāraya; पर 'chief *or* principal (thing)' is very frequently employed in this way as the terminal element of a compound.

14. पुंसः genitive singular of पुमन् 'a man', a consonant stem of three degrees. The strong stem is पुमांस्, the weakest पुंस् (as here) and the middle पुम्. The declension is formed perfectly regularly from these stems. It is here a synonym of पुरुषस्य of śloka 60.

15. In summary, we may say that, from dwelling on the objects of the senses, an individual experiences a sevenfold concatenation of conditions, *viz.,* attachment (सङ्ग) to the objects, a desire (काम) to have them, anger (क्रोध) when this desire is thwarted or unfulfilled, infatuation with the desires (सम्मोह) which results in confusion of memory (स्मृतिविभ्रम), which, in turn, nullifies the formation of a disciplined attitude of mind (बुद्धिनाश). This lack of mental attitude with its concomitant irresolution leads to the ruination of the individual.

16. बुद्धिः here cannot mean 'mental attitude' since a proper or disciplined mental attitude is itself a *prerequisite* for the achievement of tranquility referred to in 64, concerning which can hardly be made made the assertion: 'when one's mind has become tranquil (प्रसन्नचेतसो), his mental attitude quickly becomes steady (आशु बुद्धिः पर्यवतिष्ठते)'. बुद्धिः here seems to have the sense of बुद्धि in the later Sāṃkhya system where it means the 'intellect' or 'ground of all intellectual processes', *i.e.*, the faculty that lies behind one's mental attitude and in whose decision-making power an individual's course of action in each particular instance finally resides. What is meant here, then, is that this highest intellectual organ becomes permanently stabilized as a result of the repeated application of a disciplined mental attitude. In this condition of absolute equilibrium it is not subject to vacillation due to the influences of desires and attachments.

17. भावना a noun formed from the causative stem of √भू 'be', which appears in the next line in अभावयतः, a negative present participle. *Literally*, then, भावना means 'a causing *or* bringing to be *or* become', *i.e.*, causing oneself to evolve or develop into a higher state through the adoption of a firmly established mental attitude. Perhaps we might translate भावना by 'cultivation' and the participle by 'not cultivating himself'.

18. नावम् accusative singular of नौ 'ship', one of only a couple of nouns ending in the diphthong *-au*. It takes the regular endings of consonant stems; before vowel endings the stem becomes नाव्. Thus, नौः, नावम्, नावा, नावे, but नौभ्याम्, नौभिः, नौषु.

19. जागर्ति third singular present of √जागृ 'be awake', listed as a root, but strictly an *intensive* form of ³√गृ 'be awake'. Intensives are made by prefixing to the root a 'strong' reduplication, here containing a long *-ā-*, and conjugating it according to a verb of class III; thus, the intensive stem of ³√गृ becomes जा- + गर् (guṇa of गृ in the singular, but गृ elsewhere) + endings. Herewith is the complete present:

	Singular	*Dual*	*Plural*
1.	जागर्मि	जागृवः	जागृमः
2.	जागर्षि	जागृथः	जागृथ
3.	जागर्ति	जागृतः	जाग्रति

Note the absence of a nasal in the third plural, as in all verbs of class III. Finally it should be observed that no intensive meaning is involved in these forms, which merely take the place of the missing present of 3√गृ.

This stanza suggests the diametrically opposite views of the 'one who is controlled' (संयमी) on the one hand and by all other beings on the other: the one who is controlled is fully awake when all others are asleep (in the darkness of their ignorance), and when the others are awake in their night of desires and attachments, the sage, who sees, *i.e.*, has the true vision of reality, sleeps.

20. अचलप्रतिष्ठं most likely 'whose stability is unwavering (while it is being filled)'; प्रतिष्ठा can also mean concretely 'a foundation', but this sense seems improbable with reference to the ocean.

21. न कामकामी possibly qualifying स 'he', the subject of आप्नोति, thus: 'he attains peace, not desiring desires', but more likely न कामकामी should be taken as beginning a *new* sentence with शान्तिमाप्नोति implied: 'he attains peace, not the one who desires desires'.

22. निःस्पृहः, निर्ममो, निरहंकारः These three adjectives formed with the adverbial prefix निस् 'away', here serving as a prefix of negation, are all bahuvrīhis made on karmadhārayas. According to the analysis employed by the Indian grammarians, निस् is expanded into an adjective by appending to it the participle गत 'gone', hence निर्गत 'gone away (निस्)'. Accordingly, निःस्पृहः would be thus analyzed: निर्गताः स्पृहाः यस्य सः 'he whose desires have gone away', and similarly with the other two compounds. Western grammarians, however, are in the habit of saying 'having away desires' or 'having desires away', which, though awkward, is thought to reflect more accurately the quasi-adjectival value of the adverb निस् as used in this type of compound.

मम in निर्ममो is, of course, the genitive of the first person pronoun अहम्, and so *literally* निर्ममो is 'he who is without (the notion) of me *or* belonging to me', *i.e.,* is free of possessiveness.

In order to understand the third compound निरहंकारः, it is necessary to know that in the Sāṃkhya philosophy, technical terms from which are plentiful enough in the Gītā, the अहंकार (*literally* 'I-maker') is an internal organ whose function is to appropriate every act of an individual to himself in one way or another, a sort of ego-izing principle. The individual referred to in this passage, however, has so far controlled himself that he has gotten quite beyond the effect of the अहंकार. Having gotten to this point of mental discipline, he has now attained to a Brahmic state (एषा ब्राह्मी स्थितिः), *i.e.*, a state of identity with Brahman or perhaps immersion in Brahman.

23. अन्तकाले 'at the final time', *viz.*, the hour of death.

24. ब्रह्मनिर्वाणम् Nirvāṇa, as is obvious from its presence here, is not a term peculiar to Buddhism, by which it was borrowed from the general Brahmanical religion that preceded Gautama Buddha and was therefore his heritage. Its etymological meaning is 'a blowing out', as of a candle or lamp due to a sudden draught. When transferred, as is sufficiently natural, to the figure of the flames of the passions, it meant their complete extinction. This condition of quietude, the extinction of all passions, clingings and attachments, is here equated with identity or absorption in Brahman.

Vocabulary

अङ्ग, *n.* a limb.

अधि-√गम् (गच्छति, class I), go unto, attain.

अनु-वि-√धा (दधाति, class III), regulate; *in pass.* अनुविधीयते yields *or* conforms to (+ *gen.*).

अन्तकाल, *m.* 'the final time', the final hour.

अभि-√नन्द् (नन्दति, class I), take pleasure in; delight in.

अभिस्नेह, *m.* desire.

अम्भस्, *n.* water.

अर्थ, *m.* an object.

अशान्त, *adj.* not peaceful *or* tranquil [negative of *ppp.* √शम् (शाम्यति, class IV)].

अशुभ, *adj.* unpleasant, disagreeable; evil.

आपूर्यमाण, *pres. pass. part.* √पृ (पृणाति, class IX), being filled up.

आशु, *adv.* quickly.

√आस् (आस्ते, class II), sit.

इन्द्रिय, *n.* an organ of sense.

उद्विग्न, *ppp.* उद्-√विज् (विजते, class VI), frightened, perturbed.

उप, सम् *or* अभि-√जन् (जायते, class IV), be born, arise.

√ऋ (ऋच्छति, class VI), reach, attain.

कामकामिन्, *adj.* 'possessing a desire of desires', desiring desires; *as m.* one who desires desires.

किम्, *adv. acc.* how?

कूर्म, *m.* a tortoise.

क्रोध, *m.* anger.

गत, *ppp.* √गम् (गच्छति, class I), gone, *then* come to, arrived at, situated in, contained in; मनोगत 'contained in the mind', in the mind, mental.

√चर् (चरति, class I), go; wander; act on (+ *acc.*).

चेतस्, *n.* the mind *or* heart.

√जागृ (जागर्ति, class II), be awake (*strictly an intensive form of* 3√गृ 'be awake'). [*v.* note 19]

तुष्ट, *ppp.* √तुष् (तुष्यति, class IV), satisfied, content.

देहिन्, *adj.* 'possessing a body'; *as m.* a living being, a person, an individual.

√द्विष् (द्वेष्टि, class II), hate, loathe.

धी, *f.* thought, mental attitude.

√ध्या (ध्यायति, class IV), think, meditate.

नाश, *m.* destruction.

निगृहीत, *ppp.* नि-√ग्रह् (गृह्णाति, class IX), 'held apart', separated, kept away.

निरहंकार, *adj.* 'free of *or* without the I-principle (अहंकार)', devoid of the sense of ego.

निराहार, *adj.* having no food, abstaining from food.

निर्मम, *adj.* 'free of *or* without (the sense of) mine *or* belong to me', free *or* devoid of possessiveness.

निर्वाण, *n.* 'a blowing out' (as of a candle or lamp), extinction. [*v.* note 24]

नि-√वृत् (वर्तते, class I), turn away, disappear.

निशा, *f.* night.

निःस्पृह, *adj.* free of *or* without desire *or* longing.

नौ, *f.* a ship.

पर, *adj.* highest; *as n. (or m.?),* the Supreme Being.

परि-अव-√स्था (तिष्ठते, class I), stand *or* be firm, become steady.

पुमन्, *m.* a man.

प्रज्ञा, *f.* wisdom, knowledge, mental attitude *or* disposition, outlook, mentality.
प्रतिष्ठा, *f.* stability.
प्रतिष्ठित, *ppp.* प्रति-√स्था (तिष्ठति, class I), standing, standing firm, fixed, established.
प्र-√नश् (नश्यति, class IV), perish.
प्र-√भाष् (भाषते, class I), speak.
प्रमाथिन्, *adj.* agitating.
प्र-√विश् (विशति, class VI), enter.
प्रसन्न, *ppp.* प्र-√सद् (सीदति, class I), tranquil, serene.
प्रसभम्, *adv.* forcibly, violently.
प्रसाद, *m.* tranquility, serenity.
प्र-√हा (जहाति, class III), leave, give up.
ब्राह्म, *adj.* of *or* relating to Brahman, concerned *or* connected with Brahman.
भय, *n.* fear.
भावना, *f.* 'a causing to be *or* become', effecting; cultivating. [*v.* note 17]
भाषा, *f.* speech, language; description, definition.
भूत, *n.* a being, creature.
भ्रंश, *m.* fall; ruin; loss.
मनस्, *n.* the mind.
√यत् (यतति, class I), strive, make an effort.
यद्वत् . . . तद्वत्, *conj.* just as . . . so.
रस, *m.* taste; flavor (as object of the sense of taste).
राग, *m.* love, affection, desire, longing.
-वर्ज, *adj.* free from, devoid; -वर्जम्, *as an indeclinable at end of cpd.* except, excluding.
वश, *m.* power, control.
वश्य, *adj.* being under one's control, submissive, obedient.
वायु, *m.* the wind.
विधेय, *adj.* compliant, subject, obedient.
वि-नि-√वृत् (वर्तते, class I), turn away; cease, disappear.
विपश्चित्, *adj.* inspired, wise, learned.
विभ्रम, *m.* moving here and there, faltering, confusion.
वि-√मुह् (मुह्यति, class IV), be confused *or* infatuated.

वियुक्त, *ppp.* वि-√युज् (युनक्ति, class VII), dis-joined, separated from, devoid of.

विषय, *m.* an object of sense.

वि-√हा (जहाति, class III), cast aside, give up; *gerund* °हाय .

वीत, *ppp.* वि-√इ (एति, class II), 'gone away', departed.

√व्रज् (व्रजति, class I), go, walk.

शान्ति, *f.* peace.

शुभ, *adj.* pleasant, agreeable; good.

संयमिन्, *adj.* 'possessing control *or* restraint', controlled, restrained.

सङ्ग, *m.* attachment.

समाधि, *m.* fixing of the mind on, deep concentration.

समुद्र, *m.* an ocean.

संमोह, *m.* stupefaction, bewilderment, infatuation.

सम्-√यम् (यच्छति, class I), hold together, hold in check, restrain; *gerund* °यम्य .

सम्-√हृ (हरति, class I), bring *or* draw together, withdraw.

सर्वशः, *adv.* wholly, altogether; from all sides.

स्थित, *ppp.* √स्था (तिष्ठति, class I), *literally* having stood, *then* standing *as opposed to going or moving,* firm, settled, constant, invariable.

स्थिति, *f.* a condition *or* state.

स्पृहा, *f.* desire, longing for (+ *loc.*).

स्मृति, *f.* the memory.

√हृ (हरति, class I), take, take away.

हानि, *f.* leaving, leaving aside, giving up, abandonment.

LESSON THIRTY-ONE

Primary and Secondary Derivation.

I. *Primary Derivation.*

We have seen how verb forms are made from roots by the addition of the thematic vowel, various suffixes (or no increment at all!) and finally the addition of personal endings. But how are declinable stems (nouns and adjectives) formed? We do not, of course, have to form these stems ourselves, as they are listed readymade, so to speak, in our glossaries and dictionaries, and we have only to add the appropriate case endings in order to make words out of the bare stems, ready to take their place in the sentence along with the verbs that we have at some pains learned to form.

Declinable stems are made from verb roots by the addition of various suffixes, a process known in our grammars as 'primary derivation'. Sometimes, however, verb roots are used as nouns *without* the appendage of a suffix, as, for example, the two root nouns धी 'thought' and भू 'earth', which we had in the prior lesson. In such instances where the root alone functions as a declinable stem, the ancient Indian grammarians, who rigorously proceeded on the principle that *all* nouns and adjectives were derived from verb roots by the addition of a suffix, logically assumed that the essential suffix had been dropped. The reason for the requirement of a suffix is that without it a verb root was, according to their view, a mere grammatical abstraction, so that a further element was needed to indicate how the bare verbal notion was to be conceived, *i.e.,* whether as an act or process or whether as performed by an agent. Moreover, a suffix was needed to impart whatever phonetic substitutions, like guṇa or vṛddhi (or no change!), were to be effected in the root in its conversion to a declinable stem. The dummy or ghost suffix, which was dropped after imparting these factors to the root, is a postulate current also among modern linguists who call it a 'zero'-suffix.[1]

Suffixes of primary derivation, which number 50 or more (!), impart to the root either the meaning of a noun of action or of a noun of agent. The latter class of derivatives that denote the agent are often adjectival or

---

[1]A zero-suffix might similarly be postulated in English to explain mutated plurals like *mice* and *lice,* whose change of root vowel from *-ou-* (*mouse, louse*) to *-i-* (*mice, lice*) can then be attributed to the phonological effect of a suffix that was subsequently dropped. This would, in fact, be *historically correct,* as the plurals of Old English *mūs* and *lūs* (from which are descended *mouse* and *louse*) were formed in prehistoric Old English by the suffix *-iz;* thus, **mūs-iz* and **lūs-iz* (from Indo-European **mūs-es* and **lūs-es*). The *-i-* of this suffix caused the *-ū-* of the prior syllable to become 'fronted' or mutated by a sort of vocalic harmony. The mutated sound, probably pronounced as *-ü-* (long!) in Modern German, was written *-ȳ-* in Old English. The modern spellings *mouse/mice* and *louse/lice* reflect later phonetic changes and orthographical habits.

participial in character. Thus, with the primary suffix *-a* are made the following nouns of action (*nomina actionis,* as they are technically called): *krodh-a* (क्रोध) 'anger' (√क्रुध् 'be angry'), *harṣ-a* (हर्ष) 'joy' (√हृष् 'be delighted'), *jay-a* (जय) 'victory' (√जि 'conquer'), *hav-a* (हव) 'a call' (√हू 'call'), *sneh-a* (स्नेह) 'love' (√स्निह् 'love'), all with guṇa strengthening of the root, and *kām-a* (काम) 'desire' (√कम् 'desire'), *bhāg-a* (भाग) 'share' (√भज् 'share') with vṛddhi strengthening. In other examples, the same suffix *-a* forms nouns (or adjectives) of agency (*nomina agentis*): *sarp-a* (सर्प) 'a serpent (literally 'a creeper', √सृप् 'creep'), *megh-a* (मेघ) 'a cloud' (*literally* 'a rain-er', √मिघ् 'make water', but originally 'drip'), *plav-a* (प्लव) 'a boat' (*literally* 'a floater', (√प्लु 'float'). As has been said, the agential class is often adjectival (or participial) in character: so, *kṣam-a* (क्षम) 'patient' (√क्षम् 'be patient'), *khād-a* (खाद) 'eating' (√खाद् 'eat'). Frequently, the nouns of action, which are basically abstract, have also a concrete meaning; thus, *bhed-a* (भेद) from √भिद् 'split' may mean 'the act of splitting' or 'what has been split, a breach *or* split'. Similarly, formed with the common suffix *-ana,* the stem *ās-ana* (आसन) from √आस् 'sit' may mean 'the act of sitting' or 'what one sits upon, a seat *or* chair'.

The roots to which these and the other primary suffixes are attached are variously treated, *i.e.,* often by guṇa or vṛddhi substitution, or reduplication. Occasionally there is no change in the root vowel, as in *yug-a* (युग) 'yoke' (√युज् 'join, yoke'). No general rule can be given concerning the treatment of the root vowel when a primary suffix is added, as it varies with the same suffix as attached to different roots (as seen in the case of *-a*) and from suffix to suffix, some exhibiting only one kind of strengthening or none at all.

The formation of primary stems is a fundamental aspect of the structure of the language. These stems number in the many thousands, constituting the greater part of its basic vocabulary. From many of them are made, by a further process of derivation, yet other stems which, because of their secondary origin are appropriately called 'secondary derivatives', and the suffixes employed to make them 'suffixes of secondary derivation' or, more simply, 'secondary suffixes'.

Why, it may be asked, is it necessary or even desirable to know how these two great classes of stems are made? Why do we need to know, for example, that the word *jñāna* (ज्ञान) 'knowledge' is formed from √ज्ञा 'know' by the addition of the primary suffix *-ana,* that it means *literally* 'the act of knowing', then more concretely 'knowledge'? This information, after all, can be had from a dictionary, and we could be spared having to learn so many more unnecessary details! By a similar logic, we may say, quite rightly too, that it is possible to drive a car without the least knowledge of its inner workings, how the engine is made, what are its parts and their functions. When something goes wrong, we would have no recourse then but to call upon someone with the knowledge that we lack. In the same way, it is possible to skirt a knowledge of these fundamental building processes in Sanskrit and simply resort to the dictionary whenever we encounter an unfamiliar word. But while the driver of a car can get along without knowing anything about its mechanism, a student of Sanskrit, fitted with so superficial a knowledge of the structure of the language, will always be without the insight or means needed to resolve difficulties and obscurities of one sort or another. A simple example may serve to show how helpful a basic knowledge of the principles of primary derivation can be in throwing light on what is obscure. The well-known word *nirvāṇa* (निर्वाण), which came into English with the advent of Buddhist studies in Western countries, has been endlessly discussed, but often by persons who are unfamiliar with its etymology and early *pre*-Buddhist use. With a knowledge of primary derivation, we readily see that it is formed from the compound root *nir-vā* (निर्वा) 'blow out' (in the intransitive sense) with the suffix *-ana* (like ज्ञान and आसन above) and that as a noun of action it means simply 'the act (*or* process) of blowing out *or* going out', whether of the flame of a candle or a lamp. When applied figuratively to the fiery passions of love and hate, etc., it clearly and simply refers to their extinction -- their 'blowing out *or* going out'. Such is the original sense, though in the later Buddhist usage it was greatly modified by metaphysical speculation.

As we have just seen in the example of *nirvāṇa,* the primary suffixes are also added to roots compounded with verbal prefixes. These compounded roots, whether with but one or two (or rarely even three) prefixes, are treated no differently with regard to the appendage of particular suffixes than the same roots without verbal prefixes. Needless to say, the meaning of these compound formulations corresponds to their meaning as verb roots with the same prefixes; *e.g., upāgam-a* (उपागम) 'a coming near, approach' reflects the meaning of √*gam* with the prefixes *upa-ā*. Sometimes, however, the noun is specialized beyond the range of the verb root with the same prefixes; thus, *vyākar-aṇa* (व्याकरण) means 'grammatical analysis, grammar', but its parent *vy-ā-*√*kṛ* (व्या-कृ) means 'undo, sever, separate, analyze' etc., but without the particularization seen in *vyākaraṇa*.

Many of the commonest primary suffixes, including those already exemplified and a few relatively unproductive ones, are given in the following list, where they are arranged alphabetically for easy reference, rather than by frequency of their appendage. The absence of a suffix -- the so-called 'zero'-suffix -- which occurs when the bare root (with root vowel modified or not) is used as a noun (or more commonly as an adjective at the end of a compound), is indicated by a double hyphen (--).

	Suffix	*Root*	*Examples*
1.	--	√*diś* 'point out'	*diś* '(cardinal) point'
		√*dviṣ* 'hate'	*dviṣ* 'enemy'
		√*dhī* 'think'	*dhī* 'thought'
		√*bhū* 'be'	*bhū* '-being; earth'
		1 √*vid* 'know'	*-vid* 'knowing'
		√*duh* 'milk'	*-duh* 'milking'
2.	*-a*	√*yuj* 'yoke'	*yug-a* 'yoke'
		√*īś* 'rule'	*īś-a* 'ruler, lord'
		√*dih* 'stroke'[2]	*deh-a* 'body'
		√*muh* 'be confused'	*moh-a* 'delusion'
		vi-√*kram* 'step out, attack'	*vi-kram-a* 'courage'
		ni-√*vas* 'dwell'	*ni-vās-a* 'dwelling'
		sam-√*tuṣ* 'be satisfied'	*saṃ-toṣ-a* 'satisfaction'
		vi-√*śiṣ* 'leave apart'	*vi-śeṣ-a* 'difference'
3.	*-an*	√*rāj* 'rule'	*rāj-an* 'rul-er, king'
		√*takṣ* 'hew, make from wood'	*takṣ-an* 'hew-er, carpenter'
		prati-√*div* 'play against'	*prati-dīv-an* 'opponent at dice'[3]
4.	*-ana*	√*dṛś* 'see'	*darś-ana* 'seeing' (also 'causing to see', *i.e.,* 'showing' from caus. stem *darś-aya-* with loss of caus. suffix *-aya-*)
		√*bhuj* 'enjoy'	*bhoj-ana* 'enjoying; food' (*lit.* 'what is enjoyed')

---

[2]Originally, 'form *or* shape' with the hand, as mud or clay; thus, *deha* etymologically means 'something formed *or* shaped'.

[3]It is not always possible to determine in the case of a derivative with a verbal prefix whether it was formed directly from the compound root or whether the prefix was added later.

	Suffix	*Root*	*Examples*
		√*sthā* 'stand'	*sthāna* (*sthā-ana*) 'standing; place'
		√*nī* 'lead'	*nay-ana* 'leading; the eye (as the 'leader')
		√*ās* 'sit'	*ās-ana* 'sitting; seat'
5.	*-as*	√*vac* 'speak'	*vac-as* 'speech'
		√*tij* 'be sharp'	*tej-as* 'sharpness, tip (of flame); splendor'
		√*tap* 'be warm'	*tap-as* 'heat; internal warmth, austerity'
		√*man* 'think'	*man-as* 'mind'
		√*cakṣ* 'look upon'	*cakṣ-as* 'eye'
		√*nam* 'bow'	*nam-as* 'bowing, obeisance'
		√*sṛ* 'flow'	*sar-as* 'lake' (*lit.* 'fluid')
6.	*-ā*	√*hiṃs* 'injure'	*hiṃs-ā* 'injury'
		√*kṣudh* 'be hungry'	*kṣudh-ā* 'hunger'
7.	*-i*	√*kṛṣ* 'plow'	*kṛṣ-i* 'plowing'
		√*ruc* 'please'	*ruc-i* 'pleasure'
		√*śuc* 'flame'	*śuc-i* 'flaming, bright'
8.	*-u*	√*sādh* 'come *or* lead straight to one's goal'	*sādh-u* 'good' (*lit.* 'leading straight to the goal')
		1√*vas* 'shine'	*vas-u* 'excellent' (*lit.* 'shining, splendid')
		√*svad* 'be savory'	*svād-u* 'savory, tasting good, sweet'
9.	*-us*	√*cakṣ* 'look upon'	*cakṣ-us* 'eye'
		√*dhan* 'set in motion'	*dhan-us* 'bow' (*lit.* 'that which sets [the arrow] in motion')
10.	*-ti*[4]	√*vac* 'speak'	*uk-ti* 'speaking'
		√*man* 'think'	*ma-ti* 'thought'
		√*śam* 'be quiet'	*śān-ti* 'quiet; peace'

[4]Before the suffix *-ti* a root takes the same form as before *-ta*, the suffix of the past passive participle; so *cf. śān-ti ~ śān-ta, ma-ti ~ ma-ta.*

	Suffix	*Root*	*Examples*
		√*jan* 'be born'	*jā-ti* 'birth'
		√*prī* 'be glad'	*prī-ti* 'pleasure'
		pra-√*kṛ* 'presuppose'	*pra-kṛ-ti* 'nature, matter' (*lit.* 'what is presupposed, *hence* original condition of things)
11.	*-tṛ*	√*dā* 'give'	*dā-tṛ* 'giver'
		√*kṛ* 'do, make'	*kar-tṛ* 'doer, maker'
12.	*-tra, -trā* (indicates the root as the instrument of the action)	√*pat* 'fly'	*pat-tra* 'wing' (*lit.* 'means of flying')
		2√*vas* 'wear'	*vas-tra* 'garment' (*lit.* 'means of dressing')
		1√*pā* 'drink'	*pā-tra* 'cup' (*lit.* 'means of drinking')
		√*śas* 'cut'	*śas-tra* 'knife, sword' (*lit.* 'means of cutting')
		√*nī* 'lead, guide'	*ne-tra* 'eye' (*lit.* 'means of leading *or* guiding')
		1√*mā* 'measure'	*mā-trā* 'measure'
		√*daṃś* 'bite'	*daṃṣ-ṭrā* 'large tooth, tusk' (*lit.* 'means of biting')
13.	*-man*	√*kṛ* 'do'	*kar-man* 'action'
		√*jan* 'be born'	*jan-man* 'birth'
		√*viś* 'enter, settle down'	*veś-man* 'dwelling' (*lit.* 'an entering, settling down, settlement')
14.	*-na,* rarely *-nā*	1√*vṛ* 'cover'	*var-ṇa* 'color' (*lit.* 'covering')
		√*yaj* 'worship'	*yaj-ña* 'worship'
		√*svap* 'sleep'	*svap-na* 'sleep'
		√*tṛṣ* 'be thirsty'	*tṛṣ-ṇā* 'thirst'
		√*yāc* 'request'	*yāc-ñā* 'request'

	Suffix	*Root*	*Examples*
15.	*-ra*	√*śak* 'be able'	*śak-ra* 'mighty' (*lit.* 'able')
		√*vaj* 'be strong'[5]	*ug-ra* 'mighty
		√*śuc* 'be bright, glow'	*śuk-ra* 'bright'
16.	*-is*	√*hu* 'offer'	*hav-is* 'oblation'
		√*jyut* 'shine'[6]	*jyot-is* 'light'
		√*ṛc* 'gleam'	*arc-is* 'flame'

II. *Secondary Derivation.*

We have already said that by 'secondary derivation' is meant the formation of noun and adjective stems from *pre-existing* stems that are made by primary derivation. By this secondary process is made an immense class of declinable stems, which taken together with those of primary origin constitute the bulk of the Sanskrit vocabulary. There are altogether at least a couple of dozen secondary suffixes, some of which are, of course, of much commoner occurrence than others. Among the most productive of these suffixes are those that form adjectives expressing *appurtenance to* or *connection with* what is denoted by the primary stem to which they are attached. While these adjectives may conveniently be literally translated by 'pertaining to, connected with *or* relating to such-and-such', probably oftener a specific adjective will be found to be less cumbersome in expressing the idea. For example, from the noun *pṛthivī* (पृथिवी) 'earth', by the addition of the suffix *-a* (with vṛddhi of the initial vowel and loss of the *-ī*) is made the adjective *pārthiva* (पार्थिव), *literally* 'pertaining to the earth', which may often be more succinctly rendered by 'terrestrial'[7]. Similarly, from *vasanta* (वसन्त) 'spring' is formed *vāsanta* (वासन्त) 'pertaining to the spring, *or* vernal' *or simply* 'of the spring'. We would surely, however, not translate वासन्तः समीरः by 'a breeze *pertaining* to the spring', but rather by 'a breeze of the spring' or better 'a spring breeze'. Often, then, a genitive phrase or part of a compound may be used in the translation of an adjective of appurtenance.

---

[5] √*vaj*, which does not occur as a productive or active root in Sanskrit, is inferred from several primary derivatives all of which have to do with 'might, strength', as *vaj-ra* 'a thunderbolt', *oj-as* 'strength'.

[6] √*jyut* is borrowed from the Prakrit equivalent of Sanskrit √*dyut* 'shine'.

[7] Used as a noun, *pārthiva* is a common word for 'king' ('one who has to do with the earth').

Appurtenance or connection may frequently denote familial descent, especially when the primary stem is a proper name. Adjectives with this implication readily function as nouns with the meaning 'descendant *or* son of so-and-so (as designated by the primary stem)'. Thus, from *aṅgiras* (अङ्गिरस्) 'Aṅgiras' is made the secondary derivative *āṅgiras-a* (आङ्गिरस), *literally* 'pertaining to (the seer) Aṅgiras', but, depending on the context, more probably to be translated by 'descendant *or* son of (the seer) Aṅgiras'. A few of the secondary suffixes are used *exclusively* to express familial descent, *i.e.,* as patronymic or metronymic suffixes, according as they may denote a male or female progenitor. For example, *-āyana* forms a number of familiarly used proper names: *Āśvalāyana* (आश्वलायन) 'descendant of Aśvala (अश्वल)', *Kāṇvāyana* (काण्वायन) 'descendant of Kaṇva (कण्व)'.

Very often adjectives of appurtenance are employed in the neuter as abstracts; so, from *puruṣa* (पुरुष) 'man' is derived *pauruṣ-a* (पौरुष) 'manly', which as a neuter noun means 'manliness, courage'. By a curious circle of meanings from that of the primary stem to that of an adjective of appurtenance used as a noun, we are often led back to the same meaning as the primary. Examples of this circular phenomenon abound, but a couple will suffice: from the primary derivative *manas* (मनस्) 'mind' is formed the secondary derivative *mānas-a* (मानस) 'pertaining to the mind, mental', which as a neuter abstract (*literally* 'what pertains to the mind') means simply 'mind', whereby we are led back in a circle to the primary stem *manas* ! Similarly, from *manus* (मनुस्) 'man' comes the secondary derivative *manuṣ-ya* (मनुष्य) 'pertaining to man, human', which, used as a noun (like our 'human'), means 'man'!

There are half a dozen secondary suffixes that exclusively denote *possession,* and some of these are of extremely frequent occurrence. Commonest of them is the suffix *-in,* which is added to nouns ending in *-a* which is dropped before the suffix, as *bal-in* (बलिन्) 'possessing strength (बल), strong', *dhan-in* (धनिन्) 'possessing wealth (धन), wealthy'. Almost as common is *-vat,* much less so its sister *-mat,* which may be added to stems in *any* final, unlike *-in;* thus, *rūpa-vat* (रूपवत्) 'possessing beauty (रूप), beautiful', *lajjā-vat* (लज्जावत्) 'possessing bashfulness (लज्जा), bashful', *aśman-vat* (अश्मन्वत्) 'possessing stones (अश्मन्), stony'; *buddhi-mat* (बुद्धिमत्) 'possessing understanding (बुद्धि), intelligent', *āyuṣ-mat* (आयुष्मत्) 'possessing (long) life (आयुस्), longlived', *paśu-mat* (पशुमत्) 'possessing cows (पशु), rich in cows'.

The suffixes *-tva* and *-tā* constitute a synonymous pair that is of ubiquitous occurrence, especially in commentaries on philosophical works. They form abstracts, neuter and feminine respectively, and as such express the condition or quality of being whatever is denoted by the stem to which they are attached. In our readings we have many times had the abstract noun *pañca-tva* (पञ्चत्व) 'five-ness' in the idiom 'go to five-ness', *i.e.,* be resolved into the five elements of which all material things consist, hence, die. Abstracts with either suffix, but much more commonly with *-tva,* can be formed practically as needed by an author.[8] Generally they are made from nouns or adjectives, as *deva-tva* (देवत्व) 'the condition of being a god (देव), god-hood', *amṛta-tva* (अमृतत्व) 'the condition of being immortal (अमृत), immortality', *puruṣa-tā* (पुरुषता) 'the quality of a person *or* human being (पुरुष)', *i.e.,* human nature.

The most important secondary suffixes, including those already mentioned, are presented below in alphabetical order, with the meanings they impart to the primary stem and examples of derivatives made with these suffixes.

---

[8]Complex ideas, equivalent to clauses in English, especially *causal* clauses, are often expressed in Sanskrit by long predicative compounds with -त्वेन or -तया appended, the subject being put in the 'subjective genitive'; as in क्षेत्राणां जलभारनिम्नावलम्बित-जलदधारासिक्ततया अचिरेण सस्यान्यवर्धन्त । 'Since the fields had been sprinkled by showers from clouds hanging low with their burden of water, the crops soon thrived', or as expressed by an ordinary causal clause (by the conjunction यत: and its correlative तत:) with the compound resolved into shorter compounds: यत: क्षेत्राणि जलभारेण निम्नावलम्बितेभ्य: जलदेभ्य: धाराभि: आसिक्तानि (अभवन्) तत: सस्यानि अचिरेण अवर्धन्त ।

	Phonetic Changes in	*Meaning Imparted to*	*Examples*	
Suffixes	*Primary Stem*	*Primary Stem*	*Primary Stem* →	*Secondary Stem*
1. *-a*	vṛddhi of first syllable	'pertaining *or* relating to, connnected with' (often used as noun, esp. in neuter as abstract)	*ayas* (अयस्) 'metal'	*āyas-a* (आयस) 'pertaining to metal, metallic
			buddha (बुद्ध) 'Buddha'	*bauddh-a* (बौद्ध) 'connected with the Buddha', as a masc. noun 'a follower of the Buddha , a Buddhist'
			sumanas (सुमनस्)[9] 'a friend'	*saumanas-a* (सौमनस) as neuter abstract 'friendliness'
	vṛddhi of first syllable + guṇa of final *-u*		*manu* (मनु) 'man'	*mānav-a* (मानव) 'pertaining to man, human', as masc. noun 'a man'
		'descended from so-and-so' (patronymics and metronymics)	*kuru* (कुरु) 'Kuru'	*kaurav-a* (कौरव) 'descendant of Kuru'

---

[9]The primary stem may be simple or compound. The strengthened syllable here is the prefix.

Suffixes	*Phonetic Changes in Primary Stem*	*Meaning Imparted to Primary Stem*	*Primary Stem* →	*Secondary Stem*
	vṛddhi of first syllable		*subhadrā* (सुभद्रा) 'Subhadrā', wife of Arjuna	*saubhadr-a* (सौभद्र) metronymic of Abhimanyu, as son of Subhadrā
			pṛthā (पृथा) 'Pṛthā', mother of Arjuna	*pārth-a* (पार्थ) 'son of Pṛthā'
2. *-āyana*	vṛddhi of first syllable	'descended from so-and-so'	*kati* (कति) 'Kati', name of a sage	*Kāty-āyana* (कात्यायन) 'Kātyāyana', a descendant of Kati
3. *-i*	vṛddhi of first syllable	'descended from so-and-so'	*marut* (मरुत्) 'the Maruts', storm-gods in the Ṛgveda	*mārut-i* (मारुति) 'descendant of the Maruts'
			satyaka (सत्यक) 'Satyaka', father of Yuyudhāna	*sātyak-i* (सात्यकि) 'son of Satyaka', patronymic of Yuyudhāna
			somadatta (सोमदत्त) 'Somadatta'	*saumadatt-i* (सौमदत्ति) 'son of Somadatta'
4. *-ika*	vṛddhi of first syllable	'pertaining to' (etc.)	*veda* (वेद) 'Veda'	*vaid-ika* (वैदिक) 'relating to the Vedas'
			dharma (धर्म) 'dharma'	*dhārm-ika* (धार्मिक) 'relating to dharma'

Suffixes	*Phonetic Changes in Primary Stem*	*Meaning Imparted to Primary Stem*	*Primary Stem* →	*Secondary Stem*
	vṛddhi of first syllable		*nyāya* (न्याय) 'Nyāya', the Indian system of logic	*naiyāy-ika*[10] (नैयायिक) 'connected with the Nyāya system', as a masc. noun 'an adherent of the Nyāya'
5. *-in*	no change	'possessing'	*pakṣa* (पक्ष) 'a wing'	*pakṣ-in* (पक्षिन्) 'possessing wings, winged', as masc. noun 'a bird'
			hasta (हस्त) 'hand'	*hastin* (हस्तिन्) 'possessing hands', as a masc. noun 'an elephant' (the hand with reference to its trunk)
6. *-īna*	no change	added to weak or weakest stem of adjectives in *-añc* with no change in meaning	*pratyañc* (प्रत्यञ्च्) 'backward, westward'	*pratīc-īna* (प्रतीचीन) 'backward, westward'

[10]When a primary stem begins with a consonant + *-y-* or *-v-* (as in *nyāya* 'logic', *vyākaraṇa* 'grammar' and *dvāra* 'door'), the *-y-* or *-v-* are treated as though they were *-i-* or *-u-* and by vṛddhi become *-ai-* and *-au-*, and a *-y-* and *-v-* are respectively inserted after the *-ai-/-au-* as a glide; hence, *naiyāy-ika* 'adherent of Nyāya', *vaiyākar-aṇa* 'a grammarian', *dauvār-ika* 'a doorkeeper'.

Suffixes	*Phonetic Changes in Primary Stem*	*Meaning Imparted to Primary Stem*	*Primary Stem* →	*Secondary Stem*
7. *-īya*	no change	added to pronoun roots to make possessive adjectives	*mad-* (मद्), *asmad-* (अस्मद्), *tvad-* (त्वद्), *yuṣmad-* (युष्मद्), *tad-* (तद्)	*mad-īya* (मदीय) 'belonging to me', *asmad-īya* (अस्मदीय) 'belonging to us', *tvad-īya* (त्वदीय) 'belonging to you' *yuṣmad-īya* (युष्मदीय) 'belonging to you (plur.)', *tad-īya* (तदीय) 'belonging to him, her, it (etc.)'
8. *-eya*	vṛddhi of first syllable	'descended from so-and-so'	*saramā* (सरमा) 'Saramā', name of a female dog belonging to Indra and the gods	*sāram-eya* (सारमेय) 'descendant of Saramā; a dog'
			kuntī (कुन्ती) 'Kuntī', also called 'Pṛthā', mother of Yudhiṣṭhira, Bhīmasena and Arjuna	*kaunt-eya* कौन्तेय) 'a son of Kuntī', metronymic of Yudhiṣṭhira, Bhīmasena and Arjuna
			draupadī (द्रौपदी) Draupadī	*draupad-eya* (द्रौपदेय) 'a son of Draupadī'

Suffixes	*Phonetic Changes in Primary Stem*	*Meaning Imparted to Primary Stem*	*Primary Stem* →	*Secondary Stem*
9. *-ka*	no change	makes diminutives, but most often added with no effect in meaning of the primary[11]	*rājan* (राजन्) 'a king'	*rāja-ka* (राजक) 'a little *or* petty king, a princeling'
			aśva (अश्व) 'a horse'	*aśva-ka* (अश्वक) 'a nag'
			putra (पुत्र) 'a son'	*putra-ka* (पुत्रक) 'a little son' as an endearing term, but often a variant of *putra*
10. *-tana*	no change	added to adverbs of time to make adjectives	*purā* (पुरा) 'formerly'	*purā-tana* (पुरातन) belonging to a former time, ancient'
			śvas (श्वस्) 'tomorrow'	*śvas-tana* (श्वस्तन) 'belonging to the morrow'
			sanā (सना) 'of old, always'	*sanā-tana* (सनातन) 'eternal'
11. *-tva*, *-tā*	no change	condition or state of the primary	*amṛta* (अमृत) 'immortal'	*amṛta-tva* (अमृतत्व) 'immortality'

[11]The suffix *-ka* is often added to bahuvrīhi compounds, without affecting their meaning, either to produce a more easily inflected stem (as एकपत्नीक 'having one wife', instead of एकपत्नि with short final to fit the अग्नि declension) or for metrical reasons, more rhythmical sound, or just at the pleasure of an author.

Suffixes	*Phonetic Changes in Primary Stem*	*Meaning Imparted to Primary Stem*	*Primary Stem* →	*Secondary Stem*
	no change		*go* (गो) 'a cow'	*go-tva* (गोत्व) 'cow-ness', the quality or condition of being a cow
			aputra (अपुत्र) 'not having a son'	*aputra-tā* (अपुत्रता) 'a condition of being without a son'
12. *-maya*	no change	'made of, consisting of, abounding in'	*kāṣṭha* (काष्ठ) 'wood'	*kāṣṭha-maya* (काष्ठमय) 'made of wood'
			tejas (तेजस्) 'splendor, majesty'	*tejo-maya* (तेजोमय) 'abounding in splendor *or* majesty'
			vāc (वाच्) 'speech'	*vāṅ-maya* (वाङ्मय) 'consisting of speech'
13. *-min, -vin*	no change	'possessing'	*go* (गो) 'a cow'	*go-min* (गोमिन्) 'possessing cows'
			sva (स्व) 'one's own (property)'	*svā-min*[12] (स्वामिन्) 'an owner, master'
			tapas (तपस्) 'austerities'	*tapas-vin* (तपस्विन्) 'practising austerities; as a masc. noun 'an ascetic'

[12]The lengthening of the vowel in *svā-* is apparently irregular.

Suffixes	*Phonetic Changes in Primary Stem*	*Meaning Imparted to Primary Stem*	*Primary Stem* →	*Secondary Stem*
	no change		*yaśas* (यशस्) 'glory'	*yaśas-vin* (यशस्विन्) 'possessing glory, glorious'
			tejas (तेजस्) 'splendor, majesty'	*tejas-vin* (तेजस्विन्) 'possessing splendor *or* majesty, splendid, majestic'
14. *-ya*	vṛddhi of first syllable	1) 'pertaining *or* relating to, connected with'	*deva* (देव) 'god'	*daiv-ya* (दैव्य) 'relating to the gods, divine'; as neut. noun 'fate'
			grīvā (ग्रीवा) 'the neck'	*graiv-ya* (ग्रैव्य) 'pertaining to the neck, cervical'
	no change		*brahman,* m. and n. (ब्रह्मन्) 'a Brahman priest' (m.), 'holy word, holy life' (n.)	*brahmaṇ-ya* (ब्रह्मण्य) 'connected with Brahman priests', so 'friendly to Brahmans' and 'pertaining *or* attached to the holy word *or* holy life', hence 'pious, religious'
			aśva (अश्व) 'a horse'	*aśv-ya* (अश्व्य) 'relating to horses, equine'
			pitṛ (पितृ) 'father'	*pitr-ya* (पित्र्य) 'relating to one's father, paternal'

Suffixes	*Phonetic Changes in Primary Stem*	*Meaning Imparted to Primary Stem*	*Primary Stem* →	*Secondary Stem*
	vṛddhi of first syllable	2) 'descended from so-and-so'	*aditi* (अदिति) 'Aditi', infinity personified as a goddess	*ādit-ya* (आदित्य) 'son of Aditi', metronymic for Mitra, Varuṇa and several other Vedic gods
		neuter abstracts	*adhipati* (अधिपति) 'overlord'	*ādhipat-ya* (आधिपत्य) 'overlordship'
			paṇḍita (पण्डित) 'a learned man, scholar'	*pāṇḍit-ya* (पाण्डित्य) 'learning, erudition'
			subhaga (सुभग) 'a fortunate *or* happy person'	*saubhāg-ya*[13] (सौभाग्य) 'happiness'
15. *-vat, -mat*	no change	'possessing'	*bhaga* (भग) 'fortune'	*bhaga-vat* (भगवत्) 'possessing (good) fortune, fortunate, blessed'
			dayā (दया) 'compassion'	*dayā-vat* (दयावत्) 'possessing compassion, compassionate'

[13]When a compound is made into a secondary derivative, *both* parts (here *su-* and *-bhaga*) are often subjected to vṛddhi; hence, *sau-bhāg-ya*.

Suffixes	*Phonetic Changes in Primary Stem*	*Meaning Imparted to Primary Stem*	*Primary Stem* →	*Secondary Stem*
	no change		*saṃtāpa* (संताप) 'sorrow'	*saṃtāpa-vat* (संतापवत्) 'possessing sorrow, sorrowful'
			aṃśu (अंशु) 'ray, beam'	*aṃśu-mat* (अंशुमत्) 'possessing rays, rich in rays, radiant', as masc. noun 'the sun'
			jyotis (ज्योतिस्) 'light'	*jyotiṣ-mat* (ज्योतिष्मत्) 'possessing light, luminous'

VI. Kṛṣṇa's Revelation (1)

श्रीभगवान् उवाच ।
पश्य मे पार्थ रूपाणि शतशो[1] ऽथ[2] सहस्रशः[1] ।
नानाविधानि दिव्यानि नानावर्णाकृतीनि च ॥ ५ ॥
पश्यादित्यान्[3] वसून्[4] रुद्रान्[5] अश्विनौ[6] मरुतस्[7] तथा ।
बहून्यदृष्टपूर्वाणि पश्याश्चर्याणि भारत[8] ॥ ६ ॥
इहैकस्थं जगत्कृत्स्नं पश्याद्य सचराचरम् ।
मम देहे[9] गुडाकेश यच्चान्यद्द्रष्टुमिच्छसि ॥ ७ ॥
न तु मां शक्यसे[10] द्रष्टुमनेनैव स्वचक्षुषा ।
दिव्यं ददामि ते चक्षुः पश्य मे योगमैश्वरम्[11] ॥ ८ ॥

संजय उवाच ।
एवमुक्त्वा ततो राजन्महायोगेश्वरो[12] हरिः ।
दर्शयामास[13] पार्थाय परमं रूपमैश्वरम् ॥ ९ ॥
अनेकवक्त्रनयनम्[14] अनेकाद्भुतदर्शनम्[14] ।
अनेकदिव्याभरणं[14] दिव्यानेकोद्यतायुधम्[14] ॥ १० ॥
दिव्यमाल्याम्बरधरं[15] दिव्यगन्धानुलेपनम्[15] ।
सर्वाश्चर्यमयं देवमनन्तं विश्वतोमुखम् ॥ ११ ॥
दिवि सूर्यसहस्रस्य भवेद्युगपदुत्थिता ।
यदि भाः[16] सदृशी सा स्याद्भासस्तस्य महात्मनः ॥ १२ ॥
तत्रैकस्थं जगत्कृत्स्नं प्रविभक्तमनेकधा[17] ।
अपश्यद्देवदेवस्य शरीरे पाण्डवस्तदा ॥ १३ ॥
ततः स विस्मयाविष्टो हृष्टरोमा धनंजयः ।
प्रणम्य शिरसा देवं कृताञ्जलिरभाषत ॥ १४ ॥

अर्जुन उवाच ।
पश्यामि देवांस्तव देव देहे सर्वांस्तथा भूतविशेषसङ्घान्[18] ।
ब्रह्माणमीशं कमलासनस्थम्[19] ऋषींश्च सर्वानुरगांश्च
दिव्यान्[20] ॥ १५ ॥
अनेकबाहूदरवक्त्रनेत्रं पश्यामि त्वां सर्वतो[21] ऽनन्तरूपम् ।
नान्तं न मध्यं न पुनस्तवादिं पश्यामि विश्वेश्वर विश्वरूप[22] ॥ १६ ॥
किरीतिनं[23] गदिनं[23] चक्रिणं[23] च तेजोराशिं सर्वतो दीप्तिमन्तम् ।
पश्यामि त्वां दुर्निरीक्ष्यं समन्ताद्[24] दीप्तानलार्कद्युतिम्[25]
अप्रमेयम् ॥ १७ ॥
त्वमक्षरं परमं वेदितव्यं[26] त्वमस्य विश्वस्य परं निधानम् ।
त्वमव्ययः शाश्वतधर्मगोप्ता सनातनस्त्वं पुरुषो[27] मतो मे ॥ १८ ॥
अनादिमध्यान्तमनन्तवीर्यमनन्तबाहुं शशिसूर्यनेत्रम् ।
पश्यामि त्वां दीप्तहुताशवक्त्रं[28] स्वतेजसा विश्वमिदं तपन्तम् ॥ १९ ॥
द्यावापृथिव्योर्[29] इदमन्तरं हि व्याप्तं त्वयैकेन दिशश्च सर्वाः[30] ।
दृष्ट्वाद्भुतं रूपमुग्रं तवेदं लोकत्रयं प्रव्यथितं महात्मन् ॥ २० ॥
अमी[31] हि त्वां सुरसङ्घा विशन्ति केचिद्भीताः प्राञ्जलयो गृणन्ति ।
स्वस्तीत्युक्त्वा[32] महर्षिसिद्धसङ्घाः[33] स्तुवन्ति त्वां स्तुतिभिः
पुष्कलाभिः ॥ २१ ॥
रुद्रादित्या वसवो ये च साध्या[34] विश्वे[35] ऽश्विनौ
मरुतश्चोष्मपाश्च[36] ।
गन्धर्वयक्षासुरसिद्धसङ्घा वीक्षन्ते त्वां विस्मिताश्चैव सर्वे ॥ २२ ॥
रूपं महत्ते बहुवक्त्रनेत्रं महाबाहो बहुबाहूरुपादम् ।
बहूदरं बहुदंष्ट्राकरालं दृष्ट्वा लोकाः प्रव्यथितास्तथाहम्[37] ॥ २३ ॥
नभःस्पृशं दीप्तमनेकवर्णं व्यात्ताननं[38] दीप्तविशालनेत्रम् ।
दृष्ट्वा हि त्वां प्रव्यथितान्तरात्मा धृतिं न विन्दामि शमं च
विष्णो ॥ २४ ॥
दंष्ट्राकरालानि च ते मुखानि दृष्ट्वैव[39] कालानलसंनिभानि[40] ।

दिशो न जाने[41] न लभे च शर्म प्रसीद देवेश जगन्निवास[42] ॥ २५ ॥
अमी च त्वां[43] धृतराष्ट्रस्य पुत्राः सर्वे सहैवावनिपालसङ्घैः ।
भीष्मो द्रोणः सूतपुत्रस्तथासौ सहास्मदीयैर्[44] अपि योधमुख्यैः[44] ॥ २६ ॥
वक्त्राणि ते त्वरमाणा विशन्ति दंष्ट्राकरालानि भयानकानि ।
केचिद्विलग्ना दशनान्तरेषु संदृश्यन्ते चूर्णितैरुत्तमाङ्गैः[45] ॥ २७ ॥
यथा नदीनां बहवो ऽम्बुवेगाः समुद्रमेवाभिमुखा द्रवन्ति ।
तथा तवामी नरलोकवीरा विशन्ति वक्त्राण्यभिविज्वलन्ति[46] ॥ २८ ॥
यथा प्रदीप्तं ज्वलनं पतङ्गा विशन्ति नाशाय समृद्धवेगाः[47] ।
तथैव नाशाय विशन्ति लोकास्तवापि वक्त्राणि समृद्धवेगाः[47] ॥ २९ ॥
लेलिह्यसे[48] ग्रसमानः समन्ताल्[49] लोकान्समग्रान्वदनैर्ज्वलद्भिः ।
तेजोभिरापूर्य जगत्समग्रं भासस्तवोग्राः प्रतपन्ति विष्णो ॥ ३० ॥

(Bhagavadgītā XI. 5-30).

Notes

At the outset of Chapter 11 of the Gītā, Arjuna requests Kṛṣṇa to reveal his 'immortal self'. The rest of the chapter consists of this revelation, partly in the words of Saṃjaya, who is describing the whole scene to Dhṛtarāṣṭra, and partly in the words of Arjuna, the sole participant in the revelation. Having witnessed the revelation, Arjuna is profoundly affected, but also filled with fear and asks Kṛṣṇa to return to his usual form.

1. शतशो/सहस्रशः The suffix -शस् (-शः), it will be recalled, is added to words of numerical character to form adverbs of quantity; so, here 'by the hundreds'/'by the thousands'.

2. अथ here means 'and', a common usage.

3. आदित्यान् *Literally*, 'the sons of Aditi', the Ādityas were really personified abstractions, whose number is variously given. The most important of the Ādityas were Mitra, personification of the Compact, and Varuṇa, personification of Truth.

4. वसून् The Vasus are a group of gods of indefinite number and function in the Ṛgveda, closely associated with the mighty Indra.

5. रुद्रान् The Rudras, whose number is also variously given, are storm gods in the Ṛgveda, the sons of Rudra (later called 'Śiva'), whence their name. They are more usually called 'Maruts' who are subsequently also mentioned in the stanza, as though, however, they were a separate group.

6. अश्विनौ As indicated by the dual ending, the Aśvins are a pair of deities in the Ṛgveda, who are especially renowned for their help to others in distress. It is interesting to note that the names of many whom they helped are specifically mentioned. The word अश्विन् is, of course, a secondary derivative meaning 'possessing horses', although they are not especially connected with horses in the Ṛgveda. The absence of any connection with horses suggests that the retention of this equine epithet is but a relic of an earlier age, when they may have been associated with horses, as seen in their apparent Greek counterparts, the horsemen Castor and Polydeuces. The Aśvins are also called 'Nāsatyas', which may be a secondary derivative with the suffix *-ya* from a lost (!) noun **nasati* meaning 'saving, rescuing', hence, 'the two who are concerned with saving *or* rescuing', so that this alternative name would indeed allude to their principal function of helping those in need.

7. मरुतस् As mentioned under note 5, the Maruts are just another name for the Rudras.

8. भारत a secondary derivative from भरत, hence, *literally* 'a descendant of Bhărata'. *Both* the Pāṇḍavas (one of whom was Arjuna) and the Kauravas, bitter enemies in the Great War of the Mahābhārata, were Bhāratas, as both traced their lineage from Bharata, the son of King Duṣṣanta (or Duṣyanta) and Śakuntalā. But the epithet is more especially applied to the Pāṇḍavas than to the Kauravas, and thus its use here.

9. मम देहे defines इहैकस्थं '(the whole world) here in one [place], in my body'.

10. शक्यसे not to be taken as passive, but as second singular middle of √शक् according to class IV. Ordinarily √शक् is conjugated in class V, but शक्यते and शक्यति occur in the epic language.

11. योगमैश्वरम् 'lordly power' or 'power as lord', a fine example of a secondary derivative, ऐश्वर being formed from ईश्वर by vṛddhi of the initial syllable and the suffix *-a* (*aiśvar-a*), before which the final vowel of the primary ईश्वर is lost. So, *literally* 'pertaining to a lord, lordly'. योग here means something like 'mystic power'.

12. महायोगेश्वरो to be resolved into महा + योगेश्वर, *not* महायोग + ईश्वर.

13. दर्शयामास Periphrastic perfect of the *causative* of √दृश् 'see': 'caused the son of Pṛthā to see . . '. Remember that causatives take a periphrastic perfect in order to retain the causative suffix *-aya-,* which does not appear in the simple perfect because the simple perfect is made directly from the reduplicated root (which from √दृश् would be ददृश्-), *not* from the causative stem (दर्शय-). Note that the primary agent of the seeing here, *viz.,* पार्थाय (a secondary derivative, by the way!), is expressed by the *dative,* not the instrumental, which is the most usual construction with causatives.

14. All four compounds are bahuvrīhis qualifying रूपम् in the prior stanza: '(his supreme form as lord), whose faces and eyes are many, whose wondrous aspects (दर्शन) are many' etc. Note that the primary derivative दर्शन (*darś-ana*) here has a concrete meaning, *i.e., not* the 'act of seeing' but 'what is seen, an aspect'.

15. दिव्यमाल्याम्बरधरं दिव्यगन्धानुलेपनम् The two compounds and सर्वाश्चर्यमयं are probably best construed with रूपम् continued from stanza 9, rather than with देवम् below; thus, '(his supreme form as lord) wearing divine garlands and garments, with divine perfumes and unguents, abounding in every wonder'. देवमनन्तं विश्वतोमुखं is in loose apposition to रूपम् with its pendant adjectives: '(his supreme form) . . ., a god, infinite, whose faces are everywhere'. Note the secondary suffix -मय in सर्वाश्चर्यमयं.

16. भा: subject of भवेद् . . .उत्थिता in the conditional clause: 'If the effulgence of . . . *should be risen up* in the heaven', *i.e.,* should appear there. The *s*-stem भास् 'effulgence' occurs in the neuter and feminine, but that it is here feminine is proved by the words सदृशी सा which refer to भा: in the apodosis: '*it* (सा) would be *like* (सदृशी)'.

17. प्रविभक्तमनेकधा 'divided up in many ways', probably meaning 'arranged in all its variety'. Formed like एकधा and अन्यधा with the adverbial suffix -धा, अनेकधा is an adverb of manner.

18. भूतविशेषसङ्घान् 'hosts of various creatures *or* beings'. As final member of a compound (भूतविशेष here), विशेष usually means 'various', provided the element it defines has a plural value, as does भूत here. If the element to which it is added has singular value, then विशेष means 'sort of *or* kind of'. So, for example, पुष्पविशेष many mean 'a sort of *or* kind of flower' or 'various flowers'. When you ask a paṇḍit or guru what flower or tree is meant by a specific floral or arboreal name, the reply will usually be पुष्पविशेष or वृक्षविशेष, which is not very helpful to the inquisitive student!

19. कमलासनस्थम् The creator-god Brahmā (note that ब्रह्माणम् is *masculine* !) is traditionally depicted seated on a lotus, whose stem issues from the navel of Viṣṇu reclining on the great serpent Anantaśeṣa (अनन्तशेष).

20. उरगांश्च दिव्यान् 'and divine serpents', as highly venerated beings on a par with the gods. उरग is a locative tatpuruṣa meaning *literally* 'going (-ग from √गम्) on its breast (उरस्)'. We would expect उरोग, but the -स् is irregularly dropped. Notice how many times various forms of the secondary derivative दिव्य have occurred in this account of Kṛṣṇa's divine manifestation. It is made from the root noun दिव् 'sky, heaven' with the suffix -य, here expressing appurtenance: 'pertaining to the heaven, divine'.

21. सर्वतो From what we said in the section on adverbs made with suffixes, we should expect सर्वत: (*sarva* + *-tas*) to mean *literally* '*from* all (sides)', but the etymological ablative sense often slips into the locative sense '*on* all (sides)', and so सर्वत: becomes a synonym of सर्वत्र (*sarva-tra*); on this usage *cf.* विश्वतो (*viśva* + *-tas*) in the compound विश्वतोमुखम् 'having his face *in* all (places or directions), facing everywhere'.

22. विश्वेश्वर विश्वरूप Note that these are vocatives!

23. किरीतिनं गदिनं चक्रिणं The किरीत 'diadem', गदा 'cudgel' and चक्र 'discus' are among the characteristic insignia of the god Viṣṇu, with whom Kṛṣṇa is

here identified. Note that the long descriptive compounds in this chapter are generally bahuvrīhis, while here, where only one feature (*e.g.,* the discus) is involved, a secondary derivative formed with the possessive suffixes *-in* and *-mat* is used.

24. समन्ताद् a synonym of सर्वत्र and also सर्वतः (when locative in value).

25. दीप्तानलार्कद्युतिम् The dvandva दीप्तानलार्क-, which forms the first member of this bahuvrīhi compound, should be taken disjunctively, *i.e.,* with the two parts connected in sense by 'or' not 'and'; thus, 'who has the brilliance of a blazing fire or the sun'. Any dvandva may be thus construed disjunctively, but the usage is much rarer than the conjunctive resolution.

26. वेदितव्यं gerundive of [1]√विद् 'know', here used as a neuter noun, *literally* 'what is to be known', *i.e.,* object of knowledge; thus, then, 'You (are) the imperishable supreme object of knowledge'.

27. पुरुषो the spirit or soul of all, the universal self; to be construed in the predicate after मतो मे 'You are regarded by me (मतो मे) as the everlasting universal self'. The enclitic pronoun मे is genitive used practically as an instrumental, as often with a past passive participle; *cf.* English 'beloved *of* me' (*i.e.*, 'beloved by me').

28. दीप्तहुताशवक्त्रं This compound is susceptible to several interpretations depending on whether its final member (वक्त्र) is taken as 'mouth' or 'face' and with singular or plural value; thus, 'whose mouth/face (*or* mouths/faces) is (*or* are) a blazing fire'. A common word for 'fire', हुताश (or हुताशन) means *literally* 'he whose food (आश or अशन) is the oblation (हुत, the past passive participle of √हु 'offer' used as a neuter noun)', an epithet of the fire-god Agni whose food was indeed the oblation cast into the fire at the sacrifice.

29. द्यावापृथिव्योर् 'of the heaven and earth', a so-called 'देवता-dvandva', one of a dozen or so dvandvas inherited from the Ṛgveda, which contain the names of two deities (देवता), *both* inflected in the dual. The first member, however, always retains the nominative-accusative form, regardless of the case of the compound; so, for example, the instrumental of the present compound is द्यावापृथिवीभ्याम् and the genitive द्यावापृथिव्योः, as seen here.

30. दिशश्च सर्वाः The sense of व्याप्तं is carried over: 'and all the directions (are pervaded)'.

31. अमी nominative masculine plural of the farther demonstrative pronoun अदः 'yon, yonder, that (afar off)'. This is the rarest of the demonstrative pronouns, only a few forms being in common use. The declension, given in Appendix II, is troublesome to learn because of the rather perplexing shifting of its stems. अमी occurs again in 26 and 28, and असौ the nominative masculine singular in 26.

32. स्वस्तीत्युक्त्वा 'having said *hail!*' As an indeclinable noun, स्वस्ति is probably based on the phrase सु अस्ति as an expression of beneficence: 'It is well [with you]', but with the implication 'May it be well with you!' The usual analysis into सु + अस्ति as an abstract noun ('being'), hence 'well-being', is doubtful as अस्ति does not occur as an abstract noun.

33. महर्षिसिद्धसङ्घाः 'throngs of great seers and perfected ones'. The Siddhas are often mentioned in Sanskrit, but it is never very clear who they are. Their name is a past passive participle of ²√सिध् (सिध्यति, class IV) 'reach one's aim', so that its literal meaning is '(those) who have reached their aim *or* goal', which suggests some sort of spiritual attainment, perhaps freedom from rebirth or blissful existence.

34. ये च साध्या 'and those who (are) the Sādhyas', a roundabout way of saying simply 'and the Sādhyas'. The identity of the Sādhyas is a problem similar to that of the Siddhas of the prior stanza. The name is a gerundive of √साध् (साधति, class I), which has practically the same meanings as √सिध् 'reach one's goal, attain one's object' and similarly. The gerundive साध्य, being a future participle, points toward something that has not yet been realized or worthy of being realized. Perhaps, then, the Sādhyas are a class of beings of a somewhat lower order than the Siddhas.

35. विश्वे short for विश्वे देवाः the 'All-gods', the name of a particular class of deities in the Ṛgveda. Apparently the All-gods, as their name suggests, originally represented the entire assemblage of gods formulated so as to be worshipped as a unit, lest any be unwittingly omitted from due magnification. In due course, however, the All-gods came to be regarded as a separate group of deities, not all-inclusive, as shown by their mention along with other deities in the Ṛgveda as well as in this passage.

36. ऊष्मपाश्च 'and the Fathers', *i.e.,* the deceased ancestors or Manes, to whom are accorded regular worship in the so-called Śrāddha ceremonies. The deceased ancestors are usually called पितर: 'Fathers', not ऊष्मपा: 'imbibers of hot vapors' as here. This curious expression apparently has reference to the meals that are offered to the Fathers during the Śrāddha rites. The primary derivative ऊष्मन्, which forms the prior member of this accusative tatpuruṣa compound, is formed with the suffix -मन् from √उष् (ओषति) 'burn' with irregular lengthening of the root vowel.

37. तथाहम् '(the worlds) [are] disturbed *as well as I*'. तथा, *literally* 'in that way', is often an equivalent of च.

38. व्यात्ताननं 'having your mouths wide open'; व्यात्त is the past passive participle of वि-आ-√दा, *literally* 'taken apart (वि-)', *i.e.,* made wide open. The ordinary past participle of √दा is दत्त, but when combined with a verbal prefix or prefixes, it often takes the reduced form -त्त.

39. दृष्ट्वैव In order to reproduce the emphasis imparted by the particle एव to दृष्ट्वा, we might say: 'No sooner have I seen . . . than I know not' etc.

40. कालानलसंनिभानि 'resembling the fire of the (final) time (काल)', *i.e.,* the conflagration at the dissolution of the universe. Since this adjective expressing a comparison qualifies मुखानि 'mouths', मुखानि must be understood to mean '(blazing) mouths', not simply 'mouths', otherwise the comparison is meaningless.

41. दिशो न जाने 'I know not the directions', probably a way of saying 'to feel disoriented'.

42. जगन्निवास a vocative: 'O abode of the world', *i.e.,* you in whom the world dwells; or 'whose abode is the world'.

43. त्वां object of विशन्ति, not expressed until the first line of the next stanza, where, however, वक्त्राणि is introduced, as though त्वां had not previously occurred; so *literally* 'enter you (त्वां)...your mouths (वक्त्राणि)'.

44. Attention should be drawn to the two secondary derivatives अस्मदीयैर् and -मुख्यैः; the first is from अस्मद् the plural stem of अहम् + the suffix *-īya* ('belonging to us'), the second from मुख 'mouth' + *-ya* ('connected with the mouth *or* front', hence 'frontal, chief, foremost'). To be noted also is the primary derivative योध 'fight-er', a noun of agent from √युध् 'fight' + the suffix *-a* with guṇa of the root vowel.

45. चूर्णितैरुत्तमाङ्गैः 'with crushed heads', *i.e.*, having crushed heads, a use of the instrumental which may be called an 'instrumental of description'. Though fairly rare and unnoticed in the grammars, this use of the instrumental is an outgrowth or extension of the 'instrumental of accompaniment'.

46. अभिविज्वलन्ति accusative neuter plural of the present participle of अभि-वि-√ज्वल् 'flame away *or* hither and thither (-वि) opposite (अभि-)', *i.e.*, opposite those entering his mouths. The participle qualifies वक्त्राणि.

47. समृद्धवेगाः probably to be translated 'with increased impetus *or* impulse', as though the force (-वेग) impelling the moths (etc.) toward the flame becomes all the greater as they near it; but the adjective has been variously interpreted.

48. लेलिह्यसे second singular middle of the intensive of √लिह् (लेढि, class II), 'lick'. Like causatives, the intensives are a derivative formation from a verb root. They impart to the root a sense of the *repetition* or *intensification* of the action expressed by the root, and so the translation will vary from one formation to another according to English idiom. The root is reduplicated with a 'strong' vowel in the reduplicative syllable, as seen here in ले-लिह्. The reduplicated stem is then declined like a verb of the third or reduplicating class (लेलेढि), or alternatively, as in लेलिह्यसे, like a middle of class IV. Intensive verbs are sometimes called 'frequentatives' because frequency or repetitive action even more than intensification is their chief value. So, we may translate लेलिह्यसे by 'you are constantly licking *or* keep licking'.

49. समन्ताल् Note the change of the final -त् of समन्तात् 'all around' to -ल् by regressive assimilation. This adverb qualifies लेलिह्यसे and adds further to its descriptive vividness.

Vocabulary

अक्षर, *adj.* undying, imperishable.

अदृष्टपूर्व, *adj.* not seen before.

अद्भुत, *adj.* wondrous, wonderful.

अद्य, *adv.* now.

अनन्त, *adj.* not having an end, endless, infinite.

अनल, *m.* fire.

अनुलेपन, *n.* an unguent.

अनेक, *adj.* 'not one', *i.e.,* more than one, many.

अनेकधा, *adv.* in many ways.

अन्तर, *n.* the space between, an interval.

अन्तरात्मन्, *m.* the heart *or* mind.

अप्रमेय, *adj.* immeasurable.

अम्बर, *n.* a garment.

अभिमुख, *adj.* having the face toward, facing.

अभि-वि-√ज्वल् (ज्वलति, class I), flame away (-वि-) against *or* opposite (अभि-).

अम्बुवेग, *m.* a torrent *or* stream.

अर्क, *m.* the sun.

अवनिपाल, *m.* 'earth-protector', a king.

अव्यय, *adj.* not subject to change, imperishable.

अश्विन्, *adj.* 'possessing horses', a horseman' *as m. dual,* the Aśvins, a pair of Ṛgvedic deities, famous for helping those in need; also called the Nāsatyas (नासत्यौ). [*v.* note 6]

असुर, *m.* a god.

आकृति, *f.* form, shape.

आदि, *m.* beginning.

आदित्य, *m.* son of Aditi; *in plur.* the Ādityas, sons of Aditi; name applied to a group of gods in the Ṛgveda who are personifications of abstractions; among the most important of the Ādityas are Varuṇa and Mitra. [*v.* note 3]

आनन, *n.* the mouth.

आ-√पृ (पृणाति, class IX), fill up; *gerund* आपूर्य.

आभरण, *n.* an ornament.

आयुध, *n.* a weapon.

आविष्ट, *ppp.* आ-√विश् (विशति, class VI), entered by, filled with.
आश्चर्य, *n.* a wonder, marvel.
आसन, *n.* the act of sitting, posture; a seat.
उग्र, *adj.* mighty; terrible.
उत्तमाङ्ग, *n.* 'the highest *or* chief part (of the body)', the head.
उदर, *n.* the belly.
उद्यत, *ppp.* उद् - √यम् (यच्छति, class I), held up, raised.
उरग, *m.* a serpent.
ऊरु, *m.* the thigh.
ऊष्मप, *m. plur.* the Fathers *or* deceased ancestors as 'imbibers of the hot vapors' of the food offered to them in ritual observances. [*v.* note 36]
एकस्थ, *adj.* standing in the same place.
ऐश्वर, *adj.* pertaining to *or* relating to a lord, lordly.
कमल, *n.* a lotus.
कराल, *adj.* dreadful.
काल, *m.* time.
किरीतिन्, *adj.* 'possessing a diadem'.
कृत्स्न, *adj.* all, whole.
गदिन्, *adj.* 'possessing a cudgel'.
गन्ध, *m.* perfume.
गन्धर्व, *m. plur.* the Gandharvas, a class of celestial musicians.
√गॄ (गृणाति, class IX), praise.
गोप्तृ, *m.* protector, guardian.
√ग्रस् (ग्रसते, class I), swallow, devour.
चक्रिन्, *adj.* 'possessing a discus'.
चक्षुस्, *n.* the eye.
चूर्णित, *ppp.* चूर्णय (*denom. verb from* चूर्ण 'powder, meal'), 'powdered', crushed.
जगत्, *n.* the world.
√ज्ञा (जानाति, जानीते, class IX), know.
√ज्वल् (ज्वलति, class I), flame, blaze.
ज्वलन, *m.* a fire.
√तप् (तपति, class I), burn (*trans. and intrans.*).
त्रय, *n.* a triad.

√त्वर् (त्वरते, class I), hurry, hasten.
दंष्ट्रा, *f.* a large tooth *or* tusk.
दर्शन, *n.* 'sight, seeing', a thing seen, an aspect.
दशन, *m.* a tooth.
√दा (ददाति, class III), give.
दिव्, *see under* द्यो.
दिव्य, *adj.* heavenly, divine.
दिश्, *f.* a (cardinal) point, direction.
दीप्त, *ppp.* √दीप् (दीप्यते, class IV), ablaze, flaming, shining.
दीप्तिमत्, *m.* 'possessing brilliance *or* radiance', brilliant, radiant.
दुर्निरीक्ष्य, *adj.* difficult to look upon.
देह, *m. or n.* the body.
द्यावापृथिवी, *f. dual* the heaven and earth. [*v.* note 29]
द्युति, *f.* lustre, brilliance.
द्यो, *f.* sky, heaven. [strong cases like गो 'cow', elsewhere दिव् before vowels and द्यु before consonants]
√द्रु (द्रवति, class I), run.
द्रोण, *m.* Droṇa, name of the general of the Kauravas.
धनंजय, *adj.* 'booty-winnning', *as m.* name of Arjuna.
-धर, *adj.* holding, wearing (*as terminal element of compound*).
धृति, *f.* firmness, firm bearing, steadiness.
नभस्, *n.* the sky.
नयन, *n.* 'leader', the eye.
नाना, *adv.* variously, differently; *as an adj. as prior member of compound*, various, different.
नानाविध, *adj.* of various sorts *or* kinds.
नाश, *m.* destruction.
निधान, *n.* 'a putting down', *then* place where something is put down, a foundation, resting-place.
नेत्र, *n.* the eye.
पतङ्ग, *m.* 'that which goes a-flying', a moth (so used here, but strictly applicable to anything that flies).
परम, *adj.* highest, supreme.
पाद, *m.* the foot.

पार्थ, *m.* son of Pṛthā, metronymic of Arjuna.
पुष्कल, *adj.* much, many.
प्र-√तप् (तपति, class I), burn away, burn up; continue to burn.
प्रदीप्त, *ppp.* प्र-√दीप् (दीप्यते, class IV), blazing.
प्र-√नम् (नमति, class I), make obeisance before (+ *acc.*).
प्रविभक्त, *ppp.* प्र-वि-√भज् (भजति, class I), divided up (प्र has intensive meaning here).
प्रव्यथित, *ppp.* प्र-√व्यथ् (व्यथते, class I), perturbed, disturbed.
प्र-√सद् (सीदति, class I), be favorably disposed to, have pity on.
प्राञ्जलि, *adj.* *literally* 'having an *añjali* before', *i.e.,* greeting reverently.
भयानक, *adj.* formidable, terrible.
भास्, *f.* light, effulgence. [unchangeable *s*-stem]
भीत, *ppp.* √भी (बिभेति, class III), afraid.
भीष्म, *m.* Bhīṣma, name of the son of Śāṃtanu and Gaṅgā, who fought on the side of the Kauravas.
भूत, *n.* a being, creature.
मत, *ppp.* √मन् (मन्यते, class IV), thought, regarded.
मरुत्, *m. plur.* the Maruts, name of a group of storm gods in the Ṛgveda, the sons of Rudra, hence also called the 'Rudras'. [*v.* note 7]
महात्मन्, *adj.* 'having a great soul', of noble nature, noble.
माल्य, *n.* a garland.
मुख्य, *adj.* chief, principal, most excellent.
यक्ष, *m. plur.* Yakṣas, name of a class of semi-divine beings, often regarded as attendants of Kubera, but also of Viṣṇu.
युगपद्, *adv.* simultaneously.
योध, *m.* a fighter, warrior.
राशि, *m.* a heap.
रुद्र, *m. plur.* the Rudras, sons of Rudra (later called Śiva), also called the 'Maruts', storm gods of the Ṛgveda. [*v.* note 5]
रोमन्, *n.* the hair.
√लभ् (लभते, class I), get.
√लिह् (लेढि, class II), lick; *intensive* लेलिह्यते 'licks constantly'.
वक्त्र, *n.* the face.
वदन, *n.* the mouth.
वर्ण, *m.* color.

वसु, *m. plur.* the Vasus, name of a troop of Vedic deities, closely associated with Indra. [*v.* note 4]

वि-√ईक्ष् (ईक्षते, class I), look upon, behold.

विलग्न, *ppp.* वि-√लग् (लगति, class I), fastened *or* attached to, clinging to; [the prefix वि here has an intensive force].

विशाल, *adj.* broad, wide, large.

विशेष, *m.* distinction, difference; kind, sort. [for use at end of compound, *v.* note 18]

विश्वतोमुख, *adj.* having the face *or* faces in all directions.

विश्वे, *m. plur.* the All-gods, more fully called विश्वे देवाः; they are a group of Vedic deities originally conceived as embracing all the gods of the pantheon, but later evolved into another class of deities, not all-comprehensive. [*v.* note 35]

विस्मय, *m.* astonishment.

वीर्य, *n.* manliness, strength.

वेग, *m.* impetus, momentum.

व्यात्त, *ppp.* वि-आ-√दा (ददाति, class III), 'taken apart', wide open.

व्याप्त, *ppp.* वि-√आप् (आप्नोति, class V), pervaded.

शम, *m.* quiet, peace.

शरीर, *n.* the body.

शर्मन्, *n.* shelter, refuge; joy.

शशिन्, *adj.* 'possessing a hare (शश)'; *as m.* the moon (as having a hare on its face, according to Indian mythology).

शाश्वत, *adj.* eternal, everlasting.

शिरस्, *n.* the head.

सङ्घ, *m.* a crowd *or* throng.

सचराचर, *adj.* 'with the movable and immovable', with moving and unmoving things (*i.e.*, all animal and plant life).

संजय, *m.* Saṃjaya, name of the blind king Dhṛtarāṣṭra's bard who reports to him the happenings on the battlefield in the war between the Pāṇḍavas and Kauravas.

सदृश, *adj.* of like appearance, like unto *or* similar to (+ *gen.*).

सनातन, *adj.* eternal, everlasting.

संनिभ, *adj.* resembling, like.

समग्र, *adj.* all.

समन्तात्, *adv.* all around.

समुद्र, *m.* a sea, ocean.

समृद्ध, *ppp.* सम्-√ऋध् (ऋध्नोति, class V), much, abundant (*literally* 'succeeded, prosperous, full-grown, well-nourished' and then attenuated to the meanings above).

सम्-√दृश् (*only in passive*), be seen, appear.

साध्य, *m. plur.* Sādhyas, name of a group of celestial beings. [*v.* note 34]

सिद्ध, *m. plur.* Siddhas, 'Perfected Ones', name of a class of demigods. [*v.* note 33]

सुर, *m.* a god.

सूतपुत्र, *m.* the charioteer's son, *viz.*, Karṇa

सूर्य, *m.* the sun.

√स्तु (स्तौति, class II), praise.

स्तुति, *f.* praise, laudation.

-स्थ, verbal of √स्था (तिष्ठति, class I), *properly* standing, *but usually attenuated in meaning,* situated, being.

-स्पृश्, *verbal of* √स्पृश् (स्पृशति, class VI), touching, reaching.

स्वस्ति, *n.* 'well-being', welfare; (*nom./acc.* used as an indeclinable), hail! May all be well (with you)!

हरि, *m.* Hari, a name of the god Viṣṇu.

हुताश, *m.* fire.

हृष्ट, *ppp.* √हृष् (हृष्यति, class IV), bristling (of hair, due to excitement).

LESSON THIRTY-TWO

1. The Cardinal and Ordinal Numerals. 2. Symbolic Word Numerals.
3. The Numerical Signs for the Word Numerals. Place Notation and the Zero. 4. Numerical Words. 5. Methods of Dating.

I. *The Cardinal and Ordinal Numerals.*

We have reserved the Sanskrit numerals and related words to the very last lesson, not because the numerals are an area that can be neglected, but because their occurrence is relatively infrequent in the sort of literature that students are most likely to read in their early study of the language. We have already had a few of the numerals under ten, the declension of द्व 'two', and the numerals for 100 and 1000. We shall now take the numerals from one to ten and all the decades (20, 30, etc.) to 1000, both the cardinals and the ordinals, and see how the intervening compound numerals (21, 22, 31, 32, etc.) are expressed.

There are two kinds of numerals to be distinguished, *viz.*, the cardinals and the ordinals. The cardinals are the *primary* (cardinal!) numerals that are used in counting (*one, three, five, ten,* etc.), whereas the ordinals are concerned with the *order* or *sequence* of things (*first, third, fifth, tenth,* etc.), hence their designation 'ordinal', *i.e.*, connected with 'order'. Here, then, are the cardinal numerals 1-19 and the decades to 100, and the corresponding ordinals in parallel columns:

	Cardinals	*Ordinals*
1.	एक one	प्रथम first
2.	द्व two	द्वितीय second
3.	त्रि three	तृतीय third
4.	चतुर् (-:) four	चतुर्थ fourth
5.	पञ्च five	पञ्चम fifth
6.	षष् six	षष्ठ sixth
7.	सप्त seven	सप्तम seventh
8.	अष्ट eight	अष्टम eighth
9.	नव nine	नवम ninth
10.	दश ten	दशम tenth
11.	एकादश eleven	→ eleventh[1]

[1]The ordinals from 11 to 19 are identical to the cardinals, except that they are declined like ordinary adjectives of the सुन्दरः, सुन्दरी, सुन्दरम् type.

12.	द्वादश twelve	→ twelfth
13.	त्रयोदश thirteen	→ thirteenth
14.	चतुर्दश fourteen	→ fourteenth
15.	पञ्चदश fifteen	→ fifteenth
16.	षोडश sixteen	→ sixteenth
17.	सप्तदश seventeen	→ seventeenth
18.	अष्टादश eighteen	→ eighteenth
19.	नवदश nineteen	→ nineteenth
20.	विंशति twenty	विंशतितम twentieth
30.	त्रिंशत् thirty	त्रिंशत्तम thirtieth
40.	चत्वारिंशत् forty	चत्वारिंशत्तम fortieth
50.	पञ्चाशत् fifty	पञ्चाशत्तम fiftieth
60.	षष्टि sixty	षष्टितम sixtieth
70.	सप्तति seventy	सप्ततितम seventieth
80.	अशीति eighty	अशीतितम eightieth
90.	नवति ninety	नवतितम ninetieth
100.	शत one hundred	शततम one hundredth
1000.	सहस्र one thousand	सहस्रतम one thousandth

Remarks: The declension of the cardinal numerals from 1 to 19 will be explained below, as they require a fairly detailed account. The decades ending in -ति (विंशति, षष्टि, सप्तति, अशीति and नवति) are *feminine nouns* declined like मति; the decades in -त् (त्रिंशत्, चत्वारिंशत् and पञ्चाशत्) are all *unchangeable* feminine consonant stems and as such take the 'regular' endings, *e.g.*, पञ्चाशत् 'fifty':

Nom.	पञ्चाशत्
Acc.	पञ्चाशतम्
Instr.	पञ्चाशता
Dat.	पञ्चाशते
Abl.	पञ्चाशत:
Gen.	पञ्चाशत:
Loc.	पञ्चाशति

The ordinals from 11 to 19, as indicated, have the *same stem* as the corresponding cardinals, but they are declined like ordinary adjectives ending in

-अ, *i.e.*, the masculine is like देव, the neuter like फल; starting with चतुर्थ 'fourth', the feminine is formed in -ई, but in -आ for the first three, *viz.*, प्रथमा, द्वितीया, तृतीया.[2] The ordinals from 20 to 90, it will have been noted, are without exception, made by adding to the cardinal the secondary suffix -तम (thus far familiar to us as the suffix of the superlative of adjectives!). However, these ordinals may *alternatively* be made from *abbreviated forms* of the cardinals; thus, instead of saying विंशतितम, we may *optionally* say विंश (declined in the same way).[3]

To express the compound numerals between the decades, the unit is *prefixed* to the decade, somewhat as in old-fashioned English when we said 'four-and-twenty, two-and-forty',[4] except that in Sanskrit the equivalent of 'and' is omitted; so, for example, पञ्चविंशति '25', नवत्रिंशत् '39'. But the numerals द्व 'two', त्रि 'three' and अष्ट 'eight' take the form द्वा, त्रयस् and अष्टा respectively before विंशति and त्रिंशत्; thus, द्वाविंशति '22', त्रयोविंशति '23', अष्टाविंशति '28', and similarly द्वात्रिंशत् '32', त्रयस्त्रिंशत् '33' and अष्टात्रिंशत् '38'. The remaining compound decades may prefix *either* द्वा *or* द्वि (!), त्रयस्(subject to sandhi change) or त्रि, अष्टा or अष्ट. Hence, we may say द्वि- or द्वापञ्चाशत् '52', त्रि- or त्रयःपञ्चाशत् '53', अष्ट- or अष्टापञ्चाशत् '58', and so on. The only exception (there is always an exception!) is अशीति '80', which does not allow the option, but *requires* द्वि, त्रि and अष्ट to be prefixed: द्व्यशीति, त्र्यशीति and अष्टाशीति.[5]

A somewhat curious practice is the placing of the adjective ऊन 'lacking, deficient' before a decadal numeral to diminish it by a specified amount. For example, if we wish to say '39', we may, instead of नवत्रिंशत्, alternatively put एकोन (एक + ऊन 'deficient by one') before चत्वारिंशत् and say एकोनचत्वारिंशत् '40 minus one'. In fact, with the compound decades in '9', this is almost the usual method, so that if the amount of the deficiency is

---

[2]In the language of the Veda, in which the former musical accent is indicated, the ordinals from 11 to 19 are distinguished from the cardinals by a difference of accent.

[3]The numerals ending in -त् (त्रिंशत्, चत्वारिंशत् and पञ्चाशत्) are abbreviated by dropping the -त्. The remaining cardinals (षष्टि, सप्तति, अशीति and नवति) replace *-i* (-इ) by *-a* (-अ).

[4]*Cf.* the nursery rhyme 'Four-and-twenty blackbirds baked in a pie'.

[5]Because of the coalescence of vowels, however, '88' would inevitably be अष्टाशीति whether अष्ट or अष्टा is prefixed!

only 'one', it may be omitted. Thus, '19' is usually expressed simply by ऊनविंशति 'twenty-minus-[one]'.[6]

Something needs now to be said regarding the declension of the first 19 cardinal numerals. एक 'one' is declined precisely like सर्व 'all', which in turn differs from the standard pronominal declension of तद् only in the nominative and accusative singular neuter where it has सर्वम् *not* सर्वद्. By reason of its meaning, the declension of एक is restricted to the singular, except when it has the indefinite meaning 'some', in which case it is declined as a plural. In addition to its fundamental meaning 'one', एक also is often attenuated to the sense of an indefinite article; एक: सैनिक: may mean 'one soldier' or 'a soldier'.

The declensions of द्व 'two', त्रि 'three', and चतुर् 'four', like एक, distinguish gender as well as case, whereas the numerals from 5 to 19 are without distinction of gender. द्व, we will recall, is declined only in the dual according to the देव/सेना/फल type, thus reflecting the distinction of gender only in the nominative and accusative, as these three types are all declined the same in the other cases of the dual. Once again here is the declension of द्व 'two':

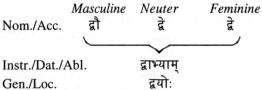

	Masculine	*Neuter*	*Feminine*
Nom./Acc.	द्वौ	द्वे	द्वे
Instr./Dat./Abl.		द्वाभ्याम्	
Gen./Loc.		द्वयोः	

The numerals त्रि 'three' and चतुर् 'four' are somewhat difficult, or at least eccentric, as they have a peculiar stem in *-ṛ* in the feminine.

[6] Students of Latin will recall that '18' and '19' are similarly expressed by *duodeviginti* and *undeviginti* (*literally* 'two from 20' and 'one from 20') respectively.

त्रि 'three'

	Masculine	*Neuter*	*Feminine*
Nom.	त्रयः	त्रीणि	तिस्रः
Acc.	त्रीन्	त्रीणि	तिस्रः
Instr.	त्रिभिः		तिसृभिः
Dat.	त्रिभ्यः		तिसृभ्यः
Abl.	त्रिभ्यः		तिसृभ्यः
Gen.	त्रयाणाम्		तिसृणाम्
Loc.	त्रिषु		तिसृषु

चतुर् 'four'

	Masculine	*Neuter*	*Feminine*
Nom.	चत्वारः	चत्वारि	चतस्रः
Acc.	चतुरः	चत्वारि	चतस्रः
Instr.	चतुर्भिः		चतसृभिः
Dat.	चतुर्भ्यः		चतसृभ्यः
Abl.	चतुर्भ्यः		चतसृभ्यः
Gen.	चतुर्णाम्		चतसृणाम्
Loc.	चतुर्षु		चतसृषु

It may be noted that the masculine and neuter of त्रि are like the types अग्नि and वारि, except in the genitive plural त्रयाणाम् instead of त्रीणाम् (to correspond with अग्नीनाम् and वारीणाम्). The feminine of both त्रि and चतुर् diverges from the stems in *-ṛ* in the nominative which is formed without guṇa of *-ṛ*, so तिस्रः, चतस्रः (*cf.* मातरः) and the accusative, which is the same as the nominative (but *cf.* मातॄः) and also the genitive which does not lengthen the *-ṛ*, so तिसृणाम्, चतसृणाम् (*cf.* मातॄणाम्). The numerals पञ्च, सप्त, नव, दश and all the compounds ending in -दश are declined alike: their nominative and accusative are without ending, and the remaining cases have the usual endings -भिः, -भ्यः, -आनाम् and -सु. Herewith is the declension of पञ्च to serve as a model:

Nom./Acc.	पञ्च
Instr.	पञ्चभिः
Dat./Abl.	पञ्चभ्यः
Gen.	पञ्चानाम्
Loc.	पञ्चसु

The numeral अष्ट 'eight' may also be declined after this model, but there is an alternative declension as follows:

Nom./Acc.	अष्टौ[7]
Instr.	अष्टाभिः
Dat./Abl.	अष्टाभ्यः
Gen.	अष्टानाम्
Loc.	अष्टासु

The inflection of षष् 'six' is nearly like that of पञ्च, सप्त, नव and दश, except for the genitive, and as the changes caused by sandhi are somewhat confusing, it is in the interest of clarity to give the full declension:

Nom./Acc.	षट्
Instr.	षड्भिः
Dat./Abl.	षड्भ्यः
Gen.	षण्णाम्
Loc.	षट्सु

Note that the genitive is formed by adding -नाम्, *not* -आनाम् (as in पञ्चानाम्, नवानाम्), with mutual assimilation, *i.e.,* the -ट् of षट् is changed to -ण् (the nasal of its own class) by *regressive* assimilation, and the न्- of the ending

[7]The two forms अष्टौ and अष्टा (in the numerical compounds and the Ṛgveda) are really *duals* which were later replaced by a paradigm fashioned upon पञ्च, सप्त, etc. The originally dual character of अष्टौ/अष्टा is reflected also in Greek *oktṓ*, Latin *octō,* Lithuanian *aštuo-nì,* and Gothic *ahtáu.* The reason for the dual apparently goes back to the practice of holding out the *four* fingers of each hand in counting, so that अष्टौ/अष्टा must have implied 'two tetrads'.

-नाम् is changed to ण्- by *progressive* assimilation: षट्-नाम् → षड्-नाम् → षण्-नाम् → षण्-णाम् (षण्णाम्).

The numerals beyond 100 (शत, *n.*) and 1000 (सहस्र, *n.*) that need concern us in so brief a survey as this are अयुत, *n.* '10,000', लक्ष, *n.* '100,000', प्रयुत, *n.* '1,000,000' and कोटि, *f.* '10,000,000'. Those who have travelled in India to any extent are surely familiar with the words 'lakh' and 'crore' in expressions like 'lakhs *or* crores of rupees'. These words (*lakh* and *crore*) are Anglo-Indian words, *viz.,* words that have come into English as spoken in India and thence spread into English generally. They have descended into the various modern vernacular languages of Northern India via the Prakrit forms लक्ख (and later लाख) and कोडि. Since these words as well as the words for the decades (विंशति, त्रिंशत्, etc.) are all nouns, they take the objects numbered in the genitive; thus, विंशत्या नागरिकाणाम् 'by 20 citizens', शतं दासीनाम् '100 female servants', बहूनि लक्षाणि रूप्यकाणाम् 'many lakhs of gold pieces', etc.[8] Alternatively, however, *instead of the genitive* the objects numbered may be put *in the same case as the numeral,* as though in explanatory apposition to it: विंशत्या नागरिकैः, शतं दास्यः, etc., as though to say 'by 20, *viz.,* citizens', '100, *viz.,* female servants'. Since the first 19 numerals (एक through नवदश) are all adjectives, they take the same case, number and gender (if gender is distinguished!) as the objects enumerated.

The multiples of the higher numerals between शत, सहस्र, लक्ष, etc. (*e.g.,* 200, 300, 5000, 6 lakhs) are formed with the cardinals (2 to 9 as required) in grammatical agreement with the higher numerals. Thus:

Nom./Acc.	द्वे शते '200'
Nom./Acc.	त्रीणि शतानि '300'
Instr.	चतुर्भिः शतैः 'by 400'
Gen.	पञ्चानां शतानाम् 'of 500'
Nom./Acc.	द्वे सहस्रे '2000'
Loc.	त्रिषु सहस्रेषु 'among 3000'
Nom./Acc.	षट् सहस्राणि '6000'
Nom./Acc.	नव लक्षाणि '9 lakhs'
Dat./Abl.	सप्तभ्यो लक्षेभ्यः 'for *or* from 7 lakhs'

8 Genitives dependent on numerals ordinarily *follow* the numerals, unlike other defining genitives which regularly precede the nouns they qualify.

When the 100's, 1000's, etc., multiplied or not, are *increased* by units, decadal numerals or higher amounts, whether the increments are simple or compound (*e.g.*, 205, 340, 1524), the most favored method of expression begins with the smaller numeral compounded either with a following उत्तर 'higher' or अधिक 'additional' to show the amount of increase by which the larger number is modified (remember qualifiers in Sanskrit come *before* what is qualified!). Thus, 'such-and-such a number higher (उत्तर) *or* additional (अधिक) by such-and-such an amount'. The compounds ending with उत्तर or अधिक may be put in grammatical agreement with the following noun or compounded with it. Following are some examples:

'113' त्रयोदशोत्तरं शतम् (literally '100 higher by 13') or
त्रयोदशोत्तरशतम् (compounded with the increment)
'645' पञ्चचत्वारिंशदधिकानि षट् शतानि or
पञ्चचत्वारिंशदधिकषट्शतानि (compounded)
'3723' त्रयोविंशत्युत्तराणि सप्तशतोत्तराणि त्रिसहस्राणि or better
the compound: त्रयोविंशत्युत्तरसप्तशतोत्तरत्रिसहस्राणि

In expressing 100 and 1000 increased by 2, 3 or 8, only the forms द्वि, त्रि and अष्ट are used (*not* the alternatives द्वा, त्रयस् and अष्टा as with the decadal numerals); thus, 102 द्विशतम्, 103 त्रिशतम, 1008 अष्टसहस्रम्.

II. *Symbolic Word Numerals.*

Many common words, which are not numerals in origin, but which can symbolically suggest a numerical value, are used in place of the first nine cardinal numerals and zero. Thus, for example, भूमि 'earth' may be used in the symbolical sense of 'one' (एक), पक्ष 'wing' or कर 'hand' in the sense of 'two' (द्व), अनुष्टुभ् 'the *anuṣṭubh* metre' in the meaning of 'eight' (अष्ट), as there are eight syllables to the *anuṣṭubh* line, and so on. This curious usage is common in giving dates in the colophons of MSS. Thus, a scribe, at the end of his copy of a particular work, may say:

इयं कृतिर्मया विक्रमसंवद्भूतग्रहर्षिसोमवर्षे लिखिता ।

'This work was copied by me in the year 1795 of the Vikrama Era'. The date here consists of the four symbolical numerals भूत '5', ग्रह '9', ऋषि '7' and सोम '1' in the form of a dvandva compound arranged in the reversed order of their digital equivalent (१७९५). As we saw in Section I above, it is usual when expressing large numbers with word numerals to begin with the units and proceed sequentially to the thousands, although the reverse order (*i.e.,* thousands to the units) is followed when the digits or figures are used.

Symbolical word numerals are especially common in poetry because there are so many synonyms for each numeral as to afford much greater freedom of expression to an author in coping with large numbers, such as occur especially in the Sanskrit astronomical and mathematical treatises, almost all of which are in metrical form.

When the symbolical numerals are used adjectivally, it is customary for the sake of clarity to add -मित 'measured by . . .' or -संख्याक 'numbering . . .' to the series of symbolical words to indicate that they are to be taken in their numeral (not their literal) sense. Thus, तस्मिन्देशे विषयगुणवसुकरशशिमिता (१२८३५) जना व्याधिनातीते संवत्सरे मृता: 'In that country 12,835 people died of disease last year'; (again note the reverse order of the digits!).

Here follows a list of the commonest words used symbolically as numerals:

zero: शून्य 'emptiness', आकाश, अभ्र 'sky, space', ख 'void'.

one: सोम, इन्दु, शशिन् 'moon', भू, भूमि 'earth', आदि 'beginning'.

two: यम 'twin', कर 'hand', नयन, नेत्र, अक्षि 'eye', भुज 'arm', पक्ष 'wing', अश्विन् in dual = 'the Aśvins', twin physicians of the gods.

three: लोक 'world' (earth, atmosphere and heaven), गुण 'constituent of primal matter' (there are three, *viz., sattva, rajas* and *tamas*), अग्नि 'fire' (there are three sacrificial fires), पुर 'city' (=त्रिपुर *three* cities of the demons, destroyed by Śiva).

four: वेद 'the Vedas' (of which there are four, *viz.,* the Ṛg-, Yajur-, Sāma- and Atharva-veda), समुद्र 'ocean' (four chief oceans being reckoned, one for each of the cardinal directions), युग 'age' (Indian tradition speaks of Four Ages, *i.e.,* the Kṛta, Tretā, Dvāpara and Kali in a descending order of morality).

five: विषय 'object of the sense' (there are five, *i.e.,* sound, touch, color, flavor and smell), इषु 'arrow' (Kāma, the god of love, has five arrows), भूत 'element' (earth, water, fire, air and ether), वायु 'vital air' (the body is said to have five vital airs or *prāṇas*).

six: ऋतु 'season' (six seasons are usually mentioned), रस 'flavor' (sweet, sour, salt, pungent, bitter, astringent), अङ्ग 'limb' (probably from the six limbs of the Veda, the so-called Vedāṅgas).

seven: ऋषि 'sage' (Indian tradition speaks of 'seven sages' सप्तर्षि), पर्वत, अग 'mountain' (there are supposed to be seven principal mountain ranges), अश्व 'horse' (the sun's chariot is drawn by seven horses).

eight: वसु (the Vasus are a group of Vedic gods numbering eight), दिग्गज 'an elephant of the compass direction' (Indian texts mention four principal directions and four intermediate ones), सर्प 'serpent' (eight serpents or Nāgas are often mentioned as being chief), गिरि 'mountain' (eight are said to surround Mount Meru), अनुष्टुभ् 'the *anuṣṭubh* metre' (which has eight syllables to the *pāda*).

nine: ग्रह 'planet' (nine planets are reckoned by Indians), निधि 'treasure' (Kubera, the god of wealth, has nine divine treasures), रन्ध्र 'opening' (nine openings in the human body are enumerated).

Various synonymous substitutions for these words occur; thus, any word that means 'mountain', for example, may theoretically be substituted for those given above (पर्वत, अग) to express the value 'seven'.

III. *The Numerical Signs for the Word Numerals. Place Notation and the Zero.*

Although the numerical signs or figures have already been several times exemplified and also employed in previous lessons in the numbering of stanzas excerpted from the Bhagavadgītā, it may be desirable for the sake of clarity to present them here in sequence and in juxtaposition with our corresponding Arabic numerals:

१ २ ३ ४ ५ ६ ७ ८ ९ ०
1 2 3 4 5 6 7 8 9 0

These figures which we are wont to call 'Arabic' are erroneously so designated, as they are Arabic only in their *immediate* origin. They are *ultimately* derived, however, along with the system of place notation, from India, whence they were transmitted to the Arabs about the eighth century A.D. The Arabs have always been aware of the Indian origin of their numerical signs and accordingly call them 'Indian', as we too, *should*. These Indian signs and the concept of place notation probably came to Europe by way of Moorish Spain. Whatever the particular route, in the course of time they displaced the cumbersome Roman numerals.

The Indian system of numerical notation involving these nine signs and zero is founded on what is called 'place notation', in which the concept of zero or a 'blank' is an indispensable ingredient. By place notation is meant that the value of the individual numerical signs is based on their position in the number. Thus, in the number 3,385 (३३८५), the *first* 3 has the value of 3,000 because it has the fourth or thousandth place from the right, whereas the *second* 3 has the value of 300, as occupying the third place, and similarly the 8 has the value of 80, and so we read the number 'three *thousand,* three *hundred, eighty*-five'. If, however, the hundreds, tens or units are *wanting* in a particular number, the blank or place that would be occupied by them is indicated by a naught or zero in order that the places of the other amounts may not be affected; thus 3,085 (३०८५), where the hundreds value is wanting, or 3,205 (३२०५) where the tens value is wanting.

On the other hand, the Roman numerical system consists of certain letters of the Roman alphabet, *viz.,* V, X, L, C, D and M, which have *fixed values without relation to their position.*[9] In writing complex numbers, the letters with the highest values are placed first, followed by the others in descending order. The number 3,385 (३३८५), which we just used in illustration of place notation, would be thus expressed in Roman numerals: MMMCCCLXXXV (M=1000, C=100, L=50, X=10, V=5), ten signs altogether, whereas the Indian method requires only four. The cumbersomeness of the Roman numerals becomes much the more apparent, however, when a simple arithmetical calculation is made, let us say the multiplication of MMMCCCLXXXV by V (five!): (MMMMM) (MMMMM) (MMMMM) (DDD) (CCCC)XXV, which then has to be simplified into XVIMDCCCCXXV! Using Indian numerals (with their place notation!), we have simply 3,385 x 5 = 16,925.[10]

IV. *Numerical Words.*

There are several groups of words in common use that are formed from the numerals and stems of numeral character (*e.g.,* बहु, सर्व, etc.) by means of secondary suffixes. They are treated below in a more or less descending order of frequency.

---

[9]There is an exception that a sign of lower value, placed before one of higher value, is subtracted from the higher; thus, IX is to be interpreted as one (I) subtracted from ten (X), hence, the combination is nine (9).

[10]The Romans used the abacus for higher arithmetical calculations.

1. *Adverbs of Manner.*

With the suffix -धा are made adverbs denoting manner as specified by the numeral or numerical stem to which it is added. Examples are: एकधा 'in one way', द्विधा 'in two ways', त्रिधा 'in three ways', चतुर्धा 'in four ways', पञ्चधा 'in five ways', षोढा 'in six ways' (for the sandhi after षष्, *cf.* षोडश 'sixteen'), सप्तधा 'in seven ways', अष्टधा 'in eight ways', नवधा 'in nine ways', दशधा 'in 10 ways', and so on with complete regularity; similarly, बहुधा and अनेकधा both 'in many ways'.

2. *Multiplicative Adverbs.*

These adverbs of fancy name denote the number of times something is done. Except for one through four, they are made from the numerical stem by adding -कृत्वस् (-:) or, much more rarely, -वारम्; thus, सकृत् 'once', द्विस् 'twice',[11] त्रिस् 'thrice', चतुस् 'four times', and from this point with -कृत्वस्, so पञ्चकृत्वस् 'five times', षट्कृत्वस् 'six times', सप्तकृत्वस् 'seven times', etc.[12]

3. *Distributive Adverbs.*

These adverbs, formed with the suffix -शस् (-:), denote 'by so-and-so many individuals, groups *or* other entities'; thus एकशस् or एकैकशस् 'one by one, singly, one at a time', द्विशस् 'in *or* by pairs, पञ्चशस् 'by fives, five at a time'; it is added also to other stems of a generally quantitative nature, as अक्षरशस् 'by syllables, syllable by syllable', ऋतुशस् 'by seasons', गणशस् 'by groups *or* crowds', सर्वशस् 'wholly' (*literally* 'by the whole').

4. *Multiplicative Adjectives and Neuter Collectives.*

With the secondary suffix -तय are made adjectives that express 'how-many-fold', *i.e.,* consisting of so many kinds; thus, त्रितय 'threefold', चतुष्टय 'fourfold', पञ्चतय 'fivefold'. All these stems may be used as collectives in the neuter, as पञ्चतय 'a group of five, a pentad', अष्टतय 'a group of eight, an octad (*or* ogdoad)'. Instead of त्रितय for 'a group of three *or* triad' and द्वितय for 'a pair *or* dyad', the primary derivatives त्रय (*tray-a*) and द्वय (*dvay-a*) are

---

[11]*Cf.* Latin *bis,* which incidentally, is the usual expression throughout Europe after a theatrical or concert performance, corresponding to our 'encore!'

[12]This -कृत्वस्, which thus functions as a suffix, is probably in origin the accusative plural of the noun कृतु, from √कृ 'do' + the primary suffix -तु, hence 'doings', *then* 'times'.

commoner. All these stems make their feminine in -ई, and in this connection we should especially note the expression त्रयी विद्या 'the threefold knowledge' or perhaps more suitably written 'The Threefold Knowledge' with reference to the Three Vedas, the Ṛg-, Sāma- and Yajur-.

V. *Methods of Dating.*

The subject of Indian chronology is complicated, and but a few general observations must suffice here. The earliest inscriptions, if they contained dates at all, were usually dated by the number of years that had elapsed since a particular ruler's coming to the throne. Sometimes, if the ruler had successors and the dynasty started by him continued on, the initial regnal year of the founder was used in dating so long as the dynasty lasted and occasionally even after its demise. But unless there is some basis for synchronizing the regnal years of a particular ruler with another fixed chronology that is generally known and accepted, as the Christian Era or the Muslim Hijrī system, regnal dates such as we have referred to are valueless to the historian.

In ancient and medieval India many systems of dating were used whose starting dates are known, *i.e.,* can be synchronized with our own system. Most of these 'eras', as they are called, are no longer in use, or if so, are only used locally, as the Nevārī Era in Nepal begun in 878 A.D. or the Lakṣmaṇa Era of Bengal begun in 1119 A.D., or in some cases only used for religious purposes, like the Buddha and Mahāvīra Eras of 544 and 528 B.C. respectively.

In 58 B.C. there came into use in the Northwest of India, now Pakistan, a means of dating later known as the 'Vikramasaṃvat' (Vikrama Era) or perhaps more commonly simply 'Saṃvat' (The Era),[13] which eventually spread throughout the subcontinent and is even today the most widely used system. Fortunately we need not be detained here by a discussion of the complicated issue of who initiated this era, why it is called 'Vikrama', and the many other points that have concerned Indian historians without satisfactory resolution. In 78 A.D. another era, known as the Śaka or Śāka Era, was started. A similar dispute has always surrounded the origin and name of this era, which, next to the Vikramasaṃvat, is the most prevalent in India nowadays.

These two eras, the Vikrama and the Śaka, are commonly employed in dating MSS, the former more commonly than the latter, occasionally both, so that any serious work with MSS requires knowing how to convert Vikrama and Śaka dates into the B.C.-A.D. system. For an *approximate equivalent and practical purposes only,* a Vikrama date may be converted by *subtracting*

---

[13]Saṃvat is a reduction of *saṃvatsara* 'year' and is indeclinable.

58 from the figure given and by *adding* 78 for the Śaka. The complicating factor, if an *accurate* conversion is needed, is that the Indian year begins in mid-March of our year and ends in mid-March of the following year, so that whether 58 or 57 is to be subtracted depends on what month is involved, *i.e.*, whether it is in the same year of our calendarial system or in the following year. If the month is *not* mentioned in the date, it is best to assume that the year has expired, in which case 57, *not* 58, would have to be subtracted. In the same way, in the case of the Śaka Era, if the date falls in one of the last three or three and a half months of the year, then 79, *not* 78, would have to be added to the figure given.

Another complicating factor in arriving at an accurate equivalent in our chronology is that in various parts of India the year began with a different month. Thus, while the Vikramasaṃvat in most parts began with the month of Caitra (चैत्र) which corresponds to our March-April, in western India it began with Kārttika (कार्त्तिक), corresponding to October-November!

The Vikrama and Śaka Eras are based on lunar months, and since a lunar month contains only 29 1/2 days, the lunar year has but 354 days, *i.e.*, approximately 12 days shorter than the solar year of 365 days. Because of this discrepancy, an extra or intercalary month had to be inserted after every 30 months in order to bring the lunar year into correspondence with the solar, otherwise the seasons would have fallen at different times with the passage of the years. Each month was divided into fortnights or *pakṣas* ('wings'), the one called the *kṛṣṇapakṣa* ('dark fortnight') going from the full moon to the new moon and hence progressively darker, the other or *śuklapakṣa* ('light fortnight') in which the new moon became full or bright. In some parts of India the months were begun with the *kṛṣṇapakṣa,* but in others with the *śuklapakṣa,* another cause of confusion and discrepancy in determining exact calendarial correspondences.

Apart from their use in dates, the names of the Indian months occasionally occur in Sanskrit texts. They are given below beginning with चैत्र. Note that the last three and a half months of the Indian year belong to the *following* year in our calendarial system.

1. चैत्र	March-April
2. वैशाख	April-May
3. ज्यैष्ठ	May-June
4. आषाढ	June-July
5. श्रावण	July-August

6. भाद्रपद	August-September
7. आश्विन	September-October
8. कार्त्तिक	October-November
9. मार्गशीर्ष	November-December
10. पौष	December-January
11. माघ	January-February
12. फाल्गुन	February-March

The names of the days of the week are based on the names of the planets which presided over them and are ultimately, at least in part, translations of the Greco-Roman names, which came to India during the Gupta period, 320 A.D.-*c.* 495. The names, all of which mean literally 'day of such-and-such a planet', are:

रविवार, भानुवार, भट्टारकवार	('day of the Sun')	Sunday
सोमवार	('day of the Moon')	Monday
मङ्गलवार, अङ्गारकवार, कुजवार	('day of Mars')	Tuesday
बुधवार, सौम्यवार	('day of Mercury')	Wednesday
बृहस्पतिवार, गुरुवार, लक्ष्मीवार	('day of Jupiter')	Thursday
शुक्रवार, भृगुवार	('day of Venus')	Friday
शनिवार	('day of Saturn')	Saturday

Instead of the element -वार 'time, day', -दिवस, -दिन or -वासर, all meaning 'day', are often found.

When dates are given in MSS, the usual sequence is:

1. The era (usually the Vikrama or Śaka);
2. the year (generally in figures, sometimes in symbolic word numerals);
3. the month;
4. the fortnight (पक्ष, whether कृष्ण or शुक्ल being indicated);
5. the lunar day (तिथि, with the figure or ordinal number);
6. the name of the day.

An example will make this clear:

संवत् १५८८ वर्षे भाद्रपदे शुक्लपक्षे एकादश्यां रविवासरे लिखितमिदं पुस्तकम् ।

'This book (*i.e.*, MS) was written on Sunday, the eleventh day [really the lunar day or *tithi*] in the light fortnight in the month of Bhādrapada in 1588 of the [Vikrama-] era [*i.e.*, 1530 A.D.]'. Many variations in this precise phraseology occur, however. Thus, sometimes the *pakṣa* is written as a compound with the name of the month (*e.g.*, आषाढकृष्णपक्षे); the word मास ('month') may be put after the name of the month (*e.g.*, वैशाखमासे). Of very frequent occurrence is the use of the abbreviations शुदि for शुक्लपक्षे and बदि or वदि for कृष्णपक्षे (*e.g.*, चैत्रशुदि for चैत्रे शुक्लपक्षे or चैत्रशुक्लपक्षे, मार्गशीर्षवदि for मार्गशीर्षे कृष्णपक्षे or मार्गशीर्षकृष्णपक्षे.[14] Note that each of these components (or compounds thereof like मार्गशीर्षकृष्णपक्षे) is put in the locative case ('locative of time when'!), except, of course, the indeclinable संवत्. Sometimes, in mentioning the name of the day, the last element -वार, -दिवस, etc. is omitted and the planet-name is put in the locative; thus, सोमे for सोमवारे, सोमदिवसे, etc. Often the dates are given with considerable economy of expression: संवत् १९०४ आषाढकृष्णद्वादश्यां भृगुवासरे ।

Often the name of the scribe who copied the MS is added in the instrumental, and to the whole may be subjoined one or more benedictory formulae, such as शुभं भवतु, मङ्गलमस्तु, कल्याणमस्तु, श्रीरस्तु, etc., all of which convey more or less the same sentiment ('May there be prosperity *or* welfare'). Occasionally the recipients of these benedictory phrases are specified, as, for example, लेखकपाठकयोः ('to the scribe and the reader').

Examples of Numerals and Numerical Words.

१) वेदरसवसुशशिभूमिसंख्याकाः सैनिका एकस्मिन्नेव दिवसे तस्मिन्युद्धक्षेत्रे द्विड्भिर्हताः ।

२) सांख्यदर्शनस्यानुसारेण[1] पञ्चविंशतिस्तत्त्वानां विद्यन्ते यथा पुरुषः प्रकृतिर्बुद्धिरहंकारो[2] मनः[3] पञ्च ज्ञानेन्द्रियाणि[4] पञ्च कर्मेन्द्रियाणि[5] पञ्च तन्मात्राणि पञ्च महाभूतानि च । बुद्धिरहंकारो मनो दशेन्द्रियाणि च त्रयोदशान्तःकरणानीत्युच्यन्ते ।

---

[14] शुदि may possibly (but not entirely convincingly) be shortened from शुद्धदिनेषु (or शुद्धदिवसेषु) 'in the bright days'; वदि or बदि may be shortened from वद्यदिनेषु or perhaps from बहुलदिनेषु, both वद्य and बहुल being synonyms for कृष्णपक्ष.

३) जैनदर्शनस्य चतुर्विंशतिर्गुरूणामासन्[6]। तेषां चरमौ वर्धमानो महावीर इति विश्रुतः पार्श्वनाथश्चास्ताम्।

४) मानवधर्मशास्त्रानुसारेण[7] चत्वारि युगानि सन्ति। तेषां चतुर्णां युगानां नामानि कृतं त्रेता द्वापरं कलिश्चेति। चत्वारि सहस्राणि वर्षाणां प्रथमं युगं कृतमित्युक्तम्। तस्य संध्या तावच्छती संध्यांशश्च तावच्छतो भवतः। अतोऽष्टशतोत्तराणि चत्वारि सहस्राणीदं युगम् (४८००)। अन्येषु त्रिषु ससंध्येषु ससंध्यांशेषु च युगेषु सहस्राणि शतानि चैकापायेन वर्तन्ते। ततः षट्शताधिकानि त्रीणि सहस्राणि त्रेतायुगम् (३६००)। चतुःशताधिके द्वे सहस्रे द्वापरयुगम् (२४००)। द्विशतोत्तरमेकं सहस्रमाधुनिकं युगं कलिरित्युच्यते (१२००)। कृतयुगे सत्यं धर्मश्च प्रभवतः[8] किं त्वनुगच्छत्सु युगेषु क्रमशः सत्यस्य धर्मस्य च ह्रासः। कलियुगेऽसत्यमधर्मो द्वेषो युद्धानि पापात्मका जनाश्च सर्वत्र भविष्यन्ति। अस्य युगस्यान्ते सर्वं जगद्विलेष्यते। प्रलयकालस्य पश्चात्सर्वलोक-पितामहो ब्रह्मा सर्वमिदं जगत्पुनः स्रक्ष्यति।

५) परमः स्वर्गः क्वास्तीति त्रिश्चतुर्वा पुत्रेण पृष्टः पिता तव हृदये विद्यत इति प्रत्यभाषत।

६) यदा गुरुरध्यायं वदति तदा शिष्योऽक्षरशः पठति।

७) मूर्खोऽविद्यायाः[9] कृष्णमेघावृतमनाः शतकृत्वः सहस्रकृत्व एव वाध्यायं श्रुत्वापि न किंचिदवगच्छति। निपुणस्तु सकृदेव श्रुत्वा सर्वं सर्वशो जानाति।

८) काश्चिन्महादेवप्रतिमा द्वादशभिर्भुजैः[10] काश्चित्तु चतुर्भिर्भुजैर्[10] अन्या द्वाभ्यामेव[10] समुपेता भवन्ति।

९) आकाशे मेघगणानागतान् दृष्ट्वा हंसा जलाशये पञ्चशः प्लवमाना मानससरोवरं सत्वरं संपतितुमुपचक्रमिरे[11]।

१०) तस्मिन्नण्डे[12] भगवान्सर्वलोकपितामहः परिवत्सरमुषित्वा स्वयमेवात्मनो ध्यानाद् द्विधाकरोत् । ताभ्यां शकलाभ्यां दिवं च भूमिं च निर्ममे ।

११) प्रलयकाले सर्वेषां लोकानां स्रष्टा ब्रह्मा चतुर्भिः शिरोभिरष्टाभिः कर्णैश्च संयुक्तो ऽनन्तशेषमहासर्पशय्यायां शयानस्य विष्णोर् नाभेर्निर्गतस्य पङ्कजस्योपरि निषीदति[13] ।

१२) कश्चिद् ब्राह्मणो ग्रामान्तराद्यज्ञच्छागमुपक्रीय मार्गे गच्छन्धूर्त-त्रयेणावलोकितः ।

१३) यथा कश्चित्सरितो बुध्नं द्रष्टुं न शक्नोति यदि जलं वायुना प्रमथितं पङ्केन पूर्णं वा भवति तथैव यदि चित्तमशुचिभिः पापैश्च दुष्टं तर्हि योगो लब्धुं तेन नरेण न शक्यते[14] । योगं प्राप्तुमष्टौ योगाङ्गान्याचरितव्यानि । प्रथममङ्गं यमो द्वितीयं नियमस्तृतीयम् आसनं चतुर्थं प्राणायामः पञ्चमं प्रत्याहारः षष्ठं धारणा सप्तमं ध्यानमष्टमं समाधिरित्येवं योगमार्गो ऽष्टधा विभज्यते ।[15]

१४) एकोना विंशतिर्नार्यः क्रीडां कर्तुं वने गताः ।
विंशतिर्गृहमायाताः शेषो व्याघ्रेण भक्षितः ॥[16]

१५) विक्रमसंवद्वेदाभ्रानुष्टुप्सोमवर्षे आषाढकृष्णपक्षे पञ्चम्यामङ्गारक-वासरे इदं[17] पुस्तकं लिखितम् ।

१६) इयं कृतिर्विक्रमसंवदिन्दुवायुदिग्गजभूमिवर्षे मार्गशीर्षशुक्लपक्षे नवम्यां चन्द्रवासरे देवशर्मणा लिखिता ।

१७) संवत् रन्ध्रपुरेषुभूमिवर्षे चैत्रशुदि प्रथमायां सोमवारे लिखितमिदम् ॥ शुभं भवतु ॥ मङ्गलमस्तु ॥

१८) संवत् १६५८ वर्षे ज्यैष्ठमासवदि तृतीयायां तिथौ[18] भृगुवासरे ॥ कल्याणमस्तु ॥

१९) संवत् १७४२ शके १६०९ पौषशुद्धे[19] एकादश्यां शनौ विश्वनाथेन लिखितो ग्रन्थः स्वार्थं परार्थं च ॥ शुभं भवतु ॥ लेखकपाठकयोः श्रीरस्तु ॥

Notes

1. The Sāṃkhya system is one of the six so-called 'orthodox' systems of Indian philosophy, which was traditionally founded by the sage Kapila. It is a dualism, which teaches matter (प्रकृति) and spirit or soul (पुरुष) as the only ultimate realities. The soul is an unchanging reality which plays no part in the evolution of the world from primal matter. It is only the ceaseless modifications of the intellect (बुद्धि), the ground of all intellectual processes, which, reflecting the pure consciousness of the soul, wrongly (*i.e.,* through ignorance) identifies the soul as participating in the world of matter. The bondage of the soul to the material world keeps the soul from its pristine independence from matter and leads to rebirth due to the continual impressions made upon the intellect.

The material world is evolved from matter by a process known as *pariṇāma* (परिणाम), whereby primal matter is *actually transformed* into the objects of reality like the body and all other material things. This view is in sharp opposition and contrast to the view of the Advaitavedānta (अद्वैतवेदान्त) philosophy, which holds that the transformation of the one absolute Brahman, the ultimate ground of all existence, is only *apparent,* like the appearance of a rope as a snake.

According to the Sāṃkhya conception, the material world is evolved by a particular progressive evolution from *prakṛti* through the interaction of its three constituent components called 'guṇas', *viz., sattva* (सत्त्व), *rajas* (रजस्) and *tamas* (तमस्). Among the evolutes are the five subtle elements called *tanmātras* (तन्मात्र) 'mere thats' -- really *potential* elements -- whence, in turn, the gross elements (महाभूत) are evolved by successive combinations of the *tanmātras.* From the five gross elements the world of objects is derived. Soul and matter with all its evolutes constitute the 25 categories or *tattvas* (तत्त्व) of the Sāṃkhya system.

2. The *ahaṃkāra* (*literally* the 'I-maker') is a physical organ of the body whose purpose it is to relate to oneself, *i.e.,* invest with a sense of 'I' or personal connection, the impressions that are supplied by the mind (मनस्) to which they have been transmitted by the sense-organs (इन्द्रियाणि). Often translated by 'ego' or 'ego-principle', the *ahaṃkāra* is the psycho-physical organ that attaches the sense of *I, me* and *mine* to perceptions.

3. The *manas* ('mind') is a lower organ that gathers the sense-data transmitted by the ten organs of knowledge and action (इन्द्रियाणि), analyzes and synthesizes them and passes them on to the intellect (बुद्धि) for some decision with regard to them.

4. The five organs of knowledge (ज्ञानेन्द्रियाणि) are the senses of sight, hearing, smell, taste and touch.

5. The five organs of action (कर्मेन्द्रियाणि) are situated in the mouth, hands, feet, anus and the sex organ and are concerned with speech, grasping, walking, excretion and reproduction.

6. The Jaina religion speaks of 24 teachers called 'Tīrthaṃkaras' (*literally* 'makers of the ford', *i.e.,* those who have crossed over the river of rebirth), the last of whom was Vardhamāna Jñātaputra, usually referred to as Mahāvīra ('Great Hero'), a contemporary of Gautama Buddha. Mahāvīra was preceded by Pārśvanātha, who flourished probably in the ninth century B.C. The others belong to prehistoric times. The Tīrthaṃkaras are also known as 'Jinas', *i.e.,* 'victors *or* conquerors', whence, by secondary derivation, is derived the term Jaina 'a follower of the (teachings of the) Jinas'.

7. The Mānavadharmaśāstra or Code of Manu is one of the chief manuals of Hindu jurisprudence and accordingly lays down social, moral and ethical injunctions as well as rules for the observation of rites and ceremonies. It begins with an account of the creation of the world, which leads to the divisions of time, in connection with which are treated the Four Ages (चत्वारि युगानि) here summarized in sentence 4. The names of the ages are apparently taken from the game of dice, in which कृत, त्रेता, द्वापर and कलि refer to the number of dots on the dice from *four* to *one* respectively in a descending order of winning throws. As applied to the Four Ages, there is a corresponding diminution of virtue from the कृत to the कलि age, reflected in the diminishing thousands of years in each, *viz.,* from 4,800 to 1,200.

8. The कृतयुग is often called the सत्ययुग to emphasize the virtue and righteousness (सत्य) that predominate in it.

9. The genitive (अ)विद्यायाः is dependent upon कृष्णमेघावृतमनाः.

10. All the instrumentals are dependent upon समुपेताः ('provided with …').

11. At the coming of the rains the *haṃsa*-birds fly far to the north to breed in Lake Mānasa at the foot of Mt. Kailāsa. Their annual migration is frequently referred to by Sanskrit poets. Incidentally, this lake is very often erroneously called (and written) Mānasarovara instead of Mānasasarovara, one of the *sa*'s being omitted by haplology, a kind of abbreviation or contraction whereby one

of two identical or similar adjacent syllables is omitted. Examples in English are *pacifism* for **pacificism, mineralogy* for **mineralology*. A startling example is the proper name *England,* which goes back to the fuller Old English *Englaland* ('Land of the Angles') which in Middle English became *Engeland* with gradual loss of one of the *la*'s.

12. The 'egg' (अण्डे) referred to here is the cosmic egg which came from the seed cast into the primal waters by Brahman in his creative aspect as Brahmā, 'the grandsire of all the worlds'. This passage is but very slightly modified from Mānavadharmaśāstra I.12-13a.

13. This depiction of Brahmā seated in the calyx of a lotus whose stem issues from the navel of Viṣṇu reclining on the serpent Anantaśeṣa is a frequent subject of sculpture in India through the centuries and also of colorful prints available in bazaars everywhere in the country.

14. योगो लब्धुं तेन नरेण न शक्यते 'yoga cannot be attained by that man'. There is no *passive* infinitive in Sanskrit, and therefore when a passive construction is used with √शक् 'be able' (which, of course, requires an infinitive to complete its sense), the passive is transferred to √शक्; thus, here लब्धुं . . .शक्यते.

15. The eight 'limbs' of yoga may be briefly defined thus:

यम 'restraint' of various kinds, such as अहिंसा ('non-injury'), सत्य ('truthfulness'), अस्तेय ('non-stealing'), etc.

नियम 'cultivation' of certain good habits, among which are purity of mind and body, contentment, austerity, religious study and meditation on God.

आसन 'posture', of which there are many kinds to be practised by the *yogin,* all of which are intended to facilitate concentration.

प्राणायाम 'regulation of breath', the purpose of which is also to help concentration.

प्रत्याहार 'retraction' of the senses from their objects.

धारणा 'attention' to an object uninterruptedly, whereby *only the object* is known by the mind.

ध्यान 'meditation', whereby the intellect ceases its modifications and clings to the one object of concentration.

समाधि 'concentration', in which state the intellect is *identified with the object* of concentration.

16. This couplet is an example of what Indians call वक्रोक्ति 'crooked speech' (वक्र 'crooked' + उक्ति 'speech'), in which the true or real meaning intended to be expressed is concealed by phraseology which suggests something else. It is a kind of pun of which Indians are very fond. The apparent meaning of the couplet is 'Nineteen (*literally* 'Twenty minus one') wives went to play in the woods; twenty came home, the remaining one was eaten by a tiger'. Since this makes no sense, a closer inspection of the words suggests an alternative explanation of the first word एकोना, as none of the other words seems amenable to an alternative explanation. If we divide एकोना into एको ना (instead of एक + ऊन: 'deficient by one'), we can take ना as the nominative singular of नृ 'man', which is declined like a noun of relationship in-*ṛ*, although its declension is defective.[15] The translation of the first line now becomes: '*One man* (एको ना) [and] twenty wives went' etc.[16]

17. Sandhi is often entirely omitted or loosely applied in colophons. We would normally write अङ्गारकवासर इदं.

18. Here तिथौ is expressed, but most often it is omitted, as in sentences 15, 16, 17 and 19.

19. पौषशुद्धे is an alternative expression for पौषशुदि or पौषशुक्लपक्षे.

Vocabulary

अक्षर, *n.* a syllable.
अङ्ग, *n.* a limb.
अण्ड, *n.* an egg.
अधर्म, *m.* unrighteousness.
अध्याय, *m.* a lesson.
अनन्तशेष, *m.* Anantaśeṣa, name of the great serpent that forms a bed or couch for Viṣṇu during the periods of the dissolution of the universe.
अनु-√गम् (गच्छति, class I), go after, follow.

---

[15]The noun नृ occurs in the compound नृलोके in stanza 48 in the following excerpt from the Gītā.

[16] This couplet is taken from Charles Rockwell Lanman, *A Sanskrit Reader,* p. 68.

अनुसार, *m.* 'a going after', conformity, accordance; *instr.* अनुसारेण + *gen.* 'in accordance with, according to'.
अन्तःकरण, *n.* an inner organ.
अन्तर, *n.* another (*at the end of a cpd.*).
अपाय, *m.* 'a going away', diminution, loss.
अव-√गम् (गच्छति, class I), understand.
अवलोकित, *ppp. of caus.* अव-√लोक् (लोकते, class I), seen.
अविद्या, *f.* ignorance.
अशुचि, *n.* impurity.
अहंकार, *m.* the I-principle in the Sāṃkhya philosophy. [*v.* note 2]
आकाश, *n.* the sky.
आचरितव्य, *gerundive of* आ-√चर् (चरति, class I), to be practised, should be practised.
आधुनिक, *adj.* present, current.
आ-√या (याति, class II), come; *ppp.* आयात.
आवृत, *ppp.* आ-√वृ (वृणोति, class V), covered over, obscured.
उप-√क्रम् (क्रमते, class I), begin.
उप-√क्री (क्रीणाति, class IX), buy; *gerund* उपक्रीय.
उपरि, *postp.* on, upon (+ *gen.*).
उषित्वा, *gerund* √वस् (वसति, class I), having stayed, remained *or* abided.
कर्ण, *m.* the ear.
कल्याण, *n.* good fortune.
कृति, *f.* a work.
कृष्ण, *adj.* dark, black.
क्रमशः, *adv.* in order, in sequence.
क्रीडा, *f.* play.
क्षेत्र, *n.* a field.
गण, *m.* a group *or* mass.
ग्रन्थ, *m.* a book.
ग्राम, *m.* a village.
चरम, *adj.* last.
चित्त, *n.* the mind.
छाग, *m.* a goat.
जगत्, *n.* the world.

जलाशय, *m.* 'a water-abode', a lake *or* pond.

√ज्ञा (जानाति, class IX), know.

ज्ञान, *n.* knowledge.

तत्त्व, *n.* 'that-ness', reality; a real (in philosophy), a category.

तन्मात्र, *n.* 'a mere that', a mere essence, a potential *or* subtle element in Sāṃkhya.

तावच्छत, *adj.* 'having *or* containing so many hundreds' (तावत् + शत).

दिव, *n.* the sky *or* heaven.

दिवस, *m.* a day.

दुष्ट, *ppp.* √दुष् (दुष्यति, class IV), spoiled.

द्विष्, *m.* an enemy.

दर्शन, *n.* 'a seeing *or* viewing', a way of looking at the world, *then* a philosophical system.

धूर्त, *m.* a rascal *or* thief.

ध्यान, *n.* meditation.

नाभि, *f.* the navel.

नारी, *f.* a woman, wife.

निपुण, *adj.* clever.

निस्-√गम् (गच्छति, class I), go out, issue forth.

निस्- 1√मा (मिमीते, class III), form, make; *perf.* °ममे.

नि-√सद् (सीदति, class I), sit down, be seated (note: स् → ष् after the -इ of नि).

पङ्क, *m. or n.* mud.

पङ्कज, *adj.* 'born in the mud', *as n.* a lotus.

√पठ् (पठति, class I), recite.

परार्थम्, *adv.* for the sake of others.

परिवत्सर, *m.* a full year.

पाठक, *m.* a reader.

पाप, *n.* sin.

पुरुष, *m.* the self *or* soul.

पूर्ण, *adj.* filled with, full of (+ *instr.*).

पृष्ट, *ppp.* √प्रछ् (पृच्छति, class VI), (having been) asked.

प्रकृति, *f.* primal matter.

प्रतिमा, *f.* an image *or* statue.

प्र-√भू (भवति, class I), be forth, ahead *or* dominant, dominate, prevail.

प्रमथित, *ppp.* प्र-√मथ् (मथ्नाति, class IX), agitated, stirred up.
प्रलय, *m.* dissolution.
√प्लु (प्लवते, class I), float, swim.
बुद्धि, *f.* the intellect in the Sāṃkhya system.
बुध्न, *n.* the bottom.
√भक्ष् (भक्षति, class I), eat; *ppp.* भक्षित.
भगवत्, *adj.* blessed, august (applied to Brahmā).
भुज, *m.* the arm (of the body).
मङ्गल, *n.* welfare, luck.
मनस्, *n.* the mind.
महाभूत, *n.* a gross element, of which there are five, *viz.,* ether, air, fire, water and earth.
मूर्ख, *m.* a fool.
मेघ, *m.* a cloud.
यज्ञ, *m.* a sacrifice.
युग, *n.* an age *or* eon.
युद्ध, *n.* a battle.
√लभ् (लभते, class I), get, attain; *infin.* लब्धुम्.
लेखक, *m.* a writer; a copyist *or* scribe.
वायु, *m.* the wind.
वि-√भज् (भजति, class I), divide.
वि-√ली (लीयते, class IV), be dissolved; *fut.* विलेष्यते.
विश्रुत, *ppp.* वि-√श्रु (शृणोति, class V), *literally* heard of far and wide (वि-), *hence* known as.
व्याघ्र, *m.* a tiger.
शकल, *n.* a piece; half of an eggshell.
शय्या, *f.* a couch *or* bed.
शिरस्, *n.* the head (of the body).
√शी (शेते, class II), lie (in sleeping *or* resting); *pres. mid. part.* शयान.
शुभ, *n.* good fortune.
श्री, *f.* prosperity, good fortune.
संयुक्त, *ppp.* सम्-√युज् (युनक्ति, class VII), joined with, provided with (+ *instr.*).
सत्वरम्, *adv.* quickly.

संध्या, *f.* morning twilight.
संध्यांश, *m.* evening twilight.
समुपेत, *ppp.* सम्-उप-√इ (एति), provided with (+ *instr.*).
सम्-√पत् (पतति, class I), fly together.
सरित्, *f.* a stream *or* river.
सर्प, *m.* a serpent.
√सृज् (सृजति, class VI), create; *fut.* स्रक्ष्यति.
सैनिक, *m.* a soldier.
स्रष्टृ, *m.* creator.
स्वार्थम्, *adv.* for one's own sake.
हृदय, *n.* the heart.
ह्रास, *m.* loss, diminution.

VII. Kṛṣṇa's Revelation (2)

अर्जुन उवाच ।

त्वमादिदेवः पुरुषः पुराणस्त्वमस्य विश्वस्य परं निधानम् ।
वेत्तासि वेद्यं च[1] परं च धाम त्वया ततं विश्वमनन्तरूप ॥ ३८ ॥
वायुर्[2] यमो[3] ऽग्निर्[4] वरुणः[5] शशाङ्कः[6] प्रजापतिस्[7] त्वं
प्रपितामहश्च[8] ।
नमो नमस्ते ऽस्तु सहस्रकृत्वः पुनश्च भूयो ऽपि नमो नमस्ते ॥ ३९ ॥
नमः पुरस्तादथ पृष्ठतस्ते नमो ऽस्तु ते सर्वत एव सर्व[9] ।
अनन्तवीर्यामितविक्रमस्[10] त्वं सर्वं समाप्नोषि ततो ऽसि सर्वः ॥ ४० ॥

पितासि लोकस्य चराचरस्य[11] त्वमस्य पूज्यश्च गुरुर्गरीयान्[12] ।
न त्वत्समो ऽस्त्यभ्यधिकः कुतो ऽन्यो लोकत्रये ऽप्यप्रतिमप्रभाव[13] ॥ ४३ ॥
तस्मात्प्रणम्य प्रणिधाय कायं प्रसादये त्वामहमीशमीड्यम् ।
पितेव पुत्रस्य[14] सखेव सख्युः[15] प्रियः प्रियायार्हसि देव सोढुम् ॥ ४४ ॥
अदृष्टपूर्वं हृषितो ऽस्मि दृष्ट्वा भयेन च प्रव्यथितं मनो मे ।
तदेव मे दर्शय देव रूपं प्रसीद देवेश जगन्निवास ॥ ४५ ॥

किरीतिनं गदिनं चक्रहस्तमिच्छामि त्वां द्रष्टुमहं तथैव ।
तेनैव रूपेण चतुर्भुजेन सहस्रबाहो भव विश्वमूर्ते ॥ ४६ ॥

श्रीभगवान् उवाच ।
मया प्रसन्नेन तवार्जुनेदं रूपं परं दर्शितमात्मयोगात् ।
तेजोमयं विश्वमनन्तमाद्यं यन्[16] मे त्वदन्येन न दृष्टपूर्वम् ॥ ४७ ॥
न वेदयज्ञाध्ययनैर्न दानैर्न च क्रियाभिर्न तपोभिरुग्रैः ।
एवंरूपः शक्य[17] अहं नृलोके द्रष्टुं त्वदन्येन कुरुप्रवीर ॥ ४८ ॥
मा ते व्यथा[18] मा च विमूढभावो[19] दृष्ट्वा रूपं घोरमीदृङ्[20] ममेदम् ।
व्यपेतभीः प्रीतमनाः पुनस्त्वं तदेव मे रूपमिदं प्रपश्य ॥ ४९ ॥

संजय उवाच ।
इत्यर्जुनं वासुदेवस्तथोक्त्वा स्वकं रूपं दर्शयामास भूयः ।
आश्वासयामास च भीतमेनं भूत्वा पुनः सौम्यवपुर्महात्मा[21] ॥ ५० ॥

अर्जुन उवाच ।
दृष्ट्वेदं मानुषं रूपं तव सौम्यं जनार्दन ।
इदानीमस्मि संवृत्तः सचेताः प्रकृतिं गतः ॥ ५१ ॥

श्रीभगवान् उवाच ।
सुदुर्दर्शमिदं रूपं दृष्टवानसि[22] यन्मम ।
देवा अप्यस्य रूपस्य नित्यं दर्शनकाङ्क्षिणः ॥ ५२ ॥
नाहं वेदैर्न तपसा न दानेन चेज्यया ।
शक्य एवंविधो द्रष्टुं दृष्टवानसि मां यथा ॥ ५३ ॥
भक्त्या त्वनन्यया शक्य अहमेवंविधोऽर्जुन ।
ज्ञातुं द्रष्टुं च तत्त्वेन प्रवेष्टुं च परंतप ॥ ५४ ॥
मत्कर्मकृन्[23] मत्परमो[24] मद्भक्तः सङ्गवर्जितः ।
निर्वैरः सर्वभूतेषु यः स मामेति पाण्डव ॥ ५५ ॥

(Bhagavadgītā XI. 38-40, 43-55).

Notes

1. वेत्तासि वेद्यं च 'You are the knower and that which is to be known (*or* the object of knowledge)'; वेत्ता is nominative singular of वेत्तृ, a primary derivative from 1√विद् 'know' formed with the agentive suffix -तृ, before which the root vowel is replaced by its guṇa substitute.

2. वायुर् Vāyu, the Vedic god of the wind. As an ordinary noun, वायु means 'the wind' and is a primary derivative of agency from √वा 'blow' and the suffix -उ with a -*y*- interposed to insulate the root from contraction with the suffix.

3. यमो Yama, the Vedic king of the departed spirits or dead, regarded as the first man to be born and hence the first to die.

4. अग्निर् Agni, the Vedic god of fire.

5. वरुण: Varuṇa, one of the most important of Vedic deities, the personification of Truth; he is one of the Ādityas or sons of Aditi, all of whom are personified abstractions.

6. शशाङ्क: 'the Moon', literally 'having a hare as its mark'; *cf.* शशि- in the compound शशिसूर्यनेत्रम् in II.19.

7. प्रजापतिस् Prajāpati ('lord of creatures'), a later Vedic god, only beginning to be mentioned in the Ṛgveda as the supreme creator of the world.

8. प्रपितामहश्च. 'and the great grandsire', Brahmā, *i.e.*, Brahman as a personal creator-god.

9. सर्व vocative! (O All!)

10. अनन्तवीर्यामितविक्रमस् An ambiguity exists here, as this may be taken as a complex compound consisting of two bahuvrīhis ('having infinite strength and unmeasured prowess'), or, alternatively, अनन्तवीर्य may be regarded as a vocative ('O you who have infinite strength') followed by the nominative अमितविक्रमस् ('you, having unmeasured prowess').

11. चराचरस्य probably most easily to be construed as a neuter collective ('the moving and unmoving') in apposition to लोकस्य, thus: 'You are the father of the world, the moving and unmoving'. Also possible would be to take चराचरस्य as an adjective of लोकस्य, thus: 'of the moving and unmoving world'.

12. गरीयान् The comparative of an adjective in Sanskrit often does not really involve a comparison, but just a very high degree of the quality the adjective expresses. गरीयान् might be translated as an 'absolute superlative' here, *viz.*, 'most venerable'. The play on the two etymologically related words, गुरुर् and गरीयान्, is, of course, lost in English. But it should be borne in mind that गुरु, the basic meaning of which is 'heavy' as opposed to 'light', figuratively means 'worthy of respect *or* honor', and it is this sense that is involved in the common use of गुरु for 'teacher'; *literally*, then, 'the venerable one'.

13. अप्रतिमप्रभाव vocative! 'O you whose power is without match'.

14. पुत्रस्य like the following सख्युः (genitive!), to be construed with सहते extracted from अर्हसि . . . सोढुम् ('please be tolerant *or* kindly disposed') in the next *pāda*. In this sense of 'be lenient *or* kindly disposed', √सह् takes the *genitive* of the person affected. Note that प्रियायाः, genitive feminine singular of प्रिया 'wife', is irregularly contracted with the initial vowel of अर्हसि; the visarga ought to have been dropped and the hiatus retained, thus: प्रियाया अर्हसि, but this sort of double sandhi is not rare in the epics. The line may be thus rendered: "As a father is tolerant of a son, a friend of a friend, a husband (प्रियः) of a wife (प्रियायाः), please be tolerant [of me], O god!"

15. सख्युः genitive singular of सखि, the declension of which is quite anomalous, differing considerably from the अग्नि-type. In the nominative and accusative singular and dual and the nominative only in the plural, सखि is replaced by सखाय् (*sakhāy-*), *i.e.,* with *-i* replaced by *-ai* (its vṛddhi substitute), which is changed to *-āy* before the vowel endings. In the nominative singular, however, the *-y* is dropped. In the instrumental and dative singular the 'regular' endings *-ā* and *-e* are added directly to सखि, yielding सख्या (*sakhy-ā*) and सख्ये (*sakhy-e*). In the ablative and dative singular the ending *-ur* (*-uḥ*), taken from the nouns of familial relationship,

is used, and finally in the locative singular the ending *-au* is added to the stem, सख्यौ (*sakhy-au*), but *cf.* अग्नौ (*agn-au*), *not* अग्न्यौ (*agny-au*). Here, then, is the whole declension for reference:

	Singular	Dual	Plural
Nom.	*sakhā* (सखा)	*sakhāy-au* (सखायौ)	*sakhāy-aḥ* (सखाय:)
Acc.	*sakhāy-am* (सखायम्)	*sakhāy-au* (सखायौ)	*sakhīn* (सखीन्)
Instr.	*sakhy-ā* (सख्या)	*sakhi-bhyām* (सखिभ्याम्)	*sakhi-bhiḥ* (सखिभि:)
Dat.	*sakhy-e* (सख्ये)	*sakhi-bhyām* (सखिभ्याम्)	*sakhi-bhyaḥ* (सखिभ्य:)
Abl.	*sakhy-uḥ* (सख्यु:)	*sakhi-bhyām* (सखिभ्याम्)	*sakhi-bhyaḥ* (सखिभ्य:)
Gen.	*sakhy-uḥ* (सख्यु:)	*sakhy-oḥ* (सख्यो:)	*sakhīnām* (सखीनाम्)
Loc.	*sakhy-au* (सख्यौ)	*sakhy-oḥ* (सख्यो:)	*sakhi-ṣu* (सखिषु)
Voc.	*sakhe* (सखे)	*sakhāy-au* (सखायौ)	*sakhāy-aḥ* (सखाय:)

16. यन्, *i.e.,* यद्, the relative refers to इदं रूपं, the intervening words तेजोमयं . . . आद्यं being pendants to रूपं: thus: 'this form -- full of radiance, all-pervading (*or* universal), infinite, being at the beginning (*i.e.,* without a beginning) -- which of me has not been seen before by another than you'. The pronoun मे 'of me' in the last *pāda* properly belongs with इदं रूपं 'this form of me', but has been brought into the relative clause where it is loosely connected with यन् ('which [form] of me').

17. शक्य (with which supply अस्मि) has a passive value, which in English has to be borne by the complementary infinitive (द्रष्टुं), as the English verbs 'can' and 'be able' are not used passively. So, we must say: '(Not by the Veda or by sacrifices) . . . (am) I able *to be seen* having such a form . . . by another than you'. The same construction with शक्य and the infinitive occurs below in stanzas 53 and 54; *cf.* also note 14 on sentence 13 in the exercise above.

18. मा ते व्यथा The imperative अस्तु has to be supplied with the prohibitive particle मा; thus, 'Let there not be perturbation on your part (ते)', and similarly with the following मा.

19. विमूढभावो *literally*, 'the condition of one who is bewildered', though in English the abstract 'bewilderment' would suffice.

20. ईदृङ्, for ईदृग्, nominative singular of ईदृश् 'such', of which -श् is replaced by -क्/-ग् according to the voiceless or voiced character of the following sound. Final -ग् before म- in external sandhi is generally changed to the guttural nasal ङ्, though it may optionally remain.

21. महात्मा This pendant nominative at the end of the stanza, so common a phenomenon in epic verse, really qualifies वासुदेवस् in the first line: 'The son of Vasudeva, having spoken thus to Arjuna . . . the noble one'.

22. दृष्टवानसि By adding the secondary suffix -वत् to the past passive participle, a past *active* participle is formed. Thus, whereas दृष्ट means 'seen', *i.e.*, having *been* seen, दृष्ट-वत् means 'having seen'. दृष्टवान् असि, then, means *literally* 'you are having seen', *i.e.*, you have seen. Just as the past passive participle (± the appropriate form of √भू or √अस्) may be used in place of a passive verb, so the past *active* participle may be employed in lieu of an active verb (imperfect, perfect or aorist). However, this *active* construction, unlike that with the past passive participle, may express the notion of a *simple past* or of a *present perfect* (*viz.*, the past formed with *has/have* in English). When the present perfect or *has/have* time sphere is meant, some form of the *present* of √अस् is expressed with the participle as in दृष्टवान् असि 'you *have* seen'. If it has the value of a simple past tense ('you saw'), no 'helping' verb is usually expressed, but if it is expressed, the imperfect or aorist of √भू (*e.g.*, अभवत्, अभूत्) is generally used.

23. मत्कर्मकृन्, for मत्कर्मकृत्, the final -त् of which may become voiced, *viz.*, -द्, before म- in external sandhi or more commonly, as here, the nasal of its own class, *viz.*, the dental -न्; *cf.* ईदृङ् for ईदृग् in stanza 49 and *v.* note 20 thereon. मत्कर्मकृन् may be translated 'performing action *in me* (मत् as equivalent of a locative)' or 'performing *my* action' (मत् as genitive).

24. मत्परमो *literally* 'having me as supreme *or* highest', intent upon me, an appositional bahuvrīhi.

Vocabulary

अग्नि, *m.* Agni, the Vedic god of fire.
अदृष्टपूर्व, *adj.* unseen before, previously unseen.
अध्ययन, *n.* study.
अनन्य, *adj.* 'not having another', undeviating, unswerving.
अप्रतिम, *adj.* not having a match, without a match *or* equal.
अभ्यधिक, *adj.* superior.
अमित, *negative of ppp.* 1√मा (मिमीते, class III), unmeasured, immeasurable.
√अर्ह् (अर्हति, class I), deserve, have a right to, be pleased to (+ *infin.*).
आदिदेव, *m.* 'god of the beginning', the first *or* primal god.
आद्य, *adj.* being at the beginning, primal.
आ-√श्वस् (श्वसिति, class II), get one's breath, become quiet; *caus.* आश्वासयति, 'causes someone to become quiet', comforts.
√इ (एति, class II), come.
इज्या, *f.* sacrifice.
ईड्य, *gerundive of* √ईड् (ईट्टे, class II), to be praised, worthy of praise.
ईदृश्, *adj.* of this sort, such.
ईश, *m.* a lord.
एवंरूप, *adj.* 'having a thus-form', having such a form, provided with such a form.
एवंविध, *adj.* of such sort, such.
-काङ्क्षिन्, *adj.* desiring, wishing (*as final member of an acc. tatpuruṣa*).
काय, *m.* the body.
किरीतिन्, *adj.* 'possessing a diadem'.
क्रिया, *f.* ceremony.
-कृत्, *verbal of* √कृ 'do' *at end of tatpuruṣa cpd.*, doing, performing.
गदिन्, *adj.* 'possessing a cudgel'.
गरीयस्, *comparative of* गुरु 'venerable'. [*v.* note 12]
घोर, *adj.* awful, dreadful.
चक्र, *n.* a wheel, a discus.

चतुर्भुज, *adj.* 'having four arms', fourarmed.

चराचर, *adj.* moving and not moving; *as n.* the moving and not moving, *i.e.*, all living things, animal and vegetal.

जनार्दन, *m.* name of Kṛṣṇa (apparently meaning 'agitator *or* tormentor of people', but the application is unclear).

तत, *ppp.* √तन् (तनोति, class VIII), extended, diffused, pervaded.

तत्त्व, *n.* 'that-ness', essence, reality, truth; *instr. as adv.* in reality, really.

त्रय, *n.* a triad, group of three.

दान, *n.* 'the act of giving', charity.

दृष्टपूर्व, *adj.* seen before *or* previously.

धाम, *n.* dwelling-place, abode.

नमस्, *n.* homage.

नित्यम्, *adv.* always, ever.

निधान, *n.* 'a putting down', *then* place where something is put down, a foundation, resting-place; substrate.

निर्वैर, *adj.* without enmity.

नृलोक, *m.* the world of men.

परंतप, *adj.* 'scorching the foe *or* scorcher of the foe', epithet of Arjuna.

पितृ, *m.* father.

पुरस्तात्, *adv.* in front, before.

पुराण, *adj.* old, ancient, age-old.

पुरुष, *m.* soul (of the universe), supreme spirit.

पूज्य, *gerundive of* √पूज् (पूजयति, class X), to be worshipped *or* venerated, worthy of worship, venerable.

पृष्ठतस्, *adv.* from the back *or* behind, behind, in the rear.

प्रकृति, *f.* original state, ordinary state *or* condition.

प्रजापति, *m.* 'lord of creatures', name of the supreme creator-god of the latest stratum of the Ṛgvedic period.

प्र-√नम् (नमति, class I), bow before (+ *acc.*). [न् is replaced by ण after प्र-.]

प्र-नि-√धा (दधाति, class III), put down (-नि-) before (प्र-). [*v.* note on प्र-√नम्]

प्र-√पश् (पश्यति, class I), see before one's eyes (प्र-).

प्रपितामह, *m.* great-grandsire, epithet of Brahmā, the later creator-god. [प्र- is employed as a prefix equivalent to 'great-' or 'grand' in words of familial relationship; *e.g.*, प्रपौत्र 'great-grandson', प्रपितृव्य '(paternal) granduncle'.]

प्रभाव, *m.* power, might.
प्र-√विश् (विशति, class VI), enter.
प्रवीर, *m.* a hero, prince.
प्रव्यथित, *ppp.* प्र-√व्यथ् (व्यथते, class I), perturbed, disturbed.
प्र-√सद् (सीदति, class I), be favorable *or* gracious; *caus.* प्रसादयति, 'causes to be favorable *or* gracious', asks the favor *or* grace of (+ *acc.*).
प्रसन्न, *ppp.* प्र-√सद् (सीदति, class I), kindly disposed to (+ *gen.*).
प्रिय, *adj.* dear; *as m.* a friend; a husband; *as f.* a wife.
प्रीत, *ppp.* √प्री (प्रीणाति, class IX), pleased.
भक्त, *ppp.* √भज् (भजति, class I), devoted.
भक्ति, *f.* devotion.
भय, *n.* fear.
भाव, *m.* condition, state.
भी, *f.* fear.
भीत, *ppp.* √भी (बिभेति, class III), *literally* 'having feared', afraid.
भूयस्, *comparative adj.* more, greater.
भूयः, *adv.* again.
मानुष, *adj.* pertaining to man, human.
मूर्ति, *f.* shape, form.
यज्ञ, *m.* worship, sacrifice.
यम, *m.* Yama, the king of the deceased in the Veda.
वपुस्, *n.* form, aspect.
वरुण, *m.* Varuṇa, the Vedic god of Truth, one of the Ādityas.
वर्जितः, *ppp. of caus.*√वृज् (वृणक्ति, class VII), devoid of, without (*at end of cpd.*).
वायु, *m.* Vāyu, the Vedic god of the wind.
वासुदेव, *m.* son of Vasudeva, patronymic of Kṛṣṇa.
विक्रम, *m.* courage, might, prowess.
विमूढ, *ppp.* वि-√मुह् (मुह्यति, class IV), bewildered, confused.
विश्व, *adj.* universal.
वीर्य, *n.* manliness, courage.
वेत्तृ, *m.* a knower.
वेद्य, *n.* object of knowledge [*gerundive of* 1√विद् 'know' used as a neuter noun].

व्यथा, *f.* agitation, perturbation.
व्यपेत, *ppp.* वि-अप-√इ (एति, class II), gone away, vanished.
शक्य, *adj.* able (+ *infin. having passive value*).
शशाङ्क, *adj.* 'having a hare as its mark', *as m.* the moon.
संवृत्त, *ppp.* सम्-√वृत् (वर्तते, class I), having become.
सखि, *m.* a comrade, friend. [for declension *v.* note 15]
सङ्ग, *m.* attachment.
सचेतस्, *adj.* conscious.
सम, *adj.* similar to *or* like.
सम्-√आप् (आप्नोति, class V), obtain *or* reach completely (सम्).
सहस्रकृत्वस्, *multiplicative adv.* a thousand-times.
सुदुर्दर्श, *adj.* very hard to look at.
√सह् (सहते, class I), be kindly towards, have patience with (+ *gen.*).
सौम्य, *adj.* mild, gentle, agreeable.
स्वक, *adj.* one's own.
हृषित, *ppp.* √हृष् (हृष्यति, class IV), bristling, horripilated (due to fear).